HISTORY OF MODERN EUROPE AND THE WORLD

HISTORY OF MODERN EUROPE AND THE WORLD

By

S.P. NANDA

ANMOL PUBLICATIONS PVT. LTD.

NEW DELHI - 110 002 (INDIA)

ANMOL PUBLICATIONS PVT. LTD.
H.O.: 4374/4B, Ansari Road, Darya Ganj,
New Delhi-110 002 (India)
Ph.: 23261597, 23278000

B.O.: No. 1015, Ist Main Road, BSK IIIrd Stage
IIIrd Phase, IIIrd Block,
Bangalore - 560 085 (India)
Visit us at: www.anmolpublications.com

History of Modern Europe and The World

First Edition, 2000

Reprint, 2006

PRINTED IN INDIA

Printed at Mehra Offset Press, Delhi.

Contents

Preface

The purpose of this book is the presentation of the *History of Europe and the World Since 1789* (The French Revolution). It is impossible within the limits of a single volume to do justice to a period so vast (1789-1950) crowded with events, fermenting with new ideas, and enriched by the triumphs of invention and discovery. This book will be of great value to students and it will also be attractive to those general readers who seek a clear presentation of this period.

The French revolution is one of the most important events in modern history. The ideas of the revolutionists–Liberty, equality and Fraternity–were admirable. Napoleon's armies by spreading revolutionary doctrines, did much to develop the feeling of nationality which is one of the chief features of 19th century history. After Waterloo Europe experienced a somewhat precarious and unstable peace which lasted nearly for forty years. Conferences were held, but two things definitely prevented any progress towards real international peace. Firstly, the rulers who were restored to their former positions showed that they had learnt little from experience, and secondly, the congress of Vienna which drew up the Paris treaty ignored national aspiration. Further, Europe during the generation which followed Waterloo (1815) was dominated by the Austrian Chancellor (Minister) Metternich, a stern and unchanging conservative. Yet, Liberal and revolutionary aspiration remain alive. In 1830 and again in 1848, popular uprising overthrew constituted authority in many parts of the continent. Meanwhile, another revolution, which was destined to affect still more profoundly the history of mankind took place. This was the industrial revolution which revolutionised the means of production.

In 1848, France became a republic again until Napoleon III imitated his uncle, the great Napoleon by converting his election as President into a personal empire, guaranteed by plebiscite. Napoleon III was instrumental in satisfying the cause of nationality both in Italy and Germany. In both the countries a particular State, Sardinia in Italy and Prussia in Germany were put at the head of the national movement. In both countries the kings of these States, had able Chief Ministers (Cavour and Bismarck) who were master in the tricky art of diplomacy. The Franco-Prussian war (1871) completed the unfication of both Italy and Germany. The peace of Frankfort which concluded the Fraco-German war, was as much an incentive to future strife as the peace of Vienna.

The development of industrialisation in Europe and the consequent growth of the population was creating a demand for raw materials and that is why the exploration of Africa was followed by such a scramble for territory that by the end of the century, it had been completely partitioned. It would hardly be an exaggeration to say that modern imperialism was a direct result of industrial revolution. Besides, a great empire which experienced a breakup in the century following the congress of Vienna was the Ottoman (Turkish) empire. The Balkan problems had much to do with the world war of 1914-18.

The 20th century witnessed the birth of the first communist State in Russia (after the great proletariat revolution in 1917) under Lenin's leadership. Before the century was halfway through its course, two world wars had been fought. After the first world war, a conference met at Paris to draw up conditions of peace. One of the most hopeful features of the settlement was the formation of the League of Nations. Hopes of a freer and happier world received many setbacks, particularly on the continent of Europe, where undermining of authority and weak Governments led to the establishment of dictatorship, which is a negation of democracy. The second World War lasted until 1945. The conclusion of hostilities was quickly followed by the formation of the United Nations, pledged to maintain international peace and security. But once again the world was divided into two military blocs led by the USA and Soviet Union respectively and the cold war fever prevailed in the world. When the world experienced ideological polarisation, India, a land of ancient civilisation proclaimed Non-alignment, which is a moral force in international politics and the movement has sought to uphold the principles of peace and disarmament.

I am indebted to numerous writers whom I have quoted frequently. I would particularly like to thank my colleagues in the Department of History, Rajendra College, Bolangir. I extend my thanks to Prof. D. Sahu,

N. Mishra, N.N. Dash, S.P. Dutta. My acknowledgements are due to the staff of Library, Rajendra College, Bolangir, for their unstinted help in procuring the necessary books and Journals. No formal thanks are enough for the members of my family. I thank Sri A.K. Sahu who typed the manuscript. Above all, I thank to Mr. J.L. Kumar, Managing Director, Anmol Publications Pvt. Ltd., New Delhi for publishing this book

–Siba Prasad Nanda

Chapter-I

Europe in the 18th Century

Socio-economic and Political Conditions of Europe–18th Century

Before we ring up the curtain on the drama of the revolution (French Revolution-1789) we must know something of the socio-economic and political conditions which prevailed not only in France, but in Europe. Eighteenth century Europe nourished the legacies of medieval European society. Society was divided into two classes, the privileged and the unprivileged. The nobility and the clergy belonged to the former category. They paid no taxes, but they still exacted feudal dues from the peasants. The clergy too were exempt from taxes and enjoyed considerable social privileges. They formed a closed class enjoying most of the benefits of the society. The masses and the middle classes constituted the unprivileged class. They were overburdened with taxation. But it was not at all a homogeneous body. Due to the advent of the industrial revolution a new class emerged in the European society known as the middle class. They were mostly industrialists, businessmen and professional people. Even they were intellectually far superior to the nobility. They had been considerably influenced by the intellectual revolution of the 18th century and formed the vanguard of the liberal and constitutional revolutions in Europe. With the growth of intellectual awakening among the unprivileged classes in Western Europe hostility towards the nobility increased. Above all the structure of European society was undeveloped and unprotected.

No single thread had united Western culture more powerfully than Christianity. The enlightenment, however, produced the first widely read and systematic assault on Christianity launched from within the ranks of the educated. The intellectuals argued that many Christian dogmas defied logic. They denounced the churches for inciting the fanaticism and intolerance that led to the horrors of the crusades, and the wars of the reformation. The leaders of the enlightenment sought to repudiate traditional Christianity and to put in its place a rational system of ethics and philosophy based on scientific truths.

In the 18th century a great number of people were chiefly agriculturists. Land was their sole property. They lived in villages. On the other hand, the nobles owned vast lands, and in most countries they were absentee landlords. The peasantry was divided into two classes, the freemen and the Serfs. The former held their lands from tenure and paid rent in cash or in kind. The Serfs had to work in the lord's farms for certain days in the week. The peasantry was extremely poor. They were subjected to various types of taxes imposed on them by the State, the lord and the church. Besides, on account of lack of scientific farming the yield per acre was meagre and peasants usually lived from hand to mouth.

The number of towns since the medieval times had gone up considerably and the middle classes were the backbone of these towns. They were flourishing industrialists and traders. In this period economy was guided by the doctrine of mercantalism. Mercantile economy sought to boost up exports and reduce imports. Free trade was antithesis of mercantalism. In the later half of the 18th century the seeds of an industrial revolution had been planted in England. Overseas commerce brought in a good deal of wealth to the business community. The market led to the growth of industry. The prospects of a lucrative trade with the colonies roused a considerable amount of international commercial rivalry.

On the eve of the French revolution absolute monarchy was the prevailing form of the Government in Europe. The kings claimed "Divine Right" to rule the subjects. According to this the king was the God's representative on earth. As such he was answerable to God only. They ruled according to hereditary dynastic right. Thus, the countries of Europe were ruled by autocrats who used to exploit the common masses along with the feudal lords. The leading royal houses in Europe were the Bourbons of France, the Hohenzollerns of Prussia, the Hapsburgs of Austria, the Romanovs of Russia and the Hanoverians of England.

Enlightened Despotism

According to Prof. Sen, "During the second half of the 18th century Europe witnesses an unprecedented enlightenment which found expression in the social, political, economic, cultural, literary, scientific and artistic aspects of life. The spirit of enquiry and criticism that had characterised the Renaissance during the 16th century continued to create an urge among the educated intelliaentsia of Europe for original thinking in various aspects of human knowledge. A good deal of criticism based on reason was made of the existing political, social, scientific system and practices.... All this led to application of reason to every aspect of human life, which gave rise to knowledge and wisdom called "Enlightenment". The chief trend of enlightenment was rationalism. Human reason was exalted above everything else and was considered to be the only key to the solution of all problems. Rationalism fostered a critical attitude which gave a rude shock to prevalent ideas and institutions. Another characteristic of the thought of the time is its humanity. By humanitarianism was meant regard for natural human rights. The 18th century enlightenment found full expression in the writings of Gibbon, Goethe, Kant, Locke, Adam Smith, Montesquiu, Voltaire, Rousseau, Diterot. Their writings had a profound influence on the minds of the rulers and the ruled in all countries. The rulers patronised the intellectual revolution and called themselves enlighten or Benevolent despots. Their motto was "Everything for the people but nothing by them". The ruler was absolute although his supremacy rested on the assumption that he should rule with an eye to the common good of the nation. The rulers ceased to be selfish. The monarchs were sincerely interested in translating the enlightened views of the philosophers into practice. Throughout Europe there was a serious tendency to increase popular education, to relieve poverty, to emancipate the serfs, to restrain the undue influence of the church etc. Fredrick, the great of Prussia, Catherine, the great of Russia, Joseph II of Austria were typical examples of benevolent despots. However, enlightened despotism failed to solve the problem of the time, which ultimately led to the American war of independnce and the French Revolution.

Austria- Prussia

Austria and Prussia are usually regarded as having been the two most important States of Europe in the 18th century. The most important ruling families in these two States were the Hapsburgs and the Hohenzollerns respectively. The Hapsburgs reigned over the Austrian dominions which included Austria, Bohemia, Syria, Carinthia, Austrian Netherlands (Belgium), Hungary and Lombardy. The Hohenzollern territories also were scattered, and included within the empire, the electorate of Brandenburg, lands on the Rhine, and some other isolated possessions in North Germany. Hapsburgs and Hoheneollerns alike aimed at uniting their separate territories in order to weld them into consolidated states. During the 18th century both Austria and Prussia were antagonistic to each other. In the 18th century, the intellectual and cultural forces of the enlightenment enabled Austria to establish an efficient system of Government. Frusted in their German territories, the Austrian Hapsburgs concentrated their attention on their Eastern States. Vienna gave them a natural power base, while catholic religiosity gradually united the ruling elites in Bohemia and Hungary with their Hapsburg kings. Charles VI, Maria Theresa, Joseph II supported the progressive and reforming elements in the nobility and Austrian administration became one of the most innovative and progressive in the continent. In Prussia, Fredrick, the Great pursued a policy of religious toleration.

Russia

Russia during the 18th century made significant strides, under various monarchs, towards joining the European State system. During the reign of Peter, the Great, the Russians established strong diplomatic ties in almost every European capitals. The Russian metal industry became vital to European development. Catherine the Great consciously pursued policies intended to reflect her understanding of the enlightenment. She promulgated a new, more secular educational system. However, all her reforms came to mean nothing to the teeming millions of Russian peasants and serfs. She kept the Church firmly under her control.

Sweden

The strongest of the Scandinavian kingdoms was Sweden. It had formerly been an important power. Gustavus III, king from 1771-92, strengthened his authority at the expense of the nobles, and aimed at recovering certain part of Finland already lost to Russia. Neither he nor his successor achieved this, and during the coming years the aim of Swedish policy was to secure compensation for lost lands by acquiring Norway from Denmark.

Italy

Italy was divided into several nominally independent States. The country lay under the influence of Austria. Naples and Sicily formed part of the Spanish dominions. In central Italy there were the Papal States with Rome as the centre.

Ottoman Kingdom

The Ottoman empire which had extended upto Hungary in the 16th century was definitely on the decline in the 18th century. It still covered the whole of Balakan peninsula and included a large number of hostile Christian subject of different nationalities. Austria and Russia took advantage of Turkish weakness and both aimed at extending their influence in the Balkan peninsula. By the end of the 18th century the complicated Eastern Question (Turkish Problems) which was the direct product of the

Ottoman empire, was already in existence.

England

During the 18th century, the Hanoverian ruled in England. It was during the rule of George I, and George II that the Whig oligarchy ruled in England. The office of the Prime Minister came into existence under Walpole. England had to fight the Jenkin ear's war, the war of Austrian succession and the seven year's war. Meanwhile, the American war of independence took place and England had to recognise the independence of the American colonies, by the treaty of Versailles. The industrial and the agrarian revolution were making a lot of progress in England and as a result England was leading Europe in the field of agriculture and industrial production. In England there was a constitutional monarchy with a parliamentary form of Government.

France

During the seven years war, France was under the Bourbon king Louis XV. France was engaged in nearly every European war of any importance during the century, and she was involved in contest with Great Britain for naval, colonial and commercial supremacy. Serious financial difficulties resulted from the wars, which did not bring to France gains proportionate to her efforts. The Bourbon kings of France and the Hapsburg rulers of Austria had been opposed to each other in European diplomacy. Sunk in vices, without military vigour, the French kings exercised no effective supervision of the great departments of State.

Thus, politically all European countries with the exception of England were ruled by absolute monarchs on the eve of the French Revolution. In the following century, there was much conflict between conservatism and the forces of liberalism and constitutionalism.

Chapter-II

The French Revolution

The French Revolution was a movement which, in the last decade of the eighteenth century, reconstructed the Government and society of France. It was an incident of that movement that the greater part of Western Europe was temporarily occupied by French armies, and the distribution of its ideas was effected alike by the provisional Government and by the spectacle of revolutionary France. Such a movement was not violently effected by the spontaneous uprising of an oppressed lower class, it was an effort of the whole population directed by men of the professional class against a discredited system of Government and aristocratic privilege. The revolution in Paris was largly conducted by lawyers, and the revolution in Europe was most widely disseminated by the son of a Corsican lawyer. Such men were accessible to the current ideas of their time, and it was from the prevailing philosophy that they drew the principles of 1789.

A mighty upheaval like the French revolution was a composite movement caused by the interaction of various forces which had long been at work. They came to a head in the reign of Louis XVI and burst into a terrific explosion. The revolution roused fervent hopes in the heart of millions within and without France. In the words of Lefebvre, " No event except the Bolshevik revolution of Russia had so much inspired men of modern times as the French revolution." The French Revolution represents a series of violent attempts and apply principles of individual liberty, social equality, and popular national sovereignty–in a word, to establish a new regime of democratic republican nationalism. It is only partially successful. While it engenders a fanatical and Quasi-religious national spirit, it serves to introduce into the nation an enduring conflict between champions and opponents of the new political, and social order. Thus, due to the French revolution Europe relapsed into twenty-five years of great disorder and upheaval which shattered its existing political structure.

The revolution affected the continent of Europe and Peoples began to say, when "France catches cold, entire Europe sneezes."

Political Causes : France was the most advanced and modern of all the continental countries in the second half of the eighteenth century. Yet, the French monarchy was still based on the idea of absolutism and "Divine right theory of kingship". The king of France still treated his realm as a collection of personal and family possession. Henry IV was the founder of the Bourbon dynasty and under him France acquired supremacy over Europe. During the second half of the seventeenth century, Louis XIV had ruled over France with great glory, But, infact, the monarchy had started to lose its strength even during his rule. The States General, i.e. the national assembly of the people had gone out of existence with the establishment of Bourbon monarchy. Under Louis XIV, the French monarchy became absolutist and bureaucratic. Under him the power of the crown reached such a height that he could claim, "the State, it is myself." Above all, Louis XIV, was an absolute monarch, and he could do as he chose, and it was for the nation to obey. The king claimed to rule by the will of God, that it, by "Divine Right", not at all by the consent of the people. Louis XIV became his own Prime Minister. Dignified yet gracious, imposing and majestic, even in trival actions, proud in his self-assurance, he impressed and overawed his subjects by his appearance and delighted them with his industry. Like his royal contemporaries he believed with all his heart in the Divine sanction of his absolutism. The king made the laws, he levied the taxes, he spent them as he saw fit, he declared wars, made peace,, contracted alliances according to his own inclination. Louis XIV's great wars and his architectural and social extravagance ultimately dissipated the riches that colbert (Finance Minister) had stored up and plunged the monarchy into that financial disorder from which it never recovered.

The Grand monarch was succeeded by his great grandson,Louis XV, who was only five years of age when his predecessor dies. He was weak and frivolous, enjoying the sweets of the royal office, while sharing the responsibilities attached to it. The consequences of a centralised Government under an incapable ruler soon manifested themselves. No doubt, Louis XV attempted to exercise direct control over the Government, with consequences only too dire for the stability of the monarchy. According to Madelin, " The king was the chief slave of a system.... which he was powerless to modify. He was the official chief but a slave chief as well, the slave, of his court, his ministry, of tradition....." Louis XV's defects quickly destroyed the popularity that he enjoyed in 1743, when his subject called him Louis the well beloved. He was no dullard, on the other hand, he had a supple mind and quick intelligence. Louis XV, was virtually the grave digger of the Bourbon monarchy. He was concerned primarily with the search of pleasure. He sought escape in a mad and vicious round of pleasures, in hunting, in gambling, in lust, in moving his court from palace to palace, in indulging his caprices, in gratifying the whims and follies of his numerous mistresses and favourites. In his gilded captivity at Court, surrounded by his parasitical courtiers, he cut himself and administration. The task of governing fell to a greedy horde of courtiers who sacrified every interest of the State in order to advance their selfish ends. A disastrous foreign policy, culminating in the humiliation of the seven years war, a capricious Government controlled by royal mistresses, a reckless prodigality of Court expenditure –all these developments opened the gates to the deluge that swept over France. The king did nothing to satiate the discontent of the people. Louis XV, reign ended in 1774 in a chorus of criticism of the monarch. The king that was once well beloved died unmourned.

Louis XVI who succeeded Louis XV in 1774 was weak–willed, though religious, pious, kind and moral. He lacked all those qualities of leadership and kingship which were required at this crucial time in the history of France, when the king was faced with a grave financial and political crisis. Louis XVI was twenty years old at his accession. He cried, "it seems the universe is falling on me," "God what a burden is mine, and they have taught me nothing." Louis was slow of sense and mind. He had many private virtues but he had no capacity to govern and to take decision at the time of need. Under him a prodigal anarchy reigned in France and the king stood a helpless spectator to it. He was moved to action not by some innate force, but by stong pressure from outside, the fears of his wife, the demand of his Ministers. The new king was entirely untrained in the arts of government. He was good, well-intentioned, he had a high standard of morality and duty, a genuine desire to serve his people. He sincerly wanted to introduce necessary reforms but failed because he had not the grit to overcome the obstinate resistance of the privileged classes whose vested interests were threatened by any scheme of reforms. Above all, he was too much under the influence of his young and beautiful queen, the Austrian princess, Marie Antoinette, who was intensly hated by the French people because she was a foreigner. She had a great deal of influence over her husband. Unfortunately the queen, though gracious and sympathetic to certain obvious types of suffering, had no political experience, little political sense, and a narrow view of life that was all the more dangerous as she came to have real power. She was gracious and vivacious, and she had a strong will, a spirit of intitiative, daring, while France was passing through a serious financial crisis and was faced with the problem of food, she was lavishly spending money on her pleasure and was absolutely unconcerned about the miseries of the people. Unfortunately, she did not understand the temperament of the French people or the spirit of the times. She was staunch to friends who deceived her, and her sympathies made her the innocent tool of ambitious factions and Court intrigues. She was proud, fivolous, impatient of all restraint, fond of pleasure and of those who ministered into it. The inefficient king was a mere tool in her hands and could not over-rule her. In the words of Robertson, " Marie Antoinette was that ingnorant, prodigal daughter of the Hapsburgs to whom France seemed only a bottomless purse to be drained for her pleasure ". She unconsciously helped to aggravate the financial situation and thus to hasten the catastrophe.

Kingns have generally been inclined to be builders, to leave imposting memorieals of their reigns in works of architecture, but no king of France ever built so much as Louis XIV. His remarkable achivement was the creation of the palace of versailles, which was the most monumental royal palace in Europe. According to Hazen "Resplended with gold and marble, glittering with mirirors, adorned with paintings, tapstries, medallions depicting the history of the reign, the triumphs of the king, the whole set in the midst of a wonderful park, itself a work of art, with endless lawns, avenues, vistas, terraces, with lakes, fountains, groves, people with marble and bronze statues, with shrubbery cut and kept in geometrical forms, all harmoniously and elaboratly combined, the palace of versailles, when completed, amaze the world by its splendor. Here lived the Court, consisting of the nobles whom Louis had cured of their war-like and independent habits, and whom he had converted into social satellites and parasites. Versailles was the paradise of the spoiled childern of fortune. The spectacle offered by the animated, aesthetic, artifical society was rare and curious." The cultural ascendancey that France had acquired under Louis XIV when the royal court at versailles was a seat the famous writers like Bossuet, Corneil, Recine etc. had been converted into a cock-pit of self-seeking nobles who were busy in exploiting the royal power to further their own interests. The royal court at versailles under the Bourbon became a place for merry making and all sorts of low pleasures. Luxury was every where the prevailing note.

The administration had been highly centralised in the 17th century and continued to be so in the 18th century. Everything in the State was decided by the council at versailles which had hardly anything to devote to the affairs of the State. The development of the central administrative system went back to the remote days of the medieval monarchy. Louis XIV didnot inaugurate the systematized organisation of the Central Government. The council at versailles was terribly over-burdened with work and so the business was allowed to accumulate and quite often by the time the council took action the political condition had changed and the orders passed by it were ineffective. Too much centralization had deprived the local officials of all initiative and unnecessary delay was caused by references to the Central Government even over trival matters. In fact, the king was assisted by five councils which framed the laws, issued the orders, and conducted the business of the State.

The only large administrative units of any significance in France in the century preceding the revolution were the generalities, or intendencies. The intendants, selected at first from the ranks of the midle class, ruled the provinces. These intendants were appointed by the king to carry on the Royal Government, each in his own district. Upon them depended in large measure the happiness or the misery of the provinces. They had the right to administer justice in all royal courts, to preside over inferior courts. They verified the accounts of their subordinate financial administrators and they had a large control over the movement of the military, calling out recruits for the regular army, and directing the activities of municipal police. The power held by the intendants and their subordinates led all thinking men of the eighteenth century to denounce the thirty tyrants of France. The weakness of the governmental system lay not with individual intendants, nor even with the intendants as a class of administrators. It lay first with the theory of Government, in the fact that the never forms of a centralised royal administration were superimposed upon a semi-feudal society in which privileged individual clung tenaciously to prerogratives and secondly with the chaos of the central administration and incompetence of Louis XVI.

According to absolutist theory all justice in France emanated from the monarch, whose officials administered it in his name in the royal courts of justice that were established throughout the entire country. The main reason for the existence of many hundred Courts of regular jurisdiction, is to be found in the procedure of selling public offices during the old regime. Below the thirteen parliaments of the realm, which were the Supreme Courts of appeal in civil and criminal cases, there existed a veritable hodgepodge of courts of primary and appellate jurisdiction. The administration of justice in different courts was cumber some,slow,costly, corrupt, and arbitrary. France had no single code of law either for civil or ccriminal cases, and no attempt was made to codify the laws. Besides, weights and measures had different names and different values as one moved from province to province. This lack of uniformity was the primary cause of confusion. The uncertainty concerning interpretation of the law and the competence of individual courts made the administration of justice not only dilatory, but also expensive. By issuing a writ, the king could remove the offender from the jurisdiction of the regular court and have him tried before any of the many courts of extraordinary royal justice. He could imprison a litigant before he was judged guilty or pardon him after he was convicted. The king could also issue writs, called "letters de cachet" (Arbitrery imprisonment without trial) by virtue of which he could imprison any subject without inquiry and trial, so long as it pleased the royal will. It is well to note that the "letter de cachet" was also used to gratify personal caprices or hatreds and that, in any case it constituted a flagrant violation of what enlightened minds then considered the most elementary personal rights of the individual. The Parliament of Paris and the twelve Parliaments were the highest Tribunals of the realm, Supreme Courts of appeal for civil and criminal cases. During the reign of the imperious Louis XIV the Parliaments passively accepted the royal edicts.

In France there was a Council of Notables besides the States General (The French parliament). This council would be called to session in circumstances of extreme necessity. When Louis XVI failed to remedy the desperate financial situation his Finance Minister summoned the council of Notables to assist the Government to raise money by levying tax, but the council refused to agree to the proposal of taxation. On the other hand the Parliament of Paris which used to record all laws passed by the kind, was asked to record the imposition of a tax levied by the king which the Parliament flatly refused to do. This was as good as a revolt of the Parliament of Paris which had already pointed out that no tax could be levied except by the States General which was the national assembly of France. This was an expression of the democratic spirit of the French Nation. Besides, the French did not have the right to hold public meetings or to form associations. Liberties which had been in vogue in England for centuries, which were the priceless heritage of the English race, were unknown in France. It is not strange that liberty and equality became the battle cry of the revolution.

Social Causes

In the pre-revolutionary period, the society was divided into two classes- the privileged and non-privileged. The privileged class included the nobility and the higher clergy and the unprivileged class included the bourgeoisie or middle class citizens, the labourers and the peasants. The privileged class enjoyed a total or patial exemption from taxation and had a monopoly of honours and emoluments. The clergy were called the first estate i.e. the first class, the clergy constituted only one percent of the popultion of the country but they were owners of one-fifth of the landed properties in France. On the other hand, they did not pay any tax to the State, rather they enjoy the right themselves to tax, the clergy through its right to tithes, the nobility through its right to exact feudal dues. Practically, the third estate bore the whole burden of taxation and were at the same time excluded from all places of authority. The unprivileged classes had no rights but were saddled with galling obligations. Thus, in a period when more and more people were talking about the equality and the natural rights of all men, the class structure in France showed glaring inequality and a wide variation in rights.

The Clergy

The clergy made up the first class or estate of France, and the Church, that is, the corporation of the clergy, was the most influential corporate body in the kingdom. It exercised an extraordinary influence in governmental administration, and held a dominant position in the life of the nation. But the first estate or clergy, was itself characterised by inequality. The high Churchmen-archbishops, bishops, abbots often enjoyed great wealth drawn from church landholdings and from tithes (A kind of religious tax). They lived with pomp and ceremony. The higher clergy monoplised all the lucrative church offices but were quite indifferent to their spiritual duties. They were recruited from the younger sons of the nobility and they conducted themselves as typical man of the world, being devoted to self-advancement and given to the pleasures, intrigues and dissipation of the court. The morals of many were scandalous, and their intellectual ability was mediocre . No doubt, some of the aristocratic churchmen were pious and hard working, but others were arrogant and worldly.

In sharp contrast, were the lower ranks of the clergy. In mode of life no less than in outlook, in birth and social status, the lower clergy were totally distinct from their ecclesiastical superiors. The lower clergy, who did the real work of spiritual consolation and instruction were wretchedly recompensated, with low income of a few hundred Frances, and they had difficulty in keeping body and soul together. The daily task of the Parish priest were many and trying. He dwelt in the midst of his flock, ate the rough food of his parishioners, wrapped his gaunt form in tattered, threadbare garments and trod the oft impassable country roads on his errands of faith and mercy. The peasants held him in high reverence and looked to him for the solution of their homely problems. In the rural villages the priest was often the guide, philosopher, and friend of his flock. Relations between the upper and lower clergy were an exchange of arrogance on the one part and open or suppressed hostility on the other. The Parish clergy demanded a voice at the periodic assemblies of the clergy, they demandned an end to the abuse of the titles, they asked for a break-up of the monopoly of promotions which the nobles guarded so jealously. They resented the insulting attitude of the upper clergy, who looked down upon them as a race apart-"dirty and ignorant". The lower clergy formed a discontented class ready to join hands with the common people against the abuses of favouritism and absolutism. Thus, the utter absence of solidarity in its own ranks weakened it from within.

The Nobility

The nobility constituted the second estate of the realm. The rank of nability was acquired by birth, by military service, by the purchase of patents of nobility, or by the possession of certain public offices. The noble in France, who constituted, the second estate, formed a heriditary caste, and they kept themselves aloof from the commoners and were very jealous of their rights. The nobility were divided into two sections, nobles by birth and nobles by office, of course there were two main classes, the nobility of the sword and the nobility of the robe. The nobility of the sword consisted of the nobles of the court and of the nobles of the provinces. At the top of the ladder were the nobles of the court, the princes of the blood and all the wealthy and distinguised noblemen who had been officially presented to the king. According to Hazen, "The nobles of the court were few in number....but they shone with peculair brilliancy, for they were the ones who lived in versailles, danced attendance upon the king, vied with each other in an eager competition for appointment in the army and navy and diplomatic service, for pensions and largesses from the royal bounty.... Everybody was jeolous of the nobles of this class,for they were the favored few, who practically monopolised all the pleasant places in the Sun. In fact, the great nobles formed a background for the king. They do not pay any direct taxes and were exempted from a number of indirect ones. Rather they levied their dues on the peasantry living on their estates and claimed exclusive hunting, shooting and fishing rights. Montesquieu acidly defined a great noble "as a man who saw the king, spoke with his ministers, and had ancestors debts, and pensions." In real influence, the nobility of robe, which included the Magistrates of the Parliaments and other soverign courts, easily outranked the more ornamental and wasterful nobles at court. In the eighteenth century the nobility of the robe became a varitiable caste, as rich commoners no longer bought posts in the judiciary. But despite, their wealth they remained a group apart, a sort of judicial clergy, holding aloof from the profane, officiating in the severe solemnity of their luxurious and imposing interiors into which none but a Magistrate may penetrate. Public opinion favored them. On the other hand, there were large number of lesser or provincial nobles who lived on their estate, patched up their crumbling mansion, and showed pride in their coats of arms, their horses, and their dogs. Many of them had small incomes, and they could cut no figure in the world of society, they had few chances to increase their prosperity. If they could ever effort to come to Paris or versailles, they were treated like country bumpkins. Their sons were trained for the army, but could never hope to rise very high because all the major appointments went to the assiduous suitors of the clique at Court. Long before 1789 the nobility was destined for destruction. The internal strife of this class destroyed its solidarity. Further, enlightened public opinion condemned the wasteful, parasitic existence of this privileged class.

The Third Estate (Bourgeoisie)

Below the privileged orders, was the vast majority of population called the third estate. But it was not a homogeneous body. It comprised the bourgeoisie or the upper middle class, the artisans and the peasants. The most powerful element of the third estate was the bourgeoisie–the merchants, bankers, businessmen, manufactures, and professional men who lived in towns or cities. They formed the well-to-do intelligent and the energetic section of the community. Even the bourgeoisie section of the third estate was superior to the clergy and nobility in education, initiative and even in wealth, but although superior to the upper classes on all counts, the bourgeoisie was not entitled to enjoy any privilege, but they had to bear the burden of the tax. Conscious that they were as good as the nobles they keenly resented the existing system under which they were made to feel in numerous ways their social inferiority. The bourgeoisie had the monopoly of all advantages, political, social and economic. They wanted abolition of state control over trade, commerce and industries. They nourished a strong grivance against the Government for the restrictions imposed on their trade. Further, this class was not in favour of the French monarchy which was being controlled by the nobility. They bought the works of the great writers of the century, mingled in the society of the salons, and joined clubs, where they discussed the new liberal and radical ideas. Their pride and self-respect were wounded by the social discrimintation and the deliberate snubs administered by the nobility. They demanded a voice in the Government. In 1788-89 their role in undermining the old regime was particularly prominent. There was growing among these bourgeoisie a sense that they did not have social esteem, political influence or economic privilegs corresponding to their wealth or eduction. They felt themselves to be the backbone of the country and the basis of its prosperity. It irked them to see a foppish noble or an idle churchman take precedence over them in society, and even escape payment of most of the taxes. Their mood was brilliantly expressed by a pamphlet written by Abbe Sieyes, which circulated on the eve of the revolution. "What is the third estate? Everything, What was it been in politics until now ? "Nothing". What does it desire? "To become something".

The Artisans

The artisans and labourers, although belonging to the third estate, were much worse off than the bourgeoisie. They were a comparatively small class because the industrial life of France was not yet highly developed. They were completely at the mercy of the rich middle class which controlled commerce and industry through guilds and similar close corporations.

The Peasants

If there was cause for discontent, the peasantry had more reason to be restive than the bourgeoisie. France was still a predominantly agricultural country, and it was on the backs of the peasantry that the other classes were borne. The condition of the peasantry, who formed by far the largest section of the population, was deplorable in the extreme. Their liveihood was most insecur, and majority of them were tenant farmers whose rights on land was precarious. The peasants had to pay rent to his feudal lord, tithes to the church and taxes to the king. They paid nearly sixty per cent of what they were able to earn. The whole burden of taxation fell with a crushing weight upon them, specially in view of the fact that the privileged orders were more or less exempt from taxation. The king claimed both direct and indirect taxes. The direct taxes comprised the taille or the land tax, a poll tax per head, and income-tax which amounted to one-twentieth of the peasants income. The State's share of taille was not fixed and was arbitrarily adjudged by the cruel tax collectors. So there was a tendency among them to live very frugally and to make no improvements in their standard of living. But whatever his status, the peasant was subject to a number of vexations burdens. If he owed no labour, he paid a quit rent. If he sold his farm, part of the price went to the lord. It he took his goods to the market, he often had to pay market fees. Under a system of benalities, his grain must be ground, his grapes pressed, and his bread baked at the lords mill, press, or oven, and a fee paid for the privilege. Only the lords could hunt, and he could and often did run his horses and dogs over the peasants new crops. Besides,, the indirect taxes comprised salt tax or gabelle, customs and excise duties and corvee or forced labour on the roads. The bulk of the kings income was derived from the masses. Three principal causes determined the steady decline in fortune of the French peasantry:

(1) sharp and continous growth in population, (2) a marked upward movement of prices, (3) the influence of the physiocrats in stimulating agrarian reforms. The peasants required only a signal to breakeout in revolt and it was their active participation that made the revolutionary movement of 1789 a success.They needed no propaganda to formulate their grievances against the established order. They wanted equality of taxation, abolition of the manorial system with all its abuses, and the local application of the tithes for education and poor relief. The peasants, who knew nothing of statecraft, who were ignorant of the destructive and subversive theories of voltaire and Rousseau, were nevertheless daily and hourly impressed with imperative necessity of reforms by the hard circumstances of their lives. They simply knew that the feudal dues would have to be abolished, that the excessive exactions of the State would have to be reduced before their lives could become tolerable.

Intellectual Causes–The influence of the French Philosophers

As France was moving towards revolution due to the desperate political, social, and economic conditions during the 18th century, there was also going on a mental preparation for revolution. The spirit of rationalism that was influencing the thought and outlook of the Europeans during the second half of the 19th century had directly contributed to prepare the French nation for the revolution of 1789. The 18th century was an age of Reason and witnessed a good deal of intellectual activity. It was an age of enlightenment and its characteristics were scepticism, Rationalism, Humanism and Deism. The writings of the philosophers had a tremendous influence on the minds of the people and created a revolutionary awakening in their mindns and formed the intellectual creed of the French revolution. The philosophers contributed a lot to the rise of intellectual revolution by their satirical writings and infused a new spirit of revolution in the people's heart. The thought of the 18th century was not only critical and solvent, it was also,itself, a new creed and, a new fanaticism. A galaxy of philosophers criticised the existing order of things in State, society, and the Church and tried to find the national basis of old traditions and institutions. According to Hazen "Literature was a lusty and passionate champion of reform and through it a flood of new ideas swept over France. Many of these ideas were of foreign origin.... The books which issued in such profusion from the facile pens and teeming brains of Montesquieu, Voltaire, Rousseau, Diderot.... and many others stirred the intellectual world to its depth. In the words of Ketlby "within the society of malcontents, working upon them and among them like leaven, were writers, stimulating them, pointing their discontent, dissolving the traditions which along held them together, voicing their grivances, giving them a leadership, and a faith, for in a land of no Parliament the men of letters had come to be the peoliticians". The philosophers focussed the people's attention to the defects in the prevalent political, social and economic systems and held out a picture of better life and living before them. According to Grant and Temperly "France held the foremost place in the world of thought.... But in reality the French were merely the leaders of a general movement, long heralded by the work of such men as Locke and Leibnitz". The philosophers put their literary ability to the practical purpose of moulding public opinion in favour of a fundamental transformation of society. Reason impelled them to attack the forces of superstition, ignorance, and folly that perpetuated an incompetent administration, a crushing financial system, a barbarous Judicial procedure, religious cruelity, and economic waste and confusion. The philosophers knew that times were out of joint because they were sensitive to obvious injustices and suffering. Indeed for all mankind, the philosophers were the standard bearers of faith that spread from France through all civilised world. Their common credo may be stated as belief in the soverignity of the people and in the rights of man. By liberty they meant civil and individual liberty, liberty of thought, and expression, by equality and fraternity they meant the abolition of special privileges for the aristocracy and the opening of carrers to talent. The State, they maintained, exists only for the benefit and the happiness of all its citizens. The philosophers were hopeful that ordinary men and women through the exercise of their reason and will could form a society in which they could develop and realize all their natural faculties. In creating the intellectual awakening in France, the following philosophers played a notable part.

Montesqieu

The true intellectual revolution in France started with Montesquieu (1689-1755). He belonged to an aristocratic family. He was only too well aware of the perils of the censorship and realized that his criticism would have to be indirect to win the approval of the wide public in the capital. This accountns for the spectacle of a serious Magistrate, a President of the Parliament of Boredeaux, penning the mildly licentious persian letters and using the literary device of having two persian travelling in Paris describe, in a correspondence with their countrymen in persia, the principal feautres of life at the French capital. in his "persian letters" he ridiculed the corruption of the court, condemned the privileges, financial administration and denounced the vices of fanaticism and intolerance. In his spirit of laws", he openly attacked the absolute monarchy of France. The "sprit of laws" was largly influenced by the English Constitution. He praised a limited

Government, a machinary of checks and balances, and admired in the English practice what he called the "separation of powers". He stressed in the "spirit of laws" that power of executive, Legislature and judiciary should be separated completely. If all these three kinds of duties are placed in the same hand then there would be no individual liberty. Montesquieu had made an original contribution to political science and the Americans adopted his ideas when they drafted their Constitution and incorporated the principle of the separation of powers in it. According to Hazen, "Montesquieu's masterpiece, "the spirit of the laws" was a storehouse of wisdom destined to the provocating of much thought, discussion and action both in France and else where".

Voltaire

The foremost champion of reason and tolerance during the 18th century and perhabs of all time was Voltaire, a master of biting satire enjoyed almost autocratic authority by rason of his powerful writing. His thought never went deep, and he has made no original contribution of importance to any side of European thought, but he was the most powerful influence in popularising ideas that Europe has ever known. His name is permanently associated with the campaign whose motto was, crush the infamous things, which was the most earnest, the most deadly in its effectiveness, and yet the most intellectually amusing offensive ever launched by a person of genius against religious authority. He was born in 1694 A.D. in a middle class family. Voltaire was a philosopher, historian, poet, dramatist and satirist of his age. In the words of Hazen "Voltaire's name has become the name of an era....His significance to his times is shown in the title men conferred on him....king Voltaire. He was a pillar of cloud by day and of fire by night for all who enlisted for the liberation of mankind". He was a prolific writer. In 1733, his observation about the Englishmen were published in a volume entitled "Letters on the English". By describing a country where opinion was free and the Government constitutional, where religious persecution was unknown, where the middle class were socially as respectable as the nobility, where civil liberties were guaranteed and men of letters were honoured, Voltaire pointed the absence of all those praise worthy features from French life. He denounced the abuses of the State, but directed his attack against the bigotry and intolerance of the Church. His ideal of Government was a benevolent despotism. He was deeply influenced by the Deistic philosophy and launched tirade against the Church and the clergy. Voltaire was not athestic and he accepted the fundamental tenets of natural religion. What he attacked were the particular dogmas, the accretions of theology, the complex mysteries and contradictory ceremonials of Christianity that through the ages had engendered fanaticism, persecution, and bloodshed, suppressed reason, and persecuted free thought. In his "philosophical dictionary," he denounced the Church as an infamous thing. All the rotton pillars of old order came under his fire. His fiery shafts did much to undermine the respect for authority and loosened the hold of the church and State on the minds of the people. Above all, his writings had a tremendous effect on millions of people not only in France but in the whole of Europe.

Rousseau

Rousseau has been righitly called the prophet of the revolution. He was the son of a Genevan watchmaker, and his education was such as is derived from a wandering life, an assortment of occupation, and an ardent, a varied, but desultory private reading. From earliest boyhood he was virtually alone in the world, undisciplined, untaught, and left to grow up without guidance. When he was sixteen years old, he ran away from his native city of Geneva, where he had apprenticed to an engraver. He was a homelses wanderer. He drifted from point to point and faileld in one occupation after another. His private life was miserable and he was a very maladjusted man. Rousseau had experienced in his own life the bitterness of poverty, and hence the offsprings of this great intellectual had to be brought up in orphanage. Both by his mode of life before and after 1749 and in the books that he wrote in rapid succession -"the origin of inequality", the new Heloise, "Emile", "the social contact", he preached a gospel of spiritual revolution. According to Hazen "Rousseau propounded his fundamental thesis that man, naturally good and just and happy, had been corrupted by the very thing he called civilisation". A society in which the few live in luxury and the many toil in wretchdness, in which a few men of rank profit by the inferiority of the great majority, in which a false education sets at naught the values of virtue and humanity, such a society is corrupt to the core. To alter it is beyond the limits of reasons power, the only society in which man can be happy is one in which he is free to follow the dictates of his spiritual being and to live in virtuous harmony with the purposes of nature. Rousseau of Geneva was neither a philosopher nor a materialist, but a visionary. He held a supreme position among all the philosophers and he influenced the society more than anybody else.

In his book' Discourse on the origin of inequality", he has analysed the inequality, dishonesty, fraud and exploitation of the modern civilisation. The political influence of Rousseau's "social contract" was incalculable, not only in France, but in all Europe. In his most famous book, "Social Contract", that revolutionary tissue of 17th century political theory and calvinist theology, he propounded a new theory of social salvation. He followed Locke's philosophy of the two treaties of Government in arguing that all men had certain natural rights and liberties, which were life, liberty, and property, and that men no longer owed obedience to any Government that failed to protect them in those rights and liberties. He said, "man was born free, but everywhere he is in chains". So back to nature was his constant cry. He should return to his primitive innocence and happiness, and destory the institution that had enslaved him. If men had the right to make the contract to establish the government they certainly had the right to break it and to replace the government if it was not just. He believed that the soverighity of the state depended on the will of the people. Laws should be the expression of the "General will". The collective will of the people, called the "General will" was the soverign power. In the justly organised society of his vision each individual would put his person and his power under the supreme direction of the "General will", and agree to act only for the common good. In renouncing his natural rights and liberties to the "General will", each individual recognised that the "General will" of the community was the real will of all the separate members of the community. Hence, people who expressed the "General will" were the soverign. This was Rousseau's famous doctrine of the social contract, which brilliantly formulated the revolutionary theory that the people are soverign and that government derive their legitimate authority from the consent of all the governed. The good state is based not on force nor on greed, but on the virtuous will of all its members. Rousseau contributed to the popular notion of modern democrasy and gave the French revolutionaries their famoaus slogan of "Liberty, Equality and Fraternity". According to ketlby, "the theory of social contract may be untenable, but it was only another way of saying that those who govern must recognise their responsibilities. The people of France were suffering because the interests of the crown were divorced from those of the state, because the noble no longer fought, and the clergy no longer prayed, because the social contract was broken..... So Rousseau become the immortal seducer of unquiet souls, the oracle of whoever feels himself misunderstood and disinherited, the philosopher of the new romanticism of self-affirmation, the evangelist of human consolation as the final measure of truth, the hot gospeller of temporal salvation, the prophet of the new coming age of secular society". Thus, Rousseau's social contract was the gospel of democracy, of the divine right to the people and the infallibility of their decisions. Lord Morley has paid glowing tribute to Rousseau in these words, "Rousseau spoke words that could never be unspoken and he kindled a hope that could never be extinguished. He made a tremendous impact upon France by his revolutionary thoughts".

The Encyclopaedists and the Physiocrats

There were also writers like Dennis Diderot, Helvetius, Holbach, Quesnai. To Diderot, perhabs, the most typical man of his age in his skepticism and hopefulness, in his inquisitiveness and his energy, fell the self-imposed task of systematizing the new knowledge. With D' Alembert, Holbach and Helvetius he carried to completion the task of editing the colossal encyclopaedie. They effected a synthesis of the essential ideas of the age of enlightnment in politics, religion, morals, metaphysics, and economics. They hated unjust things, condemned slavery, inequality of taxation, corruption of justice and the wastefulness of war. The encyclopaedie was a more successful vehicle for the propagation of the spirit and the ideals of the philosophers. The government was terrified by the fearless thought of the encyclopoedist. The encyclopaedie reflected the scepticism and rationalism of the enlightened age. They possessed power of conversion and indomitable perseverence and they had an ardent desire for the improvement of mankind. Similarly, the economic system of France was strongly criticised by a group of economists also known as physiocrats. They bitterly condemned the prevailing doctrine of mercantalism and state interference in trade and commerce. They advocated complete free trade. Their central doctrine, from which the name physiocrats was derived was the belief held by the founder of their school, that the land was the sole source of wealth. Free production and free distribution was their goal, and the only regulation they recognised was that supplied by the natural law of supply and demand and by man's enlightened self-interest. However, the physiocrats believed in the regeneration of society through the enlightened action of one central authority. Their writings had great influence on the course of the French revolution.

Historians hold divergent opinion as regards the responsibility of the philosophers for the outbreak of the French Revolution. The philosophers made the middle classes conscious both of their grivances and of their power, and they supplied a new basis of authority in their doctrines of civil liberty and constitutional self government. The philosopher's new ideas and theories upset men's convictions and changed their outlook. According to Mallet, "The seeds sown by these remarkable writers fell upon fruitful soil....Thinkers were full of illusions, fulll of hope". The philosophers created an atmosphere of freedom of thought. Their writings exposed the evils of the old regime, focused public attention upon them, compelled discussion and aroused the passion of the people. The philosophers prepared the people's mind for a revolutionary change. But according to Thomson "The connection between the ideas of the French philosophers and the outbreak of the French revolution is remote and indirect". In the words of Hazen

"The revolution was not caused by the philosophers, but by the conditions and evils of the national life and by the mistakes of the government". Still the general influence of the new philosophy of enlightenment was enormous. Through the salons, it penetrated into the French academy. Though the revolution was the out come of realities it cannot be denied that without the help of enlightenment it could never have arisen". According to Hazen, "They did not cause the revolution, but they exposed the causes brilliantly, focussed attention upon them, compelled discussion and aroused passion". In fact, the mental revolution became the foundation of the French revolution.

Financial Causes

The finances of France were in a deplorable state. Almost half of the interest on the national debt and expenditure were always larger than receipts. The rulers regarded the national income as their personal income. The French Government spent beyond its means in profitless war. The royal household was guilty of extravagent expenses in feasts and keeping vast number of jobless servants. The Bourbon's love for war, mismanagement, and mal-administration also affected the royal treasury otherwise, and the national debts of France had gone quite high. The debt steadily grew and to meet the chronic deficit the Government was forced to resort to the sale of offices, new loans etc. On the eve of the outbreak of the French revolution. France was under the teeth of a severe inflation. The new monarch Louis XVI was virtuous but dull witted, well-meaning, but lacking in decision. The common people bore the burnt of taxation. They paid both direct and indirect taxes. Nearly fifty per cent of their income was snatched away in taxation.

The policy of taxation was full of anomaly. Those who were the wealthiest and therefore the best able to support the state were the very ones who paid the least. Further, the internal and local customs hampered free circulation of goods from one part of the country to the other. The imposition of local customs not only harassed trade but also multiplied the price of goods. The taxation system was shockingly unjust and scandalously oppressive. Besides the method of realising the revenue was also faulty. The revenue was collected not by state officials but by private individuals and companies. The revenue collector used to realise more than that was due from the farmers but deposited in royal treasurey only a part of it and thus, appropriated a good amount for their own use. On the one hand, the expenses of the state on wars and luxuries went on mounting, on the other its resources were limited and had already been completely drained. When Louis XVI ascended the throne, France was on the verge of bankruptcy. But in spite of that France joined the war of American independence. French participation in the war of American independence up-set the finances of the country, without a change in the fiscal system the government could not pay its way, for the noble would not pay, while the commons could not pay. On the other hand, the French Government persistently followed a policy of meeting the deficit by raising public loans at a high rate of interest. The only way to cure these ills was to increase direct tax on the people who enjoyed immunity from payment of taxation. Both the king and the nobles failed to appreciate the gravity of the financial crisis and did not realize that if the ship of state foundered on the rock of financial bankruptcy, the nobles would also sink along with the king. The nobles remained adament, and the king continued to vacillate. To a Bishop or a noble it seemed ridiculous to expect a high born person to pay taxes like a merchant or a peasant. The privileged classes were so entrenched in the courts, the church, and the government, and so well defended by law, tradition, and precedent, that they were able to block any attempt to alter the existing system. Thus, at his succession Louis XVI was faced with a serious financial situation. So the king entrusted the management of the finance to a man of rare ability and he was none else than Turgot.

Turgot

The king Louis XVI appointed Turgot as his Finance Minister. His charecter and his writings had already made him wellknown, and he had valuable experience as intendant of the province of Limous-in. On the subject of finances his mind was made up. In the first place he would institute a policy of the strictest retrenchment. In a letter to the king he outlined his views, "No bankruptcy, no new taxes, and no loans". He hoped to extricate the national finances by two processes, by effecting economics, and by developing public wealth so that the receipts would be larger. By rigid economy he did effect gratifying savings for the treasury, though his example did not influence the monarch to cut down royal pensions and gifts and court expenditure. He proposed industry and commerce were to be unshackled, and tax burden rendered less crushing on the lower classes by transferring a propertionate share of it to the nobles and clergy. The peasants were to be freed from forced labour, but by these he only stirred up opposition. He was strongly opposed by the nobles and the clergy. His enemies, led by Marie Antoinette, prevailed upon Louis XVI to dismiss him (Turgot). Finanlly he was dismissed in 1776 and Louis XVI called upon the most famous of the bankers Necker to take charge of finance.

Necker

The man summoned was the Genevan banker, Necker. He was well-known in Paris as a hard headed swiss banker. He was a skillful financier, but not a great statesman. During his five years in office (1776-81) Necker sought to apply business methods to government finances. At first he resorted to new loans and administrative reforms. He suppressed many unnecessary offices, simplified the accounting system. He published a financial report, showing the income and the expenditures of the state. It mentioned the sources of income but at the same time it drew the attention of the masses to the colossal expenditure at court. The royal circle regarded the step as dangerous, and Necker was dismissed from office.

Calonne

In 1783, the king appointed Calonne, an experienced intendant and a highly intelligent and resourceful person, to the pivotal position of controller general (Finance Minister). Meanwhile France was engaged in still another big war, the war of American independence. Due to the French involvement in the American war of independence the French treasury heavily indebted at the beginning of the war, was on the verge of bankruptcy at its close. He warned the nobles of the impending catastrophe, but the latter would not surrender their privileges. His great mostrum for financial ailment was the restoration of public confidence, and he averred the best way to restore confidence, was to give the appearance of prosperity. Therefore, he threw economy to the winds and expanded the credit of the government by borrowing from the capitalist To Quote Hazen, "A men who wishes to borrow must appear to be rich, and to appear rich he must dazzle by spending freely". Thus, an artificial prosperity set in, and towards 1786 the process of deflation had set in, and the confidence of the capitalists vanished more rapidly than it had been restored. On his advice the king invited the meeting of the assembly of the Notabales to meet in 1787. They were not a constitutional body, nor representative in any way. They consisted of members of the privileged classes. The Assembly of the notables recommended to summoned the States General to solve the question of taxation.

THE SUMMONING OF THE STATES GENERAL AND FALL OF THE OLD REGIME

The importance of the financial situation now became political, and deficit grew steadily larger, and the notables met and did nothing. Calonne fell and was succeeded by Brienne. The conflict now shifted back to the

Parliaments, where the lawyers, in the novel character of popular heroes, rejected every proprosal of the crown. The Parliament of Paris extended its activities from the bare confirmation of decrees to à more active interference with executive acts, its example was followed by the provincial Parliaments and assemblies. The Parliament of Paris, in unintentional self-effacement, demanded a summons of the states General, and the king assented dubiously. Brienne fell, and Necker returned to office. The well-intentioned Louis XVI finanlly yielded to the popular demand and summoned the States-General (Assembly) to meet in versailles on May 1, 1789. The States-General or the feudal Parliament of France was a three chambered body composed of the elected representatives of the three orders, the clergy, the nobles and the commons. Its last meeting had taken place in 1614. It consisted when it met of 308 clergy, 285 nobles, and 621 deputies of the third Estate. When it was revived at a time of great national crisis, the question of its constitution assumed paramount importance. Whenever it was summoned, the three estate met, deliberated and voted separately and the votes of any two estate could out-weight the votes of the third estate, irrespective of the strength of each estate. The first two chambers being composed of the privileged classes, the third estate, i.e., the commons were left in a permanent minority, so the action of the privileged orders had always been decisive. There was objection to this now, since, with two against one, it left the nation exactly where it had been, in the power of the privileged classes. They could veto anything that the third estate wanted.

In 1788-89 elections to the several estates were held throughout France. In accordance with old customs, and royal request, the electors drafted reports on the conditions of their respective localities and recommendations for their representatives and for the Government. These recommendations for reform were called cahiers. A large number of cahiers were unanimous in supporting a monarachical form of government and in demanding reforms and abolishing inequalities. When the States General met at versailles in May 1789, neither the king nor his ministers had worked out a programme for it. As soon as the States General met, two grave issues raised their heads. Firstly, the third estate demanded a joint session of all the three estate. In the past they had sat separately. Secondly, the third estate demanded voting by "Heads" and not by "order", i.e., the three estates should not vote separately, but that all the estates should vote together and the majority decision should be final and binding. At the outset the king welcomed the members of the States General, and apparently expected them to devote themselves to financial problems. The king neither assured a constitution for the country, nor he spoke a word about the voting right. The people felt discontented and the king by his weak policy diverted their attention towards revolt. A conflict between the orders began on May 6 mainly relating to an important question, should the voting be by order or by members? The members of the third estate demanded that the three orders were to meet as a single chamber in which each individual should have a vote. The commons at any rate determined to fight for a single house. The members of the thirid estate wished all the delegates to meet together and to vote by head or as individuals, so that their extra numbers would give them real power. The clergy and the nobles offered a stubborn resistance. The third estate invited the other orders to sit with it and to work together for the reformation of France. At last the third estate took the momentous step of declaring itself the National Assembly on June 17,1789. The action was no doubt revolutionary as it was not sanctioned by the Constitution of France.

Tennis Court Oath

On June 20, 1789, the king closed the assembly hall in order to prevent the session of the national assembly. The members of the third estate took a revolutionary step. Led by Abbe Sieyes and Mirabeau, they proceeded to a large near by building used normally as a tennis court. There a memorable session occured, 600 deputies surging round Bailly, their president, whom they had lifted on to a table, and taking, with right hands stretched out to heaven, the oath which was to shake the monarchy, an oath never to allow themselves to be dissolved until the constitution had been established and set on a firm foundation. This tennis court oath was the actual beginning of the French Revolution, for in it the representatives of the third estate were going against the orders of the king and far beyond the purposes for which they had been summoned.

On 23rd June, 1789 occured the royal session and the king declared the acts of the third estate as illegal. He further declared that the three orders should meet separately. The king left the hall, the nobles followed than the clergy. The commons remained behind in a gloomy silence. This was one of solemn, critical moments of history. Suddenly the master of ceremonies advanced and said, "His majesty requestes the deputies of the third estate to withdraw". At this Mirabeau, a noble who had cast in his lot with the people, gave vent to a very strong experession hurling defiance at king's orders, and with thunderous voice exclaimed, "Go tell your master that we are here by the will of the people and that we shall not leave except at the point of baynot". The king perceiving the firm resolution of the commoners, gave way and ordered the clergy and nobility to join the third estate, and thus the formation of the National Assembly was completed. So by the end of June 1789, the stage was set for a radical alteration in the traditional political institutions and social structure of France. In fact, it was the first scence of the drama.

The Fall of Bastille

The next scene of the drama was laid in Paris. Before the assembly could proceed with its labours, it had to face still another change of front on the part of the king. For early in July 1789, a gradual transfer of royal troops from the Eastern frontier to the vicinity of Paris and versailles indicated that the king was preparing to use force against the assembly. The assembly at once requested the removal of troops. In reply the king dismissed the popular Minister Necker, which alarmed the common men to a great extent. Paris was on the side of the assembly, and when the news of the dismissal of Necker arrived it took fire. The destiny of the revolution lay in the hands of the Parisians. The excitement in Paris became feverish when one of the fiery revolutionary journalists, Desmoulins, denounced the impending massacre of patriots. He exclaimed, "We have only one course of action to rush to arms". The crowd rushed out and paraded the streets. From shop to shop the swelling crowed scurried in quest of arms, its rank increased by many lawless recruits and by the French guard. The mob was unchecked all through the night of July 12, breaking into shops and pilfering. Finally, on July 14, the mob attacked the Bastille, a hateful symbol of despotism and oppression. Within a few hours the mob was in possession of the Bastille, and the defenders, most of whom were mercenaries were slaughtered. The fall of the Bastille was everywhere regarded in France as a triumph of liberty and produced a widespread enthusiasm. On 15th July, the king came before the assembly to report that he had ordered the royal troops to leave versailles, and on the following day he recognised the new Muncipal government of Paris. The king recognised Bailly as the mayor of Paris and Lafayette as commander of the National guard. The French celebrate July 14, as the anniversary of the birth of their popular freedom.

When the news of the fall of Bastille came, the anarchy reigned in the provinces. The news that the Bastille had fallen only acccentuated the panic and anarchy by making the fears more credible and encouraging the violance of the peasants. The rural police were powerless to curb the anarchy. The proprietors of feudal land were not the sole victims of the great fear, for the artisans in the towns also rose against their old oppressors, harsh judges, corrupt officials, moneylenders, and grasping merchants. Monasteries were pillaged, landowers were murdered, intendants left their posts and courts ceased to function. The old regime was infact crumbling.

The fall of the Bastille rendered Paris practically independent of royal control, for during the period of disorder, prominent citizens organised their own government. The local government, the commune, as it was called, was made up of those elected representatives of the various sections of Paris who had chosen the city's delegates to the estate general. The king also confirmed the appointment of liberal Lafayette as commander of the National guard, Louis XVI put on a red white and blue cockade combining the red and blue of the capital city with the white of the Bourbons, the new national tricolour of France. In a memorable session of the National assembly on the 4th of August, 1789, the nobles voluntarily surrendered their feudal rights and privileges. Rights of hunting, corvees, and other customary services were abolished and tithes were abandoned, class distinction were abolished and the principle of equality was declared to be the basis of the state and society. In an indescribable and sustained movement of interested and disinterested self-sacrifice, deputy after deputy arose to renounce his special rights and privileges on the alter of his country. In their joy the deputies decided to proclaim Louis XVI "the restorer of French liberty". Hence, the last relic of feudalism swept out of France. On the whole, the August decrees outlined a comprehensive program of social, economic, and religious reforms.

Later on, the king refused to accept the work of August. He even furtively started concentrating troops, while the people were gripped with a new uneasiness they had to face, the harsh reality of hunger. The people prompted by radical journalists, demand that the king should be kept away from versailles to save him from the corrupt influence of the court on October 5 was presented a strange spectacle. A long line of the poorest women of Paris, riotous with hunger and rage, armed with sticks and clubs, screaming Bread, bread, bread were straggling along the 12 miles of high way from Paris to versailles. It was said that they were going to demand the reduction of the price of bread. Lafayette with his National guard followed them. The day passed over with petitions and demonstrations that did not seem of great importance. But soon after midnight, the palace was penetrated by the crowd. The king and queen were in some danger, but the arrival of Lafayette secured their personal safety.

Lafayett tried to hold them back. The royal soldiers were sent back to the barracks. He thought that he would be able to protect royalty. However, some miscreants escaped into the palace and killed the queen's bodyguard. The people clamoured that the king should return with them to Paris. And the king, as usual, thought it wisest to yield. On 6 October he left versailles, came to the tulleries once the palace of the medieval kings of France. The women shouted "We are bringing back the backer, the backer's wife, and the backer's son". To versailles the French royal family never returned. The Parisian installed Louis XVI in the palace of the tulleries, and thenceforth he was virtually their prisoner. Paris henceforth, enveloped and controlled the Government of France.

THE ACHIVEMENTS OF THE CONSTITUENT (NATIONAL) ASSEMBLY–1788-91

While the political situation in the country was fast degenerating into anarchy and peasants indulged in violence and hooliganism against the nobles, the National assembly realised the danger of letting lawlessness have the better of their commonsense–order must be restored somehow, otherwise the country would be ruined. So during its August session it passed a number of reforms which completely destroyed all emblems of the ancient regime. And the National assembly setabout framing the future Constitution of France. Henceforth, the body came to be known as the constitutent assembly, as its chief work was the making of a constitution. A great work of the assembly was the proclamation of individual rights and liberties. The old society and Government of France were disappearing. On what basis should the new be erected? Great Britain had its Magna carta, America had its declaration of independence. France was now given a "Declaration of the Rights of man and of the citizen". This document which reflected the spirit of Rousseau's philosophy, and incorporated some of the British and American provisions, became the platform of the French revolution. According to Grant and Temperley. "The representatives of the French people, organised in the National assembly, considering that ignorance, forgetfulness or contempt of the rights of man are the sole causes of the public miseries and of the corruption of governments, have resolved to setforth in a solemn declaration the natural, inalienable, and scared rights of man, in order that this declaration being ever present to all the members of the social body, may unceasingly remind them of their rights and their duties, in order that the acts of the legislative power may be each moment compared with the aim of every political institution and thereby may be more respected, and in order that the demands of the citizens, grounded henceforth upon simple and incontestable principles, may always take the direction of maintaining the constitution and the welfare of all". In consequence, the National Assembly recognises and declares, the following rights of man and of the citizen.

Man are born and remain free and equal in rights, social distinctions can be based only upon public utility. The constitution said that man has natural rights which cannot be taken away by anybody. They are liberty, property, security and resistance to oppression. Liberty consists in the power to do aything that does not injure others. Soverignity resided in the nation only. Law is the expression of the general will. No man can be accused, arrested, or detained except in the cases determined by the law. All citizens were equal before law and they had a right to enjoy equal oppertunity in society. No individual shall exploit the others. The free communication of ideas and opinions is one of the most precious of the rights of man, every citizens then can freely speak, write, and print, subject to responsibility for the abuse of this freedom in thecases determined by law. The property of any people cannot be usurped without payment of proper compensation. Society has the right to call for an account from every public agent of its administration. According to Grant andTemperley, "For a quarter of a century the declaration of the Rights of man was the watchword and charter of all the reformers and revolutionists of Europe". It certainly remained a charter of liberation throughout the 19th century. It has been remarked that the Declaration of the Rights of man was the death certificate of the old regime. While the English Parliament in its declaration of Right enunciated simply the historic and legal Rights of Englishmen against the crown, France based her action on universal principles, and in her declaration made herself the spokesman of the human race. The general, theoretical principles of French, English and American liberal thought of the 18th century were clearly stated in the preamble. These principles which were universal in their appeal, recognising neither national boundary lines nor distinctions of race, colour or creed, and emphasising the soverign nations right to resist the oppression of irresponsible Governments carried a singular appeal to contemporaries. On the other hand, the propertlyless workers and peasant did become free, but then remained defenseless against their more prosperous fellow citizens : Besides the rights of association and petition, were not recognised. Unfortunately no reference was made about the duties of the citizens. Aboveall, in the words of Hazen, "During the past century, many a nation aspiring to liberty has sought its principles in this French Declaration".

The New Constitution

The constituent assembly worked out a constitution which was finally adopted in 1791. It was the first written constitution France had everhad . The form of government was to be monarchical. The executive power was entrusted to a heriditary monarch. Louis XVI was declared "King of the French by the grace of God and the will of the Nation". In theory, the power that the constitution gave him was of considerable importance. In practice, the exercise of his power was hedged in by many restrictions. He was the supreme commander of the army and navy. The king was to choose his own ministers who, however, not to sit in the Legislature. The executive and the Legislature were rigidly separated. He appointed ambassoders, but found the direction of foreign policy largly in the hands of the deputies of the assembly. He could not declare war without the consent of the Legislature. He was given only a suspensive veto. By this veto power he could delay the passing of a measure by holding it up until it had been passed by three successive assemblies. The king has been declared the supreme head of the administration of the kingdom, yet he can change nothing without the decision of the assembly. It is no exaggeration to state that the new constitution organised a middle class Government within the framework of a constitutional monarchy.

The legislative power was given to a single assembly of 745 members to be elected for a term of two years. The members of the assembly were to be elected on the votes of active citizens. The powers given to the legislative assembly made it the strongest political authority in the State. The assembly alone could initiate and vote the laws. It controlled public expenditures. The assembly supervised the ministry and directed the diplomacy of the State. The constitution divided the population into two classes, active and passive citizens. Only members of the former class were given the right to vote and the distinction was based upon differences in wealth. Hence, political rights were made a monopoly of the well-to-do, for the new constitution did away with privileges based upon birth, but respected those arsing out of financial prosperity. Thus, the franchise was limited by a property qualification which excluded from the vote the great majority of the artisans of the towns.

The administrative organization was also completely remodelled. A new, uniform and simple administrative system was established. France was divided into 83 departments, each department into Districts, each district into cantons, and each canton into Communes. More likely, the deputies were concerned with establishing a new territorial unit that would make local administration simple and efficient. The central administration had no direct agent of its own in the local administrations. The affairs of every department were to be managed by an elected council. The decentralisation of the administrative organisation was most pronounced in the municipalities. In the words of Hazen, "France from being a highly centralised state, became one highly decentralised".

The reorganisation of Judicial administration was effected in the same spirit as that of the administrative service of the Government. Torture and Letter-de-catchet were abolished. A new hierarchy of elected Judges replaced the former Magistrates. Judical procedure was greatly simplified. The Jury system was introduced.

Financial Measures

The financial crisis which had precipitated the revolution grew steadily worse. The assembly could not ignore the financial difficulties which had been the occasion for its meeting. The assembly abolished the taxes of the old regime, except the stamp duty. The treasury was empty and the financial burden of the state higher than ever, as the liquidation of the old regime and the establishment of the new administrative system increased the public indebtedness. Taxes were imposed on trade and industry and the guilds were abolished. The assembly also established charity workshops for the poor. Moved by a sense of national need, the assembly tried to solve the financial problem at the expense of the Church. The assembly nationalised the Church property and paper notes called assignats were issued on the security of this property. But it resulted in devaluation. Since the paper money could be used to buy the confiscated land, it served as a mechanism by which the middle class and peasants acquired the properties the state had seized. The economic and financial consequences of the assignats policy were less happy.

Civil Constitution of the Clergy

To the deputies, who had been educated by the clergy, a separation of Church and State was unthinkable.The legislation concerning the tithes and the ecclesiastical lands forced the state to assume the financial obligations of the Church. The vast resources of the Church seemed to offer a means of escape from the bankruptcy which threatened the state, politically the Church should not be a state within a state. On the other hand the philosophers in general agreed that the state could not exist without religion. Further, the political traditions emphasised the subordination of the Church to the State. Accordingly, the monasteries and monkish living houses were abolished. As a pertial indemnity for the confiscation of Church property, the state undertook to pay the salaries of the clergy, who were made dependent on the state. The stipends of the clergy were rearranged. The assembly decided to reorganise the government of the Church. By the civil constitution of the clergy, Bishops and priests were to be elected by popular vote and were to be paid by the state. This new law was denounced by the pope. The assembly answered, the denunciation of the pope by enforcing on all clergy on oath of obedience to the king, the law and the nation. The church was split into two sections, the dissidents and the constitutionalists. In other words those who consented were called the juring and those who refused, the non-juring clergy. The assembly also refused to allow the Bishops to form a national council.

But no error of the constituent assembly was so disastrous in its effect as the civil constitution of the clergy. It divided the people of France in their feeling to-wards the revolution. The seeds of division were sown throughout the country and they produced actual civil war before long. Sharp protests were raised. Louis XVI unwillingly gave his sanction to the decree on the clerical oath. The civil constitution of the clergy alienated the faithful catholics and antagonised the papacy. Some priests incited the devout to work against the revolutionary trend. Many left the country to swelled the numbers of the emigrees. The civil constitution of the clergy had disastrous results on the course of the revolution. Sporadic violence in some parts of the country complicated the situation. Fundamentally a religious protest, the opposition of the faithful catholics to the impious laws gradually became a counter-revolutionary war against the revolution, a war led by staunch royalists. The religious laws did more than any other single act of the constituent assembly to develop the counter revolution.

Louis XVI was extremely dissatisfied with the provision of limited monarchy and the civil constitution of the clergy, and the planned to escape from Paris. Disguised as a servent of his childrens governess, he escaped with the queen and his children unnoticed from the Tuileries. But he was recognised and arrested at varennes. His attempted flights and subsequent capture sealed his fate. He was denounced as an enemy of the country, in league with the emigres, who now were egging foreign countries to invade France. Hence, the fidelity of the people to the cause of monarchy was shaken. The flight of the king was responsible for the birth of a Republican party.

According to Madelin, "The huge work of reform unique in history was.... very poor and fragile in construction". With reference to the work of the constitutent assembly Mirabeau remarked. "The disorganisation of the kingdom could not have been better planned". The power left to the king was too weak to be efficient. Declaration of rights of man was impractical. The sanctity of private property was taken for granted but it was not defined. After proclaiming in the Declaration, “Man are born and remain free and equal in rights”, the assembly contradicted itself by refusing to grant suffrage rights to all Frenchmen. Further, it was not proper to divide the citizens into active and passive. The king has been declared the supreme head of the administration of the kingdom, yet he can change nothing without the decision of the assembly. The king had also no right to dissolve the assembly. The executive and Legislature were so sharply separated that communication between king's ministers and representatives of the people was well-nigh impossible. Besides, the plan of a unicameral Legislature and the system of election in the case of judges proved unsatisfactory. The civil constitution of the clergy created religious struggle in the country. The over issue of assignats upset the national credit system. The bourgeoisie retained their power to rule by preserving the Franchise for their class. Babeuf remarked, "In place of commons, clergy and nobles, now there is, the rich, the richer, and the richest". But the sum total of the achievements of the National Assembly was the destruction of the old order and its substitution by a new one based on the principles of nationalism and soverignity of the people. The first phase of the revolution marked the end of absolute manarchy and the introduction of limited monarchy. The most abiding part of its work was the sweeping away of the old social system, of privilege and inequality. On 30th September, 1791 a self-denying ordinance was passed by the National Assembly and it was dissolved. The assembly voted that none of its members should be eligible to the next Legislature.

Mirabeau

Mirabeau is beyond comparison thae most notable figure in the early history of the French Revolution: Born in 1748 he ought to have been the prime of manhood when elected to the States General, but violent excesses of everykind had not merely undermined a robust constitution but had inspired general mistrust of his character. He was so much defamed among the nobles that he could not be elected as a representative of the first estate. He was elected by the voters of Aix and Marsellies to the State-General. Regarded with suspecion and received with insults his splendid eloquence and ripe political judgement quickly impressed the assembly. He was a denouncer of autocracy but a supporter of constitutional monarchy. His courage and resource in the crisis of 23 June established his preeminence among a crowd of inexperienced mediocrities, and from that day until his death he mostly dominated the constituent assembly. His democratic principles made him a leader in the parliamentary phase of the Revolution, but his ambition for authority and his instinct for public order led him to attach himself as an adviser to the court. He wanted the king to lead the revolution along constitutional paths. But his policy of states-manlike compromises was impossible with an inert king, a jealous assembly and populace leavened by Rousseau's doctrine. He had no sympathy with the ancien regime, and his supreme desire was to convince the king that the break with the past was irreparable, and to reconcile him to the new order. Not that he desired any weakening of the executive authority. On the contrary, a strong executive was to his mind the first necessity of Government, but its strength must be derived from the willing assent of the people and from harmonious cooperation with the people's representative in the assembly. But unfortunately for France, Mirabeau was not appreciated. Distrusted by the court as the champion of the people, despised by democrats as the bribed ally of the monarchy, he never succeeded in acquiring a commanding influence. Mirabeau's settlement was nothing but a judicious compromise, but the situation of France was not adapted to compromise, and the future lay with men of absolute views. He died in 1791 and with him perished the greatest man of the revolutionary epoch and the last hope of the French monarchy.

The Legislative Assembly (1791-92)

The legislative assembly met on October 1, 1791, in accordance with the provision of the new constitution. The assembly derived its charecter from two facts, the constituent with singular self-denial had excluded its own members from seeking reelection, and the primary election for the legislature had been held in the week before the flight of varnnes. It resulted that its members were largly inexperienced, and that they did not adequately represent the Republican temper, which especially in Paris had grown up since the king's unfortunate execution. The legislative assembly was weak, and the real influence on the course of events was to be found rather in the newspapers and in the clubs than on its benches. The destinies of France were committed to men, mostly young lawyers, who were full of theories but devoid of experience. According to Ketlby, "It was a new generation of young revolutionaries dazzled by dreams of unprecedented oppertunities, lured by the glamour of Paris....".

The new representatives-745 in number - were divided into several parties. The Right consisted of the constitutionalists better known as the Feuillants, a name derived from their club which met in the convent of the Feuillants. They posed as the defender of the Constitution of 1791 and maintained friendly relations with the court. They rested on the support of Lafayette, the National Guard, and the middle classes. The left was divided into two factions, the Girondins and the Jacobines. The Girondins derived its name from the fact that its leaders came from the department of Gironde. They were primarily passionate enthusiasts, full of zeal and possessed of a marvellous eloquence. They accepted the monarchy for the moment they regarded the Republic as the ideal. Their main support was to be found outside of Paris in the provinces and country districts. They were more democratic than the members of the Jacobine party but they condemned the mob rule. Their chief leaders were Brissot, Buzot, Dumoureiz, Madam Rolland. The Girondins soon became the darlings of all those zealous patriots for whom the Jacobines were too dirty, and the Feuillants were too lukewarm. On the other hand, the Jacobins had originated as a society of friends of the constitution, with such moderates at Mirabeau, Sieyes,

Lafayette. The members of the party used to meet in the Church of Jacob in Paris. The Jacobin club grew steadily more radical as revolution progressed and as its more conservative members eliminated. The Jacobins were ardent advocates of Rousseau's doctrine of sovereign right of the people. They believed that popular movements were highest expression of law. The Jacobin club had its daughter societies spread all over France. Subsequently under the leadership of Robespierre, it had become quite as radical as the cordelier. Though both the Girondins and the Jacobins were Republicans, yet both were separated poles apart. The Girondins were doctrinaries, the Jacobins were realists, the former believed in decentralisation, whereas, the latter were strong advocates of centralisation, the Girondists were in favour of foreign war, the Jacobines advocated the necessity of internal consolidation. The Cordelier club had been organised as a society of friends of the rights of man and of citizens and from the start it was radical. Its members were recruited from the lower orders of the society and so it was the hotbed of Republicanism. The members of this club were crude and rude but tremendously energetic. The ideologies of this club wre imbued with terrorism and it worked as a breeding ground of extremists. Their chief leaders were Marat, Danton, Desmoulins.

The new chamber was confronted by a score of difficulties, among the most pressing were those presented by the position of the Non-Juring clergy and of the Nobles who had fled from France. A large number of nobles led by count of Artois, the king's younger brother, had fled the country. The emigres were concentrated in coblentz on the eastern frontier. They had been egging on their supporters in France to overthrow the new constitution, as well as canvassing European powers to interven on their bahalf and the king's inorder to save the monarchy. The assembly passed decrees sentencing to death all the emigres who had not returned to France by January 1, 1792; and ordering all priests to take the oath within a week under penalty of forfeiture of their livings or pensions. The question of the church touched the king's conscience, so he voted the decrees of the assembly. On the other hand, the emigres continued their appeals to the German powers to arrest by force of arms a movement which not only threatened France but every constituted government in Europe. The royal veto led to a violent quarrel of the assembly with the king. The vetoing of these measures offended public opinion and shook the faith of the people in the sincerity of the King's promise to support the constitution. The populace became violent and surrounded the Tulleries, the royal palce and tried to force the king to withdraw his veto on the measures against the emigres and the clergy who would not abide by the civil constitution of the clergy. In this way the revolution was gradually passing into the

hands of the mob. Further, the difficulties of the limited monarchy were complicated by an embarrassing foreign situation. Is it possible that under any circumstances the revolutionary movement started in 1789 could have been confined to France ? It is a forgone conclusion that the conflagration lighted in Paris quickly engulphed the whole of Europe into the vortex of flames. Besides, the French did not remain satisfied with the realization of their ideas and principles in their own country, they became eager to disseminate the truth in other lands.

The dispute of Europe with the revolution originated in two matters of political deail; the feudal rights retained by imperial princess in Alsace under the peace of westphalia, and the Papel enclave of Avignon. In fact, the German princess had a number of rights guaranteed by the peace of Westphalia. These princess were dissatisfied with the decree of the French assembly which abolished all feudal dues and tithes, and they appealed to the German Diet. Austria supported the claim of the German princess and supported the restoration of these rights. Another aggressive act of the French was the annexation of Avignon which, though geographically belonged to France, had been subject to the Papacy since the 14th century. It was certainly a breach of international law. Further, the militant temper received its impulse from the policy of the Court. The queen, whose devotion to Austria was redoubled by her experience of France, never ceased to appeal for foreign help. Her correspondence made no pretence of patriotism, and her hopes lay with the mobilised emigres behind the Rhine. The flight to Varness branded the royal couple as a willing emigre, it became known that he had consented to purchase foreign aid with a partition of France, and it was obvious that he preferred an invasion to the revolution. Besides, the chief grivance of the French was that despite their representation, Emperor Leopold had not dispersed the French emigres from the German soil. Many nobles had fled from France, in fear and had taken up their residence in the bordering German States. These emigres were trying to induce foreign powers to interven in French affairs and restore the old regime. Meanwhile, in August, 1791, the emperor of Austria and the king of Prussia unfortunately issued the declaration of Pilnitz. This famous document maintained that the position of the king of France was a matter of concern to all European sovereigns. It demanded that the German princes should be reinstated in the feudal right in Alsace. This threat of foreign invasion infuriated the French people and increased their distrust of the king. In spite of all these war might not have resulted if the chief political factions in France had not desired it. The Girondins wanted war because they were ambitious for power and popularity. They wanted war to unmask the king. Open war would end the equivocal situation and force Louis XVI to form a Girondin ministry to prosecute the war against tyrant. The Girondists believed war would discredit the monarchy and result in the establishment of a French Republic and the general triumph of revolutionary ideas all over Europe. Only radicals like Marat, Robespierre, opposed war for fear it might lead to military dictatorship. But the Girondists after obtaining control of the government demanded that the Emperor of Austria withdraw his troops from the French frontier and expel the emigres from his territories. As no action was taken by the Austrian emperor, the Girondist ministers prevailed upon Louis XVI to declar war in April 1792. On the other hand the countries of Europe, mainly England, Spain, Holland were in favour of peace. However, the campaign of 1792 was the first stage in a vast conflict which was destined to rage throughout Europe for twenty three years. In fact, it was the beginning of an international contest between the forces if Revolution and those of the old order. The war began disastrously for the French. Their attack upon Austrian Belgium failed and their troops suffered reverses at the hands of the combined Austro Prussian armies. Yet, the French felt that they were fighting for a cause, the cause of equality, liberty and nationalsim. Among the French, patriotic enthusiasm rose to fever heat. But their armies were ill-organised and indisciplined.

On June 20, 1792, a Paris mob burst into the Tulleries, and for four hours surged round the king. The lives of the king and queen were saved only by their own calm and dignified courage. The riot dwindled into failure, but a beginning had been made, and Jacobins and Girondists set themselves to instigate another attack, which after some abortive outbreak finally took place on August 10. On 25th July Prussia formally declared war, and a few days letter, the Prussian Commander, the Duke of Brunswick issued from coblentz a manifesto to the French people. He summoned all authorities in France to submit to their lawful sovereign, declared that the whole French Nation would be held individually responsible for any resistance offered to the allied armies, and threatened Paris with demolition if any outrage were committed upon the king or the royal family. This foolish manifesto sealed the fate of the French monarchy. The French response was the insurrection of August 9-10-1792. On those days the proletariat and the extreme element in the bourgeoisie of Paris revolted against the constitutional monarchy. The Tulleries were sacked and the king's swiss guard butchered in the street. On 10th August the king was suspended from his function. The Girondist ministers were restored, and Danton, the real author of the 10th of August, 1792, became the minister of justice. The mob led by the Jacobins overthrew the Municipal Government of Paris and organised a new commune (city council), and the revolutionary commune of Paris controlled the capital. Danton decided that the way to stop the enemy was to terrify the royalist. The advance of the allies created a panic. Meanwhile, the Jacobins in a fit of insane passion carried out a series of organised massacres. For five long days, an armed band of assasins, burst upon the prisons when the suspected royalists had been dragged and hecked to pieces more than thousand men and women. There was no discrimination of rank, sex or age. These atrocities were known as the September Massacres. Marat invited the provinces to follow the brilliant example of Paris. It must be added that in the midst of the massacres Danton threw himself into task of organising the national defence. The Prussians were defeated at Valmy and their advance was checked. France was saved from her immediate danger. With Valmy the tide turned, on 6th of November Dumouriez won a brilliant victory on the Belgians at Jemappes, and the Austrian Netherlands were in the hands of the French Republic. The armies of the Republic were in possession of Belgium, Savoy, Nice, and had got a firm grip on the middle of Rhine. Thus, the Republican regimed in France was established in place of Monarchy.

THE NATIONAL CONVENTION (SEPTEMBER 21, 1792-OCTOBER 26, 1795)

The National convention, which was third and decisive Parliament of the revolution, met whilst the Prussian guns were trained on the hill of Valmy. The convention was opened on September 21 and resolved by acclamation that Royalty was abolished in France. De facto, of course, the monarchy had come to an inglorious end on August 10, Now De jure, although only the deputies from Paris had been instructed to vote for the abolition, all the deputies recognised the accomplished fact. They also passed a decree stipulating that all public documents were to be dated from year 1 of the French republic. The state which was symbolised royal absolutism in Europe was now a republic. The convention decreed that the republic was one and indivisible and place life and property under the safeguard of the new government. During the next three years the convention performed the two fold work of consolidating the revolution within France and of waging successful foreign war. The National convention was faced with the following problems, what should be done with the king? How to deal with internal disorder? and to draw up a new constitution. But the prime duty of the convention was to repel the invasion. Further, internationaly the royalists and the anti revolutionaries began to rise in revolts. However, a committee was appointed to draw up a constitution. Its work was long postponed as the convention was distracted by a frenzied quarrel that broke out between the Girondists and the Jacobins. Most of the Girondists were moderate Republicans and were imbued with great missionary zeal to spread the principles of the revolution. They were well-to-do bourgeoisie who commanded a good deal of influence in the provinces but were opposed by the Parisian commune. On the other hand, the Jacobins or the mountanists were extremist revolutionaries. They wanted to establish a social and political democracy. Their sole aim was to save France and they were ready to adopt any means to further that end. Their strength lay in their alliance with the commune. Their leaders Danton, Robespierre and Carnot were exceptionally good orator and organisers. Between them, occupying the seats of the center, were the great majority of the deputies, the man of the plain. They had no fixed policy and took decision on the merit of the issues under consideration. The Girondists were at first supreme in the convention but it soon passed under the control of the Jacobins.

The convention having unanimously voted that royalty is abolished in France, the question arose as to what should be done with Louis XVI? The Jacobins led by Robespierre wanted to execute the king even without trial. The Girondists attempted interpose delay, and suggested that the king's fate should be decided by a vote of the whole nation. But the mob became impatient. After a trial which was a parody of Justice, the king was found guilty of treason, and by a small majority his death was voted. On 21st January, 1793 the sentence was executed. Thus died upon the scaffold, with calm courage and unruffled dignity, one of the kindliest, most unselfish and best intentioned of French kings. His execution was both a crime and a blunder. Robespierre said, "Louis must die, because the country must live".

A wave of indignation swept France, the king's execution caused violent outbursts in different parts of the country. A civil war of spasmodic nature, but of considerable proportions, had broken out in France. In the west, in Brittany and Lavendee, both the Catholic church and the old nobility, had a greater hold upon the people than in any other part of France. When the decree of February was published, by which conscripts for the Republican armies were to be raised by lot among them, the peasants rose in revolt. It was aimed against the tyranny of the Jacobins and of the commune of Paris. Further, the Republicans in France adopted an aggressive attitude and challenged the existing order in Europe. They issued propagandist decrees calling upon all peoples to rise in revolt against their rulers. Thus, republican France proclaimed a war against monarchical Europe. The French nation will treat as enemies the peoples who, refusing or renouncing liberty and equality, are desirous of preserving their prince and privileged castes, or of entering into communication with them, Louis XVI's execution came as a rude shock to the monarachical countries of Europe. The edict of Fraternity, the opening of the scheldt, and the execution of Louis XVI provoked the monarchs of Europe. Austria and Prussia were already in the war path. Great Britain organised the first coalition which brought together Austria, Prussia, Holland, Spain, Sardinia and Great Britian. Three important developments had convinced Europe that the French revolution was a devastating menace to established governments. The acts of military aggression were being rationalised in terms of a universal crusade to liberate all oppressed peoples. And the Revolutionists had executed the king. To crush the menace of the armed doctrine of the French revolution became a matter of life and death to all legitimate government. England took the lead in organising the European opposition, because England's position was most seriously threatened. The opening of scheldt was a serious blow to her commercial classes. The French occupation of Austrian Netherland was a direct military menace to England herself, while French conquest in general destroyed the political equilibrium in Europe. Besides, the radical movement in England was assuming alarming propertions. Pitt's solution of this complex of domestic and foreign problems was to direct public opinion in favour of patriotic war to protect England's legitimate rights. For a brief time the allied armies threatened to overwhelm France, they reoccupied Belgium, and the Rhine provinces and took the road towards Paris. Dumouriez, suffered defeat at the hands of the Austrians at Neerwinden, the English besieged Dunkirk, while the Spaniards conquered Rousillon. But under the experienced leadership of carnot, and with the enthusiastic support of his fellow Jacobins, the convention inaugurated a militarism which was quite novel in the world's annals. The militarism of carnot and the Jacobins was based on the principle of the nation in arms. Gradually the country cleared of foreign enemies. It will suffice to point out that when the National convention finally adjourned, the first coalition was in process of dissolution.

At this national crisis the convention formed two committees and inititated an unusually strict and repressive rule which is known as "Reign of Terror". The reign of terror was an emergency despotism, a dictatorship of distress. It was born of the idea that only by establishing despotism civil war could be stopped, unity restored and the country would be in a position to defend itself against foreign invasion. The object of this step was to provide a strong government so as to concentrate the full force of the nation upon the problem of national salvation. The reverses which France had initially suffered, accentuated the bitterness of feeling between the Girondists and the Jacobins. The Girondists wanted to punish the men who were responsible for the September massacres and to restrict the supremacy of the Paris commune. On the other hand, Marat, Robespierre, were resolved on the annihilation of the Girondists. The Jacobins took every advantage of France's desperate need and of the feebleness of the Girondists. They had become converts to the war, for they saw that in a state of siege their own aims could best be realised together with the welfare of the country. They bought popularity by adopting the economic programme of the streets, they taxed the rich, guaranteed the right to work, fixed a maximum price for bread. They were of the opinion that Paris is the centre of light. They organised an insurrection against the Girondists and the infuritated mob of Paris invaded the convention and compelled it to arrest Girondists leaders. Finally, the Girondists fell, as they were unpractical idealists. The fall of the Girondists left the Jacobins supreme. Thus, the Jacobins became the masters of the convention. This was responsible for the inauguration of a reign of terror under dominance of the dreaded three, Robespierre, Danton and Marat.

The Reign of Terror and the Jacobin Dictatorship

The Jacobins under Robespierre established the Reign of Terror to crush all internal insurrections and opposition. It was the darkest and the most terrible period of the revolution. France was faced with the dreadful prospects of formidable invasion from without. So an extraordinary and emergency constitution was adopted by the national convention to establish a strong government. The need of the hour was to enforce patriotism in the dark hours of foreign invasion. Hence, it was deemed necessary in order to suppressed rebillion by the royalists and to create a sense of loyality to revolution among the people. The reign of terror was a necessity to establish that momentary despotism of liberty which was indispensable to crush the despotism of kings. As a matter of fact, the reign of terror was but an incident, though an awful incident, in a great political and social upheaval.

The machinary of this provisional government consisted of two important committees, appointed by the convention, the committee of public safty and the Committee of General security, also representatives a mission, and on the Revolutionary Tribunal. The national convention entrusted the supreme executive authority of France to a special committee, composed of Nine (later twelve) of its members, who were styled the committee of public safety. This small body was the cornerstone and indeed the very soul of the terror. It directed the Ministers of State, appointed the local officials, and undertook the administration of the whole country. All executive authority was vested in the committee of public safety. It directed all internal and external policies. The chief agencies of the committee of public safety in conducting terrorism were the committee of General security and the Revolutionary Tribunal. The committee of General security was given police power in order to maintain order throughout the country. The Revolutionary Tribunal was an extraordinary criminal court, created for the speedy trial of the suspects. No appeal could be taken from its decision. The convention enacted the law of suspects to enable the committee of the General security and the Revolutionary Tribunals to try all those who were suspected of hostility to the convention. Thousands of royalists were sent to the guillotine, to the accompaniment of popular mob frenzy. This law was so loosely and vaguly worded, it indicated so many classes of individuals that under its provisions practically any one in France could be arrested and sent before the Revolutionary Tribunal. All case which were sent to the Revolutionary Tribunal were punished by death by guillotine. Danton once said, "Let us be terrible in order to dispense the people from being terrible". The most prominent of the victims were Marie Antoinette, Madame Roland, Duke of orleans. The terror spread to the provinces. The city of Lyons, which ventured to resist the revolutionary government, was partially demolished. The authorities began by shooting each one individually, and many were mowed down in batches by canon fire. Similarly the revolt at Lavandee was suppressed with ruthless severity which resulted in burning of villages. The rebillions in the provinces were suppressed with merciles rigour and examplary punishment. The terror struck real terror into the hearts of the rebels and anarchy was brought under control Danton who was an able leader propcsed to stop the bloodshed after the end of external fear, but Robespierre guillotined him for treason. With the death of Danton France lost a statesman who could possibly has dominated the ccurse of events. The fall of Danton led to absolute domination of Robespierre, the lean lawyer from Arras. The man was of the type of Lenin, a fanatical believer in an inspired text. As KarlMarx was to the Russian, so was Rousseau to the French revolutionary. Robespierre was a pedantic follower of Rousseau. He now proceeded to Usher in the reign of virtue contemplated by Rousseau. For four months Robespierre was practically dictator, and signalized his brief passage in power by staging a new religion, that of the supreme being, and by rendering the Revolutionary Tribunal more murderous than ever. At last an opposition was organised against Robespierre and the convention out lawed him, and he was executed on July 28, 1794. The death of Robespierre ended the terror. However, the purpose of the terror, was already achived. The revolution was preserved in France.

The reaction which took place in Frence after the death of Robespierre is known as Thermidorian (one of the month of the revolutionary calander corresponding to July) reaction. According to Fisher; "The long nightmare was over, the hateful epidemic of butchery, came to a sudden end. Moderates seized the wheel of power. The dark miasma of suspicion which had poisoned the political life of Paris passed away. In her sudden deliverance from fear and humilation the country swungback into the sunlight of gaiety and hope. No more fanatical gloom! no more ravings of a blood thirsty press! no more guillotining of the brave, the good, the beautiful, the innocent! Frivolity resumed its long-interrupted reign. But if France ceased to be a terrorist state, she remained revolutionary". The reign of terror gradually came to an end. The reign of terror and Paris commune were dissolved. All the subordinate machinary of the reign of terror was abolished. The external dangers being averted, there was no necessity for a bloody repression of suspects. A committee was formed to draft a constitution, which was also known as the constitution of the year third. The constitution was a bourgeoisie document. Its principal feature were a Parliament of two chambers and an executive of five directors. Universal sufferage was abolished, the payment of taxes became necessary qualifications for voters. To avert the possibility of a monarchist Legislature the convention decreed that 2/3 of the new Legislatures should be chosen from amongst the deputies of the presents convention. But an insurrection was organised against the convention by the wealthier people, in reality a royalist project. The convention entrusted its defence to Barras, who, on the other hand called to his aid a little corsican officier, Napolean Bonparte. He dispersed the mob, and the insurgents were mowed down. The convention was saved and an astounding carrer was began. On October 26, 1795, the convention declared itself dissolved. Thus, ended an important scene of the French revolution.

Achievements of the Convention

All through the period of the reign of terror, the national convention pursued radical social objectives and even socialist policies in economic matters. The convention had put a king to death, and had established a republic. It roused great national enthusiasm in the country and the French men, women and children rose in support of the motherland. Carnot's militant nationalism produced the most efficient army in Europe. It had stilled party strifes by expelling the Girondist leaders, had organised a strong provisional government and had set up a reign of terror to rootout all anti-re-volutionary elements within France. It confiscated the property of emigres for the benefit of the state and the lower classes. Large landed estate were broken up and offered for sale in small plots and on easy terms. The enemies of France wre driven away from the French border and the French national army achived great victories. It passed certain basic social reforms like the abolition of imprisonment for debt, protection of women's claim to property, and abolition of Negro slavary in the French colonies. The convention attempted to fix the price of necessities at a fair level, and threatened profiteering merchants with the guillotine. The convention gave to the world the metric system which is the most perfect system of weights and measure. It worked at the civil code which aimed at founding the whole social life on the principle of equality. Regarding education, it proposed that the French language should be the sole language of national instruction. It established one central school in each department, and the convention was most successful in its organisation of higher education. The convention was hostile to the Roman Catholic Church whose doctrines and dogmas had been ridiculed by the rational philosophers. Hence, under the influence of the atheists, the churches were closed, and christianity was suppressed. The worship of Reason took its place. The christian calender was substituted by a new revolutionary calender. The national convention marked the second stage of the revolution, the gains of the revolution were consolidated. Monarchy and feudalism had been abolished. It also framed a new Constitution for France.

Danton, Robespierre

Danton was the son of a farmer, he had studied law, purchased a position as advocate of the royal council, and acquired, before the outbreak of the revolution, a reputation as a man of liberal taste. It was patriotism rather than ambition that threw him into politics. A Frenchman to his backbone, he was a volcano that erupted with flood of lava, purest and truest flames as well. He was ambitious but uncalculating. He is neither an egoist, nor a scholastic theoretician like his contemporaries. Less radical and more statesmanlike was Danton, who has been called a middle class Mirabeau. He was brought to the fore in the early days of the revolution through Mirabeau's favour, and like his patron he was a person of powerful physique and stentorian voice, a clever debator and a moving orator. He was the leader of the revolutionary commune which was established in Paris. When Paris was threatened by the advancing prussian troops, it was Danto who roused the patriotic enthusiasm of the populace. He was the founder of the cordelier club and later on enrolled himself as a member of the Jacobin club and supported the cause of Republicanism. He was rough and courageous, but neither venal nor bloodthirsty. He was responsible for the september massacres. As the minister for justice he had a respondibility to save the lives of the prisoners. But he showed a cynical indifference to protect the prisoners from the mob violence. As a member of the committee of public safety, he stood for a strong centralised government and tried to mitigate the bitterness of party strifes. He rejected the Girondin idea of a crusade against the monarchs of Europe. When the danger of external attack on France was over, he proposed to Robspierre to end the reign of terror. For this he was excluded from the committee of public safety. In fact he was not bloodthirsty by nature. On 5th April, 1794 he was guillotined. Before his death he said to the executioner," show my head to the people it is worth it". With his death France lost a statesman who could possibly have dominated the course of events. According to Thomson,"Not a great man, not a good man,.... but a man with great good and heroic moments".

The lean lawyers from Arras, the Apostle of Rousseau, a classmate of Desmoullins, a man of fixed ideas, became a member of the committee of public safety in 1793 and for one year, memorable for its military glories, was the real ruler of France and the master spirit of Europe. Mirabeau had prophesised about Robespierre,"That man will go far, he believes what he says". He was a political missionary like Oliver cromwell and he was determined to crush the corrupt. He was cold and grave without any spark of humour. He read Rousseau from cover to cover and believed in the philosopher's doctrine with all his mind and heart. He was sure that they would regenerate Frence and all mankind. He was a member of the Jacobin club. Though he was attached to the middle class, but throughout his life he pleaded the cause of the commoners. By the withdrawl of conservative members from the Jacobin club he became the virtual leader of the party. The ease of his oratory, the violence of his views, coupled with a great dexterity in the arts of politicial management, made him almost from the first a leader among the Jacobins. He was the master of the Paris revolutionary machine. It proved a most effective instrument for radical propaganda, and Robespierre was its oracle. He was essentially a dreamer, bit pedantic, and a bit of a fob. He proclaimed himself to be the champion of morality and a living martyr to the Republic. He took a leading part in the organisation of the reign of terror. Danton's fall led to Robespierre's dictatorship. In the words of Thomson, "he stood for all that Jacobinism means in modern history and in his own carrer he personified the Jacobin impulses.He hated alike the anarchical excesses and revolting atheism of the Hebertists, as well as the policy of moderation advocated by the Dantonists. At last the man-eating tiger overreached himself by a law (the law of 22 prairial) which threatened the life of every member of the convention, for the legislator were deprived of their immunity, and the last feeble safeguards for the protection of persons for political offences were swept away. His policy was to methodise the terror by crushing factions whose (Dantonists) clemency might ruin or whose (Hebertists) excesses might degrade the republic. Finally, the convention passed a resoltion against Robespierre and ordered his arrest on the charge of treason and he was guillotined on 28th July, 1794. In fact he was a man of virtue, a hater of women, and incorruptible in the midst of bribers and the bribed. In the opinion of many scholars he sacrificed the revolution at the alter of his personal ambition.

The Directory (1795-1799)

The intervened between the high effort of the convention and the military dignity of the consulate, he ignoble episode of the Directory. The new constitutional government of the executive directory and the two legislative councils took office on October 27, 1795. No elections were to be held, no replacement of Directors to be made until 1797. Thus, the Government had 18 months to liqudidate the revolution and the war. But the Directory of the five, which had executive power under the new constitution, was ill-fated from birth. The men who successfully became Directors were, except for the patriotic organising genius of carnot, disreputable and self seeking politicians of little ability. Madelin writes, "the Directory was the most incompetent and the most corrupt government that was ever set up in France". The new ruling class which backed the measures of the Directory, included businessmen and financial speculators, army contracters, and land owning peasants, that had profited most from the revolution and war. Their aims were a constitutional parliamentary system on a narrow social basis, moderate in action, and so devised as to prevent personal dictatorship. But the Directory which attempted to maintain its authority by a series a coups, came inevitably to rest its existance upon the army, it was improvident. When that support was withdrawn from it, the government collapsed.

A manifesto issued by the Directors shortly after they assumed office outlined their domestic programme. Their first concern was with the restoration of political stability, to wage active war upon royalism, stimulate patriotism, to crush all factions, extinguish partisan feelings and all desires for vengeance, to make concord reign. This was an oppertunist and conservative programme. Meanwhile a new peril was rising in the capital, the consipiracy of the radical malcontents of Paris to overthrew the government. The malcontents consisted of former radical Jacobin deputies of the convention who had personal grivances against the members of the administration. In 1795, in resistance to the new constitution of the Directory, a political club, was formed called the society of the pantheon. It attracted many former Jacobins and its leader was Francois Noel Babeuf, an embittered and fanatical young agitator. Babeuf, a petty official before 1789 and a revolutionary journalist since, had gradually evolved a crude communistic philosophy. In his journal, the tribune, he began Preach to his ill-digested, makeshift creed of the community of goods and the abolition of private ownership. The Babouvists proposed to revive the Jacobin constitution of 1793, and to proclaim a Republic of equals, in which a communistic organisation of society would abolish the growing gulf between rich and poor. The movement of Babeuf was intended by its organiser to secure a crude form of communism and to add to the political revolution of 1789 a social and economic revolution of 1796. In 1796 they completed their plans for an insurrection. But a traitor revealed their plot to the Directory, and the directory swooped down their leaders. The consipirators were arrested and were brought to trial. Babeuf was guillotined. The execution of Babeuf made him the last famous martyr of the white terror.

Another problem which the directory was called upon to solve was that of reorganising the religious and moral foundation of society. For the benefit of the masses the government sought to give the new vigor to the rites of the civic religion. But the government was miserably poor to give an artificial prop to decaying faith. Another problem which the Directory had to meet was that of restoring financial stability. When the government entered upon its functions, the treasury was empty, and money was lacking for the barest needs of the administration. The returns from taxations were far from sufficient. In a desperate effort to stabilise the budget, it sharply curtailed expenditures and reorganised the services of the internal debt. But the Directory failed to adopt a clear cut policy which would satisfy either the merchants and financiers who clamoured for a return to free trade and laissez Faire (Free trade or let alone). The government was almost bankarupt, and the financial distress multiplied the sufferings of the people. Moreover, the economic policy of the government was dependent upon its foreign policy. In the words of Riker, "The rule of the Directors proved to be one of the most vicious government that France had ever endured".

The Foreign Policy of the Directory

The object of the Directory was to end the war and guarantee the security of France. By the beginning of 1796 France's only active enemies on land were Austria and Sardinia and at sea Great Britain. Prussia, Spain, Holland had already signed peace treaties to with the republic. The North German States had been neutral. England's own situation was such that pitt, did not hesitate to listen to offer of peace of the other two states of the first coalition, Austria relied upon the assistance of Russiana tyroops, but Russia reserved her forces for her affairs in poland. However, the directory was able to concentrate all its efforts on the war against Austria. So the major operations were to be on the continent against Austria in Germany and Italy, and against English shipping on the North sea. An offensive was designed by carnot, which threatened the Austrian positions with a simultaneous French advance by the valley of the Main and the Plain of Northern Italy. Public interest was concentrated on the commands of jordan and Moreau, which were to operate in Western Germany, whilst the army of Italy was expected to effect a secondary diversion on the Alpine frontier. The influence of Barras secured the Italian command of Napoleon Bonaparte, who was familiar with, the practice of mountain warfare on the mediterranean littoral. Bonaparte remained in Paris for 9 days after his appointment and married two days before his departure for the South.

To the miserably clad, unpaid, inactive, and half famished soldiers Bonaparte addressed the first of his striring proclaimations, "Soldiers you are naked and hungry. The government owes you much but can give you nothing. Your patience and your courage are admirable, but they can win you neither glory nor prestige, I will lead you to the most fertile plains in the world. Rich provinces and great cities will be in your power, there you will find honour, glory, and riches....". The soldiers responded enthusisatically, dazzed by his promises and electrified by his vibrant power. Napoleon crossed and Alps mountain and defeated the army of Sardinia. He compelled the king of Sardinia to sue for an armistice. Peace was concluded and Sardinia renounced the Austrian alliance, Ceded Savoy and Nice to France. Having put the Sardinians out of action Napoleon now turned upon the Austrians, forced a passage over the bridge of Lodi and entered Milan. The second phase of the Italian campaign opened with the siege of the Austrians in the citadel of Mantua, which heldout longer than seven months and blocked Bonaparte's advance towards vienna. Again and again the Austrians attempted to relieve it, but they were defeated in the battle of Arcola, Rivoli and finally Mantua surrendered on 2nd February, 1797. The immediate aftermath was the signing of a peace treaty with the pope. By the traty of Tolentino, the Pope recognised the French annexations of Avignon, agreed to an indemnity of fifteen million Francs, and ceded Ancona and the legation of Bologna, and the Romagna. Rome was saved for the Papacy, but France gained control of the Adriatic. In June 1796 he reorganised Northern and central Italy into the cisalpine Republic. Genoa was converted into Ligurian Republic in strict dependence upon Grance. The victorious conqueror, by a rapid march came within the striking distance of Vienna. This sudden move frightened emperor Francis II of Austria, and so he concluded a peace with Napoleon by the treaty of Campo Formio (1797).

By this treaty Austria recognised the French possession of Belgium.

She agreed to cede two third of the imperial territory on the left bank of the Rhine to France. So the province of Rhine was handed over to France. Austria recognised the cisalpine republic. The republic of venice was annihilated and its territories partitioned. Continental venetia East of the Adige, Istria and Dalmatia were annexed to Austria. The treaty of campo Formio was at once a triumph for Bonaparte. Bonaparte had won for France the scientific frontier. He had established the domination of France in Italy and in Holland, and he had planted the French flag in the Ionians island. The acquisition of the Ionian island by France is the key to his policy. They were a stepping stone to Egypt, as Bonaparte believed was the key to the conflict between France and England. It marked the end of the first round of conflict between France and Europe and brought about the collapse of the first coalition. Napoleon's fame as a brilliant general rose very high. This treaty was the decisive step in the policy which gave France not only the Rhine boundary, but the dominant position in Germany and Iitaly. Further, the French influence increased considerably through the formation of the following republics- Batavian Republic (Lombardy), Ligurian republic(Genoa), the Roman republic (Papal States), Helvetic republic, (Switzerland) and Parthenopean republic (Naples and Sicily). The treaty left England without an ally in Europe. England had to struggle against the ever increasing power of France.

After the treaty of CampoFormio the struggle between England and France continued. England had been the center of the coalition, the paymistress of the coalition, the constant fomentor of trouble. Napoleon returned to France and the Directors gave a splendid welcome to Napoleon Bonaparte. His popularity was too disquieting and his very presence in the capital overshadowed the existence of the Government. At the formal reception of the Directory Barras exhorted him to crown his achivements by a conquest of England. Accordingly Bonaparte was appointed general of the army of England. The Directory wished him to attempt the invasion of England, but Bonaparte decided that this was impracticable, and he preferred paradoxically to attack England in Egypt. Accoding to Bonaparte, "I know that if I remain here, I shall soon be discarded. Everything wears out here. ....This little Europe gives scant oppertunity for more. I must go to the East. It is there that the great glory can be won". The Directors were glad to get him so far away from Paris, where his popularity was burdensome. Besides, Napoleon wanted to cut off the communication of the British possession in the East. So the war fleet sat sail from Toulon on May 19, 1798.

On the way to Alexandria he risked a surprised attack upon the island of Malta, and captured the formidable fortress. On July 1, 1798, the

French forces landed at Aboukierbay in Egypt and captured Alexandria. Napoleon reached Egypt and defeated the Mamelukes at the battle of the pyramids. In order to please the followers of Islam Nepoleon declared himself a devotee of the prophet and he declared later on, " I was a Mohammedan in Egypt, I shall be catholic in France for the good of the people". However, a single Naval defeat ruined his enterprise. Nelson, the British admiral, had learned the true destination of the French fleet. From Sicily he sailed towards Egypt, and on August 1, 1798 he surprised the anchored French fleet in Aboukir bay generally known as the battle of the Nile and destroyed it. By this one stroke England became mistress of the sea. The communications of the French forces with France were cut, and Napoleon became a prisoner in the land that he had conquered. Napolean crossed into Syria, but could not capture the mudhole of Acre which was ably defended by the British. His dreams of Eastern conquests were shattered. His hopes of expelling the English from India were also frustrated. In the meanwhile he got urgent summons from the Directory to return and he sailed for France.

Fall of the Directory

On October 9, 1799, Napoleon effected a safe landing at Frejus in Southern France, and proceeded towards Paris. The Venture of Napoleon had dazzled the imagination of the French and, by contrast, revealed the nullity of the existing government. His long trip from Frejus to Paris was a splendid triumph. The public gazed with awe to the new caeser, who had conquered in the East as brilliantly as he had in Italy. The crowds were so thick that his carriage could barely advance. The glory that he had sought in the East was his. What would he make of it? He had revealed his secret thoughts on that subject. Do you believe that it is to increase the grandeur of the lawyers in the Directory.... that I win triumph in Italy. They need glory, the satisfaction of their vanity, but as for liberty, they know nothing abaout it. The nation needs a leader, a leader made illustrious by glory". He knew that the moment had come. He established contact with Sieyes, contact established, agreement followed. The corrupt and high handed rule of the Directory in France coupled with its bankruptcy destroyed its popularity. There was no popular esteem left for this body anywhere in the country. The directors were greedy, selfish, corrupt and immoral. There were constant plots and intrigues hatched by the royalist as well as by the extremists in the Legislature against the directory. The foreign policy of the Directory was as unprincipled as its domestic policy was weak and unpopular. The European nations were alarmed by the policy of the Directory and they formed a second coalition against France. Further, the

Government of the Directory was tyrannical without being efficient. The Directors could not cope with the deteriorating political and financial conditions. The issue of assignats or paper money in large number had led to inflation and financial crisis. Even the Directors were not united and could not solve the internal problem. The capitalists were alarmed by its policy of forced loan, the working class people resented, the suppression of Babeuf plan, while the religious feeling of the provinces was outraged by the persecution of Catholicism. The government was incompetent, corrupt and unsuccessful. The need of the hour was a strong military government. Riker has rightly remarked, "Public opinion was tired of political agitation, tired of endless elections, tired of disorders....". The French people wanted a stable government. Napoleon correctly understood the general sentiment of the Frenchmen. In the hour of darkness Napoleon appeared as a saviour.

A consipiracy was planned. The Legislature was to be transferred to St. Cloud, and in that suburban seclusion a provisional government was to be imposed upon it by the exercise of military pressure. Hence, on the false pretext of a Jacobine consipiracy the councils had been transferred. The members of the council demanded detáils concerning a plot against the republic which the consipirators had given as the cause for the transfer of the council of Paris to St. Cloud, Nepoleon entered in the assembly but he was opposed with these slogan, "Outlaw him". According to Hazen, "pandemonium reigned. He received blows....his coat torn, his face bleeding". Lucien Bonaparte (Brother of Napoleon, President of the council) took in the situation at a glance and saved the day for the consipirators. He summoned the troops to expel the "brigands" who were in control of the hall. Then, turning towards Napoleon, he swore to plunge his sword into his brother's heart if ever the latter plotted against the liberty of the French people. The melodrama worked. The deputies escaped before the soldiers entered the hall. The plot was consummated. So the park of St. Cloud witnessed on a dull winter evening the last scence of the French revolution. Thus, on 10th November the reign of the Direcitory came to an end. In the words of Thomson,"The coup succeeded because neither assemblies nor Directory had any popular esteem left, and the population as a whole accepted the accomplished fact with little resistance. Confident from below, power from above, and for Napoleon to adopt it to his own views of the situation, which required his personal autocracy endorsed by popular plebiscite.....On Christimas eve, 1799, only a decade after the revolution began, the prophecy of Edmund Burke was completely fulfilled in the formal inauguration of the consulate". All through France the coup-de-detat was acclaimed as the dawn of a new era. The councils voted the abolition of the Directory and appointed three consuls, Sieyes, Ducoes, and General Napoleon Bonaparte. The Republic still existed in name actually the rule of the man on horseback had begun. Ten years of revolution had culminated in the rule of a military adventurer.

The Results of the Frence Revolution

The French revolution spread like waves all over Europe and no country was immune from its influence. Certainly, in the history of Europe, the French revolution was of great inspirational value. The revolution released dynamic and explosive of the old established order in politics, economics, social life, diplomacy and war. In England democrats welcomed that the established absolutist monarchy was at last yielding to the need for constitutional reforms The revolutionaries feeling that they were conducting a revolution on behalf of all man kind.

It swept awaya the evils and anomalies of the old regime and thereby freed the people from the tyranny of the king, the nobles and the Church. Monarchical absolutism was a thing of the past. The relics of feudalism were buried. Autocratic monarchy, arbitrary arrests, aristocratic privileges became a thing of the past. The Church had been subordinated to the state. A uniform and efficient system of administration had been introduced, laws had been codified. Taxation was shared by all and it was fairly distributed on all sections of society. Feudalism was dead and the emergence of a free land owning peasantry was a permanent result of the revolution. Right to vote, right to assemble, freedom of the press, freedom of religion which were advocated in the writings of the philosophers were all accepted. The opposition to the slave trade and the attempts to reform the condition of prisons illustrate the stimulus given to humanitarianism by the revolution. The ideal of political democracy deeply impressed the Frenchmen.

The revolution burst the boundaries of France, carrying with it new ideas of social and political organisation and thus in the long run helped to refashion Europe on new principles. In Netherland, Germany, Italy which had passed under direct French rule there were established a centralised state, equality before the law, and an individualistic state. England was also receptive to the revolutionary ideas. Leaders like Tompaine, Thomas Hardy, welcome the revolution as the greatest event since the American war of independence. Even moderate Tory government, led by pitt, the younger, had sought to introduce many financial and administrative reforms. The ideals of liberty, equality and fraternity spread a lasting impression among the masses of the conquered states.

Equality, liberty and fraternity, the three ideals of the revolution, entered into the consciousness of the French people and received permanence.The revolution, brought the ideal of legal equality, social equality, carrer upon to talents, uniformity of law and justice, Freedom of speech, freedom of thought and rule of law. On the restored Bourbon monarchy after the end of the revolution, the influences of these principles were deep enough. In the society, the privileges as well as the predominance of the clergy and the nobility were abolished and equality of all persons were established. The cardinal idea was that of liberty, an idea which found expression in the famous Declaration of rights. Liberty, personal and political, became a universal creed. Personal liberty implied the abolition of serfdom. Political liberty implied the abolition of exclusive political privileges and despotism, however, benevolent. Further, the example set by the French revolution in establishing social equality was infectious. The influences of democrasy and nationalism in the modern history were the results of the revolution. It was the urge of national patriotism that for a time made the French invincible in Europe. This was destined to act as a most important force in reshaping the boundaries of Europe. Henceforth peoples, long broken up into fragments by the arbitrary power dispositions of absolute rulers would strive to attain political unity and to secure a government which should be the expression of national will. The uprising of the German people in their war of liberation was a manifestation of nationalism. The history of Europe in the 19th century is the story of the triumph of nationalism in Belgium, Italy, Germany and the Balkan peninsula. As a result of the revolution the people of Europe acquired an experience which opened before the thinkers of later days new lines of thinking. Administration of law and justice became more uniform. By a series of radical measures the revolution established a sound economic system based upon social and economic justice. An era of religious liberty and equality was established as a result of changes in the French Church leading to the subordination of the Church to the State. Thus, the forces let loose by the revolution are potent even to this day and are working out visibly or invisibly the destinies of the nations of the world. Victor Hugo has rightly pointed out, "Revolution is the larva of civilisation".

Chapter-III
Napolean Bonaparte

Early Career

The accident of a successful coup d'etat provided France (in a cold winter evening of November 1799) with the strongest government that it had known since the death of Louis XIV. The corrupt administration of the directory and the excesses committed by the radicals made France tired to both the moderates and the radicals. There was a common desire for peace and security. Opportunity lay before a soldier of genius who choose to seize them. Napoleon was the supreme opportunist, and he had a keen insight into the forces at work. He did not care for the means to attain the ends and the coup d'etat placed supreme power in the hand of Napoleon Bonaparte.

If ever a country needed a dictator, France did in 1799. Ten years of revolution had produced disorder, strife, and insecurity. On the other hand, the French people were determined to preserve the benefits of the revolution namely equality before the law, the carrer open to talents etc. The French army equally determined to keep the natural frontiers which it had conquered. Thus, the dictator for which the country yearned needed a peculiar combination of qualities. He must be a revolutionary, a successful general, and a statesman without being a party man. Napoleon was the man born for the task. Never before in modern times has an epoch been so shaped by a single personality as the first fifteen years of the 19th century were shaped by Napoleon Bonaparte. During that decade and a half the whole continent of Europe was knit together by the struggle which arose out of his ambitions.

The French revolution would never have exercised such a profound influence over modern civilisation had not its spirit been personified by Napoleon, and carried into every country of Europe by the armies which he commanded, sweeping away the cobwebs of feudalism as with the rushing mighty wind. The way had already been prepared by the National convention. On anarchy they had superimposed a despotism, and when the convention fell the only power that remained standing was the army. Napoleon succeeded to the heritage of caeser and Cromwell, his oppertunity is clear and his success intelligible. By his aid the convention had triumphed, on his strong arm the Directory was to lean, in him the revolution was to find both consummation and contradiction. For Napoleon Bonaparte was at once the embodiment of the principles of the revolution, and the representative of the reaction against them.

Very often he exhibited Machia-Vellian traits. He could easily roused his soldiers with a battle cry leading to inevitable victory and send home a report that might be the envy of newspaper correspondents–a report splattered with heroic names. At times he was totally cynical. He was welcomed as a liberator with enthusiasm and flowers, he gave the Milanese freedom from Austrian domination, he patronised their artists and men of letters. A few days later he imposed a levy of twenty million Francs and despatched wagons of their works of art to France. Having planted a tree of liberty in the square of St.Mark and placed a copy of the Declaration of the rights of man beneath the paw of the venetian lion, the French handned the city over to the Austrian enemy, the leader of the crusade against revolutionary France since 1792 ! in return France gained Lombary and the Austrian Netherlands. Despite his demonic belief in his own destiny and over-weening confidence, he suffered all the while from inferiority complex. The ruling class of Europe detested Napoleon since he was a product of revolutionary France. Metternich referred to him as "Revolution incarnet". Yet, there was something in him that ticked off and that which enabled him to dominate the stage of Europe for nearly 20 yeas.

The story of the corsican boy who made himself Emperor of France is one of the most romantic episode in history. Napoleon Bonaparte was born on 15th August, 1769, in Ajaccio, Corsica, a short time after the island had been sold by Genoa to France. Rousseau wrote "I have a presentiment that this little island will someday astonish Europe." There was born the boy, Napoleon, who justified the prediction. His family belonged to the impoverished patriotic Corsican nobility, and the youthful Bonaparte dreamed romantically of leading his people to a reconquest of their independence. But thanks to his father's belated conversion to a pro-French attitude, the slenderness of the family purse was overcome. A friend of his father found to have the boy educated at state expense at various military schools in France. There the influences of his Corsican heridity and the dominant charecteristics of his own personality manifested themselves. An alien in a foreign land he was driven inwards on himself. Napoleon became tacit turn and meditative, an omnivorous reader and a diligent student particularlyr of history and geography. There was no holidays at the military school and the boys could not leave the school to see their parents. At school the young Napoleon was marked by a precocious sense of responsibility towards his work and his family, by a growing contempt for his fellows, who despised his poverty, and laughed at his foreign accent and name. "The youngster is made of granite, but there is a volcano inside", said one of his teachers. He (Napoleon) found that the French despised the Corsicans. He reacted by becoming solitary and studious. His feelings were all the stronger for being an exile, and he longed to avenge his countrymen at the expense of the French Government that was paying for his education. Once he wrote to his mother "I do not have any friend except the books". During his student carrer he hated France and dreamed of a war of independence for Corsica. He wrote to an exiled patriot, "I was born when my country was dying.....My cradle was surrounded, from the very day of my birth, by the cries of the dying, the groans of oppression, and the tears of despair". After passing from the military school, he served as a Lieutenant in the French army.

The revolution dramatically changed his prospects. On August 10, 1792, at Paris, he had his first experience with a revolutionary mob, an experience which left him with an unconquerable aversion for demagogus, and their radical follower. In 1793 a final dispute with Paoli, the venerable patriotic leader of Corsicans, forced Bonaparts and his family with his adopted country and become an ardent patriot and jacobin. Towards the end of 1793 he took a distinguished part in recapturing Toulon from the English. As a reward the government promoted the young officer to Brigadier general. He defended the government from the attack of Parisian mob in 1795. Napoleon was rewarded with the command of the army of the interior. In March 1796, he obtained his heart's dream, the command of the army of Italy. The Italian campaign was the dawn of his carrer and his accession to the French throne was its logical result. Two days before his marriage with Josephine, he was appointed to the command of Italy. That command marks the real beginning of Bonaparte's political carrer, and a turning point in the history of the war.

Napoleon was only five feet two inches tall, his gesture were brusque, while his glance annihilated resistance, even the blustering Augereau (a soldire) confessed that he was struck down by that terribel eye. The army of Italy resented the appointment of a Junior. But when this slender, round shouldered small and sickly looking young man appeared they saw instantly that they had a master. He was imperious and laconic. "The more

I saw of him", recorded one who knew him well,"the more he intimidated me. I always felt that no emotion of the heart could act upon him....I felt that his spirit was a cold and biting sword that froze as it wounded". He was marvelously gifted. His brain was a wonderful organ, swift in its processes, tenacious in its grip, lucid, tireless, and it was served by an incredibly accurate memory. He won his battles in his head before he won them in the field. He said of himself, "Different matters are stored away in my brain as in a chest of drawers. When I wish to interrupt a piece of work I close that drawer and open another. None of them get mixed...." His intellectual gifts were as varied as vast, imagination, clearness of vision telescopic over the widest horizon, and microscopic into the minutest detail, terrific power of concentration, a resistless impulse to employ his mind in absorbing knowledge and in cordinating it for action. He rarely smiled, he never laughed, his conversation was generally monologue, but brilliant, animated. He had a magnificent talent as stage manager and actor, setting the scenes, playing the parts consummately in all the varied ceremonies in which he was necessarily involved. He won the devotion and admiration of his soldiers by the glamour of his victories. He was as little as he was big.

Ten years of revolution had culminated in the rule of a military adventurer. France tamely accepted the warrior who had made himself master of the republic. Other men (Danton, Robespierre) had stood on the swift wheel of French affairs during the previous decade, but the effort of scrambling to the top had left them without power to stay there. Affairs had never moved faster than in 1799, and the years that followed. According to Hazen, "By a successful coup detat the famous young warrior had clutched at power....Fate had trembled dangerously in the balance on that grey, Sunday afternoon, but the gambler had won. His thin sallow face, his sharp, metallic voice, his imperious gesture....his long disorder hair became a part of the history of the times. Manifesting the intensely vivid impression which he had made upon his age and was to deepen". Such was the man who effected the Coup d'etat of 18 Brumaire (November 1799).

Rise of Napoleonic Dictatorship–Causes

Napoleon was the child of the revolution. He owed his rapid rise from obscurity to political power to the events of the revolution and the oppertunities that they threw open. When he seized power by Coup, it coincided with the success of the revolution and political vulnerability. After he became the first consul, he stressed that he was the heir to the revolution and he had stabilised the principles on which it began. He thought that his principal task was to close the romance of the revolution.

He retained some achivements of the revolution. He organised the ancient regime, and he consolidated the revolution.

His success was due in large part to the extraordinary oppertunity which French politics at that time offered. He was thorougly convinced of his own abilities. He was a masterful oppertunist. The momentum of the revolutionary movement in France had burned itself out, and the time was now ripe for a popular soldier with a genius for organisation to take over authority. Fatalistic and even superstitious, Napoleon believed that he was a "man of destiny". Napoleon was unscrupulous. According to Hayes, "Knowing what he desired, he was ready to employ any means to attain his ends". No love for theories or principles, no fear of God or man, no sentimental aversion to bloodshed, nothing could deter him from striving to ralize his vaulting but self centered ambition.

He combined in him love for order and authority as a soldier and a hatred for the ancien regime as an offspring of the revolution. Royalists and reactionaries, moderates and republicans, all saw in the overthrow of the Directory the possibility of the opening of a new era satisfactory to their several interest, hopeful for their divergent aims. The royalists regarded it as a step towards the restoration of the Bourbons, the moderate Republicans imagained that it might establish liberty. But the masses saw in it, the triumph of the strong man who would restore order in France. Infact, the popular general, who understood the art of conciliating the soldiery, and possessed the true spirit of command, and who knew how to draw the eyes of all men upon himself.

The people of France willingly accepted Napoleon as their master, because they wanted a strong ruler, independent of party, because they were tired of the Directory and its incompetence. No one shed a drop of tear for the fall of the directory. Abbe sieyes, who was one of the Director desired to make experiment with a new constitution on a new principle, "Confidence from below and power from above". He joined hand with Napoleon to organize the Coup of November 1799 which led to the rise of Napoleon. France turned to Napoleon at a moment at which he was resolving to rescue France. According to Riker, "Public opinion in France was tired of political agitation, tired of endless elections, tired of disorders...." Ten years of revolutionary turmoil had dimmed the fire of political idealism and made the citizen indifferent to plots both Red" and "White", predisposing them to accept the accomplished fact, whether it was legal or illegal. They were ready to support any leader who would maintain the advantages that they had gained and restore tranquillity. Napoleon himself, ever a superb realist, struck the correct pose. He was not overthrowing the republic,on the contrary, he was consolidating it. He once remarked, "My policy is to govern in accordance with the wishes of the great majority". It was generally felt, here was the man who can reconcile liberty with order. He once said; "what the French want is glory and the satisfaction of their vanity, as for liberty they have no conception".He possessed an effective means of satisfying his ambition. He was heir to the militarism of the French revolution, and he made himself the idol of the soldiers.

Napoleon had no desire to restore the Bourbons and feudalism, on the contrary the destruction of the ancien regime was the presupposition of all his work. Privilege, once for all, was abolished, and free competition had taken its place. Natural and social inequality remained; but legal inequality was abolished. He took no account of birth or political antecedents, talents and loyality to himself were his sole criterion of merit. Of his Marshals, Massena was the son of a wine merchants, Ney of a cooper, Augereau of a mason. Napoleon said, "I do not believe, that the French love liberty and equality. The French have not been sentiment honour. That sentiment must be nourished, they must have distinctions". Napoleon realized equality, liberty he did not attempt to realize at all. When he said, "I am the revolution, he meant it, and it followed that the revolution was not liberty. It was he who delivered France from anarchy". The people didnot really want liberty any more than they wanted equality, even if they wanted it, they were not for it, even if they were fit for it, they should not have it. He once said, power is my mistress. I love it as a musician loves his violin, I love it as an artist:. France was at once his country and his property, and duty conspired with interest to support his absolute control. Napoleon had remarked, "They seek to destory the revolution in my person...I am the French revolution, and I must defend it".

THE CONSULATE

The Consulate and its Constitution :

The overthrow of the directory necessitated the revision of the constitution. A provisional consulate was appointed to draw up a new constitution. The provisional government lasted only unitl 13th December, 1799 on that day the new constitution of the year VIII was promulgated. Drafted by the prince of constitution mongers, Abbe Sieyes, it seemed the most fantastic scheme ever evolved out of the brain of a doctrinaire. Externally it retained the liberal forms of the revolution, in reality it organised a strongly autocratic and paternalistic regime. It concealed Napoleon's military dictatorship, under the veil of a popular forms. The scheme, despite lip homage to democratic ideas, virtually extinguished popular representation.

The executive power was vested in three consuls. They were elected for ten years. The post of the first consul was given to Napoleon Bonaparte. The first consul enjoyed unlimited power. He proposed legislation. The first consul appointed the Ministers, the ambassoders, the officers of the army and the navy. He appointed all the Magistrates of civil and criminal courts. He also signed treaties subject to the ratification of the legislatiive assemblies. Thus, he controlled the military and diplomatic service and the general administration with out being responsible for his actions to the legislative assemblies. The other two consuls (Sieyes and Ducos) were mere assistants. In 1802 Napoleon was appointed first consul for life.

The legislative power was divided among four bodies whose effectiveness was restricted by an elaborate system of checks and balances. The first consul appointed a council of state whose main work was to propose legislation. Since it was appointed by the first consul, all initiative in legislation rested with the first consul. The tribunate, composed of 100 members, could discuss and criticise proposals brought beforeit, but could not vote upon them. The legislative body of 300 members, listen in silence to the proposals of law which were brought before it and voted for their acceptness or rejection without discussing them. The three consuls appointed the senate consisting of 60 members whose main functions were to appoint tribunes and legislators and to act as the custodian of the constitution.

France, weary of revolution and afraid of counter-revolution, eagerly surrendered its liberties into the hands of the man (Napoleon Bonaparte) who promised it security and order. The constitution was ratified by a popular plebiscite. According to Cobban. "The real motive power of the great machine was the first counsul. Other institutions were devised to mask the transition from liberty to despotism". The constitution as drawn up by the consulate was a mere sham. The constitution had a liberal facade, but it built up the autocratic regime of one man Napoleon Bonaparte. It organised the rule of the drillmaster who had no other conception of government than that of a nation yielding prompt obedience to his commands. Napoleon began to act as an absolute monarch in the garb of the constitution. France was a republic in name but in fact the government became a veiled monarchy. The hastily drawnup constitution sounded the death knell of Republican government.

Reforms Under The Consulate

Napoleon's genious was not confined to the battle fields and conquest, in internal administration as well he showed his versality. His success against the European coalition and conquest of a vast empire gave him unprecedented popularity. The name of Napoleon acquired a hypnotic influence on the people of France. He addressed himself to the establishment of strong, efficient, and orderly administration and in order to do what he set up an autocratic rule. His aim was to bring out order and peace out of the prevailing confusion that had been the supreme need of the hour. According to Fisher, "He found Chaos and left order, Inherited mutiny and created discipline....Napoleon was a voltairean". It was his task to reconcile the new France with the old. His government was a scientific despotism based on plebiscits. Throughout his carrer Napoleon professed himself to be the son cf the revolution, the champion of the ideals of equality, liberty and Fraternity. It was to the revolution that he owned his position in France, and it was to France that he claimed to be preserving the fruits of the revolution. But he laid greater stress on equality than liberty. He declared. "What the French people want is equality not liberty". According to Hayes, "Napoleon interpreted Fraternity in a national rather than international sense". The abosolute power which he had secured was employed with indefatigable energy in the work of reorganisation. The revolutionary experiment in democrasy had issued at the cost of liberty. As an administrator and reformer Napoleon was to some extent influenced by the contempoary philosophers. From hisitory of Sparta, Switzerland, England, he learnt the lessons about the need for the establishment of welfare state and reforms for the well-being of the people. In his reforms he was guided by four distinct aims, namely, to establish equality and fraternity in the social and economic life of France, to strengthen the central government, to reduce the rights and powers of the self governing institutions, and to leave behind him a fame which would be fondly remembered by the posterity. According to Thomson, "Napoleon brought to the task of reorganiation the qualities of swift decision and action,the same concentration upon essentials which had already brought him success in war. The spirit behind the great reforms of the consulate at home was the transference of the methods of Bonaparte the general to the tasks of Bonaparte the statesman".

The Administrative System

The system of local self government established in 1790 had failed. The communes had proved insubordinate to the central authorities and the individual citizens to their communal officials. The latter were ignorant, incompetent, and corrupt. Napoleon once said, "Since 1790 the 36,000 communes represent 36,000 orphan girls, neglected for ten years by the muncipal guardians of the convention and the Directory. A change of Mayors, counsellors has means, as a rule, nothing but a change in a method of robbery, there has been robbery of the roads, robbery of the personal effects of the commune". This state of things Napoleon set himself to remedy by a system of centralised administration. The departments were divided into arrondissments, over each department set a prefect, over each arrondissment a sub-prefect, over each commune a Mayor. To assist the prefect, a general council was established, and in similar fashion, the sub-prefect had the aid of a district council and the mayor of a muncipal council. These officers were appointed by the Government. However, the councils had no real authority. In this way the centralisation of the old regime was reestablished. The prefect took the place of the former intendent, and the result was practical efficiency at the cost of local initiative. Even the police in big cities was also controlled by the central government. This highly centralised administration of the country afforded the people little direct voice in public affairs, but it possessed the advantage of assuring prompt and uniform execution of governmental decrees. Further, he sought to enlist the sympathy of every section of the community by doing away with all party distinctions. The emigres and the nonjuring clergy were sympathetically treated. For him the revolutionary past was over, and he had no intention of rekindling the fires of ancient passions.

Financial Reconstruction

French finance was in no better condition in 1799 that it had been ten years earlier. Napoleon wanted to guard his regime against any financial crisis. The assignats (paper currency) had already been repudiated in 1797. The trade and commerce were badly affected. The government of France was on the verge of bankruptcy. To stabilize the financial condition of the consulate, severe economy was introduced in public expenditure previously. The taxes were not realised properly. Napoleon himself appointed the tax collectors, instituted a court for the verification of their accounts, bound them by caution money, and was inexorable to all corruption. Henceforth, there are no arrears and no malversation. Corrupt and inefficient officials were punished severely. The Bank of France was established in 1800 and "a sinking fund" was instituted. According to Hayes,"the bank of France is one of the soundest financial institution in the world". During the consulate too bagan the industrial regeneration of France. He took special care to protect French products against foreign competition. Serious efforts were made to stimulate industrial production. A society for the encouragement of National industry was founded. Napoleon's interest in industrial production was as well received by the workers as it was by the manufacturers.He abolished the guild system. The legislation against striking workmen was strengthened. The working class were among Napoleon's enthusiastic supporters, because they had good wages and steady employment. A special find called the extraordinary domain was raised from indemnities imposed on the defeated countries to meet the expenses of the army. So Napoleon's war ere not at all great drains on the French exchequer. He made his enemies pay the expenses of the war.

The Press

The liberty of the press had been one of the principles of the revolution. How little it had been realized in practice may be illustrated by the following decree of the convention, "Whoever shall be convicted of having composed or printed works which urge the dissolution of the national representation, the reestablishment of the monarchy or of any other power incompatible with the soverignity of the people, shall be brought before the special tribunal and punished with death". He subjected journals and books to censorship, prohibited printed and publishing except under licence, and revoked the licence if anything was produced, contrary to the duties of subject towards the sovereign and the security of the state. Hostile opinion was thus silenced. But that was not enough. Favourable opinion must be created, and created by education.

Education

Nepoleon's conception of education was purely political. He regarded it as a machinary for the production of efficient subjects. He said, "there will never be a fixed political state of things in this country until we have a body of teachers instructed on established pricniples. So long as the people are not taught from their earliest years, whether they ought to be republicans, royalists, or christians, the state cannot properly be called a nation". In accordance with this principle he drew up his scheme of education. Napoleon reared an imposing state system of public instruction. Every commune would have a primary school under the supervision of the prefect or sub prefect, secondary or Grammer schools were to provide special training in French, Latin, and elementary science, and , whether supported by public or private enterprise. Every town, as far as possible, would have a high school. Technical schools would be opened under the control of the government. He established a single university, with a corporate existance and independent property, its officers were a grand master, a chancellor, and a treasurer, all appointed by the emperor, and they were assisted by a council, composed of ten permanent members, nominated by the emperor. To this body was entrusted the absolute control of higher as well as elementary education. Every teacher and official in the public colleges and schools was nominated by the Grand master. Private schools already existing were swept into the system, and they wre only allowed to give instruction up to a acertain standard. All teachings was based on the principles of christinanity, loyality to the head of the state, and obedience to the rules of the university. The Catholic seminaries were subjected to severe restrictions, only one was allowed to exist in each department for these the university drew up the regulations and supplied the teachers. Napoleon said, "Our boys must be neither bigot nor sceptics. They must conform to the state of the nation and of society". The curriculum was adjusted to this conception. The end of education was not man, it was Napoleon and the state. But lack of funds and shortage of lay teachers were responsible for a large number of private Catholic schools.

Legal Reforms

Napoleon's greatest claim as the benefactor of mankind rests primarily on his legal codes. These codes became the most effective instruments in spreading the ideas of the French revolution. It is an attempt to contain the laws of France within the smallest possible compass and in a form at once clear, logical and complete. The constitution of 1791 had promised a uniform national code, the National convention had already begun it, but the preoccupations of the leading revolutionaries, delayed its completion. The code Napoleon, which came into effect in 1804 and is still the law of France, was a brief, clear collection of leagal principles. It hammered out a synthesis between the liberal, customary, and natural law of the revolution, and the Roman law which under the directory had been revived in reaction against the revolution. The code Napoleon assured all Frenchmen equality before law, regardless of rank, riches, or religion. Businessmen applauded the abolition of internal customs barrier, the benefits of a uniforms system of weights, measures, and coinage, the improvement in roads, harbours etc. The peasants were grateful for the abolition of feudal dues. Besides, proprietors who had acquired land confiscated from the Church or from exiled no less could thank Napoleon for legalising their titles of ownership. Napoleon codified the laws and the following codes were compiled; civil code, code of civil procedure, code of criminal procedure, penal code and commercial code. Out of these five, the civil code is most widely acclaimed. He supported absolute authority of the father over wife and children alike. The father had the right on the income of his sons, and the property of the father was to be distributed equally among the sons. Complete freedom was not granted to women. He once said, "the only job of a woman is to marry and to give birth to children". The code Napoleon preserved the chief social conquest of the revolution, such as civil equality, religious toleration,equality of inheritance, emancipation of serfs, abolition of feudalism and privilege. The code confimed the rights of private property.

According to Hayes, "Bonaparte was rightly hailed as a second justinian ("Roman law giver).

Concordat with Church

Nepoleon himself had no pronounced religious beliefs. If not an agnostic, he was at the most a vague deist. He said, "Let them call me a papist, I am nothing, I was a Mohammedan in Egypt, I shall be a Catholic here for the good of the people...I do not believe in religions... It was by becoming a Catholics that I terminated the vendean war, by becoming a Musalman that I obtained a footing in Egypt,.... and had I to govern a nation of Jews, I would rebuild solomon's temple". Religion was to him only a useful political instrument, a national imaginative focus, a social cement, a safety valve. He said, "The people must have a religion, and the religion must be in the hands of the government". He had a lively sense of the political importance of religion. His aim was to end the religious strife of the revolution and find a realistic settlement. He wanted to separate royalism from Catholicism.

The Civil Constitution of the clergy had created a breach with the pope. He wanted to befriend the pope, as a vast majority of Frenchmen were Catholics, and Napoleon wanted their political support because a large number of them backed the future Louis XVIII. He believed that the control of religion must be vested in the sovereign. To effect this end Napoleon had recourse to the Pope. He said, "if the pope had not existed, I should have had to create him for this occasion". In the world empire to which he aspired it was necessary that the soul aswell as the body, the spiritual as well as the temporal powers, should be subject to his domination. It was in this spirit that he concluded the concordat of 1801. By it Catholicism was recognised as the religion of the great majority of the French people. The Pope accepted the work of the revolution and reconciled himself to the confiscation of Church property and the suppression of the monasteries. All the officials of the church would received their salaries and take on oath of loyalty to the government.. The Pope agreed that all existing bishops would resign, and that in the future, bishops nominated by the French Government would be instituted by the Pope. The bishops would appoint the priests. The non-juring clergy were released from prison. Thus, the Catholic church was reestablished though not in its pre-revolutionary power. It was made dependent on the state. By this compromise the papacy was protected against Bonaparte's threat to secularise the state, while Napoleon succeeded in defeating the pope's desire to have catholicism declared the State religion. The schism between the church and the state was healed. But the religious settlement proved to be among the less durable of his achivements. In the words of Thomson,"it was not a synthesis, but a compromise, and like many compromises it left both extremes dissatisfied".

Others

Napoleon initated some of the good features of the age of Louis XIV. He inaugurated a vast series of public works, Roads were constructed, canals were dug, French manufactures fostered by a system of production, the Lyons silk industry was revived, agriculture was improved by the new methods from England. The principal sea ports, both naval and commercial were enlarged and fortified. State palaces were redecorated. Monuments were erected. The city of Paris was beautified. The Louvre museum was completed and adorned with works of art which Bonaparte captured as fruits of victory from Italy, Spain and the Netherland. During the consulate,Paris was begining to lay claim to a position as the pleasure city of Europe. Napoleon also created a new aristocracy of merit by institutions, "the legion of Honour". The legion of honour enabled Napoleon to flatter the varity and reward the merit of loyal followers by distributing medals carrying with them a comfortable annuity for the recipients. A new class of nobility was created and it constituted a great pillar of support for the empire. Further, he tried to restore the French colonial empire. He prevailed upon the Spanish government to recede to France the territory of Louisiana.

Conclusion

In his work of reorganising the institutions of France, Napoleon showed himself at once the heir of the revolution and the product of the reaction against it. He trampled upon liberty which was one of the three great ideas of the revolution. Behind a screen of popular deceptions he restored absolution in France both in theory and in practice. His remark, "I am the revolution", is partially true. His reforms were in accordance with the principles of the revolution insofar as equality is concerned. By throwing "carrers open to talent", he secured to all equal oppertunities and thus ignored any privileged caste. According to Thomson, "The dictatorship of Napoleon in France was a utilitarian, efficient, industrious, hard headed government.... it lacked fanaticism and passions of the rule of Robespierre...". He harmonized old order with the new. The code Napoleon was one of his most enduring achivements. In the words of Fisher, "If the conquests of Napoleon were ephemeral, his civilian work in France was built upon granite". He consolidated the revolution by securing to its people its more valued fruits. He purged the revolution of its excesses and conciliated all section of the people. Hayes remarks, "The memoirs represented Napoleon in the light of a true son and heir of the revolution, who had been raised by the will of the French people to great power in order that he might substantiate, the revolutionary ideas of liberty, equality and fraternity". He carried out far-reaching reforms which ushered in an era of progress and prosperity. But the so-called first empire was different from the French Bourbon monarchy. It was efficient and depended on the willing support of the people.

Foreign policy of the Consulate

At the moment when Bonaparte became first conusul, the republic was still at war with Austria and, England. He urgently needed peace to carry through his reorganisation of France, and all the belligerents were weary of war, but the Austrian emperor could not abandon the ancient imperial provinces on the left bank of the Rhine. And England had for centuries made it the chief end of her policy to keep France out of Belgium, while the French would never consent to giveup those conquests of the revolutionary wars.

The first consul prepared second Italian campaign against Austria. Having sent Moreau to attack the Austrians from Germany, Napoleon set out to meet them in Italy. He accomplished one of the famous exploits, the crossing of the great St. Bernard pass, and unexpectedly appeared before the Austrians. He defeated the Austrians at Marengo in 1800. Moreau, a French general also won a victory over the Austrians at Hohenlinden which opened the road to vienna. The Austrian emperor Francis II was forced to sue for peace. In 1801 both France and Austria concluded a treaty at Luneville. By the peace of Luneville, the emperor of Austria accepted the treaty of Campo formio and agreed that Rhine should remain the boundary of France on the east. The Austrian emperor had to recognise the Batavian, cis-Alpine and Helvetic republics established by Napoleon.

The people acquiesced in his dictatorship because they were weary of the atrocities of the revolution. The administrative, judical, financial organisation and the great codes are still in force. When Napoleon assumd the government the opinion of the country was with him, he was the crying need. Neither it can be said that he destroyed, all that he did was to substitute despotism for anarchy. But despotism was the condition of reorganisation, and as such it was welcomed by a people distracted by a decade of revolution. But they centralise the administration and making it more efficient he did much to organise, the ancient regime. In this respect he may be looked upon as the destroyer of the revolution. He deprived the Departments of all powers of self government and emphasised a reaction towards the old system of intendants by a law which imposed a prefect and a sub prefect on every department. The principle of election was subordinated to that of selection. Inspite of all these Napoleon proved himself to be one of the greatest social reformers. So it has been rightly remarked, "If the conquest of Napoleon were ephemeral, his civilian work in France was built upon granite".

In 1802 Napoleon became the consul for life which was the penultimate step towards assumption of imperial crown by him. He once said, "I found the crown of France lying on the ground and I picked it up with my sword". In 1803 when the toyalist began to conspire against him, Napoleon was invested with the imperial title inorder to render security to his life and to give the new regime permanance. The senate adopted the proposal for investing Napoleon with imperial status, which was supported by the people of France unanimously in a plebiscite. The senate passed a decree, saying, the government of the republic is entrusted to an emperor. He was crowned with great pomp. So once again France had a monarchical form of government with an emperor as. Thus, Britain was for the second time left to carry on the struggle single handed. In order to ensure that France would not get supplied and raw materials from abroad, England claimed the right to search netural ships. Russia, Sweden, Denmark and Prussia protested against this and formed the Northern league and declared war on Great Britain. So the Armed Neutrality was revived at the instigation of Napoleon. The object of this league was to prevent England from searching netural ships of French goods. When this league was formed the English fleet under Nelson bomarded Copenhagen (Denmark's capital) and captured Danish fleet. This victory and the assassination of Czar Paul of Russia, broke up the Armed neturality. Command of the sea also led to the final extinction of French power in Egypt. Both sides were by this time convinced that it was useless to prolong the contest between a whale and an elephant. So the two agreed to make the peace of Amiens. (1802) By the peace of Amiens, England restored all colonial conquests to the French except Trinidad and Ceylon. French got back West Indian islands. France withdrew her control from the dominions of the pope and Naples in Italy. England recognised the new government of France. England promised to restore Malta to the knights of St. John. Both France and England withdrew from Egypt. Both the powers were to sail their ships freely round the cape of Good hope. Apparently the peace of Amiens was a great triumph for Napoleon Bonaparte. The treaty was more in the nature of a truce than a settlement. It was made because both sides were weary of warfare. Napoleon was given a free hand to impose his own policy on Europe. Great Britain did not succeed in crushing France and the French mastery on land was maintained. But this one sided settlement cannot prove lasting. No doubt, both sides needed peace, but neither was really willing to pay the price demanded by other. Hence, after sometime war again brokeout in Europe.

FOREIGN POLICY OF NAPOLEON (1804-1807)

The establishment of the French empire (1804) was an event of European importance, it was the last phase of the revolution. The revolution was crystallized in the empire. Napoleon imposed the revolution on Europe, and it is the importance of the empire that under his direction that movement was extended over the whole continent. The empire was not an interruption but an extention of the revolution. Until the peace of Tilsit the monarchies of Europe were united against France by a common hostility to the revolution. The empire, which was the personal predominance of Napoleon, was an incident in the history of the revolution, it was the revolution in its Europen aspect. When the empire succeeded to the consulate, it inherited the international situation which had been created earlier.

According to Hazen, "Napoleon wanted to make France a "La Grande" Nation of Europe and for this a spirited foreign policy of Constant militarism was very essential", In fact he dazzled the people of France by his victories. The key of his foreign policy was to smash the British power. It was his duty as the heir of the revolution to defend the prize which the armies of revolution had own. He was inspired by the example of Alexander, the Great and Caeser. He wanted to leave his name to the posterity as a world conqueror. The main object of Napoleon were the colonial expansion, revival of the ancient glory of France, and the strengthening of the military power of the country. But the key of his foreign policy was to smash the British power and to exercise effective pressure upon England in three ways, by the suppression of British trade, the capture of British colonies, and the invasion of England.

The truce with England secured by the treaty of Amiens proved to be of short duration. He complained that England declined to evacuate Malta, on the otherhand, the English demanded that France should evacuate Holland and Switzerland. Further, when Napoleon extended French influence along the Rhine, Britain was threatened with the loss of valuable commercial privileges in all those region. The British were also hostile to any French attempt for the revival of the French colonial empire. A large majority of people in England were hostile to the French revolution and its atrocities and they regarded Napoleon as an heir of the revolution. France also refused to renew the Anglo-French commercial treaty, Napoleon was extremely annoyed that the British government allowed journals to attack him verbally and to ridicule him in caricature. But the actual casusbelli was Malta and when the negotiation on Malta brokedown, war between France and England also brokeout. Napoleon welcomed the renewal of war. During the year 1803-04, made elaborate preparations for an armed invasion of Great Britain He assembled near Boulogne the finest war machine in history. In England these preparations aroused much alarm. The most important step that Britain took to meet the crisis was to recall pitt, the younger (Prime minister) to power in place of the incompetent Addington. The only countermove that pitt could make to build up another of those craking coalition machines, as Napoleon contemptuously called them. No doubt, Napoleon's actions had offended most of the other powers. Prussia was alarmed by his occupation of Hanover. Austria was perturbed by his activities in Italy, the Czar (Russia) was shocked by the Judicial murder of d'Enghien. But it was difficult to bring them to the point of actually declaring war, as they were all, handicapped by money. But pitt was the real bone of the third coalition, which was formed in 1805 by England, Russia, Austria and Sweden to overthrow Napoleon.

The Trafalgar Campaign (1805)

The main intention of the campaign of 1805 centred in the attempt of Napoleon to achieve the supreme object of his military ambition,. the invasion of England. A large number of ships, boats, frigates etc. were collected, villeneuve, the French admiral, was to sail from Toulon to join the Spanish fleet at cadiz. The two fleets would than sail for the west Indies to attack British shipping and trade. The French were certain that they would be pursued by Nelson (British Admiral) to the West Indies. While on the high seas, they would give Nelson the slip and sail back to France and in conjunction with the fleet at Brest invade England. But unfortunately the fleet of Brest could not unite with them due to the presence of Nelson in sea. Nelson pursued the French fleet and defeated it decisively at the battle of Trafelgar in 1805. Lord Nelson lost his life in the conflict, but from that day to the close of the Napoleonic era, British supremacy on the high sea was not seriously challenged. This victory destroyed the French naval power. The victory at Trafalgar was decisive in determining the continuation of England's mastery on the seas.

War Agaianst Austria

The fighting on the continent against Austria was brief and decisive, and Napoleon's victories resulted in significant modification of the political balance in Europe. Napoleon advanced towards Austria and reached near Danube and surrounded the Austrian army at Ulm on 20th October, 1805. He then entered Vienna. On December 2, 1805 Napoleon won perhabs his

,most famour victory, the battle of Austerlitz against the Austrians, on the first anniversary of his coronations as emperor. After the battle of Austerlitz, pitt, the younger said, "Roll up the map of Europe, it will not be wanted these ten years". Napoleon wrote,: "The battle of Austerlitz is the most splendid of all I have fought." The defeat of Austria was complete, and it was acknowledged by the terms of pressburg. The immediate result of Austerlitz was the enforced withdrawl of Austria from the third coalition. By the treaty of pressburg Austria ceded venetia, Istria and Dalmatia to France. Austria gave tyrol to Bavaria. The Austrian emperor Frances II renounced his suzerainty over Bavaria and wurttemburg which were converted into independent kingdoms. Now Austria was reduced to a second class power.

Reconstruction of Germany

After Austerlitz Napoleon's title of Emperor began to take on a new meaning. After the treaty of pressburg, Napoleon assumed the role of a second charlemagne and began to surrounded himself with a chain of dependent kingdoms. The time had now come for the final reconstruction of Germany, long contemplated by Napoleon, and on July 19, 1806 the confederation of the Rhine was formally proclaimed under his protectorate. This included 16 German states, of which the largest were Bavaria, wurttemburg and Baden. It was to have a sort of shadow Diet (parliament) at Frankfort, but it was to look to him as protector. It was to have no independent foreign policy, and it was to furnish contingents to Napoleon's army. Napoleon declared himself the president of this confederation. On 1 August 1806 France formally declared that she no longer recognised the Holy Roman Empire and on August 6, 1806, that Venerable institution came to a dishonoured end. The Holy Roman Empire had long since ceased to be effective, but it was atleast a symbol of German unity, and its dissolution marked the attainment of an end for which France had been struggling for centuries. By erasing a mazy network of internal frontiers, Napoleon unconsciously took an important step in the direction of German unity. The complicated political map of Germany was greatly simplified. The old Germany was gone for ever.

War Against Prussia

Prussia which had so far remained neutral finally joined the third coalition. Because Prussia regarded the creation of the confederation of the Rhine with great apprehension. Further, there was a good deal of suspense over the fate of Hanover. The upper classes in Prussia were far less dispose to truckle to the conqueror than their king, and they found a leader in the high spirited queen Louise. Then came a crowing insult. After the death of pitt, a coalition ministry had been formed in England, with fox at the foreign office. Fox had always maintained that Bonaparte was more sinned against than sinning, and he took the first oppetunity to open negotiations for peace. But these negotiations ended in failure. On the otherhand, Napoleon intimated that he would hand back Hanover to king George provided that Britian would consent to sicily being restored to the kingdom of Naples. When these discussion leaked out, the torrent of fury that arose in Prussia carried away even the Prussian king Fredrick william. Appealing for the support of Austria, Russia and England, he mobilised his army against France. Napoleon had watched the mechinations of the Prussian rulling class with close attention. He absolutely prepared when the rupture came. Without waiting for assistance from the Russians who were coming up, the Prussian army, under Brunswick advanced against the veterans of Napoleon. According to Hayes, "The resulting battle of Jena and Auerstadt proved the superiority of Napoleon's army over the Prussian, they marked not only a disastrous defeat but the total collapse of the Prussian army and the destruction of the military prestige acquired under Fredrick the Great". Napoleon entered Berlin and the Prussian resistance was completely crushed.

War with Russia

The conquest of Europe was incomplete, and the result of Jena had produced no effect on the resistance of Russia. Russia was a more formidable oppenent than Prussia. Now the fighting was shifted to the vast swampy polish plains of East Prussia, where the great desolate stretches, the bitter cold of the approaching winter, and scarcity of food became great obstacles in the path of the invaders. In 1807 the French Army fought a fierce battle with the Russians in the battle field of Eyleau. But it was a drawn battle. On June 14, 1807 Napoleon defeated the Russians at Friendland, and the great fortress of Danzigand Konigsberg fell into his hands. The tser Alexander I at once sued for peace.

The Peace of Tilsit (1807)

Napoleon met tsar Alexander I on a raft in the river Niemen and the latter was very deeply impressed by the formers personality. Alenander's first words were, "I hate the English as much as you do",to which Napoleon replied, "in that case peace is as good as made". Both the emperors conversed in the most dulcet, rapturous way, "why did not we two meet earlier", said the tsar. By the treaty of Tilsit the Czar recognised the confederation of the Rhine, now augmented by a Prussian territories west of the Elbe. Prussian Poland was formed into a grand Duchy of Warsaw, with the elector of

Saxony as its ruler. Russia was to observe the Berlin decree. Both the emperor had divided Europe between each other. Russia was not compelled to pay any compensation, but she was given a free hand to extend its empire in Finland and Turkey. Purssia was dismembered. Purssian Army was reduced to 42,000 army. A heavy war indemnity was imposed on Prussia. Russia was to restore the Ionian islands to France and to make common cause with her if England did not come to terms with France. Both Prussia and Russia recognised the new kingdoms created by Napoleon. In secret articles Prussia was required to close her harbors to the English and take common action with France and Russia against the mistress of the Sea. Such was Tilsit, which left each monarchy with the comforting feeling that he had outwitted the other. The year 1807 marked the highest watermark of the French glory. Napoleon was at the zenith of his truimph. According to Riker, "Tilsit was in a sense, the turning point of his (Napoleon's) fortune". The third coalaition collapsed and Napoleon had broken Prussia and gained full military control over Germany from one end to the other. Above all, the power and prestige of Napoleon reached its climax at the time of the treaty of Tilsit.

The Continental Blockade

Napoleon found it impossible to make a direct attack upon England, so he sought to bring England to terms by indirect means. No doubt, the military effort which accompanied the revolution had resulted under the direction of Napoleon in the conquest of Europe. By the creation of a group of subordinate governments the emperor of the French became the effective soverign of all Europe. The continent from Paris to Warsaw was governed by a single executive. Napoleon's general became regent, his brothers became kings, and his national government became continental dominion. But his most obstinate enemy was England and Napoleon was bent upon bringing England to her knees. For this he introduced the continental system. Ever since Trafalgar had made invasion impossible, he had been turning over in his mind a scheme for starving Britian into surrender. The industrial revolution was in full swing there. No longer self supporting economically, the country was dependent on international trade for its very existence. If that trade were cut off there would ensure a financial crisis, in which starving mobs would overthrow the government and insist on an immediate peace-on Napoleon's term. So, as Napoleon was bent upon briging England to her knees, he decided to launch a commercial war against her. The continental system is the term that Napoleon himself applied to that set of measures by means of which he confidently expected to ruin English economic prosperity. At the moment that Napoleon formally established the continental blockade, he was in sufficient control of Europe. His system was a Europen confederation of states under his domination. By establishing a continental blockade against English products, Napoleon could inflict a crushing blow upon the English economic system. In sheer contempt, he called the English a nation of shopkeepers which had become rich on account of her trade. Hence, he decided to wage on economic war against England. But the idea of compulsory regulation of commercial policy was not new and the theory underlying it was older than the revolution. It was certainly not the brain child of Napoleon, rather it had its rootos in the 18th century economic doctrine of mercantalism. Following the mercantile theory that a country was strong insofar as its exports exceeded its imports, and that the mothe country should have the monopoly of trade with its own colonies. Since 1793 till the close of the Napoleonic era the commercial relations between the two countries consistently followed the older traditions of blockade. The revolutionary government passed severe decrees for the exclusion of British manufactured products from French markets. With Napoleon's seizure of power in 1799 the commercial war between France and England grew more severe. Napoleon thought by closing the continent to the English and forcing them to buy their food-stuffs from France, paying for them in metallic currency, he would deplete the gold reserves of the Bank of England. English credit system would then collapse, and France would emerge victorious. Such was the Napoleonic conception of the commercial war. From 1803 Napoleon made sincere efforts to close the Europen sea-board to British trade.

After his victory at Austerlitz Napoleon was free to promote his plan of conquering the sea by the land, that is, of using his military domination on the continent to close European markets to the English. From 1806 to 1814 the struggle between Napoleon and England was an economic endurance test. In the Berlin decree (November 1806) Napoleon proclaimed a state of blockade against the British isles and closed French and allied ports to ships coming from Great Britain or its colonies. As this decree was binding upon all of France's allies and dependencies, it virtually established , a cordon against British commerce. The prohibition of trade with England was also felt by the neturals in Europe. The British Government retaliated by issuing the orders-in-council in November 1807. According to it all the ports of France and its allies were declared closed. Because of British supremacy on the seas, the neutrals, suffered more keenly from the British order than they did from the more sweeping Berlin decree. The English government was mainly concerned with forcing goods,whether colonial or manufactured, British or enemy, upon the continent via a British port. The order in council was wholly consistent with the traditional English policy of commercial warfare. The next move in the commercial struggle lay with Napoleon, who retorted to the new orders in council with the Milan decree of December 17,1807. His decree stated that every vassel that put in at any port in Great Britain or in its colonies and possessions and paid duty would be held lawful prize if captured by a French warship. The Milan decree was the logical conclusion of Napoleon's policy of forbidding the export of British goods on neutral vessels. England was now totally cutoff from the continent and isolated from all save its colonies. The Fontaimbieau decree was made on 18th October, 1810. It was declared by his decree that the goods confiscated would be burnt publicly. A court of law was also established to punish those found guilty of violating the commercial rules. According to Grant and Temperley; "Napoleon by his military power excluded Great Britian from trade with Europe. Grate Britain by her navy now cut off France and her allies from trade with the rest of the world."

Results of the Continental Blockade

The commercial war fare continued till the fall of Napoleon. The continental system, prevented the entry of English goods into the continental country. It inflicted much damage upon British trade by the closing of European markets to British goods. The English commerce had suffered much due to the continental blockade but Napoleon brought about his own ruin by using this economic weapon against England. The success of the continental system depended upon its being applied universally; if any port in the continent was open to receive British merchandise the system was bound to fail. Portugal, which had always been friendly with Great Britain was reluctant to exclude British trade, and Napoleon determined to enforce the system in that land. After the conclusion of the treaty of Tilsit England was apprehending that Napoleon might seize the Danish fleet and used it against Great Britain. But a British squdron visited copenhagen in 1807, bombarded the city, and captured the Danish fleet. The Pope announced that in the application of the continental system he would remain completely neutral. This enraged Napoleon and at once he occupied the Papal states and kept the Pope under surveillance. Napoleon incorporated Holland into France as Holland did not follow the continental system completely. France also failed to prevent the massive smuggling of British goods in Europe. Further, France had no capacity to met the European demands. The economic warfare involved Great Britain in a war with the neutral powers particularly with Denmark, and the British navy defeated the Danish fleet. The English blockade of the continent was so complete,that the prices of consumer goods shot up and soon there was shortage of food on the continent. People had to suffer terrible hardships and the continental system became very unpopular. Smuggling of British goods became common and defeated the purpose of the continental system. The people began to hate him for his selfish and tyrannical rule. Napoleons pride and ego were the chief reasons for the failure of the continental system. The continental system was based on the fundamental error that Napoleon's subject would sacrifice their personal comforts to enable him to crush his hated enemy, England which was economically indispensable to Europe. The seizures of British goods excited popular feeling to a pitch of fury against the French military agents. Due to shortage of foodstuff and the possibility of internal insurrection, several countries refused to adhere to the continental system. Portugal was the first to give a lead to other European nations. In the application of the continental system, Russia gradually became unwilling and there developed sharp differences between Russia and France. Russia opened her ports to the English ships, and Napoleon marched against her for this breach of terms of the treaty of Tilsit.

According to David Thomson, "The result of continental blockade was impoverishment of the allies of France and their consequent hatred for Napoleon". France and its allies and to face difficulty in meeting their daily needs. Napoleon was fully aware of this fact but being obstinate, he did not budge an inch. The allies of Napolean encouraged smuggling and so made the system ineffective. Napoleon himself many times purchased shoes, and over coats from Great Britain. The continental system hit the Dutch trade very adversely and in the interests of his subjects Louis Napoleon refused to accept it. Napoleon's system inflicted temporary hardships upon Great Britain, but it failed of any permanent effects. It did not in any way retard the rapid rate of British industrial development. The British navy was supreme at sea and successfuly carried out a blockade of Europe and almost starved France and her allies. Portugal defied Napoleon and precipitated the Peninsular war. By putting pressure upon the Czar to end the neutral and smuggling trade in the Southern Baltic, Napoleon only increased the tension between France and Russia. The continental system of Napoleon was the principal tragedy in the drama of his fall. It failed disastrously and Napoleon could not take any advantage from this scheme. The system failed and it proved Napoleon's incapacity as a statesman, and gave a fatal blow to his empire. So the continental system was a great blunder of Napoleon.

The Peninsular War (1808-1814)

The treaty of Tilsit with Russia in 1807 marked the highest Watermark of Napoleon's fortune. If the Sun of his fortune had reached the meridian in 1807 it was also followed by setting of the sun from 1808. The first protest against Napoleon's continental system came from portugal. For over a 100 years Portugal had been linked in close trade relations with England. Napoleon asked Portugal, an old ally of England, to accept the Berlin decrees and to close her ports to British trade. Prince John, the regent of the small country, protested, finally refused, and appealed to Great Britain for help. Therefore, Napoleon arranged with Spain for the conquest and partition of Portugal. But in reality he had no such intentions, it was a mere bluff. French troops under Junot invaded portugal through spain and occupied Lisbon. The Portuguese royal family fled to Brazil.

Napoleon's design against Portugal was part of his larger scheme for the enslavement of Spain. It was unlikely that Napoleon proposed to invade portugal in the interest of Spain without retaining some benefits for France, that benefit was the inclusion of Spain itself within the area of French control. In the Court of the Spanish Bourbons was a situation which Napoleon could utilise in order to have his way in both portugal and Spain. The king, Charles IV, was utterly incompetent, the queen was grossly immoral, her favorite and paramour, Godoy, was the real power behind the throne. The nation despised this precious trio, but hoped for better times under the heir apparent, prince Ferdinand. Mismanagement, slackness, and corruption had made the Spanish government so weak that it was doubtful whether it would be able to exclude British goods from its ports. So, Napoleon decided to sweep it away, and replace the Bourbon by an efficient Bonaparte. According to Hazen, "By a treacherous and hypocritical diplomacy he contrived to get Charles IV, the queen, Gody, and Ferdinand to come to Bayonne in Southern France. No hungry spider ever viewed more cooly a more helpless prey entangled in his web." There, after sardonically watching a degrading family squabble, he bullied Ferdinand and Cajoled charles into surrendering into his hands their claims to the throne. He then announced that he had assigned the vacant throne to his brother Joseph, king of Naples. At this there was a wild outburst of patriotic rage in Spain. To impose his yoke upon a people, loosly united among themselves, intensely provincial in sentiment, and long insured to querrilla warfare, proved to be no easy task. To Napoleon himself the uprising of a people was a strange phenomenon, as yet undreamt of his philosophy. No sooner was Joseph nominated to Madrid than Spain blazed forth into angry resistance. As a nation, the Spaniards were too backward to appreciate the boons which Napoleon offered them. Moveover, they were the most catholic nation in Europe, and Napoleon's attempt to bully the Pope into supporting the continentala system made him appear in their eyes a sort of anti christ. Committees or Juntas were speedily organised in the different provinces, and troops were enrolled. The Spanish rising had opened a new chapter in the historyrof the Napoleonic era.

Great Britain offered to help both Spain and portugal in their struggle against Napoleon, and Arthur wellesley (Later on Wellington) was appointed British commander. Sir Arthur Wellesley landed in Portugal, and won a brilliant victory at Vimiero. Junot was compelled to evacuate Portugal. Portugal ceased to be a French province and became a British base. In December 1808 Napoleon personally assumed command of the French forces in the Peninsula. He reinstated Joseph in Madrid and drove the main British army out of Spain. But the difficulties which impeded French military operations in the Peninsula were well-nigh insurmountable. The nature of the country furrnished several obstacles. According to Hayes, "Farms were poor,settlements sparse, provisions scarce, the French army found difficulty in following their usual practice of living off the land. The succession of fairly high mountain ranges... prevented Campaigning on the large scale to which Napoleonic tactics were best adapted, and put a premium upon loose, irregular querrilla fighting, in which the Spaniards were adepts." Meanwhile, Duke of Wellington defeated the French in the battle of Talavera.

Napoleon appointed Massena to reconquer Portugal. Wellesley's policy was to cut off the French lines of communication and to strave them, and to construct a triple line of defence called the lines of Torres vedras. Massena advanced but was defeated at Busaco. Then wellesley retired behind the lines of Torres vedras. The lines to Torres Vedras played a very significant part in the French defeat and marked the turning point in the Peninsular war. The French found themselves helpless against Wellesley's strategy. The English again defeated Massena at Albuera. Napoleon was immensly pained at the failures of Massena, so he appointed Marmont in his place to fight against Spain and Portugal. In 1812 Napoleon was distracted by the effort of the Russian expedition and so Wellington was in a better position to develop an offensive campaign. In 1812 Wellington with his allied British and Spanish troops won a notable victory at Salamanca, captured Madrid and drove Joseph and the French to Valencia. The Spanish patriots drafted a liberal constitution for Spain, based on the soverignity of the people. The king was allowed only a suspensive veto. This written constitution, next in age to the American and the French became a model for later liberal constitutions throughout Southern Europe.

In 1813 Soult, with the flower of the French Army, was withdrawn to

Germany. Wellington was now at last ready to make the decisive movement which was to drive the French armies out of Spain. Moving rapidly North, he threatened the only great military road from Madrid to the Pyreness. Wellington defeated Joseph severly at Vittoria. The great struggle was virtually at an end. Wellington followed up his success on French soil in 1814. But by this time the French cause was already lost, for Napoleon had abdicated and the allied forces occupied paris. According to Marriot, "Thanks to the dogged patriotism of the Spanish Juntas, thanks to the splendid tenacity and skill of Wellington, Napoleon had been compelled to keep a large army in the Peninsula which would have been invaluable on the Elbe. Though he described the struggle as a war of priests and monks,...but it acted as a running sore." Later on Napoleon admitted that the "Spanaish ulcer had ruined him". His Spanish enterprise was his first step towards ruin. In the words of Grant and Temperley, "The Spanish war has been well called the cancer that drained away the strength of Napoleon". But long before the Spanish war was ended the centre of interest, diplomatic and military, had shifted E..st wards.

Results

Marriot writes, "Europe was taught that Napoleon was not invincble", He underestimated the strength of the Spanish national resistance and this mistake led to serious reverses. The Spaniards resorted to querrilla war fare and as the French armies were strangers to the geographical conditions of Spain, hence they could not chase the querrilla soldiers. Spain is mountainous and poor, so it was difficult for the French to secure food and transport for a large army. Besides, he could not take part in the Spanish campaign fully as he was preoccupied with the problems of central Europe. He left the task to his generals whose Jealousies prevented concerted action at many critical junctures. Further, Napoleon's action in Spain provoked a national spirit. They had a slogan “Spain is for the Spaniards”. He failed to Cope with the nationalistic feelings of the Spaniards. Napoleon's attempt to conquer Spain brought about his own downfall. To Cope with a hydraheaded resistance he had to keep enormous armis in Spain. Naturally it drained his resources. With the Spanish rising the national reaction began and its effect was seen in the immense immpulse given to the national movement in Germany. Napoleon not only suffered a defeat in Spain but the myth of his invincibility was broken.

The Moscow Campaign and The War of Liberation (1812-14)

The collapse of the French empire was preceded by the breakdown of the Franco-Russian alliance. The bankrupty of the system of Tilsit had been demonstrated by the unenthusiastic cooperation of Russia in the continmental system, and it was emphasised by every development of French policy. Russian enthusiasm for the French alliance was steadily diminished by the intolerable pressure of the continental system on a country whose natural market was Great Britain. Napoleon's role in the revival of Poland by creating the Grand Dutchy of Warsaw was resented by the czar. The Czar resolved to reestablish the Russian control of Poland. The czar had begun to repent of the treaty of Tilsit almost as soon as he got back to St. Petes burg. His mother, who had great influence over him, loathed Bonparte and hated to see her son in alliance with such a low born adventurer. On the other hand, Napoleon was more anxious than ever to maintain the alliance. So he presuaded Alexander (the Czar) to come to a conference at Erfurt in 1808. For a week the Thuringian capital was ablaze with uniforms. The social festivities were on a magnificent scale, but the diplomatic result did not go much beyond Tilsit. The czar was to received Finland and the Danubian principalities, and in return to recognise the Napoleon dynasty in Spain. The interview at Erfurt had merely checked for a few weeks the process of disillusionment which had been going on in Alexander's mind ever since Tilsit. There had always been a anti-Bonaparte party at his Court, headed by his mother, and a number of circumstances strengthened its influence during the next few years.

Napoleon's policy in European Turky was an important factor in embittering his relations with the Czar. At Tilsit he had dangled before Alexander the spectacle of a Turkish empire partitioned between France and Russia. And at Erfurt he had consented to Russia's retention of the two Danubian principalities (Moldavia and Wallachia) at the conclusion of the war between Russia and Turky. But contrary to those promises, agents of the emperor were stiffening the resistance of the Turks of the Russian armies and preventing the speedy end of hostilities. Napoleon's intention concerning Balkans are not entirely clear. It is certain that his earlier declarations at Tilsit and Erfurt were gesture to beguile Alexander into false security.

The rift between Russia and France was completed by the Czar's refusal to increase the rigours of Napoleon's economic blockade of England. The Russian merchants had protested more and more vigorously over the rupture of direct commercial relations with England. In 1810, Napoleon summoned the Czar to confiscate neutral ships in Russian ports on the ground that they carried only British goods, but the Czar refused. Had Napoleon been willing to make the necessary concession concerning Poland and the Balkans, it is likely that Alexander would not have made an open issue of the continental system. On December 31, 1810, the Czar issued a decree which favoured the entry of Neutral ships into Russian ports. Further, Napoleon had occupied oldenburg in order to implement his scheme of continental system effectively. The king of oldenburg was the brother-in-law of the Czar, hence the Czar was annoyed. Further, the prizes with which the Russian concurrence had been purchased at Tilsit were shown to be largly illusory, because the annexation of Finland was a disappointing compensation. It even appeared from the advance of French policy in the affairs of Sweden that Napoleon had adopted a hostile attitude towards the Baltic ambitions of Russia. Bernadotte, a French General was adopted as the Napoleonic candidate for the Swedish throne. His election alienated Alexander and indicated the creation in Sweden of a second Poland, where French influence might support Scandinavian nationalism against Russian expansion further, Napoleon proposed a matrimonial alliance with the sister of the Czar which was rejected by the latter. On the other hand, the Czar was annoyed, when Napoleon married a Hapsburg princess of Austria. Meanwhile, the Russian ultimatum demanded permission to trade with neutral, and the evacuation of Prussia and Swedish pomerania. The emperor declined to withdraw from the position imposed upon him by the continental system, and replied with the diplomatic preparations for a war. The French alliance was imposed upon Prussia and Austria. On the other hand, Russian diplomacy prepared for the war by an alliance with Sweden, a coalition in the traditional form with Turky of the treaty of Bucharest, which liberated the Russian forces in the Danube valley.

In June 1812, Napoleon crossed the Niemen river and began an invasion of Russia. His forces were superior to the Russian in numbers, organisation and equipment. But the Russians adopted the Policy of not fighting but constantly retreating, luring the enemy farther and farther into a country which they took care to devastate as they retired, leaving no provisions for the invaders. Unable to defeat or capture his foe, Napoleon penetrated even deeper into Russia. Only once the Russians venture to fight under kutusoff at Borodino. The battle was one of the bloodiest of the whole epoch. The Russians were defeated, and they retreated, leaving the road open to Moscow. Napoleon entered the city of Moscow with great pomp, but on the same night the city was ablaze. Napoleon found Moscow practically deserted. To Napoleon's growing dismay, the Tsar continued to keep silence. For five long weeks of suspense Napoleon tarried in the doomed city, and finally on october 18, he gave the order for the retreat.

The Napoleonic retreat from Moscow is one of the most horrible episodes in history. The Napoleonic Moscow campaign surmounted the Russian summer, the retreat was confronted with the Russian winter. The first check came when Kutusov blocked Napoleon's retreat along the southern and the shorter route to smolensk and forced him to fall back along the line of his advance. On the heels of the French, as they made their way past the charnel house at Borodino, were Kutusov and the Cossocks, before them the on coming winter, in their midst, hunger, cold, and despair. According to Hazen, "The scenes that accompanied the flight and rout were of unutterable woe, culminating in the hideous tragedy of the crossing of the Beresina (River), the bridge breaking down under the wild confusion of men fighting to get across, horses frightened,, the way blocked by carts and wagons, the pontoons raked by the fire of the Russian artillery". Marshal Ney fought valiant rearguard actions to save the demoralised French army, but the retreat became a rout. This ill--fated expedition shattered the military power of Napoleon and encouraged the powers of central Europe to shake off his domination.

The War of Liberation- 1813

The disastrous retreat from Moscow considerably demoralised the French Army and lowered Napoleon's prestige in Europe. Prussia took advantage of the debacle. A resurrection marked the history of Prussia. It was Fichte, the famous philosopher, who first preached the duty of patriotism. A league of virtue was formed to encourage self- improvement, mental, moral and physical.

Men of letters came to the realisation that the bases of the Prussian State would have to be widened if Prussia were to regain her place among the great states. The intellectual preparation for this regeneration had been begun in the days preceding the military catastrophe at Jena. The shock of the French revolutionary armies carrying their new gospel of equality shattered the old indifference of German intellectuals to public life and the concerns of the ordinary individual. The Prussian king appointed Stein as chief minister. His first edict emancipated all serfs and allowed peasants to buy land from nobles. He encouraged local self government and established a system of popular education. Equally drastic reforms were carried out in the army by scharnhorst. The old system based upon privilege and caste distinction was abolished. The Prussian State was modernised and centralised. Intellectual liberty found expression in the new university of Berlin, where the Prussian professors studiously avoided the cosmopolitianism of the French intellectuals. All these reforms produced a new awakening of the patriotic spirit and a determination to liberate Prussia from the shackles of Napoelon. By the treaty of Kalisch, Prussia and Russia joined together and declared war on Napoleon. Driven by an overwheliming national impulse the Prussian king had apple to the people and the response was spontaneous. Prussia declared war of liberation against

France. Napoleon avanced into Sazony, and he attacked the allied Russians and Prussians at Lutzen. He defeated them, but was unable to followup his advantage for want of horseman. He gained another fruitless victory at Bautzen and recovered Dresden. Napoleon accepted the pact of pleswitz, according to it the hostilities were suspended for seven weeks. This proved a fatal error on his part.

Austria played a waiting game. Austria had not the same aims as prussia and Russia. Francis (Emperor of Austria) did not want to see his son-in-law dethroned or his daughter begging her bread. What he wanted was to recover his lost provinces. He disliked the popular pan-Germanism, which was now spreading outside Prussia, for nationalist sentiment would be fatal to the coherence of the Austrian empire. So he got the allies to support a draft proposal for peace. He proposed that the confederation of Rhine and the grand duchy of Warsaw were to be abolished. Prussia was to recover what she had lost at Tilsit, Austria should get back all her Italian possession. Napoleon was furious. "So you too want war" he said frowningly to Metternich. "Well, you shall have it. I have beaten the Russians at Bautzen, now you wish your turn to come. Be it so, the rendezvous shall be in Vienna". Austria joined the European coalition. Prussia, Russia, Austria, England and Sweden were prominent members of the fourth coalition against Napoleon. At Dresden in August 1813, he won his last spectacular victory against the Austrian army. But he was overwhelmed by the allies and was decisively defeateat at the battle of Leipzig or the battle of the Nations. Leipzig sealed his fate. The emperpor had lost not only 200,000 men, but all the outlying provinces of his empire. The Italians and the Dutch threw up his rule. The confederation of the Rhine was ruined, and Jerome was forced to flee from west-Phalia. Spain was wholly lost. Austria recovered the Tyrol and Illyrian provinces and occupid Venetia and Switzerland. Metternich, the Austrian chancellor, induced the others to agree to one more effort to save Napoleon from complete ruin. By the proposals of Frank fort they offered him the Rhine and Alps as his eastward frontier. Napoleon should recognise the independence of Germany, Italy, Holland and Spain. The terms were highly favourable as they secured to France of objects of her traditional foreign policy. But Napoleon refused them.

Allied Invasion of France

So the allies invaded France from all directions. The allies made the treaty of chaumont pledging not to make peace individually. Wellington invaded from Spain, Prussia under Blucher from the Rhine, Austria under Schwarzenburg from Switzerland, and Bernadotte, from the North-East. But Napoleon displayed some remarkable genius, the same indomitable will, as had charecterized his earliest campaigns. But he was hopelessly outnumbered, and Napoleon could not prolonged the resistance indefinitely and on March 31, 1814, the allies entered Paris. The allies made a personal treaty known as the treaty of Fountainebleau in 1814 with Napoleon. He was forced to abdicate unconditionally. He was allowed to retain his title of emperor but henceforth, he was to rule only over Elba. An annual pension of two million Franc was granted to him and his wife Maria Louise would get the Duchy of Parma. According to Hazen; "He said farewell to the old guard in the courtyard of the palace of Fontainebeau, Kissing the flag of France....". "Nothing but sobbing was heard in all the ranks" wrote one of the soldiers who saw the scene, "and I can say that I too shed tears when I saw my emperpr depart". Napoleon retired to Elba in April 1814 and Louis XVIII, brother of Louis XVI, was restored to his ancestral throne and the allied made the first treaty of Paris with him.

First Treaty of Paris

By the first treaty of Paris it was agreed that the Bourbons were restored to the French throne. French boundaries were reduced to what they were in 1792, No army of occupation was sent to France and no indemnity was imposed on her. The treaty of Paris proved beneficial for France. Thus, the allies reestablished the rule of the Bourbons in France on the principles of legitimacy which was propounded by Tailyrand. Time alone would show whether or not the new monarchy and its supporters could regulate their actions by the terms of the treaty of Paris.

Having regulated the future of France, the powers met at Vienna, to celebrate with social festivities from the dread figure which had overshadowed them fifteen years. The representatives of the four chief victors tried to settle matters among themselves. But Talleyrand had no intention of allowing himself and his country to be thus slighted. His master card in the diplomatic game was to sow discord among the other powers. The victors quarrelled over the spoils of victory. This dissension among the allies combined with the news that the French people were discontented with the reactionary tendency of Louis XVIII's government, encouraged Napoleon to try conclusions once more with united Europe. When discussions were at their height, the congress was started by the news that Napoleon had escaped from Elba and had returned to France.

Hundred Days and the Battle of Waterloo-1815

At the end of February, 1815 he (Napoleon) left Elba and landed in the South of France with about a thousand men. According to Hazen; "The return of Napoleon from Elba will always remain one of the most romantic episodes of history". People welcomed him again with the familiar shout "Long live emperor". But his appeal was particularly to the army, to which he issue one of his stirring bulletins; "Soldiers, your general, called to the throne by the choice of the people, and raised on your shields, has comeback to you, come and join him. I am sprung from the revolution. I am come to save the people from the slavery into which priests and nobles would plunge them". When troops were sent to arrest him he stepped forward and, opening the familiar grey over-coat, exclaimed, "Here I am, you know me,if there is a soldier among you who wishes to shoot his emperor, let him do it." The soldiers broke into cheers and surged round him. As soon as he reached France he declared' "I have come back to safeguard the citizens of France....I will safeguard the land of the peasants....I will not let the feudalism establish itself again....I will try to safeguard the benefits of the revolution". Louis XVIII fled from the Tuileries. Meanwhile, Napoleon was reorganising his army. The tightlipped, laconic, tireless, spartan man of action had degenerated into a plump, easy going and slumberous, and he seemed to be haunted by memories of these dark days at Fontaninebleau a year before, when his trusted Marshals had deserted him. What was the happiest period of your life as emperor? Some one asked him at St.Helena. "The march from Cannes to Paris" was the quick reply quoted from C.D. Hazen.

When the dignitaries at the Congress of Vienna heard of his escape from Elba they immediatedly united against this disturber of the peace of Europe. The allies sent their armies to France to overthrow Napoleon. The allies organised two armies to face Napoleon. The Duke of Wellington and Marshall Blucher were appointed the Chief Commanders of the armies. Russia and Prussia sent supporting troops. He (Napoleon) resolved to attack before his enemies had time enough to effect their union. The Duke of Wellington chose his ground at Waterloo (Belgium) with his usual skill, where he could screen his reserves on the farside of a slope. There, on a hot sunday on June 18, 1815, Napoleon was disastrously defeated and the Sun of Austerlitz set for ever. The last act of the tragedy ended an epoch. Napoleon said desperately; "I ought to have died at Waterloo, but the misfortune is that when a man seeks death most, he can not find it. Men were killed around me before behind and everywhere. But there was no bullet for me. Napoleon at first intended to escape to America, but he found the coast closely watched by British Warships, and decided that it would be more dignified to surrender. The allies delegated to England the thankless task of acting as his gaoler, and he was eventually sent to St. Helena, a rocky island in the South Atlantic. There he died of cancer in May 1821. The epic of Napoleon was ended, but the glory of the Napoleonic legend was yet to be.

The allies made the second peace of Paris with France. According to the peace of Paris, French boundaries were reduced to what they were in 1790, and a heavy indemnity was imposed on France. An army of occupation was sent to France to stay till the indemnity was paid. The Bourbons restored, but absolute monarchy was not restored. The principles of the revolution had triumphed over abolutism. According to Hayes; "The Napoleonic empire was shortlived but it had tremendous importance in spreading throughout Europe certain novel principles which it inherited from the French revolution. There are particularly significant individualaism, secularism and Nationalism".

CAUSES OF NAPOLEON'S DOWNFALL AND AN ESTIMATE OF NAPOLEON

Napoleon, the "son of the Revolution", and the "man of Destiny", succeeded in conquering a vast empire, but the maintenance of so vast a dominion depended upon unerring skill. His hold on Europe during 1799-1815 was complete and the destiny of Europe depended on his whims and fancies. He touched the zenith of his power at the time of the treaty of Tilsit in 1807. Napoleon was essentially a soldier and his love of domination in the long run alienated the whole of Europe and roused bitter national animosity against which he could do nothing. Several other factors were responsible for his rapid downfall.

Napoleon's empire was based upon force and maintained by force. There was no common loyality to the emperor. It is true that Napoleon had been able through force or favour to dictate a multitude of princes, but a soon as either of these methods ceased to be effective, his artificial domination over Europe began to show sign of crack. His insatiable ambition blinded him to the sense of what is practicable or not, and so led him to stretch his power to the breaking point. He wanted to establish a vast empire under his sway. He was aware that it was not an easy task but he didnot give up his efforts. He often rejected the advice of his worthy ministers. Napoleon was not prepared to come to terms with his enemies and as hope did not leave him till the end, there was no possibility of a compromise and peace. He continued to believe to the end that he was the "man of destiny". Later on he became boastful. During his intervention in Spain he wrote; "I may find the pillars of Hercules in Spain, but I shall not find the limits of my power.... I have seen nothing so cowardly as these Spanish nobles and troops". It was his judgement that degenerated him. He suffered from a megalomania which deprived him of practical sense. He thought that there was nothing that he could not master. Therefore, he was himself responsible for his own downfall. His extraordinary ability proved of no avail when he forgot that "to err is human."

Napoleon's power was based on his armed strength, His empire was based on force, and it could be maintained only by force. He was not as great a genius of campaigning in the final stages of the conflict, as he was in the Italian campaign , or in the battle of Austerlitz. Further conscription which he had to introduce to fight his enemies, was no popular. The new army lacked the ardour of those who had won the battles of Austerlitz and Jena. Moreover, Napoleon posted his armies in the countries under him and forced them to meet the expenses of his armies. It generated hatred in the subdued countries for Napoleon. The grand army of Napoleon became more and more haterogeneous and consequently lost its fighting effectiveness. During the famous Moscow campaign, the French army was haterogeneous, consisting of Germans, Poles, Italians, etc., who were not imbued with the revolutionary spirit of the French and hence they were not as zealous fighters as the French. They had no nationalistic spirit for France.

Napoleon missed several oppertunities of retaining his power. On the eve of the war of liberation and after his defeat at Leipzig, the allies offered him very liberal terms, which he refused to accept. Metternich urged him at Dresden to accept the terms, But Napoleon asked "what is it you wish of me"? That I should dishonour myself ? Never, I shall know how to die.... your sovereigns who were born on the thrones may get beaten twenty times and yet return to their capitals. I canot, for I rose to power through the camp". It was a great blunder on his part, particularly when he had lost to heavily in men powers in the Russian campaign and the war of liberation.

Napoleon's Government became a police state which denied liberty and individual freedom. As he was the symbol of absolutism, he did not allow the people to participate in the affairs of the government. Further, by a series of conquests he had established a vast empire, but the people of the conquered territories regarded him as an alien. The people began to oppose his autocratic rule. The French revolution had given rise to nationalism all over Europe, and all nations aspired to be independent and sovereign. But when Napoleon began to depose the legitimate rulers, and placed his own kinsmen on the thrones of conquered territories, their national self respect was hurt. They revolted against Napoleon who was regarded as a usurper trying to enslave them for his personal glorification. The Spanish rising inspired other nationalities to rise and opposed Napoleon. The spirit of nationalism which had already manifested itself in Spain, spread like a contagion over to Germany. The Germans under Fredrick William of Prussia joined hands with Russia and began the war of liberation in 1813.

By his policy of conquest and the introduction of continental system he created for too many enemies. The promulgation of the continental system was a leap in the dark. The blockade of the continental parts caused a dislocation of trade and thereby raised the prices of the articles of common necessity. Napoleon had a motive behind his plan, that is, to get the continental markets for the French in a very serious conflict with European powers. Without sufficient naval strength at his command it was futile for Napoleon to close all the continental ports to the British ships. The continental countries depended on England for their supplies of the finished goods. Under such circumstances, the continental ports were only theoretically closed. Smuggling in every shape and form went on. The continental system roused a great feeling of disloyality towards Napoleon, for it was practically ruining the economy of most of continental countries. It finally led to breach with allies like portugal, Spain, Russia. Subsequently, there were revolts in these countries and involved in wars on all sides. The Pope rejected the continental scheme of Napoleon. Napoleon demanded that the Papal ports should be closed against British ships but the Pope replied that he would remain neutral. There upon Napoleon imprisoned the Pope and annexed his territories. This gratuitous affornt to the Pope shocked the Catholic sentiment of Europe and did much to snake the fabric of Napoleon's power.

Napoleon himself admitted that it was the Spanish ulcer that ruined him. It was his determination to exclude English goods from Portugal and Spain that forced him to interfere with these countries. Napoleon abused the Spanish hospitalities by taking advantage of the Spanish permission to send his army across Spain in order to attack Portugal, but he conquered Spain as well. Further, he placed his brother on the Spanish throne. This roused the national spirit of the Spaniards which ultimately led to the peninsular war and this was the beginning of the end of Napoleon. Napoleon had to learn that the roused spirit of nationalism cannot be conquered. It was the rising tide of nationalism which was considered as one of the most important causes of his down fall.

Napoleon's invasion of Russia in 1812 was a blunder. Between the peace of Tilsit and the Russian expedition there was an increasing estrangement of feelingss between Napoleon and the Czar. The rupture of this alliance led to the collapse of his imperial structure and was the most important causes of his downfall. The Czar's support to the continental system was withdrawn, so Napoleon led an expedition against Russia which brought untold sufferings to Napoleon and his men. The Russian snow, the inhospitable climate and attack of the cossacks became the cause of his failure. The Russian disaster encouraged the powers to combine against him, and this combination eventually proved fatal to him.

Napoleon's kind treatment of his relatives was also partly responsible for his failure. He was most unhappy regarding the attitude of his brothers. They did not prove even loyal to Napoleon and often acted, treacherously. Further, although Napoleon was the child of the revolution, he was the child who killed the mother. He did not care for the principles of liberty and fraternity. He centralised everything in his own hands and thereby destroyed the initiative of the people. Complete censorship was imposed on the press. He tried to impose a military discipline on the people. He was the last and greatest of the autocratic legislators who worked in a unfree age.

Napoleon had annoyed England by his own faults. He wanted to crush England but could not be successful to that end for want of a powerful Navy. Besides, a large majority of Englishmen regarded Napoleon as an heir of the revolution trying to spread it abroad by force. The British were hostile to any French attempt for the revival of the French colonial empire. England played a major role in building up anti-Napoleonic spirit. The British navy carried out a successful campaign against Napoleon and they could send help to portugal and Spain during the Peninsular War. According to Fisher, "The downfall of Napoleon is a trilogy of which Moscow, Leipzig, Fontainebleau are the successive pieces and waterloo the epilogue". Fate also played a trick with Naploleon in the battle of waterloo which dealt the final blow t o Napoleon's power.

An Estimate of Napoleon Bonaparte

It is very difficult to form an accurate estimate of Napoleon Bonaparte, for there are many point in his carrer and charecter about which widely different opinions will always be held. His charecter and personality are still a riddle for the scholars. According to Gottschalk, "Napoleon Bonaparte is, perhabs, the most written about individual in history....". In fact, he was one of the greatest ruler in the world. Above all, he was a versatile genius. He ranks with Alexander, Caesar and chrelemagne as one of the greatest personality in world history. Alexander Hellenised the civilisation of his day, charlemagne ploughed and sowed the soil of Europe, making it receptive for the most superb of all secular ideals, that of nationality, and Napoleon tore up the system of absolutism and propagated the modern conception of Individual rights.

Napoleon rendered great services to France. The difference between the France of 1799 and 1815 was the work of Napoleon. The administration was unitary and homogeneous. The Napoleonic era was not only conspicuous for the struggle for the mastery of Europe, it was also marked by significant developments in politics, and society. His victories saved France from foreign enemies. He established a strong central government and thereby saved France from anarchy. He found chaos and left order." He gave France a sound system of laws. Napoleon introduced a civil code in France. Once he said, I shall not be known for my victories, but my civil code would make me immortal". He promoted education and took active steps to improve trade and industry. He issued no paper money and imposed no income tax. As a ruler he may be called an enlighten despot. His strong government ensured political order. Napoleon carried out the principles of social equality by throwing carrers open to talent. He maintained that, "He was the child of the revolution". Napoleon emphasised the principle of equality and recruited his servants on the basis of merit. He gave permanence to the influence of the French revolution. According to Riker; "Napoleon was the last of a series of benevolent despots, he was at the same time one of the first of great modern statesmen. He valued ability...". The despotism of Napoleon vanished with himself, leaving behind a tradition, but his centralisation remained as the expression of modern France.

The growth of nationalities in Europe was one of the results of Napoleon's work in Europe. He had no particular interest in providing encouragement to the spirit of nationalism but some of his acts contributed to the growth of nationalism. He simplified the map of Germany, but it really served the cause of German Nation. The formation of the grand duchy of Warsaw helped in the rise of nationalism in Poland. He will always be remembered as one who laid the foundation of a new social order in Europe by sweeping away the evils arising out of feudal society and medieval system of law.

Napoleon was an excellent military organiser. He was a born solider and he had a great love for war. In order to stabilise his position in France, he won a series of dazzling victories. His first italian campaign has remined in the eyes of military man ever since, a masterpiece, a classical example of the art of war. He won ascendancy over the soldier. He was a source of inspiration to the soldiers. He used to infuse a spirit of bravery into cowards. Napoleon's proclaimations to his army were masterpieces. He once said; "Soldiers I am satisfied with you....you have adorned your eagle with immortal glory" once he said to his generals, "There is no need of being disappointed. The results of war are ever changing, whatever we have lost to day, it can be regained- tomarrow." He never lost his mental equilibrium. He was not disturbed by the decimation of his vast army in the Moscow campaign and again devoted himself to its reorganisation.

Mapoleon loved work, and no man in Europe, and few in all history, have labored as he did. He was an industrious person. He said, work is my element, for which I was born and fitted". He could himself work more than 18 hours a day. During the battle of Waterloo, he said, "I have known the limits of the power of my legs and arms. I have never discovered those of my power of work". Besides, Napoleon was a great orator, and a writer. According to Fisher, "He was the prince of Journalists, the father of war correspondence". He was a man of learning. He had studied almost all the works of the French philosophers. He read history extensively, regarding it as the torch of truth.

But critics are of the opinion that Napoleon was the tyrant of Europe. He was not contented with the natural frontier of France. He desired to follow in the footsteps of both Alexander, the great and charlemagne. His ambition was unlimited. He had an ambition to leave his name to the posterity as a great conqueror. Domination of Europe beckoned him. But his victories in successive battles made him proud and haughty. His egoism became a mania and consequently refused to listen to the advice of others. No doubt, he initiated many reforms but took away the liberty of the people which marred the spirit of the reforms. The principle of nationalism a great ideal of the revolution was buried under his imperialism. He curtailed individaul liberty, freedom of speech, and freedom of press. Napoleonic State became a police state. His government was a veiled autocracy. As a soldier, he firmly believed in authority and order. Accoroding to Fisher; "It is a paradox to assert that Napoleon had any intention of educating a German nation. The confederation of Rhine was an old device of French diplomacy (French diplomacy ... that). That these states should develop an independent one was the last thing which Napoleon intended". His suppression of political liberty in the conquered country made his rule hateful. Further, his policy of interference also proved detrimental to France's interests and turned Russia, Prussia, Spain, Austria into his enemies. Napoleon thought himself to be a great politician and diplomat and often acted treacherously with his friends. His attitude towards his allies was of high handed treachery. He was determined to use all means, fair or foul to win. Further, in order to satisfy his soaring ambitions, he perpetrated several blunders and did not care for the consequences. His extraordinary ability proved of no avil when he forgot that to err is human. Inspite of all his shortcomings, Napoleon still commanded popularity in France. He stood for the restoration of peace and confidence. By his reforms, Napoleon purged the revolution of Chaotic forces. The Code Napoleon was one of his most enduring achivements, by which he will always be remembered by the posterity.

Chapter IV

The Congress of Vienna and the Concert of Europe

Ninenteenth century history begins with the fall of Napoleon. For a quarter of a century Europe had been in a turmoil of war and revolution, with frontiers shifting from year to year, and during more than half that time it had been swayed by the will of one man. But the overthrow of Napoleon brought with it one of the most complicated problems ever presented to statesmen. As all the nations of Europe has been profoundly affected by his enterprises so all were profoundly affected by his fall. The old monarchcies now reasserted their "Divine right", and concerted measures to repress revolutionary movements where ever and in whatever forms they might appear. In fact, they tried to put the clock back to 1789, so far as seemed safe and convenient. But what the French revolution and Napoleon stood for could not be contained as it happened to be the inevitabale force and factor of the emerging Europe. For a short while there was a eull because of Metternich. But popular impulses towards national unity and constitutional government continued to ferment beneath the surface and to splutter from time to tiime, Until, in 1848 there was a terrific explosion. According to Thomson, "There existed within Europe a further tension between forces of continuity and forces of change.....The conflicts between these opposing forces were to dominate the generation after Waterloo".

The four great powers (England, Russia, Austria and Prussia) which had combined to overthrow Napoleon regarded the conflict "as war to end war". As they had sent Napoleon to Elba they set to make the world safe, not for democrasy, but for legitimacy. A Congress of European diplomats was summoned to meet at Vienna to give peace to a tired and timid generation and to deal with a number of political problems consequent upon the upheavels caused by the wars of revlolutionary France and those of the Napolenic period. The victors resettled the frontiers of Europe at the congress of Vienna, the later stages of the process being interrupted by the "Hundred days". They then reassembled at Paris to revise the terms to be imposed on France to prevent any revival of Bonapartism. Much of the work of the congress was done through committee, and some parts of the settlement were the results of negotiations and intrigues carried on within small groups. Therefore, many of the Vienna decisions, had been reached before the congress opened. But what should be the future government and boundaries of France? The war waged by Revolutionary France and Napoleon had completely changed the politiical map of Europe. The upheaval of the last 25 years had brought about vast political changes in the boundaries of European states. Therefore the congress had to redraw the political map of Europe. Further, the diplomats were of the opinion that the revolutionary feelings were like contagious disease. So the suppression of these feelings was also an intricate problem to be dealt with.

The Congress of Vienna was one of the most important diplomatic gathering in the history of Europe. Never since the Congress of Westphalia. (1648) had an assembly of all European powers met to consider questions of European importance. All big and small countries of Europe, except Turky, were invited, Vienna was chosen as the venue of the congress in view of the leading part played by Austria in the final overthrow of Napoleon. The congress was a pageant, and was associated with much gaiety, feasting and merrymaking. The brilliance of the congress is almost proverbial, Emperors, kings, princess, generals, proud nobleman, and a swarm of lesser notables assembled at the Austrian capital to forget the tribulations of the past, and to lay the ghost of Bonapartism. The care free dancing, the lavish entertainment, the theatricals, the charming masquerades, and the merryhunting parties were at once a foil for and an instrument of the intensely serious business that had brought these grandees of Europe to Vienna. Their's was indeed a sober task, the task of settling the fate of territories and people liberated from Napoleon's control. In what spirit did the diplomats shoulder their responsibilities to millions of people, to the generation yet unborn that would be bound by their decisions? Would they satisfy the hopes of enlightenmen? But the victors over Napoleon could not break throught the hardshell of their fears, fears of revolutionary ideas which Napoleon had translated into new institutions. They regarded themselves as the saviors of Europan civilisation, and their mission as to undo the work of the revolution, and, so far as possible, restore the political system of Europe to the condition in which it had founded itself in 1789.

Leading Personalities

The representatives who influenced most of the decisions of the congress were Tsar Alexander I, Emperor Francis I, king Fredrick William III, Metternich, the Austrian chancellor, Lord Castlereagh, the British representative, and Talleyrand, the French Minister. Czar Alexander I of Russia was generous by nature, and a great idealist dreamer who was swayed at times by the high ideals of the gospel of christianity. He was the most illustrious and most enigmatical figures at the congress. He was a curious combination of shrewdness with mysticism, ambition with compassion. He granted a constitution to Poland and checked the vindictive zeal of those who wanted to impose very severe terms upon France. He stood for a just and fair settlement. The part that he had played in the defeat of Napoleon gave him an authority in European affairs. But he had neither the diplomatic astuteness nor the cynical persistance of Metternich. By nature Alexander was unstable well intentioned, a susceptible, imaginative, egoist, and an unpractical inconsistent idealist. According to Ketebley, "Emperor Francis I of Austria played the host, an unpretending figure in a shabby blue coat, a dull egoist", He was obstinate and reactionary in his outlook. "Keep yourselves to what is old, for that is good", was his principle. King Fredrick William III of Prussia was slow, timid and weak and a great traditionalist. Metternich, the chancellor of Austria,presided over the congress and soon became its guiding spirit. He exerted his influence with great success in promoting the interests of Austria and give a reactionary turn to the policy of the congress. He was the central figure in European diplomacy. His personal charm and social gifts, his diplomatic experience, his astute insight into men, gave him an ascendancy at the congress. He was a great reactionary and the most vehement opponent of liberalism. According to Keteleby, "He could swim like a fish in the sparkling whirlpool of Vienna. No one knew so well as he how to carry through a political intrigues between dinner and a masked ball". His first intention was to restore, as far as practicable, the political and territorial status quo of 1792. He distrusted all innovations and new ideas and tried his best to maintain the old order. The British representatives were castlereagh and Wellington. Castlereagh was essentially liberal in his outlook, Who wielded considerable influence in brining about compromises, when there were deadlocks among the allies. But neither in his thinking nor in his actions could he find place for those principles of national independence and popular institutions which had become potent during the generation of upheavel from 1789-1815. Castlereagh was most anxious to achive a moderate and generally agreed settlement, because British interests lay in a peaceful Europe with which trade could be established. The delegate of France was

Talleyrand. He was shrewd, cunning and quick to take advantage of the differences among the allies. He saved France ably and saved her from utter humiliation by flattery, and intrigue. It was due to the able diplomacy of Talleyrand, France was in no way less powerful than any other European power at that time.

The Problems Before the Congress

After such a great upheaval as that caused by Napoleon the most important task before the congress was that of territorial settlement. The congress aimed at suppressing all revolutionary movements, where ever they raised their head. The congress tried to suppress liberalism in Europe by means of the concert of Europe. Further, France should not be allowed to disturb the peace of Europe, and hence she should be surrounded by strong and powerful states on her frontiers. But of all the questions that divided the negotiators, the thorniest was the settlement of the rival claims to the grand duchy of Warsaw and the kingdom of Saxony. By arrangements concluded in 1813 Prussia agreed to Alexander's plan of joining the territcry of Warsaw to the polish territory acquired by Russia in the partitions in order to restore the kingdom of Poland. The Czar's intention were to grant a liberal constitution to the new kingdom and bind it by a personal union with Russia. In return Russia promised her support to the Prussian claim upon the territory of Saxony. In the bitter dispute that brokeout over this territorial deal, castlereagh played his not unfamiliar role of mediator with great courage. Uppermost in his mind was one consideration, to establish a strong central Europe that would be as much a bulwork against Russian aggression from the East as against French threat from the West. To establish this central bulwork, a federation of German States was necessary. Such was the goal towards which castlereagh moved. His path was difficult, for with the Austrian diplomats objecting to the Russo-Prussian agreement and the Prussian, and the Russians adopting a menancing tone, the possibility of war as a solution was great. The climax of the dispute was reached in January 1815, when castlereagh admitted Talleyrand in the armed mediation and arranged a secretreaty which bound Austria England and France, if attacked by Prussia. This measure insured the success of castlereagh's compromise solution. The main issue of the Saxon and polish question were soon settled, It was the shock of the startling news of Napoleon's escape from Elba that compelled the powers to compose their differences and to arrange an acceptable compromise. By the treaty of Vienna, signed in June 1815, a few days before the decisive battle of Waterloo, the territorial rearrangement of Europe was made.

Principles of the Congress

The Congress of Vienna, resumed its task which had been interrupted by Napoleon's escape from Elba. The main work of the congress was the redistribution of territories that France had been forced to relinquish. Further, they sought to make a territorial rearrangement calculated to make Europe safe against future French aggression and from the infection of the revolutionary ideas. Their deliberations were guided by three principles, that of Balance of Power, that of legitimacy and that of compensation. By the principle of legitimacy the diplomats wanted to retain statusqo in respect of the territorial redistribution of Europe. Legitimacy meant the restoration of the pre-revolutionary dynasties and governments overthrown by Napoleon. But it must be noted than even the principle of legitimacy was not consistently applied, for it had to be greatly compromised by the more arbitrary principle of compensation and the fear of the future rise of France. The second principle, the balance of power was a time honoured political practice of Europe. All measures were adopted to ensure the prevention of France's rising into menacing strength in the future. In the Congres of Vienna, a balance or parity of strength was to be maintained between France and her neighbours. The allies who had, after immense effort and sacrifice, overthrown Napoleon, felt that they should have their reward. As in the Napoleonic wars the victor powers had to suffer huge losses, they wanted to aggrandize themselves by way of compensation for the losses suffered or reward for their sacrifices. The big powers were rewarded for the sacrifices they had made for the overthrow of Napoleon. In many cases the principle of legitimacy was compromised by the necessity of providing compensations to the victors at the cost of the defeated party. In the distribution of such rewards, no uniform principles could be followed. In order to reward one country, territories from other country had to be taken. Further, the congress which was dominated by absolute monarchs was hostile to republics and so the republics of Genoa and Venice were not restored. The big four powers also formed the Holy alliance to defend the statusquo of 1815.

Territorial Settlement

According to the second treaty of Paris, France was to go back to her boundaries as they were in 1790. The Bourbons were restored and Louis XVIII returned to his ancestral throne. France was to pay a heavy amount as indemnity to the victorious allies. The allied army was to remain in occupation of France till the payment of reparation. France was also compelled to restore the works of art brought by Napoleon from the conquered territories. Old dynasties were restored to the various countries according to the doctrine of legitimacy. The king of piedmont was restored to the throne of Piedmont. The Hapsburg princess were restored to the central duchies (Parma,Mod-ena and Tuscany) of Italy. The House of orange was reestablished in Holland. The Swiss confederation was restored with most of its territories. The Pope was also restored with all his possessions in Italy. The Vienna settlement restored the Bourbons in Spain. The House of Braganza was restored to the throne of portugal. The principle of legitimacy was applied with great flexibility in Germany. Germany was formed into a loose confederation of thirtynine states whose affairs were to be controlled by a federal Diet under the presidency of Austria. The Diet was composed not of the representatives of the people but of the delegates appointed by the different states. The Bourbon Ferdinand was restored to the kingdom of two sicilies.

Though France was treated leniently at the Congress of Vienna, but steps were taken to ring her round with a girdle of strong states as bulworks against her future aggression. So the principle of Balance of Power was applied with the intention of protecting Europe from future French aggression. On the North Eastrn border of France, Belgium (Formerly an Austrian province), was joined to Holland as one kingdom under the House of orange. On the South Eastern border of France, Switzerland received three cantons (Districts). Prussia was given the territories of the Rhine so that she might be the chief sentinal to hold France in check in the East. The kingdom of Sardinia-Piedmont was strengthened by the acquisition of Genoa so that it might be stronger to resist French aggression in the South East. Thus, France was surrounded by a ring of States which would not easily succumb to French aggression. With the intention to maintain balance of power, England and Austria opposed the Prussian occupation of Saxony and Russian occupation of Poland.

The Victorious allies were rewarded according to the principle of compensation. Prussia was considerably enlarged by the addition of the following territories, she retained posen and corridor in Poland, Sweden gave her pomerania. Two-fifth of Saxony was annexed by her.

She also recovered her Rhenish provinces and cologne and Treves. Norway was taken from Denmark and joined with Sweden. Austria was compensated for the loss of Austrian Netherlands by the cession of Lombardy and Venetia in Italy. She also got the Tyrol from Bavaria and recovered the Illyrian provinces along the Eastern Coast of the Adriatic. She got Galicia from Poland. Russia emerged from the congress with goodly number of additions. She retained Finland, Bessarabia, Turkish territories in the South West and most of the Grand Dutchy of Warsaw. Russia now extended farther Westward into Europe than ever, and could speak with greater weight in the European affairs. She also got major part of Poland. The expansion of the colonial empire was the main interest of England. In the congress of Vienna she was rewarded with valuable colonies, she got Heligoland in the North sea, Malta and Ionian islands in the Mediterranen. England retained Trinidad from Spain,Mauritius and Tobago from France and Ceylon and the Cape of Good Hope from Holland. She become the greatest colonial power in Europe. In Italy, Austrian interests determined the territorial arrangement. Austria received Lombardy and Venetia as Compensation. The king of Piedmont was restored to his own kingdom. The Pope was restored to the Papal Kingdom. The Hapsburg princnes were restored to the central duchies. Bourbon Ferdinand was restored to the kingdom of Naples and Sicily. No Central Government was created in Italy and she became "a geographical expression". As regards the settlement in Germany, it was decided not to restore all the petty states which existed before the French revolution. This arrangement was made due to the influence of Metternich who did not want a united Germaney.

Criticism

No provisions were made to revise or modify any of the terms of the settlement of Vienna. Consequently, the settlement at Vienna was the point of departure for the history of the century, (1815-1914), in which the aspirations of the nationalists and the liberals were largly realized. For the settlement along the lines of restoration, compensations, and guarantees gave the measure of the fears of the conservative soverings and diplomats. It attempted to elevate the natural desire for response and tranquillity into a principle of statesmanship,and it failed because it ignored or disregarded the new forces which the revolution had released.

It is said that the Congress of Vienna was not a congress but it was merely the meeting of the victors to divide the spoils of the vanquished. According to Hazen; "The congress of Vienna was a congress of aristocrats, to whom the ideas of nationality and democracy as proclaimed by the French revolution were incomprehensible. The rulers rearranged Europe according to their own desires, disposing of it as if it were their own personal property". Great pharases, such as "the reconstruction of social order", "the regeneration of the political system of Europe", "a durable peace based upon a Just division of power", were used by the dilomats of Vienna in order to impress the peoples of Europe". But the real object of the congress was to divide among the conquerors the spoils of the conquered. Infact, there was an unseemly scramble for grabbing the territories of the Vanquished by the victors.

The political ideas of the European rulers were derived from the

18th century, and at the Congress of Vienna there was much talk of the principle of legitimacy, which is known in English history as divine right. The revolutionary and Napoleonic period was generally regarded as a long nightmare, and left behind a strong prejudice not only against revolutionary principles but against the freedom of thought. The peacemakers at Vienna were suspecious of intellectual activity, and rigorously checked the free expressionof opinion. In this way they were supported by the Catholic Church and whose teaching hadbeen questioned by scholars and revolutionaries alike clerical control of education and thought was restored,particularly in Austria, Italy and Spain.

The Vienna treaty only protected the interests of the big powers and neglected that of others. According to Hayes; "in the settlement of Vienna there was little that was permanent and much that was temporary". France, Belgium, Germany, Poland were totally dissatisfied with the result of the peace settlement. So the peace agreement of 1815 was branded as a great deception and betrayal.

In their attempt to find a just equilibrium they erected safeguards both internal and external against France and made a sort of neutralisation of the powers of Russia, Austria and Prussia. They reverted to the outworn and exploded notions of Balance of power and the dynastic interests. This was indeed due to their anxiety to restore peace, yet it must be noted that they made a great mistake by regarding the French revolution only as a passing phase. The congress did not show any respect to the new born principles of liberalism and democracy. In the name of legitimacy, every where in Europe,Monarchical and despotic regimes of the old ruling houses were restored. Here in lay their lack of political wisdon and foresight and the history of rest of the 19th century is but the struggle for the destruction of the foundation laid at vienna. In the words of Hayes, "The Vienna settlement was defective in sofar as the people were regarded as to many pawns in the game of dynastic aggrandizement". Further, according to Curtwell; "It was hypocritical not to extend the doctrine of legitimacy to Republics". Though the avowed object of the settlement was the restoration of the old order and existing rights, the smaller states were ruthlessly sacrificed for the benefit of the larger. In Germany the smaller states were cut and carved out to suit Austrian or Prussian convenience.

The settlement of Vienna completely ingored the principle of nationality inorder to uphold the principle of legitimacy, or to maintain the balance of power. Nothing was done to satisfy the aspirations of Poland. Italy was placed under foreign ruler, Belgium and Holland which wre opposed in race, and historical traditions, were united under the House of orange purely in the interests of European equilbrium. Norway was united with Sweden much against the wishes of her people. German unity could not be achieved and the German patriots felt terribly frustrated. So everywhere the spirit of nationalism was crushed under the heels of reactionary monarchs. Thus, the seeds of discontent were inherent in the very nature and basis of the settlemen of Vienna.

The Congress of Vienna was a Congress of aristocrats, to whom the ideas of democrasy as proclaimed by the French revolution were incomprehensible. No representative of the people of any country was invited to this conference while taking the decisions the congress ignored the feelings of the common people. The liberal and democratic regimes setup during the revolution were destroyed by the order of the congress. The rulers rearranged Europe according to their own sweet will. There could be no settlement because they ignored the factors that alone would make the settlement permanent.

Although the work of the Congress of Vienna was reactionary, nonetheless it marks not only the close of an old epoch but the beginning of a new. True, that many blunders were committed, little foresight was shown and important principles were ignored. But certain things must not be forgotton, that the diplomats had to undertake the reconstruction of Europe on the old and cumbered site, that had no clean state to start their work upon. They were also bound by pledges and treaties previously made. Besides they could not be expected to legislate for centuries. Some of its territorial adjustment were pregnant with important consequences. Thus, an unconscious step was taken towards Italian unity. According to Thompson; "it was on the whole, a reasonable and statesman–like settlement". No doubt, the peacemakers ignored the ideas of nationality and democracy but in the words of Thompson, "it would be wrong to blame the makers of the settlement for failing to appreciate the power of nationalism and liberalism, which few realised in 1815". It was the first occasion when the representatives of almost all the countries of Europe had gathered at one place to solve the international problems. It gave birth to the feeling of international cooperation. According to Ketlby; "The Vienna Congress sought to protect Europe against a revival of French militarism, it provided a guaranteed order, and initiated a policy of settling future disputes, and it bradly on Metternich's principle of a balanced European society of five major powers, and so well distributed were its stresses and strains that no major war disturbed Europe for forty years". Further,it set the example of settling European questions by mutual negotiation through a congress. According to Thompson; "Vienna had the practical merit of giving Europe nearly half a century of comparative peace, and this was what most Europeans most feverntly wanted in 1815".

The Concert of Europe

The work of the Congress having been completed to the satisfaction of the Tsar and Metternich, they now wanted to establish an institution to safeguard the peace of Europe and to ensure that revolutionary and liberal movements would not raise their heads in any part of the continent. The Vienna treaties were entrusted to the collective guarantee of the powers, but the experience of the last 20 years had aroused a desire for greater international security and for some machinary for mutual protection. Hence, the so-called peace makers attempted one of the most interesting political experiments of the century. They tried to give practical shape to the idea of the concert of Europe. It was the first attempt of its kind at international government. It inaugurated the system of diplomacy by conferences which was a new departure from the old system of individual diplomacy. However, the idea of a concert of European powers was not a new one. The idea of a concert of Europe was suggested by the Austrian Chancellor, Kaunitz, in 1791 and it found expression in the treaty of Chaumont which was made in 1814 by England, Russia, Austria and Prussia. Accordingly, the four allied powers pleaded themselves to maintain by force, for a period a twenty years, the arrangements reached at Chaumont, Vienna and Paris. This undertaking created the so-called concert of Europe, because the four powers also agreed to periodic meeting of their representatives for the purpose of consulting upon their common interests and for the considerations of the measures most salutary for the maintenance of the peace of Europe. The concert of Europe had two distinct parts, the Holy alliance and the quadruple alliance.

The Holy Alliance

The Czar Alexander I was a man of deep religious feelings, and he proposed that the chief powers of Europe should enter into an alliance with a view of conducting the affairs of Europe upon christian principles. In fact the French revolution had a deep impact on the mind of the Czar who was an intensely devout person and he wanted to make sure that an irreligious revolution would not again engulf Europe. He wanted the rulers of the different states to guide their mutual conduct on the basis of christian virtues, namely, peace, charity and faith. This strange document was the work of the Czar who was easily influenced by theories based on religion. The Holy alliance was not a treaty, it was a solemn declaration initiated by Alexander and affirmed by the soverigns of Europe. So under his inspiration Russia, Austria and Prussia organised themselves in to a Holy alliance whose ostensible object was to exhort their subjects to live according to the teachings of Christianity. In fact, to please the tsar, Austria and Prussia accepted these high sounding platitudes, but they had no faith in them.

The Holy alliance, appealing to the old notion of the unity of Christiandom, Presupposed a community of like minded states. Its importance lies in the fact that it had in its the germs of the idea of international cooperation for peace. The Holy alliance presents some points of similarity to the united Nations of the present day. In its original form the Holy alliance was neither insinc-ere nor anti-liberal. According to Fisher, "the Holy alliance sought to unite the conservatives and reactionary rulers of Europe together". The real aim of the Holy alliance was to suppress all liberal movements.

Metternich called the Holy alliance, “a philanthropic aspiration clothed in religious garb, an overflow of the pietistic feelings of Emperor Alexander". In his memoris Metternich asserted that the main motive of Austria and Prussia in signing the alliance was to please the Czar, which they could afford to do because of the meaninglessness of the whole scheme. In the words of Hayes; "The eventual failure of the Holy alliance to ameliorate political and social conditions was due not so much to a want of its author or to any criminal charecter in its purpose as to the vagueness of its signatories to give it more than lip service". Hardly anyone except Alexander regarded it seriously. To Castlereagh" it was a piece of sublim mysticism and nonsense." He feared that England might be involved into dangerous and unforseen commitments by signing such a document. The Pope denounced it as the work of "a heretic". Talleyrand, dismissed it as a ludicrous contract. Since no other great power sincerely believed in its principles, the Holy alliance was a dead letter from the beginning. According to Ketelby; "It was shortlived figment of Alexander's imagination, a moral gesture, a pious aspiration....". But certainly, the Holy alliance was a symbol of the political ideal of the Europe of the day.

The Quadruple Alliance

The quadruple alliance of November 1815, was of far greater importance. Austria, Prussia, England and Russia undertook to uphold, by common action clearly defined, the second treaty of Paris, infact, the alliance was designed to extend, for twenty years, the war time collaboration between the four principal enemies of France. Moreover, meetings were to be held at intervals to discuss general policy. The signatories to the alliance agreed to act jointly, as a concert of Europe, to solve international disputes. According to Article VI of the quadruple alliance; "In order to consolidate the connections which at the present moment so closely unite the four sovereigns, the high contracting parties have agreed to renew at fixed intervals, either under their own auspices or by their representative ministers, meetings consecrated to great common objects and the examination of such measure as at each one of these epoches shall be judged most salutary for the peace and prosperity of the nations, and the far the maintenance of the peace of Europe". The concert of Europe was established with the purpose of putting into practice the settlement of Vienna and to maintain the statusquo, i.e., the condition of the pre-revolutionary period. The main objectives of the quadruple alliance were as follows; to maintain general peace in Europe. To make sure that Napoleon did not again endanger peace. To ensure that the second treaty of Paris was not upset and to keep the revolutionary French ideas in check and to maintain the balance of power. To meet at intervals of mutual consultation to solve international disputes. Metternich, the chancellor of Austria was the guide and leader at the congress of Vienna. He realised that if the spirit of democracy and nationalism would spread into his country then it would be broken up into a number of smaller states, for Austria had a mixed population. Metternich was guided by the Austrial interests and wanted to suppress these ideas. The concert of Europe, therefore, became an instrument of repression, a sort of an international police force in the handns of Metternich for the suppression of the liberal forces in Europe. The quardruple alliance remained inforce for ten years (1815-25) and this period is called the age of conferences in the history of Europe. Five conferences were held during this period at different venues, which were Aix-La-Chapelle (1818), Troppau (1820 A.D), Laibach (1821), Verona (1822) and St. Petersburg (1825).

The Congress of Aix-La-Chapelle (1818-A.D)

The first meeting of the quardruple allies took place at Aix-La-Chapelle in 1818, where they agreed, since arrangements for payment of reparations had been made, to withdraw the army of occupation and invite France to join in future meetings. They invited France to join the quintuple alliance to preserve the peace, but at the same time secretly renewed the old quadruple alliance as a safeguard against her. The most important object for which the quadruple alliance had been made had now disappeared since there was no danger of France upsetting the peace of Europe. The Holy alliance powers now suggested that the alliance should continue to carry out the following objects. They should police Europe and suppress all revolutionary movements wherever they raised their heads and they should meet periodically. On the other hand, Great Britain proposed that the powers should not intervene in the internal affairs of a country and they should meet only when there was a special problem to disucss. Metternich and the Tsar wanted to use the concert of Europe as an instrument of repression of all liberal movements, but England was not in favour of this policy.

The concert successfully adjudicate in the disputes of smaller states. The ruler of Monaco was ordered to improve the administrative system of his country. They called king Bernadotte of Sweden to account for ignoring treaty rights with regard to Norway and Denmark. The congress decided to grant the title of king to the elector of Hesse in Germany. The question of succession in Baden was solved. But before the congress was dissolved, however, signs had already appeared of the divergent interests and mutual jealousies which were to paralyse action and break-up the concert of Europe. First was the question of the rebellious South American colonies of Spain. The Ruler of Spain wanted to supporess the revolt and he sought the help of the allied powers. France and Russia wanted to help Spain, but England opposed it. She protested that her trade in Spanish America would be disturbed by restoration of Spanish authority. Metternich supported the British stand and the question was postponed for the time being.

Congress of Troppau (1820 A.D.)

At Aix-La-Chapelle there was a perceptible rift in the lute. The rift became wider at the next congress. The congress of Troppau was summoned as there were liberal movements in Spain and the kingdom of two sicillies. During the penisular war, the Spanish patriots had drafted a liberal constitution, but in 1815 the king abrogated the constitution and restored absolutism. In 1820, Colone Riego, a Spanish patriot revolted at Cadiz and soon the revolt spread to the whole of Spain. Finally, the Spainish king was forced to restored the old constitution. Czar Alexander I was horrified at this news. He hated democracy and feared that if the movement spread elsewhere no monarch would be safe. Russia offered armed assistance to the Spanish king to suppress the revolt in Spain. Castlereagh pointed out that the Spanish revolution was an internal affair of Spain and it was outside the Jurisdiction of the concert. England took her stand on the policy of non-interference in the internal affairs of other countries. Metternich sided with castlereagh because his hatred of revolution was balanced by his fear of Russian aggrandizement. Within a short time the example of Spain was followed in Portugal, Naples and Piedmant. In each of the existing governments were overthrown and constitution modelled on the Spanish constitution was adopted. The revolution in Naples and Piedmont directly menaced the Austrian domination in Italy and this made Metternich very uneasy. So Metternich summoned the meeting of the concert at Troppau.

The three Holy alliance powers Austria, Prussia and Russia condemned the revolutionary movement in Spain and Italy. They drew up a protocol, "asserting that if a state undergo a change of government due to revolution, the results of which threaten other states, the powers should be ready to use force to bring back the guilty state into the bosom of the great alliance". The protocol laid down, the principle of Joint intervention. On the otherhand England reaffirmed the British policy of non-intervention. Inspite of the strict opposition of England, the principle of interference was endorsed.

The Congress of Laibach (1821)

The third congress was held at Laibach in 1821. Austria was allowed to send her troops to Naples to suppress the revolt. The congress recognised the predominant interest of Austria in Italy. The Austrian armies restored the kings in Naples and piedmont to absolute power.

The Congress of Verona (1822)

The liberals in Italy had been checked by Austria, but in Spain the king was still controlled by his insurgent subjects, and the Greeks revolted in March 1821, against the Turks. Tsar Alexander I was anxious to go to war with Turky in support of the Christian Greeks.

But to Metternich, the idea of the balance of power was more important than the preservation of Greece. He wanted to maintain the integrity of Turky against Russian aggression. Austria was supported by Great Britain. They agree to summon one more congress where they hoped to prevent Alexander from taking any action against Turky. Before the congress met at Verona in 1822 disturbances in Spain assumed serious proportion. Henceforth, the Congress of Verona was soon occupied with Spain rather than with Greece. France insisted on interfering in Spain to restore the absolute monarchy and claimed the moral support of the allied powers. By then castlereagh had committed suicide and was succeeded by George Canning, whose hostility to congresses and projects of armed intervention in other states was even more than castlereagh's. But Britain could not prevent French intervention in Spain. A French army entered Spain, suppressed the revolt of the people and restored king Ferdinand to absolute power. England withdrew from the congress. Verona congress marked the completion of breach between Britain and her partners in the Quadruple alliance. The Success of the concert in Spain led to the reopening of the question of the Spanish American colonies. But England was determined to prevent the project of concerts intervention in Latin America Canning officially recognised the independence of the Spanish American colonies. So with the intention to forestall Spanish intervention in her colonies in South America,canning turned to the united States. American President Monroe issued his famour message, Later known as "Monre doctrine". According to the Monroe doctrine; "Our policy, in regard to Europe... is not to interfere in the internal concerns of any of its powers, to consider the government de facto as the legitimate government for us, to cultivate friendly relations with it, and to preserve those relations by a frank, firm policy..... It is impossible that the allied powers should extend their political system to any portion of either continent, North and South America without endangering our peace and happiness...". Due to Monroe doctrine and the determined attitude of canning,Metternich's policy of intervention had to be abandoned.

Great Britain as champion of the liberal movements, played a notable part in arresting the reactionary policy of the Holy alliance. The experiment of co-operation between the great states thus brokedown under the strain of the Italian and Spanish rebillions, owing to the divergent views of Britain and the Eastern powers. In 1824 the Czar attempted to call a congress over the question of Turky and Greece, but Canning flatly declined to call a congress over the question of Turky and Greece. In January 1825 the last meeting among the four great powers (France, Russia, Prussia and Austria) took place at St. Petrsburg. But the conference broke up without accomplishing anything. Nevertheless, the idea of a European concert did not disappear. Conferences were occasionally called through out the century to deal with problems as they arose, and a valuable tradition of meeting common difficulties by common action had been established.

Causes of the Failure of the Concert

The great powers of Europe which met together to resolve disputes among themselves and to preserve a certain balance of power in the continent met with little success. But after a short period , of ten years, this system came to an end. By 1823 the outcome of the congress system was the disintegration of the diplomatic alliances made in 1814 and the hardening of the position of both the forces of conservatism and the forces of change.

Autocracy and constitutionalism cannot go together. England with her parliamentary institutions found herself unable to pull on with the autocratic powers of Europe. The concert of Europe, viewed by the conservatives powers as dam against revolution. Metternich and the Czar tried to convert the concert into a machinary to enforce despotic system in Europe. The members of the concert had no homogeneous character. The concert of Europe brokeup on the divergent interests of the powers, on irreconcilable differences of constitutional outlook, and on the absence of any agreed principles of political faith. The concert could not satisfactorily function as an agency for international cooperation because of the mutual jealousy of the powers. England set her face against the principle of intervention adopted by the congress of Troppau. The congress system became a trade union of kings to suppress the liberties of the people. There was no internal harmony among the powers.

The concert of Europe wanted to maintain the staus quo, that is the political condition of the pre-revolutionary era by sheer force. But the institutions and systems which time had discarded could not be retained by this method. As the concert of Europe went against the very ideas contributed by the French revolution, it could not succeed in the long run. The concert was following a policy which was against the forces of liberalism released by the French revolution, but it could not keep these forces down for all time. Besides,it was the only fear of France that urged the European powers with divergent interests to come together. But when the French danger was over, the unity among the allies was gone and every power decided to deal individually with her diplomacy. Further, the concert neglected the small powers of Europe. The big powers always ignored the interests and rights of the small states. So the alliance could not be successful towards getting any support from these small states.

The Monroe doctrine was considered as an important factor which had contributed to the failure of the concert of Europe. The American President Munro warned the European power against any interference in any part of the American continent and made it clear that America was for the Americans. This damped the spirit of the concert of Europe. This moral defeat was also a cause of the failure of the concert of Europe.

But the congress system was the first serious experiment in international government. The Periodical meetings of the concert served useful purposes by adjustment of mutual interests of powers and settlement of disputes. According to Thomson; " The congress system of Europe could meet together from time to time to resolve disputes among them, it.... helped to keep peace". In the decades that followed 1825, the examples of the concert was emulated. Though the concert was dead, its spirit survived. It was successful in its attempt to established peace and security in Europe. It gave rise to a new feeling of internationalism. Above all, the concert successfully prevent the wars in Europe for a period of forty years.

Chapter-V

The Industrial Revolution

The industrial revolution, a movement the early phases of which took place in England between 1770-1825 and in continental Europe 1815, changed fundamentally the industrial, commercial, political and social life of the Western World. The term industrial revolution refers to the shift from an agririan, handicraft, labour intensive economy to one dominated by machine manufacture, specialisation of tasks, factories, a freer flow of capital, and the concentration of people in cities. For contemporaries of the industrial revolution, the application of machine to humas-tasks seemed the most significant change taking place. According to Devies, "The industrial revolution, a term which is used to express the change which was responsible for the adoption of system of making things on a large scale in factories with the aid of stem power, as opposed to the old system, which was generally followed up to the middle of the 18th century, of making goods in the cottage or shops of the workers", The large scale and basic nature of the changes introduced in a period of about sixty years justifies the term Revolution, although the scientific and economic background extends for centuries into the past, and the movement is still going forward at a rate perhabs geater today than ever before. But industrial progress did not proceed everywhere at the same pace. The changes that began in England in the mididle of the 18th century did not start in France until the French revolution. In the latter half of the 18th century, it originated in England where political and economic conditions were most suitable for its germination. It enriched her and gave her a lead over all other European countries. It spread to the main continent of Europe almost fifty years later. The industrial revolution is truely a revolution without boundaries and, thus far, without an end in sight. The-term industrial revolution was first coined by the French writer Blanqui in 1837, which was later on popularised by the British historian Arnold Toynbee. Blanqui has pointed out that the French revolution and the industrial revolution have brought a world of change in political, social and economic outlook in the 19th century.

The Background of Industrial Revolution

The process of industrialisation began in Western Europe for a number of reasons. Western Europe was wealthier than much of the world, and his wealth had accumulated slowly over the centuries. The widespread production of diverse rural handcrafts, for the preceding two centuries provided the foundation for the rapid expansion of trade. This expansion resulted from an aggressive search for new markets rather than from new methods of production. So the resources of the new world both human and material fueled Europe's accumulation of wealth.

In the middle of the 18th century the customs of economic life were little different from those of the middle ages. In agriculture, the inefficient "Open field" system prevailed. Each peasant cultivated strips of land, into which the large arable fields were divided, and grazed his livestock on the common or uncultivated pasture land that was free to all. Fertilisation of soil, rotation of crops, and controlled breeding of live stock were unknown. One-third of the cultivated land lay fallow every year. Crop yields were poor.

Etymologically the word manufacture means "make of hand" , and of upto 17th, century handicraft was the only method of production. In the 18th century the industry was carried on chiefly in the home with simple hand tools requiring little outlay of money. Production of goods was essentially production for use, not production for profit in a free market, since the market was small and local. Further, travel and transportation were slow and difficult. Little money was in circulation. The rigid class stratification of society and the illiteracy of the mass of the population prevented most men from improving their condition by enterprise. And government was monarchial or oligarchic.

Causes of the Industrial Revolution

In the 18th century many innovations in agricultural methods and organisation brought far reaching changes that foreshadowed and promoted the industrial revolution. By the 18th century, traditional patterns of farming were breaking up. Agriculture became more and more a capitalist enterprise, production was undertaken for the market, Land freed from traditional obligations became just another commodity to be bought and sold. Peasants freed from manorial obligations joined the ranks of enterpreneurs and tenants, all farming produce for the market. Further, the enclosure movement greatly improved agricultural efficiency and the total crop yield of land but deprived large numbers of small peasants of their livelihoods and forced them to migrate to the cities in search of employment. Besides, the earning of the rich landlords increased considerably and they had plenty of agricultural capital to invest in new industries.

The expansion of commerce which was the result of the discoveries of new lands and new sea routes led to greater demand for manufactured commodities. These commodities were sent out to new countries where from raw materials were procured. Export of manufactured commodities and earning of huge profits led to accumulation of capital. All this broadened the oppertunities of large scale manufacture. Expansion of commerce accelerated industry. There was a great urge among the Western countries to earn profits through export of manufactured goods.

The enormous European population growth of the 18th century provided with both consumers and labour. Most of this growth took place after the middle of the century and continued into the 19th century. The population expanded rapidly for several factors. The number of births increased. The number of deaths from war,famine, and disease declined at the same time. More efficient agriculture and better food distribution reduced malutrition, which meant more births, and fewer deaths.

Conditions in England were favourable for the beginning of the industrial revolution. England had achived a higher degree of national unity and political stability than other European countries. In the 18th century England had become the leading maritime and colonial power of the world. Her colonial and naval supremacy provided incentive for the development of the industry as the colonies provided raw materials as well as markets for the manufactured goods. Great Britain also possessed many natural advantages. Her coast line offered excellent harbours. Her climate was innvigorating and promoted habits of industry. Her natural resources were abundant. There were coal and iron mines in close proximity and the exploitation of these resources proved to be a great stimulant to the development of industries. The role played by private enterprise in England's economic development was extraordinary and unique, but the state played a part as well Parliament created a climate favourable to economic expansion. The state aided industrialisation by providing law, order, and protection of private property. As a natural corollary England emerged as the leading capitalist nation in the 18th century. The joint stock company was highly developed. England became the financial metropoli's made England so rich and of the world. The engines of the industrial revolution which made England so rich and powerful that she was able to stand the strain of Nepoleonic wars. No other country in Europe, was pregnant with so many potentialities for industrial development. Aboveall, the disorder on the continent attending the French revolution and the Napoleonic wars delayed the acceptness of the industrial revolution in France, Germany and the low countries.

For two centuris there had ben steady accumulation of scientific knowledge. The progress of science revolutionised the methods of production. In the later half of the 18th century the coal industry was fast reaching its limits, as water prevented the plumbing of lower levels of the coal mines. So there was need for more powerful engines to pump out the water from the lower level of the coal mines. The spirit of inventiveness had been one of the major aspects of the renaissance. The 16th and the 17th centuries were full of practical inventions. Technological inventions helped the ignition of industrial revolution.

Scientific Inventions and Growth of Mechanical Industries

The industrial revolution brought a change from handicrafts to machine manufacture and from human or animal power to other forms of energy such as steam.

The spinning wheel had early come into Western Europe from India and its operation had been improved by Leonardo da-Vinci. As early as 1589 knitting by hand was substituted by an Englishmen which herealded the industrial revolution in England. It was the cotton textile industry that received the first momentum from the outburst of inventions. John kay's (1733) flying shuttle speeded up the process of weaving and thus increased the demand for thread. James Hargreaves Spinning Jenny (1767), followed by Arkwright's waterframe (a water power operated spinning machine 1769), and Crompton's spinning mule (1779) supplied the demand for thread and created a surplus. Cartwright's Power loom (1785) improved weaving methods and thus restored the balance between spinning and weaving. Whitney's cotton gin (1793) made available a large cheap supply of raw cotton for spinning. Invention of these textile machinaries revolutionised the woolen and cotton textiles industries.

By far the most important invention of the industrial revolution was the steam engine which revolutionised industry and mining. Steam as motive had a distinct advantage over water power. It was no longer necessary to install factories near waterfalls. James Watt studied Newcomen's steam engine and removed its defects and invented a new engine with a separate condenser. Use of steam as power was a revolutionary step in the technological improvement which led to industrial revolution. Steam replaced horse and water power in the textile industry also. James Watt began to produce steam engines for industrial purposes. George Stephenson invented steam locomative engine (1825). The steam printing press (1814) decreased the cost of printed matter and facilitated the spread of universal education.

Early in the 18th century Abraham Darby made experiments in the substitution of coke (made from coal) from Charcol (From wood) for the reduction of iron-ore. In 1760 John Smeaton improved the Darby process by the addition of a waterpower driven air blast that improved the quality and yield of coke. About 1784 Henry cort introduced the puddling process for the purification of pig iron made with coke. From this time forward coal and iron went hand in hand with steam as the foundation of industrialisation. later developments of Prime importance were the invention (1859) of the "Bessemer process" and of the open hearth process for the large scale manufacture of steel.

Changes in mining textiles, Mettallurgy, speeded change in other industries, especially transportation and communications. Major road building took place in the 18th century in England and France. John Metcalfe, John Macdom made tremendous improvements in road making Rail roads were so successful that in mid 19th century England, roads became mere auxiliaries to the railways were a great born to mankind. A penny posal system was introduced in Great Britain in 1840. But the greatest improvement was the practically instantaneous communication by electricity introduced with Morse's telegraph (1837). The development of electrical science late in the 19th century led to the invention of Bell's telephone (1876) and Marconi's Wireless (1896).

In the second phase of industrial Revolution the invention of machinaries was particularly important. Among hundreds of machines, processs, and scientific principles may be mentioned, Faradays's discovery of electromagnetic introduction (1831), Large scale preservation of food by canning (1845) Daguerre's invention of photography (1839) Ericsson's screw propellor, Good years rubber vulcanisation (1844). Agriculture also received a new spurt due to the use of machinaries and chemicals. Thus, there was a radical change in the process and method of production in diverse fields which changed the outlook and life of the people.

Effects of the Industrial Revolution/Economic Results

The old method of small production in the home with one's own tools could not meet the competition of machine production, and the cost of machinary was prohibitive to the individual workers. Hence, arose the factory system, i.e., large scale production in factories using machines owned by the employer. The factory systems stimulated the growth of division of labour and of mass production through standardisation of processes and parts.

As a result of the industrial revolution a large variety of articles which were unknown in the centuries preceding the 18th, began to be manufactured in large quantities to satsify the growing needs of mankind. Particulary Significant was the rise of the producer's goods industry as distinguished from the consumers goods industry. The increasing productiveness of the macnines led to an enormous total increase in wealth, but the surplus was concentrated in the hands of a few rich men. In the long run the total increase in wealth led to a general rise in standard of living.

Formerly, capitalists invested their capital in trade and commerce. But as a result of the industrial revolution, when large scale factories began to develop, the mercantile capital, i.e., the capital invested in commerce was now being invested in the establishment of industries. So the mercantile capital was converted into industrial capital. Huge capital was being invested by capitalists in the manufacture of finished goods. Large scale industries replaced small scale production.

The great problem of the capitalists was the profitable investment of their wealth. The development of multiplied productivity required an ever larger market for the disposal of the product. Hence, arose in the later 19th century, when domestic markets begun to reach a saturation point, the pressure for imperialist expansion and sphere of influence in the undeveloped part of the world. As production for profit in a free market replaced production for use, and as innovations of method upset the balance in established industries, the phenomena of large scale booms and depressions introduced a new element into economic life. The industrial revolution enormously accelerated the movement towards international economic dependence that had begun with the commercial revolution of the 16th and 17th centuries. The entire world became a market place. Dislocation of industry in any part of the world often has important repercussions in countries thousands of miles away.

Social Results

`The changes in agricultural production, business organisation, and technology had revolutionary consequences for society and polities. People were drawn from the countryside into cities. Industrialisation made the world smaller. The whole world was drawn into commerce, and, ultimately, manufacturing at a dizzying speed. Because of the industrial revolution, a vast urban proletariat grewup, property less, largly illiterate, and entirely dependent upon wage earning for a living. The industrial revolution gave rise to a number of industrial towns, unfortunately, their development was most unplanned. In the factoried themselves men and machinens were crowded together, and outside the factories, the tenements of the workers grew like mushrooms with out any plan. The overcrowed towns lacked the barest sanitary amenities. They were smoky, filthy and unhealthy. The living togehter of men and women in these small dark dungeons led to several moral vices.

The industrial capitalists found it more profitable to employ women and children in their factories. Children of pauper parents were farmed out to factory owners on terms that amounted to slavery, unprotected even by the property interest that mitigated the rigors of true slavery, and were literally worked to death. Long hours of work in insanitary conditions affected their health. Later, the government had to pass laws forbidding the employment of women and children in hazardous industrial enterprises where their health was likely to be undermined. Besides, as the supply of labour, considered as a commodity, was usually in excess of the demand, and because the workers were without any independent means of subsistance, the fear of loss of the job became a constant specter in the workers mind. Mass unemployment became one of the greatest social problems arising from the industrial revolution. A far reaching consequence of the industrial revolution was the development of highly efficient mechanised weapons that rendered war immensely more destructive and dangerous to civilised progress.

The industrial revolution destroyed forever the old division of society into clergy, nobility and commoners. The development of industry and commerce caused a corresponding development of a bourgeoisie, a middle class comprised people of common birth who engaged in trade and other capitalist ventures. The middle class was made up of several economic layers. From the 18th century on, as industry and commerce developed, the middle class grew in size. But its increased size did not bring increased power. Throughout the 18th and 19th centurries, the middle class struggled against this entrenched social structure to end political, social and economic discrimination. During the 19th century, the social changes resulting from industrialisation brought the mididle class greater power and social respectability. As industrial wealth became more important, the middle class became more influential. Industiralisation also sharpened the distinctions between the middle class and the labouring class.

Political Results

Thepolitical effects of the industrial revolution were complementary to the social and economic effects. So long the landed aristocracy used to enjoy all political rights and privileges and philosophers used to preach the ideal of democracy. The working class movement that only trade unionism would not be enough to improve their condition. They realised that they could remedy the evils of the working classes life and working conditions by acquiring political rights and influencing legislation of the country. Thus began working class movement for acquisition of political rights. In England the working class movement succeeded in getting right of representation in the Parliament. The success of working class movement was not enough to remedy all grivances of the working class. This gave rise to the demand for democratic government on economic basis that is for socialism.

Another political effect of great consequence was the colonial expansion by different European countries in comparatively backward ones. Demand for more raw materials and markets for finished goods led to a scramble for colonial expansion.

Cultural Results

The social and economic changes made by the industrial revolution stimulated the growth of the science of economics or political economy, it was usually called 19th century economic thinking stems chiefly from Adam Smith whose "Wealth of Nations" (1776) argued for non-interference by government with business. Smith held that each man is the best judge of his own economic affairs. He championed the doctrine of Laissez Faire (Free Trade). This Laissez Faire doctrine appealed to the new capitalists of the industrial revolution. The idea of Smith were developed by the school of classical economists, the leaders of which were Malthus, Ricardo, James Mill. Malthus formulated his principle of population, which asserted that any improvement in the economic condition of the poor would be counter balanced by an increase in population. Ricardo enunciated the celebrated "Iron law of wages". Against the terrible, if cheerful, pessimism of the individualist economists arose the socialists, who refused to accept as irrenediable the blood bad conditions brought by the industrial Revolution. The socialists like St. Simaon,Blanc,created a public opinion against the system of free trade, which demanded better working conditions, a higher standard of living, and a greater freedom for women and children. The industrial revolution stimulated scientific investigation. The profession of engineering became indispensable to the new applied science appealed to the imagination of the common man. Besides, the mass-circulation newspaper, the automobile, the motion picture all products of the industrial revolution have supplied man with a whole new set of interests, and far more than the arguments of philosophical agnosticism have brought about the secularisation of view point and widespread religious indifferentism that is characteristic of contemporary life.

Thus, the industrial revolution which took place during the second half of the 18th century brought about an unprecedented change in the economic and political life of the world.

Chapter- VI

The Era of Metternich

A clash between the forces unleashed by the French revolution and the traditional outlook of the old regime took place during the years 1815 through 1848. The period opened with the Congress of Vienna, which drewup a peace settlement after the defeat of Napoleon, and closed with the revolution that swept across most of Europe in 1848. The forces of conservatism trimphed with the restoration of old order. Monarchs still held the reins of political power. Aristocrats, retained their traditional hold over the army and administration, controlled the local government and enjoyed tax exemption. Determined to enforce respect for traditional authority and to smother liberal ideals, the conservative ruling elites resorted to censorship, secret police and armed force. However, inspired by the revolutionary principles of liberty, equality and fraternity, liberals and nationalists continued to engage in revolutionary activity. The old bottles could not indefinitely hold the new wine.

Charecteristic of the Era

The period from 1815-48 has usually been called the "Era of Metternich" because the policies and influence of prince Clemens Metternich, Austrian Chancellor and foreign Minister, were dominant in continental Europe. He established his moral dictatorship over central Europe. Belonging to the old order of Courts, Metternich hated the new forces of nationalism and liberalism. He regarded liberalism as a dangerorus disease carried by middle class malcontents. Metternich believed that domestic order and international stability depended on rule by monarchy and respect for aristocracy. The misguided liberals belief that society could be reshaped according to the ideals of liberty and equality, (said Metternich), had led to twentyfive years of revolution, terror and war. To restore stability and peace, the old Europe must suppress liberal ideas, and quash the first sign of revolution. Metternich strongly opposed the principle of nationality, as it would disrupt the Austrian empire which was inhabited by a number of nationals like Germans, Magyars, Czechs, poles etc. He believed if these ethnic groups became infected with the nationalist virus, they would shatter the Hapsburg empire. A highly cultured, multi-lingual and cosmopolitan aristocrat, Metternich considered himself the defender of European civilisation. He was a bitter enemy of the Nation States. He felt that by arousing the masses, nationalism could undermine the foundations of the European civilisation that the cherished.

Metternich was the apostle of conservatism. Govern and change nothing was his watchword. He was an ardent supporter of absolutism. He was determined to end the chaos of the Napoleonic period and restore stability to Europe. He sought a settlement that would avoid the destructiveness of a general war, Metternich stood for the maintenance of the statusquo in Europe.

His Career And Character

Metternich was born in 1773 in a noble family. He studied in the university of Strassburg. The matrimonial alliance with the grand daughter of the Austrian chancellor enchanced the prestige of Mettrnich. He came into contact with high officers, politicians and the rulers of other countries of Europe. When he was hardly 36 (1809) he was appointed the chancellor of Austria and he occupied that position for nearly 40 years. According to Hazen, "He was a man of high rank, wealthy, polished, blending social accomplishment with literary and scientific pretentions,....He was the prince of diplomatists, thoroughly at ease amid all the intriguing of European politics." He had a hand in Napoleon's defeat at Leipzig. He presided over the Vienna Congress. Metternich considered himself as the most important figure of the continent of his time. According to Ketelby, "He could swim like a fish in the sparkling whirlpool of Vienna. No one knew so well as he how to carry through a political intrigue between dinner and a masked ball." He sought to base Austrian stability on a balanced European society, a general presonal magnetism of his character, his sociability, his diplomatic experience, his power of Judging man's character and above all his ability to tackle most intricate problems gave him an ascendancy all over Europe. His ideal was a reactionary Europe propped up under the hagemony of Austria. Metternich was a great egoist and a cynic who did never change his convictions and had a firm belief in his infallibility. He is known as the chief architect of European convervatism which arrested the constitutional progress of Europe from 1825-48. There was not a single drop of modesty in his character. He said, "my position is such that all eyes, all expectations are directed to that point where I happen to be.... He said, "I have come to the world too early or for late. Earlier I should have enjoyed the age, later I should have helped to reconstruct it. Today I have to give my life to propping up mouldering institutions." The exigencies of the domestic situation forced Metternich to make Austria the conservative barrier to all the progressive movements in Europe to devote the whole resources of the monarchy to a life long struggle with Jacobinism- the spirit of revolutionary unrest. He regarded reforms as an incentive to revolution. He hated Parliament and representative system of government. He said "Democracy could only change day light into darkest night". Metternich defined himself as a man of statusquo. According to Fisher, "Metternich had engaging presence, a cool head, a vast comprehension of affairs,a firm and patriotic will. His prestige as a liberator of his country and as the principal artificer of the new Europe was immense.... In the counsels of autocrats his was the directing mind so that the period between 1815-48 has not unjustly been called the "age of Metternich". He saw no mean between revolution and autocracy and since revolution was odious he set himself to repress that which is the soul of human life, i.e., society, the very spirit of liberty". As per Prof. Phillips, "For a tired and timid generation, he was a necessary man, and it was his misfortune that he survived his usefulness and failed to recognise that while he himself was growing old and feeble, the world was renewing its youth". In fact, he was a prisoner of the age. He has been branded as an oppertunist, but he pursued a policy of conservatism in order to preserve the Austrian domination. He knew that the mult-racial Hapsburg empire would go to pieces if the new born ideas of liberalism and nationality were allowed to play- of course, he was supporting an ideal which had been rejected by history.

Metternich System

Metternich was an Austrian Minister and Austrian interests influenced his internal and external policies. In pursuance of his aims he adopted a reactionary and conservative policy and instituted a system of Government popularly known as the "Metternich system "to strengthen his hold over the Austrian empire. He realised that if the influences of the French revolution particularly those of democracy and nationalism would spread into Austria which had a people of various racial origin, then Austria's political unity would be lost. He, therefore, was determined not to allow the forces of nationalism and democracy to make any headway within Austria. He followed a double policy of prevention and suppression- prevention of the spread of the revolutionary forces within Austria and to suppress any expression of these forces in Europe.

Metternich wanted to control the minds and ideas of the younger generation and so he instituded a strict control over univesity education. Texbooks were censored and professors were screened lest they might impart liberal ideas, political meetings of students were banned. Spies kept a secret watch on the activities of the professors and students. Political science and history were removed from the curriculm. The press was muzzled and could not publish any liberal news. To stop the infiltration of liaberal ideas, frontiers were closely guarded. The people in general and students in particular were not allowed to travel abroad so that they might not infected with revolutionary ideas. Persons suspected of liberal tendencies were imprisoned without trial. The police system was strengthened to keep all liberal movements in check. In Europe he wanted to maintain the reactionary system of government. Maintenance of the status quo in Europe was the main principle of the foreign policy of Metternich. The concert of Europe was formed with this end in view. According to Hayes, "To combat the dangner of infiltration of revolutionary ideas from abroad, he created a wall of tariff and censors around the Hapsburg lands. To prevent the rise of liberalism at home, he rigidly supervised the press....Even the slight liberalism in Giriliparzer's drama was detected by the government censors and Austria's foremost dramatist cynically ceased to write. It was only music which escaped Metternich interference".

Metternich and the Austrian Empire

Metternich followed a reactionary policy in Austria–Hungary. In the application of his system within Austria he kept everything unaltered, did not allow any reform measures to be undertaken, and followed a policy of autocracy and reaction. Control of the press, educational system and other similar measure, he kept Austria free from the influences of democracy and nationalism. His had negative policy. Prevention was the key note of internal administration. "Govern and change nothing was the beginning and the ending of his programme. According to Francis II, the Austrian emperor, "I also have any estates, I have maintained their constitution and donot worry them, but if they go too far, I snap my fingures at them and send them home.... He who serves me must teach what I command".

Austria was composed of heterogeneous nationalities, like the Germans, Czechs, Italians and others, who spoke dififerent languages and had different political institutions. It was well high impossible to fuse the various nationalities among them was bound to lead to the disruption of the empire. In Austria, the people were divided into three classes, the nobles, the bourgeoisie and the peasants. Besides, the people were mostly agriculturists and industries were in a very primitive state. In short, absolutism in government, feudalism in society, special privilegee for the favoured few, oppression and misery for the masses, such was the condition of Austria upto 1848. The monarchy discouraged all initiative and enterprise on the part of the servants, and the cumbrous machinary of the state was practically at a standstill. The Austrian system of government, was nothing more or less than stagnation in every direction. Neither industry nor commerce flourished. Education was at a alow level. The very heterogeneous nature of the state and the economic backwardness of the people provided a rich enough soil for the seeds of the revolutionary principles of liberty, equality and fraternity to germinate and grow. Under the circumstances only an arbitrary government could keep the various nationalities together. According to Marx, "A constitution and a free press for Austria were things considered unattainable, administrative reforms, extention of the rights of the provincial Diets, admission of foreign books, and a less severe censorship–the loyal and humble desires of these good Austrians hardly go any further". The various nationalities of the empire, were kept under control by Metternich's garrisoning methods and so there were not serious national or constitutional uprising upto 1848.

Metternich and German Confederation

In spite of the wishes and efforts of the German patriots, a loose confederation was created in Germany as that was the only thing in the interests of Austria. Metternich did not favour a unified Germany.. Because he did not want to encourage the establishment of nation states. Austria would not allow German unity under Prussian leadership, as that would undermine her influence in Germany, as the Hapsburgs had been leaders of Germany for centuries. The 38 soverign States of the German confederation would be used by Austria to serve her own ends. Metternich's main motive was to stop the tidal flow of the revolutionary principles in Germany. The German patriots felt frustrated since a unified independent German State was not created and liberal constitutions were not granted by the German princes. The liberals were extremely disatisfied and universities were the chief centres of discontent. In 1817 some students at Wartburg burned various symbol of the old regime. Two years later, a conservative spy named Kotzbue was assassinated by a liberal student. This event gave Metternich an oppertunity for action. He summoned a meeting of German statesmen at Carlsbad and secured the promulgation of the resulting carlsbad decrees by the Diet of the German confederation. Censorship was imposed on the press. All societies were banned. No constitution inconsistent with the monarchical principle was to be granted. Liberalism was crushed and reaction become the order of the day.

Metternich said, "It is the prime duty of every ruler to continue suppressing and crushing all the efforts of the nationalists....". Metternich's hold over Germany was so great that the revolution of 1830 and minor reactions in a limited number uprising and the rulers were forced a grant a constitution on the model of the French charter of 1814. But Metternich soon intervened and suppressed, the revolts. This state of affairs continued upto 1848 when the Metternich regime ended.

Metternich and the Rest of Europe

No less complete was Metternich's influence in Italy. Austria ruled in the north, Hapsburg princes and the Pope in the centrer, and the Bourbon Ferdinand in the South. All joined in re-establising the old regime. When the news of the successful Spanish revolution of 1820 reached Italy, the Patriots of Italy were highly stumulated. The congresses of the concert of Europe were convened at Troppau and Laibach. The Austrian soldiers were sent to Naples and the ruler was restored to absolute power. Police, troops and spies held down all liberal agitation and the fact that in much of Italy the repressive hand was a foreign one made it irksome to Italian liberals and nationalists. In the opinion of Mazzini, "Country, liberty, brotherhood all are wrested from them, their facilities are mutilated, curbed, chained within a narrow circle traced for them by men who are strangers to their tendencies, to their wants, their tradition is broken under the care of an Austrian Corporal, their immortal soul feudatory to the stupid Caprices of a man seated on a throne at Vienna." Only in the kingdom of Sardinia was there a ruler with exclusively Italian interests. Officially all Italy was conservative and reactionary.

During the early part of the era, Metternich could count on the support of the so-called concert of Europe. The concert under Metternich's guidance, dealt with threats to peace by a series of conferences. These conferences became the means for the suppression of liberal movements within the various countries. At Troppau, Russia and Prussia formally agreed with Austria to Act joinly against revolutionary disturbances. From this decision England dissented, and henceforth, the concert was practically a continental affairs.

Ferdinand II was restored in Spain in 1815. He followed a reactionary policy and cancelled the liberal constitution of 1812. In 1820 there was a revolt in Spain. Ferdinand hypocritically agreed but he corresponded with the great powers. The reactionary powers of Europe saw the haunting spectre of the revolution in Spain. The congress of Verana authorised France to interven in Spain. Metternich was happy when Ferdinand was restored to absolute power.

The February revolution in France (1848) profoundly affected the fortune of Austria. Revolt occured throughout the Austrian domains. On March 13, 1848, a turbulent mob of students and workers clashed with police in the strects of Vienna. Metternich called out the civil guard to disperse the crowed, but it refused. Finally, the white haired old Minister presented his resignation. His residence was already sacked and burning, on March 14, 1848 he hurridly departed from Vienna for London. Metternich, the veteran foe of revolution was fleeing for his life before a revolution. According to Hazen, "Metternich who for 39 years had stood at the head of the Austrian State, who was the very source of reaction, pitiless, masterful was now forced to resign, flee in disguise from Austria to England, to witness the whole system crash completely beneath the onslaught of the very forces for which he had for a generation shown contempt".

Failure of Metternich System

Metternich succeeded in following his policy of reaction for long years from 1815 to 1848. But his policy both within Austria and all over Europe was too narrow, unstatesmanly and destructive. "Metternich system" ran counter to the contemporary progressive ideas. While the spirit of nationalism, liberalism and democracy had been fast influencing the minds of the people, the Metternich system sought to suppress it by force. Under the muffling blanket of Metternich's conservative system, liberalism and nationalism were concealed but not eliminated. He could crush the revolutionaries but he could not repress their spirit and ideas. The revolutionary principles of equality, liberty and fraternity triumphed over his conservatism in 1848, Metternich system was negative and oppertunist. Prevention was the sum of his policy. But it only retarted but could not avert the day of reckoning. The British and French support of the Belgian patriots in the struggle for Belgain independence, the independence of the Spanish colonies in America and the war of Greek independence weakened Metternich;s hold on Europe. The Monroe doctrine (1823) was another blow to Metternich's theory of intervention. According to Marx, "There was a slow underground movement going on which baffled all Metternich's efforts. The wealth and influence of the trading middle class increased ....The new commercial and manufacturing population came everywhere into collision with the old feudal institutions ....." The impact of the revolution of 1848 was so severe in Austria that Metternich system came to an end. According to Hazen, "The effect produced by the announcement of Metternich's fall was prodogious. It was the most astounding piece of news Europe had received since waterloo. His fall was correctly heralded as the fall of a system hitherto impregnable". However, the period of Metternich was a period in which Europe wanted peace rather than liberty. Metternich system maintained peace in Europe for at least 30 years. Had Europe been involved in war or revolutionary struggle after the peace of Vienna it would have been disastrous for whole of Europe. In sofar as Austria was concerned Metternich saved unity of the country inhabited by people of different races. Metternich was an Austrian Minister and Austrian interests guided his policy. He advised his master to adopt a policy of evolutionary conservatism, but due to blind conservatism, of the emperor, he failed. He said, "I am giving my life to support a tottering structure .... I have come in this world either too early or too late". According to Thompson, "Metternich was neither a bigot nor a papalist. He had a firm and patriotic will. Metternich imposed his conservatism system in Europe for the sake of balance of power". In the opinion of Ketelby, "Metternich's repressive policy was justified because it had a higher purpose, the protection of Austria from disruptive nationalist movements. Behind his oppertunism, there lay the logical defensible principle, preservation of Austrian empire.

Chapter-VII

France (1815-30)

(Restoration, Reaction and Revolution)
(The July Monarchy and the February Revolution–1848)

Louis XVIII

At the fall of Napoleon, the Bourbon line of kings was restored in France in the person of Louis XVIII, brother of Louis XVI. He followed a policy of compromise and reconcilation. France experienced a compromise between the revolution and the ancient monarchy. It was based on the "Divine right of kings", yet it limited their (King's) power by a written constitution, it admitted Catholicism as the State religion, yet tolerated other creeds, it retained the nobility as a separate order, yet refused to restore their original status. Louis XVIII, cold blooded, sceptical, free from illusions, free from the passion of revenge, indolent by nature, he desired to avoid conflicts and to enjoy his power in peace. He dared not to undo the work of the revolution and therfore retained much of its work. He realised from the outset the impossibility of reviving the pre-revolutionary regime. He saw that the day of the absolute monarchy had passed forever in France. The monarchy must be constitutional. The king recognising that he must compromise with the spirit of the age, and hence issued the constitutional charter in 1814.

The Charter

The restoration opened with a promise of moderation. In 1814 the king issued the charter, accompanied by a preamble which indicates his attitude to the revolution. He says, "It was our duty according to the example of the kings, our predecessors, to appreciate the results of the constantly increasing progress of enlightenment, the new relations that this progress has introduced into society, the direction impressed upon opinion for half a century, and the grave alterations which have ensued. We have recognised that the wish of our subjects for a constitutional charter was the expression of a real need". The king thus frankly admitted the conditions imposed by the events of the revolution, the constitution he published was liberal compared with the despotism of Napoleon. It was a pact between the king and his poeple.

At the head of the state stood the king inviolable in person. He controlled the administrative system by the appointment of the prefects, subprefects and mayors. The constitution was his own creation, and in it he had reserved for himself the initiation of laws and the right of veto. There were two houses of Legislature, a chamber of peers, consisting of an ulimited number of members nominated by the king, and a chamber of deputies. The former was to sit in secret, and besides, its legislative functions, shared with the king and the chamber of deputies, was to act as a court of Justice. The chamber of deputies was to consist of persons who paid not less than 1000 Franc a year in direct taxation elected in the department by persons paying 300 Francs in direct taxation. It was to be elected for five years, but one-fifth of its members were to retire annually. Napoleonic nobility was placed on an equality with the old nobility. Property confiscated during the revolution was not to be restored. The legion of honour was retained. The civil liberties of the Frenchmen were assured by the charter. Religious toleration was proclaimed. All people of France will be considered equal before the law. No person could be imprisoned without a fair trial and trial by jury was guaranteed to all. All class distinctions and privileges were abolished. It has been rightly pointed out that the charter is a treaty of peace between the two parties into which France has been divided, a treaty by which both parties yield some of their pretentions in order to work together for the glory of their country". From the position of the king it might appear to follow that representative government would be as much force under the restoration as it had been under Napoleon, but this was not the case. In spite of the restricted electorate, in spite of the pressure, the government could put upon the voters, inspite of the modification of the electoral law, it was not found possible to secure a stable and permanent majority under the control of the king. The chamber tended constantly to be either more liberal or more reactionary than he, (The king) and it was the obstinate and repeated return of a majority hostile to the policy of the crown that led to the coup d'etat and the revolution of 1830. On paper the charter preserved many of the principles of the revolution, though it failed to maintain them in fact. Frenchmen were declared to be equal before the law, yet this vaunted equality of the people did not exit, the right of voting were restricted to men of certain degrees of wealth. Yet, the charter remained the constitution of France up to 1848.

The Position of Political Parties

The "Hundred days" (of Napoleon) made the position of the restored king much more difficult than before. In 1814 the allied had pretended that the French nation was eager to welcome the Bourbons, but in 1815 this was no longer possible. Hence the humiliating precautions imposed in the second treaty of Paris-humiliation which made it patriotic for Frenchment to despise the monarchy which had been forced to accept them. After Napoleon's final defeat at Waterloo in 1815, the allies who brought him (Louis XVIII) in their baggage train, once again restored Louis XVIII to the throne of France.

France at this time was divided into three main political parties, the Ultra-Royalists, the Moderates and the Radicals (left). The restoration of the Bourbon dynasty to the throne of France furnished the signal for the outbreak of political strife. Those nobles and clergy who had fled from France to other countries to save their lives during the course of the revolution were called the Ultra-royalists. Their leader was count of Artois. The Ultra-royalists were the obstinate and relentless enemies of the French revolution, inflexibly resolved not only to stem the rising tide of liberalism, but to turn back the whole course of French historical development into reactionary channels. They represented the traditional policy of the emigres who had always repudiated the revolution. The leading idea of the Ultra-royalists programme was nothing less than to revive the old order. They were fighting for the privileges of their own order. According to Hazen, "More eager to restore the former glory of the crown, the former rank of the clergy and the nobles, more bitter towards the new ideas than the king himself, they were the ultra-royalists or ultras-men more royalisst than the king, as they claimed. They saw in the revolution only robbery and sacrilege and gross injustice to themselves. They bitterly assailed Louis XVIII for granting the charter, a dangerous concesion to the revolution–meanwhile desiring to nullify its liberal provisions as far as possible".

In opposition to the Ultra-royalists were the moderate elements, pledged to defend the revolution and continue it without revolutionary spirit. They dreamt of an alliance between order and liberty, between legitimacy and the revolution. They stood by the charter granted by the king in 1814 and were loyal to the crown. There was also a party or a number of parties, of the left Republicans, Bonapartists, and other discontented groups. These groups wanted revive the republic. At the beginning of the reign they were in a hopeless minority.

Chief Events of the Reign of Louis XVIII

A general election was held in 1815, and it resulted in the ultras commanding a majority in the chamber of deputies, although the moderates prevailed in the chamber of peers. The leader of the Ultra-Royalist party was the king's brother, the count of Artois, who regarded any concession to democracy as a bargain with the devil. He demanded that the charter should be withdrawn, that the property confiscated under the revoluion should be restored, and that Bonapartists should be prosecuted. They procured the dismissal of Talleyrand and Fouche, despite the fact that these two former minister of Napoleon had done more than any body else to make the restoration possible. This was followed by an outbreak of royalist fanaticism known as the "White terror" At Marseilles, a royalist mob attacked the Bonapartists. The movement spread to other departments in the south. Rioting went on in a large scale and the government did nothing to curb it. A number of leaders of the revolution including marshal ney the bravest of the brave were killed. The chamber demanded repressive measures of various kinds from the king and got them. The king now took a decisive step, and he dissolved the chamber. In the election, the ultra majority was swept away and a large majority of moderates royalists was returned. And from 1816-20 the Government of France was able to advance along more liberal lines. The two Chief Ministers, Richelieu (1816-18) and Decazes (1818-20), both convinced adherent of the Bourbon monarchy.

The Work of the Moderates and the Murder of the Duke De Berry

The first Prime Minister under the restored French monarchy was the Duke de Richelieu. Though an aristocrat who had lost everything in the revolution and had been many years in exile, he was too high-minded to bear ill-will towards his fellow countrymen. He tried to rule in the spirit of the charter, to restore confidence and to make the government financially solvent. Richelieu continued in office until 1818, and during this period France was able to pay off the indemnity imposed by the second treaty of Paris. The Government of France appeared to be so stable that the army of occupation was withdiawn by the allies in 1818. He changed the electoral law in favour of the moderates, but the growing strength of the party of the left, however brought about the retirement of Rechelieu in 1818 and Decazes was placed at the head of the government.

The programme of Decazes was expressed in the formula, "Royalise France and nationalise the monarchy". His policy was conceived on liberal lines. Press censorship was relaxed, but this law pleased neither of the extreme parties. The army was reorganised and measures were introduced tɔ raise the French Army. A new electoral law was passed, lowering the Qualification of members, and this was more favourable to the bourgeoisie.

In 1820 the Duke de Berry was assassinated on the step of the opera house by an anti-Bourbon fanatic named Louvel. The Duke was the second son of the count of Artois. The murder was the act of an isolated fanatic, but the ultras trans-fixed with horror, were not slow to charge the responsibility for the dastardly deed upon the weakness of the king and the liberalising policy of his Minister. One of the ultras said, "I saw the dagger that pierced the duke de Berry, it was a liberal idea." "Either Decazes must retire before the reigning dynasty", said another ultras, or "the race of our kings must retreat before him". The murder of the Duke roused great indignation. According to Schevill, "The assassination in 1820 of his (Louis XVIII) nephew and ultimate heir, the Duke of Berry, shook him (Louis XVIII) profoundly. Although the murder was the deed of a fanatic, who had acted an his own initiative, the courtiers insisted clamorously that the real responsibility rested with the liberal ministry. Louis therefore replaced it with a ministry of ultras".

Richelieu returned to office for a short time, but he was unable to stem the tide of reaction which had set in. The electoral law was revised to the marked advantage of the ultras. The censorship of the press was restored and an electoral law passed which suppressed secret ballot. By the end of 1821 Richelieu gave place to villele, an able statesman but a pronounced reactionary, who held office till the end of 1827.

Ministry of Villele (1821-27)

The ministry of villele lasted from 1821-27. It was a period of ascendancy for the ultras, not that the minister belonged, except in name, to their party, but that he was unable to resist the pressure they brought to bear. Civil liberties were curtailed, the press censorship was strengthened, a new and heavy tariff was drawn up, and public education was placed under the control of the university, which was itself directed by a Bishop. The tenure of the chamber of Deputies was extended. A new electoral law discriminating against the bourgeoisie was passed. Meanwhile a French expedition, with the sanction of the Holy alliance, entered Spain and restored the absolute power of Ferdinand VII. According to Hayes; "It was a strange irony of fate that the French arms which had so recently carried the message of liberty, equality and fraternity to the peoples of Europe, should be the weapon of divine right of monarchs on behalf of conservatism and reaction". In 1824 Louis XVIII died and was succeeded by his younger brother, the count of Artois, who ascended the throne with the title of Charles X.

The Reign of Charles X (1824-30)

The charecteristics of the new king were well known. He was the convinced leader of the reactionaries in France. He had been the bitter opponent of his brother's liberalism. The coronation of the king revealed the temper of the reign. Charles X personified the spirit of the emiges who had sickened the Courts of Europe with their claims and pretentions during the consulate and empire. His wooden-headed bigotry led him into a course of action which brought the monarchy to ruin within six years. His brother had tempered his legitimism with shrewd common sense, but Charles despised compromise. He had indeed learnt nothing and forgotton nothing since 1789, and would have boasted of this as honourable staunchness to principles. He revived the elaborate court ceremonial of Louis XIV. France was treated to a spectacle of medival mummery that amused and at the same time disgusted a people that had never been known to lack an appreciation of the ridiculous. According to Hayes; "It had been the count of Artois, who with Marie Antoinette had engineered the Court intrigues against the revolution in its earliest stage. It had been he who had headed the emigration of the nobles and the clergy when their privileges were threatened by the revolution. It was he who was never tired of agitating against the revolutionaries and against Napoleon, and it was he who, on the triumphant return of his family and of the emigres, ecouraged the ultra royalists in acts of retaliation".

When he ascended the throne in 1824, the ultras under villele were still in power in the Legislature. Secure for the moment of his parliamentary majority, and strengthened by the accession of Charles X, Villele could now bring forward the measures embodied in the Ultra-royalist programme. The most important was the indemnification of the emigres. But it was impossible after an interval of thirty years to disposses the new owners of the soil. So an alternative device was adopted to satisfy the claims of the emigres. The rate of interest on the national debt was reduced from 5 to 4 per cent, and the economy thus effected enabled the government to compensate the old nobility for the losses they had sustained by the sequestration of their possessions. Further an institution of the Roman Catholic was established, the aim of which was to encourage the powers of the Church. The Jesuits were allowed to returned to France. One of the important Act passed by the villele ministry was designed to make the press the creature of the executive. No newspaper was to appear without the sanction of the crown. The contents of the newspaper were to be censured by the government. Even an attempt was made to pass a new law by which the liberty of the press was to be completely ended. Villele also tried to alter the civil code of Napoleon which provided equal share of property among all sons, but this law was defeated in the upper-house. And when in 1827 the king was reviewing the national guard, the soliders greeted him with such persistent cries of "Down with the ministry". A Bill was promptly passed for the disbandment of the force. But the effect of the disbandment was fatal. Such attempts to muzzle the opposition merely embittered it. The rising tide of discontent began to wash away the government's majority in the chamber, and in 1828, the king disolved the chamber. The result was a terrible shock.

Ministry of Martignac (1827-29)

In 1828 Martignac was appointed as the Prime Minister and the new man was too liberal for the king and too conservative for the chamber. He wass a man of ability, moderation and experience. Some useful work was done. The press censorship was relaxed, the excluded professors restored to their posts, the clerical control of education was abolished, and a considerable measure of local self-government was proposed. The reactionists were furious and the progressives were not appeased. The Martignac ministry was defeated in the chamber, and the king dismissed it with the chareteristic remark; "I always said there was nothing to be done with these liberals".

Ministry of Polignac 1829

Polignac, an ex-emigre, formed the ministry but he was very reactionary and was intensly hated by the moderates. Polignac was a devout Catholic who shaped his course by visions of saints, and this divine guidance was urgently required, for his own mental capacity was exteremely limited. His colleagues were men of the same kidney, for his Minister of Justice had taken a prominent part in the massacres of the white terror, and his minister for war had deserted from the French Army on the eve of Waterloo. Such a ministry was a challenge not only to every liberal minded man in France, but to the powers which had guaranteed the charter as a safe guard against revolution. Charles X was now determined to make no more concessions, but to impose his own will upon the chamber and the country. The king said, "There is time to call a halt". The ministry looked upon constitutional goverment as something foul and shameful. A vigorous policy of reaction was followed, which aroused such a degree of oppositon that the Chamber of Deputies petitioned the king to dismiss polignac. The liberal deputies had protested in an address to the crown against a ministry holding office when it was not backed by a parliamentary majority. The king interpreted the liberal protest as an insult and dissolved the chamber. In the fresh election the government lost over fifty seats and was in a hopeless minority. A crisis had arisen. Had charles dismissed polignac he might have preserved his crown. He preferred to act under an article of the Charter which empowered him to issue ordinances for the safety of the State.

July Ordinances 25th July, 1830

On 25th July, 1830, the king published four ordinances. The first prohibited the issue of newspaper without the assent of the government, secondly, the Chamber of deputies was dissoved, thirdly, a great change was made in the eligibility for the voters was made more rigid. Fourthly, it was declared that the new elections would be held in september 1830. France was momentarily stunned, but Paris quickly recovered.

The next day Paris, at the instigation of the Journalists broke out in revolt and erected barricades. Crowds assembled in the streets of Paris, raised the tricolour (Revolutionary flag), seized the Hotel de Ville, and a provisional government was set up. The king now sought to revoke the ordinances, but it was too late. After a futile attempt to save his dynasty by abdicating in favour of his grandson, the duke of Bordeaux, he passed into exile. What kind of government was to be established now? Some wanted a republican form, other's a monarchy. Finally, under the guidance of Lafayette, it was decided to offer the crown to Louis Philippe, the Duke of Orleans. For the moment, France was committed to yet another constitutional experiment, conceived and largly initiated by doctrinaires who knew more about the history of England than the temper of France.

Importance of the Revolution

The July revolution released an extra ferment of ideas and passions which continued to work long after the revolution. The revolution involved the overthrow of the principle of Divine Right in France. The soverignity of the people was reasserted and the attempts made by Charles X to revive the old order were frustrated. According to Lipson; "The task of the French revolution of 1789 which remained incomplete hitherto was now completed by this revolution. Now the fundamentals of the revolutionary ideology-equality, secularism and constitutional liberty became secure for ever". The civil rights of the people were reaffirmed and the reactionary government had to yield to liberalism. The hopes of the ultras were extinguished. Further,echoes of the revolution were heard in Belgium, Spain, Poland, Italy and the revolution marks the definite reversal of one feature of the Vienna settlement. The sparks of revolution from the furnace of

France Flew far and wide. It proved to be a signal of the dowfall of the system of Metternich and gave a new form to the principle of the Balance of Power.

July Revolution of 1830 and its Reaction in Europe

The influence of the revolution of 1830 was felt all over Europe. It was the signal for widespread popular movement which for a short time seemed to threaten the whole stucture erected in 1815 at Vienna. According to Thompson; "The revolutions that took-place all over Europe between 1815 and 1830 made considerable breaches in the political and territorial settlement of 1815". The attempt of Charles X of France was destroyed by the July revolution. France not only discarded the legitimist dynasty which was imposed on her by the Congress of 1815, she gave up the conservative path of the Bourbons and moved in the path of liberalism. According to Fisher; "Sparks from the Paris furnace flew fast and far among the unsound timbers of Congress of Europe Sneezes". The Belgians rose against the Dutch, the poles against the Russians, the Carbonaro against the priestly governance of the Papal states. A wild clamour for a war of liberation to be undertaken in the grand old revolutionary manner in relief of suffering people ran along the Paris pavements. Metternich's immediate impulse was to organise a coaliation Louis Philippe, king of the barricades, but for various factors this was impractiable.

Belgium

At the Congress of Vienna (1815) Belgium was annexed to Holland in order to create a strong state on the North-Eastern bondery of France. The principle of nationality was thrown to the winds and against their wishes the Beligians were united with the Dutch. But it was easier to declare these two peoples formally united under one ruler than to make them in any real sense a single nation. Though it might seem that the peoples of this little corner of Europe must be essentially homogeneous, such was not at all the case. There were lines of Cleavage which made fusion impossible. They spoke different languages and formed two distinct nations with separate cultures and traditions. The Dutch were protestant while the Beligians were Catholics. The Dutch lived by overseas trade and had valuable colonies, while the Belgians were mainly agricultural and industrial producers. The Dutch who had been independent since 1609 looked down upon the Belgians as inferior to themselves. William I (King of Netherland) tried to impose the Dutch language, and Dutch officials on the Belgians who were execluded from high official posts. Thus, the relations between the Dutch and the Belgians were very strained and there was great disaffection among the latter.

The embers of discontent were smouldering ever since the union (1815), and when the means of the successful revolution in Franch reached Brussels, they were fanned into a conflagration. There was street fighting in Brussels and the revolution spread rapidly. The royal troops were driven out and on October 4, 1830, Belgium declared itself independent. A congress was summoned to determine the future form of government. It decided in favour of a monarchy, adopted a liberal constitution, and elected Leopald of Coburg as king.

Naturally the powers could not ignore all this, for they had themselves created and guaranteed the union which the Belgians had broken up. The Czar was all for intervening in the cause of the legitimate rights of a fellow sovereign, and the king of Prussia mobilised-an army on the frontier. But Louis Philippe of France who was riding the crest of French nationalism warned Russia against intervention in Belgium. Lord Palmerstone, the British foreign minister sysmpathised with the Belgian cause and was in favour of recognising Belgian independence. Austria was busy with the insurrection in Italy. At a conference in London, Rusia, Prussia, Austria, France and England recognised the independence of Belgium. The final settlement came in 1832 when the five powers agreed to guarantee the neutrality of the new kingdom. The king of Holland indignantly protested, and invaded Belgium, but the appearance of a French Army, compelled him to retire. Thus, a new state had arisen in Europe, as a resuit of revolution.

The Revolt of Poland

The successful revolutions in France and Belgium inspired others which had very different results. In the Congress of Vienna most of the area of Poland was given to Russia. Alexander I had in the first flush of his liberal enthusiasm made his polish provinces into a constitutional kingdom separate from autocratic Russia, with its own army and legal system. But the polish nobles were not satisfied. They complained because the Czar had not included in the kingdom certain former possessions of Poland such as Lativia and Lithuania, and the army officers formed a secret society to work for a greater Poland. This provoked Alexander to restrict the liberties which he had granted under the constitution of 1815. His successor Nicholas I went further, he nullified the constitutions by refusing to convoke the Diet (Parliament).

The news of the July revolution sent a wave of enthusiasm and hope among the poles and they began to dream of their independence. The poles revolted in Warsaw (Poland's capital) and killed many Russians. This revolt was so powerful that constantine, the Russian Governor of

Poland fled the country. Russia declared war, and the poles fought with great bravery, but without good leadership. The Poles were hopelessly outnumberred and the revolt was suppressed. Terrible atrocities were perpetrated on them. The constitution of 1815 was annulled. Poland ceased to exist as a separate kingdom and became merely a province of the Russian empire. The insurgants were brutally punished. But it remind Europe of the existence of a body of national sentiment, which was still strong.

Reaction in Other Countries

Vienna, Prague and Budapest remained quiet, but there were liberal rising in Saxony, Hanover and Hesse, where the princess were forced to grant liberal constitutions similar to the French charter of 1814. But Austria was in no mood to tolerate the blosoming of German liberalism. Meternich at once called the meeting of the Federal Diet and passed several repressive ordinances. Severe restrictions were imposed on the press, speech and writings. In Hesse and Hanover the constitution were soon abrogated and in Saxony it was made ineffective.

The revolutionary wave also reached Italy. The secret societies become active. After the July revolution in France revolution raged in Italy. But these were quickly suppressed by the armed intervention of Austria, which from its Vantage point of Lombarday kept a strict watch upon all movements in Italy. The kings of the different state were again enthroned. The only result of the revolution of 1830, for Italy, was an increased hatred of the Austrians. In Spain and Portugal liberal constitutions were granted within a few years of the July revolution. It may, however, be noted that this was due more to the internal conditions than to the effects of the July revolution. The July revolution had its indirect influence on England. The reform act of 1832 was passed, for the Tories realised that the forces of liberalism were irresistable. The July revolution led to the succesful assertion of the principles of liberalism and nationality. It was certainly an event of resounding importance to Europe. Above all, the revolution had far-reaching consequences beneficial to the cause of the people.

(THE JULY MONARCHY–THE FEBRUARY REVOLUTION) (1830–48)

1848 is often called the year of revolution, for throughout Europe, uprising for political liberty and nation-hood took place. The economic crisis had intensified political and national unrest. A financial crisis precipitated by over-speculation had caused terrible food shortages. The common people blamed their governments for their misery and sought redress. Although economic hardship aggravated discontent with the existing regimes, but it was absence of

·liberty, which was most deeply resented by the peoples of Europe and led them to take up arms. An uprising in Paris set in motion the revolutionary tidal wave that was to engulf much of Europe in 1848.

It is the fatal vice of revolutions that one can never fortell their course or predict their issues. In 1830, as in 1789, those who initiated the movement planned one thing, but circumstance gave birth to another. On each occasion an attempt was made to establish the political soverignity of the people, but each time it ended in fiasco. According to Fisher, "The monarchy of Louis Philippe, after a life of 18 years, perished as it had been born, in a Paris revolution. To a logical people like the French there was a fundamental flaw in a regime which was neither true monarchy, nor true republic, nor true empire, but a hybrid, without the historical glamour of the legitimate crown, or the democratic appeal of the republic, or the military renown of the house of Bonaparte. ...The kind bourgeoisie king with his large sentimental umbrella and his obtrusive domestic virtues was condemned by the common citizen as a bore."

The Government of July was a Government of compromise, it was continuous with the restoration by its form, but divided from it by its origin. What issued form the revolution of 1830 was not a change in the constitution, but a change in the person of the monarch. That change, however, involved a new theory of the monarchy. Louis XVIII and Charles X had rested upon their legitimacy, they represented the tradition of centuries, of which the revolution was an impertinent interruption. This tradition was the source of their strength and also of their weakness. Their tendency was inevitably towards reaction, and to this tendency they succumbed. The policy which had ruined Charles X could not be that of Louis Philippe. He had no heriditary title to the throne and no support in the pre-revolutionary past. According to Metternich; "Louis Philippe finds himself at the accession to the throne in an untenable position, for the basis upon which his authority rests consists only of empty theories. His throne lacks the weights of the plebiscite which was behind all the forms of government from 1792 to 1801, lacks the tremendous support of historical right, which was behind the restoration, lacks the popular force of the republic, the military glory of the empire, the genius and the arm of, Napoleon and the Bourbon support of a principle. Its durability will rest solely upon accidents". The basis of Louis Philippe's throne was middle classes, who possessed the monopoly of power, and with whose aid he ruled France from 1830 to 1848. They had wrested the fruits of victory out of the hands of the populace which had borne the heat of the struggle, and had established the july monarchy in order to consolidate their position in the community as the governing class.

Louis Philippe, son of Philippe Egalite (Orlean dynasty–Junior Branch of the Bourbon), had been connected with the Jacobin club, and had fought at valmy and Jemappes. Later he had fled to Switzerland, where he earned his living as an usher. At the restoration he had returned to France and had lived thence forth as a private citizen, a courteous and unpretending gentleman of means, patronising art, attached to his family, careful of his investments and walking the streets at his ease with an umbrella under his arm. He walked the streets of Paris alone, talked and drank with workman and sent his sons to the public schools to associate with the sons of the middle class, a delicate compliment fully appreciated by the latter. He had no illusions, no theories and no enthusiasms. He had seen the catastrophe of the revolution, and he had no belief in republican or royalists formula. What he did believe in was his own experience and judgement, and it was in reliance upon this that he accepted the throne of France. He was the bourgeois king, the creation of the middle classes. He received the Crown at Hotel de ville, under the sponsorship of lafayette and was confirmed in his dignity, and approved by popular demonstration. The basis of the new system was a kind of tacit contract between the king and the nation. His policy was one of "Golden mean", neither aristocratic nor democratic, but moderate. By temperament he was averse to change and the pity was that he failed to recognise that times were changing. His policy of stagnation eventually brought about his downfall.

Characteristics of the Liberal Monarchy

The new monarchy was essentially a bourgeois monarchy, and it depended on the support of the middle classes and not of the whole nation. But inorder to win the support of the people, Louis Philippe adopted and introduced some symbols of liberalism. The king declared himself to be the king of the French instead the king of France. He relaxed press censorship. The franchise was slightly extended. Those people who were 30 years old and paid 500 Francs as taxe to the government were declared eligible for the membership of the house of Deputies. He replaced the Bourbon white flag with the revolutionary tricolour. The members of the chamber of peers were to be nominated by the king from the assemblage of the officers of high rank. The recognition of Roman Catholicism as the state religion was withdrawn. The national guards was agian established. In foreign affairs, France sympathised with liberal movements abroad.

Opposition to Louis Philippe

The king was faced with many difficulties. The root of them was the fact that he had gained the throne without the cordial support of the bulk of the nation. Though the French people had resented the anchromistic posing of Charles X, they had not wanted to go so far as to dethrone him. The revolution had been carried through by a few thousand workmen and students of Paris, and the settlement had been devised by a still smaller number of middle class politicians. The unorganised masses of the nation had merely shrugged their shoulders and accepted the fait accompli. Louis Philippe had to meet opposition both from the right and the left. The legitimists wanted a Bourbon prince, and considered Louis Philippe as a usurper. The Bonapartists recalled the glories of Napoleon and had no love for a king whose foreign policy was peaceful. His moderat policy estranged the republicans. It was only the constitutionalists who supported him. As the king was dependent on them for support, the orleanist monarchy became a middle class monarchy. This angered the other parties who in derision, gave Louis the derisive sobriquet, "Citizen king". It was a bourgeois monarchy hated alike by the republicans and socialists for its extremely conservative policy. The former criticised the government as undemocratic, while the latter denounced it as capitalistic. The leading political parties tried to overthrow his government by frequent revolts. The first revolt brokeout in the city of Lyons. There was a legitimist insurrection of 1832, inspired by the Duchesse de Berry who sought to stir up Lavandee on behalf of her son. There were republican riots in Paris. At the same time there were the premature attempt of Louis Napoleon to size the crown by exciting revolts at Strassburg. These movements showed the danger of the forces arrayed against Louis Philippe. The government adopted vigorous measures for the suppression of these revolts. Louis Philippe passed a series of repressive laws called the September laws (1935) in order to eliminate all oppositon. The September laws were successful in their immediate aim, France was governed for 18 years by an aristocracy of wealth.

Even more menacing was the industrial situation. During the July monarchy France experienced the first birth *pangs* of the economic revolution. Rapid industrial changes produced their intellectual reaction. It was on an industrial rather than a political rock, that the orleanist monarchy foundered.

Louis Philippe's Policy of Changing Ministry

Louis Philippe would have been a good deal firmer on his throne if he had a solid majority in Parliament, but the groups of politicians who had momentarily joined forces to make him king soon fell asunder. The first ten years of the reign were crowded with polincidents, the king trying various combination of ministers in the hope of finding one which would both carry out his policy and command a majority in the chamber. Of the half-dozen ministries which held office during this decade, the most notable were that of Casmir-perier (1831-32) which definitely established the monarchy by repressing disorder and gaining recognition from the powers and that of Marshal Soult (1832-36) which chained up republicanism by the laws of September. Thiers came into power for a few months in 1836, but his anxiety to pursue a more spirited foreign policy alarmed the king and in September 1836, he gave place to count Mole. This ministry was shaken by the theatrical attempt of prince Louis Napoleon to raise the Bonapartist flag at Strassburg and by a simultaneous Republican outbreak at Vendome. After a breif experiment with Thiers, Louis Philippe found a man of his choice Guizot who controlled the helm of affairs till 1848. Guizot's outlook was coloured by the rigid calvinism in which he was brought up. Under the empire he had made a mark as Lecturer and writer on history. When the Bourbons were restored in 1815 he became leader of the doctrinaires who adopted the creed of English Toryism. Driven out of politics by the victory of the ultras (1820) he had gained reelection for the Chamber of 1830, and had taken the lead among the deputie who offered the throne to Louis Philippe. The chief traits of his political character were his belief in a franchise restricted to the rich, his contemptuous in-difference to popular clamour and his Tory view that the king ought to play a vital part in the conduct of the government. He declared his policy in the following words; "We have to prevent the flood of revolution in France, we shall adopt such a liberal policy with other countries, so that there should be no interference in their internal affairs, I want to maintain peace everywhere and always".

The Rise of the Napoleonic Legend

In the romantic memories which Napoleon dictated at St. Helena, he represented himself as embodying the revolution, and as having been on the verge of setting up a truely democratic regime when he was thwarted by jealous reactionaries. After the great man's deah many frenchmen began to look back on the empire through rose-tinted spectacles. Forgetting its cost in blood and tears and treasure, they (the French men) only remembered its glory. They recalled that whereever Napoleon's armies went, they aroused national spirit, sweptaway fedual cobwebs, opened the carrier to the talents, had checked priestly domination. In order to gain popularity the liberal monarchy encouraged the cultivation of the Napoleonic legend. Napoleon was hailed as a great national hero. Napoleon's glorious achievements were magnified. Poets and Philosophers like victor Hugo and Beranger sang his praises and roused popular admiration or the

magnificent exploits of the Emperor. Louis Philippe's patronage of the Napoleonic legend was a grave blunder, as he unconsciously encouraged opposition of his own regime. For since the death of Napoleon Bonaparte, the only possible Bonapatist claimant was Louis Napoleon, son of the one time king of Holland, an unattractive young man with short legs, a pasty complexion and leaden eyes. He was a strange, studious, ruminating young man, full of dreams and expedients, and possessed by a firm conviction that he was destined to revive his uncle's line in France. Twice, first in 1836, and again in 1840, he had made a dash for the French crown. The government paid him the compliment of a state trial for treason. Louis Napoleon seized the oppertunity to make a speech which was a manifesto to the nation. He said in the Chamber, "For the first time in my life, I am at last able to make my voice heard in France...I represent before you a soverignity of the people, the cause is that of the empire, the defeat is Waterloo". He was imprisoned but he escaped t
England where he bided his time to grasp a suitable
oppertunity while the Napoleonic legend continued to be cultivated in France. According to Marriot, "The seeds of the disorder to which Louis Phillipe ultimately succumbed were already sown, the virus was inflecting the whole body politic. But operation was slow and subtle".

Rise of Socialism

The Philosophy of 1789 had been egalitarian in its conception of political and personal rights, but had not attempted to abolish private property, nor to protect the artisans standard of comfort, nor to interfere with the liberaty of industrial exploitation. Socialism, though it was not a plant of recent growth had never before made itself felt as a potent factor in French politics. The theory of socialism had long been discussed in the saloon and the classrooms, but never until 1848, did it descend into the streets and inspire the political action of the mob.

One of the acts of the revolution of 1789 had been to abolish the trade corporations. These bodies represented an economic organisation which had prevailed throughout Europe for many centuries, it was their function to limit the number of labourers, or of master in a trade, to secure good and uniform work, and to value it at a fair price. The revolution (1789) abolished these. The revolution thus effected in the organisation of trade was contemporaneous with the transition from the old to the new industry. By the removal of legal restriction the number of apprentices increased indefinitely, and the rate of wages was lowered in propertion, commercial crisis became severe and frequent. According to Louis Blank; "Strife of producers among themselves for the conquest of the market, of labourer among themselves for the conquest of employment, of the manufacturer against the workmen to determine the rate of wages, of the poor man against the machine that is destined to destroy him by starvation–such, under the name of competition, were the characteristics of the situation."

Socialism was a product of the first revolution, though the word was not invented till later. According to Fisher; "Socialism, which is as old as poverty itself, takes different forms in different mind". Artisans and their families had participated in the great revolutionary outbreak of 1789, and had defended the barricades in 1830. These people felt betrayed by the regime of Louis Philippe, which had brought them neither political representation nor economic reform. The factory workers and artisans were becoming attracted to socialist thinkers who attacked capitalism and called for state programme to deal with poverty. On the other hand, the July, monarchy was essentially an employer's regime". There was no hope of factory acts, the governments only reply to agitation with stern repression in the name of order. Thus, the working class were eager for schemes to overturn the capitalist system which seemed to be the cause of their misery. St. Simon was the first to announced a socialistic scheme for the reorganisation of society. He believed that the state should own the means of production and should organise industry on the principle of "Labour according to capacity and reward according to services". Sismondi attacked the doctrine of Laissez Faire. It was a young journalist named Louis Blank who first gave socialism a definite programme. In a Pamphlet called L'organisation du travail, he maintained that the state ought to organise production and provide its citizen with work and wages. He declared, "All economic evils would vanish if the governemnt would furnish workers in each industry with funds to start "national workshops", to be controlled by the workers themselves. To Blank such political reforms as the extention of the franchies were important mainly as a means of creating a truely democratic government which would bring about a social and economic transformation on these lines. A poor harvest and an international financial crisis, which drastically curtailed French factory production, aggravated the misery of the working class. Prevented by law from striking, unable to meet the financial requirements for voting and afflicted with unemployment, the urban workers wanted relief. Alexis de Tocqueville in a speech, captured the mood of the the working class; "Do you not here them unceasingly that all that is above them is incapable and unworthy of governing them, that the present distribution of goods throughout the world is unjust, that property rests on a foundation which is not an equitable foundation? And do you not realise that when such opinions take root, when they sink deeply into the masses, they are bound to bring with them sooner or later...a most formidable revolution". A German, Stein, wrote; "The time for purely political movement in France is past; the next revolution must inevitably be a social revolution". The rise of socialism considerably weakened the foundation on which the edifice of the bourgeois monarchy had been constructed. As years rolled by, the red menace became graver and garver.

Foreign Policy

Louis Philippe's foreign policy was dull and colourless. It did not satisfy the French sentiment for glory abroad. Lamertine remarked; "France as a nation is bored". Louis Phillipe as a liberal monarch supported the cause of Belgian nationalists against the oppression of the Dutch. The successful intervention by Louis Philippe certainly enhanced his prestige, but his glory was shortlived, for, when the Belgians offered the crown to his son, the duke of Nemorous, he was balked by the British opposition and had to decline the offer. This signalled the decline of the international prestige of France.

In 1839 the Eastern question was reopened by the restless ambition of Mehment Ali, the Pasha of Egypt Mehment Ali was not only anxious to throw off the Turkish Suzerainty in Egypt, but had alterior designs upon constantinople itself. To satisfy popular clamour he placed thiers as the head of the ministry, who had pleaded himself to champion the cause of Mehment Ali, as a matter of great patriotic interest. Meanwhile, England, Austria, Prussia and Russia formed the quardruple alliance and supported Turkey. France found herself in a position of inglorious isolation. A war between France and the quadruple alliance seemed imminent for the sake of Mehment Ali. But Louis Philippe thought that discretion was the better part of valour. Their's resigned, and for the the second time England had imposed his will upon Europe, and inflicted a damaging blow upon the prestige of the orleans monarchy.

Louis Phillippe began to realise that something must be done to reestablish his credit in Europe. He wanted to divert the attention of his people from internal unrest to foreign glory. He decided to have a family compact with Spain. The marriages of Isabella, the girl queen of Spain and her sister Marie Louisa were a matter of European importance. Louis Philippe wanted to see a member of his family on the Spanish throne, but England objected to any revival of family compact. In 1843 Lord Aberdeen (Foreign minister of England) agreed with Louis Philippe to a compromise on the subject. That England would not object to infanta (Marie Louisa) marrying a French prince, provided that queen Isabella was already married and had a child to succeed her on the throne. But Louis Philippe went back on his words and the two siters, Isabella and Louisa were married on the same day. It was a disgusting piece of trickery. It brought about estrangement with England. The net result of this muddle-headed policy was that France was completely isolated in Europe.

Louis Philippe tried to make up for the loss of British Friendship by carrying favour with Metternich over a crisis which had recently arisen in Switzerland. This little country was a loose confederation of tiny cantons which varied in race, speech and religion. A struggle broke out between the liberal party which wanted to build up a more unified state and a Catholic party headed by the jesuits. The liberal party had control of most of the cantos. The Catholic cantons formed a league called the Sonderbund. The Swiss Federal assembly decreed the liquidation of the Sonderbund and the expulsion of jesuits from Switzerland. The Catholic cantons appealed to the powers against a violation of the cantonal liberties which had been guaranteed by the congress of Vienna. Louis Philippe in the hope of breaking his isolation and making an alliance with Austria supported the reactionary aontons. Palemerstone, the British foreign Minister opposed it and proposed that the Swiss should be allowed to settle their internal affairs, palmerstone kept the ring for the protestant cantons, warded off the interference of the powers. The Sonderbund was dissolved, the federal union was consolidated, and Switzerland was finally delivered from the dangers of foreign interference. Louis Philippe had once again to eat humble pie. The July monarchy had stripped itself of the last shred of its claim to be "liberal", without achieving anything at all.

Ministry of Guizot and the Revolution-1848

After the resignation of Thiers, Guizot now became the Chief Minister, with the elevation of Guizot to the leading position in the government, France attained ministerial stability. Eminent as a professor, an historian, and an orator, he was a man of strong and rigid mind, holding certain political principles with the tenacity of a mathmatician. In a world of change he remained immutable. To preserve peace within and peace without, was his programme.

There was no more friction between and the king ministry, for Guizot was his mouth, the organ through which his policy was expressed. And Guizot was conservatism incarnate. The constitutional monarchy created by the revolution of July was his political idea, and he would not sanction the least alteration in it. Democracy in the modern sense of the term he regarded as red ruin and the breaking up of laws. Moreover, the government was scrupulous in its adherence to parliamentary forms, in which Guizot was a strict believer. To preserve the system and keep himself in power

Guizot acted on the motto of Walpole's, Quieta non movere-"let slipping dog lie", avoid trouble everywhere and always. And his method of controlling Parliament was equally wlapolian-indirect corruption by means of patronage. More than half the deputies held government post or contracts. Before 1848 not less than one-third of the deputies had become place-holders under the government. A deputy said; "What is the chamber, a great bazar, where everyone barters conscience, or what passed for his conscience, in exchange for a place or an office". Corruption was rampant everywhere and infected every branch of the administration. Several gross scandals were brought to light in the last years of the July monarchy.

Such a system was a mockery. According to a member of the Parliament, "What have they done for the past seven years, Nothing, nothing, nothing." France was ashamed of its government, above all, France was bored. The old king and his ministers might, Ostrich-like, stick their heads in the sand, but this did nothing to avert the fate that was stalking them. Of course, the reign of Louis Philippe is famous for some constructive measures in the areas of education, religions and the government tried to follow a policy of neutrality. Though the right of imparting the primary education was given to the Church but the schools were kept under the strict control of the government. Further, factory legislation were made and childrens were prohibited from working in the factory. But these never came into practice due to the oppressive policy or Guizot. By 1847, however, the middle class monarchy of Louis Phillippe became very unpopular with all sections of the people. Under the leadership of Barrot and La martine, a campaign for parliamentary reform was launched.

The position of the or-leans monarchy had gradually deteriorated, and while enemies multiplied, friends grew more and more apathetic. Yet down to February 1848, nobody supposed that the existance of the monarch was seriously threatened. For sometime past the cry in favour of parliamentary reform had been gaining in volume. The liberal, and republicans demand a change in the composition of the chamber of deputies, and an enlargement of th suffrage, parliamentary and electoral reform. Against both these proposition, Guizot resolutely set his face. To prove this falsity of this assertion, the opposition insituted a series of reform banqets (after-dinner speech) which addressed by the reformers. A reform banquet scheduled to meet on 22nd February, 1848 was banned, but the angry students and workers were not to be cowed down. Bonfires were lighted in the streets. Barricades were constructed and street fighting followed. Some shots were fired. The government called out the National guard. It refused to march against the insurgents. Some of the members of Sthe guard began to shout, "Long live Reform", "Down with Guizot". The king frightened at this alarming development, dismissed Guizot from office. Had he done this twenty-four hour earlier there would have been no revolution, but it was too late. In the evening of February 23, Paris was illuminated and the trouble seemed ended. But the republicans were determined to take advantage of the excitement to gain their own ends. They made a hostile demonstratin before Guizot's residence. Some unknown person fired a shot at the guards, and the guards instantly replied and more than 26 person died. The Republicans placed the bodies of some men who had been killed in the rioting on lorries and paraded them through the streets to arose the horror and indignation of the multitude. The ghastly spectacle aroused every where the angriest passion. Barricades were put up in the streets of Paris. The cries of long live reform, heard the day before, now gave way the more Ominus cries of "Long live the Republic". Finally, on February 24, the king abdicated in favour of his grandson. For during the afternoon, Louis Blanc and his friends had taken possession of Hotel de Ville, where they proclaimed a socialist Republic and set up a provisional government. For a few hours it seemed as if an armed conflict would break out between the faction of the tricolour and the faction of the red flag, but this was averted through the tactful mediation of Lamartine. Finally, the leaders proclaimed a Republic and ordered elections to an assembly, which was to draft a new constitutions.

Chapter-VIII

France:
From Republic to Empire (1848-52)
and
From Empire to Republic (1852-70)

–Echoes of the Revolution of 1848
–Napoleon III–The Second Empire–1852-70

The February revolution marked the final victory of the French bourgeoisie. The revolution of 1848 was extraordinarily swift, entirely unexpected and extremely radical. Lamartine, one of the prominent leader of the revoltion proclaimed the republic on 26th February, 1848 in the following words: "Royalty is abolished. The Republic is proclaimed. The people will exercise their political rights."

The Provisional Government

The fall of the Orleans monarchy in February 1848 had shown once more how difficult it is to control the course of revolution when once it was been unleashed. Liberals had merely wanted to force Louis Philippe to dismiss Guizot, but the republicans had carried the movement on the drive the old king himself into exile. From the very outset there were grave differences of opinion among the members of the provisional government. The moderates led by Lamartine, were anxious to regard their functions as strictly provisional. On the other hand, Louis Blanc and the Reds were determined to accept the clamour of the parisian mob as the voice of the people of France, and to commit the country irrevocably to a socialist republic. The provisional government, divided as it was into socialists and anti-socialists, ran the risk of all coaltions, that of being reduced to impotence by internal dissensions.

The government was to hold office while arrangements were being made for a constituent assembly which was to provide France with a new republican constitution. Meanwhile, the doctrine of socialism spread repidly among the working class of Paris. Now that the heavy hand of the Orleans censorship was removed, many democratic clubs sprang into existence to spread the gospel which promised the working man a fairer share of the produce of his labour. And the socialist leaders had the same formidable means of coercing the government which the Jacobins had in 1792-94–the armed mob of Paris. On the very first day of its existance the provisional government was intimidated by a mob into promising to provide work for all. But the "NATIONAL WORKSHOP" now set up was totally unlike that which Blank had proposed. As a matter of fact it was organised, inspite of his protests, by a non-socialist member of the government who wanted to demonstrate its fallacy. The government engaged the workmen in unproductive tasks like excavation for public works and no differentiation was made between artisan and artisans and cobblers, carpenters, smiths worked together and a uniform rate of two Francs a day was paid as wages to them. The work was unsuitable to many of the workers, and the scheme failed. The experiment wasted the public money, accomplished nothing useful and led to a stereet war. The socialists blamed the government. According to Hazen; "Louis Blank wished to have every man practise his own trade, in real factories started by state aid. They should be engaged in productive enterprise...Instead of this the government simply set men of the most varied sorts...to labour upon unproductive tasks...This was properly no system of production, but was merely a system of relief for the unemployed, who were very numerous. Owing to the fact that many factories had to close because of the generally disturbed state of affairs. This experiment wasted the public money accomplished nothing useful, and led to a street war...".

The Constituent Assembly and the June Days

When the constituent assembly met, it was obvious that a stiff struggle was at hand. The rift between the republicans and the socialists became wider with the election of constituent assembly in April 1848. It had a predominantly republican majority, it appointed a provisional government consisting of five persons with Lamartine as its head. The assembly showed at once that it was bitterly opposed to the socialists. The government, believing that the National workshops were breeding spots of socialism, resolved to root them out. The socialist leaders lost no time in planning the overthrow of a regime which threatened to thwart their hopes. The "dole-drawers" (unemployed workers) took up the challenge with a boldness, born of despair, better, they said, die by a bullet than by slow starvation. They drew up barricades and turned the city of Paris into a formidable citadel defended by armed insurgents. The assembly gave full powers to General cavignac (Minister of War) and that stern republican acted with ruthless determination. During four June days (June 23-26, 1848) the most fearful street fighting paris had ever know went on behind a baffling network of barricades. General cavignac put down the revolt with an iron hand. Thousands of national guards poured in from the provinces by train to defend the cause of law, order and property. Thousands of socialists were massacred and the insurrection was put down ruthlessly. Thus did the republic triumph over socialism, but in destroying socialism it destory itself. Cavignac was virtually the ruler of France, until the election of the president of the republic. His supreme object was to save it from legitimists and Bonapartists on the one side and from th communists on the other.

The New Constitution

The constituent assembly had appointed a committee to draft a new constitution, which after prolonged discussion in the assembly finally became law on October 28, 1848. Its special features were as follows-The Legislature was to consist of a single chamber elected on universal adult suffrage for a period of three years. The executive was vested in a President, elected directly by universal suffrage for 4 years. He was to have a suspensive veto on legislatin and to appoint his Ministers. The President alone had the right to propose legislation and to negotiate or ratify treaties with foreign powers.

Louis Bonaparte and the Presidential Election

The presidential election was fixed for December 10, 1848. There are five condidates, Louis Bonaparte, Cavignac, Ledru Rollin, Raspail, Lamertine, but the real choice was between Cavignac and Louis Napoleon. Lamartime was despised as a mere talker, cavignac was hated as the slayer of the working men in Paris, Rollin was distrusted as a socialist. Louis Bonaparte was the nephew of the great Napoleon. Since the death of the Duke de Reichstadt he had been the recognised head of the family. In that capacity he had made two attempts to establish himself in France, one in 1836, the other in 1840, both had ended in failure. In 1846 he escaped to England, where he was living when the revolution broke out in France. Throughout his curious carrier, a consipirator in Italy, a Prisoner in France, a country gentleman in England, at once an adventurer, a student and a visionary thinker, he had been dominated by one conception, that of his own predestined empire. He wrote; "In all my adventures, I have been governed by one principle. I believe that from time to time men are created whom I will call providencial, in whose hands the destinies of the country are placed. I believe my self to be one of those men. If I am mistaken, I may perish uselessly, if I am right, providence will enable me to fulfill my mission...But, living or dying, I will serve France." According to a contemporary, "He was impressed, with a perfect conviction that he was destined to end the revolution and to restore France to prosperity under a Bonaparte dynasty". The revolution of 1848 was his oppertunity. France, infact, was waiting for the regime of a Bonaparte. The political power had been transferred from the middle class to the peasants, and the peasants were dominated by two passions, the hatred of feudalism and the love of order. And the name of Napoleon was a guarantee of both. Moreover, to the mass of the nation, the very name Napoleon was like a magic spell, peace and prosperity was Bonaparte's programme. Louis Napoleon was elected president by an overwhelming majority.

The first stage to the empire was accomplished, and the President solemnly took his oath to the republic. He said: "The votes of the nation, and the oath which I have just taken, control my future conduct. My duty is clear, I will fulfill it as a man of honour. I shall regard as enemies of the country all those who endeavour to change by illegal means that which France had established". He further said: "I seek with pleasure all oppertunities which may bring me into contact with this great and generous people which has elected me, for, believe me, my most devoted friends are not in the palace, but under the thatch, not under cloth of gold, but in the workshop and the field...that my fibre respond to yours and that we have the same interests, the same instinct". On becoming president he assured the people of France that he would always respect the soverignity of the people". The party of order (A conservative anti-socialist organisation) established a majority in the new Legislature. In order to strengthen his hold on the government, he tried to suppress the republicans on the one hand and appase the workmen, the Roman Catholics, and the Democrats on the other. He put down a Republican insurrection, public meeting forbidden and Republican Journals were suppressed. The interests of the workmen were safeguarded. Every remnant of Bonapartist sentiment was sedulously cultivated. Further, he ensured the support of the catholic party by restoring the control of the Church over education.

The Coup D'etat of December, 1851

Although Louis Napoleon had sworn to remain faithful to the Republic, he aimed at reviving the monarchy and making his power permanent. His election in preference to a Republican candidate revealed to him that the vast majority of the French people disliked the republic. So he began to lay plans for his own ascendency. He adroitly utlised a dispute with the Assembly which displayed a monarchical tendency. Louis Napoleon asked the assembly to revise the constitution, particularly the clause which prohibited the re-election of the President after four years. The assembly refused and a real tussel ensued between the President and the assembly. There were many person in France who started thinking in terms of settling up a monarchy. To quote one: "If there could be anything absolutely new under the Sun, it would be spectacle which France offers to the world today. It is filled with monarchists who cannot establish a monarchy and who groan under the weight of a Republic which has no republicans to defend it. In the midst of this confusion only two personage remain standing, Louis Napoleon and the mountain, two things only are possible, a new revolution or a dictatorship. It is evident to me that force must bring about a solution". He gathered round him a clique of unscrupulous adventurers whose fortunes would be depended on his own, and appointed them to responsible posts in the Army, the ministry and the police. Above all, he contrived to make people feel that he was the only man who could save socieyt from the Reds. On the evening in secret conclave to make the final arrangements for the forcible overthrow of the constitution. Before morning all the politicians likely to oppose the change were arrested in the beds, and the walls of Paris had been placerded with a proclaimation. The President announced that he had dissolved the assembly as a hot bed of plots against democracy. On 2nd December, 1851, on the anniversary of the battle of Austerlitz, he staged a coup d'etat. The chamber of deputies was guarded by troops, all Journals were suppressed, and placards appeared in every prominent place announcing the dissolution of the assembly, the establishment of a new government, and an immediate appeal to the people for the ratification of the change. Thus, the prince-President was left master of the situations, and so weary was the Nation that when the promise plebiscite was held they approved the new regime. He restored the imperial eagles to the regiments of the army and was hailed by the troops with cries of "Vive l'empereur". Within a year of the coup d'etat the Senate (which under the revised constitution, he had himself nominated) invited him to become heriditary emperor of France, and he asumed the title of Napoleon III.

Echoes of the Revolution of 1848

The political earthquacke of 1848 had shaken the foundation of autocracy all over Europe, and the succeeding generations were encouraged to strike effective blow at the tottering structure. The triumph of democratic revolution in France in 1848 sent a thrill of hope throughout Erope and released the pent up feelings of liberalism everwhere. Nationalism and constitutionalism, the demand for racial unity and demand for parliamentary government, were like two gases which together form an explosive mixture. Engendered by the French revolution of 1789-94, they had been repressed by the reaction which followed the fall of Napoleon, but there had been repeated splutterings of explosion, and in 1848 it was as if a spark had been brought into a coal-mine full of fire-damp. The whole system of reaction which had succeeded waterloo and which had come to be personified in the imperturbable Metternich, crashed in unutterable confusion. The great mid-century uprising of the peoples had begun the most widespread convulsion Europe was destined to know untill 1914. And the storm center of this convulsion was Vienna.

Austria

The Hapsburg (Austrian) empire, the product of dynastic marriage and inheritance, had no common nationality or language, it was held together only by the reigning Hapsburg dynasty, its army and its bureaucracy. The ethnic compositon of the empire was enormously complex. The German constituted about 25 per cent of the empire's population, the Magyars predominated in the Hungarian lands of the empire. The great bulk of the population consisted of Slaves-Czechs, Poles, Slovaks, Slovenes, Croats, Serbs, Ruthenians, Italians, Rumanians. The Hapsburg dynasty, aided by the army and German dominated civil service, prevented the multinational empire from collapsing into anarchy. The society was organised on the feudal pattern where the nobles enjoyed numerous privileges and were exempted from taxes. The masses by and large were ignorant, illeterate and superstitious politically, the hold of Metternich, the implacable foe of liberalism was supreme. But in spite of all these, signs of political unrest and upheaval were not wanting. The middle classes and the industrialists with a sprinkling of liberal and advanced nobles, formed a nucleus of the revolutionary movement in the Austrian empire.

In 1848, revolution spread throughout the Austrian empire. Aroused by the abdication of Louis Philippe, Viennese liberals denounced Hapsburg absolutism and demanded a constitution, relaxation of censorship, and restrictions on the police. The authorities used force that was strong enough to arouse the insurrectionists and create martyrs but not strong enough to subdue them. Confused and intimidated by the revolutionaries, the government allowed freedom of the press, accepted Metternich's resignation, and promised a constitution. The constitutional assembly was convened and it voted the abolition of serfdom. Meanwhile, revolts in other part of the empire, Bohemia, Hungary, and northern Italy added to the distress of the monarchy.

The most serious threat to the Hapsburg realm came from the Magyars in Hungary. Hungary, though it had formed an integral part of the Hapsburg empire since 1699 had never been completely incorporated in Austria, but it had preserved its own national Parliament. In recent years there had been a distinct revival of national spirit among the Magyars. Men like Stephen Szechenyi, a great Hungarian noble and Francis Deak, were foremost in promoting moderate liberal reforms, the use of the Magyars language, parliamentary reform and a responsible ministry, equalisation of taxation, the abolition of serfdom and so forth. Bitterly opposed to these constitutional liberals, was Louis Kossuth, a nationalist agitator, an impassioned orator, a reckless demagogue. He was true liberal and was the very incarnation of the democratic ideas. A liberal and democratic party, nourished on the ideas of Western Europe, led by Louis Kossuth. He kept the spirit of opposition burning year after year by his orations in the Diet (Parliament) and his writings in his journal, "the pestiHirlap." He had been demanding the use of Magyar in place of Latin as the official language, and the employment of Hungarians in the administration. Kossuth's impassioned appeals were made directly to the people. In a famous speech delivered on March 3, 1848, he developed this idea; "The suffocating vapour of heavy curse hangs over us, and out of the charnel house of the cabinet of Vienna a pestilential wind sweeps by, benumbing our sense and exercising a deadening effect on our national spirit.... It is our task to establish a happier future on the brotherhood of all the Austrian races, and to substitute for the union enforced by baynots and police the enduring bond of a free constitution". The Hungarian Diet at pressburg passed a number of laws of far-reaching importance and these laws were know as MARCH LAWS (1848). It provided for annual Parliaments, triennial elections, a responsible ministry, manhood suffrage, equality of taxation, freedom of the press, religious equality, a national flag, and local control of the Hungarian Army. The Austrian emperor confirmed the new constitution. In the spiing of 1849, the Hungarians renounced their allegiance to the Hapsburg and proclaimed Hungary an independent state with Kossuth as President.

The Bohemian movement was an expression of Czech nationalism against German domination. The Czech intellectual palacky became the spirit of the Czech liberation movement. In 1848 young Chechs met at Prague and presented a petition to the emperor and demanding a constitutional government. The Austrian emperor conceded the demands of the Czechs. But soon differences arose between the Czechs and the

Germans. Soon after the revolution of 1848, there was a nationalist upheavel among the Czechs, and they demanded equality with the Germans. In June 1848, the Czechs summoned a Pan-Slavic Congress in Prague to countermand the demands of the Germans. General Windischgratz Bombarded Prague and reestablished Hapsburg authority.

In case of Hungary the Hapsburg rulers took advantage of the ethnic animosities inside and outside Hungary. They encouraged Rumanians and South slavs to resist the new Hungarian Government. When Hapsburg forces moved against the Magyars, they were joined by the South slaves, whose nationalist aspiration had been flouted by the Hungarians. Meanwhile, Austria appointed Jellachich, a fiercey anti-Magyar, as viceroy of croatia. He also appealed to Czar Nicholas I for help. The czar complied, fearing that a successful revolt by the Hungarian might lead the poles to rise up against their Russian overlords. The Hungarians fought with extraordinary courage but were overcome by superior might. Kossuth and other rebel leaders went into exile. Thus, through division and alliance, the Hapsburgs prevented the disintegration of the empire. The revolution of Austria, Hungary and Bohemia were mercilessly crushed. Austria was saved from this terrible crisis by the loyalty of her soldiers who remained attached to the cause of the emperor, and by the rivalry of the different races of the empir. The intervention of the Czar Nicholas I sealed the fate of the revolution. Further, liberalism was not broad-based and it was confined only to the middle class intellectuals. The bulk of the masses were still loyal to the old tradition.

Italy: Continued Fragmentation

Italian nationalists eager to end the humiliation of Hapsburg occupation and domination and to unite the desperate states into a unified and liberal nation, also rose in rebillion in 1848. Revolution broke out in Sicily in 1848. Bowing to the revolutionaries demands, king Ferdinand II of Naples granted a liberal constitution. The grand duke of Tuscany, king Charles Albert of Piedmont, and Pope Pius IX, also felt compelled to introduce liberal reforms. Then the revolution spread to the Hapsburg lands in the North. The peoples of Milan, built barricades and stood ready to fight the Austrian oppressor. After five glorious days (March 18-22) of street fighting, the Austrians withdrew. The people of Milan had liberated their city, Venice also declared itself free. King Charles Albert, who hoped to acquire Lomabrdy and Venetia declared war on Austria. Intimidated by the insurrections, the ruling princess of the Italian States and Hapsburg Austria had lost the first round. But soon the forces of reaction recovered and reasserted their authority. The Austrians defeated the Sardinians and reoccupied Milan. Revolutionary disorder in Rome had forced the Pope to flee and the revolutionaries proclaimed Rome, a Republic. Heeding the Popes call for assistance, Louis Napoleon attacked Rome, destroyed the infant republic and allowed the Pope to return. Venice was bombarded by the Austrians, and it surrendered. Reactionary princess still ruled in Italy, the Hapsburg occupation persisted in the North. Italy was still a fragmented nation.

The German States–Liberalism Discredited

It is not surprising that when the news of the fall of Louis Philippe in Paris was followed by that of Metternich in Vienna the effect was electrical. The flight of Metternich was regarded as the most important event in European affairs since the battle of Waterloo. Revolutionary movement spread from State to State throghout the German confederation. There was a general demand for constitutional liberty within the State, while a strong body of advanced opinion throughout the time was ripe for the achievement of German unity. During March and April 1848 the traditional rulers in Baden, Wurttermburg, Bavaria, Saxony, Hanover and other States made concessions to the liberals, eased censorship, established Jury systems, framed constitutions, and formed Parliaments. Wild demonstrations were held in Berlin with the cries of liberty and equality. King Fredrick William IV called a provisional diet to consider a new constitution. In a collision between the police and the mob about 200 men were killed (March 18, 1848). The king tried to pacify the mob by expressing his regret at what had happened and issued a proclaimation on March 21 to the effect that Prussia had been merged in Germany. At the same time arrangements were made by a few liberals who met at Heidelbarg at the invitation of Von Gagern the Minister of Hesse for a vor-Parliament to meet in Franckfort. The vor-Parliament met on March 31, and resolved to have a German federation, with two chambers. The details were to be settled at a national constituent assembly elected by universal suffrage. The Frankfort Parliament met on (May 18, 1848) under the presidency of Von Gagern. Much time was wasted in discussion, and they took about six months to settle the fundamental rights of the people. It was decided by a majority that only the German speaking states would be included in the German empire and that the king of Prussia would be offered the title of the emperor of the Germans. But when the offer was made Fredrick William IV declined to accept it at the hands of the people. Baffled in its attempt to bring about unity the Frankfort parliament was dissolved. Thus, German liberalism had failed to unite Germany or to create a constitutional government dominated by the middle class. Liberalism, never securely rooted in

Germany, was discredited. Prussian humiliation was complete, Austria was as triumphant in the German confederation as in her own dominions.

The influence of the revolution was also felt in other countries. The first flush of success no doubt died out in most cases, but some good come out of it. Feudalism disappeared, taxes were distributed among the different classes more equitably, and the people were better prepared for democratic government. The political earthquake of 1848 had shaken the foundation of autocracy all over Europe, and the succeeding generations were encouraged to strike effective blow at the tottering structure. The age of revolution initiated by the French revolution 1789 had ended. In the words of Palmer; "The revolution of 1848 had deposited some deeply laid time bomb, class hatred and national jealousy, Pan-Germanism and Pan-Slavism, a dictatorship in France, and last but not the least, the philosophy of Karl Marx".

However, the revolutionary tide rolled back and Europe relapsed into the old condition. The various races in Austrian empire could not unite and their interests clashed. Want to unity prevented the coordination of efforts. Owing to the lack of an able leadership, the movement could not be properly organised, hence they were mercilessly put down by the autocratic powers. Besides, Liberalism was not broad-based, it was confined only to the middle class intellectuals, and the industrial proletariat. The bulk of the masses were still loyal to the old tradition. As the nobles were hostile to revolutionary changes, so they opposed the revolution. According to Grant and Temerley "Sentimental liberalism...failed before the iron-hand and naked force of authority". However, the political earthquake of 1848 had shaken the foundation of autocracy all over Europe.

Napoleon III
The Second Empire (1852-1870)

It was the Napoleonic legend, the fear of the red (Socialist) menace, the blunder of the Republican Legislature, and his (Napoleon III's) own skillful maneuvers, which enabled Louis Napoleon to overthrow the second empire was coloured by the fact that Napoleon III was a "crowned adventurer". He had many qualifications for the role, for he was mixture of brooding dreamer, cunning consipirator and bold gambler. He was the great imperial Sphinx, an enigma to France and Europe. A French historian says that one-half of him was Machiavelli and the other-half was Don Quixote. Victor Hugo branded him as "little Napoleon". His economy of words created an illusion of his depth of thought. Despite his unromantic appearance, he had an innate distinction of manner and personal charm. He knew how to forget past injuries. Napoleon III dogged faith in his star, it was his destiny to rule France-never wavered through the long years of exile, ridicule and imprisonment, and his belief that France needed Bonapartism was perfectly sincere. But he could never shake off the effects of the violence and trickery by which he had gained his throne, and he was always dependent on the shady adventurers who had been his fellow consipirations in the coup d'etat. The second empire was a queer combination of autocracy and democracy. The most essentail article of Bonapartism was public order and security, and the plebsicite had shown how fervently France desired these blessings. Thus, though a lover of liberty, he had to suppress every sign of disorder. If this was despotism, it was enlightened despotism. Before the establishment of the second empire, he delivered a speech for his countryement, in which he tried to make his programme clear, "Nevertheless there is a fear to which I ought to reply. In a spirit of mistrust certain people say. 'The empire is war', I say, "The empire is peace...". I confess, however, that...I have many conquests to make...I wish to conquer to religion, to morality, to prosperity and part of the population...We have immense districts of Virgin soil to clear, roads to open, harbours to dig, rivers to render navigable, our network of railways to complete...We have everywhere ruins to restore, false gods to overthrow, truths to establish in triumph. This is how I should understand the empire, if the empire is to be reestablished. Such are the conquests that I mediate, and all of you who surrounds me, who desire like myself, the welfare of our country, you are my soldiers". With all his heart he identify himself with the great transforming movement of the age, the industrial revolution, and was resolved to shower France with its mainifold blessings.

His Domestic Policy

Louis Napoleon owed his elevation to the magic of a great name and so he had to live upto the tradition of his great uncle. According to Lipson; "The name Napoleon stands within for order and the welfare of the people...The reconciliation of order with liberty, in other words, the political eduction of the people, constituted the design and purpose of Napoleon III's domestic policy. The first condition of a stable government is full recognition of its authority...". The constitution he set up, was modelled upon that of the consulate of his uncle. It disguished his absolute power and personal predominance under republican forms.

The political institutions of the empire were largly based on those of the consulate. The emperor stood at the head of a vast centralised administrative system which covered every part of France and concentrated in his hands enormous executive authority. The emperor had the control of peace and war, the nomination of all officials, including the Ministers and the council of state, and exclusive right to initiate legislation and summon, prorogue, or dissolve the legislative body. The legislative body was elected by universal suffrage for a maximum period of six years. Its function was to discuss, and adopt or reject, the laws submitted to it by the Ministers, but it had no power of amendment. The senate was to act as guardian of law and to interpret the constitution. Local government was concentrated in the hands of the prefects, who were themselves the nominees of the emperor.

Faithful to his leading idea of progress based on conservatism, the emperor had fairly endeavoured to recouncile his popular dictatorship with liberty. He was sincerely anxious to reconcile order with liberty. To stifle criticism the press was muzzled and newspapers rigorously supervised. The police force was reorganised with the object of making it more thorough and efficient. In order to control elections the government bore the expenses of official candidates. All candidates had to taken an oath of fidelity to the emperor. The fundamental idea underlying the Napoleonic regime was that of inverted democracy, caesarism founded upon a Plebiscite.

Social and Economic Reforms

The emperor was favourably impressed by the contemporary vogue of liberalism. In politics he was hardly a liberal but in economics he was even more liberal than Louis Philippe. Legislation deesigned to aid business was the order of the day. Every kind of encouragement was afforded to industry, means of communication were improved, roads, canals, and harbours were constructed. The formation of stock companies was made easier. The stock exchange, became ever more active as the capital market boomed. A system of savings banks was established. Two great central banks, the credit foncier and the credit mobiliser, were established. Simultaneously, land banks were also established. The tradition of high tariffs was broken, when Napoleon III cut the French import duties to a maximum of 30 per cent in the cobden treaty with Great Britian. The number of agricultural socities was increased, horse breeding was encouraged, land was brought into cultivation by draining the marshes. Napoleon III also sponsored a remarkable series of public works to stimulate industry and commerce and to provide employment for labour. Paris was rebuilt and made more spacious, more splendid and more defensible. Broad boulevards and magnificent public buildings were constructed in Paris. Nor was he indifferent to the more special interests of the working class, by a law of 1864 he legalised combinations of labourers, he organised free law for the poor, opened free parks, developed schemes of insurance for old age and accident, and encouraged provident and co-operative societies. Subsidies were given to the inn-keepers to guarantee cheap bread to the workers. The right of the workers to strike was recognised by a law.

Napoleon III consistently followed a policy of keeping the catholic in good humour.. The clergy had greeted with enthusiasm the advent of the empire. during his reign, most of the educational institutions were connected with the Church. The clergy were appointed in the universities and public schools. Financial assistance was given to the Church by the government. France maintained French troops at Rome for the protection of the Pope, and in general posed as the champion of Catholic christianity.

However, upto 1860 Napoleon III was practically a dictator of France. The year 1860 was a turning point in the history of the second empire. He adopted a policy of liberalism after 1860. Upto 1860 France was charecterised by a suppression of political liberty through censorship, secret police and a sham constitution. To make up for the loss of liberty, it emphasised material well-being. Later on, control on the press and public meetings was related. Elections become fair than before. According to Marriot, "Within ten years of the beginning of his rule, he fulfilled to a certain extent the promise that he had made to the people in Bordeaux, namely, of making France a great nation". The Legislature was given complete freedom of debate. However, discontent mounted against him and failure in foreign policy aggravted it. The second empire, like the first, went down before a foreign (Germany) foe. Leipzig was echoed by Sedan.

The Foreign Policy of Napoleon III

Napoleon III's foreign policy was self contradictory. He was a declared votary of nationalism, and aimed at tearing up the treaties of 1815. It was his nationalism, and his name, which attracted the French masses to him after they had gotton rid of the unatriotic bourgeois monarchy, and which led him to the post of president and then of emperor. His nationalism and romanticism made him the object of constant pleas for active assistance in forwarding the freedom and unity of oppressed nationalities in Europe. Liberal patriots throughout the continent looked to him for support. Further, the glories of the first empire and the grand achievements of his great uncle always inspired him immensely. His support of nationalism abroad, was to same extent inspired by the desire to gain compensation for services rendered by him. Besides, he wanted to make France a powerful country in Europe. He understood the sentiment of the nation and adopted a vigorous foreign policy. But Napoleon III was pacific at heart. He was a product of mid nineteenth century liberalism. He lacked the martial zeal of the born soldier and he had an un-Napoleonic aversion to the smell of gunpowder and the sight of bloodshed. But the carrier of Napoleon III was so full of inconsistencies that it is difficult to form a correct estimate of it. He had declared that empire is peace, but peace was inconsistent with glory which the Fench people expected from him. Napoleon III was torn by conflicting sentiments and forces and his subsequent policy became one of Meddle and Muddle. Nodoubt, he dazzled France for sometime, but he puzzled entire Europe. Napoleon III was impelled to war by the circumstances of his rises to power and by the nature of the policy he chose to follow in order to retain power. Revolutionary schemes of foreign policy floated like storm driven clouds accross the surface of his unquiet spirit. According to Fisher: "He had certain gift of political perspective, and could paint on the canvas of the future with a bold sweep of the brush...his figure had no anatomy, and were like the creations of the delettante artist who has excused himself from the tough and technical discipline of his head full of untested faniful and contradictory policies, his capacity unequal to the execution of his opaque and fluctuating designs".

The Crimean War (1854-56)

In the first decade of his reign Napoleon III's enterprises in the field of foreign affairs greatly enhanced the international prestige of France. He intervened in the crimean war in 1854. Quarrels at the holy places in palestine between Catholic and Orthodox monks provided the spark for igniting the train of ill-feeling between France and Russia. The Czar considered Napoleon III as an upstart. On the otherhand the French had not forgotton the Russian compaign of 1812 and wanted to have their revenge on the Russians: Further, Napoleon wanted to pacify the French Catholics who bitterly resented the Czar's internal affairs of the ottoman empire. The French liberal detested the Czar's autocracy. So by going to war against Russia, Napoleon hoped to win over the support of both the Catholic and liberal at home. The Crimean war broke out due to various other causes (For details please see-Eastern Question). The French troops fought side by side with British soldiers. Russia was compelled to came to terms and Napoleon had the satisfaction of dictating the peace of Paris (1856). The Crimean war greatly enhanced the emperor's prestige. Though France gained little by the Crimean war, Napoleon personally gained much. Upto 1854 his position in Europe was far from assured, the Crimean war established it, and until the advent of Bismarck his influence upon the continent was almost supreme. The political isolation of France in Europe was broken. Napoleon earned great popularity with the French Catholics.

Napoleon III and The Problem of Italian Unity

Napoleon III's Italian policy was a turning point in the history of the second empire. According to Hayes; "Cavour was urging Napoleon to aid Sardinia in expelling Austria from the Peninsula and creating a free and united state for Italy. The emperor was receptive, his uncle had erected a kingdom of Italy, he himself had been a carbonaro, the Bonaparts had Italian blood in their veins, Austria had given no active assistance to France in the Crimean war, A war with Austria for the unification of Italy would be popular with French liberals, and Napoleon III might get some tangible compensation for French effort. Yet the emperor hesitated...a united Italy might prove to be a strong and perhaps dangerous rival to France, many French Catholics were heeding the protests of the Pope against any Italian unification which might deprive him of his temporal power". No wonder, Napoleon was on the horns of a dilemma. However, his in decision was ended when an attempt was made on his life by Orisini, an Italian patriot.

Without consulting his ministers, Napoleon III arranged to meet Cavour at a secret meeting at Plombiers. It was agreed between them that Napoleon III was to help piedmont to drive out the Austrians from Lombardy and Venetia, and France was to get Nice and Savoy as compensation. In 1859 Sardinia-Piedmont declared war against Austria and France helped piedmont in the war. But all on a sudden he stopped the war and made an armistice with Austria (Villafranca) By it Austria was to cede Lombardy to piedmont–Sardinia. But shortly after, he supported the annexationist movement in central Italy (Parma, Modena, Tuscany) to be united with Sardinia. He obtain Nice and Savoy. On the whole, Napoleon III's Italian policy marked the beginning of the end of his dominating role in Europe.

Napoleon's intervention in the Italian struggle caused very far-reaching reactions in France. Napoleon's intervention in Italy earned him the antagonism of Austria. Piedmont and the Italian patriots were annoyed to a great extent, as he had let them down at a crucial hour. His annexation of Savoy and Nice roused a good deal of distrust in England. On the otherhand, the liberals of France were angry because he wanted to uphold the power of the Pope. Thus, his Italian policy could please neither the Italians, nor the liberals, or the Roman Catholics of France.

Napoleon III espoused the cause of nationalism abroad in the hope of winning the support of the liberal party at home. In the Balkans he supported the national movements in Wallachia and Moldavia. On the eve of his intervention in Italy, he prevailed upon the great powers to permit Moldavia and Wallachia to elect their own parliaments, and choose their own reigning princes. In 1861 both Moldavia and Wallachia elected Prince Alexander Cuza as their head. It was owing to his influence that the two principalities were united in to a single state called Rumania.

The Polish Revolt

In 1863 he sought to champion the cause of polish nationalism. In this year polish patriots stirred by recent nationalist event in Italy and Rumania, and rose in revolt against Russia and appealed to Napoleon III for assistance. His position forced him to do something for the insurgents, for nationalism was always an essential article of his creed, and the poles (being Catholics and Republicans) had the support of both the opposing factions in the French Nation. Britian also wanted to check the Czar, but she could not agree with France upon the joint action which alone would have been effective. So Napoleon sent a strongly worded note protesting at the Czar's failure to give Poland the separate constitution promised by his Predecessor. Russia took advantage of Bismarck's offer of support to refuse all discussion of the polish question with France. The poles were left, despairing and unfriended, to be overwhelmed by Russian soldiery. As Napoleon could not follow up his strong words by acts, the result of this meddlesome policy was to alienate the Czar.

Then came the affair of the Danish duchies (Scheles-wig, Holestein). By this time (1864-65) Napoleon was so deeply involved in his mexican adventure that he did not dare to do more than put forward mild proposals, but Bismarck's contemptuous disregard of them was sufficiently humiliating.

Failure in Mexico

Napoleon was greatly disturbed by the growing criticism of his home and foreign policies, therefore he wanted to achieve something spectacular in the foreign field to divert the attention of his critics. The troubled water of Mexican politics offered a good opportunity to him to carve out a colonial empire. Napoleon wanted to glorify the empire. France and other European powers had grivances against the Mexican government for the unjust treatment of their citizens resident there. Further, the Mexican government repudiated the debts which it owed to France, England and Spain, and in 1861 the government by an arbitrary decree suspended all payments of interest on bonds to foreign creditors. The French, British and Spanish government sent a joint expedition to compel the Mexicans to fulfill their obligations. But the restless and imaginative adventurer on the throne of France espied a chance for a grandiose scheme of expansion. He saw in a rosy vision of the future a Mexican empire under French influence to be an outlet for French commerce, and a restoration of the French interest in the American continent. The moment was opportune, as the United States of America was busy with the civil war and was not in a position to enforce the Monroe doctrine and stop European interference in the affairs of the American countries. As soon as the British and Spanish governments realised Napoleon's ulterior aims they withdraw their contingents. In 1862 the dissident Maxican minority helped the French and president Juarez (of....Mexican Republic) was driven out and Mexico was proclaimed a monarchy. The crown was offered to Maximillan, brother of the Austrian emperor. Napoleon III supported him with French soldiers, in the expectation that he would undo the anti-ecclesiastical work of Juarez and grant economic concessions to French men. But Maximillian was unpopular with the Mexican nationalists and guerilla warfar continued. Meanwhile the ending of the civil war in America (1865) enabled the American government to reassert the Monroe doctrine. Napoleon III was not prepared to risk a war with America and recalled his forces leaving Maximilian to the mercy of Mexicans (Later on he was shot dead). The Mexican enterprise of Napoleon proved to be a veritable boomerang. The great ideas of his reign proved disastrous. He was bitterly criticised by both the Catholics and the liberals for leaving Maximilian to his doom. His preoccupation in Mexico did not give him an opportunity to intervene actively in the Prusso-Danish (1863-64) or the Austro-Prussian wars (1866) with the result that he unconsciously helped Prussia to strengthen her position. Its disastrous failure was a great blow to the French prestige abroad. The Mexican episode gained Napoleon a bad name as a wild and unprincipled schemer, and for five years it was a perpetual drain on his reserves of men and money. Thus, the Mexican enterprise proved a vertitable boomerang against Napoleon III.

Napoleon III and German Unity

In his desperate anxiety to please the French nation by some sort of acquisition to set off against all these rebuffs, Napoleon now entered into secret negotiations for the purchase of Luxemburg. Napoleon was sympathetic to German nationalism because he hoped that by supporting Prussia he would gain more territory as compensation. Bismarck, the Prussian chancellor, wanted to make sure of French neutrality in the event of a war between Prussia and Austria. Bismarck was perfecting plans for the expulsion of Austria from Germany and the establishment of a National State under the Hohenzollern king of Prussia. In 1865, Bismarck had an interview with Napoleon III at Biarritz. The Prussian statesman knew how to work upon the French emperor's romantic attachment to the principle of nationality, upon his personal vanity, and upon his desperate readiness to clutch at any chance to obtain a little glory for France. On the other hand, napoleon was not afraid of Prussian compensation and even urged Italy to conclude a treaty with Prussia against Austria. He was under the impression that a war between Austria and Prussia would be a long drawn out affairs. And then at a suitable opportunity he would intervene in the struggle and dictate his own conditions to both and extract favourable terms for France. The German war came suddenly in 1866. The war was short and decisive, so short that it is known as the seven weeks war, and so decisive that Austria was obliged to cede Venetia to Italy. Napoleon missed the greatest opportunity of his life. Had he intervened in the war, he would have become the master of the situation. The Austrian defeat at Sadowa was regarded by the French as a humiliating defeat and there were cries for the revenge of Sadowa. Napoleon III got no compensation for France. Napoleon made grotesque miscalculations as to the duration and result of the Austro-Prussian war, and by his ill-timed requests for compensation on the Rhine he merely strengthened Prussia's hold over the rest of Germany and embittered the South German States against himself. When this was refused he suggested that Bismarck should support him in annexing Belgium, in defiance of the guarnatee of Belgian neutrality which the powers had given in 1839. Bismarck returned an evasive reply and kept Napoleon's despatch by him for use on some future occasion. For a while he thought he might secure Luxemburg. The States of Luxemburg was nearly as complicated as that of the Danish duchies. The king of Holland was its heriditary grand duke, yet it belonged to the German confederation. And ever since 1815 a Prussian garrison had occupied its fortress as a safeguard against a French attack on Germany. In 1867 Napoleon III negotiated with the Dutch king for the purchase of the grand duchy, the king (Holland) was willing, but Bismarck objected. Eventually a settlement was made by a conference of the powers in London (1867). Luxemburg was declared a neutral State and the Prussian garrison was to be withdrawn. Once again poor Napoleon had to go empty away.

Napoleon's diplomatic defeat at the hands of Bis Marck discredited him in the eyes of the republicans. The emperor sought to regain his popularity by making his government more liberal and from time to time dribbled out concessions and reforms. But the opposition grew steadily. At last he persuaded himself to believe that it was only by a resounding military success over Prussia that he would be able to stabilise his shaky throne and rehabilitate French prestige in Europe. On one matter it was still possible for any French government to command the almost unanimous support of Frenchmen. That was the matter of political unification of Germany. French liberals detested Prussia as a reactionary power, French

Catholics disliked Prussia as a protestan State. The Frenchmen were fearful of the sudden emergence of Prussia as a strong State. Feelings ran high and there were demands for revenge. But Napoleon III had no stomach for a war with Prussia. He knew that France stood isolated in Europe. But Sadowa made Franco-German war almost inevitable. On the other hand, to wage war with Germany would be a big gamble for Napoleon, Yet such a gamble seemed to be the only recourse left to him. Bismarck who was spoiling for a war with France very cleverly manipulated the political situation and the relations between France and Prussia deteriorated over the question of the Spanish succession (For details please see German unification Movement) National feelings were roused to a high pitch and Napoleon had to bow before the wishes of the national. The press of both countries fanned the flames with furious diatribes. Napoleon was nothing like so eager for war as the people around him, for he was not misled by the optimistic reports of the generals as to the efficiency of the army, but he had not the moral strength to withstand them. Further, he was carried away by his high-spirited empress, who regarded war against Prussia as a crusade against protestanism, and looked for a glorious prestige that would restore the waning prestige of the empire. War was declared on 15th July, 1870. The French armies were no match for the Prussians and Napoleon was defeated at Sedan. The French began full of flamboyant confidence, with an attack on the upper Rhine which they hoped would bring in Austira and the South German States on their side. But everything went wrong for them. Bismarck had played his card so well, that the South German States threw in their lot with Prussia. Besides, the readiness of the French army for war had been overestimated. Moreover, the high command was honey combed with personal jealousies, self-seeking and favouritism-fatal weaknesses when pitted against German discipline, efficiency and forethought. And Napoleon's attempt to take supreme command resulted in hesitation, delay and intrigue. The news of Sedan was the signal for a revolution in Paris. The ministry resigned, a Republic was proclaimed. But it could not save France and after a siege of four months, paris surrendered on 28th January, 1871, by the armistice of Versailles.

An Estimate of Napoleon III

It has been remarked that history and historians have done scant justice to Napoleon III. The carrier of Napoleon was so full of contrasts and inconsistencies that it is difficult to form a correct estimate of it. He was the great imperial sphinx, an engima to France and Europe. From the circumstances of his rise to power, he seems a dark and dangerous plotters, stopping at nothing to gain his end. True that Napoleon III had raised high hopes in the minds of the French people by holding before them the traditions of Napoleon Bonapate. The revival of Napoleonic tradition roused feelings which were not within the power of Napoleon III to fulfill. He was a prisoner of indecision. Napoleon III promised that his empire meant peace, but his whole reign was full of wars. He dazzled France, he puzzled Europe and was in the end neither trusted nor understood. He had no concerted plan. On the one hand he work hard to promote the French industries, on the other he tried to satiate the people by free trade treaty. Napoleon earned prestige for France by joining the crimean war but lost more than what he had gained by his failure in Mexico. His sudden withdrawl from the war of Italian liberation movement earned him the hatred of Italian liberals. In the age of realpolitic his romanticism was unreal. The German and Italian Nation State remained as a perpetual problem to French security. Napoleon III handled his foreign policy as a naive. His failure to check Bismark in defeating Austria in the Austro-Prussian war was rightly considered by the French nation as tantamount to French defeat. Even after this Napoleon III did not try to find allies as a measure of safety against the probable attack by Germany. He allowed himself to be overruled by popular enthusiasm for war with Prussia knowing fully well that the French army was ill organised, ill-equipped and hopelessly outnumbered by the Prussians. The tragedy of Napoleon III is that he lived on after his reconstructive aims were achieved. The apex of his life had been reached by 1860. His foreign policy after a striking beginning also turned to failure.

But in internal affairs Napoleon brought prosperity to his people and the industrial revolution in France gathered great momentum. He was responsible for a great economic development in France. He was the architect of the cobden treaty (A commercial treaty with England). He was a man of ideas and vision. Napoleon For-saw the possiblities of the Suez and Panama canals when men of the day looked upon such project as chimerical. He extended the French colonial empire. In France he left behind indelible traces. It will be unfair to regard Napoleon III as a total failure. His patronage to the nationalities of Europe altered the political map of 1815. Another factor has to be considered before any conclusion can be drawn, and it is that Napoleon III had to deal with the greatest statesman of the 19th century-Bismarck.

Chapter-IX

The Unification of Italy

Italy from the fall of the Roman empire until the establishment of the Napoleonic Kingdom, was a mere "geographical expression". She could not be called a nation any more than a stack of timber can be called a ship. In the middle ages great parts were played on the stage of European politics by the city-States of Italy, by Venice and Genoa, by Milan and Florence. But Italy did not exist. At the close of the middle ages, Italy became the cockpit of Europe, where foreign powers contended for mastery. Her native princess sacrificed national aspirations at the alter of self-aggrandizement. Not until the latter half of the 18th century did Italy attain some degree of tranquillity, and the calm which the age of the enlightened despots brought to Italy was the repose not of quiet happiness but a miserable inertia, a hopeless torpidity of soul.

In the early part of the 19th century, Italy consisted of several separate States. In the south, a Bourbon king ruled the kingdom of the two sicilies, the Pope governed the Papal State in Central Italy, Hapsburg Austria ruled Lombardy and venetia in the North. Hapsburg princess subservient to Austria ruled the duchies of Parma, Modena and Tuscany. Only piedmont and Sardinia were governed by an Italian dynasty, the house of savoy.

Besides all these political divisions, Italy was divided economically and culturally. Throughout the penisula, attachment to the local region was stronger than devotion to national unity. Economic ties between North and South were weak. Except for the middle class, most Italians clung to the values of the old regime. Believing that society was ordered by God, they accepted without question rule by prince and Pope and rejected the values associated with the French Revolution.

During the wars of the French revolution, France had occupied Italy. The French eliminated many barriers to trade among the Italian States. The French had given the Italian States constitutions, representative assemblies, and the concept of the State as a community of citizens. The foreign French rule in Italy awakened the idea of nationhood among the Italians. Napoleon sowed the seeds of national unity in Italy. Napoleon contributed to Italian more than a political prophecy. Napoleon brought to Italy the fruits of the Franch revolution in the extinction of feudalism and the overthrow of the social structure based upon it. According to Marriot; "He overthrew the splendid hope of a united Italy, and his policy was uniformly directed towards its achievements". Indeed, Murat, though a Frenchman, is still revered by Italians as the earliest champion of her union. However, the hands of the clock were set back by the diplomatists at Vienna. The congress of Vienna opens with an attempt by the diplomats of Europe to bridle the forces unloosed by the revolution and by Napoloeon. The settlements of Vienna were made to adjust the territorial ambitions of Great powers, not to satisfy the claims of nationalities. At the Vienna congress national aspirations were ignored, and Italy was treated as a pawn in the diplomatic game. Austria emerged as the sole arbiter of Italian destinies. According to Hazen; "Italy became again a collection of small States...Each of the restored princes was an absolute monarch. Italy had neither unity nor constitutional forms, nor any semblance of popular participation in the government...".

The problem with which Italian patriots were faced inthe 19th century was two fold, the establishment of unity and the development of constitutional government in a land which contained many petty States, in all of which absolute government prevailed. The governments were mostly corrupt, and the people were ignorant and superstitious and they had not learned the necessity for concerted action. But the greatest difficulties to be overcome by those who schemed for Italian unity were the power of Austria and the power of the Pope. Austria was ever watchful against any spark of Italian nationalisan. The military might of Austria was strong enough to crush any liberation movement in Italy. On the other hand, the Pope presented an even more formidable obstacle to unity, since any attempt to deprive him of control over the States of the Church might be met by spiritual penalties, and ex-communication presented real terror to an ignorant peasantry. Newspapers were censored, and public meetings were suppressed. Above all, the country was full of provincialis, localism and regionalism.

An expanding intellectual elite, through novels, poetry, and works of history awakened interest in Italy's glorious part. They insisted that a people who had built the Roman empire and had produced the Renaissance must not remain weak and divided. These sentiments appealed particularly to the middle class. The Italian poets and philosophers were responsible for a new movements, called the "Risorgimento" or literary and national revival, which glorified the achievement of the old Roman empire, and inspired the present day generation to achieve independence and unity. The idea of the thinkers like Gioberti, Balbo, D'Azeglio created a stirring among the Italian intellectuals. This is, in fact, the begining of the Italian Risorgimento or Resurrection. The intellectuals created a good deal of mental preparation of the Italians and articulated their aspiration for independence. According to Hazen, "No political party was organised, but a general state of mind was created which held that Italy must become independent, which meant that Austrian influence must be eliminated, and that the Italians could do this themselves, if they only would. The Watch-Word was given by Charles Albert, king of piedmont, as he said, "Italia Fara da se", Italy will do it alone.

The Carbonari Movement

The settlement of Italy as made by the Congress of Vienna was highly disappointing to the patriots of Italy. The impulse towards unity and liberalism they had received from Napoleon could not, however be wiped-out by tyrannical repression. Thus, secret societies kept alive the hopes for liberty and independence from foreign rule in the period after 1815. The most important of these societies was the carbonaries (Charcol burners). But the Carbonari movement was far from a mass movement. The Carbonari had a strong base in South Italy. In 1820, the Carbonari, its members drawn largly from the middle class and the army, enjoyed a few months of triumps in the kingdom of the two sicilies. Supported by the army and Militia, they forced king Ferdinand I to grant a constitution. But Austria suppressed the constitutional government in Naples. But the Carbonari movement did not die down after its failure of the rising in 1820. According to Hazen, "they plotted new insurrections which virtually brokout in 1830-31." But, again the Austrians suppressed the insurrection by the Carbonari in the Papal kingdom. In spite of the failure they served a useful purpose by keeping alive the spirit of patriotism.

There had been serious disagreement among Italian patriots about methods of achieving national unity. Mazzini and his supporters advocated the establishment of a Republic. Another method had been advocated by a piedmontese priest named Gioberti, who sought to reconcile nationalism and liberalism with traditional religion, and proposed a federation of existing Italian States under the presidency of the Pope. A third group of Nationalists had urged the creation for all Italy of a liberal constitutional monarchy under the king of Piedmont-Sardinia. The wave of revolution in Europe in 1830, when Charles X lost the throne of France and, Belgium declared herself independent of Holland, encouraged renewed out-breaks in Italy. On this occasion disturbances occured in central Italy. The rulers of Parma and Modena were expelled, and a considerable rising brokeout in the Papal states. The Italians for a time hoped for French support, but Louis Philippe was disinclined to risk his newly won crown in a war with Austria, whose prompt action was again successful in putting down the rebels. It was again made clear that local iisings, of indefinite aim and with limited support, would be powerless to achieve Italian unity and independence.

Mazzini and the Young Italy (1805-72)

According to Ketelby; "For within a prison cell of Savona, amid the infinities of the sky and the sea, drawing a mingled inspiration from a scanty library of his own choice, an ardent young patriot, a Carbonaro, Guiseppe Mazzini, had seen the vision of a regenerated Italy and heard a call to leadership. Thence ensured the society of "Young Italy", which, with its more definite aims and a more inspired direction, soon superseded the Carbonari as the nucleus of nationalist revolution".

Three great leaders of devoted patriotism and of excellent thoughts though dissimilar parts stand in the forefront of the Italian Risor-gimento-Mazzini, Garibaldi and Cavour. Each of them in his own way rendered valuable services to the cause of his country. Mazzini was the Prophet of Italian unity, Garibaldi its sword and cavour its brain. Fifteen years of reaction, broken only by sporadic and seemingly fruitless insurrections, had crushed the spirit of Italy. Many of her bravest sons were languishing in dungeons. The Carbonari had proved their incapacity for leadership. One man in Italy faced these facts. Born in Genoa, in 1805 Mazzini had been impressed, even as a child, by the misery and degradation of his country and had resolved to dedicate his life to the cause of Italian liberation. Even in his boyhood he was morbidly impressed with the unhappiness of his country. He says; "In the midst of the noisy tumultuous life of the student around me I was somber and absorbed and appeared like one suddenly grown old. I childishly determined to dress always in black, fancying myself in mourning for my country". As Mazzini grew up all his inclinations were towards a literary life. But he perceived, that for men conscious of an unfulfilled duty as citizens, the production of great literature is impossible. According to Mazzini, "Without a country and without liberty we might perhaps produced some prophets of art, but no vital art. Therefore it was better for us to consecrate our lives to the solution of the problem. Are we to have a country? And if were successful, the art of Italy would bloom and flourish over our graves". He joined the Carbonari, not because he approved even then of their methods, but because atleast they were a revolutionary organisation. Mazzini wrote; "We are a people, known from time immemorial by the same name as the people of Italy. ...We have no flag, no political name, no rank among European nations. We have no common centre, no common market. We are dismembered into eight States, all independent of one another, without alliance, without unity of aim. ...And all these states among which we are partitioned are ruled by despotic governments...all these States tamely submit to Austrian influence". When the wave of revolution swept the Italian peninsula in 1830, Mazzini also took a leading part in it, but was arrested and later exiled.

The fire of patriotism kept burning within him and in 1831, he founded a new party called the "Young Italy", destined to be an important factor in making the new Italy. Its programme was definite and ambitious. The Austrians were to be expelled, Italy to be liberated and unified, and a reform papacy was to assume the moral leadership of the world. He said, "Revolution must be made by the people and for the people". According to Hazen, "The society must be a secret organisation, but it must not be a body of consipirators, it must be educative, proselyting, seeking to win Italians by its moral and intellectual fervor to an idealistic view of life, a self-sacrificing sense of duty". He was fully confident of the strength of the youth. He said "Place youth at the head of the insurgent multitude, you know not the secreat of the power hidden in these youthful hearts, nor the magic influence exercised on the masses by the voice of youth. You will find among the young a host of apostles, of the new religion". With Mazzini the liberation and unification of Italy was indeed a new religion appealing to the loftiest emotions, entailing complete self-sacrifice, and the young were to be it apostles. His task was to educate the Italian nation to realize that it was a nation and not a geographical expression. He made the creed of Italian unity a living faith. Mazzini gave new force to the crusade against Austria and made the national movement a religion of the Italians. By 1833 the society reckoned 60,000 members. Branches were found everywhere. At a time when the obstacles seemed insuperable, when but few Italians dreamed of unity, Mazzini declared it was practicable ideal. He said; "The one thing wanting to 20 millions of Italians, desirous of emancipating them-selves, is not power but faith." But his work proved ineffective. He was dogmatic, intolerant and impractical. But he is one of the chief of the makers of Italy.

Italy and the Revolution of 1848

Throughout the period 1830-48 a strong under-current of opposition was developing in Italy towards the despotism of Austria. The people of Italy received a fresh impulse in 1846 when Pius, IX, a man of liberal views, was elected to the papal chair. He was believed to be well disposed to the ideas of the patriots and to lean definitely towards liberalism. His first act was to issue an amnesty for political prisoners, and this was followed by other liberal reforms such as the relaxation of the press, the modification of the ecclesiastical character of the government. These measures were received with unbounded enthusiasm and Pius IX became immensly popular. The Pope's example was followed in some other Italian states, notably in piedmont, where the king Charles Albert, abolished the censhorship of the press and proclaimed a new constitution. He said; "If providence sends us a war of Italian independence, I will mount my horse...I will place myself at the head of an army...What a glorious day it will be in which we can raise the cry of a war for the independence of Italy." King Ferdinand granted a liberal constitution in the Kingdom of two Sicilies. Such was the condition of Italy at the opening of 1848.

The news of the rising in Paris, followed by the news of the revolution in Vienna and the flight of Metternich sent a thrill of hope throughout Italy. In March 1848 rebellion against the Austrians broke out in Milan. After several days of desperate finghting the Austrian army under Radetzky, was driven out of the city. The rest of Lombardy and Venetia joined the revolt. A universal impulse stirred all Italy. There arose a wide demand for war to terminate Austrian domination. Italian patriotic feeling was at fever heat, and for the first time the rising appeared to be national rather then local in character. Charles Albert, supported by the Pope, the grand duke of Tuscany, Lombardy and the kingdom of two Sicilies, declared war on Austria in March 1848. But unfortunately, the Pope torn by conflicting sentiments, declared his opposition to a war with a Catholic power, while Ferdinand of Naples recalled his army to put down a revolt in his capital. Charles Albert was now left alone to fight against Austria. Radetzky, the Austrian general defeated charles Albert at the decisive battle of Custozza in July 1848. The following year (1849) Charles Albert made a further effort, but was defeated at Novara, Charles Albert then abdicated the throne of Sardinia infavour of his son victor Emmanuel.

The Pope's desertion was bitterly resented by the Italian patriots who under the leadership of Mazzini invaded the papal state, and the Pope fled away. A constituent assembly was summoned and it declared Rome a republic. The entire catholic world was flabbergasted at the Pope's despositon, and the Austrian and French troops restored the Papal authority in June 1849. The Austrians recaptured all the revolted territory. But though a failure, the struggle of the Italians was not althogether fruitless. For the first time they had combined in the name of Italian nationalism. Neapolitans had shed blood for Venice, Lombards for Rome, and piedmontese for all

Italy. Though the attempts of the Italian patriots were thus unsuccessful, an inspiring example had been set, and there remained as a powerful gathering ground for a future effort, the constitutional monarchy of piedmont-Sardinia under the able, liberal, and intensely Italian minded Victor Emmanuel. The efforts of 1848 had not only made Italy conscious of her nationsalism, but had given the national cause a dynasty to represent it, and a people to defend it.

The greatest hurdle in the unification of Italy was the near total dominance of Austria over the whole peninsula. When Europe was shaken by liberal and romantic revolts in 1820, 1830 and 1848, Italy too had experienced popular upheavals. Every time Austria had put down the fire of revolt. The most humiliating defeat for the liberal constitutionalists occured in 1848. King Charles Albert (Piedmont-Sardinia) was defeated at custozza and Novara. He was succeeded by victor Emmnuel. Despite the persistent opposition of Austria, the new king retained the constitution which was sanctioned by Charles Albert. This event made him gain favour in the eyes of all patriots. Thus, piedmont, the only state in Italy that had a constitution, became a liberal oasis in the desert of despotism. She became the bacon of liberty. Piedmont became a model state, and when the time came, the Italians of other states would recognise her leadership. Victor Emmanuel had no great intellectual gifts, and his private life was far from examplary, but his plain, vigorous common sense and his steadfast devotion to the cause of Italy enabled him to play a vital part in the drama about to be unfolded. His kingdom became an assylum for political refugees from the other provinces, and the feeling grew stronger as the years went by that the ultimate deliverance of Italy would come from this direction. That hope was intensified when the king took as Chief Minister count camillo Cavour (1852), for Cavour proved himself one of the ablest statesmen of modern time.

Count Camillo Benso Di Cavour

Cavour was born at Turin on August 10, 1810. He belonged by descent to one of the smallest and proudest aristocracies in Europe. As a younger son of his family he was destined for the army, but a soldiers life was not congenial to him. He resigned his commission in 1831, and for the next seventeen years lived the life of a country gentleman developing his estate. Later on, he took to Journalism and edited a newspaper, "the Risorgimento", in which he advocated the cause of liberal Reform in Piedmont. He was anxious to play a part in politics himself, though he saw no chance in a country as yet without representative institutions. He said; "If I were an Englishman, by this time I should be somethng, and my name would not be wholly unknown." He had travelled widely and had studied the political life of France and of England particularly. Owing to his independent thinking, and high ideals Cavour became much popular among Italians. Cavour was an admirer of English Parliamentary system. Night after night he sat in the galleries of the House of Commons and studied the parliamentary proceedngs of England. He was an ardent believer in parliamentary government and said, "Italy must make herself by means of liberty". In 1848, Charles Albert announced the concesion of a constitution for piedmont and in the first Parliament Cavour took his seat as a member of Turin. He declared that "it was the mission of the Sardinian State to gather to herself all the living forces of Italy and lead our mother country to those high destinies where unto she is called". He held subordinate office in 1850 and was Prime Minister in 1852. He remained in these posts, with a brief interruption until his death in 1861.

Cavour had imbided the English liberalism of the day, individualism, material progress, a constitutional king, and a Parliament representing the educated classes to promote liberty in ecclessiastical and economic matters. Realism was the note of his whole policy. He said, "Piedmot must begin by raising herself, by reestablishing in Europe, as well as in Italy, a position and a credit equal to her ambition". As premier, Cavour strove to promote the material welfare of his state in accordance with the English liberal model. Tariffs were lowered. The building of factories and the importation of machinary were encouraged. Roads were improved and railways constructed. A new army of 90,000 soldiers with a better discipline was organised. At the same time, Cavour sought to lessen the influence of the Church by restricting its privileges. He expelled the Jesuits from the country and suppressed many monastic establishment. He organised a national society with the object of enlisting the support of other Italian States for piedmont. Its motto was independence and unity, out with the Austrians and the Pope". Cavour's talent was versatile, and he was not a romantic like Mazzini. His internal measures which alone would have given him as an able minister of modern enlightment-were eclipsed by his brilliant foreign policy.

Cavour believed as did all patriots, that Austria must be driven out of Italy before any Italian regeneration could be achieved. According to Ketelbey, "Cavour's whole policy was dominated by an inflexible ambition to effect the emancipation of Italy from Austria. It was based upon the fundamental assumption that only by European support and foreign alliance could his great end be achieved. By European diplomacy and war, Italian unity must be lifted out of enervating obscurity of Austrian domestic politics...it must became European question on which the power should fight." Till now it was the proud boast of the nationalists that Italy acting alone would be able to work out its own salvation. "Italia Fara da Se" (italy will act by herself) was the motto of earlier movements. The failure of these movements had convinced Cavour that alone Italy, by her unaided efforts would not be able to reach the desired goal. Hence it became the business of Cavour's policy to secure the sympathy of the great powers. Cavour, like Bismark, was an exponent of real-politike, that is, government and state policy be divorced from moral consideration. While being dictated only be the exigencies of power and latter to be Judged only by success of failure. According to Ketelby, "No cause was more blessed in leaders of devoted patriotism and of excellence though dissimilar parts than that of the Italian Risorgimento. But Mazzini, its fervent though unpractical apostle, and Garibbaldi its soldier and knight-errant, might have been martyrs of a barren hope without Cavour, the real creator of Italian unity".

Cavour's Role in Crimean War (1854-56)

The Crimean War had provided Cavour with the opportunity for one of his skillful diplomatic strokes. Italy indeed had no interests in the issues between Russia and the allies. But the enemies of Russia were much in need of help and support. He persuaded the king to join England and France against Russia as a means of bringing the Italian question before the great powers. A token force of 15,000 Piedmontese troops were sent to crimea. A Piedmontese soldier said, "Out of this mud (Crima), Italy will be made," and the words expressed the essential aims of Cavour. Cavour's calculations were fulfilled. In the peace Congress of Paris cavoured claimed a place. The diplomatic position of Sardinia was established. Cavour's assurance was justified. The Italian question has become for a future a European question. According to Marriot, "the cause of Italy has not been defended by demagogues, revolutionists and party men, but has been discussed before the congress by the plenipotentiaries of the great powers". He declared in the peace congress that the root cause of the problems of Italy was the influence and dominance of Austria. He said, "Austria is the arch enemy of Italian independence, the permanent danger to the only free nation of Italy, the nation which I have the honour to represent". The crime-an episode was the turning point in the fortunes of Cavour, of Sardinia and of Italy. Sardinia now was a recognised part of the diplomatic web of Europe. Cavour was recognised as among the ablest of European diplomatists. Cavour returned from Paris with no material advantage gained, but his moral victory was complete.

Napoleon III and Italy

Cavour reaped the fruits of his foresight a few years later in the pact of plombiers. Cavour turned to France, and in the emperor he found the ally whose encouratgement and military support were indispensable for the furtherance of his schemes. Napoleon III was induced by a variety of motives to assume an active part in the Italian movement. He was sprung from an Italian house. The French emperor was known to be sympathetic towards a country where he had fought as a Carbonaro. Mingled with personal inclinations and unfeigned interest in the Italian cause were his imperial ambitions. He was the inheritor of the Napoleonic traditions, and wanted to be the champions of all oppressed nationalities. Moreover, he had a strong heriditary reason for seeking to discredit the settlement of 1815. As an astute diplomat Cavour also dangled the bait before Napoleon's eyes with consummate adroitness. The bait was swallowed. Napoleon's efforts were seconded by an unexpected incident, the attempt to murder the emperor by an Italian named Orsini. The incident for a time seemed fatal to Cavour's hope. But Cavour pointed out that revolutionary crime like that were but the misguided acts of ardent spirit driven to desperation by the oppressive rule of Austria. His arguments were reinforced by orsini's dying appeal to the emperor to deliver Italy. Npoleon was impressed by the adjurations which Orsini addressed to hm by from the jail. Napoleon III sent a message to Cavour. Cavour wrote to a friend, "The drama approaches its crisis". He met the emperor on July 21-22, 1858 at Plombiers.

France promised to support Sadinia in a war with Austria on condition that Cavour provided a pretext, which would justify France's action in the eyes of Europe. If the allies were victorious, Italy would be constituted into a confederation consisting of following states under the presidency of the Pope, A northern kingdom under victor Emmanuel II, consisting of Sardinia-Piedmont, Lombardy, Venetia, Parma and parts of the Papal States. A central kingdom including Tuscany and part of the Papal States, Rome directly under the Pope, and the kingdom of two sicilies. France, would received Savoy and Nice as "Compensation". Napoleon was to arrange diplomatic isolation of Austria on the eve of war. Finally, victor Emmanuel was to give his daughter in marriage to the emperor's cousin prince Jerome. Cavour said, "Whether we like it or not our destinies depend upon France."

Cavour's immediate problem was to bring about war in such a way that Austria would be appear to be the aggressor. By increasing the Piedmontese forces and concentrating the troops near the border of Lombardy he succeeded in arousing Austrian apprehensions. The British government offered it mediation to settle the Italian question. But to Cavour's delight, Austria presented an ultimatum bidding piedmont to disarm. Cavour refused and Austria declared war. Cavour said,"the die is cast and we have made history." Piedmont was regarded by others as merely defending herself from an unprovoked attack. The war of Italian liberation began in 1859 and the French army led by Napoleon III joined Sardinia against Austira. The latter were victorious in two great battles that of Magenta and Solferino. The allies occupied Lombardy. The Italians were eagerly following up their victory when they were thunderstruck by the news that Napoleon had signed an armistice with Francis Joseph (Austria) at villafrance on 12th July, 1859.

The Villafrance Armistice

According to Lipson; "But misfortune still continue to mar the destinies of Italy, for the moment she was about to drain her cup of triumph, it was again dashed from her lips". To Piedmont and to the nationalists throughout Italy Napoleon's move wore only one appearance, it was a desertion and betrayal. As per the villafrance armistice. An Italian confederation should be created under the presidency of the Pope. Austria should cede Lombardy to France and France would give it to Piedmont. Venetia would remain with Austria. The rulers in central duchies should be restored. But why had Napoleon stopped in the middle of a successful campaign. There were several reasons. Unaccustomed to the grim realities of war, his nerve had been shaken by the sights of the Battle fiedl of solferino. He was alarmed at the exuberance of Italian nationalism. He was unconsciously creating a united Italy on the border of France and the French were hostile to the idea of establishing a powerful neighbour who might prove dangerous later. Several of the German States were showing sign of coming to the support of Austria. The situation in France was becoming serious. The Catholic party in France took on a menacing attitude, when it appeared that the Papacy was to suffer for the benefit of Piedmont. Besides, the French losses had been heavy and the Austrian forces were strongly intrenched in Venetia. According to Napoleon, "To secure Italian independence I made war against the wish of Europe, as soon as the fortune of my own country seemed to be endangered I made peace".

Expansion of Piedmont

The news of the peace came as a cruel disappointment to the Italians, dashing their hopes just as they were apparently to be realised. In intense indignation at the faithlessness of Napoleon III, overwrought by the excessive strain under which he had long been laboring, Cavour lost his self control, urged desperate measures upon the king and when they were declined, in a fit of rage therw up his office. Victor Emmanuel's judgement at this critical moment was more sound than Cavour's. He clerly saw that it was wiser to take what one could get, and bide the future than to imperil all by some rash course of action. The armistice was followed by the treaty of Zurich. The news of the evacuation of Lombardy by the Austrians has been the signal for the explosion of popular feeling in the central duchies and parma, Modena and Tuscany rose in revolt, and expelled their rulers. But according to the treaty of Zurich, the old rulers were to be restored. In 1860 parma, Modena and Tuscany had resolved by Plebiscite to unite themselves with Piedmont under the house of Savoy. But would victor Emmanuel venture to accept such an accession of territory? Would the powers permit the fusion? Cavour who had returned to ofice fully realised that the annexation of the central duchies cold only be done with the consent of Napoleon III. So he offered him Savoy and Nice. At this juncture, Great Britain gave powerful moral support to Italian aspirations. Europe accepted the accomplished fact. Victor Emmanuel accepted the soverignity thus offered him, and on April 2, 1860, the first Parliament of the enlarged kingdom met at Turin. According to Hazen, "This was the most important change in the political system of Europe since 1815...It constituted the most damaging breach made thus far in the work of the congress had decided was to be a mere geographical expression was now a nation in formation". But Nepoleon's fill had still to be paid. To surrender to France the cradle of his race (Savoy and Nice) was for Emanuel the sacrifice most painful to his heart. Because of it Garbibaldi cried, "You have made me a foreigner in the land of my birth". By the annexation of Savoy and nice, Napoleon lost the gratitude of the Italians.

Thus, the first advance towards Italian unity had been made. To Cavour it was a mere stepping stone. He said, "They have stopped me from making Italy by revolution from the south." From princes and foreign alliances Cavour turned to Garbaldi. With the utmost diplomatic cooperation and ingenuity Cavour embarked upon one of the most important enterprises in the history of Italian unification.

Cavour took took full advantage of the grave political discontent against the reactionary Pope and Francis II, the Bourbon king of the two sicilies. He exploited the serious political unrest in the kingdom of the two Sicilies and secretly encouraged the patriots there to revolt against Francis II.

Garibaldi (1807-1882) An Introduction

Garibaldi, born in 1807 at Nice, appeared and reappeared as the most strange and startling personality of 19th century Italy. By nature he was freedom loving, Romantic and poetical. He believed in Italy as the saints believed in God. According to Trevelyan; "He acquired just enough book learning to feed his freedom loving and poetic disposition, but not enough to train his mind". Destined by his parents for the priesthood, he preferred the sea, and for many years he lived a roving and adventurous sailor's life. He was introduced to Mazzini and joined the "young Italy" society. Garibaldi described his ideas about Mazzini, as such, "He alone watched when all around slept, he alone kept and led the sacred flame". He took part in the unsuccessful insurrection organised by Mazzini in Savoy in 1834, and as a result was condemn to death. He managed to escape to South America, where for the next 14 years, he was an exile. Returning to Italy, a romantic figure in "Red Shirt", Garibaldi led a volunteer army of 3000 personal followers in the Sardinian war of 1848 against Austria, and later he joined Mazzini in his invasion of Rome in 1849. But after its failure he fled to the united States of America. In 1854, he returned once more to Italy, awaiting an opportunity to strike for national liberty. In 1856 he met Cavour and he was converted to the cause of the Sardinian monarchy although Garibaldi remianed Republican at heart. In 1859 the consipirators of Sicily appealed to Garibaldi for help. He accepted the invitation in the name of Italy and victor Emmanuel. At that time Cavour too played his card. When revolution broke out in Sicily in 1860, Garibaldi appealed to Cavour and the king for authorisation and help Cavour was caught in a dilemma.

Garibaldi and the Conquest of Naples and Sicily

When the patriots in Sicily revolted against the reactionary Francis II, Garibaldi saw his opportunity and with a band of his thousand soldiers he sailed from Genoa. Piedmont officially was at peace with Francis II, so Cavour could not openly extend help to Garibaldi, and though he outwardly denounced him, Secretly he encouraged the Red Shirt invasion. In May 1860 Garibaldi landed in Sicily while he was given protection by a small British naval squadrom. At this point it was fortunate for the movement that palmerston, Russel and Gladstone had come in to power in Britain, for if the members of this liberal triumvirate were in hearty agreement about little else, they were all keen supporters of the Risorgimento. The British Mediterranean squadron ought by international law to have prevented a filibustering attack an a friendly state, but the admiral in command had orders to remain neutral, and as a matter of fact the mere presence of British ships in the neighbourhood paralysed the Neapolitan gun boats while Garibaldi and his thousand landed at Marshala. His magnatic personality enthralled everybody. His ragged enthusiasts defeated a Neapolitan army of twice its strength, and within a few weeks all the island was in his power. At palermo he proclaimed himself dictator in the name of victor Emmanuel. This brilliant success of Garibaldi posed a problem for Cavour. It was certain that Garibaldi would cross over to the mainland. But such an advance was sure to lead to a war with France, for Rome was protected by French garrison. Moreover, there was always the possibility that Garibaldi, who was at heart a Republican, might be prevailed upon by the extremists to give the movement a Republican Character. Cavour declared, "Italy must be saved from foreigners, evil principles and mad man". Cavour decided to intervene. Assuring himself that Napoleon III would not interfere so long as Rome was resepected, he despatched victor-Emmanuel at the head of royal troops to forestall Garibaldi. Using some hostile moves on the part of the Pope as a pretext, victor Emmanuel invaded the Papal States and occupied Umria and Marches. He then moved towards the South to meet the Red Shirts at Naples. Garibaldi had met with an unexpected check from the Neapolitan army. Meanwhile plebiscites having been held in Sicily, Naples, Umria and Marches, the people everwhere voted for union with the kingdom of Sardinia and piedmont, Garibaldi surrendered his power and his army to victor Emmanuel. Their combined armies defeated the Neapolitan forces at Capua. The conquest of Sicily and Naples was now complete Garibaldi had added to his master's crown a new and more brilliant jewel and then, refusing all rewards and decorations, he went quietly away to his island home in Caprera. The kingdom of Sardinia had expanded into the Kingdom of Italy. Victor Emmanuel II was proclaimed king of Italy. In 1861 the first Italian Parliament representing all italy except Rome and Venetia met at Turin. In brief, Garibaldi turned history in to an epoch and politics into a romance. If Mazzini was the soul, Cavour the brain of new Italy, Garibaldi was surely its swords. Meanwhile Cavour passed away on 6th June, 1861. But his task was done. Italy was united and had a liberal constitution.

Completion of Union

Only two States were now wanting to complete the unification Italy-Venetia held by the Austrians and Rome held by the Pope with the assistance of the French army. In 1865 the Italian government offered to buy Venetia from Austria, but the offer was refused. It therefore turned to Prussia, which was preparing for the struggle with Austria for the leadership of Germany and was anxious both to gain Italy's aid against Austria and also ensure the neutrality of Napoleon III. Almost immediately afterwards Austria offered, through Napoleon to give Venetia to Italy, if she would remain neutral in the coming struggle, but La Marmora, Cavours successor refused the offer. In April 1866, Italy made an offensive and defensive alliance whereby, in the event of war breaking out within three months, Italy should assist Prussia, and if victorious, she was to be rewarded with the annexation of Venetia. They were defeated in the actual fighting, but the necessity of retaining large bodies of Austrian troops in Venetia contributed to the Prussian victory at Sadowa, and in the peace which followed Venetia was ceded to Italy. The Venetian plebiscite was almost unanimously infavour of Annexation to Italy.

The Franco-German war (1870-71) afforded Italy an opportunity to obtain Rome. Napoleon III was compelled to withdraw the French troops in order to put them into the field against Prussia victor Emmanuel seized the oppertunity and, despite some resistance from Papal troops, entered the city which became his capital and Pope Pius IX withdrew into the Vatican. In this manner Rome, while remaining the central seat of Catholic Christianity, became also the capital of the new born Italian state. At last the unification of Italy reached its completion, a thing accomplished by Mazzini's moral enthusiasm, Garbaldi's sword, Cavour's diplomacy and victor Emmanuel's tact and good sense.

Estimate of Cavour

According to Hazen;-"Cavour", said Lord Palmerston, in the British House of Commons, "left a name to point a moral and adorn a tale". The moral was, that a man of transcendent talent, indomitable industry, inextinguishable partriotism could overcome difficulties which seemed insurmountable, and confer the greatest, the most inestimable benefits on his country. The tale with which his memory would be associated was the most extraordinary, the most romantic, in the annals of the world. A people which had seemed dead had arisen to new and vigorous life, breaking the spell which bound it, and showing itself worthy of a new splendid destiny." Under his skillful guidance Italy, which for centuries had been a mere geographical expression, became a political entity and a national state. According to Phillips; "Italy as a nation is the legacy, the life work of Cavour. Others have been devoted to the national liberation, he knew how to bring it into the sphere of possibilities, he kept it pure of any factious spirit, he led it away from barren Utopia, kept it clear of reckless conspiracies, steered straight between rebels and reactions, and gave it an organised force, a flag, a government, and foreign allies". His contribution to the making of Italy was immeasurable. He saved Italy from reaction and revolution. Cavour said, "The emancipation of the peoples cannot result from mere plots...it will be a necessary consequence of the progress of civilisation". The unification of Italy demanded not merely the expulsion of Austria but the extinction of many princely houses and the destruction of the temporal power of the Pope. He said, "Italian nationality would not come from military or democratic revolution but from the combined action of all national rulers of Italy". Besides, he employed his diplomatic ability in securing the sympathy and support of the great powers. It was his great achievement to turn into one current all the available forces of the time-Napoleon's ambition, Mazzini's inspiration and Garibaldi's sword. In fact, he was a master diplomat of his age. Cavour was a democrat of liberal school. He once said, "I always feel strongest when parliament is sitting...I am the son of liberty and to her I owe all that I am. It a veil is to be placed on her statue, it is not for me to do it". He was a follower of the British parliamentary system. If there has been no Cavour, to win the confidence, sympathy and support of Europe, Mazzini's efforts would have run to waste unquestionable insurrections, and Garibaldi's feat of arms must have added one more chapter to the history of unproductive patriotism. By his diplomatic skill Cavour converted a mere goegraphical expression in a powerful unified state. Cavour did not live to see the complete unification of Italy. According to Lipson; "He lived long enough to create the Italy of the Italians, and to earn the undying gratitude of the Italian people".

Chapter-X

Unification of Germany (1815-71)

The German Empire (1871-90) and the Role of Bismarck

One of the most remarkable changes of the 19th century was the transformation of Germany, from a loose confederation into an imposing empire. The unification of Germany was facilitated by forces, factors and personalities. The most important force was the cultural renaissance of Germany, which witnessed eminent musicians, men of letters and philosophers. The romantic movements awakened national feelings. By examining the language, literature and folkways of their people, romantic thinkers instilled a sense of national pride in their compatriots. Herder conceived the idea of the Voksgeist (The soul of the people). His emphasis on the unique of a people stimulated a national consciousness among the Germans. The romantics were the earlies apostless of German nationalism. Most German romantics expressed hostility to the liberal ideals of the French revolution. On the otherhand, Fichte and Hegal exalted the conception of the state and the historical role of the men of letters who made Pan-Germanism articulate and who preserved Germany from provincialism which threatened to engulf her. The chief intellectual support for the regeneration of Prussia and the growth of nationalism in Germany came from the universities. Behind this activity lay the spirit of liberation evoked by the revolutionary and Napolenic storms. This influenced the statesmen to a great extent. Under the guidance of Scharnhorst German army was reorganised. Under the guidance of Hardenburg and Stein the machinary of government was overhauled. Prussian victory at Leipzig, became a patriotic legend. The German liberals drew their spiritual force from literature enriched by Lessing, Herder, Goethe. The Philosophy of Kant and Fichte influenced them not a little. But the people of Germany were greatly dissatisfied with the provisions of the Vienna settlement. Upto 1806 the German States had been bound together in a loose union called the Holy Roman empire. According to Voltaire, "It was neither holy nor Roman or empire". That had been succeeded by the confederation of the Rhine, a creation of Napoleon. it is one of the ironies of history that Napoleon was the creator of Modern Germany. In the Congress of Vienna it was replaced by the establishment of the German confederation, composed of 38 states, under the presidency of Austria. The confederation was a union of princes, not of peoples. The liberals of Germany eager for national unity, thus suffered a severe defeat at Vienna. The Post-Vienna era were years of restlessness. The German liberals were indignant at the great deception of Vienna. The people of Germany never accepted the decisions of the Vienna Congress by heart and soul. Nickolson has observed : "The high hopes of the nationalists and liberals were doomed to disappointment, the oppertunity was missed to create a German confederation which might well have been liberal, civilised and human, the unity of Germany could thereafter only be forge by Blood and Iron".

Depotic government prevailed in most of the states of the confederation. In the Austrian empire Metternich, the chancellor, had to face the problem of ruling peoples of many races, languages and religion. He felt that it was possible to do so with success only by setting himself against any change. Things were to be left as they were, and no reform of any kind was to be attempted. By a strict censorship of the press, by controlling the teaching of the universities, by suppressing revolutionary movements, Metternich succeeded for many years in maintaining the ancien regime. To a great extent he succeeded in imposing a similar system of repression upon the German confederation. Fredrick William III, king of Prussia could have been expected to lead the patriotic and liberal forces in Germany, but even he fell under the influence of Metternich and consequently joined hands with him to suppress all signs of nationalism and liberalism in the country. The disappointment of liberals was intense. The chief seat of disaffection was found in the universities. According to Sybel, "The young heroes returning from the war fill the universities with their patriotic indignation, and by the founding of societies of students (Burschenschaften), representing all the universities, they sought to fill all the educated youth of Germany with their enthusiasm for unity, justice and freedom. These societies, for the most part cherished ambitions which were thoroughly ideal. They did not look to the overthrow of present conditions, but relied upon the training of rising generation. By moral elevation and patriotic inspirations, they hoped to lead the state to the future to the great goal of national unity. To be sure, their nations of this future state were generally indefinite and were mere unpractical fancies, indeed, this enthusiasm rose in some groups to the pitch of wild fanaticism, so that they were even ready to seize sword and dagger for tyrannicide. Yet such enthusiasts never succeeded in securing in the societies at large any great following for their project".

A characteristic feature of German history is the influence which scholars and men of letters have exerted upon the development of Germany. The students of Jena university had during the Napoleonic wars founded a society called Burschenschaft, whose purpose was the inculcation an intense national patriotism, the constant exaltation of the ideal of a common Fatherland, Within two years the organisation had obtained a footing in 16 universities. Metternich, to whom the union of all Germans in one Germany was an infamous object, watched with growing apprehension the spread of revolutionary doctrines among the youth of Germany. The Burschenschaft took a decision to hold a festival at Wartburg, an old castle in Weimer on 18-19th October, 1817 to celebrate the fourth anniversary of the battle of Leipzig and three hundredth anniversary of Luther's Quarrel with the Church of Rome. There was a good deal of patriotic oratory, aspiration for political freedom and unity were expressed, and some reactionary books were burnt. Later-on in 1819, a student named Karl Sand, killed a dramatist and journalist Kotzebue, who was hated in university circle as a Russian spy. Metternich decided to take full advantage of the circumstances. He immediately summoned a meeting of the German princess at Carlsbad, where decrees were drawn up for the suppression of liberalism throughout the German confederation.

Carlsbad Decree 1819

The Carlsbad conference is an important turning point in the history of central Europe. These decrees were the work of Austria, seconded by Prussia. They signified in German history the suppression of liberty for a generation. They really determined the political system of Germay until 1848. By the Carlsbad decrees, the Government of Austria became the head of an all powerful German police system. The decrees passed by the Federal Diet, inaugurated an era of repression and riveted the yoke of despotism upon Germany. The Carlsbad decrees provided for a vigorous censorship of the press, and subjected the professors and students of the universities to a close goverment supervision. All teachers who should propagate harmful doctrines, should be removed from their positions. The student societies were suppressed. The students who were expelled from one university were not to be admitted into another. Provision were made for a central commission of investigation to supervise the working of the decrees. another provision was directed against the establishment of any further constitutions of a popular character. The Carlsbad decrees were rigidly enforced. Police spies were actively engaged in trying to discover traces of Liberal opinions. Men were imprisoned or exiled on mere suspicion. By such means Metternich succeeded imposing on the German confederation the system which he had already brought to perfection in the Austrian empire.

The Zollverein

In this gathering gloom the nationalists only hope centred on the attitude of Prussia. But she was not in a position to challenge the leadership of Austria, as she was politically and economically not strong. If Prussia was to realise the hopes of the German patariots, she must first put her own house in order and strenghten her-self economically and politically. During the first half of the 19th century Germany was, economically and commercially, the most backward country in Western Europe. The country as a whole had not yet emerged from the agrarian stage. The fiscal arrangements of prussia reflected and accentuated the peculiarities of her political evolution. No where were duties uniformed. The first step towards uniformity in the Prussian dominions was taken by the enactment of the tariff reform Law of May 28, 1818 on the advice of a Prussian economist Massen. Under this act he abolished all internal customs and established free trade throughout her territories. In order to check smuggling the tariff was lowered. Thus, internally Prussia became for the first time an economic and commercial unit, while her external tariff was the most liberal in continental Europe. Having established a common tariff system throughout her kingdom, Prussia invited the other German States to enter into a tariff union with her. The smaller States of North Germany were, as usual, suspicious of any suggestion made by their powerful neighbour, but at length they were convinced of the advantages of the proposal and most of them joined the custom union or Zolleverein. A few years later a rival custom union was formed in South Germany under Bavarian leadership and a third one was established in central Germany on the proposal of Saxony. In course of time these groups amalgamated, and by 1842 the Zollverein, under Prussian leadership included most of the states in the confederation. Thus, it was the commercial union under prussia which ultimately drew most of the German states excluding Austria.

Trade and industry flourished by leaps and bounds and the merchants were thankful for the abolition of the numerous internal barriers which had hampered trade. German territories, excluding Austria became one economic entity. Economic unity, thus created, removed the political barriers and paved the way for German political unity and community of material interests, stimulated the growth of national feeling and fostered national feeling and fostered national consciousness. The Zollverein was an economic weapon in prussia's political struggle for primacy in Germany. The zollverein made the German states and the people accustomed to cooperation without Austria, it taught them the advantage of prussian leadership. The Zollverein has brought the sentiment of German nationality out of the regions of hope into those of positive and material interests. The custom union helped to satisfy the interests of the rising mercantile and manufacturing bourgeois class. They desired even more the support and protection in foreign lands which only a powerful country could ensure. According to Hazen; "The interest of German history between 1830 and 1848 does not lie in the evolution of political liberty, for political repression and absolutism were the order of the day. It lies rather in growth along economic lines, in intellectual achivements outside the domain of politics and in those movements of opinion and of racial aspiration which rendered so notable and far-reaching the vast turmoil of 1848". The general feeling in Germany towards the Zollverein is that it is the first step towards what is called the Germanization of the people. By a community of interests, on commercial and trading questions it has prepared the way for a political nationality. It has been rightly pointed out that, "Germany was made by coal and iron, before it was united by Blood and Iron".

The July Revolution of 1830 had its echo in Germany where isolated outbreaks of popular movements took place in many of the States. There were demands for the grant of liberal constitutions and the same were conceded by the rulers of many states. The net result was that while Prussia remained unchanged, the smaller states got liberal constitutions. Metternich was able once again to establish his hold over Germany.

The Revolution of 1848 and the Frankfurt Parliament

Under Fredrick William III (1797-1840) no change had been made in the political institutions of Germany. In 1840 Fredrick William IV succeeded Fredrick William III. Fredrick William IV was well meaning but weak willed sentimentalists. He had long been intending to make some concession to constitutionalism and pan-Germanism, but these impulses had hitherto been checked by the ingrained absolutist traditions of the Hohenzollern dynasty, and by the influence of Metternich. The fall of the orleans monarchy, followed by that of Metternich, frightened him into immediate action. In other words, the French revolution of 1848 had its repercussions in Germany. King William IV announced the abolition of the censorship and the establishment of parliamentary goverment for all the prussian dominions. When the Berlin populace heard this, a crowd gathered outside the palace, partly to congratulate the king on the concessions, and partly to gain confirmation of them. A chance shot by one of the guards killed a civilian where upon the crowd lost its temper and began a street fight in which barricades were thrown up and a score of lives were lost. Fredrick William IV was overcome with grief at the untoward turn of events, and the effect of it on his sensitive and unstable mind was to make him surrender to the demands of the liberals more completely than ever. He promised that he would give whole-hearted support to the scheme for a pan-German constitution and to assume the leadership of "a free and new born German nation". In March 1848, the German nationalists met at Heidelberg and decided to convene a German national Diet, elected by universal adult suffrage to draft a new federal constitution.

Frankfort Parliament

In May 1848 about 600 elected members assembled in the city of Frankfort. Their mission was the drafting of a constitution for united Germany. According to Ketelby; "it was the flower of the revolutionary democratic nationalism of 1848". The lawyers and professors who met at Frankfort to devise a new federal constitution had no experience of getting things done in a Parliament. The task before the Parliament was threefold to achive German unity, to draft a constitution for the united Germany and to adopt the fundamental rights of the German nation. The delegates spent the first six weeks in designing a provisional government, with an Austrian archduke as imperial vicar. The Frankfort Parliament adopted the fundamental rights of the German nation but the other two problems were awaiting solution, what was to be the relationship between Austria and prussia in the new State? and what territories should be included in the German union? At last, it was decided that only German States which were under the possession of Austria should be included in the new German nations.It was further decided that Germany should be a heriditary empire and the king of prussia would be the president of the new Federation.

Meanwhile a delegation was sent to the prussian king on behalf of the Parliament. But Fredrick William temperamentally conservative, Romantically loyal to the Hapsburg, mistrustful of democratic forces and religiously imbued with Divine Right, he found himself in a cruel dilemma. Finally, he refused the offer of the Parliament, as he was not prepared to be "a serf of the revolution". He would wear no "crown of shame". Thus, Fredrick William missed the oppertunity of achiving German unity in 1849.

Prussia had been responsible for the failure of the Frankfort assembly to achive the union of Germany. The liberal movement in Germany collapsed.

Marx and Engles called it as "an assembly of old women". But infact, liberalism had been primarily a bourgeois movement. It was of the sentimental and romantic order. Its leaders generally were men without political experience. They treated the problems of politics from the angle of theories. Further the members could not take firm decisions on important issues and wasted time in useless discussion. The triumph of the conserva-tives in Austria sealed the fate of the assembly. It was Austria who bitterly opposed the decision of the Parliament. Above all, Fredrick William decli-ned to accept the imperial crown of united Germany. No doubt, the sense of German unity was checked but in nosense destroyed by an reaction after 1848.

The movement for a united Germany was not yet at an end. In 1849 Fredrick William invited the representatives of other states to Berlin, and to them he suggested the formation of a closer German union under prussian leadership. Saxony and Hanover assented at first, and with prussia formed the league of the three kings. But when it was proposed to summon another German national parliament, Hanover and Saxony left the league of the three kings. But Fredrick william undaunted, went ahead and a meeting of the parliament of prussian league was summoned to meet at Erfurt in March 1850. The Erfurt parliament met, but it accomplished no more than its predecessor at Frankfort.

Austria was now recovered from her internal troubles to intervene. Her new chancellor, Schwarzenberg, summoned a meeting of the Diet of the old German confederation. At this stage a crisis in Hesse-Cassel offered an oppertunity for a trial of strength between Austria and prussia. The Elector of Hesse-Cassel, a member of the prussian union, had annulled the constitution which he had granted to his people in 1848. His subjects revolted and appealed to prussia. On the other hand, the Elector appealed to the diet of the German confederation. If the king of prussia failed to support the people of Hesse his league would collapse and if he would take up arms on their behalf a war would begin which would involve the question of the future of Germany. Fredrick William shrank from the appeal to the sword. Meanwhile Austrian troops subjugated the Hessians.

Olmutz : Convention

Fredrick William's humiliation was complete at the convention of olmutz (November 1850). Schwarzenberg dictated his own terms to the Prussian king. The Austrian right to protect Hesse was recognised. Fredrick William dissolved the Prussian league and the old German confederation was restored. Fredrick William by his timidity had let down the cause of German unity. Prussia purchased an inglorious submission at olmutz at the price of complete submission. Among the spectators of these transactions was a young pomeranian squire, a member of the Berlin parliament, and he was otto Von Bismarck, destined to be one of the greatest figure in prussian history.

In spite of the recent failure of prussia to lead the national movement she was the only power fitted for the leadership of Germany. The Zolleverein had established her economic leadership in Germany and bound the smaller states to her by strong ties of material interests. Prussia was the only State in Germany which could challange the might of Austria, the greatest obstacle to German unity. Further, the princess of Germany were very zealous of their position and were not likely to favour any movement which would endanger it. They leant upon the support of Austria for the maintenance of their position. So no new adjustment of relations with them was practicable unless Austria was removed from the scene. A large measure of German unity was destined to come in little more than 20 years, but the political ideals of liberalism were doomed to wait much longer before they realized any real triumph on German soil.

William I-Otto Von Bismarck- and German Unification

In 1857, Fredrick William IV became insane, and William his brother was called upon to shoulder the responsibility of the state as regent. In 1861 Fredrick William died, and William I became king of prussia. He was a frank and simple-minded soldier to whom all political trickery was abhorrent. He had all the Hohenzollern faith in divine right. Politically he was a bigot, he believed in the established order, but William I combined liberal sympathies in detail with rigid conservatism in essentials. He detested the constitution set up by his brother in 1850, but as long as it was the law of the land he loyally tried to carry it out. He allowed free election to the Reichstag and appointed a liberal ministry. But he had little interest in the business of government. His entire lifetime has been spent in the army, which he loved passionately. William I believed that Prussia's destinies were dependent upon her army. He said that, whoever wishes to rule Germany must conquer it and that cannot be done by pharases. There was reason to think that Prussia required a stronger army. The humiliation of Olmutz was fresh in his mind. The history of Prussia was predominantly military, and there could be no thought of changing the character of the state. The king was assisted at this juncture by one of the makers of modern prussia, the war Minister Von Roon. This true organiser of vicotry had a religious belief in the destiny of prussia and of Germany, and a deep conviction that the Prussian army was the instrument through which Prussia must accomplish her destiny.

King William I and Von Roon, his war minister, devised a series of army reforms which involved the formation of 39 new regiments, and service for three years with the colours and four years in the reserve. The difficulty was that the scheme involved increased expense, and for this the constitution required the consent of the Reichstag (Lower house of the German parliament). The progressive majority in the Parliament objected to the three years service. Then came the general elections of 1861, which gave a majority to the party of progress. The middle classes, who had the greatest electoral power, were strongly opposed to militarism. Annoyed by some contemptuous remarks of Von Roon, the new chamber rejected the budget which provided for the increased army estimates. A constitutional crisis followed. An open conflict between the king and parliament seemed imminent. The king had three alternatives, he could either abrogate the constitution or dissolve the legislature and rule like an autocrat. He could give up the idea of carrying out army reforms or he could abdicate. Von Roon felt that Bismarck was the one man who might pilot prussia through the great storm that threatened. He induced the king to get rid of his present ministry, and to entrust the government into Bismarck's hands. Bismarck was very unpopular as an ultra-monarchist who didnot disguise his contempt for parliamentary rule, and for a time king william hesitated to defy public opinion. Bismarck was at that time prussian diplomatic representative at Paris. When Bismarck was summoned to the palace he found the king with a written abdication before him on the table, but before the end of the interview, the document was torn up. The new president (Bismarck) declared on his side unyeilding opposition to parliamentary claims. He said, "I will rather perish with the king, than foresake your majesty in the contest with parliamentary government."

Otto Von Bismarck

The man now entered upon the stage of European politics was one of the most remarkable character of his century. Bismarck whose life from 1815-1898 practically covered the 19th century, was the greatest man the age produced. By birth, breeding and outlook he was a "Junker"- a Prussian squire. Born in 1815, he came of a noble family in Brandenburg. Educated at the gymnasium of Berlin and at the universities of Gottingen and Berlin, Bismarck was destined for a diplomatic carrer. In 1845 he became a member of the provincial diet of pomerania, which he represented in the imperial Diet of Berlin in 1847. During the revolutinary year (1848) he revealed himself as a strong conservative and devoted to the monarchical idea. He said, "my historical sympathies remained on the side of authority. He shared the prevailing sentiment infavour of German unity, but in the methods to be followed he held very different views from the mass of his contemporaries. Bismarck wanted to strengthen the king of Prussia unlike

Cavour in Italy, Bismarck was enraged when the king granted a constitution to Prussia. He hated democracy as he hated Parliament and constitution. He said; "I look for Prussian honour in Prussia's abstinence before all things from every shameful union with democracy". He was opposed to the acceptness of the Frankfurt Crown. He wanted German union but not at the cost of the Prussian monarchy, the Prussian army or the prussian tradition. He said, "We all wish that the prussian eagle should spread out its wings as guardian and ruler from Munich to the Donnersberg Diet. Prussians we are and Prussians we will remain". The failure of the Parliament of Frankfurt, filled him with a savage joy. Above all, he believed in force rather than abstractions.

In 1851 he joined the diplomatic service and from 1851-59 was a member of the German diet. As early as 1853 he told his government that there was no room in Germany for both Prussia and Austria. From 1859-62 he was prussian ambassader to Russia and in 1862 he was transferred to paris in the same capacity. So he was able to correctly asses the weakness and strength of both Russian and France. His great opportunity came when he was called upon by the king to head the ministry. As Minister President, Bismarck's views were in perfect consonance with those of his king William I. They were two fold, Prussia must take the lead in the matter of German unification and oust Austria from the German confederation by force. And Germany must be Prussianised, rather than that Prussia should loose its identity in Germany. For the inevitable struggle with Austria, he steadily prepared. He developed friendship with the minor sovereigns by strenthening their economic ties with Prussia.

The appointment of Bismarck–a bully and an absolutist–merely lashed the opposition to greater rage, but Bismarck was unmoved. He said; "Germany is looking not to prussia's liberalism, but to her power–– The great questions of the day will not be decided by speeches and majority resolutions, but by Blood and Iron". At first he tried to woo the liberal members of the parliament, but when they didnot respond favourably he ignored the parliament and continued to build up the army in the teeth of bitter antagonism. He governed the state without a legal budget. The liberals barked, but didnot bite, and Bismarck, undaunted, went along with his scheme. According to ketelby, "Bismarck was an artist in politics, selecting and moulding his material to his designs, and oppertunist of means, not of ends, grasping his chances with acute vision and a nice calculation, utilising them without scruple as they suited his purpose".

Bismarck had definite aims, Germany must be united and the unification must be effected under the dominant leadership of Prussia. But Prussia would never be able to assume the leadership of Germany as long as there was Austria to thwart her projects. Hence Austria must go, and as She would not go voluntarily, war was necessary. So he now pursued a policy to isolate Austria. He began by courting the friendship of Napoleon III, the enemy of Austria, and for the purpose, concluded a commercial treaty with France, and giving her favourable terms. Bismarck offered prussian help to Russia in 1863, at the time of the polish revolt. He said, "Prussia must never let Russia's friendship wax cold. Her alliance is the cheapest among all continental alliances, for the eyes of Russia are turned only towards East". Having built up the army and assured himself of Russian neutrality, Bismarck now set about to achive his cherished aim, the unification of Germany under Prussian leadership. He was fully aware that the process of German unification could only be achived by wars and he was now ready for the impending struggle. In order to strengthen her hold on the German confederation, Austria proposed to hold a congress of the princes at Frankfort and invited Prussia to attend it. He insisted that King William I of Prussia should not attend the congress of German princes which, had summoned to consider proposals for the reform of the German conferation. The king was anxious to accept Austria's invitation to attend, but Bismarck with great difficult dissuaded him. Due to Prussia's refusal the congress came to nothing. Bismarck wrecked Austria's plan of reforming the fund. Thus Bismarck scored a diplomatic victory and now precipitated a crisis which led to a war with Denmark

The Schleswing and Holstein Question

According to Hazen, "The German empire was the result of the policy of "Blood and Iron" as carried out by Prussia in three wars which were crowded in to the brief perid of six years, the war with Denmark in 1864, with Austria in 1866, and with France in 1870, the last two of which were largly the results of Bismarck's will and his diplomataic ingenuity and unscrupulousness, and the first of which he exploited consummately for, the advantage of Prussia". The Schleswig- Holstein question has become a byward for obscurity. It is like some intricate trial at law where the opinion of the onlooker changes with the addresses of the differnt advocates. The Duchies of schleswig and Holstein were attached to Denmark for Centuries together. TheDuke of Schleswig-Holstein became the king of Denmark by heriditary right, but the duchies maintained their separate government. The population of Holstein was mainly German, and in Schleswing, half the population was German. Holstein was a member of the German confederation, but not Schleswig. The two duchies were, according to the German theory indissolubly united. In 1460 count christian of oldenburg, who in 1448 had become king of Denmark was elected duke of Schleswing and Holstein, by the estates of those duchies. But the union between the crown of Denmark and the duchies was not organic, and its personal nature was still further emphasised by the Lex Regia of 1665. The personal union continued until the death of Fredrick VII in 1863.

The Danes, had made strenuous efforts to get the duchies organically in-corporated in the kingdom. The duchies, however, resisted incorporation, and in 1848 rose under Fredrick of Augustenburg, prince of Schleswig - Holstein, and declared their independence. - Holstein were thus caught up in the great wave of national enthusiasm which was now sweeping over Germany, and henceforth their fate was intricably interwoven with the destinies of the German nation. The dispute threatened to develop into a major catastrophe and the great powers intervened. By the protocol of London, the following agreement was reached, Fredrick VII, king of Denmark was recognised as the Duke of Schleswig and Holstein, but the Duchies must remain separate. The position of Holstein as a member of the German confederatin was not touched. The Duke of Augustenburg renounced his claim on payment of a handsome compensation. This compromise proved unworkable, and the relations between the German confederation and Denmark grew more and more strained. The controversy regarding the Duchies was extremly nebulous. Palmerston remarked that only three people were fully acquainted with the truth, the prince concert of England, who was dead, a German professor, who was in a lunatic asylum, and himself, but, he had forgotton it.

In 1855 king Fredrick annexed Schleswig to the Danish kingdom. By a royal charter schleswig was absorbed in the Danish kingdom in March 1863, and although Holstein still maintained its independent position, it was exploited financially in the interest of the whole State. This involved a two fold infringement of the treaty of London, firstly Holstein was not consulted in the matter, and secondly the rights of the German confederation were disregarded. Besides, the two Duchies, there was the question of succession to the throne as king Fredrick VII was childless. These questions were taken up at the Diet of Frankfort and it urged Denmark to withdraw the charter of 1863. In the matter of succession the Diet supported the claims of Fredrick, the Duke of Augustenburg.

The matter became complicated when Fredrick VII died on November 15, 1863. Prince Christian of Gluckesburg ascended the throne of Denmarak, but the assemblies of the Duchies announced their separation from Denmark, and proclaimed Fredrick, the Duke of Augustenburg as their ruler. The new king of Denmark put the draft constitution in force in violation of the London treaty and in opposition to the wishes of the German confedration. This gave Bismark an oppertunity which he well know how to turn to the benefit of prussia. The events of 1848 had shown that prussia needed an ally in the event of European interference. He therefore induced Austria, whose fears of Napoleon's Italian - policy made her anxious to cultivate the friendship of prussia, to accept the proposal for a joint intervention in the duchies. In interfereing in this affair, he was guaging European opinion and the extent to which they could be isolated. If victory comes it would help him silence his opponents in prussia. The joint Austro-prussian exercise against Denmark would negate the idea of German confederation as legally Austria and Prussia had no right to declare war without the sanction of the Diet of German confederation. Bismark calculated that the arrangement of the Duchies after victory would contain germs of discord between Austria and prussia providing him in the future an oppertunity to drive-out Austria from Germany. And finally he coveted the duchies. According to Marriot, "Bismark could count, thanks to Poland, on the active sympathy of Russia, upon the stupidity of the Hapsburg, upon the anxiety of Lord Russel to avoid war at any price. Even Napoleon looked kindly upon Prussia's action if it was calculated to embroil her with Austria". He had no wish to march the Diet. As a signatory of the London treaty he was bound in advance to recognise christian, on the risk of giving offence to England and Russia. It was no attraction for him that the young pretender (Duke of Auguestenburg), a liberal and a friend of crown prince, should rule over a new German state which would certainly act as a check upon prussia. He wanted the duchies for his master. Then both Austria and Prussia entered strong protests against the infringement by Denmark of the arrangement of 1852, and delivered an ultimatum to her, demanding the repeal of the constitution recently, proclaimed. But as the Danish king refused to consider the ultimatum, Prussia and Austria declared war. An Austro-Prussian army invaded (January, 1864) Denmark and completely defeated the Danes, and compelled christian to sue for peace. By the treaty of Vienna the Danish ruler ceded his rights over schleswig and Holstein and over the small duchy of Lauenburg to the victorious German powers. According to Grant and Temperly, "In these tangled events lie the beginnings of that condition of things in Europe which led at once to two major European wars and then forty years later to the first world war. Europe failed France and France failed England and both failed Europe. The triumph lay with Bismark alone. He had laid his hand on the heart of Frnace and detected the inertia of England. He held Russia by the memories of the polish question".

After Denmark's defeat, Austria and Prussia tried to decide the ultimate disposition of the territory. What Austria wanted was a joint Austrian and prussia-n occupation of the disputed regions. But the future of Schleswig and Holstein was kept vague, purposely, because Bismark forsaw the cause of a conflict between Austria and Prussia over their future status. The lesser German princess supported by Austria wanted the duchies to be united under the duke of Augustenburg and to remain with the confederation. But prussia maintained that by the traty of Vienna she and Austria alone had the right to decide the future of the duchies. At the same time Bismark agreed to recognise the Duke of Augustenburg on terms which would have meant the complete subjection of the new principality to Prussia, in foreign affairs and military organisation. The Duke refused the offer. War seemed imminent between the two great German powers. But in August 1865 the convention of Gastein "plastered over the cracks" and the partners divided their spoil. Prussia was to administer schleswig, and Austria Holstein.

The convention of Gastein was a great diplomataic triumph for Bismark. It gave Bismark splendid opportunity to engineer irritating plot against Austrian Rule.

The Austro - Prussian War - 1866

The Schleswig - Holstein Question was a mere stepping stone, and Bismark had not lost sight of his aim of driving Austria from Germany. He wanted to expel Austria from the German confederation in order to achive German unification. The Gastein arrangement contained many seeds of discord out of which would give prussia the hagemony of Germany.

Austria under the Hapsburgs had been enjoying the leadership of the German States for centuries together. The rise of the Hohenzollerns in Prussia in the 19th century brought a strong rival into the field. The ascendency of Austria was bitter-ly resented by the Germans because she had been responsible for the supression of all liberal movements. The Prussians felt that they would not be able to remove Austria from this ascendency unless Prussia became a strong military state. The leadership of Germany was offered to Prussia by the Frankfort Parliament during the revolution of 1848. But king Fredrick William IV was afraid of Austria, and did not venture to ignore the dignity of the emperor. But his son William I was a man of different type. In the war of Italian independence William I offered the services of the Prussian army to Emperor Francis Joseph of Austria against France on condition that he himself should be placed at the head of the whole federal forces of Germany. The emperor refused the offer and William I considered refusal as an attempt on the part of the emperor to prevent Prussia from becoming more important in Germany. The personal and political relations of the two rulers were thus embittered, and the war dealt a heavy blow at prestige of Austria - king

William I therefore resolved to perfect his army scheme. Bismark, the new minister fully sympathised with the ideas of the king, and had realised during his stay at Frankfort that Austria was the determined enemy of Prussia. Austria must be driven out from Germany to make Prussia the leading power and this was possible only by means of war. With this object in view he began to cultivate the friendship of the minor sovereigns, and to adopt a more independent and bolder diplomacy in the wider Eurpean sphere. The Schleswig–Holstein question afforded an oppertunity to pickup a quarrel with Austria.

In 1862 Bismark made his famous "Blood and Iron" speech clearly stressing the need of a war with Austria. So one may take 1862 as the date line from with Bismark nourished the idea of a war with Austria. But, infact, Bismark spread his diplomatic net after the convention of Gastein with a view to force Austria out of Germany. The Gastein arrangements with regard to the duchies contained many germs of discord, out of which Bismark deliberately set himself to produce a war that would yield the final conclusion to the problem of Germany. Further, in order to achive German unification, Bismark wanted to expel Austria from the German confederation. But the confederation had been created by the Congress of Vienna. So any attempt to dislodge Austria from her leadership of confederation was likely to invite foreign intervention. So, before embarking on a war with Austria, Bismark desired to isolate Austria. He turned to diplomacy, and the result was an interview with Napoleon III, and an alliance with Italy. The attitude of France he regarded as most important, Consequently, he took occassion to seek a conference with Napoleon III at Biarritz (October 1865). Nobody knows what exactly passed there, but there is little doubt that Napoleon encouraged Bismark to proceed with his scheme for an onslaught on Austria in conjuction with Italy, and suggested possible cession of Rhineland territory to France to balance Prussia's gains. Bismark played on the vanity of Napoleon III and his love of nationalism and dangled before him all sorts of baits. He proposed that he might allow Napoleon to annex Belgium or Luxemburg, or even the Rhenish provinces if he remained neutral in a struggle between Austria and Prussia. But nothing was committed to paper, and Napoleon's apparent neutrality was gained. According to Ketlby, "Bismark seems to have freely offered what did not belong to him–His aim was clear enough - to secure French neutrality without any awkward bills of exchange which might be presented for payment". With regard to Russia, Bismark had played his moves in the political game of chess long before, in the St. Petersburg days, in the crimean war, and in the polish rising, and he now counted on the close understanding which he had established with the tsar to bear its fruit. The attitude of Great Britain towards German nationalism which was symbolised by Prussia was one of sympathy and by introducing a policy of free trade, Bismark further won over British support. In April 1866 victor Emmanuel (Italy) came to terms with Bismark. Italy was to declare war on Austria if war broke out between Austria and Prussia within the next three months.

Bismarck's preliminary preparations for the decisive conflict with Austia were now complete. It was not difficult on the part of Bismarck to find pretexts. The treaty of Gastein proved a most convenient aid. Prussia protested vigorously against Austria's method of administering Holestein. Austria resented the criticism. Relations between the two powers thus became strained to the point. Bismarck did not want to declare war on Austria on the issue of the two duchies; instead, he preferred to be fighting for the question of the reform of the German confederation, and therefore in April 1866, Prussia proposed the following reforms in the German diet: - A German national Parliament should be elected on universal suffrage, Austria should be excluded from it. The new confederation should negotiate a special treaty with Austria. The supreme command of the army of the new confederation shoul be vested in Prussia. By shifting the ground of dispute he hoodwinked the powers and averted their intervention. Bismarck was still waiting for the provocaion to come from Austria. Finally, Austria brought the Schleshing-Holstein Qustion before the Diet. At once Bismarck declared that this was a breach of the treaty of Gastein. Austria moved in the Diet that the federal forces be sent against Prussia. Prussia, thereupon, seceded from the confedration and declared war (16th June, 1866) upon Austria, appearing to take up arms in self-defence.

The Seven Weeks War

The war was short and sharp. It lasted less than two months. Von Roon's preparations had been made with meticulous care, the machinery of mobilisation worked efficiently, and the new"needle-Gun" with which the Prussian infantry were armed proved immensely superior to the old fashioned weapon still used by their opponents. Hanover and Saxony lay helpless in the prussian grasp before they realised that the war had begun. At the great battle of Koniggratz (3rd July, 1866) Or Sadowa, the Austrians were decisively defeated. The result of the campaign might have been very different but for the fact that an Austrian army corps was engaged in Italy. The defeat of the Italians at Custozza had very little effect on the course of the war. Bismarck fearing the intervention of powers, pressed for speedy negotiations with Austria. The war was closed by the treaty of prague signed in 1866.

The Treaty of Prague and its Results

The negotiations were conducted through the mediation of Naoleon III. He had expected that Austria would be successful aftera severe struggle in which both combatants would be so exhausted that he would be able to dictate practically what terms he chose, and in a position to claim valuable terrirorial concessions for France. Prussia's overwhelming success came as a thunderclap to him, and sadowa was almost as great a disaster for France as for Austria. As matters stood, Bismarck held all the cards in the diplomatic game, and he played them with masterly astuteness. According to ketelbey, "The day after Sadowa Bismarck had already remarked. Now is the time to restore the old friendship with Austria–My chief concern was to avoid anything which would impair our future relationships with Austria". Hence he offered very liberal terms to Austira- Schleswig and Holstein were to go to prussia, The German confederation was dissolved and a North German state under the leadership of Prussia was established. A very small war indemnity was imposed on Austria. Venetia was annexed by Italy. The southern Geman States were to be permitted to form an association of their own.

Having exclued Austria from Germany, Bismarck proceeded to make a new organisation of the German States on the basis of Prussian supermacy. In order to give formal effect to this supermacy, Prussia laid before the North German States the draft of a treaty which was eventually accepted by twenty two states. A constitution drafted by their plenipotentiaries at Berlin was approved by a constituent assembly, and was than submitted to and accepted by the Parliament of each separate state. The king of Prussia was heriditary head of the confederation. He appointed its officials and controlled them through the Chancellor. The Chancellor was not a prime minister dependent on the support of an assembly. He dependent wholly upon the king. Bismarck became the first Chancellor of the North German confederation. The council of the Confederation (Budesrat) consisted of the representatives of the different states of the confederation. They represented the government. The Reichstag or the lower house would be composed of 297 members elected on the basis of universal suffrage for three years. Most significantly, Bismarck, the Chancellor was the keystone of the new constitutional arch. The Austro-Prussian war opened a new epoch in central Europe. When Bismarck returned to Berlin he was greeted with enthusiastic cheers. Prussians were so intoxicated by the sense of power emanating from the mighty military machine which his policy had given them that it required the miseries of the great war to sober them. Henceforward, Bismarck could rely on the support of the bulk of the nation in his work for the consolidation of Germany under Prussia. All on a suden Prussia sprang to the front as a great military power and her astounding victory profoundly altered the historic balance of power. The Prussian victory had a profuond impact on political life within Prussia. Bismarck was the man of the hour, the great hero who had extended Prussia's power. Bismarck recognised the great appeal of nationalism and used it to expand Prussia's power over other German States and to strengthened Prussia's voice in European affairs. By heralding his state as a champion of unification, Bismarck gained the support of Nationalists throughout Germany. Prussia's victory over Austria, therefore, was a triumph for conservatism and nationalism and a defeat for liberalism. The liberal struggle for constitutional government in prussia collapsed. Enthralled by Bismarck's achivement, many liberals abandoned liberalism and threw their support behind the authoritarian prussian state.

The war had equally decisive effects in Austria. The shock of defeat had shaken the ramshackle empire to its foundations. Several attempts had been made since 1848 to reform each of the provinces and a central council of the empire were created to advise on financial matter. But the Magyars would not be satisfied with anything short of their old national independence under the Hapsburg monarchy. Theyrefused to send representative to the central council and remained in a state bordering on rebillion. There is litle doubt that if the war of 1866 had gone on a little langer Bismarck would have stirred them into breaking away from the empire. The Slav peoples - Czechs, poles, Serbs and crats - were also restless and the emperor now realised that the only way to hold his empire together would be to admit the Hungarians to a partnership in ruling these subject races. An outcome of the war which had even more momentous consequences was Bismarck's friendly hint to Austria that, as Prussia could no longer allow her to dominate Germany, she should turn her attention to the Balkan peninsula.

Napoleon entirely failed to extract any advantage for France out of the Prussian wars with Denmark and Austria was made a grave matter of reproach in the French chamber. According to Marshal Randon, "It is France search for compensation came too late. The French demand for a Rhenish palatinate, Hesse, for Belgium and Luxemburg, unsupported by force, were rejected with impunity. The Austro-prussian war augmented the unpopularity of Napoleon III. The estrangment between France and Prussia prepared the way for the Franco-prussian war.

Further, by the terms of the treaty of prague, Italy had acquired venetia and thereby advanced one step further towards her complete union.

The Franco-prussian war 1870-71

Prussia emerged from the war with Austria as the leading power in the North German confederation. The prussian king controlled the armies and foreign affairs of the states within the confederation. To complete the unification of Germany, Bismarck would have to draw the south German states into the new German confedration. But the south German states, Catholic and hostile to Prussian authoritarianism, feared being absorbed by Prussia. Bismarck hoped that a war between Prussia and France would ignite the nationalist feeling of the South German, causing them to overlook the differences that separated them from Prussia. The creation of a powerful North German confederation had frightened the French, and the prospect that the South German States might one day add their strength to the new Germany was terrifying. Both France and Prussia had parties who advocated war. In France, a party small in numbers, but in-fluencial and clamorous, consisting mainly of clericals, were thirsting to get even with prussia for the gains which Bismarck had not allowed France to share, while in Germany Bismarck forsaw that such a war would be the best means of carrying through the final stage of his great design to weld all Germany together under prussian hegemony.

To France the triumph of Prussia was a most disagreeable surprise. Sadowa had upset all the calculation of Napoleon III. He had expected a long drawn and evenly balanced struggle which would give him an oppertunity of intervention at the right moment and would enable him to extract some territorial gains. But the rapidity of Prussian victory dissipated all his hopes. The French people felt that it was France that was beaten at sadowa. On the other hand Bismarck realised that a Franco-Prussian war must take place before the construction of a united Germany. Bismarck declared that a war with France would succeed that with Austria, lay in the logic of History. The growing tension of public opinion in France and Germany could only have been relieved by a cordial reapproachment between their rulers. But there was no possibility of this, and a single spark sufficed to set the two countries aflame.

Meanwhile, Bismarck had been busy even before the treaty of prague was signed, staging the next series of diplomataic manoeuvres which would complete the political unification of Germany. He signed treaties with Bavaria and other Southern States that opened them to Prussian influence. Prussia, resented the sense of grivance felt by France. An occasion for dispute was speedily grabbed. Napoleon III, egged on by his ministers, made a proposal to Bismarck in pursuance of the vague promise made by him at Biarritz before the Austro-Prussian war. This was rejected. Then Napoleon III turned to the idea of Belgium. Another dangerous document in the French ambassoder's handwritting was added to Bismarck's collection.

Napoleon's Belgium demand was also met with a smiilar rebuff.

Then Napoleon III made his last bid for Luxemburg, which was with the king of Holland. For some time it was a member of the German confederation and the Zollverein. France demanded the removal of Prussian troops. Holland showed its williangness to sell it provided the king of prussia gave his consent. Bismarck kept quiet and soon passion were roused in Germany. The Germans cried that the land which was essentially German must not fall into the hands of herditary enemies. The king of Holland now refused to sell it, and Napoleon complained that Bismarck had duped him. The failure of Napoleon's attempts to secure compensations lashed the temper of the French people to fury and they talked of revenging Sadowa. When this affair came to be known to European powers, they were shocked by the chicanery of France. Prussia suggested a European congress. Luxemburg was declared a neutral state. But the crisis passed off without war. However, anti-prussian feeling had been mounting France.

Bismarck wanted that France should be isolated before a war on France could be declared. The international situation was highly favourable to his plan and Bismarck took advantage of the situation. Bismarck made an alliance with Russia. In order to ensure her neutrality, Bismarck suggested to the star that prussia would raise no objection if Russia denounced the Black sea clause of the treaty of Paris, Further, Russia had not forgotton Napoleon's III's part in the crimean war. He had also taken care to secure the goodwill of Austria by treating her with great leniency and moderation after sadowa. Austria preferred to remain neutral in a possible Franco-Prussian war. Italy was grateful to Prussia for the annexation of venetia in 1866, but she was annoyed with France, because French troops still garrisoned Rome. Bismarck suggested to Italy that in the event of a French defeat, the French troops would be withdrawn from Rome which she could occupy at the oppertune moment. Thus, he secured the neutrality of Italy, Britain was alarmed by the French unscrupulousness. Thereby he ensured English neutrality in a Franco-prussian conflict. He also secured the support of the Southern German states by revealing to them Napoleon's design on the palatinate. One by one the countries of Europe declared their neutrality. Deiplomatically France was isolated.

Immediate Cause of the War–The Question of Spanish Succession

By the beginning of 1870 the Prussian preparations were complete, and all that Bismarck needed was a suitable reason for war. It came over an issue with which neither Germany not France had any direct concern. Queen Isabella of Spa-in whose reign had begun with the unsavoury incident of the Spanish marriages, had made herself impossible as a sovereign. Pleasure loving, ignorant, wilful and superstitious, she had fallen under the influence of a reactionary clique of clerics and courtiers. Meanwhile, Marshal prim raised the standard of revolt at Cadiz (Spain, September 1868) and he was supported by most of the best elements of the nation especially the ammy. The Bourbon queen Isabella fled to France, and a national assembly met at madrid to provide the country with a new form of government. As a republic seemed likely to offend the crowned heads of Europe, it was finally decided to set up a constitutional monarchy. But there was difficulty in finding an eligible prince willing to take over the vaccant throne, until at last an invitation was sent to leopold of Hohenzollern–Sigmariangen. He was a very distant relative of the king of Prussia. When king William (Prussia) gave his consent as head of the family, it seemed as if the matter was settled. France vehemently opposed the candidacy of leopold, for his accession might lead to Prussian influence being extended into spain. William, seeking to preserve the peace, urged prince Leopold to withdraw his name from consideration. So leopold withdrew his acceptness of the crown. Not satisfied with this, Napoleon III instructed his ambassoder Benedetti to seek another interview with king william (Now taking the waters at Ems) and demanded an explicit undertaking that he would never renew the candidature of Leopold or any other relatives in future. Even now the king refused to take offence, he merely sent a message to Benedetti to the effect that, as the prince had withdrawn there was no point in any further discussion of the matter.

Ems Despatch

Bismarck was in despair, the diplomatic structure, constructed with infinite patience and pains, was like to fall about his ears, he decided to resign. The truculent attitude of France was just the pretext for war that he was seeking, and here was the king throwing the opportunity away. On the afternoon of 13th July, 1871 he was gloomily discussing the situation in Berlin with Roon and Moltke when a telegram arrived from king William describing the recent incident. Bismarck saw his chance. In a few minutes his message was ready for the press. By publising the telegram with certain passages deleted he made it appear that the king had been insulted and had refused any further communication with the ambassador in term that could only be a prelude to war. There was great excitement in Paris also at the publication of the report and the Ems despatch had the effect of a "Red rag on the gallic bull". As far as Prussia was concerned the die was cast. In Paris there was the wildest excitement among the populace. The press of both countries fanned the flames with furious diatribes. France felt insulted and clamoured for war to avenge her honour. There were, of course greatey and deeper causes of war then Bismarck's doctoring's of the Ems telegram, but it was the communication prepared by Bismarck for the press at the Berlin dinner table which actually set alight the flames of the great war. On 19th July, 1871, France declared war on Prussia.

The South German States joined Prussia in the war against France. The German army commanded as one unit by Moltke, organised with scientific precision, and equipped with superior artillery and supplies, at once moved smoothly into action. The cumbersome French war machine, lacking clear leadership and surprisingly ilI-equipped for action, creaked and split before the concentrapted power of the German attack. The French suffered reverses after reverses in the battle field. Napoleon tried to check the advance of the Germans at the fateful field of sedon. On 2nd September, 1870. French soldiers surrendered at Sedan and Napoleon III was imprisoned by the Germans. After the victorious German armies rapidly marched on Paris which they encircled and besieged. After a heroic resistance for five months Paris was compelled to capitulate for want of supplies. Finally, the treaty of Frankfort closed the war in 1871. On January 18, 1871 at Versailles, the German princess granted the title of German Kaiser (Emperor) to William I. It was 170 years to a day since Fredrick had assumed the kingly crown of Prussia.

Treaty of Frankfort and the results of the Franco-Prussian War

According to Hazen, "The treaty of Frankfort remained the open sore of Europe after 1871. France could never forget or forgive the deep humiliation caused to it". The provisions of the treaty were severe, France had to cede the provinces of Alsace and Lorraine. France agreed to pay large war indemnity and to allow the German troops to hold a part of France until it was paid.

The Franco-German war completed the unification of Germany. The war made Germany mistress of Europe and Bismarck master of Germany. Germany took her place among the nations. The great victories, won by the united efforts of the states of the north and the south, created the desire for a permanent union, and accordingly king William I of Prussia was proclaimed German emperor. Germany was organised a federal government with an upper house Bundesrath composed of the delegates of the several states and a second house called the Reichstag, elected by the people on the basis of direct and universal suffrage. Thus, German unification had been achived and the dream of German patriots had come true. A powerful nation had arisen in central Europe. The people were educated, discplined, and efficient, its industries and commerce were rapidly expanding, Metternich's fear had been realised, a Germany dominated by prussia had upset the balance of power.

The Franco-Prussian war led to the final completion of the Italian unity. Franch forces were with-drawn from Rome after their defeat, and it was occupied by the forces of piedmont. The historic city of Rome became the capital of italy and the unity of Italy was now materialised. Russia also took advantage of this war and repudiated the Black sea clause of the treaty of Paris 1856.

In France this war led to the creation of a Republic and led to the collapse of the second empire. Republicanism truimphed on Bonapartism. The treaty of Frankfort sowed the seeds of hostility between France and Germany. The Frano-German hostility became one of the main events in the 19th century European politics. Of course, this hostility led to the first world war. Thus, Bismarck completed the unification of Germany, Prussia, prussianised Germany as a result of her "Blood and Iron" policy.

The German Empire-1871-1890

The foundation of the German empire was the most important European event of the 19th century. The result of the unification was a German empire that enabled Prussia to control all the German States and European politics aswell. The birth of Germany Created an entirely new center of gravity in international affairs and represents as complete a break with the Europe (1815-71) as that era represents a break with the ancien regime of pre-French revolutionary days.

The most pressing European problem of the priod 1871-1914 was that of adjusting the old European system to the new Germany- According to Marriot, "For more than two hundred years Paris had been the capital of continental Europe — Europe has lost a mistress and gained a master. The master's home was in Berlin.

The new German empire which emerged from the Franco-German war was no more revival of the Holy Roman empire, with its meaningless and empty claims of universal rule, but a new national state, brought about by successful wars. The next step was to give this state a corporate life, for obstacle to unity were numerous. Among them the non-German elements in the populatin, the religious animosities of catholics and protestants, the jealousy between the land owning class and the middle class of industrialists who had for some time been pushing themselves to the front, and the rise of the working class to political consciousness.

For nearly twenty years Germany was to be ruled by the two men who had brought her into existence.

Though William I was a fine character, but he was 74 years of age, and was content to give a free hand to Bismarck. The real ruler of the country, the director of home and foreign policy alike, was Bismarck. Nobody could have been more fitted than he was to complete the work which he had begun so well. His prestige was enormous, his understanding of the obstacles to unity and the real weaknessess of the Federal empire was very great. He had to build up the political, legal and financial institutions necessary in a new state. His first business was to give imperial Germany a constitution. The constitution of the North German confederation needed little amendment to adapt it to Germany as a whole. On April 14, 1871, the new constitution was promulgated.

The Constitution

The king of Prussia was given the title of German emperor with the power to control the military and political policies of the State. The emperor was the head of the army and navy. He appointed the chancellor, declared wars and made peace treaties with other countries.

The favoured position of Prussia was further strengthened by providing for the emperor's appointment of an impreial chancellor who remained in office during the pleasure of the emperor. The chancellor was the agent of the emperor. The chancellor was the sole responsible official of the state and only the kaiser could get rid of him. The chancellor could address the Reichstag, preside over Bundesrat, and he proposed legislation and executed it.

The legislature consisted of the Bundesrat or imperial council and the Reichstag. The Bundesrat represented not the people of the empire, but the states. Membership in the Bundesrat was not the same for each state but varied according to its size and importance, and all the delegates from a single state voted as a unit. Hence, Prussia with 17 out of 61 votes had a predominating position. On the other hand, the Reichstag or popular house elected by manhood suffrage by the people of whole empire. The election of 236 of the 397 representatives to the Reichstag from Prussia, gave that state a decided advantage in this house also. The aristocratic Bundesrat was the real law making body and it fixed the imperial budget, audited the accounts between the empire and the States and supervised the collection of customs and revenue generally. The Reichstag had no power over the executive branch of the goverment. It was scarcly more than a debating society in which public affairs were discussed but not acted upon.

There was one great federal Supreme Court, the Reichgericht. It exercised original jurisdiction in cases of treason, and was a court of appeal on points of imperial law from the state court.

Unlike Great Britain and France, Germany took hardly any steps towards democracy. Bismarck, Germany's greatest statesman, was an implacable enemy of democratic ideas, and Germany had no long tradition of legal resistance ot the encroachment of the rights of the individual. For the French revolution watchwords of liberty, equality and fraternity, the Germans may be said to have substituted the ideals of system, efficiency and discipline. Their great historical hero was the enlighten diving right monarch, Fredrick, the great. For the long parlimentary tradition of such an institution as the British House of common, the Germans had no feeling. The Legislatures were merely vested with law making powers and they could not overthrow a government by adverse vote. The Reichstag in appearance was democratic, but in reality its power was limited. It had no control over the chancellor. On the other hand, the Bundesrat was a monarchical institution. No equality was maintained between the states in so far as their representatives were concerned. The Government of Germany was not in any real sense parliamentary. And so aristocracy and feudalism flourish not as in Russia. In the late 19th century Germany seemed to many observers in democratic countries to be a huge anachronism, its science and industries leading the world, but its politics sleeping in the 18th century. The empire was in fact Prussianised Germany.

Domestic Policy of Bismarck

In home affairs Bismarck was less the artist and more the dictator. His chief aim was to consolidate and strengthen the empire and to crush its enemies.

There were five important political parties in Germany during Bismarck's chancellorship. Bismarck had the support of the bourgeois national liberal party, and of the free conservative party, which was mainly composed of Prussian landlords. The other major parties were the old conservative, made of largly of old fashioned Prussian squires, Lutheran clergymen and army officers, and the progressive party, drawn chiefly from middle class liberals. The former was too Prussian to sympathise with Bismarck's all German mood, and too reactionary to approve his gesture towards democracy. On the whole, however, they went along with him on most matters. But the progressive, who were pacifist and wanted a really democratic and liberal government, were a thorn in Bismarck's flesh. The Catholic or center party opposed the nationalistic policies and supported the idea of particularism (States Rights), Bismarck opposed the catholics for several reasons.

Bismarck adopted a policy of Germanization towards the submerged nationalities which were included in the German empire, the three and a half million poles on the Eastern frontier, the Danes of North Schleswig, and the nearly two million French men of Alsace and Lorraine. Every attempt was made by him to assimilate these foreigners in the German system. Through process of acculturation, Bismarck tried to neutralise their anti-German attitude. But in fact the Germanising efforts seem merely to have fostered their own national self-consciousness.

Bismarck reformed the legal system of Germany with the help of the Jurist, Delbruck. The laws were codified. Imperial coinage supplanted the coins of the various states and an imperial bank was set up. An imperial railway Bureau unified the state rail road, and coordinated them with the military, postal and telegraph services. At the same time compulsory military service was enforced all over Germany. The peace strength of the German army was fixed at 4 lakhs.

Bismarck's Quarrel with the Catholics–Kultur Kampf or Battle for Civilasation

Almost the only rebuff that Bismarck Experienced during his forty years of public life was in a struggle with the catholic church. This was in essence a renewal of the great "investiture contest" between the popes and Emperors of middle ages–the claim of the state to control the chuch pitted against the chuch's claim to spiritual independence. In this new form it became known as the kulturkampf, owing to an expression used by one of Bismarck's supporters that it was a struggle (Kampf) for civilisation (Kultur).

The circumstances which give rise to it were three fold. Firstly, Prussia was traditionally hostile to cataholicism because, in the long struggle for the mastery of Germany, German Catholics had naturally become extremely active among the industrial working classes, organising them in christian social unions to agitate for reforms, shorter working hours, Sunday rest, factory inspection. This gave great offence to the industrial magnets, who were among the chancellor's chief supporters. Thirdly, Bismarck's ideal was an all powerful government directing all aspects of the national life for its own ends, but the Prussian constitution made the clergy practically independent of the state. Bismarck wanted to control this spiritual gendarmerie, with their vast influence over the minds of their flocks. Besides, the catholic party of Germany was quite powerful. It always received inspiration from the pope and opposed Bismarck. Meanwhile, Pope Pius IX issued the syllabus of Errors and the doctrine of Papal infallibility. By the syllabus, the pope condemned almost all the modern political doctrines as irreligious. In the infallibility decree it was said that the pope cannot err when he defines a dogma. On the promulgation of the dogma a conflict broke out between the church and the state. The promulgation of the decree gave such offence to some German catholics that, headed by a famous theologian and professor named Dollinger they formed them-selves into a separate sect. These old catholics were persecuted by the orthodox clergy and appealed to the government for a support. A religious war was shortly in progress, which grew more bitter every year. Bismarck was in no mood to tolerate papal intervention in state affairs. The German liberals condemned the papal syllabus and supported Bismarck. Prof Virchow named this conflict as a battle of culture because he hoped that the struggle would liberate the German educational system from the control of the Church. Bismarck was determined to subordinate the Church to the State and embarked upon a vigorous anti-clerical policy.

His failure to negotiate a settlement with Rome evoked from the chancellor the famous utternance: "To canossa we shall not go, either in the flesh or in the spirit". He severed diplomatic relations with the vatican, wrested the control of education out of ecclesiastical hands by appointing lay inspectors of schools. He made civil marriage compulsory throughout the empire. Then a series of laws (Known as the May laws because they were passed in the Mays of 1873-75) placed the clergies and their seminaries under state control. It forbade Cataholic priests to coerce individuals by public excommunicataion, it required candidates for the ministry to pass a state examination in general knowledge and to study theology for three years at a Geman university. It ordered the compulsory notification of all ecclesiastical appointments. He made marriage a civil contract and withheld the stipends of all priests who refused to declare their submission to these regulation. Clergy who actively opposed were expelled from their benefices and even imprisoned. This religious discord was in full swing and it continued for about nine years.

Pope Pius IX condemned the May laws root and branch. During these years Bismarck was in alliance with the National liberals. During these years the catholics offered non-violent passive resistance. The result was that the cataholics (the centres) party largly increased their representation in the Reichstag. The long term hope of Bismarck that there might come in to existence a German national chuch did not materialise. Meanwhile other questions were becoming prominent of the econimic and social character, and Bismarck wished to handle them. Particularly, requiring attention in his opinion, and that of William I, was a new and most menacing party, the socialist. Bismarack therefore prepared to retreat. Further, the centre party grew so strong that Bismarck found that he would not be able to carry on the government unless he came to terms with it. Luckily, Pope Pius IX died in 1878 and his successor Leo XIII was a liberal man. He made pact with Bismarck, according to which diplomatic relations were restored between Germany and the Papal States. Bismarck suspended the operation of the May laws, later on they were quietly repealed. The expelled clergy gradually returned to their livings. By 1887 the only traces left of the struggle were the right of the government to inspect all schools, and the permanent establishment of a strong catholic party in the Reichstag. "So Bismarck went to canossa, though by a slow process, but he went there, and then described his journey as a compromise".

Bismarck and Socialism

Bismarck's withdrawl from the contest with the chruch was connected with the beginning of another political campaign against socialism. The industrial revolution had come upon Germany with a rush, causing overcrowded towns, and wages sometimes as low as 8s. for a week of 72 hours. One of the most notable feataures of mass production, in Germany as elsewhere, was the recurrence of trade depression, causing wides-pread unemployment and destitution. One such slump came in 1874, as a result of war indemnity from France, which stimulated a too rapid expansion followed by disaster bankrupticies. All this gave a great stimulus to the socialist movement which had appeared in Germany during the sixties. In the Rhine provinces the leader was Lasalle, who adopted much of the teaching of Louis Blanc, but in Saxony, under Leibknecht, the prevailing doctrine was Marxism - far more drastic and revolutionary. Bismarck looked upon their aims and methods as destructive of the state and the existing social order. Meanwhile, both the parties of Lasalle and Leibknecht united together in 1875 which came to be known as the united social Democratic party. In the election of 1877 the number of socialist deputies increassd to 12. Bismarck regarded the socialist principles as the enemy of the State. Bismarck sought to supress the growing tide of socialism in two ways–to crush it by force and to kill it by kindness. Two attempts on the life of the emperor in 1878, though neither of the assailants was a member of the socialist party, gave an excuse for rushing through severe laws of repression. According to Hayes, "The doctrines which these socialists preached--revolution, class conflict, thorough going social and political democracy, abolition of private property, internationalism and pacifism, were the very opposites of Bismarck's ideas and to him they seemed destructive of the state, the family and civilisataion itself". Bismarck forced through the Reichstag a number of exceptionally severe laws for the suppression of every kind of socialist organisation. In 1878 a law of great severity intended to stamp out completely all socialist propaganda was passed by the imperial parliament. It forbade all associations, meeting and publications having for their object the subversion of the social order, or in which socialistic tendencies should appear. The meetings of the socialists were prohibited, their publication suppressed, their funds confiscated and their leaders arrested. Extensive powers were granted to the police to arrest and deport any suspected person. But secret socities sprang up, and meetings which could not be held in Germany were held outside in Switzerland. Bismarck was defeated by the socialists as he had been by the catholics. In 1881 it won twelve seats in the Reichstag, and by 1890, it was thirty five.

Bismarck also tried to wean the working man from the socialist party by an experiment in state socialism, as it has been called, by proving that the imperial government was alive to its responsibilities towards the artisan class, and would take steps to ensure its welfare. As a junker landlord he Bismark had no great sympathy for the new industrial capitalists. Bismarck thought that by removing the most acute economic grivances of the laboring class, he could make it loyal to the State and immune to socialist propaganda. He introduced a number of legislations for the welfare of the working class. According to Hazen. "Bismarck was a pioneer in this field". The method by which Bismarck proposed to improve the condition of the working class was by an elaborate and comprehensive system against the misfortunes and vicisitudes of life against old age, sickness, accident and incapacity. It was his desire that any workingman incapacitated in any of these ways should not be exposed to the possibility of becoming a pauper, but should receive a pension from the state. In 1883 a law established insurance for workers against sickness. The next year employers were compelled to insure their employees against accidents. In 1887 the labor of women and children was drastically limited, the hours of work were restricted in various industries. Sunday was set aside as a day of rest. In 1889 arrangements were made to insure labours against old age and inability to work. Thus, by 1890 the German workers were better protected against exploitation. It is rightly pointed out that this socialist legislation went a long way in making Germany one of the leading countries of the world in the industrial field. Bismarck's experiment became the model for the social legislation of England and France. So Dawson calls him the first social reformer of the century.

Policy of Protection

Bismarck brought about a profound change in the financial and industrial policy of Germany by inducing parliament to abandon the policy of a low tariff and comparative free trade, and to adopt a system of high tariff and pronounced protection. He was probably the first statesmen of the principle of free trade. With that adject in view, he gave up his alliance with the National Liberals and joined the centre party. In Germany there set in towards the end of 1870's period of agricultural depression which hit the landed interest. The agriculturists demanded protection against the competition of the new world. Moreover, the imperial finances were as hard hit as those of individuals. The French indemnity had proved a doubtful blessing to Germany, it had inflated the currency, raised prices. Bismarck accordingly had recourse to a tariff, alike to give him a revenue and to afford protection to agriculture and industry. By an Act of 1879, a wall of high tariff was created against the foreign imports to protect the German farm products and domestic manufactures. Bismarck's tariff policy had the effect of strengthening the Central Governments and tightening the bonds of the empire. The result of the policy of protection was that the infant industries of Germany were protected and after the lapse of sometime were able not only to their own legs but also compete in every nook and corner of the world. Due to the protection policy, employment increased, wages rose, the output of shipping increased and exports rose. His fiscal policy gave a powerful stimulus to the rising party of social democrats and forced him to come to terms with the catholics. But the tariffs certainly strengthened the government and unified the empire.

Colonial Policy

Bismarck declared in 1871 that Germany was a "satiated country". But soon after the formation of the empire there arose within Germany a demand for colonies. Bismarck opposed it for a long time on the ground that it would complicate his continental diplomacy. But soon after 1880 the importance of overseas territories as markets and as sources of raw materials led him to change his views. The change in the policy of Bismarck was largly a result of the adoption of the policy of protection and active governmental encouragement of manufactures and commerce. The patriots also demanded colonies to add to the glory of their country. Further, Germany needed colonies to settle her rising population. In 1879, a German trading company got some privileges in the Island of Samoa and in 1882, the German colonial union was formed. In 1884, Bismarck adopted a vigorous colonial policy. In 1884 Germany seized a number of points in Africa, in South West Africa, Togoland, Cameroon, East Africa, the Marshal Islands, a part of New Guinea. Thus, Germany joined in the European scramble for the partition of Africa.

Bismarck's Foreign Policy (1871-1894)

In foreign affairs Bismarck remained as ever the supreme artist, both as a statesman and as a diplomat. It was said about him that he was the only man who could juggle with five balls (Austria, England, France, Russia and Itally) of which atleast two were always in the air. With the establishment of the German empire which stood out as the foremost military power, Bismarck as its first chancellor logically relied on the same means to insure the Hohenzollern German empire's preservation. The international situation from 1871-90 was favourable to Germany which Bismarck exploited to the utmost. Germany, he declared was a "satiated" country. Feeling sure that peace would best serve the purposes of Germany he directed his diplomacy towards the avoidance of war and the maintenance of the statusquo. He who had before so fundamentally disturbed the balance of power that was established at Vienna had now become the preserver of a new Balance of power that had been established at Sadowa and Sedan. But he realised that the chief menace of German security was the implacable enemity of France. The loss of Alsace–Lorraine was felt in France as a bitter national humiliation and a spirit of revenge animated all sections of the French people. The keystone of Bismarck's foreign policy was to keep France diplomatically isolated so that she might not secure allies with whose help she might wage a war of revenge on Germany. He realised that the creation of the German empire in central Europe had disturb the balance of power. So any further German expansion would be opposed by the European power, hence Bismarck decided to consolidate the gains. He tried to win over Russia, Austria, England and Italy to his side and kept France isolated, because singly she would not be able to defeat Germany. Hence, he raised no objection to the establishment of a republic in France, because both Russia and Austria abhorred Republican governments. He encourage colonial rivalry between France and England and thereby ensured that there would be no Anglo-French alliance against Germany. He took pains to cultivate the friendship of Great Britain and the two countries were on good terms down to the end of Bismarck's administration. Once Bimsarck declared, there was no reason for war between a land rat and a water rat.

Three Emperors League

The two powers whose friendship Bismarck desired most were Russia and Austria. He knew that any other power which desired a clash with Germany could realy on French suport, and therefore, aimed to isolate France, and in particular to prevent an alliance between her and Austria or Russia. To do this endeavoured to attach these two countries to Germany, and his success is the measure of his consummate ability as a stateman and a diplomatist. His own moderation and foresight in 1866 were now of great assistance, as was the personal friendship of the emperor william I for Francis Joseph (Austria) and the Czar Alexander II (Russia). The prospects of a permanent alliance were strengthened by the fact that, how eyer divergent their interests in other directions, on one point their interests were identical. It was an easy task for Bismarck to persuade Austria and Russia that the revolutionary unrest manifested in the paris commune, German social Democracy, and Russian Nihilism threatened the structure of autocracy in all monarchical countries alike. He exploited, the fears of the conservative powers in order to build-up another Holy alliance. He now arranged for an exchange of ceremonial visits between the German and Austrian emperors. At Berlin the Czar was also present, and there the leauge of the three emperors was arranged in 1872. This resulted in the entente understanding known as the Dreikaiserbund or the three emperors league, but the term is misleading. No actual treaty was concluded, but the three emperors agreed to work together for the maintenance of the boundaries recently laid down, the settlement of problems arising out from the Eastern question, and the repression of revolutionary movement in Europe. The understanding formed the solid bed-rock of German diplomacy. According to Lipson, "Bismarck said that I have thrown a bridge across to Vienna, without breaking down that older one to st. petesburg.

Dual Alliance 1879

In 1874 and 1875 there were war scares caused by Bismarck's desire to provoke a preventive war with France before she should ally with Russia, but the latter, supported by Britian, made it clear that she would not stand by and see France attacked. Faced by such coalition, Bismarck withdrew from his bullying position.

The reopening of the Eastern Question in 1875 made it impossible for Bismarck to continue his policy of a close understanding between Russia, Austria and Germany. In 1876 he refused to give the Czar a guarantee that Germany would remain neutral in the event of war between Russia and Austria, because he did not wish to desert Austria and leave Russia the dominant power in the Balkans.

The Congress of Berlin 1878 caused further disappointment to Russia. After the Russo–Turkish war of 1877, Russia established her ascendency in the balkans by the treaty of sanstefano and Austria demanded a revision of the treaty. On Bismarck's mediation an international congress was held in Berlin (1878) Bismarck who pretended to act as the honest broker in dividing the spoils of war in the balkans favoured Austria which was allowed to keep Bosnia and Herzegovina to maintain order. But the greater Bulgaria, a protegee, of Russia was dismembered. According to the statement of a Russian. "The congress of Berlin is a consipiracy against the Russian people and Russia has been crucified. A fool's cap and bells have been set upon her head". Russia attributed her failure to obtain the fruits of her victories to Bismarck's support of Austria, and the Czar withdrew from the Dreikaiserbund. A regrouping of the powers followed.

In August 1879, Bismarck met Andrassy, the Austrian Chancellor at Gastein and an alliance betterly known as the Dual alliance between the two empires was concluded. Its terms were to be kept secret, and not untill 1888 were they officially published. The compact provided that if either ally were attacked by Russia, the other must assist it with all its forces. If any power, other than Russia, were the assailant, than the ally was to observe neutrality, and was not bound to mobilise until Russia entered the field. According to Marriot, "In plain English if France attacked Germany, Austria must contain Russia".

Revival of the Three Emperor's League 1881

Bismarck was anxious not to break with Russia altogether, for she must at all costs be prevented from seeking alliance with France. In this he had with him the emperor William I, who did not wish for an anti-Russian policy and had Austrian alliance. The new Czar, Alexander III, who ascended the throne in 1881 after the assassination of his father, felt the growing isolation of Russia. Being an autocrat himself he had no love for democratic republican France. Further, Bismarck wanted to reinsure his safety by striving to arrest the alienation of Russia and to restore friendly relations with her. As he declared, "he must keep the private-wire open to St. Petersburg although the public wire had broken." Finally, the Dreikaiserbund was renewed. Austria, Germany and Russia agreed that if any one of them was at war with a fourth power, the other two would observe benevolent neutrality. Russia recognised Austrian interests in the Balkans. Austria promised not to oppose the union of Eastern Rumelia with Bulgaria.They agreed to insist on Turky to enforece her rule on the straits.

The Triple Alliance 1882

In May, 1882, the Dual alliance became a triple alliance by the accession of Italy. This was a remarkable achivement on the part of Bismarck, for it seemed that Italy could have little common with either of the Gemanic nations, on the contrary, her hostility to Austria arising from memories of gaining Italian irredenta was obvious. There was acute rivalry between France and Italy over Tunisia in North Africa Bismarck exploited this rivalry and at one stage hinted to Italy that she should annex it, at another he encouraged France to do so, partly to compensate her for her loss of Alsace and Lorraine. So when France occupied it in 1881, Italy was terribly indignant. Her resentment further accentuated by the demand of the clerical party to France for the restoration of the temporal power of the Pope. Italy was thus thrown into the lap of the Dual alliance and it became a Triple alliance. Italy agreed to support Germany in the event of her being attacked by France, in return for the promise of support from Germany and Austria if she were attacked by France. In case Russia attacked Germany or Austria, with the help of France, Italy would also assist her allies. This treaty was to be effective for five years and it was to be kept as a secret treaty.

The conclusion of the triple alliance constituted a vetriable tripumph for Bismarck. According to Marriot, "Henceforward, German hegemony in central Europe moved securly on the pivotal point of the Tripple alliance, which grew into the one grand combination in the European State system, with which all other possible combinations or entente had to reckon". The triple alliance brought considerable benefit for each of the contracting parties. The triple alliance did not supersede the Dual alliance but Guaranteed Itally against attack by France, while it freed Austria from the dread of a stabl in the back in the event of war with Russia. Serbia and Rumania, by separate treaties, jointed the powers of the Triple alliance in forming a formidable central European block, designed by Bismarck to maintain the status quo.

The Re-insurance Treaty (1884,1887)

Bismarck had failed to keep Russia, Austria and Germany united together on account of Austro-Russian rivalry in the Balkans. But he was eager to keep Russia detached from France. Meanwhile, the tsar's proposal for a Franco–Russian alliance alarmed Bismarck. Hence, he wanted to ensure Russian neutrality if a war broke out between Germany and France. So he concluded the Re-insurance Treaty by which Russia promised to remain neutral if France attacked Germany, and recognised Bulgaria as being within the Russain sphere of influence. No permanent change of territory was to take place in the Balkans without Germany being consulated. The new Friendship of Russia and Germany prevented an Austro-Russian war and a Franco Russian coalition. Thus did Bismarck isolate France and made Germany the arbiter of the international relations of Europe.

The Mediterranean Agreement

Germany and Austria had agreed to differ on the Bulgarian question, and the latter looked around for assistance in checking Russia's ambition in the Balkans. At the same time Italy was disturbed at the growing influence of Boulanger in France, so that when in 1887 the Triple alliance came to be renewed additional agreement were added. Austria and Italy agreed that the existing position in the Near East should be maintained. Another agreement between Germany and Italy stipulated that if France should move to extend her North African terrirtories, Germany would assist Italy in any war that might follow. Italy had further strengthened her position by coming to an understanding with Britain to maintain the statusquo in the mediterranean.

Relations with England

Bismarck maintained freindly relations with England. Bismarck rightly pointed out that there was no reason for a war between a land rat and sea rat, with a view to avoid any conflict with Britain. Bismarck discouraged the growth of the German navy and her colonies. Bismarck did not take any interest in the Eastern question, as he knew that it would create ill-feeling between England and Germany. He was not prepared to risk war with England. On the other hand Anglo-French and Anglo-Russian rivalry often gave him weeks of excellent and profitable sports. On the other hand, England was also maintaining the policy of splendid isolation upto the end of 19th century. Further, there was colonial rivalry between France and England. Bismarck wanted to conclude a treaty with England but Salisbury (British Prime Minister) did not accept his offer. Had Salisbury concluded a treaty with Bismarck, the first world war would have been averted.

Bismarck's authority depended on the confidence of the sovereign whom he had served so long. When Williiam I died in March, 1888, his successor Fredrick II was a dying man and lived only three months more. Yet there was at first no divergence of views between Bismarck and the new Kaiser William II. In 1889, Bismarck asked Salisbury for a definite treaty pledging the two countries to mutual support against an attack by France, but Salisbury was afraid of public opinion. The real cause of conflict between Bismarck and William II was that while the former was determined to maintained his control over the affairs of the state, the latter was determined to snatch away the same. To quote William II himself, "There is only one master in his country, and I am he". The two man parted in a spirit of bitter hatred. Finally, Bismarck submitted his resignation on 20th March, 1890.

Thus, the year 1890 marked the end of the remarkable carrer of Bismarck.

Estimate of Bismarck

According to Marriot, "In the history of the 19th century, Bismarck will always claimed a foremost place, in the sphere of diplomacy no one except cavour could dispute his claim to the first place. That he was a great patriot will be denied only by those to whom patriotism is an exploded superstition. He desired to see Germany united–Germany must be made not by the merging of Prussia in Germany, but by the merging of Germany in prussia. That was Bismarck's supreme aim, and that was his remarkbale achivement." Bismarck had made prussia supreme in Germany and Germay supreme upon the continent of Europe. Before his fall Bismarck had built up for Germany a complicated protective system of alliance and counter - alliance. He had secured Russian neutrality in case of an Austrian attack upon Germany. Austrian neutrality incase of a Russian attack, Italian support against a French attack. It was a complicated system of juggling that needed a Bismarck to work it. Bismarck had wanted war as a means to unify Germany. But after unity had been achived, he wanted peace to consolidate the gains. In pursuit of the object he displayed the same subtlety and dexterity as had charecterised his previous diplomatic carrer. He kept peace and made Europe keep peace as long as he held office. he held in his hands all the string of international policy and manipulated them of to the advantage of Germany. According to marriot, "Every move in a complicated game was carefully planned from the out-set, calculated assistance to Russia in 1863, a quarrel picked with Denmark–– the rupture with Austria and the dissolution of the Bund–– the luring of the emperor Napoleon III–the crushing German victory, the formation of the new German empire–the sequence was logical and unbroken". It is indeed true that he was a strong believer in militarism and relied upon a policy of blood and iron in achiving his object, but he was never a rank jingoist.

According to Ketelby: "But he left for his successor difficult and entangled problems of international relationships. Kaiser William II showed no dipolamtic skill in their handling, but Bismarck himself must bear considerable responsibility for raising or aggravating them." However, he was considered to be the architect of European politics and left his great impression on the era which came to be known as the "Age of Bismarck". Bismarck was an enlightened oppertunits. He believed in the maxim "end justify the means".

He never concealed his plan to establish Prussian predominance in Germany. In shaping the domestic affairs of Germany, Bismarck showed the abilities of a sound statesman. He inaugurated a new economic policy in Germany. He reformed currency, banking and offered protection to German industries. Bismarck's policy of state socialism was a new experiment. Bismarck diplayed a high order of constructive statesmanship which resulted in securing to Germany prosperity at home and predominance abroad. Above all, as a statesman, Bismarck is one of the greatest figure in German history.

Chapter-XI

The Eastern Question

(1815-1914)

The Eastern or Near Eastern or the Balkan Peninsular has always been a international question since ancient times. In one form or another it has furnished the background of European politics. The Ottoman Turks had conquered the Balkan peninsula in the 15th century. The mighty Turkish Empire had once been a terror to Europe. The Ottoman Turks in the prime of their strength had ruled over the entire Balkan peninsula (Asia Minor, Syria, Mesopotamia, Arabia, Egypt, North Coast of Africa). It stretched like a huge crescent round the Eastern and Southeren shores of the Mediterranean from the Adriatic nearly to Spain. There were bitter wars between the Turks and the christian rulers. In 1682 the Turks over-ran Hungary and in 1683 appeared at the very gates of Vienna. But John III, the king of poland defeated the Turks, and the Turkish conquests was halted. With this defeat began a steady decline of the Turkish empire. This stady and gradual fall of the Turkish empire gave rise to an "intractable and interwoven tangle of conflicting interests" and to "the problem of filling-up the vacuum created by the gradual disappearance of the Turkish empire from Europe". The gradual decadence of the Turkish empire raised a number of Knotty problems of international concern, which came to be expressed by the term Eastern question. A Russian diplomat has defined the problem in the following words ; "This damned Eastern Question is like a gout. sometimes it takes you in the leg, some times it nips your hand. One is lucky if it does not fly to the stomach". According to Marriot, "The Turks conquered the peoples of the Balkan peninsula, Serbs, Bulgars, Greeks, and Romans, but the sultan never absorb them. This feataure differentitates the Ottoman conquest from most others of which Europe has had experience. As a result of that conquest, the Balkan kingdoms were destroyed, and the

Balkan peoples were politically buried beneath the supr-incumbent mass of ottoman Turks. But notwithstanding the incubus, the peoples survived, and in the 19th century they reemerged, and one after another, re-established independent kingdoms" In the 19th century, the Eastern Question had four imprtant aspects - the decline of Turky, the aggrandizement of Russia, the national ambition of the Balkan people, and the policy of the European powers about East Europe.

In the 19th century Turkish decline became a historical fact. The government of the Sultan was inefficient, and its mechanism of control of its agents deplorably defective. A process of dismemberment was going-on in Turky. A large loosely organised state was being broken up by the personal ambition of its agents. Further, difference of religious belief was made the basis of the state. The population was divided into two classes, the Muslims and the non-Muslims. The government had never attemped to fuse the two elements. The Balkan christians suffered under the intolerant rule of the Muslim government. In the age of nationality and liberalism, the Turkish autocracy appeared as an anachronism. In the 19th Century the wave of nationalism, liberty, equality and fraternity had already swept across Europe after 1789. Stirrings of nationalism and liberty appeaed in most of the parts of European Ottoman empire. Above all, built up by the sword, Turkish dominion was maintained only by the sword. No ties of common sentiment knit together–conquerors and conquered, and the Turks always remained isolated in the midst of a subjected population.

The problem of the Eastern Question appeared in the 18th century, but then the interest aroused by Turky's weakness and the Southward expansion of Russia at her (Turky's) expense was not general enough to make it a matter of European diplomacy. Russia, since the days of peter, the Great and Catherine, the Great, had been trying to expand Southward at the cost of Turky, and saw in her steady decline, a suitable opportunity to achieve her aim. In the reign of peter, the great, Russia for the first time became conscious of cutting an outlet to the Black sea through the Turkish region. If Russia could penetrate the Black sea region, she could cut a passage through the straits (Bosphorus and Dardanelles) into the ice-free waters of the Mediterranean. Besides, Russia was too anxious to assist the slav peoples of the peninsula. Russia stood forth as the champion of the slav nationality, as well as the protector of the orthodox church. Russia posed herself as the legitimate heir to the Byzantine empire. Russia fished in the troubled waters of the Blakan peninsula and by the treaty of Kutchuk-Kainardji (1774) acquired the right to protect the christian subjects of the sultan.

The policy of Russia converted Austria into a rival and enemy. In the eyes of Austria, Russian ascendancy in the Balkans foreshadowed a great slav empire which would one day absorb all the Slaves of South Eastern Europe. Hence, the integriety of the Hapsburg monarchy seemed bound up with the integrity of the Turkish dominions. On the otherhand, the British and French suffered from Russo-Phobia and would not allow Russia to expand southward, because they feared that Russian influence in the Blakans and her control of the Mediterranean might endanger their communications with the East, England upheed the doctrine of Turkish integrity, which meant preservation of the status-quo in the Near East. While the European powers successfully warded off the perils which threatned Turky from without, they could not prevent the foundations of the Ottoman empire being slowly undermined by the internal weaknesses. Thus, the problem which Europe was called upon to solve in the 19th century was that of obtaining for the small christian nations relief from Turkish misrule without sanctioning an extention of Russian influence, and it was complicated by the Jealousies and suspicions existing among the great powers, and later among the Balkan States.

Nationalist Rising in Serbia

It was the Serbs, who struck first blow for Balkan freedom. A struggle began in 1804 under the leadership of Kara (Black) George, a man of peasant birth. In 1805 Kara George at the head of an oddly assorted peasant army drove the Turkish pasha from Belgrade. He cooperated with the Russians in the war which they waged against the Ottoman empire and by the resulting treaty of Bucharest (1812), the Ottoman Sultan, was obliged to recognise Kara George's government. The Turks recovered Serbia and kara George fled the country. But the rising was renewed under Milosh Obrenovitch, who in 1820 secured recognition from the Sultan as prince of the Serbians. Backed by Russia he continued to press for Serbian independence. By 1829 further concessions were granted to the Serbs and later on complete autonomy of the Serbs was recognised.

The Greek War of Independece (1821-32)

The insurrection of the Greeks in 1821 opened a new phase in the development of the Eastern Question. The Greeks were of three types. The inhabitants of the mainland, the Morea, were half-civilised peasants much given to banditry, the people of the isles of the archipelago were mostly occupied in sea-trading or piracy according to individual taste and the Greeks of the Dispersion were mainly prosperous merchants living in constantinople, Odessa, Paris and London. The Sultan ruled his Greek subjects through their priests, at the head of whom was the patriarch of constantinople. Slavonia and Albanian elements were predominate in their very mixed descent, but geographically and linguistically they preserved the memory of "Glory that was Greece".

The Greeks were a cultured people and they had not forgotton their, ancient glory though they had degenerated considerably. A national awakening roused by poets and philosophers like Korias and Rhegas infused a new spirit in them. The Greek language was purified, a love of old classic Greek was instilled in the people, and natinal songs roused a wave of Phil-Hellenism in them. Birth of national spirit lit the fire of liberty among them. Besides, the Greeks enjoyed greater political autonomy than any of the other christian subjects of the porte (Turkish Sultan). They were allowed to retain their traditional village autonomy and their orthodox church. The tolerant rule of the Turks bred in the heart of the Greeks a spirit of independence. To the Greek revival the French revolution also contributed. Ideas of liberty and nationality began penetrate the Balkans. Dormant memories of sometime greatness began to stir both slaves and Greeks. In 1814, in the Russian city of Odessa was founded a Greek revolutionary society named Philike Hetairia (Association of friends). The society was founded with the object of disseminating nationalist doctrines and fostering insurrection against the Turks. Their hopes rose high when Ali pasha, the Turkish governor of Janina, rebelled against the Sultan in 1821.

The first Greek revolt took place under Alexander Hypsilanti in the principalities of Moldavia and Wallachia in 1821. The news of the Greek rising came to the diplomatists at Laibach (Congress) as a bolt from the blue. But he did not receive the expected help from Russia and was defeated by the Turks. He fled to Hungary where he died as a prisoner in 1828. The rising was suppressed by the Turks. The priests of the Greek Church fanned the flame of revolution. The Ottomans in the Morea were exterminated by the Greeks. The Turks took the revange by killing the Greek Christians in constantinople. The patriarch, the head of the Greek orthodox Church was hanged by the Turks in his pontif dress. This created a strong indignation among the Christian nations. Thereafter national and religious feelings were stirred to their depths in Russia which was the protector of the Christian people. The cry for a crusade rent the sky. In many European countries socities were formed for the purpose of assisting the Greeks with money and troops. For some years both sides carried on the conflict with the utmost barbarity. According to Hayes; "The Greek revolt appealed to the imagination of Europe. Classicists saw in it a revival of the ancient glories of Hellas. Romanticists perceived in it a valorous struggle for national freedom. Liberals beheld in it a popular uprising on behalf of liberty.

Conservatives pictured it as the climax of the long series of Crusades by Christians against muslims. Youthful volunteers flocked to the Greek standard from every country of Eruope. ...Lord Byron gave pen, fortune, and life for Greek independence".

In 1824, the Sultan, Mahmud summoned to his aid his powerful vassal Mehemet Ali, the pasha of Egypt. The Pasha sent a fleet and army under Ibrahim (His Son) to assist the Sultan in the suppression of the revolt. The Morea was recovered, and few places remained to be reconquered. The Governments of Europe were perplexed by the Greek revolt. Meanwhile, Alexander, the Tsar of Russia had made of his mind that he most at all costs save his coreligionists from extinction, but the Tsar died in 1825. He was succeeded by his brother Nicholas I, a selfconfident realist, who placed the interests of Russia a long way before the vague principles of morality which cast such a spell over Alexander. He at once announced that he intended to check the Turks whether he had the support of the other powers or not, Canning, the British foreign minister, alarmed, lest Russia should declare war on the porte on her own account, proposed the joint intervention of the two powers. Finally, Russia, France and England sent a note according to the treaty of London demanding armistice. The three powers proposed in the treaty that the Greeks should be granted autonomy, but should be required to pay an annual tribute to Turky. They pledged to end the war, and were prepared to take some effective measures if Turky did not give any satisfactory reply. When the Sultan refused to accept demands of the allies, the combined fleet of the allies destroyed the Turko-Egyptian fleet at Navarino. The battle of Navarino was accidental, but it was decisive, as it rendered hopeless any further efforts of the Turks to suppress the Greeks revolt, it also registered a distinct setback to Metternich's policy. Wellington ignored canning's diplomacy and withdrew from the war and allowed Russia to fight against the Turks single handed.

The Treaty of Adrianople (1829)

On 20th December, 1827, the Sultan declared a holy war on Russia, Russian forces occupied the principalities (Moldavia and Wallachia) and the Russian fleet entered the Dardanelles, and they reached Adrianople. The Sultan was now forced to sued for peace. By the treaty of Adrianople in 1829, Greece was recognised as a self-governing state under Turkish overlordship. However, the Greeks refused to accept this as a solution of the problem, and in 1832 the kingdom of Greece was recognised as fully independent, with Otto of Bavaria as king. Autonomy was granted to the Serbs. Practical autonomy was conceded to the principalities of Moldavia and Wallachia under Russian protection. Russian title to Georgia and caucaus was recognised. Thus, the treaty of Adrianople was an important milestone in the dismemberment of the Ottoman empire. By the convention of London in 1832, the treaty of Adrianople was confirmed.

Significance of the Greeks War of Independence

The significance of the Greek war of independence was far too extensive. It demonstrated the interest of the great powers in the Nera East. The Greek war undoubtedly augmented Russian influence in the Near East. The treaty of Adrianople confirmed territorial, commercial and political rights of Russia in the principalities. Russia claimed all credit for the independence of Greece. The principle of nationality triumphed over the principle of legitimacy. The liberation of Greece was the first example of the triumph of nationalism. The example of Greece was followed by other nations in the Balkan. The Greek war of independence initiated the process of the dismemberment of the Ottoman empire. The policy of the European powers to resist Russia and protect Turky was marked by the treaty of Adrianople. It was due to the Greek war of independence, the first successful blow was administered to the autocratic Governments of Europe.

The Eastern Question (1829-1854)

The Greek war had an important sequel. After the Greek war of independence, Russia gained a victory. Britain was preoccupied with the independence of Belgium. And France favoured Mehmet Ali. Mehemet Ali was an ambitious viceroy and he was determined to strengthen his hold at the expense of the Turkish empire. Mehmet Ali, dissatisfied with create as a reward for services rendered to the porte, attacked Syria in 1831, and by the end of 1832 no Turkish force barred his way to constantinople. To prevent constantinople from falling into the hands of the rebels, the sultan failing to obtain help from other powers, accepted a Russian offer of assitence. Russian troops landed on the northern shore of Bosphorus in 1833. This roused the jealousy of the French and the British who vigorously protested to the Sultan for seeking Russian help and demanded its withdrawl. But the Tsar refused to withdrew until Ibrahim (Son of Mehmet Ali) retreated. Russian troops were sent for the defence of constantinople, to the dismay of England and France, who now urged the Sultan to come to terms. He did so, granting Syria to Mehmet Ali, and the Russian troops withdrew. On the other hand, Russia induced the Sultan to sign the treaty of unkiar-Skelessi (1833). It had an important secret clause whereby the starits of Dardanelles were closed on the demand of Russia to war vessels of all nations. This treaty marked the Zenith of Russian influence in Turkish affairs and placed the ottoman empire under the military protection of Russia. The treaty of unkiar-Skelessi was a turning point in the attitude of England towards Russia.

In 1839 the Sultan tried to regain Syria and ordered his army to march against Mehmet Ali. But Egypt routed the Turkish armies at Nessib and the Turkish fleet deserted to the Egyptians. In the Turko-Egyptian conflict, the interests of the great power clashed. France in order to extend her influence in Egypt, supported Mehmet Ali. Palmerston, who at this time was foreign secretary in Great Britain realised that, in the absence of British intervention, Russian influence would further extend over the crumbling empire (Ottoman empire) while an Egyptian victory would go far towards establishing that French influence in Egypt and Syria which was threatened forty years earlier, and which was prevented by the victory of Nelson at the battle of the Nile. His policy was to maintain the integrity of Turkey and to prevent Russia from making capital out of the troubled situation by isolated interference. Britain despatched a fleet to blockade Alexandria as a warning to Mehmet Ali, and proposed a conference of power to impose terms upon Mehmet Ali. Consequently, by the convention of London, a quadruple alliance between Great Britain, Austria, Prussia and Russia was formed. France, whose government still supported Mehmet Ali, was not a party to these negotiations and resented them bitterly. Mehmet Ali, depending upon the promises of help of the French Government, disregarded the warning. However the successful operation of the allied fleet compelled Mehmet Ali to submit and to accept the treaty of London (1841).

Under that treaty, the Sultan agreed to confer upon Mehmet Ali, the heriditary Pashalik of Egypt, (and for his life only), and the administration of Southern Syria., including the fortress of St. John of Acre. The Dardanelles were to be closed to the Warships of all nations in time of war. This clause tore up the treaty of unkier Skellessi and thus saved Turkey from dangerous dependence on Russia. Thus, the four European powers (Russia, England, Austria and Prussia) became the guarantors of Turkish integriety. Turky was rescued alike from the open hostility of Mehmet Ali and from the interested friendship of the Czar. The prestige of Great Britain was revived and an understanding was reached between England and Russia. The treaty of London was a great triumph for palmerston and he made it clear that England would tolerate neither the Russian protectorate over Turkey, nor the French protectorate over Egypt. France at the moment stood isolated and her national pride was wounded. No further development of the Eastern question occured and ten years later a petty religious dispute reopened the Eastern question. Dispute in palestine between the clergy of the Roman

Catholic Church and those of the Greek orthodox Church brought the Eastern question to the forefront again and led ultimately to the crimean war.

The Crimean War (1854-56)

As per a statesmen, "All that we here everyday of "the week" (Newspaper) about the decay of the Turkish empire, and its being a dead body or a sapless trunk, and so forth, is pure nonsense. No compromise was possible when the Czar said the Turk was a dying man and plamerston answered non-sense! There in lay the germ of the Crimean war". For 40 years there had been no great war, a long period of peace than Europe had enjoyed for centureis. The great exhibition in Hyde Park (1851, London) was intended to draw the nations still closer together, and Napoleon III at the outset of his regin declared, empire means peace. yet two years later Europe was once more convulsed by war. The underlying cause of it was a revival of the Eastern question.

The crimean war occupies a peculiar place of importance in European history. It has been remarked that the crimean war was in general sense the watershed of European history. After the second treaty of London, Mehmet Ali disappeared from the political stage. The young Sultan, Abdul Medjid, relieved from external pressure, had an opportunity of putting his own house in order. The Sultan granted a charter of liberties, promising security of life, property and honour to every subject irrespective of his religion, creed or nationality. The army too was reorganised and education was encouraged. These reforms infused a new spirit among the Turks but concession served only to whet the appetite for reform. According to Marriot, "The war of creeds blazed out more fiercly than ever, and each sect in turn applied to its external protector, the orthodox to the Czar, the catholics to France. The Quarrels of the Greeks (Orthodox) and Latins (Catholics), were indeed, not the least important among the many contributory causes which issued in the great European conflagration known to as the crimen war".

Rusia wanted the dissolution of the Turkish empire. During a State visit to London, Nicholas, the Czar had a talk with the British foreign minister and he (Nicholas) repeated his proposal of partition of Turkey. But the British foreign ministry did not agree with the Czarist view that fall of Turkey was imminent. The maintenance of the intergrity of Turkey was the traditional British policy and there was no desire to change it. The conversation created a deep distrust of the designs of Russia. It was unfortuneate that England did not sympathetically consider the Czar's proposals. The English government was not prepared to accept the Czar's proposals, for a large majority of Englishmen suffered from Russo-Phobia and were afraid of her expansionist designs. Moreover, having enjoyed a liberal democratic government in their own country, they had an inherent distrust of Russia, which to them was the corner-stone of despotism in the East. Besides, England feared that if Russia was successful in increasing her influence over the Turkish empire, she might create a great hindrance for the British empire situated in India. Lord Palmerston, an influential minister in the Birtish cabinet believed that Russia was eager to upset the balance, so he felt the need of a war with Russia. The British press created an ill-informed public opinion in England infavour of the war. "If ever a war was made by ill-informed but ardent public opinion against better judgement, it was the crimean war".

The great powers to the north of the Danube watched events with anxiety in which ambition and fear both played a part. The empire of Austria owed its origin to the necessity of barring the way against an invader from the lower course of the Danube, and its whole life was closely bound up with resistance to the Turkish power. Fear of the Turkish power had been followed by another–the fear of the power (Russia) which might take Turky's place in the Balkan peninsula. Thus, Austria feared the designs and ambitions of Russia in the Balkan. Austria was opposed to Russia's aggradizement on Turkey.

At this posture of events a quarrel brokeout between the monks of the Greek church and the Latin monks over the custody of the Holy place in Jerusalem. (The christian church is divided into many sects. The Latin or the catholic church is headed by the Pope of Rome, and the orthodox Greek Church is headed by the patriarch of constantinople). Upto the middle of the 18th century the Latin monks (Catholics) were recognised by the Sultan as the guardians of the holy shrines. But during the French revolution the Greek monks had encroached upon the rights of their latin rivals. For decades both the Greeks and the Latins had been using the Church. But while the Greeks had the key of the great door, the Catholics had the key of the side door only. The Catholics now demanded the key of the great door and claimed the guardianship of other holy places. Napoleon III of France, solely for reasons of prestige and glory, seeking to win the French Catholic support, demanded full restoration of the righs of Catholic monks. The Sultan reluctantly conceded to these demands. As expected, it provoked Russia. The Czar Nicholas loathed Napoleon III partly as an upstart and partly as a Bonaparte. Not wanting his power to be supplanted in the Near East by that of the French renegade, the Czar demanded the Turks to withdraw all concessions. Napoleon III saw the dispute a golden oppertunity of humbling Russia and of winning the support of the Catholic party at home. A war with Russia in support of the Latin Monks would suit the purpose to a nicety. Besides, a victory over Russia would gratify French national pride by avenging the humiliation of Moscow. Nicholas, on the otherhand, sought to attain the traditional object of Russia's policy under the cover of the struggle over the Holy places, Meanwhile, the Sultan conceded the French demands, but in doing so invited the wrath of the Czar, who demanded their immediate rejection.

In March, 1853 the Czar despatched to constantinople prince Menschikoff, one of the most prominent figure in the Russian court. He was Charged not only to obtain full satisfaction in regard to the Holy places, but to demand from the Sultan a virtual recognition of the Russian protectorate over all the Orthodox subjects of the porte. Menschikoff's militant attitude unnerved the Sultan and he turned to the English for guidance and advice. Lord strratford-de-Redcliffe, the British ambassorder to Turkey, was a shrewed politician and had gained the confidence of the Sultan. He did not allow the grass to grow under his feet. He induced the porte to give satisfaction to Russia on the question of the Holy places. But the concession made by the porte effected no improvement in the diplomatic situation. Lord Startford advised the porte to refuse the protectorate claimed byRussia over the Christian subjects of the Sultan, which would inevitably lead to loss of independence. In May 1853 Menschikoff left constantinople in protest against this decision. The withdrawl of Meanchikoff from constantinople was a serious step. On July 21, 1853 a Russian army occupied the principalities (Moldavia and Wallachia) Russia there upon announced to the powers that the occupation was not intended as an act of war, but as a material guarantee for the concession of her just demands. Diplomacy made a last attempt to prevent the outbreak of hostilities. A conference of powers (England, France, Austria and Prussia) met at Vienna and drawup a declaration known a the Vienna note. It aimed at Protecting the christian population of the Balkans without admitting the right of Russia to interfere. The Tsar accepted it, but the Sultan encouraged by Redcliffe rejected it on October 5, 1853, the Porte demanded from Russia the Evacuation of the principalities within 15 days, and on October 23, 1853 Turkey declared war.

Russia and the western powers still remained at peace, and the Tsar declared that, despite the Turkish declaration of war, he would not take the offensive in the principalities. The Turks attacked vigorously on the Danube, and the Russian Black sea fleet retaliated by the entire destruction of a Turkish squadron in the boy of Sinope was the immediate prelude to the European war. England and France sent a joint ultimatum to Russia demanding the evacuation of Moldavia and Wallachia. As Russia refused to comply with the demand, both France and England decalred war upon Russia in 1854. Later on, Sardinia-piedmont also joined them. The fighting was primarily confined to crimea and the principal target was Sebastopol. At the battles of Alma. Balaklava, inkerman nothing decisive happened. Storms, blizzards, cholera, and malarial fever took their dreadful toll. While the soldiers toiled and suffered in the trenches amidst crimean winter, the diplomatists were busy at Vienna, and they presented a memorandum to the Russian embodying four points as follows. The exclusive protectorate exercised by Russia over the principalities and Serbia was to cease. The navigation of the Danube was to be free. The preponderance of Russia in the Black sea was to be terminated. And Russia was to renounce all pretensions to a protectorate over the Christian subjects of the porte. Notwithstanding the diplomatic activity, the war went on. But the death of Czar Nicholas I, the prime author of the war, led to negotiations for peace. Both the parties were unwilling to prolonged the war and met in Paris in 1856 to resolve the tangle.

The Treaty of Paris, March 1856

The crimean war came to a close by the peace of Paris, Accroding to the terms of the treaty, the Black sea declared neutralised and opened to the merchant ships of all nations. The Dardanelles was closed to all Warships. Construction of aresenals on the shores of the Black sea was forbidden. All conquests were restored. Russia evacuated part of Bessarabia which was ceded to Moldavia. Russia also returned kars to the Turks. Russia promised not to interfere in the interal affairs of Turkey. Freedom of Moldavia, Wallachia and Serbia under the nominal suzerainty of the Sultan was guaranteed, by the great powers, Russia was made to give up her claims to act as the guardina of the Greek christian subjects of the Sultan. The powers affirmed the independence of Turkey. The powers engaged themselves to guarantee the integrity and independence of Turkey. Turkey was admitted to the consert of Europe. By an addendum to the peace treaty, changes were made in the international maritime law and the powers renounced their right to seize enemy goods carried by neutral ships.

A Critical Note

According to Marriot, "The crimean war if not a crime, was atleast a blunder and it might have been avoided." As a solution of the Eastern question, the war was a total failure. Their's the French Minister lamented that the war was fought to give the key of Grotto to a few wretched monks. So far was the solution of problems of the Eastern question was concerned, the crimean was proved to be a useless war. David Thomson has rightly remarked "It was a fumbling war, probably unnecesary, largly futile, certainly extravagant, yet rich in unintended consequences." The treaty of

Paris was riddled with short lived solutions. The real objective of treaty were never fulfilled but the indirect consequences emanating from the treaty were very important and some unwittingly initiated beneficial developments. The principal objectives of the treaty were containment of the disintegration of the ottoman empire and keeping away Russians from the scene. Russia repudiated the Black sea clauses in 1871. The treaty only postponed Russia's advance against constantinople, it did not destroy Russian ambitions. Hopes of Reform within the Ottoman empire were also belied. Though the objectives of the treaty were never fulfilled, its intended consequences were of importance in Europe. In a sense Turky was the greatest gainer by the Crimean war. She obtained a new lease of life under the protection of the power, her territorial integrity was guaranteed. In repudiating the exclusive protectorship of Russia, the powers assumed a responsibility for the good government of the Christian subjects of the porte which the sultan could ignore only at his peril. The treaty was a great rebuff to Russia. Her expansionist designs received a setback. She was kept back from the Danube by the cession of Bessarbia to Moldavia, and from the Black sea which was neutralised. But though the direct results of the crimean war were barren, its indirect results greatly influenced Europe. It has been remarked that the crimean war was in general sense "the watershed of European history."

Probably the greatest gainer by the war, excepting the porte, was Italy. The intervention of Sardinia in the war not only gave her a place in the concert of Europe, but the right as well as the oppertunity to champion the cause of Italian liberation. In the words of Ketelbey; "Out of the mud of crimea a new Italy was made and less obviously a new Germany". The unification of Italy under the piedmont-Sardinia-house served as a great impulse to the Germans for unification. Though France gained little by the crime-an war, Napoleon gained much. His position was far from assured in Europe, and the crimean war established it. Until the advent of Bismarck his influence upon the continent was supreme. Austria was neutral during the war. But she pursued a policy of hostility towards Russia, who was a sincere friend of Austria during the Hungarian revolt 1848-49. The result was that on times of her need in the subsequent period of her war with Prussia she did not get any help from Russia. Bismarck took advantage of the situation and began to court the friendship of the Czar in order to further his project of ousting Austria from Germany. The war also marked the begining of a new epoch in the history of Russia. It gave a new turn to Russian expansion. The expansion checked in Europe, was transferred to central Asia where she began to push forward with giant strides. The Czar introduced modern reforms in various spheres of Russian life. But one of the important results of the war was the revelation of the weakness of Britain as a military factor in European politics. The war proved that the British economic development and political evolution were not accompained by any corresponding growth in her military strength. Further, at Paris, the powers agreed upon rules governing sea warfare, a development soon grew into the Hague conventions on land warfare, and the general convention on prisoners of war. Europe in the decade after 1848, stood at the parting of the ways. The old concert was dying, the balance of power was beginming to shift, and the new era of realism was dawning Besides, another important development was the begining of a hospital reform under Florence Nightingale, the lady with the lamp. But the crimean war broke the spell of peace in Europe. And within 20 years the Eastern question was again troubling the peace of Europe.

The Eastern Question Upto 1878 from the Treaty of Paris to the Treaty of Berlin-1878

The Crimean war registered a definite set-back to the policy of Russia in the Near-East. It also gave an opportunity to the Sultan to put his house in order. Nothing was done to ameliorate the lot of the Christian subjects. They were continued to be subjected to religious persecution and war victim of Turkish tyranny, mal-administration and fiscal oppression. The superficial calm which had reigned in the Midle East was shattered by a new wave of nationalism called pan-slavism, which aimed at the emancipation of the slav subjects of the sultan. Meanwhile, the union of Moldavia and Wallachia into one kingdom under the name of Rumania came into existence. (1863) Besides, Russia's interest in the Balkan peninsula was traditional. In 1865 she encouraged the people of crete to rise in revolt against Turkish over-lordship. During the Franco-Prussian war (1870) Russia made her reentry in the near Eastern politics by violating the maritime clauses of the treaty of Paris. Further, Turkish mis-government in the European provinces had become a crying scandal. The subject peoples groaned under the oppressiveness and uncertainty of a fiscal system which was as ruinous to the sovereign as it was hurtful to the subject. Eastern question once more entered upon an acute phase. The increasing restlessness of the subject states of Turkey due to their growing nationalist aspirations and the disappointment of all hopes of Turkish revival, certainly precipitated a crisis. In 1875 the Eastern Question was reopened by the outbreak of insurrection among the people of Bosnia and Herzegovina. Then it spread to their kinsmen in Serbia and Montenegro.

The Ottoman goverment was inefficient that the movement continued unchecked, and Austria became alarmed lest it should spread to her own

South Slavs. With the cooperation of Russia and Prussia, count Andrassy drewup a memorandum, which suggested the following remedies. Full recognition should be guaranteed to the christian religion and religious persecution must cease forthwith. In Bosnia and Herzegovina, the economic condition of peasants should be improved by turning them into free proprietors of land. The system of farming the taxes should be abolished. France and Italy signified their agreement with this line of policy. The Sultan accepted the protest and promised reforms. However, the efforts of the diplomatists were foiled, by the attitude of the insurgents. Meanwhile, revolt brokeout in Bulgaria, but an energetic Turkish governor crushed the movement and followed up his success by atrocities designed to cow the people from repeating their attempt. Some fanatic Turks murdered the French and German consults in Salonika. The situation becoming critical. The three emperors of Austria, Prussia and Russia met at Berlin and drewup the famous Berlin memorandum in which they demanded an armistice for two months, the repatriation of Bosnian exiles and fugitives and the removal of Turkish troops from Bosnia. France and Italy gave their assent to the note, but Disraeli refused to be a party to it.

Russo-Turkish War-1877

The situation was now getting more serious. Serbia declared war against Turky on June 30, 1876 Montenegro also joined the war against Turky on July 1876. In Bulgaria about a hundred officials had been murdered and in retaliation the Turkish soldiers had wiped out about 80 villages, and killed many peoples. The Bulgar atroctities created a great indignation in Christian Europe. The affairs in Turkey had also taken a new turn, Sultan Abdul Aziz was deposed and the new Sultan Abdul Hamid had been placed upon the throne by the "Young Turk" party and agreed to an armistice. The Serbians rejected the offer on account of the hard conditions. The Czar in order to avoid hostilities sent General Ignatieff to constantinopole to demand an immediate armistice. But the prospects of peace was shattered by Disraeli (The British Prime Minister), who announced that England was ready to interfere on behalf of Turkey. Russia now made preparations for war. But before declaring war another attempt was made to settle the differences. A conference of the powers met at constantinple and the sultan promised to introduce reforms and did not desire to surrender his sovereign rights over his own subjects. The conference therefore came to an abrupt end. The promised reforms never came about, and Russia had no alternative than to declare war. Before declaring war she sought the help of Germany and Austria. Germany refused to give any help but Austria promised to remain neutral. The attitude of England was inexplicable. The war continued till January 31, 1878, when the Sultan on the arrival of the Russians at Adrianople sued for peace. The terms were embodied in the treaty of San-Stefano on March 3, 1878.

The Treaty of San Stefano

The treaty recognised Rumania, Serbia and Montenegro as independent States, created Bulgaria an autonomous State, provided a christian governor inBosnia and Herzegovina and confined the Ottoman empire in Europe to constantinopole. Russia was to get Dobrudja and some territories in Northern Armenia, in addition to a large indemnity. It was stipulated that Rumania would exchange Bessarabia for Dobrudja and the Turkish fortress in the Danube would be destroyed. It marked the end of the Ottoman empire in Europe. It was a great Russian victory and her influence in the Balkans was restored. But the Greeks opposed the creation of a greater Bulgaria, Rumania was angy at the loss of Bessarbia. The powers were indignant at the publication of the terms of the treaty. They did not like that the problem of the Near East be settled without reference to them. The creation of a greater Bulgaria was Vehemently resented. Further, England denounced the treaty and ordered her fleet to proceed to the Dardanelles. Russia in retaliation threatened to occupy constantinopole. The situation was very alarming, but on the request of the Sultan, the British fleet withdrew and the tension relaxed. But England demanded a revision of the treaty of San Stefano to be made by the European powers. Austria also sided with England in this demand. The warlike attitude of England compelled Russia to agree to refere the settlement of the Turkish question to a congress of European powers. Bismarck, who presided over the congress, promised to play the part of an "Honest Broker". But the congress was dominated by Disraeli (The British Prime Minister).

(Treaty of Berlin-1878)
Provisions

By the provisions of the treaty of Berlin, Greater Bulgaria of San-Stefano was split into three parts. Bulgaria proper from the Danube to the Balkans was made an autonomous state under the Suzerainty of Turkey. Eastern Rumelia south of the Balkans was created a self-governing province under a christian governor. And Macedonia remained under direct rule of Turkey.

Montenegro gained access to the sea and Serbia obtained uskub and Monastri. The independence of Montenegro, Serbia and Rumania was recognised. Bosnia and Herzegovina were to be occupied by Austria indefinitely, with the privilege of garrisoning Novibazare. Russia was paid an indemnity and was given Bessarbia in Europe and Batoum, Kars and Ardahan in Northern Armenia but she gave up her claims to Bayazid. The Danube was neutralised. The porte agreed to undertake extensive reforms in create, Macedonia, and Armenia where lived a large number of Christians. The Jews in Rumania was granted political franchise. Greece was promised an increase in territory to be adjusted later on. England by a separate treaty with Turkey, secured the control of cyprus. To satisfy the objections of France and italy, they were allowed to occupy Tunis and Tripoli respectively.

Significance of the Treaty

If the pece of Paris had maintained the integrity of theTurkish empire, the treaty of Berlin dissolved it, which the powers at least pretend to maintain. The treaty of Berlin did not satisfy the nationalist sentiments of the Balkans. The statesment who design the treaty of Berlin were guilty of disregarding the principles of nationality. The Slaves were terribly disappointed with the occupation of Bosnia and Herzegovina by Austira. The divisions of Bulgaria was a cruel blow to the national aspiration of the Bulgars. It was made to please Austria who feared that the Big Bulgaria of the treaty of Sanstefano would be a satellite of Russia–and might be an obstacle in the future Austrian expansion towards the west.

When the British representative, Disraeli and Lord Salisbury, returned home, the Prime Minister declared that they had obtained "peace with honour". It is to be presumed that Disraeli, by this pharase, meant that British interests in the East had been maintained and that war with Russia had been averted. In the light of subsequent development it is doubtful if the settlement can be regarded as a satisfactory solution of the problem. It was a wrong estimation of Disraeli that Turky would make reforms to improve the condition of the christians. Soon the Balkan powers began to quarrel between themselves. The Balkans, fermenting with national unrest, remained a centre of disorders, rivalries and intrigues. According to Gooch, "The treaty provided no permanent settlement of the tangled problem of the Balkans and most of its signatories left Berlin smarting under a sense of disappointment...Serbia lamented the transfer of Bosnia from the nerveless grasp of constantinopole to the tighter grip of the Hapsburg (Austria), Greece contrasted the nebulous recognition of her claims with substantial awards to her Balkan rivals, and finally Russia saw the precious fruits of her struggle and sacrifices turned off from her by Disraeli and Andressy with the assent, if not indeed, the encouragement of Bismarck, while Austria pocketed Bosnia and Hezegovina as rewards for her inglorious neutrality".

Beconsfield (Disraeli) inflicted a serious check on Russia in Europe, but one of the main defects of the treaty of Berlin was that Russian activity was transferred from the Bosphorous to the frontier of India that added to the worries of the British Government. Lord Salisbury view was that in the congress of Berlin, Great Britain "backed the wrong horse". At the same time, the conduct of Bismarck during the congress of Berlin alienated Russia from Germany. The bitter Russian propaganda against Bismarck was one of the important causes which forced Bismarck to enter into the Austro-German alliance of 1879. It is also pointed out that by ousting Russia from the Balkans, Disraeli introduced Austria-Hungary into the same area. Austria was given the right to occupy and administer Bosnia which caused a bitter rivalry between Austria and Russia. This in the long run gave rise to complication which directly led to the first world war. In the words of Thompson; "The settlement reached at the congress of Berlin had the remarkable outcome that it left each power dissatisfied and more anxious than before–International tension was increased, not eased by the events of these years. The new balance of power now clearly centred on Germany and she was destined to preserve the peace for another whole generation. But it was doomed to be a most uneasy and unstable peace subject to recurrent crises and threats of war. The next general European congress met 40 years later, not in Berlin but in Paris and at it there were to be no representatives of the Dreikaiserbund."

From the Treaty of Berlin (1878) to the Treaty of Bucharest 1913

The affairs of the Balkans after 1878 became more and more complex and began to revealed developments most disquieting to international peace. These developments were due partly to the unsatisfactory character of the treaty of Berlin, partly to the fierce nationalism of the Balkan peoples and partly to the rivalry of the great powers for the control of the Balkan States. No doubt, the treaty of Berlin created a few new States, but the nationalist aspirations of these states still remained unsatisfied. So long as these states did not attain full self government and national unity, the knotty problems of the Balkan remained unsolved. As their claims often overlapped, the Balkan region provided a spectacle of increasing unrest, and frequent wars. Besides the Turkish Sultan Hamid II was an inefficient and weak as devoid of statesmanlike qualities. His short-sighted policy and backward administration increased the urge for independence among the Balkans all the more. The young Turks, a progressive party which had been originally formed in 1891 in Geneva, was now a potent factor in Turkish politics. Further, at the congress of Berlin Bismarck had acted as an "honest broker" and Germany had made no demands on Turkey. Hence, the porte (Sultan) was deeply impressed by the Germans. A period of close diplomatic and economic cooperation began between Germany and Turkey. The treaty of Berlin had given Austria an increased interest in the Balkans by allowing her to occupy Bosnia and Herzegovina. This occupation was a great blow to Serbian national aspirations. An armed conflict seemed imminent. Germany and Austria supported each other on the problems of Turkey. On the other hand, Italy was against the expansion of Austria in South and England wanted to set Turkey free from Russian influence. Naturally the Eastern question became more and more complicated.

It has already been said that the Berlin treaty did not solve the problems of the Balkan States. Big Bulgaria was split by the Berlin congress, but this division did not last long and in 1885 Bulgaria and Rumelia got themselves united. Simultaneously, the Berlin congress had kept Macedonia under Turkey which was a gross disregard of the nationalist sentiments of the Macedonians. It was not only a short sighted un-statesmanlike policy followed by the leaders in the Berlin congress but was contrary to human consideratin to leave the Macedonians under the tyrannical rule of the Turkish government.

The union of the two Bulgairas excited the jealousy of Serbia. She declared war against Bulgaria on the ground that the Bulgarian aggrandisement thereatened the Balance of power in the Balkans. In the conflict that followed Serbia was badly beaten by the Bulgarians.

Greece had become independent of Turkey in 1833. Otto, son of the king of Bavaria had become king of Greece. During his long rule he appointed a large number of Bavarian in Greece. This caused a great resentment among the Greeks. Otto followed autocratic policy which led to revolt in Greece. Otto had to abdicate Greece. His successor George I succeeded in getting Thesaly, but for getting create from Turky, Greece had to declare war against Turkey. Finally, Turkey agreed to return create to Greece, keeping a nominal suzerainty over it.

The Balkan Wars (1912,1913)

Meanwhile, the idea of establishing a league among the christian nations of the Balkans had been mooted in the past, but on account of their political rivalries it had so far been beyond the pale of realization. But in 1812, it was within the realm of practical politics as Serbia, Greece, Bulgaria were anxious about the future of Macedonia. The Common hostility to the Turks now bound them together. Venizoles, the Minister of Greece was a masterly statesman. He formed the Balkan league in 1912. The Balkan league comprised Serbia., Bulgaria, Greece and Montenegro. The members of the Balkan league were roused by Turkish misrule in Macedonia and wanted to save their brethren from Turkish tyranny. They pressed for the execution of reforms in Macedonia and when Turkey refused to concede their demands, they declared war against Turkey. The combined forces defeated the Turkish troops in different parts of the Turkish empire and occupied a considerable areas of Turkey. Turkish empire in Europe virtually collapsed. The victories of the Balkan states forced Turkey to come to terms and the war was brought to a close in 1913 by the treaty of London. According to the London treaty, Turkey ceded almost all her European territory. She was left with constantinopole and a small area round it. Macedonia was partitioned among Serbia, Bulgaria and Greece. Montenegro was not allowed to retain scutari. And a new state of Albania was formed criticising the treaty of London, Marriot has written, "The European concert congratulated itself upon a remarkable achievement, the problem which for centuries had confronted Europe had been solved. The clouds which had threatened the peace of Europe had been dissipated, the end of the Ottoman empire long foreseen and long dreaded as the certain prelude to Armageddon, had come and come in the best possible way, young nations of high promise had been brought to the birth, the older nations were united, as never before, in bonds of amity and goodwill".

After the first Balkan wars, Bulgaria felt very sore over the distribution of the spoils of war. As a result of the treaty of London, Serbia acquired uskub and Monastir, but lost her gains in Albania. Serbia now demanded compensation from Bulgaria for the loss of her territory in Albania, and claimed a part on the Aegean. Both Greece and Bulgaira were dissatisfied over the partition of Macedonia. Consequently, relations between Bulgaria on the one side and Serbia, Greece and Rumania on the other deteriorated. An offensive and defensive alliance between Greece and Serbia was made against Bulgaria. Bulgaria attacked serbia. Meanwhile, Rumania and Turkey declared war on Bulgaria. Surrounded by enemies on all sides she sued for peace. And the second Balkan war came to an end by the treaty of Bucharest. As per the treaty, Rumania got a large strip of Dobrudja including the fortress of Silistria. Greece acquired southern Macedonia, Salonika and Epirus. Serbia got central macedonia and the Eastern half of Novibazar. And Montenegro got the Western half of Novibazar.

Results of the Balkan Wars

According to Grant and Temperley, "No single event influenced the outbreak of war in 1914 more than the Balkan wars of 1912-13, the overthrow of the Turks caused an immediate danger, for it affected the balance of power in the present...Serbia added a million to her population, erased the humiliation of the Bosnia annexation and triumphanatly asserted her prestige in an out burst of the pan-serb and yogoslave enthusiasm, which swept Dalmatia. Bosnia like a prairie fire...The prestige gained by Greece and Rumania was only second to that of Serbia. All three States now looked forward to a time when each flag would cover all their kinsmen in the Balkans...A perpetually increasing nationalistic agitation in Austria, Hungary and Turkey, where such agitatin was so dangerous was the direct result of the Balkan war". In fact, the Balkan wars were a prelude to the European war of 1914.

Serbia now regarded war against Austria-Hungary, as inevitable, Extreme Serbian nationalists formed the "Black hand society", a secret organisation dedicated to effecting the restroration of Bosnia-Herezegovina to the motehrland. The war cannot be said to have solved the Balkan problems. The second war was a fratricidal one and intensified the rivalries among the Balkan states. Bulgaria felt a deep grudge against her neighbours who had deprived her of territories and looked to Austria and Turkey as possible allies. Russian influence in the Balkans was strengthened since– Turkey lay crushed. The rivalry of the great powers and the growing nationalism in the Balkan region proved a prelude to much greater conflict. The Balkan wars also led to Dissolution of Turkish empire in Europe. In June 1914, the archduke Francis Ferdinand, the heir to the throne of Austria, was murdered at Sarajevo, the capital of Bosnia. The incident provided Austria with an ideal pretext, since she chose to regard the murder as inspired by the Serbian Government. Russia promised to halp Serbia, whereas Germany took up arms on behalf of Austria. Thus, the European war began.

Chapter-XII

The Expansion of Europe

From the long perspective, European history has been one of expansion. In the 16th century, Europeans conquered and settled substantial regions of the Americas. From the 16th to the 18th centuries, Europeans made inroads in South-East Asia and Africa from lucrative trade in spcies, silks; etc. For much of the 19th century, Europeans showed little interest in adding to the remnants of the 18th century empires. Advocates of free trade argued that commerce would go to whichever country could produce the best goods most cheaply. Efforts to add colonies would be better expanded in improving industry, they said. "They also hoped Europeans had grown too civilised to flight over trade networks. Nonetheless, European influence over the rest of the world grew in the 19th century. As European nations industrialised, world trade expanded greatly. The expansion of world trade and the spread of Western ideas along with Western technology continued to take place even without extension of political empire. Yet at the end of the century, the European presence shifted abruptly from commercial penetration to active conquest, political control, and exploitation of previously untouched territories. Europeans confronted each other, willing to fight over stretches of desert or rain forest. Asians and Africans who could not resolve conflicts among themselves found their lives controlled and land occupied. In the last two decades of the 19th century, European nations very rapidly laid claim to Africa, seizing goods, annexing territories, and carving-out empires. Westerners exploited the weakness of the Japanese and Chinese dynasties, forcing commercial concessions and the cession of treaty ports to gain economic and political advantage in the Far-East.

The Emergence of New Imperialism

What accounted for the struggle of Europeans to claim and control the entire world? The new imperialism (to differentiate it from the colonialism of settlement and trade of the 16th to 18th centuries) was a direst result of industrialisation. With intensified economic activity and competition, Europeans struggled for raw materials, markets for their commodities, and places to invest their capital. In the late 19th century, many politicians and industrialists believed that the only way their nation could ensure the economic necessities was the annexation of overseas territories. Captains of industry defended the new empires.

The economic justifications of imperialism are inseparable from the intensely nationalistic ones. Newly unified States, Germany and Italy demanded colonies as recognition of their great power status. Having lost ingloriously to Prussia in 1870, France also turned overseas, hoping to recoup some prestige. Many leaders hoped that a policy of imperialism would win them the loyality of their own people. The nationalistic competition between the Europeans led them to extend their power struggle to Africa and Asia. Far away from their European boundaries, leaders acquired territories for strategic reasons.

The most extreme ideological expression of nationalism was social Darwinism, with its image of national vitality and competition between fit and unfit. Social Darwinists advocated empire. To these elitists, all white men were better fit than non-whites to prevail in the struggle for dominance. Social Darwinists thought their nation the best, which sparked their competitive enthusiasm. Further, many believed that the extension of empire, and industrial civilisation would raise backward peoples up the ladder of evolution and civilisation. Many Westerners believed it was their duty as christians to set an example and to educate others. They thought the extension of the world market economy would create alternatives to the ancient occupations of war, pillage, and enslavement of the vanquished.

Some of the passion for imperialism was sparked by interest in exotic places. At the turn of the 19th century, the expeditions by Mungo park, a Scottish explorer, on the Niger river in West Africa stimulated the romantic imagination. The explorations of Livings-tone in the congo basin and of the Richard Burton fascinated many Europeans. In the 19th century expenditions were a matter of adventure. Sponsored by national geographic and exploratory societies and encouraged by their nations military, explorers captured the public imagination. Besides, the fiction of Rudyard Kipling and Haggard stimulated the passion for far away places and unknown peoples.

European Expansion in Asia

The story of European imerialism in Asia is complicated. In India, China and Japan, powerful kingdoms arrived. The Asian Kingdoms possessed a sense of cultural unity arising from tradition and from loyality to the great religious and ethical system of Hinduism, Buddhism, Islam and Confucianism. When as a result of industrialisation in the 19th century the Europeans came in much greater numbers with greater power, the Chinese and Mughals empires were weakened by internal problems. Indian, Chinese and Japanese cultural identities were not nationalism as Europeans knew it, but within a short time, resentment of European domination developed into national feeling, unifying diverse social and religious communities.

CHINA

For centuries the Chinese had held aloof from Europeans and had been content to live simple lives and enjoyed their own culture. The isolation of China which had been maintained except for a few instances such as Marcopolo's sojourn, the visit of Portuguese merchants at Macao, and the presence of the Birtish in Canton, was threatened after 1840 by improved means of communication, by the Eastward expansion of the European powers, and by the filteiing of European ideas into China.

The attempt of the English merchants to import opium into China from India resulted in a war between Great Britain and China. The British were successful in their attacks upon the Chainese ports, and the treaty of Nanking (1842), which provided for the opening of Amoy, Ningpo, and Shanghai to foreing trade, was accepted by the emperor. But the murder of a French missionary and the seizure of a British ship caused these powers to oppose China in 1856. A treaty was arranged which gave Great Britain foothold near Hongkong, opened six more ports to trade, allowed foreign ministers to resides at pecking, and promised the protection of Christian missionaries in China.

The Chinese empire consisted of the 18th provinces of China proper, the three provinces of Manchuria, Korea and Mongolia, the provinces of Sinkiang, Tibet and several States in Indo-China. On all sides China was menaced by foreign enemies. Russia obtained important territories on both sides of the Amur river, East of the Ussuri river, and north of Korea. A port of the province of Sinkiang was later annexed.

The Sino-Japanese (China-Japan) was (1894-95) which was caused by Japanese interference in Korea was won by Japan. The treaty of Shimonoseki provided that an indemnity was to be paid to Japan. Formosa and Liao-Tung peninsula were given to Japan, and Korea became independent of Japan. But the treaty of Shi–Monoseki (1895) was opposed by Russia because of her own designs on this territory. Japan gave up all except the island of formosa and accepted an additional indemnity.

The Germans proceeded to take Kiao-Chau (1897) as a German base, and France took Kwang-Chow Wan (1898). Russia gained important privileges in Pecking, the right to build the trans-Siberian railway across Manchuria, and a lease on the much desired port Arthur on the Liaotung peninsula. Great Britain stepped in and occupied wei-hai-wei (1898) in order to watch Russia.

The Russo-Japanese was (1904-05) was caused by Russia's humiliation of Japan at the end of the Sino-Japanese was and by attempt of Russia to annex Manchuria. Russia was badly defeated, and by the treaty of portsmouth she gave up her lease of the Liao-tung peninsula to Japan.

The French interfered in Indo-China (Vietnam) Between 1862 and 1885, France obtained complete control over Cochin-China and a protectorate over Cambodia and Annam. The British control of India made it possible for Great Britain to extend her influence to the North and East. Burma, a tributary State of China was annexed outright, and the independent states of Nepal and Bhutan came under British influence. Despite the attempt of China to retain her control over Tibet, England extended her power over outer Tibet.

China Under the Manchus

The Government of China was administered by a divine right emperor assisted by a group of mandarins who carried on the actual administration. The government failed to reorganise the army and as a result, the Japanese defeated the Chinese. It was not until 1898 the emperor Kwangsu instituted some reforms which would partially Europeanized China. Later on, the emperor was dethrone and his aunt, the Doweager empress Tzu-Hsi, became the real ruler and the champion of reaction. The reactionaries formed a society of "Boxers" dedicated to the stamping out of the foreign devils. The Boxor rebillion (1900) was crushed with great brutality. Meanwhile, a young China party under Sun-Yat-Sen inaugurated a Republication movement, and in a successful revolution, they overthrew the Manchu dynastry and established a Republic (1912).

JAPAN

Japan, like China was opened to the West against its will. The Japanese had expelled Europeans in the 17th century and kept isolated for the next two centuries. By the 1850's social dissension in Japan and foreign pressure combined to force the country to admit outside trade. Americans in particular refused to accept Japanese prohibitions on commercial and religions contacts. Like China, Japan succumbed to superior techn-logical power. In 1853, commodore perry sailed into Tokyo bay, making a show of American strength and forcing the Japanese to sign a number of treaties that granted westerners extraterritoriality and control over tariffs. A flood of unrest was unleashed. The Warrior nobility, the Samurai, who feared for their social status, attacked foreigners. The Samurai thought that trade would enhance the status of merchants a social class they despired. In response to Samurai belligerence, a fleet of U.S. and European ships attacked and destroyed Japanese fortresses. A group of Samurai seized the government, determined to preserve Japan's independence. This takeover– the Meiji restroration of 1867, returned power to the emperor, or Meiji from the feudal aristocracy that had ruled in his name for nearly 700 years. The new government enacted a series of reforms turning Japan into a powerful modern unitary state. All classes were made equal before the law. Universal military service was required, as in France and Germany, which diminished social privileges, and helped to imbue Japanese of all classes with nationalism. The Meiji regime introduced modern industry and economic competition. The government built defense industries, backed heavy industry, and developed a modern communication system. During the 1880's, it sold factories to wealthy family monopolies, "the Zaibatsu," which came to dominate the Japanese economy. Within little more than a generation of the Meiji restoration, Japan moved from economic backwardness to a place among the top ten industrial nations.

By 1900, Japan ended the humiliating treaties with the West and become an imperialist power in its own right. It had own Taiwan and Korea in its war with China (1894-95). Finally, in 1904, conflict over influence in Manchuria brought Japan and Russia to war, which Japan won. The Victory of an Asian power over a Western power had a tremendous impact on Asian nationalists. Japan's victory inspired anti-western movements throughout Asia. Japan earned the respect of the imperialists. The first alliance that Britain negotiated when it moved from a policy of splendid isolation was the 1902 naval alliance with Japan. In the first world war Japan fought on the side of the allies.

In the 19th century European gained control and influence in South East and Central Asia. In South East Asia, the French claimed Indo-China (Vietnam, Laos, Cambodia) in a war with China (1883-85). Indo-China was a prosperous country, but it traded mostly with Asia. Some individuals profited economically from the colony, but as a whole France was indifferent to its new acquisition. French expansion might have continued into Siam (Thailand). But it remained an area of conflict between France and England until Entente Cordial was concluded in 1904.

The Dutch controlled the Islands of Java, Sumatra, parts of Borneo and new Guinea. A profitable trade with these islands was carried on by the Dutch.

The Hawaiian islands were obtained in 1898 by America, and as a result of the Spanish-American war, the Philliopine islands were annexed.

The European Partition of Africa

The race for acquiring colonise in Africa went on side by side with the European expansion in Asia, Africa was regarded as the Dark continent and not much was known about its people or natural resources till the beginning of the 19th century. As late as 1880, European nations ruled only a tenth of the continent. By 1914, Europeans had claimed all of Africa except Liberia, Ethiopia. The only great powers that did not play a part in carving of Africa were Russia, Austria-Hungary and the United States. European powers had occasionally been involved in Africa early in the century. The French had moved into Algeria in 1830. During the Napoleonic wars the British had gained capetown in South Africa. But the Dutch farmer's or "Boers", resented the British rule, and they migrated to the North and established the Boer Republic of Orange Freestate and Transval. The two Southern States of Napal and Cope colony remained under British control. Upto 1870 great power interest in Africa seemed marginal. Then the astounding activities of Leopold II, King of Belgium, changed the picture. In 1876, as a private entrepreneur, he formed the international association for the exploration and civilisation of central Africa. Leopold sent Henry Stanley to the Congo river basin to establish trading posts, signed treaties with the Chiefs, and claim the territory for the association. Business enterprise was fostered. Leopold II and his capitalist associates reaped a fortune in the Congo, but the cruelty of their methods of exploitation shocked the conscience of the entire civilised world. Finally, reforms were instituted as a result of British and Belgian criticism of the treatment of the natives, and Leopold II turned the Congo Free-State over to the Belgiam Parliament (1908).

The same reason that prompted imperialism in Asia and America were paramount in Africa. Cecil Rhodes and Luderitz began to occupy territory and to claim it for the mother country. Up and down the continent they went on carving out colonies. In order to prevent serious disputes over African territory, the leading powers arrived at certain understanding.

In the partition of Africa Britain secured the lion's share which includes the best regions of the continent. In the North she controlled Egypt where from she extended her sway over the Sudan. The acquisition of British East Africa, followed by the protectorate over uganda, gave her a continuous stretch of territory from the Indian Ocean to the Mediterranean. At the southern end of the continent there were four colonies, viz., the

Cape of Good Hope, Natal, Transval, and the Organge river colony, all united since 1910 in the union of South Africa. North of this union was the protectorate of Bechuana-land and to its North again extends Rhodesia reaching the boundary of German East Africa. Thus pushing north-wards from the Cape colony, the British came to control an unbroken sweep of territory upto lake Tanganyika, and but for German East Africa, her empire would have extended in a continuous stretch from the Cape to Cairo. Her holdings in other parts of Africa included Gambia, the Gold coast, Sierra Leona and Nigeria on the West and part of Somaliland on the East coast of Africa.

The French already held a few possessions on the West coast of Africa, but they were not content with their colonial empire in Africa and desired to increase their influence along the North coast. Their eyes were specially focuss-ed on Algeria, Tunisia and Morrocco. Under Louis Philippe, the conquest of Algeria was completed.

Tunisia was coveted by both the French and Italians and consequently there was acute rivalry over it between them. The Bay of Tunis was in-debt to France and the administration was very inefficient and corrupt and there was no hope of the repayment of the French debt. France and Italy therefore, intervened in the internal affairs of Tunisia to set the administration in order. At the Congress of Berlin in 1878 Bismarck hinted to France that she could establish her protectorate over Tunisia. Further, relations between Algeria and Tunisia were not cordial and Tunisian tribesmen had aggressive designs on Algeria. In order to suppress them, the French attacked Tunisia in 1881, occupied it and declared it a protectorate. Italy was indignant, England suprised but Germany approved the French action. By the treaty of Bardo the great powers accepted the French protectorate over Tunisia. In 1883 the French colonised Madagascar. But Morocco was a bone of contention between France and Germany. But as result of an argreement with England, France was allowed to establish her protectorate over Morocco.

Portugal also shared in the scramble. She expanded her decaying coastal stations south of the Belgian Cango, and these developed into the large province of Angola. On the West coast she had also founded the colony of Mozambique. She tried to connect her Eastern and Western possession by securing a belt of portu-guess territory right across Africa, but British rivalry forced her to call a halt.

Italy whose ambitions had been thwarted in Tunisia by France felt Frustrated. But she too had her share of the Scramble in Africa. In 1882, she occupied Assab which finally led to her acquisition of Eritrea in 1885. In 1911-12 Tripoli and Cyrenaica were also annexed by her. These two provinces became the Italian colony of Libya.

Germany had achieved her unity in 1871 and so she had been left behind in the race for the acquisition of colonies. Besides, Bismarck at First was against any colonial enterprise. It was only after the industrial revolution in Germany that she began to feel the need of raw material and foreign markets and finding suitable settlements for her increasing population. Bismarck now followed a forward policy. Within a short time Germany established her colonies in German South-West Africa, Togoland, Camerun on the West and German East Africa.

Europe in the Americas

The old colonial system had planted in the new world French, English, Spanish, and Protuguese States which were similar to the mother countries in many respects. The new imperialism sought avenues to profitable investment in the New world (America).

After its war for independance (1775-83), the United States spent the next century in expanding her natural boundaries. The expansion of the United States, territorially, was accompanied by economic growth. Rich natural resources and cheap immigrant labour helped to make the United States a great industrial nation.

During the 16th century Spanish nobles and gentlemen adventurers created an American empire for their nation. Cortez in Mexico (152), Pizarro in Peru (1531), Mendoza in the Argentine (1535), Memendez in Florida pushed out the frontier of Spanish territory. By 1575, the Spaniards, organised politically in the vice-royalities of New Spain and Peru were exploting the resources of central and South America, christianizing thousands of the natives and sending a steady stream of gold and silver to Europe.

The small number of Europeans living in the republics prevented the successful application of democrating government. Revolutions were frequent and the natives were easily influenced by politicians and military leaders. Costa Rica which had a large Spanish population, was the only state which was able to maintain peace and prosperity in central America. Revolutions and civil wars were common. The Countries of Argentine, Brazil, and Chile prospered under stable government. Trade and industry were fostered and immigration from Europe were welcomed.

The industrial revolution acted as a great spur to colonial activity. And to a large extent, the colonies were exploited for the benefit of the mother country, but this exploitation certaintly provided employment to a number of inhabitants of the colonies. Surplus industrial capital in Europe found profitable investment in the colonies.

In America, South Africa, India, Australia, a large number of European settlements were founded. It was literally an expansion of Europe. The Europeans profess the christian religion, and the people of the colonies also adopted. European culture and social customs to a very large degree. Europeanisation also took place in Asia, Africa where western civilisation tried to superimpose itself on the old and ancient civilisation of the East. Western civilisation also affected political thought. Besides, with the European expansion in Africa began a new chapter of humantarian activity. Slave trade was abolished and the African tribes came under the influence of christrianity and received the benefits of Western education.

In the 19th century colonisation or imperial expansion was carried out peacefully, though not without acrimonious disputes. But its effects on international situation were profound. Affairs in Egypt and Sudan almost led England and France to the brink of war. Italy quarreled with France over Tunisia and was driven into the triple alliance by her colonial disappointments. Morocco was a bone of contention between the French and the Germans. The strained relations between the two were one of the causes of the Catastrophe of the first world war. Russian expansion in Asia specially in the direction of Persia and Afghanistan, was a source of anxiety to England and made the relations between the two countries very bitter. Thus, expansion in Asia and Africa led to an entente and perhaps to war in 1914.

World War I was a turning point in the history of imperialism. Britain and France divided the German colonial spoils. But the origins of decolonisation date from the postwar era. Less than three decades later, World War II exhausted the European colonial power. Today almost a century after the rapid division of the world among the European powers and decades after the decolonisation of most of the world, the results of imperialism persist, but imperialism has left a legacy of deep animosity in countries of Asia, Africa and Latin America. Imperialism has been source of great bitterness to former colonial peoples. World War II may have brought an end to the age of Western imperialism, but the world's dependence on Western industry and technology has not diminished.

Chapter-XIII
Russia Since 1815

Russia occupies a peculiar place in the European polity. Upto the beginning of the 18th century she contributed almost nothing to the political, intellectual, and social life of Europe. In the 18th century, under such aggressive and ambitious sovereigns as peter, the Great and Catherine, the Great, Russia emerged as an important European power. It was Peter, the Great who gave to his country a veneer of Western civilisation, he opened a window towards the west by his Baltic campaigns. In respect of Government, of social structure and of economic development, Russia was purely medieval. The Czar was not merely Emperor but autocrat of all the Russians. The administration was a highly centralised autocracy, and power was concentrated in the hands of the Czar. Russia possessed neither a loyal and intelligent nobility of independent means nor an enterprising well-to-do-middle class, it also lacked the creative competition of free citizens. For several centuries the state itself had taken over the responsibility for mobilizing resources, growing all powerful, while reducing its subjects to pawns. Even in the early 19th century, only two classes of people were said to exist in the Russian empire, the servitors of the tsar-army officers, officials, and the landed nobility from which they sprang–and the serfs who served the servitors.

In the words of Lipson; "At the opening of the 19th century Russia was still a semi-Asiatic State". In 1850, when England and France were developed industrial countries dominated by the Bourgeois and profoundly stirred by the forces of economic and political liberalism, Russia was a "Backward" country with a medieval social and economic structure. Because of her great physical size it was impossible for any other nation to cause much military damage, but since her resources were undeveloped and her social organisation antiquated, she could not threaten the domination of Europe. Her interests in the Black sea region brought her into conflict with the Turks and, through the Turks, with England and France, while her racial connections with the Slavic peoples of the Balkans made her a rival of Austria-Hungry, but until the beginning of the 20th century these international difficulties were of a local character. Towards the end of the 19th century, however, the industrial revolution began to effect a "Westernization" of Russia. During the later half of the 19th century when Russia abolished Serfdom and started the industrialization of the country, it brought revolutionary and liberal ideas in its wake. However, this does not mean that Russia didnot play a prominent part in the foreign affairs of Europe. The facts remains that she was counted to be a great power and her every move on the chessboard of international affairs was watched with interest, fear and danger.

Alexander I :

Alexander I might well be termed a Schizophrinic Hamlet, Born on December 23, 1777, he was a classic example of human contradictions and inconsistencies. His early education was entrusted to saltrykov, who instilled in the boy the principles of autocracy. Later his principal tutor was Fredric Harpe, a Swiss Republican and admirer of Rousseau, who tentalized the imagination of the young heir with reason, justice, equality, humanity and other noble notions of the French enlightenment. Alexander acquired his grandmoter's (Catherine II's) mannerisms. The new emperor was an unstable dreamer and a misfit, a sterile liberal and a stubborn drill master, a person of sincerity and a practitioner of hypocrisy. This unusual soverign has been called the "enigmatic Tsar", a sphinx, and crowned Hamlet".

Alexander I, who became Tsar in 1801, was a deeply religious temperament and was inclined to follow a policy of reform. At the time of the Congress of Vienna he was looked upon as the most liberal minded of the monarchs of Europe. He was known to be in sympathy with the granting of constitutions to the nations of Europe, he set the example to other monarchs by granting a constitution to Poland, which was made a separate kingdom with himself as king and was connected with Russia only through his own person. An elected diet (Parliament) was established in Poland and was endows with extensive powers. In his Government of Russia, the Tsar wished to improve the state of the country. He tried to check corruption among public officials. Alexander I also realised the necessity of improving the condition of the serfs. He established technical and primary schools, he abolished capital punishment for nobles, clergy, and merchants. But the later years of his reign witnessed a sharp reaction. The pupil of Laharpe came under the domination of Metternich. Metternich regarded reform as an incentive to revolution. Metternich won the tsar over to the side of repression. Stern repression was the only means of averting a repetition of the horros which France had witnessed. The tsar was converted and henceforth he was an autocrat.

The Decembrist Movement

Though the defeat of Napoleon greatly consolidated Russia'a international standing, it did not fulfil the hopes of the country's gallent defenders who wanted to be freed from Serfdom. "We saved our country from a tyrant, returning campaigner grumbled, only to again be tyranised by our masters". In Russia there was no middle class saturated with liberal ideas, to lead the revolt against the government, and the peasants themselves were too cowed to furnish leaders from their midst. But in the years immediatly following the Napoleonic wars their cause found champions in unexpected quarters.

Disappointment with the course of Alexander's reign played an important role in the emergence of the first Russian revolutionary group, which came to be known after its unsuccessful uprising in December 1825 as the Decem-brists. Most of the Decembrists were army officers often from aristocratic familiers and elite regiments. Essentially the Decembrists were liberals in the tradition of the enlightment and the French revolution, and they wanted to establish constitutionalism and basic freedoms in Russia and to abolish serfdom. At first the liberals who later became Decembrists were eager to cooperate with the government on the road of progress. Their early societies, the union of salvation founded in 1816 and the union of welfare which replaced it were concerned with such issues as the development of Philanthrophy, education, and the civic spirit in Russia rather than with military rebillion. But as reaction grew and hopes for a liberal tranfornation from above faded away, did the more stubborn liberals begin to think seriously of change by force and to talk of revolution and regicide.

The tsar, Alexander I died unexpectedly in November 1825. Though the heir-apparent was his (Nicholas's) elder brother constantion, but long before Alexander's death he had secretly abdicated in favour of his brother Nicholas. The plotters who had planned their uprising for 1826 were at first put out by this development. But they soon gained heart and decided to capitalise on what they thought an opportune occasion. It was decided to start the uprising on December 26, when the troops were to swear allegiance to the new tsar on senate square in St. Petersburg. The plan was for the troops to refuse to do this and compel the senate to issue a manifesto to the Russian people, which would proclaim the abolition of the autocracy, transfer power into the hand of a provisional revolutionary government, abolish serfdom, and other democratic liberties. The regiments were not the only force behind the uprising. All the ordinary people of St. Petersburg rose up. Vast crowds thronged senate square and the adjacent streets. When Nicholas and his retinue dared showed their faces, the workers building the Cathedral of St. Isaac Chased them away. But the initiators of the uprising acted indecisively and played for time. For this reason, the new tsar Nicholas I was able to seize the initiative. He ordered loyal troops to fire on the mutineers with Cannons. By nightfall everything was over. Fresh snow was shovelled over the pools of blood and the bodies of the dead were tossed into the river beneath the ice. The Decembrist revolt as it is called after the month in which it took place was most harshly suppressed. The December consipiracy had no possible chance of success. Hatched in the Salons of the capital, headed by officers of the quards, and inspired much more by docrinaire philosophy than by practical grivances, it had no popular support behind it, and collapsed at the first sign of vigour on the part of the government. Yet, according to Lipson; "The blood of martyrs waters the seeds of liberty, and the Decembrists had shown that the sufferings of the Russian people did not pass unheeded, but were capable of raising up patriots willing to pour out their blood for the regeneration of their country".

Nicholas I (1825-55)

Nicholas I, who ruled Russia for 30 years, was brought up to be a soldier, not a tsar. He looked upon the empire to which he had so unexpectedly succeeded as a military command. Disciplined, obedience was the rule of his life. The new tsar regarded western Europe as a Godless, democratic, anarchy. He believed, Russia had nothing to learn from the west. Orthodoxy, autocracy, Nationality became the official motto of the new reign. Nicholas I stood for a distinctive slavic civilisation. He encouraged Russian literature and culture but sternly excluded foreign books and the liberal influences of the west. He began with merciless suppression of rebellious liberal outbreak among his troops at St. Petersburg-the socalled Decembrist revolt. He was of the opinion that, "Everything for the poeple, nothing by the people". The Decembrist rebellion at the beginning of Nicholas's reign only hardened the men emperor's basic views as well as his determination to fight revolution to the end. The new regime became preminetly one of militarism and bureaucracy. In 1826 he set up the third section of the imperial chancery for the detection and summary punishment of any one who advocated political or social novelities. It is pointed out that the record of the third section (Administrative Rule) is one of the darkest pages in the history of Russia. The chief of police was the head of the third section and he was given an unlimited power of arresting, deporting and making away with any one whom pleased without any restriction whatever. He tried to save his subjects from the infection of the liberal ideas of Western Europe. He put restrictions on foreign travels by the Russians. New restrictions curtailed university autonomy and academic freedom. Constitutional law and philosophy were eliminated from the curricula. Censorship reached ridiculous proportions. Determined to preserve autocracy, afraid to abolish serfdom and suspecious of all independent initiative and popular participation, the emperor and his government could not introduce the much needed fundamental reforms. In practice as well as in theory they looked backward. This was how Russia was ruled, under the thirty year's reaction of Nicholas I. The years of Nicholas's reign was a period of revolution in western and central Europe, when monarchs everywhere either fled from their places or granted the revolutionaries demands while mobs stormed at their gates. No revolution occured in Holy Russia, however, although a polish rising, led by Czartoryski and the army, flared up in 1830 and deposed constantine. The rising was suppressed. In 1848-49, the climatic years of European revolution, Nicholas was able to despatch his loyal troops to Hungary to help restore the authority of his neighbour and partner in the Holy alliance (1815), they emperor of Austria. Not content with being the policeman of his own empire, Nicholas became known as the "Genderme of Europe", a title which he accepted with equanimity and some pride.

Nicholas, however, is best remembered in European history for his policy towards poland, for the assistance which he gave to Austria in repressing the revolutionary movement of 1848, and not least for the part he took in advancing the interests of Russia in the Near-East. In foreign policy he followed the traditional policy of aggradndisement at the expense of the Ottoman empire. Russia's interest in the affairs of this ramshackle empire derived from a variety of motives, the ultimate aim of which was to annexe constantinople. This had been the purpose of Catherine's Greek project but the project had not been realised during the life time of Catherine. Nicholas's reign began with revolts by both the Rumanians and the Greeks against their Turkish overlords. For reasons of their own both England and France decided to support the Greeks and Nicholas was able to intervene without opposition. But when after the untoward event of Navarino, England and France retired, Nicholas on his own account declared war upon Turky and compelled her to recognise the independence of Greece by the treaty of Adrianople. He, thus, made Russian influence predominant in constantinople. After the Greek war of independence, Mehmet Ali (Sultan of Egypt) was given the island of crete for his services. But Mehmet Ali was not satisfied with the prize and taking advantage of the weakness of the sultan, he occupied Syria and Asia Minor. When he seemed to threaten constantinople, the Sultan asked for Russian help. It was in these circumstances, the treaty of unkiar-Skelessi was signed in 1833. By this treaty Turky agreed to allow Russia a controlling authority in the Dardanelles.

For some years the poles had been discontended, and in 1830 a polich insurrection brokeout. A revolutionary government was set up in Poland. But the Russian stamped out the revolt ruthlessly. The polish constitution was abolished, and in 1832 the country was united with Russia. Further, Russia was untouched by the wave of revolutionary enthusiasm which rolled over Europe in 1848, and it was due to Russian intervention that the Hungarian revolt was crushed in 1849. But shortly afterwards he was secretly prosposing to England a partition of the Ottoman empire and was astentatiously claiming a virtual protectorate over all orthodox Christians within it over this question, and doubtless for the fulfillment of far reaching designs, he was again to war with the Turks in 1853. This time Britain and France and (Sardinia) intervened to protect the Ottoman empire against Russian aggression. The resulting struggle, the crimean war took place from 1854-56. (*For details see Eastern question–crimean war*) The Crimean war killed the tsar Nicholas I, it certainly averted the progress of Russia towards constantinople, and it also had an important effect upon the domestic situation in Russia. The war had been the principal agent in precipitating the turbulent state in which his (Nicholas I's) reign closed. The war also served to reveal the inefficiency and the corruption of the administration. To Russia the Crimean war was not merely a defeat but a disillusionment. It discredited the authocratic rule of the tsar and exposed the whole system of administration to serve criticism. The people were profoundly stirred and the need for immediate constitutional and social reforms was felt. According to Lipson, "Awake, O Russia! Devoured by foreign enemies, crushed by slavery, shamfully oppressed by stupid authorities and spies, awaken from your long sleep of ignorance and apathy! –– Stand forward calmly before the throne of the despot, and demand from him on account of the national disaster". The catastrophe of the crimean was underlined the pressing need for fundamental reforms in Russia as well as the fact that the hour was late.

Alexander II, The Czar Liberator

Alexander II stepped to the throne of imperial Russia in a time of crisis. The nation was fighting a losing, costly war against an arry of powerful allies, the liberals were becoming more and more strident in their agitations for reforms, the peasants more and more sullen and insubordinate, and the nobles, on whome the regime leaned so heavily were beset by rumors and fears- fears of losing their estates, their power and privileges. The era of reforms was at hand, and the masses had reason to believe that in Alexander II they had their liberators.

The new emperor was not, like his predecessor, a crowned drill-Sergent, and the character of his administration was from the outset more humane and enlightened. Alexander's preliminary measures seemed intended to pave the way for the complete reversion of his father's policy. The new tsar remarked; "We have to thank the war for opening our eyes to the dark sides of our political and social organisation–". The tsar felt that reform was a medicine that was required to restore the health of mother. Russia was because of his various liberal reforms and particularly for abolishing serfdom that Alexander is known as tsar the liberator.

In the crimean war, Russia was defeated largly due to administrative mismanagement. The new tsar wanted to remove these defects and to introduce liberal measures in the administration of the country. He understood it clearly that the whole of Europe had been deeply influenced by the forces of democracy and nationalism and it would not be possible for Russia to continue to follow the autocractic rule of the time of Nicholas I. Alexander II, therefore, determined to introduce liberal measures and reduce the autocratic system of his father. But in doing so Alexander was careful not to reduce the power of the tsar. He released the Decembrist, the rebels who took part in a rebillion in 1825 during his father's rule. Besides, for economic regeneration of the country Alexander II encouraged the establishment of new industries. The tsar made improvements in roads and transport arrangements. Railways had been further extended and the existing railways had been repaired and improved. All this helped to improve the economic activities of the country as well as fast movement of the army. He took measures for reorganising and strenthening the Russian army and the navy.

Russian Serfdom and its Abolition

Alexander's most memorable achievement was the emacipation of the Russian peasant. Russia was overwhelmingly an agricultural country, and when Alexander came to the throne the majority of his subjects were still in a condition of serfdom. Under the system of serfdom, as developed in Russia, the position of the peasants was sorry. They were attached to the soil, that is, without their lords consent they could not leave the estate on which they were born, and the transfer of an estate from one lord to another automatically transferred the peasants allegiance. To their lord, the peasants paid dues, for him they performed manual labour. Unde serfdom, the mass of peasants remained almost wholly illeterate and quite unable to improve their minds. The exisance of a vast servile population debased the country and stagnated Russian life. Serf revolts hampered the progress of the country. Soviet scholar claims that peasant rebillions played the decisive role in the emacipation of the serfs. Besides, rising in rebillion, serfs ran away from their masters. On occasion large military detachment had to be sent to intercept them. A growing sentiment for emancipation, based on moral grounds, also contributed to the abolition of serfdom. The Decembrists, the Slavophiles, the Westernizers, and supporters of nationality, together with other thinking Russians, all wanted the abolition of serfdom. As education developed in Russia, and especially as Russian literature came into its own, humane feelings and attitudes became more widespread. Infact, on the eve of the abolition of serdom in Russia, virtually no one defended that institution. Further, the crimean was provided additional evidence of the deficiencies and dangers of serfdom which found reflection both in the poor physical condition and listlesness of the recruits and in the general economic and technological backwardness of the country. At the time of the coronation, about a year after his assumption of power, Alexander II addressing the gentry of Moscow, made the celebrated statement that it would be better to begin to abolish serfdom from above than to wait until it would begin to abolish itself from below, and asked the gentry to consider the matter. Although the government experienced great difficulty in eliciting any initiative from the landlords on the subject of emancipation, it finally managed to seize upon an offer by the gentry of the three Lithuanian provinces to discuss emancipation without land. The Czar appointed a secret committee to prepare a plan of emancipation of serfs of whole Russia. Then by a policy of cautions and compromise he overcame the dogged opposition of the selfish landlords and promulgated the famous edict of emancipation..

Emancipation Edict

The edict of emancipation abolished serfdom and liberated over 40 millions of the Russian people at one stroke. The land problem had been solved by a compromise. Serfs were to be set free without compensation to the landlords. They were to receive the plots of land immediately surrounding their houses. How much more they retained of the land which they had formerly tilled depended upon the landlord's readiness to part with it and the decisions of local arbitrators. For the loss of this land the landowner would be generously compensated. Four-fifths of this sum would be advanced immediately by the state in cash or bonds. The remaining one-fifth must be paid by the peasant, who would repay the outstanding sum to the state over a period of 49 years. The tsar was satisfied with this scheme, because both land-owners and serfs received something from it. To have liberated the serfs without land would have made the probability of revolution even more imminent. Of course, the land was not vested with individual serfs. But the village mirs got the land as a whole and controlled it.

The emancipation of the serfs can be called a great reform and in the words of a historian, "The emancipation of the serfs is one of the greatest legislative act in history." The Moral value of the emancipation was certainly tremendous. It is regarded as the beginning of modernisation is Russia. Yet, the emancipation reform also deserves thorough critiscism. Many peasants found themselves in a worse economic plight than before. The land allowed to the former serfs turned out to be insufficient, and for whatever land they got they were burdened with longterm installment payment of the money which the government advanced as compensation to nobles. The edict did not fulfil the expectations of the serfs. They found themselves subjected to the village mirs (village community) instead of the lords. The treatment of emancipated peasants by the State authorities was often harsh and corrupt. The financial arrangement proved unrealistic and impossible to execute. It has been remarked wisely, that the edict of Alexander II liberated the peasants from the nobles only to make them serfs of the state. The emancipation reform disappointed Russian redicals, who considered it inadequate, and it also, apparently, failed to satisfy the peasantry. However, the edict of emancipation was a highly salutary measure as it profoundly altered the social and legal organisation of Russia for the better. The edict of emancipation virtually revolutionised the Russian society. By releasing the serfs from the landed slavery, Alexander II went down in the history of Russia as Czar, the liberator.

Other Reforms

The emancipation of the serfs made other fundamental changes much more feasible. Alexander II turned next to the reform of local government, to the establishment of the so-called Zemstvo. For centuries local government had remained a particularly weak aspect of Russian administration and life. A new law enacted in January 1864, represented a strong modernisation and democratisation of local government, as well as a far-reaching effort on the part of the state to meet the many pressing needs of rural Russia and to do this largly by stimulating local initiative and activity. Institutions of self-government, Zemstvo assemblies and boards, were created at both the district and provincial levels-the word Zemstvo itself connotes land, country or people, as distinct from the Central Government. The Zemstvo or local councils were elected by the people representing all classes of the community. These district councils in their turn elected provincial councils. These local bodies were entrusted with the duties of repairing roads and bridges, of supervising sanitation and primary education and of taking measures against famine. According to Wallace; "The Zemstvo has done a great deal to provide medical and primary education for the common people and it had improved wonderfully the conditions of the hospitals, lunatic assylumus and other benevolent institutions committed to its charge––". The Zemstvos gave Russia an apprenticeship in self-government. Alexander II had unintentionally laid the foundations of constitutional government in Russia. The Zemstvos proved to be the training school in political education.

At the end of 1864, the year that saw the beginning of the Zemstvos administration, another major change was enacted into law, the reform of the legal system. The Russian judiciary needed reform probably even more than the local government did. Archaic, bureaucratic, cumbersome, corrupt, based on the class system rather than on the principle of equality before the law, and relying entirely on a written and secret procedure, the cld system was thoroughly hated by thinking Russians. The legislation of 1864 marked a decisive break with that part of the Russian past. The most significant single aspect of the reform was the separation of the courts from the administration. Instead of constituting a part of the bureaucracy, the judiciary became an independent branch of government. Judges were not to be dismissed or transferred, except by Court action. Judicial procedure acquired a largely public and oral charecter instead of the former bureaucratic secrecy. The contending parties were to present their cases in Court and have adequate legal support. The Courts were organised into a single unified system with the senate at the apex. Locally, justice was to be administered by Justices of peace who were to be appointed by the District and Town councils. All classes were to be equal before the law and, except where the offence was political or committed by an official, trial by Jury was in criminal cases to be the rule.

The overhauling of educational institutions was imperative. The post-1848 repressions had left Russia with practically no elementary schools. Secondary schools were inadequate, and the universities were crippled. The statute (Parliamentary acts), declared that elementary schools were opend to all social classes, and that their aim was the strenthening of the religious and moral understanding of the people and the dissemination of the essentials of useful knowledge. To attain these objectives, the statute recommended the teaching of reading, writing, arithmetic, religion. Secondary education fared better. The statute of 1864 established two types of secondary schools, classical gymnasiums or traditional schools, and pro-gymnasium, patterned after the popular German schools. By the same statute autonomy of the university was restored, reduced the power of the regional government curator, removed most of the restrictions instituted against universities under Nicholas I. But later on by an Act of 1874, the autonomy of the universities was curtailed. The Act imposed strict control over teachers, and prohibited the use of books without prior authorisation from the ministry of education. The educational reform was followed in 1865 by a slight relaxation of the rigid censorship exercised by the government over the press, but press prosecutions continued to be numerous, and newspapers, journal showing liberal sympathies were suppressed on slight provocation.

The great reforms went a long way toward transforming Russia. To be sure, the empire of the tsars remained an autocracy, but changed in many other aspects. Vastly important in themselves, the government's reforms also helped to bring about sweeping economic and social changes. The growth of capitalism in Russia, the evolution of peasantry, the decline of the gentry, the rise of the proletariats-all were affected by Alexander II's legislation. Indeed Russia begain to take long strides on the road to becoming a modern nation.

By 1865, however, ten years after his accession, the reforming spirit of Alexander II was spent. He had never been in heart a liberal. The era of great reforms did fail in one crucial respect, it left unaltered the power of the Emperor. This deliberate oversight eventually undermined all the reforming statutes, led to dissatisfaction, and invited the growth of reaction, repression, terror and revolution.

Polish Revolt 1863

The accession of an apparently liberal tsar had aroused the hopes of the poles. But Alexander was no true liberal. He acted in the spirit of benevolent despotism. He did not regard the objects of polish aspiration as either necessary or desirable, and he determined to make no concession. In 1863 the poles precipitated open rebellion at Warsaw against the Russian Government. But it was merely a struggle of ill-armed pariots against regular troops, and it was marked by no real battle. From the nations of Western Europe, the polich leaders received only sympathy, within a year of its out break the revort was crushed with great severity. It was followed by the complete incorporation of Poland in the Russian empire.

The Nihilist Movement

Within his own lifetime and as the consequence of his actions Alexander II met the fate which can so often befall men who challange the dead hand of tradition and release the forces of change. He asked for cooperation but received instead impatient criticism. Reactionaries reproached him for stirring up trouble. As though to prove their pessimism justified, both peasants and reforming nobles grumbled that he had not done enough for them. His least tolerant critics came from the student population however. In 1861, just after emancipation, university students in St. Petersburg, Moscow, and Kazan demonstrated against everything from the examination system to the conditions of the serfs. These students were members of a new wave in Russia. Less disciplined and repressed than their parents, they were more outspoken in their criticism of the regime and more extreme in their ideas for the future. Even their appearance was designed to draw attention to them and to mark them out as rebels against tradition. They wore long hair and beards, slouch hats, and long scarves draped negligently around their necks and shoulders. To the older generation they appeared rootless, despising everything and believing in nothing. The novelist Turgenev coined a name for them which was to stick, Nihilists. The term Nihilist, as applied to Russian revolutionists, was first introduced by Turgeneve in his novel, "Fathers and Sons". Its principal character, Bazarov (The Son) was intended to portray a new type than coming into prominence among the younger generation of the Sixties. Whereas the "Fathers" (Of the forties) grewup on German idealistic philosophy and romanticism in general, with its emphasis on metaphysical, religious, and historical approached to reality. Nihilism was a fundamental rebellion against accepted values, against abstract thought and family control, against lyric religion and rhetoric. The earnest young men and women of the 1860's wanted to cut through every polite veener, to get rid of all conventional sham. What they usually considered real included the natural and physical sciences, simple and sincere human relations, and a society based on knowledge and reason rather ignorance, prejudice, exploitation, and oppression. They discarded the doctrine of "Art for Art's sake". To them, "A shoemaker is superior to Raphael" (An artist) because the former makes useful things, while the latter makes things that are of no use at all". Nihilism has been described by Stepniak as a struggle for the emancipation of intelligence from every kind of dependence, the fundamental principle of Nihilism, properly socalled was absolute individualism. Its Motto was "Go among the people" and its followers carried out the Motto literally. Ardent young enthusiasts of both sexes went among working people to educate them in radical principles of

Nihilism. They were very much influenced by the ideas of Karl Marx. The tsarist government let loose iron handed repression on the Nihilists and several Nihilists were exiled to Siberia. Though the Nihilists were but few in numbers, their energy, fearlessness, and devotion to their cause made them extremely formidable. The Nihilists resorted to conspirary and assassination. It was a bomb thrown by the Nihilists that killed Alexander II in March 1881. Although the hopes of the liberals in Russia were dashed, the Nihilist movement did not end.

Foreign Policy

The foreign policy of Alexander II began with the termination of the Crimean war and the treaty of Paris, possibly the Nadir of the Russian position in Europe in the 19th century, and it did much to restore Russian prestige. Notably, the Russian fought a successful war (Russo-Turish war, 1877) against Turky and largly redrew the map of the Balkans. Also, in the course of the reign, the empire of the Romanovs made a sweeping expansion in the Far-East and central Asia. But the changing pattern of power relations in Europe, fundamentally affected by the unification of Germany, which the tsarist goverment helped more than hindered, was in many ways less favourable to the State of the Romanovs in 1881 than it had been fifty years earlier.

(For details see Eastern question-Crimean war to Berlin Congress, unification of Germany)

Alexander III (1881-94)

The spirit of the reign of Alexander III was one of shock, and its direction one of reaction. The shock was caused by the assassination of his father and the reaction was attributable to Alexander's advisers. Alexander III was a strong and unimgaginative man who had never approved of the reforms of his father's reign and now became even more certain that it was his duty to repair the damage which had been done to tsardom. His reign because of its assault against revolutionaries and reformers, became known as the "Era of counter-Reforms". The new ruler was determined to suppress revolution and to maintain autocracy. The first proclaimation of his reign declared that, "The voice of God orders us to stand boldly by the task of governing relying on divine providence, with faith in the strength and truth of autocratic power, which we have been called to confirm and protect for the good of the people, against all encroachment". The new tsar was under the influence of pobiedonostseff, procurator of the Holy Synod, a man who utterly abhored all forms of constitutional government. According to Lipson, "He pronounced constitutional government to be the great political lie which dominates our age, and defined Parliament as merely an institution serving for the satisfaction of the personal ambition, vanity and self-interest of its members. It was indeed one of the greatest illustrations of human delusion, while democracy was the most complicated and the most burdensome system of Government recorded in the history of humanity."

Temporary regulations to protect state security and public order, gave officials in designated areas broad authority in dealing with the press and with people who could threaten public order. Summary search, arrest, imprionement, exile and trial by court-martial became common occurance. St. Petersburg, Moscow, and several other parts of the country were placed in the extra ordinary emergency status. Alexander III's Government enacted counter reforms meant to curb the sweping changes introduced by Alexander II and to buttress the centralised, bureaucratic, and class nature of the Russian system. New press regulations made the existence of radical journals impossible and the life of a mildly liberal press precarious. The university statute of 1884, which replaced the more liberal statue of 1863, virtually abolished university autonomy and also emphasised that Students were to be considered as individual visitors, who had no right to form organisations. The judiciary was directly brought under the control of the adminstration and the independence of the judges was abolished.

Alexander III in order to complete the reactionary system of his government sought to bring the emancipated serfs under the landlords. The landlords were given the duty of policing over the people. Breach of contact by the labourers was made criminal offence. Formerly the justices of the peace were elected. Alexander III abolished this system and appointed a new class of officers called Land captains and entrusted upon them the duty of maintaining peace and order. The land captains were all appointed from the landlords. The executive and the judicial departments were again united, the result was that justice became nothing better than injustice.

The Government also made certain significant changes in the Zemstvo system. The previous classification of land holders that of 1864, had been based on the form of property, so that members of the gentry and other Russians who happend to hold land in individual ownership were not distinguished. In 1890 the members of the gentry became a distrinct group. Peasants, on the other hand could thenceforth elect only candidates for Zemstvo seats, the governors making appointments to district Zemstvo assemblies from these candidates, as recommended by land captains.

The reign of Alexander III also witnessed increased pressure on non-orthodox denominations and a growth of the policy of Russification.

The policy of Russification sought to impose the Russian language and the orthodox faith on non-Russians of the empire so as to make them loyal Russians. The schools of the poles were completely Russianised. They were not allowed to sell their land to non-Russians. In Lithuania the Catholics were discriminated and their marriages and their children were treated as illegitimate. In Estonia and Lativia, Russian was made the official language. The Jews were also persecuted with great severity. It was laid down in 1890 that all Jews living in the interior of Russia were to migrate to the western provinces. They were even not allowed to own or lease land. They were put under the strict control of the Government. The Jews were also excluded from the legal profession, the Zemstvos, and municipal self-government.

But in the field of industrial development Alexander III's reign formed a landmark in the history of Russia. Before Alexander III industries in Russia meant only cottage industries. But under Alexander III the liberal patronage of industry, trade and commerce gave rise to various new industries. Under the guidance of Witte, who became Minister of Finance, industrial development began. Russia possessed vast natural resources, and it was Witte's ambition to set-up industries which should be based on the raw materials which Russia itself could supply. Protective duties were established to guard against foreign competition, and transport facilities were provided by the construction of railways. Capital was needed, however, and was supplied in large amount by French financers. Heavy duties were imposed on foreign goods and foreign capitalists were encouraged to establish their industries and invest money in Russia. Besides, the means of communication developed in Russia to a great extent. The construction of the Trans-Siberian railway line was one of the greatest achievement during the reign of Alexander III. The establishment of factories brought large number of workmen together and promote the growth of large towns. The labour problems,–wages, hours, and conditions of work-which had appeared elsewhere sprang up in Russia. Efforts were made to form labour unions, strikes occured, and the discontent of workmen afforded oppertunities for the spread of revolutionary propaganda. The condition of the workers in Russia was desperate and police repression was savage. Russia presented the Marxist golden opportunity. Among the first to realize this was Gerorge Plekhanov, a member of the first Nihilist generation. In 1883 he founded in Geneva a party called the liberation of Labour, which was uncompromisingly Marxist in its programme. By the end of the century it was becoming active in Russia itself and the younger ulyanov, betterly known as V. I. Lenin, was one of Plekhanov's keenest disciple.

Foreign Policy

Alexander III did not add vast territories to the Russian empire. Still his achievements in foreign policy were monumental. The changes which had taken place in foreign policy constituted no less a revolution than that which was taking place within Russia. Indeed, a dramatic transformation had taken place in the European balance of power since the end of the crimean war. The three emperors league which had ceased to function after the congress of Berlin was revived. The new ruler of Bulgaria, a German prince, proved an unwilling vassal of the tsar. Russian agents kidnapped the Bulgarian prince in the early years of Alexander III's reign and forced his abdication, but once again the west intervened and Russia was forced to accept diplomatic defeact. Despite the efforts of both Gorchakov (Russian foreign Minister) and Bismarck, these crisis put a considerable strain upon the league of the three emperors. Bismarck concluded a separate alliance with Austria which secretly promised support in the event of an attack by Russia. Though, Bismarck tried to repair the damage by a treaty of reinsurance with Russia in 1887, the relationship could not be the same again. Towards the end of the reign of Alexander III Russia faced a bitter situation and she was once again isolated in Europe.

One country however had stood aside from the anti-Russian coalition. This was France. France was an old enemy and also a republic by defination therefore anathema to the tsar, but diplomacy makes strange bed fellows and Russia think in terms of a French alliance to bring them both out of isolation. The Finance Minister provided additional reasons for establishing good relations with France. Russia needed capital for the industrialisation therefore, drew the Republic and the autocracy together. In 1894 a formal alliance was concluded between the two states. It was restricted to mutual defence against Germany and Austria. Thus, Russia and France had ended a century of hostility.

Nicholas II (1894-1917)

Alexander III died in 1894 and like almost every tsar of Muscovy, he left behind not only domestric and foreign problems of considerable magnitude, but an heir unprepared to assume the burdens of power of Nicholas II so it can be said that he was totally unprepared. No wonder Nicholas II has often been compared to Louis XVI (France). The last tsar possessed certain attractive qualities, such as simplicity, modesty and devotion to his family. But these positive personal traits mattered little in a situation that demanded strength, determination and vision. It may be argued that another peter the Great could have saved the Romanovs and imperial Russia. There can be no doubt that Nicholas II did not.

In fact, he proved to be both narrow-minded and weak, unable to remove reactionary blinders very often, unworthy ministers made crucial decision that the soverign failed to understand fully. Later in the reign, the Empress, the reactionary hysterical, and wilful German princess Alexandra, became the power behind the throne, and with her even such an incredible person as Rasputin could rise to the position of greatest influence in the state. A good man, but a miserable ruler (Nicholas II) lost in the moment of crisis.

Reaction continued unimpeded. The new emperor who had been a pupil of Pobedonstsev, realied on the Holy Synod, and on other reactionarises. The government continued to apply and extend the temporary regulation to supervise the press with utmost severity, and as best it could to control and often restrict education. The Zemstvo experienced further curtailment of their jurisdiction. Religious persecution grew and Russian sectarian suffered the most. Many of them were exiled. The State also confiscated the estates and charity fund of the Armenian Church. The position of the jews too underwent further deterioration. But the case of Finland represented in many respects the most telling instance of the folly of Russification. Finland, acquired from Sweden during the reign of Alexander I, had been regarded as a separate grand duchy, with the tsar as Grand Duke. Its union with Russia was merely in the person of the tsar. It was more prosperous than Russia. But in 1899 Nicholas II diminished the power of the Finish Diet (Finland's Parliament). The Finns protested.

Meanwhile, the rapid indusrialistion of Russia, with its usual by-products of problems, made many converts to Marxism among university students and radical intellectuals. In 1900 the news paper Iskra (The Spark) began operation in Germany in order to serve as a major forum for the party. The socialist revolutionary party also made its appearance during the early years of Nicholas II's reign. At the end of 19th century liberal nobles, teachers, doctors were in favour of a change. University students also surged to the fore as a potential force under Nicholas II. Underneath the restlessness of students, of the Zemstvo liberals, and of the profesional revolutionries, boiled an active Volcano of peasant discontent. Further, another force that came to troble the regime of Nicholas II was industrial labour. But the most important force to arise and challenge the Russian regime at the turn of the century was the militant nationalism of non-Russian peoples of the empire. A direct result of long years of aggressive Russification caused discontentment among the non-Russians. All these uncoordinated but discontented forces converged in 1905 to produce a revolution.

The Russo-Japanese War (1904-05)

Nicholas II's policy did not contribute to peace. Aggressiveness and adventurous involvement characterized Russian behaviour in the Far-East around the turn of the century, which culminated in the Russo-Japanese war. The construction of the Trans-Siberian railroad (1891-1903) entirely justified in terms of the needs of Siberia, serve also to link Russia to Manchuria, China, Korea and even indirectly to Japan. Japan had just gone through a remarkable modernization and in 1894-95 (Sino-Japanese war) it fought and defeated China, obtaining by the treaty of Shimonoseki the Chinese territory of Formosa, and the Liaotung peninsula. Meanwhile Russia concluded a secret agreement with China, Whereby in return for guaranteeing Chinese territory against outside aggression, and Russia obtained the right to construct a rail road through Manchuria to the coast. While Russia had legitimate commercial and other interests in Asia–for one thing, selling the product of its factories in the East when they could not compete in the West, and while upto that point Russian imperialism in the Far-East had limited itself to peaceful penetration, the situation became increasingly tense. Moreover, Russia responded to new oppertunities more and more aggressively. Thus, when the murder of two German missionaries in 1897 led to the German acquisition of kiaochow through a 99 years lease, Nicholas II obtained a 25 year lease of the Southern part of Liaotung peninsula with port Arthus. Following the so-called Boxar rebellion (1900-01) of the exasperated Chinese against foreigners, which Russian forces helped to suppress, tsarist troops remained in Manchuria on the pretext that local conditions represented a threat to the rail road. Besides, a group of adventurers with strong connections at the Russian. Court began to promote a scheme of timber concessions on the Yalu river meant to serve a vehicle for Russian penetration into Korea. The foreign office failed to control Russian policy in the Far-East. On the other hand, Japan proved to be a more skillful aggressor. Offering partition, which would give the Russian Northern Manchuria and the Japanse gauged the futility of negotiating, chose their time well, and on Feburary 8, 1904, attacked successfully the unsuspecting Russian fleet in the outer harbor of port Arther-thus accomplishing the original pearl Harbor. What followed, turned out to be a humiliating war for the Russians. The Russians colossus suffered defeat after defeat from the Japanese pigmy. This outcome, resulted from ample causes, Japan was ready, well-organised, and in effect more modern than Russia, while Russia was disorganised, and handicapped by a lack of popular support. Japan enjoyed an alliance with Great Britian, whereas, Russia found itself diplomatically isolated. Finally, on May 27-29, 1905, Japan defeated Russia in the battle of Tsushima strait. An armistice followed soon after Tsushima. President Theodore Roosevelt aranged a peace conference at Portsmouth, New-Hampshite in 1905. The provisions of the treaty of portsmouth reflected the skillful diplomacy of witte (Russia Minister). By this treaty, Russia recognised a paramount Japanese interest in Korea and ceded to Japan its lease of the Liaotung Peninsula, the Southern part of the rail road upto chang-Chun, and the half of the island of Sakhalin. And both the countries agreed to restore Manchuria to China.

The 1905 Revolution-Bloody Sunday

The Russo-Japanese war exposed the decay of the monarchy, the mediocrity of the ruling elite, its inability to express the interests of the dominant class, let alone the country's interests. In short, it was the last Straw. The people's patience was exhausted. In late December 1904, there took place in St. Petersburg what at first seemed an inconspicuous event but which was to become the starting point of great upheavals. The management of the putilov plant sacked four of its workers. The other workers stood by them. When there demands were not met they called a strike, Lateron all the factory workers in St. Petersburg struck in solidarity. At that time the workers still believed in a just tsar, who would protect them from the factory owners. They decided to draw up a petition in which they would state their grivances, and present it to the star. All the workers of St. Petersburg attended the meetings held to discuss this petition. Learning about it Nicholas II fled pancic- stricken to his country estate. On 22nd January, 1905, the workers arranged a procession in St. Petersburg under the leadership of father Gapon in order to present their demands to the tsar of Russia. Carrying Church banners and portraits of the tsar and chanting prayers and the royal anthem, the factory workers converged on the winter palace to see the tsar. However, the peaceful character of the procession did not deter the tsarist butchers. The troops fired point-blank at the people falling prostrate in the dirty, blood-stained snow. They shot them down from the back and mounted, sword-swininging Cossacks chopped down all who rushed to take refuge under arch ways. Desperate the stunned with horror, several columns broke through to the winter palace where they were met by volleys of gunfire. This day January 22 has gone down in history as "Bloody Sunday". The news of Bloody Sunday shocked Russian and world public opinion. To pacify the enraged country, Nicholas II promised to convene a consulative assembly of selected representatives to assist in the discussion of legislative bills. But on May Day 1905, political working class stikes took place under the slogan of "Down with autocracy". At length the tsar decided upon a change of policy, and in August 1905 he announced the forthcoming establishment in Russia of a Duma or elected assembly. But the franchise on which it was to be elected was so narrow that it was impossible to regard the Duma as representative of the Russian people. The tsar also made further concessions. But before the Duma was elected its power were severely restricted. The largest party in it, the constitutional democrats, demanded that ministers should be responsible to the Duma, but the Court was unwilling to make concessions. And the usual methods of repression, arrest, exile, and death followed.

At the elections of the second Duma extreme measurer were resorted inorder to secure the choice of official candidates. Meanwhile, the Czar appointed Stolypin (Minister) who was a man of great courage and far more practical than the other Russian officials. He put down lawlessness with a heavy hand and manipulated election in order to obtain a Duma which would side with the Government. The third Duma was not opposed to the government and its most important achievement was the passing of an important law which ended the system of holding village lands in common. But the 4th Duma was more reactionary than its predecessor. The constitutional experiment in Russia appeared to be of little value, when the great was began in 1914 autocratic government still existed in Russia. Finally, in 1917 the great Russian Revolution took place which witnessed the death of the starist Government.

RUSSIAN REVOLUTION-1917
(Its Causes and Results)

The Russian revolution of 1917 proved to be one of the major formative international influences of the 20th century and the communism from which it derived was a development of the essentially international creed of socialism which, cutting across national loyalities, called on workers of all countries to unite. Yet, contrary to the predictions of Karl Marx, the first successful communist revolution took place in a country whose economy was among the most backward in Europe. It is, thus, necessary to look for the formative shaping of communism as much in Russian history as in the particular theories of European socialism and the teachings of Karl Marx from which it stemmed. But certainly it has proved to be one of the greatest social upheaval since the French revolution (1789).

Russia in the opening of the 20th century was in many ways materially prosperous, its economy was expanding, its foreign trade increasing with industrialisation, its population growing. The Siberian lands, "The New America", were being opened up. Yet against this was to be a set of darker picture. The economic and financial reforms effected by the able minister

Witte had been sound enough but their product had been dissipated in the disastrous war of 1904-05 with Japan, which Witte bitterly opposed. The rapid growth of factories and towns brought harsh exploitation which, with poor wages and housing and inadequate enforcement of protection laws, gave rise to Dickension conditions of living for many Russian workers. In the misery of urban poverty, revolutionary ideas, made rapid headway. The peasants, in their turn, were oppressed and obessed by the need for land. For the middle classes, the new century opened in a mood of disillusionment and foreboding. It was the period when Tolstoy turned from the world to seek a richer fulfilment in the ideal of the simple life, and Chekhov has depicted the isolation of the individual of intelligence and goodwill in a society whose standards were hostile, cramping and alien. The closing years of the tsarist regime saw a great flowering of the arts. Yet, the predominant mood seemed to many observers in Russia to be one of decadence, expressed in a popular literature which was strongely prone to apocalyptic vision, and to prophecy of doom or a golden age to come.

During the eighties and nineties of the 19th century the industrialisation of Russia began to make great progress. Towns multiplied and factories began to spring up like mushrooms. Capitalists and urban proletariate arose and with them also arose new problems of factory life and the new outlook of the town workers. It was from this class that the message of socialism met with a hearty response. In the nineties the teachings of Marx were popularised and spread by radicals like Gorky. In 1883, Plekhanow (Later to be the mentor of Lenin) founded a Marxist group from the Liberation of labour from which evolved the Russian social Democratic party, with its emphasis on the urban working man. Its secret publication Iskra (The Spark) was edited by Plekhanov. The movement, conspiratorial and underground in face of government repression, went to work mainly among students and working men. After the Congress held in London in 1903, the social Democratic party divided under the impact of Lenin's powerful personality, into Mensheviks (The minority), led by Martov, and the Bolsheviks (The majority), led by Lenin. The Bolsheviks stood for extreme measures and were eager to establish a dictatorship of the proletariat.

The rule of Nicholas II was as autocratic as it was inefficient. The political condition of the country was unstable, censorship was notorious and the police system ruthless, Nicholas was well-intentioned but weak. He was much liberal to his subjects, but he was heavily influenced by his wife the empress Alexandra. Nicholas had inherited a conception of autocracy which combined the more extreme forms of divine right, with a mystical tradition rooted in a Muscovite and Byzantine past. When the neurotic and obessive empress admitted the disreputable Rasputin (A monk) to her confidence, the last elements of the tsar's independence of action faded. Able ministers gave place to non-entities. He lacked the qualities required for independent political judgement and action.

Any enquiry into the origins of Russian revolution must inevitably take into account the late survival of Serfdom in Russia and the problems which followed its abolition by tsar Alexander II. The servile system reached its climax in Russia in the late 18th century. A material and a spiritual gulf separated rich from poor. The peasants belonged to an older Russian tradition whose roots lay in the shadows of a dark past. Untouched by education, they lived in a world dominated by superstition and conservatism. Alexander's most cherished reform (Emancipation of the serf), in effect, a potent cause of the revolution of 1917. What it destroyed was nothing less than a whole social structure, without providing a sound basis of new one.

The lot of the landed peasant was more complex. The landlords were hand–somely compensated at once. The vagaries of officialdom and the rapacity of some landlords meant that many peasants received unworkable units of land for possession of which they now found themselves burdened with redemption payments for heavier than their dues under the old system. As the 19th century ended, the agrarian situation was one of the Russian governments most pressing problems. Between 1905-1914 successive ministers tried to produce a new land policy, to encourage consolidated farms and the practice of a more modern agriculture. When war (First World War) came, Russian agriculture was still largly dependent on the wooden plough and on a primitive, under fed peasantry rooted in the habits of the thought of the past. And ahead lay the stern communist experiments in collectivisation. The emancipation of 1861 had destroyed a social order and created new economic problems.

The socialist revolutionaries were the party of the peasants, they were heirs to the Narodnik or populist tradition which in the 1870's had produced a good deal of revolutionary terrorism. The Narodnik movement, part terrorist part reformist, had died out when the peasants failed to rise in revolt subsequently the socialist Revolutionary party emerged, founded on the pattern of European left-wing parties, and affiliated in 1903, to the second socialist international. Their programme included political and social reform, with the main emphasis on the land for the peasant. Their tendency to utopianism seems to make them akin to the tradition of the English radicals.

As in France, the material revolution in Russia was preceded by a revolution in the realm of ideas. In spite of the attempts of the tsar to seal

Russia hermetically against the liberal ideas of the west, the influence of West European thought filtered into Russia. A wave of realism was ushered in Russian literature by Tolstoy, Chekhov, Gorky. The novels of Turgeneve, Dostoievsky profoundly stirred the imagination of young Russia. The writters pleaded on behalf of radical social reforms. The writings of the intelligentsia generated a passion among the people for fairness and justice. Impelled by the new monumental human passion, the scholars gave such a dynamism to radicalism and revolutionary movements that when the tsarist state and the old order collapsed they came down with a thunder clap.

The defeat of the Russian Army in the Crimean war, the Russo-Japanese war, revealed to the Russians the utter inefficiency of the tsarist government. The autocratic Government of Russia did not provide essential facilities to the army. Besides, the bureaucracy of Russia was also responsible for the revolution. They never thought of the problems of the masses. Resentment spread all over the country, as corruption and nepotism became the order of the day. In 1905, the deep political and social discontent in Russia, exacerbated by the defeats suffered on the war against Japan in 1904-05, erupted in a great revolutionary movement. This was heralded by the massacre in St. Petersburg of a large number of workers and others who had come intending a peaceful demonstration before the tsar's winter palace, a massacre which earned for 22nd January the name bloody Sunday". The Zemstvos demanded reforms, the workmen struck work, and the peasantry plundered the landlords. Though the revolution of 1905 failed but it created a deep crack in the edifice of the tsarist autocracy.

Although the country was materially ill-equipped, Russia entered the 1914 war more patriotically united than the divisions of the preceding years might have led anyuone to expect. In the precarious balance of Russian opinion, however, the one reverse, the tsarist government could not afford was military defeat and that, after initial enthusiasm, came in swift and disastrous measure. The great German offensives, cruelly exposed the inadequacies of the tsarist government. Russia could not be saved by the numbers and heroism of men alone. By 1916, the frustration of defeat, the shortage of food, the appalling casualities and the humiliation of retreat lay heavily upon the Russian people. The liberals pressed urgently for government reform. The revolutionaries were also at work, inciting desertion from the ranks of the army and organising strikes in the factories. From exile, Lenin called on workers everywhere to lay down their arms and refuse to continue to fight in the capitalist, imperialist cause. Supported by well-disciplined Bolshevik party, Lenin kept vigilant control over all what was happining in Russia. He was a practical genius. Lenin Vehemenely opposed the policy of Russification by the tsar. By January 1917, civil and military authority in Russia was virtually at breaking point. Everywhere there was utter confusion as refugees, deserters, workers on strike, and peasants taking advantage of the confusion to start the seizure of land, contributed to the disintegration of order. When bread riot broke out on 8th March, 1917, in petrograd, they acted as the focus of revolutionary insurrection, within four days the city was effectively in revolutionary hands. The tsarist system virtually crumbled away and Nicholas II abdicated on March 1917 and the Duma set up a provisional government.

The February (Or March according to the new style calender) revolution and the collapse of the Romanov dynasty, obliged the opposition groups to redefine their aims. The constitutional democrats joined with moderate right wing elements in the Duma formed the provisional government under prince LVOV, who was succeeded later in the year by the moderate socialist, Kerensky. But without popular support the provisional government was doomed from the start. The Bolsheviks were oppossed to war and they sought to establish the dictatorship of the proletariat. They established petrograd Soviet, an elected council of Workers, peasants, and soldier's deputies. The soldiers influenced by the pacifist propaganda of the Bolsheviks refused to fight. In vain Kerensky continued to offer the liberal panacea of constitutional reform but by now the provisional government had shown it could offer neither successful war nor successful revolution. The Romanovs had gone, now Kerensky passed unmourned from the scene. On 26th October (or November) the Bolsheviks stepped into fill the void created by the disappearance of opposition. Lenin became the unrival master of Russia. Lenin is still remembered in history as the father of the Bolshevik revolution and the creator of new Russia.

Significance of the Russian Revolution

Russian revolution is a symbolic continuation of the French Revolution because the latter was the revolution of the bourgeoisie against the absolute feudal order and arbitrary monarchy. It was a Marxist-Socialist revolution, aiming to install a dictatorship of the proletariat, which after withering away, would lead to the communist ideal known as communism.

The Russian revolution of 1917 and the later development of Russia internally made a profound impression upon the world. The rise of communist Russia is an event of great consequences in the world history. Marx and Engles visualised the proletarian revolution sweeping over all of Europe. Though tsarist Russia was not ripe for proletariat revolution as the industrial base of Russia was of meagre nature. However, in the lead that was given by the revolutionaries, workers played a prominent part and that too those of the workers who were sufficiently indoctrinated in the Marxist thought. The example and propaganda of the Bolshevik revolution helped to found communist parties in different countries that were pro-Russian. These were federated in 1919 in a third international (comintern), with head`quarters at Moscow. Through the comintern, Russia directed the policies and activities of communist parties in Germany, France, Italy, and most other countries on the European continent. Socialism has been made feasible only by the success of the Russian revolution. Russian achievement in the economic activity as piloted by the plans has captivated the imagination of a great number of nations in the world. In other words, the importance of the Russian Revolution lies in the fact that the capitalist societies have to continue fighting their own creation since socialism is a direct product of the capitalists system. Socialism is a logical extention of democratic tradition. The Russian Revolution is a monunmental landmark in the emancipation of man. According to Marx; "All the previous political changes were the work of minorities and every political change led to change in the group of exploiters since in every political change a specific group of exploiters gained control of the means of production. Added to this, the whole super structure of man as embodied in the institutions, systems, principles, values, arts and science only served the ends of the economically dominant section of a society, while the Have-nots were made to believe that the whole superstructure was for their own good. The whole superstructure as sustained by the Haves could be ended in the era of communism since the means of production would be owned by the whole society—".

The immediate importance of the Russian revolution was the stance taken by it on the future of subject nationalist Lenin advised the nationalist leaders in various colonies to keep emancipation of their colonies as the first goal. The Russian revolution had tremendous impact in the economic sphere of the country. The ruthless exploitation of human material did in fact produce remarkable developments. Agriculture and industry developed on an unprecedental scale. All properties, factories, lands, banks were nationalised and private properties were declared illegal. Production and distribution systems were nationalised. Thus imperialism was substituted by socialism. The committees of workers were formed to manage the sytems of production and distribution. Further, the birth of communist Russia alarmed the democratic western world. As an ideology communism differed from democracy on many basic issues. Thus there began an ideological conflict between communist Russia and the democratic States like England, France and America.

Chapter-XIV

Era of William II

(1888-1914)

From 1888 to 1914 the Emperor-King William II occupied the chief position in Germany and in Prussia, Preserving Prussia's leadership in Germany, and Germany's prestige in Europe. He was a convinced imperialist, Kaiser William II was intensely patriotic. His character was a mixture of inordinate ambition, high imagination, superficiality and impulsiveness. He was a strange mixture of opposites and had a firm faith in the theory of "the Divine Right of King". He was opposed to democratic sentiments. William II was determined to rule as well as to reign. Probably he was the ablest of the Hohenzollerns since Fredrick, the Great. His aim appeared to be to make Germany dominant not only in Europe but throughout the world, and the chief interest of his reign is concerned with his foreign policy, which led to the Great war of 1914-19.

According to Marriot, "Contemporary have the choice of two contradictory portraits of William II, the one delineating a strong willed, clear sighted ruler, a true scion of the stock which produced a greater elector, a Fredrick the Great, the other showing as a man of bluffing character and curiously, contradictory impulses, imperious rather than strong, a prodigal of fine words but barren in achievements, imagining himself a master craftsman in diplomacy, but in truth a sorry burgher at once generous and crafty, pious but unprincipled––a proud autocrat but the slave of a military clique––". Kaiser William II's childhood covered the period of prussia's golden age. The letters that Kaiser William II had in his early youth written to Bismarck were full of admiration. But on his accession to the throne, Kaiser found that the personal preponderance of Bismarck in the administration and his influence upon the ministers and officials of the state were so great that Kaiser was left with no practical power. To check

Bismarck, William II ordered that henceforth the cabinet minister should have access to him directly rather than through the chancellor as the custom earlier. By 1890 estrangement between Bismarck and the Kaiser reached the position of no return. Finally, the emperor demanded and received Bismarck's resignation. William II dropped the pilot (Bismarck).

William II appointed General Caprivi, an able soldier whose capacity had for many years been recognised by Bismarck, as successor to the iron chancellor, but the policy of the Government henceforth was determined by the emperor. Caprivi, with the help of the National liberals, fostered colonial expansion. But he was hated by the Prussian aristocracy. It was during his time that Heligoland was exchanged for Zanzibar in 1890. His dismissal was demanded by the Prussian conservatives and he resigned in 1894.

In 1894 Caprivi was succeeded as chancellor by Hohenlohe, who held office for six years. The period was remarkable for the development of German naval power, colonies were obtained in the pacific, and a concession on the Shantung Peninsula in China was acquired. The development of land armaments was supplemented with a naval force that rivaled Great Britain. The rise of German navy was due to increased imperialism, the development of nationalism, and the activities of admiral Tirpitz as Secretary of State for the navy. Kaiser William II said, "The future of Germany lies on sea". A naval base resulted from the acquisition of Heligoland and the completion of the Kaiser Wilhelm canel connecting the North and Baltic seas. In 1897 a definite programme of naval construction was drawn-up and approved, and a Navy legue was found. More ambitious naval schemes was put forward in 1900 and the admitted aim of the government and the Navy league was to challenge the naval supremacy of Great Britain. The result was the Anglo-French entente of 1904.

Bulow was chancellor from 1900 to 1909. A good-deal of opposition to the government was maintained in the Reichstag, mainly on account of the increasing taxation necessary for naval construction. A constitutional crisis of the first magnitude occured on 1908, when William II granted an interview to a representative of Daily Telegraph". The publication in that Journal of the Emperor's personal views without reference to his ministers, provoked an outburst of indignation from all parties in the empire. The first and second Moroccan crisis took place during the chancellorship of Bulow. In 1909 Hollweg became the chancellor. The coming of a new chancellor did not mean a change in policy, but rather a continuance of the old, because the real chancellor was the emperor. The chief interest of the period lay in the growing tension in foreign affairs.

The reign of William II was marked by the accelerating tempo of

Germany's industrialisation. Between 1888-1913, the number of German engaged in manufacture and commerce increased. This economic development was greatly promoted by Bismarck's policy of protection. By developing the coal mines of Ruhr, Silesia, and the Saar, Germany became one of the great coal producing countries of the world. During the reign of William II, the roads and railways were also improved.

William II adopted a concilliatory policy towards the socialists and allowed the repressive laws against the socialists to lapse. Taking an advantage of the liberal attitude of the emperor, the socialists began to organise themselves. The emperor realising the futility of palliative measures determined to revive coercion, but his attempts failed as the Reichstag rejected his proposals.

The young Kaiser discarded Bismarck's idea of Germany as a "Satiated power". He said "Nothing must go anywhere in the world in which Germany does not play a role." He had a firm faith in the superiority of German race. He further said, "Germany was peopled by Teutonic race which was destined to dominate Europen and the World." After "Dropping the Pilot", Kaiser William II in his eagerness to take share in the welt-politik", i.e., world politics, he embarked upon a vigorous policy of colonial expansion in Africa and the Far-East and of active participation in the affairs of the Near East. This policy directly led to an ambitious naval programme. Such an ambitious policy involved the complete breakdown of Bismarck's system of alliances and led to diplomatic developments highly prejudical to Germany. The Keynote of Bismarck's policy had been to isolate France and to keep Russia in good humour. But the Kaiser wanted to strengthened the alliance with Austria at the cost of Russian friendship. William II nourished doubt about the value of Russian alliance. So he allowed the Reinsurance treaty with Russia to lapse. He there by drove Russia into the arms of France. So, Russia turned towards France and concluded the Franco-Russian dual alliance in 1891. The Frano-Russian alliance was a blow to the Bismarckian system.

In 1890-91 Britain which then was friendless in the international field, proposed a friendly alliance with Germany. Kaiser William II spurned the offer and there by lot the chance of earning even greater goodwill of Britain. For the first few years Kaiser did not enter into any open opposition to Britain as a result of which he could obtain Heligoland. Another reason for the British support of the German colonial supremacy in central Africa was the bitterness in the relations between France and England which led the latter to check French colonial expansion in central Africa by supporting Germany. But the Kaiser did not realise the situation, on the contrary, he secretly supported the Boers when Britian was engaged in the Boer war. He even sent a telegram of congratulation to President Kruger of Transval on the victory of the Boers against the British. The development of the Bagdad railway under German auspices was also looked upon with great apprehension by Great Britain as it involved a menace to British interests in the East. Further although Germany had began to acquire colonies under Bismarck, that great statesmen was primarily a continentalist. His diplomatic skill was quite equal to the task of allaying the irritation caused by England by the appearance of a new aspirant to the colonial empire. But the Kaiser was a zealous imperialist and his words, "our future lies on the water," touched Great Britain at her most tender point. In spite of that England maintained friendly relations with Germany, as she had many outstanding causes of friction with France and Russia. In 1901, England again offered to discuss the outstanding problems with Germany. But the negotiation for alliance between Germany and England brokedown due to the Kaiser's ambitious policy. As there was increasing estrangement between England and Germany, it naturally brought England and France nearer each other. In 1904 the Anglo-French convention was signed. Finally, an alliance known as Triple entente among England, France and Russia was signed. Thus, as a result of his (William II) mishandling of foreign affairs, William II began to lose the safeguards which Bismack had provided for the safety of the German empire.

Bismarck was primarily a continentalist and he had only a limited enthusiasm for colonial enterprises. But William II with his ideas of world politics and world-traffic, embarked upon a vigorous colonial policy. In the Far-East, Kiao-Cho was acquired from China in 1897 as compensation for the murder of two German missionaries. In 1890 the caroline islands were purchased from Spain. Germany's real aim was world domination. When France tried to establish her protectorate over Morocco, Kaiser William II intervened and assured protection to Morrocco. However, the Morocco crisis was solved in the Algeciras conference in 1906. But in 1911, Germany created another international crisis by sending German ship panther to Agadir in Morocco. But England openly supported France at Morocco. The radical foreign policy of the Kaiser William II led Germany on to war.

Chapter-XV

The First World War

(1914-1918)

The war which began in 1914, was in many ways entirely novel in human history. It was the first war on a scale large enough to dislocate that international economy which had grown up during the 19th century, the first between European nations which collectively controlled most of the rest of the world. It was fought with determination and desperation, because belligerents believed that they fought for survival. The great wars, got so utterly out of hand as an instrument of policy that it demanded unlimited liability. According to Thomson: "Its greatest novelty, historically, was a remarkable disparity between the ends sought, the price paid, and the results obtained". By 1914 the balance of power in Europe had been so successfully restored that the nicety of its equilibrium was in itself a menace to peace. Each power, had consistently aimed not at an equal balance but at preponderance for itself and its allies. Each wanted, to enjoy a margin of preponderance great enough to give it at least security against aggression. According to an English Journalist: "The stage which Europe had reached was that of semi-internationalism which organised the nations into two groups but provided no bridge between them. There could scarcely have been worse conditions for either peace or war. The quilibrium was so delicate that a puff of wind might destroy it––". The murder of Archuke Ferdinand provided the great powers, the occassion to test their strength, and this precipitated a world war.

The great war of 1914-18 was not the result of any sudden incident. The stage for it had been set during last years of the 19th century and the first few years of the twentieth. The great war of 1914 was the culmination of the developments that had been going on for more than a generation. Its causes are to be sought in the conjunction and intermingling of various forces and tendencies which had been at work for long time among the nations of Europe.

The Alliance System

The defeat of France by Prussia in 1870-71 and the formation of the German empire gave to Germany the unquestioned predominance in continental Europe. But Bismarck feared a recovery by France and a war of revenge. So he formed the three emperors league (1872). But conflicting interests between Russia and Austria in the Balkan made a further renewal of the three emperor's league impossible, but Bismarck concluded a secret agreement with Russia, known as the Re-insurance treaty (1887). In the re-insurance treaty, Bismarck sold out Austria's interests in the Balkans in return for Russia's promise not to aid France in a Franco-German war. But Caprivi, who followed Bismarck as German chancellor, allowed the re-insurance treaty to lapse. Bismarck also entered into alliance with Austria in 1879 (Dual alliance). But Germany was all along apprehensive of the designs of France. Italy, on the other hand, felt aggrived, when Tunis was appropriated by France. So that German diplomat persuaded Italy to join into a triple alliance with Germany and Austria-Hungary (1882). This alliance continued till it was dissolved by the defection of Italy in 1915.

Bismark was dismissed by Kaiser William II in 1890, and henceforth German foreign policy underwent a great change. The new Kaiser refused to renew the treaty with Russia. She (Russia) thus turned to France who had also no other friend at that time. When the re-insurance treaty expired in 1890, Russia was glad to form an alliance with France. There seemed to be something unnatural in a partnership between the most reactionary despotism (Russia) and the most enlightened republic (France) in Europe, but each of them saw in the Triple alliance (Germany, Austria-Hungary and Italy) a permanent obstruction to its dearest hopes-France to the recovery of Alsace-Lorraine, and Russia to the acquisition of constantinople. In 1894 the Frano-Russian agreement was turned into a formal military convention stipulating in what circumstances and with what forces each would give military support to the other. Henceforth, Europe was divided into two groups, the Triple alliance and the Franco-Russian alliance. But the antagonism between these two combinations was not so marked in the beginning.

On the other hand, Great Britain continued outside the alliance system and for some years pursued a policy of "Splendid isolation". She had conflicts of interests with all the continental powers. Her rivalry with France in Africa came to the very verge of war in 1898 over the Fashoda incident. Her relations with Russia kept in a strained State by Rusia's activities in Persia, Afganistan, and the Far-East. Germany was vigorously challenging her old time commercial supremacy. In 1900-1902, Great Britain, repeatedly approached Germany with offers of an understanding, but Germany refused the offers. Rebuffed by Germany, the British turned first to Japan, with whom they signed a treaty in 1902, and then to France, with whom they reached an understanding (Entente Cordiale) in 1904. Both England and France had been traditional enemies for hundreds of years. But the failure of the British reapproachment with Germany, the determination of Germany on a naval building programme, the changed attitude towards Britain on the part of the French Government after the French elections of 1902, all contributed to a change of front. Finally, a deal was arranged between France and England, and the essence of which was that Britain promised the French a free hand in Morocco in return for French recognition of Britains' virtual conquest of Egypt. Although this agreement was merely a statement of harmony and not an alliance, it was of great importance in ending Anglo-French rivalry and was consequently a terrific blow to the Triple alliance. The Entente is of vital importance as making the abandonment by Britain of her policy of isolation in world affairs and her realisation of the seriousness of Germany's Challange to her sea-power. Moreover, it led to an improvement of Anglo-Russian relations and prepared the way for the Tripple Entente of 1907.

Despite the Anglo-French entente, relations between Britain and Russia remained strained, and during the Russo-Japanese war, British public opinion openly favoured Japan. After the war overtures were made from both sides and France naturally used all her influence to bring Britain and Russia together. The adoption of a form of democratic parliamentary government in Russia (1906) helped to create a better feeling in Britain, and in 1907, a convention was signed removing the causes of antagonism. Spheres of influence in Persia were agreed upon, and the two powers engaged to preserve the integrity of both Afghanistan and Tibet. Thus, a new grouping of powers came into existence which would have seemed impossible twenty years before. Germany's policy had created its own opposition. Hence forward till 1914, Europe was divided into two armed camps. Each nations were linked by a maze of treaties, conventions, agreements and understandings. Thus, the shifting and maneuvering of international diplomacy had at least brought about the necessary condition for a world war.

Secret Diplomacy

The anarchic condition of international relations was aggravated by the practice of secret diplomacy, which lent itself to all kinds of corruption and double-dealing. An atmosphere of fear and suspecion was created.

Forgery, lying and corruption reigned in every foreign office throughout the world. International morlity sank very low. No nation knew when it might be sold out by its allies, what plots might be forming in its back. Men perfectly honourable in their private lives were willing to lie shamelessly in the service of their countries. Such instances of international duplicity as Bismarck's negotiation of the Reinsurance treaty, Italy's nullification of the triple alliance bring to mind the prevalence of conspiracy and Machiavellianism in the dealings among great states and show why no nation felt it could trust any other.

Economic Imperialism

Economic imperialism leads to international rivalries. World history during the 19th and 20th centuries was charecterised by a struggle for markets, for sources of raw materials and fields for investment of surplus capital and for settlement. The imperialistic rivalries, exacerbated nationalist feelings and led to endless friction among the great powers. Particularly keen in the decade before world war I was the commercial competition between Germany and Great Britain. The efforts to establish protectorate and sphere of influence in various parts of the world resulted in bad blood among nations. There were also tariff wars between various countries.

Ultra Nationalism

The spirit of nationalism or the emotional desire for unity and political independence among peoples having a common language and a common racial and cultural heritage is a very old force in human civilisation. Throughout the 18th century, nationalism continued to grow, and it received an immense impetus from the French revolution and the Napoleonic wars. At the Congress of Vienna nationalism was largely diregarded in favour of legitimacy. During the 19th century the Vienna settlement was revised, in most cases by violent nationalistic upsurgence. But there remained in the period 1871-1914 many unsatisfied nationalistic ambitions, and the agitation of these ambitions, combined with the manouvering of the great powers to take advantage of the situation constituted a constant meance to peace. Nationalism in its chronic form assumed the aspects of pan-Germanism, pan-Slavism and revenge. The people of France had decided to regain the provinces of Alsace and Lorraine from Germany. Similarly, Trentino and Trieste remained part of the Austrain empire after the unification Italy, although the majority of the population was Italian. Austria-Hungary and Italy, although joined together in the triple alliance, coul dnot be real friends as long as this source of irritation continued. On the other hand, the internal politics of the Balkan states was also affected by the feeling of extremist nationalism.

Chauvinism and Militarism

Very often, newspapers in all countries tried to inflame nationalist feelings by misrepresenting the situation in other countries. Politicians, hungry for applause and votes, exploited a never failing reservoir of popularity by vain-glorious boasting about the achivements and historic destinies of their countries. Each nation had its war cult and its popular literature praising military glory. The pressure of the Chauvinists was such that even pacifically statesmen were carried along by the current and forced to adopt aggressive policies against their better judgements.

The rising nationalist sentiments, the increasing tension among the powers and the existence of the two rival systems of alliances, produced a deep sense of insecurity in the minds of the powers. Germany greatly increased the size of her standing army. In all the continental countries, peace time conscription (Universal military training) was in Vogue. In the meantime the progress of science and the industrial revolution were multiplying the effectiveness of weapons and continually adding to the cost and complexity of the modern military machine. Each nation believed itself to be arming in self-defense. An important cause of the growing estrangement between Great Britain and Germany in the years 1900-14 was the German effort to create a large navy, which Britain regarded as a direct threat to her national safety. Further, questions of governmental policy came to be decided more and more by the necessities of the general staff and their plans for war.

Role of Kaiser William II

William II became the Kaiser (Emperor) of Germany in 1888 and German foreign policy underwent a radical change. Difference of opinion between Kaiser William II and Bismarck became so keen both in respect of internal and external affairs that in 1890 Bismarck had to resign. Kaiser William II was imbued with on out of date belief in "Divine Right" which went to his head like strong wine. Vain, exuberant, impulsive, restless, gifted with superficial cleverness and unbounded self-confidence, he enjoyed his position more than any other man that was ever born to an imperial throne. The young Kaiser announced in so many words that henceforth there was going to be only one master in Germany-himself. He ignored the chancellor and when Bismark played his well tried card of resignation, it was accepted with insulting alacrity. All Europe was aghast at the temerity of the inexperienced captain in thus dropping the pilot who had steered the ship of the empire with such triumphant success since its lauching, but he had no qualms of self-distrust.

Kaiser William II was a man of high ambitions. He said; "Germany is not a satiated country but a nation capable of infinite expansion. Germany's destiny was not merely European, but world wide". Germany was on the point of threatening the European balance of power under the aggressive nationalism of the German Kaiser, William II. According to Hazen: "The reign of William II was notable for the remarkable expansion of industry and commerce which rendered Germany the redoubtable rival of England–– William II desired that Germany should be strong on the sea, that she might act with decision in any part of the world, that her diplomacy, which was permeated with the ideas that nothing great should be done in world politics anywhere, in Europe, Asia and Africa, without her consent, might be supported by a formidable navy. To make that fleet powerful was a growing pre-occupation of the emperior". His dreams of welt-politic (World politics), his naval and colonial ambitions and his policy in Turky and Africa led to the formation of the Triple entente among England, France and Russia. His attitude in the Moroccan crisis was most provocative. German admirals and generals followed in the footsteps of their master. Admiral Tipnitz and General Von Moltke claimed that they could sweep England, France and Russia aside if they had their way. This sabre-rattling of the German army and naval officers overawed the politicians in their own country and created a good deal of distrust abroad. William II's unsatisfied imperialist ambition was the chief source of international frictions and crises that presaged the outbreak of the great war.

Lack of International Institution

Historians of the first decade of the 20th century dwelt much on the material prosperity of the world. While the general optimism had substantial grounds, it is difficult on the part of the Post-war generation to see civilisation and progress as the essential charecteristics of the period. We are more inclined to see the sinister forces that were slowly working forward to a world Catastrophe. There was anarchy in the international relations. Although there was a code of international law and morality, there was no power to enforce the same. Many resolutions were passed at the Hague conferences of 1899 and 1907 but those were observed by the various states according to their convenience. There was no institution of international nature which could make efforts to evoid the possibility of the war. Every state considered itself to be sovereign and did not regard itself to be bound by its international commitments.

Colonialism and Imperialism

One of the remarkable features of the 19th century was the feverish attempt of the European powers to extend their control over the non-European world. The outcry for colonies and sphere of influence is strikingly illustrated by the scramble for Africa. Foreign policy tends more and more to become world policy and the whole world is now the field of active diplomacy. As the century progressed, several factors combined to create a new impetus for colonial expansion. This revival of imperialism, was largely, the result of the new economic conditions produced by the industrial revolution. With the growing industrialisation came large scale production which demanded new markets. The improvement in transportation and communication brought about by modern science made it much easier to acquire and govern distant overseas regions. Further, colonies held promise of draining off surplus population of unemployed classes and of new opportunities of new investment of surplus capital with prospects of greater returns. The spirit of national pride and hunger for prestige supplied a very strong incentive to colonial expansion. This spirit was strong in the two new States of Italy and Germany. With the entry of these two States the competition for overseas possessions became keener. The scramble for colonies produced bitter disputes and international rivalries which often threatened to develop into armed conflicts.

International Crisis 1905-14

After the separation of Europe into two armed groups diplomatic incidents became increasingly dangerous, more likely to develop into crisis, which might involve the whole continent in war. During the ten years following the entente between Britain and France an series of incident occured.

Moroccan Crisis 1905-06

The formation of the entente cordiale was a shock to German diplomacy. Determining not to be left out of the settlement of the Moroccan question, the German Minister, Holstein, sent the Kaiser on a visit to Tangier in March 1905. The Kaiser made a speech recognising the independent soverignity of Morocco, and Germany demanded an international conference to settle the future of the country. Delcasse, the French Foreign Minister resented this challange and advocated war with Germany. But Russia was exhausted by her war with Japan and because of internal disorder she was in no condition to fight, while Great Britain, though offering strong diplomatic support, did not definitely commit herself. The French finally submitted to the German pressure. This was regarded as a humiliating defeat for French diplomacy. At the Algeciras conference, the Germans found themselves out-voted. At the Algeciras conference,

France and Spain were granted limited powers of control and the integrity of Morocco was reaffirmed. The Moroccan crisis strengthened the bonds of union between Britain and France.

The Bjorko Pact

Germany had felt the need for support. Even Russia, broken by the defeats of the Russo-Japanese war, was not to be despised at this juncture. At Bjorka in the Baltic, in 1905, the Kaiser obtained the personal pledge of the Czar to a draft treaty guaranteeing mutual support if either was attacked by a European power. The Kaiser was delighted, feeling that he had formed a new block (Russia, Germany, France, Italy, Austria-Hungry). But Russian statesmen realised that France would never consent to such an arrangement and forced the Czar to repudiate the pact.

The Second Moroccan Crisis 1911 Or (The Agadier Crisis)

The Conference of Algeciras was not followed by improvement in the internal conditions of Morocco, where disorders and misgovernment continued. In 1911, the tribes in and around Fez rose in rebellion which the sultan was unable to suppress. When French troops were sent to suppress it, Germany protested against the occupation of the capital. At the end of June the German Gunboat panther was sent to Agadier at the request of German firms for the protection of their lives and property. After France had protested against Germany's action, negotiations began. Only when Britain let it be clearly known that in the event of war she would support France did Germany modify her demand. Eventually, French protectorate over Morocco was recognised by Germany, and in return France ceded to Germany a large part of the Congo.

The Tripolitan War 1911-12

Italy had been disappointed of territory in North Africa when the French seized Tunis, and afterwards turned her attention to the north-East part of the continent and there secured Eritreas and part of Somaliland. Her attempt in 1896 at the conquest of Abyssinia had failed, but anticipating the imminent breakup of the Turkish dominions she obtained in advance the consent of France, Russia and Britain to her annexation of Tripoli. The young Turk revolution and the activities of Germany in Turky caused Italy to prepare to hasten the event, and the Agadier crisis presented the opportunity when the other powers were too pre-occupied to raise any objection. In 1911, Italy declared war on Turky. In October 1912, the attack of the Balkan league on Turky caused the latter to make peace hurridly, and by the treaty of Lausanne to cede Tripoli (Libya) to Italy. The effects of the Tripolitan war were far-reaching. Germany was indignant at Italy's action. It marked a stage on the road by which Italy went from the Triple alliance to join the entente, while Turky came gradually to occupy the Vaccant position by the side of Germany and Austria.

The Balkan Problems

No single event influenced the outbreak of the war in 1914 more than the Balkan wars of 1912-13. The clash of interests of the great powers in the Balkan peninsula was the most outstanding cause of the first world war.The clash of national forces in the Balkan peninsula had led to one crisis after another all through the 19th century.

Bosnia and Herzegovina had been adminstered by Austria-Hungary since 1878, although the provinces were nominally part of the Ottoman empire. In 1908 taking advantage of a revolution at constantinople, the Austrian foreign minister and his Russian counterpart arranged a deal by which Austria was to annex Bosnia and Herzegovina and Russia was to obtain the opening of the straits to Russian battleships. The annexation aroused the greatest resentment in Serbia, where ardent Pan-Slavists had been nourishing plans for a greater Serbia to include the South Slaves of Bosnia. But the annexation of the provinces blocked Serbia's access to the Adriatic and facilitated Austria's penetration in the Balkan regions. Henceforward Serbia was the centre of a Pan-Slav agitation directed towards the break-up of the Dual monarchy. For some months war seemed imminent between Austria-Hungary and Serbia. The Balkan tangle was further complicated by the unqualified support of Russia to Serbia. Russia, a slav nation, herself encouraged Serbian nationalism and Pan-Slavism. Since 1908 both Serbia and Russia harboured the most evil design against Austria. The Crux of the Balkan problem lay in the rival aspirations of Austria-Hungary and Serbia supported by Russia. The hostile Serbian press campaign and the subversive activities of the Slav terrorists had in turn caused extreme hostility in Austria. The Balkan problem was further complicated by the fact that Germany had been expanding her influence in the Ottoman empire. Germany's Turkish policy, and particularly the construction of the Berlin-Baghdad railway was bitterly resented by Russia. Germany and Austria-Hungary had been trying to isolate Serbia in the Balkans.

The Balkan wars of 1912-13 revealed the anti-Serbian attitude of Austria. She followed a most uncompromising attitude towards the ambitions of Serbia and did her best to block the expansion. It was at her instance that the powers erected Albania as an autonomous state in order to prevent

Serbia from obtaining an outlet to the sea. Austria complelled Serbia to evacuate various Adriatic towns which the Serbians had conquered from the Turks. The second Balkan crisis brought war within a measurable distances. Though it was averted, but it greatly intensified the Austro-Serbian feud. The nationalistic serbs redoubled their Pan-Serb agitation. Throughout the period of the Balkan wars, the European diplomats were kept in a state of nervous excitement. A tremendous military preparedness fever swept the continent.

Assassination of Archduke Francis Ferdinand

On June 28, 1914, the Archduke Francis Ferdinand, heir-apparent to the throne of Austria-Hungary, and his wife were assassinated at Sarajevo, the capital of Bosnia, by a fanatic Serb patriot princip, (a member of the Serbian terrorist society Black Hand), a south slave Austrian subject. The assassination, inspired by Pan-Slav sentiment and planned in Belgarde, was an incident in the long feud between the Serbs and Austria-Hungary that had lasted since 1903. The Austrian Government ordered an investigation, and though, the report contained no evidence of the Serbians government's complicity, decided to present an ultimatum. Having obtained the blank cheque from Germany, Austria delivered an ultimatum to Serbia containing ten humiliating damands. In the ten demands, Austria had demanded a guarantee of good behaviour in the future, dissolution of secret societies, immediate suppression of Anti-Austrian propaganda, etc. On July 25 1914, Serbia made a reply to the Austrian ultimatum, conciliatory in tone, but practically rejecting as destructive of Serbian Soverignity (those requring that Serbia accept the collaboration of Austrian officials is Serbia for supressing the subversive movements and for investigation of the Sarjevo murder). Austria pronounced the reply unsatisfactory and broke off diplomatic relations with Serbia. The French Statemen confined themselves to a stand firm, united front policy which they hoped would frightened the Germans into a peaceful diplomatic retreat. Russia was determined to prevent an Austria triumph.

On July 28, 1914, Austria declared war on Serbia, Meanwhile, Serbia had appealed to Russia for support and Czar had ordered "measure preliminary to mobilization". The crisis was deepening and Europe was heading towards a catastrophe. The Kaiser made a last minute effort to localise the conflict, but it was too late. The Russian mobilization forced mobilization by Germany. On 2nd August, the threat of war between Germany and France grew very grave and on 3rd August, 1914, Germany declared war on France. It was still doubtful whether Britain would take part. The British fleet was in readiness, and grey (the British Foreign

Secretary) asked the French and German government whether they would respect Belgian neutrality. The German reply was evasive. News of the German demand for a free passage through Belgium came next day, and on August 4, 1914, British ultimatum was sent to Germany. On 4th August, Great Britain declared war on Germany. Few or none of those responsible for foreign policy wanted war. But diplomacy had long been a game of bluff backed by a show of force, and in 1914 Austria was prepared to risk a general war to get her way, and Russia was prepared to resist her. The complexity of Europe's military machines reduced the chances of peace. The ambitions, the fears, and the hatred of the two groups (Allies and Axis) had plunged the world in darkness. According to Grey, "The lamps are going out all over Europe, we shall not see them lit again in our life time".

Results

The war that was waged from 1914-18 differed from earlier wars in many respect. Artillery was used to a greater extent than on any previous occassion. It was said, and probably with truth, that the amount of ammunition consumed in a single day would have been sufficient to serve for a whole compaign in a 19th century war. At sea, mines and torpedoes used with deadly effect in the blowing-up of ships, while, as submarines came more and more into use, many ingenious devices were invented to combat them. For the first time war was carried on in the air. The casualties sustained during the war were much more numerous than in any previous war. It would be useless to attempt to form an accurate estimate of the number of those killed and wounded on all fronts and in all armies.

The world war proved to be a mighty accelrator of events. It was said by Lenin that it destroyed the Hohenzollern of Prussia, the Hapsburg of Austria, and the Romanv of Russia. The first world war uprooted the autocracy and monarchy from almost all the countries of Europe. Another important results of the war was the spread of democracy. Germany and Austria adopted democratic constitutions, while in Russia the democratic movement became entangled with Bolshevism. The new states that had been created, setup republication constitutions with a parliamentary government based upon democratic franchises. War provided an incentive to the cause of women in getting the right of Franchise.

As the war developed by 1918 into a full scale world war, it affected most parts of the world. In 1917, when the French armies mutinied large sections of the most important front depended on British contingents drawn from various parts of her empire. By 1918 more than a Quarter million Indians were on the battle line. Their immense contribution, in turn, made the war a stage in the decline of colonialism. Not only in India but the demand for self determination came to be heard in the Middle East which became a storm centre of politics after 1919.

With the surrender of Germany on 11th November, 1918, the first world war came to an end. At the beginning of 1919, the leaders of the victorious nations, numbering 32, gathered in Paris, the capital of France, in a conference, famous as the peace conference of Paris. Actual business of peace was conducted by the so called "Big Four". It was a conference of the victorious powers to punish the defeated nations. The treaty which was forced upon defeated Germany is famous as the treaty of Versailles. For Germany, the treaty of Versailles was the most humiliating treaty. The treaty of Versailles became a direct cause of the second world war.

Post-war Europe was confronted with a variety of perplexing problems, and in many cases democracy was found incapable of coping with them. The anti-democratic forces like Fascism, Nazism and Bolshevism gave rise to dictatorships. In the Fascist States the fundamental ideas of democracy such as freedom of the press and participation of the people in the government, were denounced as a source of weakness and were consequently repudiated. Power was assumed by an individual who proclaimed himself as the representative of the state and who allowed neither opposition nor criticism.

A bright result of the first world war was the formation of the league of nations at the end of the war. President Wilson of America thought of a lasting peace in future by bringing into existence a world organisation for peace. As a result, the Paris peace conference worked for the formation of an organisation to be known as the league of Nations. It was founded to promote international peace and security, to maintain just and honourable relations among the nations.

The economic consequences of the war were even more serious than its political aftermath. The territorial losses of Germany caused a major economic shock among the defeated powers. France and Belgium suffered from the devastation of their industrial regions. In Eastern Europe, lack of seeds, fertilizers, and agricultural implements resulted in a marked decline of farm production. All the powers had lost foreign markets. And a general return to protective tariffs retarded recovery everywhere.

The Prices of all goods and commodities shot up considerably due to the decrease of production. Owing to the heavy amount of loans the countries had to issue paper currencies and it led to the inflation of money.

Total war affected the civilian populations which soon began to suffer food shortage and diseases caused by malnutrition. The optimism of the 19th century with its belief in automatic progress could scarcely survive a war which left many million widows and orphans. The war had a deep effect on customs and manners.

The labourer had played an important role in the war. After the end of the war, they put their demands before the Government to provide them with necessary facilities of life. The reawakening of the labour class was an important consequence of the world war. The concept of socialism was a by-product of the first world war. The principle of socialism became popular in all countries of Europe.

Another factor that promoted post-war instability was finance. The western allies were indebted to the United States. This caused problem in international financial affairs in the post-war period. The effects of the post-war economic crisis were felt in many ways. Unemployment never much of a problem in the past, now assumed alarming propertions. All the major countries from Europe suffered inflation.

It is thus clear that the first world war ended an era but the respite proved to be too short. The second world war broke out in 1939. The devastating global wars ravaging the world within four decades is a matter of great significance. The war led to profound consequences in the social, cultural and economic fields. The first world war put an end to the era of supremacy of Europe on the world stage. The disillusionment heralded a loss of faith in liberal-democratic values that contributed to the widespread popularity of the Fascist ideologies in the post-war world. Having lost confidence in the power of reason to solve the problems of the human community, in liberal doctrines of individual freedom, and in the instiutions of parliamentary democracy, many people turned to Fascism as a saving faith. Far from making the world safe for democracy as the liberals had hoped, the first world war gave rise to totalitarian movements that would nearly destroy democracy.

Chapter XVI

Paris Peace Settlement

(1919)

Forty-nine months of desperate war, cataclysmic experience had transformed the political structure of Europe, undermined its socio-economic foundations and reduced its influence in world affairs. The war destroyed many beautiful cities, caused distress to the millions and good deal of humanity suffered the pangs of starvation, poverty and hopelessness. The old world of Europe had disappeared. Consumed in the furnace of war, Europe had become a mass of molten mental, and had to be reshaped new. At the same time how many millions would have to struggle with health permanently impaired, how many women would have to bear alone the responsibility of rearing their families because the fathers had been killed, these were samples of the many questions that could never be answered. In fact the war was a test of strength and the Axis powers lost the war. Monarchy tumbled down in many countries, a spectore of communism hunting Europe. In an atmosphere poisoned by memories of the carnage in the battle fields, and the crushing burdens laid upon posterity, the statesmen met at Paris. The interest now shifted from the battle-fields to the chancelleries, and the diplomats resumed the place from which they had ben ousted by the Generals. The slogan of 'the war to end war' commanded universal support. The task of dealing with the defeated nations and of attempting to build a more secure world, was undertaken by the victors. The peace conference opened in January 1919 at Paris, with clemenceaus as President. On June 28, 1919 in the hall of mirrors in the stately old palace of Louix XIV, the treaty of versailles was signed by representatives of Germany and of thirty-one nations leagued against Germany. The scene was that in which in 1871 the Hohenzollern empire had been proclaimed, and the date was that on which in 1914, the archduke Ferdinand had been assassinated. Thus, the first world war formally ended on the fifth anniversary of the immediate occasion of its beginning.

Venue of the Meeting

In order to liquidate the war and to restore peace and tranquility, a Congress of the victors was summoned on 18th January, 1919, in Paris which was the venue of the congress. The choice of the French capital marked, symbolically, the centre of gravity of the bloc of western liberal, democratic powers. It also ensured that the tiger of France, the aged French premier clemenceau by courtesy became the President of the conference, and that French influences in general should bear strongly upon its whole atmosphere and spirit. Of course, vindictive tone of the Paris press and the slogan of 'no mercy to Germany' made Paris a nightmare. Only the allied and associated governments represented in the Paris peace conference. The three major omissions in the conference were the neutral powers, communist Russia, and the defeated axis powers. The exclusion of these states proved the basic weaknesses of the settlement. Any how, despite the important omission, it was the first great world peace conference. The organisation of the conference recognised a clear distinction between belligerent powers with general interests which were only the big five (The USA, Britain, France, Italy and Japan), and belligerent powers with special interests comprised all other belligerent states. The big five sent five delegates each. As the conference was large and its agenda varied, and as the war had been a war of the great powers, control was exercised by the council of Ten. This select body made all the preliminary and initial arrangements for the conduct of the conference. It soon, however, broke-down into two bodies, the council of five and the council of four (consisting of President Wilson, Clemenceau, Lloyd George and Orlando). Japan and Italy lost interest in the proceeding of the conference, so ultimately the "Big three" determined the proceeding. No doubt they were a contrasted trio, but the most important things they had in common were that they were leaders of democratic countries, and therefore sensitive to national feeling at home. The organisation of the work of the conference was inevitably elaborate. But the great fault of the political leaders was their failure to draft a plan of procedure. Fifty-Eight commissions were set up to deal with different aspects, but all important decisions were finally made by the "Big Three". All smaller powers were relagated to playing minor roles in the conference.

Leaders of the Conference

The peace Congress after its formal inauguration met rarely. So the real work was done by special committee of diplomate and it was done in privacy. It was no easy task to reconcile differences of opinion and policy among the thirty-two delegations and to preserve a united front on the part of all the allied and associated governments. President Woodro Wilson, who had set his heart upon for forming a permanent league of nations, felt obliged to make concession to his fellow negotiators in order to enlist their support for his pet project. Wilson was the representative of the most powerful nation in the world, whether thought of in terms of manpower or of economic resources. He enjoyed a high personal prestige because, before America had entered the war, his pronouncements had seemed to express, as no one else had done, the aims and hopes of the fighting nations. The various nations had found themselves at war for immediate objectives, like the preservation of Belgium's neutrality, or the possession of Alsace-Lorraine or the like.

Though, a professional politician of no little skill, Wilson had his early carrier in academic spheres and he believed in the power of ideas to influence human affairs. The moral sense which motivated him was partly the product of his own outlook and training, partly that of the detachment which distance lent to his American view of Europe and of the world. His contribution to the settlement was influenced by the ambiguity of his position in American domestic politics. By Europeans he was acclaimed as the saviour of a war-wrecked continent. Great crowds greeted his arrival in Paris and set great store by his presence there, but they knew little of the American back-ground of his visit to Europe. Among masses of people, on both sides of fighting lines, Wilson was revered as a kind of prophet who held the solution of the world's problem. This placed upon him a terrible responsibility, and one of the most crucial questions of the day was whether he had the character and the equipment of knowledge sufficient to enable him to do all that was expected of him. He had been a university professor of political science and something of the classroom and the study seemed always to remain with him. That is to say, he was too prone to consider the theory and logic of the question without taking into account sufficiently its personal and practical elements. This was a serious handicap to a statesman who would have to deal with shrewd and nimble-witted politicians in solving the most complex political problems in Europe. He was further handicapped by having only a limited understanding of what those problems were.

Wilson's 14 Point

The USA emerged from the war as creditor of her victorious but exhausted allies. She had achieved in four years of war an industrial expansion equal to that of the previous quarter of a century. The senate elections of 1918 had brought Republican victories and had deprived Wilson of the support of a majority of his own democrat members in the senate. He was well aware of the amount of opposition to his role as a world statesman and mediator. Wilson brought to the conference table an element of idealism which was in strong contrast to the cross-currents of motive at work in post-war Europe. The Wilsonian programme had been outlined to congress on 8 January 1918". What we demand in this war.... It is that the world be made fit and safe to live in, and particularly that it be made safe for every peace loving nation, wishes to live its own free life, determined its own institutions..." These aims had been summarised in 14 points which included (1) abolition of secret diplomacy, (2) Free navigation at sea for all nations in war and peace, (3) removal of economic barriers between states, (4) all round reduction of armaments, (5) impartial adjustment of colonial claims in the interest of population concerned, (6) evacuation of Russian territory, (7) restoration of Belgium, (8) liberation of France and restoration of Alsace-Lorraine, (9) readjustment of Italian frontiers along lines of nationality, (10) self-government to the people of Austria-Hungary, (11) Rumania, Serbia to be evacuated and Serbia given access to the sea, (12) self-government to the non-Turkish people of the Turkish empire and permanent opening of Daranelles, (13) an independent Poland with secure access to the sea, and (14) a general association of nations to preserve peace. It was thus as the hopeful architest of world peace that Wilson arrived in Paris in 1919. He made another addition to the general principle, "impartial justice meted out must involve no discrimination between those to whom we wish to be just and those to whom we do not wish to be just". These fomulations of peace aims were endorsed by the allied governments and were made the basis on which the German Government accepted the armistice. But later on when the big powers sat on the conference table they found that their basic interest opposed to each other.

In Clemenceau and Lloyd George, Wilson faced two vivid and contrasted opponents. Clemenceau was the oldest of all the statesman at versailles. He was able to remember the Franco-prussian war vividly, and the humiliation of the French defeat at the hands of Germany, and he was conscious of the destruction wrought by the German in France's north-eastern provinces. He typified France's attitude, and had the confidence of his fellow countryman, he summarised in himself the intense hostility of the French towards the Germans. To him the conference had only one purpose, to produce a treaty that would give to France complete security against any future danger from Germany, and would restrore to France her lost provinces, Alsace-Lorraine. This could be done by depriving Germany of her armed forces and by crippling her economic resources so that never again would she become wealthy enough either to compete with her neighbours in trade or to threaten their peace. He wanted immediate compensation for French losses in the recent war. It was a typical 'Tigerish' attitude, little concerned with theories that did not affect him or his people, but fiercely adamant where their interests were concerned. No one can doubt that he spoke for France alone.

Lloyd George had the difficult task of trying to reconcile Wilson's indealism and clemenceau's revenge. He had a considerable backing at home, having been confirmed in his position as Prime Minister in the election in 1919, Which saw his return to power, by a massive majority, amid such slogans as "Make Germany pay". As a war time Prime Minister and as a politician seeking popularity, he went to the conference with many ideas for future peace. He had made known his war aims, "we want peace, which will be just but not vindictive. We want a stern peace.... The crime demands it. But its severity must be designed not to grafity venegeance but to vindicate justice". Reparations were imposed upon Germany to make her pay for the war. Lloyd George wished to scale them down, but he got little assistance from the Americans and met down-right hostility from the French. He certainly raised his voice for moderation in Paris, urging his counterparts to act as impartial arbiters, forgetful of the passion of wars. But the British Prime Minister was a controversial figure with a capacity for attacking a bad press. Goodwill towards the defeated was not a popular cause and he was attacked in both press and Parliament for his lack of ruthlessness. At the same time, the rigid, fiery nationalist clemenceau, was against the equally rigid theorist, Wilson, and could never have agreed upon any question, had not the supplied, quick-witted Lloyd George been present to find a compromise to appease both. In this sense he was the king-pin of the whole conference.

Among these three diplomatic giants, the fourth figure at the conference was the Italian representative, Vittoriao Orlando. He was a learned and eloquent diplomat, who had no command over English. He felt dejected when his territorial claim was flouted in the Paris peace conference, though it was promised in the treaty of London. He left the conference in the midst of the conference.

Problems of Making a Peace Settlement

The peace makers had to work within limits and conditions that existed before it met. One of these limitations was the terms of secret treaties. Italy and Rumania, before entering the war, had made bargains with Britain and France about territories that they were to receive when victory was attained. The treaty of London which was signed in 1915 promised some territories such as Trieste and South Tyrol. Such promises had now to be matched with the later statements. Wilson had stated that Italy's frontiers should be along clearly recognisable lines of nationality, and he protested that the treaty of London, previously secret did not uphold this principle. Another treaty which would bind the allies was the one which they had made in 1916 with Rumania whereby she was promised considerable territories including Transylvania, Bukovina. Another fact facing the conference when it wanted to adjust state boundaries was that is several instances local population already had mad their own decisions in the matter. One of the thorniest problems was what should be done with the Austro-Hungarian empire and its complicated populations. But, by the time the conference met, the empire no longer existed. It was split-up into its elements. At the end of may 1918 the Czeches declared themselves independent. Similarly Yugoslavia came into existence. The allies had intended to enforce severe terms upon Germany and Austria. The question therefore arose whether the new nationalist states were to be treated as guilty because parts of them had been within the empire. Similarly, the Bolshevik revolution and its ideals created panic among the powers. A necessity was felt to bring a change in the approach of the allies towards Germany in order to keep Eastern Europe safe from the revolutionary wave of Russia. Above all, when the peace conference met, it was soon obvious that a settlement would be difficult because of the differing allied views about how to treat the defeated powers. France wanted a harsh peace to ruin Germany--Economically and militarily, so that she could never again threaten French frontiers. Britain was in favour of a less severe settlement enabling Germany to recover quickly so that she could resume her role as a major customer for British goods. USA had earlier been in favour of a lenient peace but Wilson's attitude changed after the German ignored his 14 points, and imposed the harsh Brest-Litovsk treaty--On Russia and he now agreed to the British and French demands for reparation and German disarmanment. He was also in favour of self-determination. Hence, there was a struggle between two conflicting ideologies in the conference namely idealism and realism. It was not a conflict between nations or personalities. The confusion that haunted the conference, haunted also the minds of men in 1919, a tension between hopes and ideals of a more orderly world as a prize to be snatched from the opportunities of victory, and the human emotion of vengeance, the natural reaction of people who had suffered oppression, and whose recent experiment nourished hatred and fear. This background of the conference was important as it helped to produce a settlement, which was harsh where it might better have been lenient. Thus, the five treaties concluded at the Paris peace conference were the treaty of versailles (June 28, 1919) with Germany, the treaty of St. German (September 10) with Austria, the treaty of Neuilly with Bulgaria, (November 27) the treaty of Trianon (June 4, 1920) with Hungary, and the treaty of Sevres (August 10, 1920) with Turkey.

Treaty of Versailles

The draft of the proposed peace treaty with Germany was lengthy document running into 15 parts and 440 articles in 230 pages. It was agreed to by the big four and endorsed by the Congress in plenary session on May 6, 1919. On the following day the German plenipotentiaries were admitted to the Congress and presented with the draft. They protested that it was intolerably severe and contradictory of the 14 points, on the basis of which they had consented to the armistice. But the allied statesmen were deaf. Then, after demonstration of protest throughout Germany, after threats of compulsion–On the part of the allies, after the resignation of the scheidemann ministry at Berlin, after several days of awful suspence, the German constituted assembly at Weimer on June 23, 1919, finally voted to accept unconditionally the allied terms of peace. On the fifth anniversary of the Sarajevo murder on June 28, 1919 the treaty of versailles was signed in the great hall of mirror, the palace of the French king at versailles where the birth of the German empire had been proclaimed in 1871. Now that its death warrant was signed, it proved that time has brought its revenge and history inscribed on her pages.

By the terms of the treaty of versailles, Alsace and Lorraine were returned to France. Belgium received Moresnet, Eupen and Malmedy, Denmark received northern Schleswig, while southern Schleswig voted to remain with Germany. Germany ceded the coal mining area of the Saar to France, as compensation for the loss of the French coal-fields during the war, for 15 years. During this period the territory would be administered by the league of nations after which its fate would be decided by a plebiscite. To independent Poland, Germany ceded posen and west Prussia. Upper silesia, as a result of Plebiscite, was divided between Poland and Germany. To provide Poland with a port, the German city of Danzing was restored to its former status as a free-city and placed under the protection of the league. The connection between Poland and Danzig was secured by the establishment of a polish corridor, which separated East Prussia from the rest of Germany. Memel was attached to the newly created state of Lithuania. In addition to territorial cessions in Europe, Germany was required to renounce all her rights and titles over her overseas possession. They comprised German south-west Africa which was given to the union of

South Africa. German West Africa consisting of Togoland and the cameroon was partitioned between France and England, German's East Africa was shared between Britain and Belgium. Its lease of Kiaochow and privileged position in the Chinese province of Shantung, were transferred to Japan. Samoa was given to Newzeland, other pacific possession was ceded to Austrialia. These former German possessions were assigned under a mandate from the league, at any rate they were held in guardianship. Germany also recognised the independence of Czechoslovakia, and renounced the treaties of Brest-Litovsk and Bucharest, which it had signed with Russia and Rumania respectively. However, the western settlement with Germany was reached, after a profound disagreement among the big three, especially in relation to the Rhine land. France demanded an indefinite control over the Rhineland as a military gurantee of French security, but the USA and Britain refused to agree for fear of creating a new Alsace and Lorraine.

Article 231 of the treaty declared that "the allied and associated governments affirm, and Germany accepts, the responsibility of Germany and her allies for causing all the loss and damage to which the allied and associated governments and their nationals have been subjected to as a consequence of the war imposed upon them by the aggression of Germany and her allies". This was the war-guilt clause. It developed from the undertaking which Germany had accepted at the armistice to pay compensation to allied civilians. In the treaty it appeared to have become an over simplified explanation of how the war began and an extension of Germany's obligation to pay compensation. The allies were guilty of slipshod wording. It was absured to suggested that Germany alone had brought the First World War. It was equally absured of the Germans to take the war guilt clause in isolation and pretend that on that alone the settlement of Europe was based, Kaiser William II was accused for a supreme offence against international morality and the sanctity of treaties. But he could not be brought to trial as Holland, where he had taken shelter, refused to surrender him to the allies. Only few war criminals were persecuted in the German court.

The treaty imposed restrictions on Germany's military strengths. The German general staff was abolished. Her army was limited and conscription being prohibited. She was to retain only six battleships, six light cruisers, twelve destroyers, and twelve torpedo boats. She could possess no submarines, no military aircrafts, and no heavy guns and built no fortifications. Neither she could import or export war materials, nor she could made or purchase poison gases, armoured cars, and tanks.

Germany was forced to acknowledge responsibility for the world war and to promise that it would make financial reparation "for all damages done to the civilian population. Germany was to reimburse Belgium with interest at 5 per cent for all the money she had borrowed from the allied government during the war. The economic resources of Germany were to be devoted directly to the physical restoration of the invaded areas. Germany agreed to make large annual coal deliveries for ten years to France, Italy and Luxemburg. Besides, a reparation commission was to be appointed by the allies to determine the total amount of reparation. Meanwhile, upto May 1, 1921, Germany was to pay, in gold, securities, ships, the equivalent of nearly £ 5,000,000,000 pound. Germany was to surrender all her merchant vessels of 1600 or more tons gross. For five years the allies were to enjoy rights and privileges over the export and import trade business of Germany. The rivers Elbe and Kiel canal of Germany were internationalised. The treaty also provided for the collection of debts and regulation of various property rights and interests, contract, patents, insurance, etc.

The Minor Peace Treaties

The treaty of versailles, imposed on Germany, established the principles that would be applied to the smaller States associated with Germany in the war. By the treaty of St. Germain, Austria was compelled to cede Trieste, Istria, and part of Tyrol to Italy, Bohemia, Moravia and part of Silesia to Czechoslovakia, Bukovina to Rumania, and Bosnia-Herzegovina, Dalmatia to Yugoslavia. The Austrians would have preferred to join their fellow-Germans in Germany but the conference, determined to keep Germany weak, specifically forbade this by a clause in the treaty stipulating that the independence of Austria is inalienable.

The treaty with Hungary was delayed until 1920 owing to internal upheavals in that country. By the provisions of the treaty of Trianon, the Hungarians then accepted, under protest, the reduction of the State which the Hapsburg emperor had formerly ruled as King of Hungary. Hungary accepted the break-up of the Austro-Hungarian empire. Austria and Hungary became separate states with no control over other lands which had formerly belonged to the Austro-Hungarian empire. Hungary was reduced in size, and the treaty imposed limitations on Hungarian armed forces. And Hungary accepted her responsibility for certain war damage. As per the treaty Slovakia was transferred to Czechoslovakia, croatia to Yugoslavia and Transylvania to Rumania. In vain, they protested that plebiscite should be held in areas now declared to be parts of Czechoslovakia, Rumania, and Yugoslavia. Many Magyars (Hungarians) now found themselves the subject of foreign government.

From Bulgaria were taken, by the treaty of Neuilly, most of the land it had acquired in the Balkan war of 1912-13 and all its conquest in the world war. Dobruja went to Rumania, the greater part of Macedonia to Yugoslavia, and the Thracian Coast, to Greece. Bulgaria promised to pay a huge amount as compensation, and to reduce its army to 33,000. The treaty made Bulgaria the weakest among the Balkan States.

At the treaty of serves the decadent Ottoman empire was compelled to accept terms in which the traditional hostility of Greece was evident. Turkey acknowedged the loss of all rights in Egypt, Sudan, Cyprus, Morocco, and Tunisia. Armenia would be a free Christian Republic under international guarantee. Smyrna, adjacent territory in the coast of Asia minor, together with Adrianople, the Peninsula of Gallipoli would be surrendered to Greece. The Dardanelles and the Bosphorus would be internationalised. The Government of Sultan Mohammed VI at constantinople agreed to the treaty of Sevres, but the Turkish national assembly at Ankara, under the leadership of Mustafa Kemal, refused to ratify it. However, this treaty was revised at the Lausanne conference.

Critique of the Peace of Paris

Had the allies missed the bus which could possibly take them along the new road to peace? Of course, the Paris peace conference must stand in history as a conspicuous failure, it was an overall failure of human intelligence and wisdom, and in part of failure of organisation and method. This was not due either to an excess of realism or a lack of idealism, but rather due to a misapplication of both. The peace of Paris did not assume the form of a pact freely negotiated between the belligerents, it was an instrument imposed at the point of bayonet by the conqueror upon a crushed foe. The peace makers had assured a new kind of peace, but they forced upon the oppression and the enslavement of a great nation. The peace treaties were an outcome of bargains and compromises between the lofty ideals of Wilson, the nationalistic demands of clemenceau, and opportunistic aims of Lloyd George. No doubt, every treaty that brings war to an end is, in some sense, a dictated peace. As Carr says "in the treaty of versailles the element of dictation was more apparent than in any previous peace treaty of modern times". Yet, the international situation that confronted the peace-makers in Paris was certainly the brutal realities of history. They had to redraw the map of central and Eastern Europe in a way, which replaced the old dynastic frontiers by the new frontiers based on realities of national grouping, of economic viability, and of military security. They had to make a settlement with Germany which, so far as they could contrive, would perpetuate a distribution of power in Europe which was unfavourable to German resurgence as an aggressive military state. Thus, they could attempt to weaken Germany permanently by depriving her of important territories in the East in the name of granting the right of self-determination to poles. Besides, the allies claimed, there must be justice for the dead and wounded, and for those who have been orphaned and bereaved. There must be justice for those millions whose homes and land, German savegery had destroyed. But somebody must suffer for the consequences of the war. Is it to be Germany or the people of allied countries? Hence, they believe that the peace they had proposed is fundamentally a peace of justice. However, the critique of the peace of Paris opined that in making settlement with Germany, the victorious powers showed little wisdom. The allies subjected the infant Weimer republic to such constant humiliation and forced it to ratify a treaty so offensive to German national sentiment that the republic came to be associated in German minds with national disgrace.

The central powers could at least disclaim responsibility for whatever mistakes had been made. They had been required only to sign the treaties, which they did under protest. They counted their losses, lamented that self-determination had not been applied properly so that, for example, the Sudetan Germans were locked inside Czechoslovakia. The Russians could regard the settlement either as irrelevent or as a capitalist plot. On the other hand, the allies left Paris hopeful, and the treaties and the league stood as monument to their energy and hope. But Wilson returned to an America swinging to the Republican and increasingly isolationists. Britain, too, seemed half to wish that it could be possible to ignore European affairs and to concentrate on domestic problems. France was uneasy, when the Americans renounced both the league and the treaties, France began a morbid brooding on her own weakness which seemed bound to end in disaster. Italy maintained that she had been cheated. Japan retired dissatisfied with her apparent lack of superiority and brooding on the differences between white and yellow.

The peace of Paris was made familiar by German propaganda in a phrase "a dictated peace". Concession was exacted from the defeated nations without raciprocity. It was not at all negotiated by process of give and take. In case of the treaty of Versailles the element of dictation was more apparent than any previous treaty of modern times. The Germans were not consulted throughout the treaty signed. They were treated as criminals, which a cultured nation could not tolerate. Even the ordinary courtesy of social intercourse were not observed. In the words of Lloyd George "the treaty of versailles are written in the blood of fallen heroes. We must carry out the edict of providence and see that the people who inflicted the war shall never be in a position to do so again". This justifies the hatred and vengenance of the allies. The defeated nations regarded the treaty as staggering to their severity and impossible of fulfilment. The wishes of the vanquished were ignored. The treaty of versailles has been criticised by the Germans as a carthagian peace. On the other hand, not only Wilson was bomboozled but Lloyd George and clemenceau had no better fate. French Parliament attacked clemenceau as he permitted the autocratic position to bully him into the surrender of French rights.

On the basis of Wilson's 14 points Germany accepted the treaty of versailles. But the allied nations applied the principle of balance of power and statusquo. They redrew the map of Europe, which replaced the old dynastic frontier. The territories of Poland included people who were indisputably not polish. Arabs were not granted independence but put under mandate. These new nations which had been carved out of the defeated powers territory created trouble in the later years. These new nations of Czechoslovakia, Yugoslavia, and Poland remain sandwiched between Germany on the west and Russia on the East and when the two monsters pressed on them in 1939 they cracked like chest-nuts. It was a fraudulent treaty as it violated the provision of Wilson's 14 point. Free navigation was forbade as the powers did not like to lose their monopoly overseas. With regard to third point all sorts of economic barrier was enforced by the allied nations upon the defeated power. No reciprocity was maintained regarding colonial question. Colonial question was not interpreted impartially and colonies of Germany was distributed among the victors. Russia was not welcomed to the family of nations. The principle of self-determination was thrown to wind in case of the defeated nations. The promise of a new life, the great human ideal for which the people had shed their blood and the fulfilment of a new international order did not find a place in the treaty of Versailles.

The economic clauses of the settlement were punitive and harsh, and had the purpose of crippling the economies of the defeated countries. Thus, the demand for reparation for war-damage inflicted by the German armies was set at astronomical figures without any consideration of how it would be possible for Germany to pay. Germany was held responsible for all damages. Germany was deprived of her colonial possession, merchant fleet, bank-balance. These led to an exhaustion of German economy. Through the imposition of a heavy reparation the allies continued the economic warfare against Germany. Churchill once said "History will characterise all these transactions as insane. They helped to breed martial curse and the economic blizzard". The victors snached-away important German minerals like iron, coal, zinc. Is it possible to expect both milk and beaf from the same cow? Even though compensation was made by Germany for all damages done to the civilian population, they had to incur stagging losses caused by the maltreatment of the prisoners of war. The treaty embodied hatred, bitterness and resentment and it was not at all based on justice. Conscription was abolished, tanks, armoured cars, military aeroplanes were forbidden incase of the defeated nations and raciprocity was not maintained in respect of disarmament. Rivers and canals were internationalised and the defeated countries forfeited the right to use their own rivers. The Germans became more aggrieved later, as it became clear that none of the other powers intended to disarm. The Germans strongly resented the disarmament clauses and they began claiming that 1 lakh troops were not enough to keep law and order at a time of political disturbance.

The treaty of versailles created the minority problem by including many Germans into Poland and Czechoslovakia. Nearly three million Germans remained in the sudeten land within the border of Czechoslovakia, about a million lived in Poland. Similarly seven million Magyars were left in Czechoslovakia and some in Rumania. Poland was created as an independent state and was given an outlet to the sea through the polish corridor of posen. The colonial people were denied their right of self-determination. Greece was enlarged at the expense of Turky. For a great power large minorities aborad may became a military advantage, usable to disrupt a neighbouring country and prepare it for attack. As Hitler was later to show, it is easy to generate agitation for irredentist lands as for irredentist minorities. The principle of self-determination was being violated in the case of the Saar, Alsace-Lorraine, Danzing, and Memel. On the subject of the colonies it was stated that the settlement of the colonial question is equally contradictory to a peace of justice. The Germans claimed that the colonies constituted valuable parts of her national capital, functioning as a market for her industries and as an outlet for her surplus population. Thus, German property was confiscated, not only but the victors whittled her physically, humiliated her emotionally, suffocated her economically and encircle her territorially. Besides, the weimer republic from the very beginning was associated in the mind of Germans with hatred to the treaty of versailles, the imposition of war-guilt clause, and the humiliation associated with it were criticised and the republic was held responsible for accepting such terms. A democracy was imposed on a monarchical state. The militarists, the nationalists, the Junkers, the Nazis criticised the republic as the architest of German misfortune. Disbanded soldiers, unemployed youths, discontented industrialists, and business magnets had no faith in the republic. And the Nazi party took advantage of the situation and created the myth that

German salvation lay in the abolition of the weimer republic. As Langsum has put it "the continuing hostile attitude of France, the quarrel over the Ruhr, the Rhineland occupation, the reparation, and the wrangling over disarmament created anger among the Germans". The treaty of versailles was the object of criticism of the national socialist party. The reparation problem was one of important causes of the economic crisis of 1930's. The middle class was reduced to the position of proletariat, their small saving was washed off, which proved to be a happy hunting ground of nationalist, socialist propaganda. The Nazi party promised employment to the unemployed. The treaty was responsible for the rise of a militant nationalism. The Germans had no respect for parliamentary institution and they preferred glory to liberty and wanted a strong man who could bring peace and prosperity. This was the condition of Germany that chose Hitler to handle dictatorial powr in Germany.

Probably the most important outcome of the Paris peace conference was the league of nations. In its main function, the prevention of another world war, the league of nations was a failure. The next twenty years were to witness the gradual decline of its influence. A serious defect was the absence of the really great powers from the league. The USA never joined, as the senate of the USA refused to approve of American enrty. Russia did not joint unitl 1934 and without the membership of the two nations, the league lacked influence. Besides, the league was associated with the peace treaties, and as these particularly the treaty of versailles, were condemned as harsh and unjust, the league suffered condemnation. The league's lack of a military force of its own was a grave weakness. For all theses reasons the league was a weak institution. It failed to ensure a peaceful future to the world.

The settlement of 1919 failed to exact from Germany an adequate military guarantee of security. France demanded indefinite control of the left bank of the river Rhine as a military guarantee of French security. But the US and Britain refused to agree, as they were afraid of French supremacy in Europe. The Rhineland was to remain in allied military control for fifteen years, and France accepted a joint Anglo-American guarantee to support France in case of future German aggression. But the guarantee lapsed due to the senate's refusal to ratify the treaty. So France embarked on a quest for more firm safeguards of national security throughout the inter-war period. The fifteen-years occupation of the Rhineland proved equally illusory. The treaty provided German imperialist the necessary time to revive their military strength. Besides, one of the most important single factors that enabled Hitlerite Germany to wage the most barbarous war in history was that Great Britain and France were at logger heads over the execution of the peace settlement. Simulataneously Hitler after his accession to power in 1933, was able to take advantage of the current views about the Versailles treaty. He declared, Germany, was forbidden to rearm by the terms of the treaty, whereas others were rearming and thus causing humiliation and danger to Germany. He withdrew Germany from the disarmament conference at Geneva. Conscription was introduced by denouncing the treaty provisions. The abrogation of the treaty of versailles continued when Hitler ordered the troops to enter the demilitarized Rhineland. Thus, the history of the period between the two world-wars can be described as the history of the infringement of the treaty of versailles. One can safely conclude that the seeds of the Second World War were sown by the peace-makers at Paris in 1919.

Chapter-XVII

The League of Nations

During the First World War the people all over the world and particularly of human souls, large-scale destruction of private and national properties, and the horror of the deadly scientific weapons created panic in the hearts of the millions. Ne weapons in the air, on land and at sea had come into its own as a means of encouraging both civilian and military morale as well as a weapon to undermine the enemy. War which has made such apparently insatiable demands in trained men, munitions and supplies required wholly new concepts of organisation and overall control and, at the same time, it imposed on civilian populations a strain. The physical scars of war healed quickly, but the more subtle psychological scars were permanent. The scale of the war and difficulty of controlling it,had tended in the end to blunt sensibilities. The peculiarities of the international situation could not be described as international anarchy, but a twilight era of mixed system. But it is a forgone conclusion that every where people became eager for peace. Hungry for permanent peace, the victors in the war created the league of nations, which formally came into existence on 10th January 1920, the same day the versailles treaty came into operation. No doubt the league of nations was the brain child of the American president Woodro Wilson, yet, he was not the first man to conceive of so noble an idea as a scheme for international cooperation, and the First World War was not the first war to stimulate such ideals. After the Napoleonic wars a hundred years previously statesmen in Europe had given much attention to the Congress system, which was designed to prevent the outbreak of future war. Wilson's idea must futher be viewed against the background of increasing international feeling. The international Red Cross and the universal postal union dated from 1864 and 1874 respectively, a number of political movements were unaffected by national boundaries, and in 1899 and 1907 international conferences on disarmament had been held at the Hague.

International organisation of the affairs of nations was becoming a real necessity and the league of nations came into formal existence in 1920, with headquarters at Geneva in Switzerland.

The Covenant and the Purposes of the League

The covenant of the league was embodied in the treaty of versailles and the other treaties of peace. It set out the basic principles and rules. There were 26 article in the covenant. Membership was to consist of the original signatories to the covenant and thereafter to any independent state which received the votes of two-thirds of the assembly. All member states pledged that they would not embark on any aggressive act against other member states. Its chief aim was to maintina peace through collective security, if one state attacked another, the member states would act together, collectively. It was to be an agency for the enforcement of certain provisions of the peace treaties. The league was to encourage international cooperation inorder to solve economic and social problem. The signatories to the covenant pledged to maintain world peace and security through international cooperation instead of resorting to war. In order to achieve these purposes, the member states required to assume certain obligations towards each other. They agreed to respect and guarantee as against external aggression, the territorial integrity and existing political independence of all members of the league. They agreed to submit their disputes to peaceful of settlement. It was also stipulated in article 16 of the covenant that the member states would impose economic blockade and would enforce military measures if necessary against any state violating the covenant. They recognise that the maintenance of peace required the reduction of national armaments.

How was the League Organised?

There were 42 member states at the beginning and 55 by 1926 when Germany was admitted. Its main organs were, assembly, council, and secretariat. The assembly was the deliberative organ, consisting of all members. The council was a small body consisting of Big powers. the Secretriat was the principal administrative organ of the league. There were, two institutions organically connected with the league but enjoy autonomy, these were the International labour organisation and the permanent court of international justice.

The Assembly

The assembly was the deliberative organ of the league. The assembly consisted of the representatives of the member states of the league. Each member states could send three delegates to the assembly. But each member states had one vote. The assembly elected its own President. Regarding the admission of new member to the league and the election of the non-permanent member of the council, the assembly decided it by a two-thirds majority. According to article 13 of the covenant, the assembly might deal at its meeting with any matter within the sphere of action of the league. In practise the assembly discharged three types of functions namely constituent, electroal and deliberative. As a constituent body, the assembly could amend the covenant by majority vote. But amendment must be unanimously approved by the council and ratified by all the member states. In exercise of its electoral function, the assembly elected non-permanent members of the council. It also elected, along with the council, every nine years the 15 Judges of the international court of Justice. It also gave its approvel to the nomination of the Secretary-General by the council. As a deliberative body the assembly considered general, political, social, economical and technical questions of international interest. The assembly had broad responsibilities and authority. It assumed many of the functions of a popularly legislative assembly. It was a forum for debate and discussion where issues could be elucidated, often expressed in the form of resolutions. It formulated the basic political and administrative policy of the league.

The Council

The council serve as the executive body of the league. It consisted of two types of members, permanent and non-permanent. Originally, Great Britain, France, Italy and Japan, to which were later added Germany and the Soviet Union as permanent members. The number of non-permanent members were 4 and eventually it increased to 11 in 1936. The tenure of the non-permanent members was fixed at three years. The council was expected to meet once in a year. Besides, it had special sessions. The presidency of the council rotated each session in alphabetical order. Each member of the council had one vote and unanimous approval was required for non-procedural decisions.

The Council could deal "with any matter within the sphere of action of the world". The most important function of the council was the settlement of disputes. It could deal with wars, or threats and punish the aggressor. To settle disputes amicably it could convene international conferences. The council had executive, administrative and supervisory functions in connection with Danzig, the Saar Vally and the mandate system. It had the responsibility for bringing about disarmament and it could also impose military sanctions. The council nominated the secretary general and accorded its approval to the appointments made by him to the subordinate posts in the secretariat. So, the council was the real pivot of the league and the source of executive decision.

The Secretariat

The covenant provided for a permanent Secretariat. It consisted of international civil service of expert officials, was the permanent and real administrative organ of the league. The head of the secretariat was the secretary-general appointed by the council with the approval of the assembly. The expenses for the maintenance of the secretariat were contributed by the member states in proportion decided by the council. While on duty the officials of the league were entitled to diplomatic privileges and immunities. In practice, the secretariat made preliminary examination of question to be taken by the council or assembly, kept records of the league and supplied information to member states about the league's activities. The secretariat was looked upon as an important feature of the league of nations. The secretary-general was authorised by the covenant to make arrangement for investigations and consideration of a dispute referred to the council at the request of one of the parties. The first secretary general Sir Eric Drummond earned great reputation as an impartial official.

The Permanent Court of International Justice

The covenant of the league provided for the establishment of a permanent court of international justice. In 1920 the council appointed a committee of jurists, and they submitted a plan. It was passed by the council and assembly with few amendments. A court was set up at the Hague. According to the statue of the permanent court of international justice, the court was to be composed of 11 Judges and 4 deputy judges. But the amendments of 1930 increased the number of judges to 15, and in 1936, the deputy judgeships were abolished. These judges were selected for a term of 9 years. The members of the court were nominated and elected through a number of ingenious devices designed to insure high professional standards. Article 31 of the statute provided for special national judges who might be chosen by parties whose nationality was not represented among the members of the court.

The court, a centralised judicial agency, was to perform two types of function. It was to be an important means of settling disputes of legal nature, such as disputes over the interpretation of treaties. It was also an organ which would advise the asembly and council on legal questions. Above all, the court had jurisdiction over such disputes as member states were willing to submit to it. In the words of Schuman, "the establishment of the permanent court of international justice was the most important and successful effort so far made to establish an international judicial Tribunal for the adjudication of controversies between states." For a period of nearly 20 years the court functioned with surprising success. As the league collapsed the permanent court ceased to function.

International Labour Organisation (ILO)

The ILO was more closely connected with the league. The ILO was a creation of the treaty of Versailles. After the First World War, the meetings of the labour associations insistent in their demands for action. Inter-allied labour group called upon governments to incorporate certain provisions in the peace treaties for the benefits of the working class peoples. Hence, the Paris peace conference decided to create a labour organisation. All members of the league also became its members. Its main objective was to promote international peace through the promotion of social justice by regulating working hours, labour supply, protection of workers against sickness, prevention of unemployment, vocational and technical education, freedom of association, technical assistance to underdeveloped countries. In fact, the chief objective of the ILO was to gain recognition for workers as human social beings. It worked under the control of a governing body consisting of 32 members. While 16 of them represented the government, 8 represented the employers and 8 represented the workers. Its term was fixed at 3 years. ILO provided an international forum for the discussion of labour legislation.

Achievements of the League

During the period between 1924 and 1930, the league of Nations achieved rare success and its prestige rose high. E.H. Carr has said "The years 1924 to 1930 were the period of the league's greatest prestige and authority". It was a period of general prosperity and co-operative relations among the major powers. No serious challenges were made to league principles, complicated political problems such as disarmament and the more effective organisation of peace were tackled with tolerance. The league's prestige began to increase from 1924 as the member state began to represent in the league council. During this period the league was able to settle certain international disputes. Besides, the league did much in the cause of international cooperation by establishing a number of social and economic organisations. When Germany was given a permanent seat on the council in 1926, the league reached its full strength. The main purpose of the league was the prevention of war by the peaceful settlement of disputes and between 1924 to 1930 the league achieve considerable success in settling some disputes. In the quarrel between Sweden and Finland over

Aland Islands, the verdict of the league went in favour of Finland and it took the responsibility of protecting the private properties of the neutralised and demilitarised citizens.

Germany protested against the attribution of Eupen and Malmedy to Belgium. But the council decided the transfer of Eupen and Malmedy to Belgium and it was confirmed by a plebiscite. The league also settled the disputes between Poland and Lithuania over Vilna and succeeded in maintaining peace between the two. Over the rival claims of Germany and Poland to the important industrial area of upper Silesia, the league decided that it should be partitioned between the two. The league successfully handled the Greco-Bulgarian dispute. The frontier between Greece and Bulgaria had been the scene of disturbances. When a commander of the Greek force was murdered Greece invaded Bulgaria. When Bulgaria appealed to the league, the council called upon Greece to withdraw her troops. A commission of inquiry was appointed to go into the matter. The Greek forces left Bulgaria and she was condemned to pay compensation to Bulgaria. The first use of a threat of employing sanctions was made in the Albania-Yugoslave crisis which arose out of alleged advance into Albanian territory by Yugoslavia troops and Albania's complaint to the council on that score. Within a week the council met and both nations gave assurances, a neutral zone was established and within a short time trouble ended. A dispute arose between Turkey and Britain over the boundary of the district of Mosul. Mosul was a district of Iraq which was given as a mandate to Britain by the league. The matter was referred to the council and it appointed a committee of investigation. On the basis of its recommendation the boundary of Mosul was fixed by the league. Though it failed to satisfy Turkey, but later on Turkey accepted it. Squabbles were settled between Peru and Colombia and between Bolivia and Paraguay. It is significant, however, that none of these decisions went against a big power. So most of its success in the period between 1924-1930 were achieved at the cost of the smaller states. But the great economic depression, the rise of Fascism in Italy, Nazism in Germany and militarism in Japan constituted a serious threat to world peace.

Prevention of war and reduction of armaments were two main task of the league, besides, the league was entrusted with some humanitarian services which it discharged with conspicuous success. During its brief existence the league accomplished certain major achievements. It published many useful reports and studies on important international issues, and thus served as a store house of facts and a clearing house of ideas about truly international affairs. For example the ILO's main purpose was to improve conditions of labour all over the world by persuading government to fix a maximum working day a week, specify adequate minimum wages, and introduce sickness and unemployment benefit and old age pensions. It collected and published a vast amount of information and many governments were prevailed upon to take action. To make provision to secure and maintain freedom of communications and of transit and equitable treatment for the commerce of all members, the league created an autonomous communications and transit organisation. It was concerned with the freedom of international transit, the simplification of passport and other travelling documents, discrimination against foreign shipping in ports, the use of inland waters, etc. The refugee organisation led by F. Nansen, the Norwegian explorer, solve the problem of many prisoners of war marooned in Russia at the end of the War. After 1933 valuable help was given to thousands fleeing from the Nazi persecution in Germany. The mandates commission supervised the Government of the territories taken from Germany and Turkey, while yet another commission was responsible for administering the Saar, which it did most efficiently, concluding by organising the 1935 plebiscite in which a large majority voted for the Saar to be returned to Germany. It provided a machinery for international co-operation in the economic field. With a view to accomplish economic reconstructions of the war-ravaged countries of the world, the league adopted a well-planned programme, the Governments of Austria, Greece, Hungary, Bulgaria were provided financial assistance to implement a plan for financial reconstruction and to set their house in order. For international economic development, the league convened an international financial conference in Brussel. The purpose of the conference was to check inflation, to control gold standard, to remove all impediments to international trade. It recommended to help industrial establishment of all state in a spirit of cooperation, to stabilise custom duties, to keep an eye upon agricultural and industrial development. The world economic conference was also summoned by league. It recommended they for co-operation and not competition must be the objective of industry, and industry should be nationalised. Due to the initiative of the league for the first time in history, the agenda of international meeting was crowded with economic questions, tariffs, depressions, access to raw materials. This was certainly a far-reaching step in the direction of greater economic collaboration. The health organisation did good work in investigatinig the causes of epidemics. It helped much in preventing cholera and plague. In 1923 a malaria commission was appointed and similar efforts were made to combat other diseases. The league also tried its best to control of traffic in women, children and the no less pernicious traffic in opium and other drugs. The production of such drugs as morphine, heroin and cocaine registered a marked decrease and the number of addicts in many countries diminished. Not only that the league also took up the campaign against slavery and set up a permanent slavery commission.

As an international organisation the responsibility of the league was vast. Apart from preserving world peace, it had also the responsibility of crating peaceful conditions in international sphere by reducing armaments of the nations of the world. The attempt of ensuring collective security through the league was indeed remarkable. At the same time the league of nations cannot be described as a super state or a federation for it had not the power of making sovereign laws. It completely depended upon the goodwill of its members for the execution of its decisions. The members of the league had agreed to restrict their freedom in certain cases for the preservation of world peace. The league cannot be called a federation or state. Rather it is an organised family of nations. But with the March of time, the financial crisis of 1929-30, Japan's well-timed attack on Manchuria in 1931 and the seizure of power by Hitler in Germany brought back the post-war tensions. Hence, the league after 1930 was a mute witness to many upheaval in world politics.

Why did the League Failed to Preserve Peace

At the time of the corfew incident in 1923, many people wondered what would happen if a powerful state were to challenge the league on a matter of major importance, for example, by invading an innocent country. How effective would the league be then? Unfortunately such challenges occurred during the 1930's, and on every occasion the league was found wanting. In 1931 the league entered upon the third period of its history. It was a period when, under the influence of economic depression and its train of unemployment, poverty and hunger, the world had to face a disastrous revival of national animosities and military aggression. The period of conflict open when, in September 1931, Japan attacked Manchuria. In quick succession, the leagues failure to check Japanese aggression in Manchuria was followed by the rise of Hitler to power in Germany, the collapse of the legue disarmament discussions, the failure of league sanctions against Italy following Mussolini's attack on Ethiopia, and German Remilitarisation of the Rhineland in clear violation of the Locarno pact. Britain and France took refuge in the council resolutions, condemning such action. When Japan bombarded openly in the town and cities of China, the council simply condemned Japanese bombing. In the words of letvinov, the western powers said to Japan "Take your plunder and peace be with you, and to China "love your aggressor, resist no evil". Hence, the league of nations prevented no major war, and it was ineffective in maintaining international order. The outbreak of Second World War was tragic testimony to this fact. Several reasons have been advanced for league's failure.

An initial disadvantage was that it was too closely linked with the versailles treaties, giving it the air of being an organisation for the benefit of the Victorious powers. In addition it had to defend the peace settlement which was far from perfect. Some of its provisions were bound to cause trouble, for example the disappointment of Italy, and the inclusion of Germans in Poland and Czechoslovakia.

The league was dealt a serious blow in 1920 when the US senate rejected both the Versailles settlement and the league. The reasons behind their decision were varied. Many Americans wanted to return to a policy of isolation and feared that membership of the league might cause them to be embroiled in another war. The Republicans, now in a majority in the senate, strongly opposed president Wilson. The league was deprived of a powerful member whose presence would have been of great psychological and financial benefits. The league had no means by which it could enforce its decision. Besides, the covenant required unanimity of the members for most substantive decisions of the council and assembly. No doubt, the league was a world organisation but that was not world wide. It was neither universal enough to achieve general concilation, nor cohesive enough to achieve decisive action as a concert of powers. The covenant provided the league with a machinery for the peaceful settlement of disputes and for the application of sanctions against a member of the league who resorted to war. The influence of the league dependent on the certainty of its sanctions against any recalcitrant state.

Germany was not allowed to join the league until 1926 and the USSR became a member only in 1934. For the first few years of the existence the league was deprived of two of the world's most important powers. Besides, in the early years the conference of ambassadors in Paris was an embarrassment. It was intended to function until the league machinery was established, but it lingered on, and on several occasions took precedence over the league. In 1920 the league supported Lithuania in her claim to vilna which had just been seized from her by the poles. But then allowed the ambassadors to award vilna to Poland. At this early stage, however, supporters of the league dismissed the incident as teething troubles.

Divergent national and state interest, which resulted in the conflict between the French and British policies as well as in the generally antagonistic policies of the great powers, had destroyed the league as an instrument of collective action on matters of major importance. To France and her allies, maintenance of the territorial status quo and French hegemony in Europe were raisond d'etra of the covenant. To France, therefore, the permanent inability to wage was was the foundation of the status quo. For Great Britain, Germany's come back as a great power in the continent with Great Britain as its holder. The conflict between the British and French conception and policies led to the creeping paralysis in the league's political activities. At the same time, England and France were so scared by Soviet cmmunism that they considered that Germany might be used as a bulwork against Soviet communism. And Germany used this fear of communism, which obessed the great powers, as a weapon with which to strengthen her own position and to defunct the league. The world economic crisis which began in 1929 contributed to the league's decline. It brought unemployment and falling living standards to most countries, and caused extreme right wing government to come to power in Japan and Germany, together with Mussolini. They refused to keep to the rules and pursued a series of actions which revealed the league's weakneses. Besides, the failure of the world disarmament conference which made under the auspices of the league was a grave disappointment. The Germans asked for equality of armaments with France. But when the French demanded that this should be postponed for eight years, Hitler was able to use the French attitude as an excuse to withdraw Germany from the conference and later from the league.

In 1931 Japanese troops invaded the Chinese territory of Manchuria. China appealed to the league which condemned Japan and ordered her troops to be withdrawn. When Japan refused, the league appointed a commission under Lord Lytton which decided that there were faults on both sides and suggested that Manchuria be governed by the league. However, Japan rejected this and withdrew from the league. The question of economic sanctions let alone military ones was not raised, because England and France had serious economic problems and were reluctant to apply a trade boycott of Japan. Japan had successfully defied the league, and its prestige was damaged though not yet fatally. The most serious blow was the Italian invasion of Abyssinia in 1935. The league condemned Italy and introduced economic sanctions which, however, did not include a ban on exports of oil, coal and steel to Italy. So half-hearted were the sanctions that Italy was able to complete the conquest of Abyssinia without too much inconvenience. A few weeks later sanctions were abandoned and Mussolini had flouted the league. Again, Britain and France must share the blame for the league's failure. Their motives were the desire not to antagonise Mussolini too much so as to keep him as an ally against the real danger, Germany. But the results were disastrous. Mussolini was annoyed by the sanctions and began to draw closer to Hitler. Thus, when aggressive States such as Japan, Italy and Germany defied the league, its members were not prepared to support it either by decisive economic measures or by war. The league was only as strong as the determination of its leading members to stand upto aggression. Unfortunately determination of that sort was sadly lacking during the 1930s.

In spite of the failure of the league to maintained world peace, yet its achievement cannot be undermined. In the words of walters "The league as a working institution is dead, but the ideals which it gave rise, have become an essential part of the political thinking of a civilised world..." The most remarkable achievement of the league was its influence in spreading the idea of international cooperation, amity and internationalism. It cannot be denied that the league had done commendable humanitrian work. If the league had failed to ensure collective security, it was due to the failure of its members to accept the principle on which the covenant of the league was based. Regarding the preservation of peace the league cannot be held responsible alone. Langsum comments. "The league failed in the end to preserve peace because it could be only what the nations made of it nothing less and nothing more". Perhaps the most important fact about the league was the very fact of its birth. Similar hopes attended the formation of the UN in 1945, itself a rebirth of the league and an institution that was to benefit from the latter's experiences.

Chapter -XVIII

The Quest for Security and the Locarno Honeymoon

The twenty years between 1919 and 1939 form one continuous period of Europe's history made up of events stretching between the two world wars. Indeed it is possible to trace the sequence of events leading step by step from the one to the other. One of the motives inspiring large numbers of statesmen and of their peoples during the years immediately following 1919 was a passionate desire to ensure that never again should the world be afflicted by war. Therefore, they busied themselves, with clearing up the residue to the effects of the 1914-1918 war and with trying to find some basis for disarmament so as to make another war less and less likely. But a series of efforts towards disarmament was coming to a futile end. The establishment of the league of nations, and its early activities, showed a genral determination to find an alternative to war for the settlement of international disputes. Yet, very soon the politicians became aware of weaknesses of the league as an instrument for peace. France, in particular still dreading a renewal of German aggression, had no confidence that the league could give her the security that she needed. This lack of confidence in the league resulted in various agreements which aimed to greater all round security. France embarked upon a search for security against another German invasion. As long as Germany remained economically and militarily powerful, it was natural for France to seek material guarantees of protection and help. The French never forgot that they might have been easily defeated in 1914, had they have been without allies when German military boots pounded on French soil. So the years following 1919 the foreign policy of France was motivated by the fear of German aggression. All French statesmen sought one goal in international affairs, security and maintenance of French hegemony over the continent. As Carr has said

"The most important and persistent single factor in European affairs in the years following 1919 was the French demand for security."

The League of Nations rested upon a general and potentially universal treaty where in signatories mutually guaranteed their collective security. Had it been considered effective for this end, separate pact and treaties would have been superfluous. But from the outset, France, feeling robbed of the material guarantees for which she had striven at the conference of Paris, sought special guarantees in treaties of alliance in Eastern Europe. France, the chief consumer of security in Europe, countered every proposal for agreed disarmament with the thesis that far from disarmament being, as the British maintained, a source and pre-requisite of security, greater security was the pre-requisite of disarmement. Britain and the US, tended to think of security as meaning security against war. The French more pessimistically, thought of it as including also security against defeat in war. Besides, France demanded the application of the principle of disarmament for security. She tried to enforce the principle of collective security through the league. But the collective security system envisaged under Article 10 of the covenant weakened when the league by an interpretative resolution left the whole matter of military assistance to the discretion of individual member states. France began to demand a general guarantee of additional security both for France and her allies. Article 16 of the league convenant stated that all member states of the league would sever all sorts of relations, economic, commercial and cultural as punitive measures against the aggressor and would render military help to the victim of aggression. But some amendments were made in the Geneva meeting to Articles 10 and 16. So the term of collective security in the league covenant became weak due to the new interpretation of those two articles. Hence, the reliance of France upon collective security system diminished.

The French obsession with security frequently irritated and alienated Great Britain and others. Yet, France received the pledge that the US and England would come to her assistance in case Germany made unprovoked attack upon her. At the same time France demanded that England should specifically state the nature of her military assistance But it was rejected by the British Government. Simultaneously, the guarantee which France accepted was diluted as the USA rejected the treaty of Versailles. So, France had to resort to a policy of force. She occupied the Ruhr region. Her real motive was to ensure her security by breaking the backbone of German industrial potentiality. But the French plan failed due to the passive resistance of the Germans. France, desperately concluded a military pact with Belguim, for security. It provided that the two countries would come to each others aid in case of German attack. She also concluded a military convention with Poland. Yet, France was mortally afraid of German resurgence and her quest for security continued without any respite. Therefore, efforts were directed to strengthen the league system of collective security through pacts.

The Draft Treaty of Mutual Assistance 1923

The first attempt to satisfy the French demand for security through the strengthening of the league system of collective security took the form of the draft treaty of mutual assistance The draft was presented to the assembly of the league in 1923 by the temporary mixed commission charge with investing the question of disarmament. It combined vague provisions for future disarmament with specific guarantee for present security. It proposed that within four days of an outbreak of hostilities the council of the league should decide which party was the aggressor, and that members of the league should be obliged to give military assistance against the aggressor. Under Article 16 of the covenant, providing for sanctions against aggression, military sanctions would thus become automatic instead of optional. The draft incorporated, the French thesis that absolute security should precede disarmament. The draft treaty was an ingenious attempt to combine the respective advantages of general guarnatee and a local system of alliances while obviating their defects. While a joint obligation was to rest upon all signatories to assist any of their members against a war of aggression which was stigmatised as an international crime. The draft treaty linked disarmament with security. But it was provided that no state or states lying outside the war zone would be asked to render military assistance to the victim of aggression. But the draft treaty was rejected by Great Britain and the British dominions, as well as by the Scandinavian States, though it was warmly welcomed by France. The draft treaty thus became a dead letter. But in 1924, a compromises was sought in the form of the "Geneva Protocol."

The Geneva Protocol, 1924

One of the difficulties of dealing with possible breaches of the peace was that the league covenant did not define "an Act of aggression". As a result, either the assembly or the council of the league would need to consider each incident between two nations as its arose and then to decide whether or not there had been such an "act". Only then could it recommend a course of action to its member states. This vagueness and waste of time would cause ineffectiveness and loss of confidence in the league. Finally, in 1924, Macdonald, the British Prime Minister, and his French counterpart Harriot, together proposed a protocol for the pacific settlement of international disputes, more commonly known as the Geneva Protocol. The Geneva Protocol may be defined as an attempt to promote disarmament by creating security, to create security by out-lawing war, to enforce the outlawry of war by uniting the world against the would be aggressor, and to base this union of mutual protection upon the fundamental principle of compulsory arbitration. The main feature of the protocol was its attempt to improve the machinery of the league as an instrument to preserve peace and prevent aggression. It sought to achieve this result by supplying an easy test of aggresion and by closing the existing gaps in the league covenant which still left the door open for war. These were mainly two, if the council should not be unanimous in its judgement on a dispute, and if the subject of the dispute were ruled to be a matter within the domestic jurisdiction of the parties. Under the protocol all disputes of a legal character were to be submitted to the permanent court of international justice. On other disputes if the council should fail to reach unanimity, it would refer the matter to a committee of arbitrators. Disputes about matters of domestic jurisdiction, though still beyond the jurisdiction of council, were to be submitted to the procedure of conciliation under Article 11. This article entitled the league to take any action that may be deemed wise and effectual to safeguard the peace of nations. No nations was to be deemed as an aggressor if it had brought the dispute before the league under Article 11. While the Geneva protocol declared aggressive war as an international crime, it supplied a satisfactory test of aggression. Besides, in order to keep the balance between security and disarmament, the protocol proposed for convening the disarmament conference on June 15, 1925.

The Geneva Protocol was based on the status quo of powers and it went out of its way to meet the French demand for security. The protocol linked the French demand of security with inviolability of the Paris settlement of 1919. So the protocol accentuated what was afterwards attacked as one of the weaknesses of the covenant, its tendency to identify security with the maintenance of the settlement. The protocol closed the major gaps in the league covenant. It left no door open whereby legal wars might ordinarily arise. The only occasions of legal wars under the protocol would be a war of self defence. Yet, it did nothing to strengthen the power of the council under Article 16 of the covenant or to make military sanctions obligatory. Hence, it did not fully satisfy the French demand for security. But again Great Britain and the British dominions began to have grave doubts. Japan wanted to use the procedure to protest at Geneva against the restrictions on Japanese immigration introduced by Canada, and Australia. Compulsory arbitration and the application of military sanctions were uncongenial to British opinion. The replacement of the labour government in 1924 by the conservatives under Baldwin killed the Geneva Protocol.

The Locarno Treaty, 1925

Confronted with this further disappointment, France reverted to her quest for specific British guarantees of her Rhineland frontier. From this policy the treaties of Locarno were born. But the first definite move was made by Stressmann, the foreign minister of Germany. In February 1925 he sent to Harriot, proposals for a peace pact which was to apply to a paricular region of Europe and was to be guaranteed by France, England, Italy and Germany. There then followed long negotiations which by early October and made sufficient progress towards arrange a meeting of representatives of the powers. This was held at Locarno, a Swiss beauty spot on lake Maggiore. French fear of German aggression was the basis of all security problems. France adopted towards Germany a stiffer attitude, and declared Germany in voluntary default on reparation. And in the teeth of Anglo-American oppositon (France) occupied the German territory of the Ruhr. Germany further aggrandised France by signing the treaty of Rapallo with the USSR. In 1922, the old fear of Russo-German alliance made the French foreign office unhappy. The French occupation of Ruhr further Germany's cup of humiliation. All these developments generaed tension between France and Germany. Besides, the guarantee against aggression provided by the league covenant was illusory. In the mean–time, the German Government had proposed that France and Germany should make a mutual pledge, with which Britain and Belgium would also be associated not to resort to war against each other for a generation. In 1925 government changes in Frances brought and Briand as the foreign secretary. It was realised that the time had come to have a political, as well as financial, settlement with Germany. France gave a provisional welcome to the German proposal revived in 1925. These developments culminated in the opening of the hsitoric conference at Locarno in Switzerland on 5th October, 1925. Negotiations progress rapidly and representatives of England, France, Germany, Italy, Czechoslovakia, Belgium and Poland concluded seven treaties which were subsequently signed at London on December 1, 1925, and ratified by all parties. These were (I) a treaty of mutual guarantee among Germany, France, Great Britain, Belgum and Italy. (II) four arbitration treaties between Germay on the one side and France, Belgium, Poland and Czechoslovakia on the other (III) two treaties of mutual guarantee between France and Poland and between France and Czechoslovakia. All these treaties constituted the Locano pact. The first treaty obligated France and Belgium on the one side and Germany on the other to renounce war against one another except in legitimate self-defense.

They also agreed to settle all their controversies by pacific means. The signatories collectively guaranteed the maintenance of the territorial status-quo resulting from the frontiers between Germany and Belgium and Germany and France as fixed by the treaty of versailles. In the event of unprovoked aggression, all the signatories including Great Britain and Italy, had pleged to come to the rescue of the victim. The four arbitration treaties obliged the parties to submit all disputes of every kind with regard to which the parties are in conflict as to their respective rights to a permanent concilation commission, arbitration, or to settlement by council. The two treaties between France and her allies provided that if Germany violated any of her obligations, the signatories would lend each other immediate aid and asssistance.

The impact of the Locarno treaties on international relations was significant. Chamberlain claimed that it marked "the real dividing line between the years of war and years of peace". The Locarno achievements were hailed as precursors of a new era in world history. It became henceforth the custom to speak of the "Locarno spirit" and it was expected to work wonders. Macdonald, a bitter critic of the treaties denounced it as a "Pigeon holed agreement". But later on he recognised its possibilities in the words that "it has been the most significant example of mass coueism that I have ever known". In the favourable atmosphere of 1925 the treaties contributed to the general pacification of Europe. They were the first attempt to recognise impartially the needs of both France and Germany. Germany was brought back into the magic circle of great powers. The treaty was hailed as the beginning of a new era in the relations between France and Germany. Locarno proved to be a mirage that dissolved almost as soon as it was glimpsed. Realism had been set a side and an atmosphere of illusion began to descent on internatinal politics. The pact provided for the German need for treaty revision and the French demand for security. It struck for the first time since the war a fair and impartial balance between France and Germany. It completed the work which Dawes plan had began by bringing Germany into the family of nations. The Locarno pact introduced a new spirit of cooperation and optimism in the international relations. Germany had refused to accept the bindings of the terms of the versailles treaty. But by voluntarily putting signature to the Locarno treaties she (Germany) took upon herself the obligations of the versailles treaty. At the time of its adoption, at any rate, the Lacarno pact was "a most effective and formidable looking scarecrow."

Britain's distinction between frontiers that she would guarantee and frontiers that she would not, undermined the general importance of the covenant. France and further overburdened herself by special obligations in Eastern Europe without partnership with Britain. There were technical absurdities, too, in the nation of planning any effective military cooperation between the general staff of Britain and France against possible German attack, if the British staff were at the same moment supposed to be concerting similar action with the Germans against a posssible French attack. All these implications were to appear later, at the time they were smothered by the prevailing mood of optimism and goodwill. Though the agreements were accepted, yet international disputes continued to exist. The pact offers only the fragile appearance of a guarantee. It is an illusion which will delude facile minds and put vigilance to sleep. The spirit of Locarno is itself a threat to the security of France. The Locarno pact by seeking to strengthen the Paris peace settlement of 1919 weakened its foundation because this implied that the obligations imposed by the versailles treaty were morally, if not legally less binding then obligations voluntarily accepted. So the Locarno pact was based on the foundation of discord and apparent Locarno concord between Germany and France was due to German's helpless financial condition. Besides, in the long run, the Locarno treaty was destructive of the versailles treaty and of the covenant. The treaty encouraged the view that Government could not be expected to take military action in defence of frontiers in which they themselves were not directly interested. Russia considered the pact as a conspiracy of the western powers against itself. In 1926 Germany signed an agreement with Russia in which both reaffirmed the treaty of Rapallo. Nationalist opinion in Germany was left with strong resentment against Geneva and with the suspicion that her return to a status of equality with other powers was more apparent than real. The shadow of a German-Soviet alliance had darkened. Yet, the Locarno pact was an event of the highest importance in Europe. Unlike treaty of versailles, it was signed by Germany voluntarily, and she was thereby recognised as the equal of other European powers, which seemed a step towards the end of Germany's bitter resentment against her conquerors.

The Pact of Paris (Kellog-Briand Pact–1928)

The process of pacification by pacts was carried still one stage further in 1928, though by then mood of optimism was already dispersing. The effort towards disaramament during the first decade after 1919 was the pact of Paris. Its most notable feature was not so much its contents as the fact that the USA was one of its signatories, thus recognising once more her connection with and responsibility towards Europe. The first step towards this end was taken by the French Minister, Aristide Briand, who on 6th April, 1927 (the tenth anniversary of the USA's entry into the war) proposed that France and the US should undertake to outlaw war, between themselves. In the USA the idea of outlawing war gained slow but wide acceptance. So much so that in December the US Secretary of State Frank B. Kellog, went further than Briand and suggested a multilateral treaty which all states could sign binding themselves "to renounce war as an instrument of national policy". It is said that the pact of Paris was born of American initiative and French courtsey. Everybody felt that international peace could never be permanent unless the traditional way of settling all international disputes by war dropped. France agreed to the American suggestion. Finally the French Government accepted the American proposal. The next party to discuss the pact with a view to joining it was Britain. British Government are willing to sign treaties provided that the British interest are safeguarded, which means, non-interference with the colonial and imperial relations of Britain. In August 1928, a few days before the assembly of the league met, representatives of the six great powers, (the USA, England, France, Italy, Germany and Japan), the other Lacarno powers (Belgium, Poland and Czechoslovakia) and the British dominions and India all met in Paris and signed what came to be known as the Kellog-Briand pact or the pact of Paris. An invitation was extended to every other states to accede to it. The pact declared that every signatory condemned 'recourse to war for the solution of international controversies and renounce it as instrument of national policy in relations with one another. And that every signatory agreed that the settlement of all disputes of whatever nature, which may arise among them, shall never be sought except by pacific means. This agreement among fifteen states to renounce war was the high watermark of inter-war pacifism. Almost every state in the world, including the USSR adhere to it. In all 65 states signed it.

The covenant had not banned war as an instrument of national policy, but it planned to punish members who indulged in such kinds of war. The pact condemned all wars, but it made no provision for punishing any. Yet, in the course of framing the pact, signatories had in fact made certain exceptions. A war of self-defence was not condemned, so the pact was not in this sense completely pacifist. Chamberlain in a letter to the US ambassador made it clear that the right to self-defence included the right to preserve the British empire. Each signatory remained the sole judge of its actions, and no machinery for enforcement was even contemplated. National sovereignty was in no way impaired. In spite of all its imperfections the pact of Paris was a considerable landmark. It symbolised the willingness of the US to undertake responsibilities for the preservation of the world peace. Besides strengthening the league's collective security system the commitment to peace by the USA and the USSR created the climate of peace and international understanding among the nations.

Above all, the pact of Paris was an imperfect document. It did impose a complete ban on war. It was agreed by all that the pact forbade only wars of aggression and did not apply to defensive wars. All these had the effect of making the pact a declaration of moral principle. The efficacy of the pact was diluted by the various reservations made by certain nations. At the same time, the pact of Paris provided no machinery by which renunciation of war as an instrument of naional policy could be conforced against a prospective aggressor state. The pact considerably undermined the importance of the league of nations, the pact constituted a great challenge to it. The pact was an expression of pious hopes, an aspiration rather than an achievements. Moreover, the pact was institutionally inadequate. No machinery for the enforcement of the pact was enforced. It dependent on the good faith of the signatory. Flagrant violations of the pact was committed by the powers. Thus, one of the chief effects of the Paris pact was the appearance of the so-called undeclared war. Norman Bentwick called it "an international kiss purely platonic promising nothing for the future." So, this was the most thorough-going undertaking in support of the peace that nations had ever made. Had the pact been observed faithfully, war would have disappeared from the world. Nonetheless, these attempts towards disarmament had their value, they showed beyond doubt that the people genuinely wished for peace with their fellows.

The plethora of pacts in these years was made possible, as well as the genuine spirit of reconcilation by the co-existance and frequent meeting of Briand, Stresemann, and Chamberlane. These three men, whose personal relation and temperaments were so harmonious, established a remarkable of confidence and friendship which in itself stabilise European affairs. Meeting in hotels, smoking one anothers cigar, learning how to reach agreement, they fused their national policies into a general policy of pacification. These conditions disappeared abrubtly when chamberlain lost office, Stresemann died and Andre replaced Briand. Above, all, the "Economic crisis", which broke at this moment, diverted the energies of statesmanship toward domestic problems.

Chapter-XIX

Rise of Nationalism in China and Turky

Nationalism in China

China is a country with a long history covering many centuries, during which her culture evolved a distinctive form of its own. The Chinese were extremely proud of their cultural attainments and this influenced China's relation with the outside world. The Chinese called their country "Tien Hua" "under the heaven" and Chung Kuo, "Middle kingdom". They looked down on all foreigners and regarded them as barbarian. During the Manchu rule the celestial empire was opened to the foreigners. This was an embarrassing confrontation. The old civilisation of China was confronted with the new Western civilisation. The Chinese imagine that the middle kingdom would provide a beacon light to the west. But China failed to meet the new challenge of the occident. Once the foreigners came they created problem both for the rulers and the ruled. The foreigners not only drained away Chinese wealth, but also ruined Chinese economy. They made war which brought humiliation to China, as well, they also made China pay for war. The foreign missionary provided a major cause for the anti-foreign sentiment. The missionary condemned everything that was Chinese. On the other hand, the Chinese continued to cling to their old 6 reliefs and faith. They considered the missionary as the advance guard of western imperialism. The "cutting of the Chinese melon" made the Chinese bitterly resent the presence of the foreigner in China, violent anti-foreign outbreak started in China since the early part of 20th century. The Boxer movement was certainly a national and patriotic outburst.

A Decade of Transition

The victory of a dwarf (Japan) over a giant (Russia) thrilled the peoples of Asia and it had an impact in China. Immediately a new constitution was made for China on the Japanese model. In spite of this the forces of revolution were gathering strength. The young Chinese, armed with Japanese diplomas returned home, hoping to get job, but they were frustrated. Naturally they turned against the establishment, and became revolutionary. Dr. Sun-Yat-Sen, father of the Chinese republic drew the attention of these students who had to suffer the nightmare of unemployment. The revolt spread quickly throughtout the southern part of China, whereas the north remained loyal to the imperial Government, January 1, 1912, the Nanking assembly, elected on Dr. Sun as the President of the new republic. On the other hand, the imperial government made Yuan-Shi-Kai as the viceroy of Hukuang province. The Republicans under Dr. Sun demanded the end of monarchy and Yuan was offered presidentship, and Yuan agreed to their conditions. Dr. Sun resigned and Yuan was elected first President by the Nanking revolutionary assembly. The internal history of China following the overthrow of the Manchu dynasty wintnessed a period of turmoil and chaos. There was Chaos and confusion every where. There were catastrophic floods and famines, fanatical anti-foreign outbursts, the political quarrels between Republicans, and the Communist. The effects of the First World War and Japan's twenty-one demands added fuel to the fire. The Chinese received the decision of the Paris peace conference as a betrayal of their national interest. There was rioting in the streets of peking. When anti-western feelings were strong in China, due to the Versailles treaty, the Soviet Union's declaration, Offering to abrogate all Russian privileges in China, created a tremendous impact on China. Russian assistance to China for fighting against foreign imperialism, encouraged the Chinese to a great extent.

The May 4th Movement

The transfer of Shantung to Japan disillusioned the Chinese intellectuals. They had put their faith on the declared war aim of the allies that they were fighting to end war for all time to come, and for self-determination of all peoples. The general indignation resulted in a protest march by the students and teachers of peking university in peking on May 4, 1919. The May 4th movement marked a watershed in the development of radical nationalism in China. The May 4th movement began as a protest against the decision arrived at versailles peace conference rudely awakened the Chinese. The students demanded that China should refuse to sign the humilating treaty. The merchants, workers, students, teachers and politician woke from their deep slumber. They believed China's salvation lay in the development of a new culture. They challenged old tradition, and the inferior status of woman. The impact of the west made the Chinese react to the past Ku Hung Ming wanted China to combine its Tao with western science. Hu Shih rejected Confucius as antiquated. Some were influenced by the idealist school of Kant and some by Marx's school of historical materialism. The intelligentia attacked the written language which contained thousands of ideograph. In order to popularise the vernacular (Paihua) as a literary medium, Hu Shih Utilised it in composition of poems, essays, histories. No doubt, years of storm and stress, marked the beginning of literary renaissance movement. It reached its height when the new writing became the vehicle for the expression of Chinese nationalism. There was a new feeling, that China must change if she was to survive as a nation. A great ferment of ideas developed, with the peking university as its focal centre. The movement was nationalist in character and directed against foreign domination. The great discontent brewing in the cities was matched by a greater discontent that pervaded rural China. Yet, rural China was unorganised and not vocal like its counterpart. Any how, the movement not only modernise China to a great extent, but also contributed to the reorganisation of the Kuomintang and the birth of the communist party. The students who flocked to foreign countries sowed the seeds of revolt against the old ways. These students undid old China.

Dr. Sun and San-Min-Chu-Yi

Dr. Sun-Yat-Sen was by no means a competent organiser. His was the carrier of a crusader, who conducted his fight with an unwavering conviction destined to win. In 1924, he delivered six lectures to his followers, and these were put in a book form and are known as San-Min-Chu-Yi or three principles of the people, and this became the bible of nationalist movements in China. Dr. Sun realised the lack of a feeling of nationalism in China. The Anti-Manchu struggle had led to the disappearance of the Manchu from the political scene, Yet China had remain divided and weak. It was weak, because it lacked a feeling of unity, of national consciousness. The individual Chinese loyalty was purely local. So he insisted on efforts being made to create a national spirit which would act as a cementing force to bind together the Chinese. He emphasised on the policy of liberation of China by the Chinese and establishment of equal rights for all. Dr. Sun genuinely desired a democratic Government for China. But as a pragmatist, he realised that a democratic government could not be introduced merely in imitation of the west. By democracy he meant initiative, referendum, recall and some indirect rights. He linked the western ideas with the Chinese system of examination and consorted to make it palatable at home. He was aware that the Chinese needed training in democratic government, So he visualised a step by step evolution of democratic polity from military Government, to transitional stage and finally to a constitutional system. He was against untested dialectical Marxism. China was an agricultural country and she had hardly any industry. Therefore, inequality could mean unequal distribution of land. His single tax idea envisaged a system of land assessment and land purchase that ensured equality and justice. He supported state socialism. Agriculture was to be made more productive to feed the rising population. He did not believe in Utopian socialism. He had been criticised by many for his lack of logic and idealism, yet, he made the feeling of nationalism as an effective force and crystalised public opinion behind a democratic movement.

Kuomingtang, Communism and Nationalism

Led by Dr. Sun, the nationalist tried their best to bring the North under the sway of Kuomintang and unify the country. The USSR extended its support for this endeavour. Russia sent M. Borodin to China to win the confidence of Dr. Sun and his associates, with the active cooperation of the Soviet advisers, the Kuomingtang was reformed and adopted the nationalist doctrine of anti-imperialism with the social and economic doctrine of agrarian and labour reform, which strengthened the Kuomingtang to a great extent. The first Congress of the reorganised Kuomingtang was held in 1924. Borod-in had set before himself the important object of transforming the Kuomingtang into a highly disciplined party. Under the guidance of the Russian, Dr. Sun set up the whampo military academy. Soon, thereafter, peking signed an agreement with Moscow, whereby the latter gave up its extra-territorial rights in China and pledged the restoration of Mongolia to the republic. Meanwhile, the communist party of China was founded. The comintern advised that the communist should join the Kuomingtang as individuals, (but no CCP-KMT amalgamation was recommended) so that Marxist might get nationalist support. In 1925 a rift in the Kuomingtang party was evident. The right wing members of the party were against the aims of the communist left wing and wanted to end the close relationship with Russia. Dr. Sun was able to hold the two camps together but after his death the differences widened. Although, he died but Sun Yat-Senism remained as a powerful force in Chinese politics.

After the death of Dr. Sun, Chiang Kai Shek (The sword arm of Sun) became the undisputed leader of the KMT. Hence, the main dramatis personae have been seen on the political stage. Soon after he became the master of the KMT, Chiang threw off the mask and the workers general union was crushed. There was a reign of terror, secret societies, which had sided with Chiang, looted and killed in working class quarters. The Shanghai coup was followed by similar coups in canton, Nanking which purged these cities of communist influence. The national Government was then officially shifted to Nanking from canton. When Chiang-Kaishek conslidated his powers, broke off relations with the Russian communists. Sino-Soviet relations further strained because of the propagandist activities of Bolshevik agent in China. The year after the break with communist, the nationalist army under Chiang captured peking. To carry out Dr. Sun's programme in which a period of tutelage was to follow the seizure of power, the KMT central executive committee was convened in 1929 and provided for a party dictatorship. But though centralised in theory, in practice rivalry within the KMT itself, Political rivals of Chiang made the task of real unification very diffficult for Chinag. But the Nationalist government secured recognition from many western States and Japan. Chiang invited US and German experts to assist in the reorganisation of the country. But the constant disorder enabled the communist to increase their numbers and replace the nationalist government by a Soviet system. Chiang waged uninterrupted warfare against the communists. However, the communists under a Hunanese and the son of the pious Buddhist mother, Mao-Tse-Tung resist the KMT. Though the KMT destroy the urban political strength of the CCP, but they developed close relatins with the restive peasants. The CCP also increased their influence among the workers. Thus, in spite of all the attempts made by Chinag-Kai-Shek to crush communism, it continued to remain as a powerful force. Chiang, even launched an all-out annihilation drive, but all ended in fiasco. Rather, the failure weakened Chiang's position.

Though the nationalist government functioned under considerable handicaps, but than its achievement in the domestic and foreign affairs was praise-worthy. The Government could accomplish many things within a short span of time and much credit for this is due to T.V. Soong, Finance Minister. The Nanking Government wanted credibility abroad, so it accepted the public debts of the earlier government. A greater achievement was the presentation of a balanced budget in a time of crisis. This had been made possible because of an enlarged income due to customs autonmy, and a rigid economy. Some progress was also made in the construction of rail road and highway. Plans were made to industrialise the Yangtze region. The nationalist government made elaborate plans to effect transformation of education. The government established schools, colleges, teachers training institution. Legislation was enacted for the organisation of labour. A matter of derogatory to the sovereignty of China was extra-territoriality, which gave the foreign power jurisdiction over their subjects in China. The powers agreed to the abolition of extra territoriality. The astonishing thing is that in spite of many difficulties, the government could endure as long as it did, and did not crack up under the overwhelming internal and external pressures. The Kuomingtang and the nationalist were instrumental in creating a feeling of nationalism among the Chinese was certainly no mean achievements.

Washington Conference–(1921-22)

The conference on limitation of armaments in the Far-East was summoned by the American President Harding in 1921. The First World War had changed the situaion in Asia and Japan had emerged as the dominant power in the pacific. All of the sea approaches from the north to the south were controlled by Japan. The possession of Saghalin and Kurile islands gave her control over the sea. Thus, she controlled all maritime access to China. Her position north of the great wall of China and Shantung province gave her the power to control peking. In establishing this supremacy, Japan had fought three successful wars, thus displacing China in Formasa and Korea, Russia in Manchuria, and Germany in Shantung. From the versailles treaty Japan had acquired from Germany, the leased territory of Kiachow in China, which caused China to withhold her signature from the treaty. She had acquired mandatory rights over all former German colonies. She had become the only great power on the border of China, and the third naval power in the world. Korea become a good field for Japanese exploitation, and Manchuria was completely under the Japanese control. But the main opposition to Japan in her Asian adventure came from the US. After the occupation of the Philippine islands, the (US) had begun to take an increasing interest in the Far-East and looked upon China as a potential market. Many were convinced that the future prosperity of the US was dependent on an enlarged participation in foreign trade. The US foreign office realised that, if Japan was unchecked, she might become a danger to American interests in the Far-East. This situation prompted the US to convene a conference at Washington in 1921, on the limitation of naval armaments and the settlement of international problems in the Far-East. Besides, England was tired of the Anglo-Japanese alliance of 1902. From 1902 England supported Japan faithfully, not only against Russia, but subsequently against the US. But the growth of American-Japanese antagonism caused much disquietude in England. There had been a growing friendliness between England and America. Of course, war necessity forced the British Government to follow a liberal approach towards Japan. In the post-war period many Englishmen desired to see the Anglo-Japanese alliance terminated, as it constituted a obstruction to the extention of British trade in China. And because of dominion, especially Canadian pressure, the Anglo-Japanese alliance was to be abrogated. And the Washington conference provided an opportunity to terminate the alliance. Besides, the Paris peace conference failes to satisfy the hopes and aspirations of China. Moreover, she was becoming very much worried at the expansion of Japan in China and the peacific region. The Japanese also acquired Shantung and mandatory rights over all former German colonies in the Far-East, and when news of these events reached China, it was greeted with violent demonstrations. Japanophil members of the government at peking were attacked as traitors. At this point, President Harding invited eight powers to attend a conference at Washington on the limitation of naval armaments and the settlement of international problems in the Far-East. The conference was attended by the US, England, Japan, France, Italy, China, Belgium, Portugal and the Netherland. Of course, Russia and Germany were not invited to the conference. Probably, Russia was not invited because of the American unwillingness to have any dealings with the unrcognised Soviet Government.

There were several motives for calling this gathering. America was anxious to check a race in naval armaments with England, and to close the confrontation between China and Japan. The US State department had realised that because of the Anglo-Japanese alliance, Britain was tending to overlook the principles of the "open door" policy. The conference set from November 1921 to February 1922 and concluded seven treaties. Two of these dealt with naval disarmament, and the remaining five, with pacific and Far-Eastern questions. Two separate treaties were signed outside the conference concerning Shantung and Yap.

Treaty Provisions

The four power pacific treaty signed on February 5, 1922 by the US, Great-Britain, Japan and France was an agreement to respect mutual rights in insular possessions and insular dominions in the region of the pacific. In case of a dispute, the powers agreed, to refer the matter to a joint conference for consideration and adjustment. The four powers bound themselves to full and frank communication in order to arrive at an understanding as to the most efficient measures to be taken if the said rights were threatened by the aggressive action of any other power. The same treaty provided for the termination of the Anglo-Japanese alliance. Pressure from the US and Canada brought to an end the alliance which for 20 years had been the cornerstone of Anglo-Japanese policy in the pacific region. The treaty was to remain in force for 10 years, subject to automatic renewal, unless, terminated by an signatory on 12 months notice. It drew the US for the first time into a limited system of consultation with other great powers on matters of common concern. And it gave a decent burial to the Anglo-Japanese alliance.

The five power treaty on the limitation of naval armament signed by the US, England, Japan, France and Italy. It called for a ten year construction holiday on capital ships, and for the scrapping of some ships already planned or being built. It limited capital ships to 35,000 tons and naval armament to sixteen inch guns. The US, England, Japan, France and Italy were to maintain a ratio in capital ships of 5.5:3:1.75:1.75 respectively. The treaty was to remain in force for 10 years, and thereafter was subject to termination on two years notice by any of the signatory powers. All the powers welcomed the respite from the race in building expensive capital ships. Article 19 of the five-power treaty provided for the maintenance of the status quo in fortifications and naval bases in the Pacific. Although every gun in the US Navy was pointed at Japan because of the heated controversies between the two countries, this agreement, promising not to fortify pago-pago, the Philippines, ruled out any naval action in the western Pacific. Engalnd was equally limited by its agreement not to fortify Hong Kong, though it was still free to build up the defenses of Singapore at its pleasure. The Americans and Britains felt that their respective countries made disastrous sacrifices in accepting these provisions. However, these limitations removed potential sources of friction and gave Japan the additional measures of security which made the Japanese Government willing to accept the inferior naval ratio.

All the powers signed the nine power treaty which gauranteed the independence and territorial integrity of China and reiterated the principle of the open door. China upon her part is prepared to give an undetaking not to lease any portion of her territory to any power. The powers also agreed not to conclude between themselves any treaty which directly affect China or the general peace in the region. All special rights, privileges, claimed by any powers also agreed to provide the fullest opportunity to China to develop and maintain for herself an effective and stable government. Besides, China's rights as a neutral are to be fully respected in future. Provision is to be made for the peaceful settlement of international disputes in the Far-East. Japan looked upon this treaty as the complete triumph of the US over Japanese diplomacy and the final blow to its drive for hegemony on the Asian continent. China benefited in a negative fashion, for she did not lose more than what she had already lost. The treaty also contained an undertaking that the unfair discriminations made in tariffs and facilities on Chinese rail roads in the past would not be resorted to in the future. Foreign wireless stations would have had to be destoryed, and foreign post offices would have had to be withdrawn from her territory. And above all the notorious 21 demands made by Japan in the post-war period, would have had to be revised.

In addition to these treaties, the Sino-Japanese agreement provided for the return to China the Kiachow territory. The US-Japanes agreement guaranteed the economic rights of the US citizens in all the Japanese mandates and guaranteed then free access to YAP, a former German possession.

The Washington conference in many respects an unhappy diplomatic denouncement for Japan. The world's sympathy for China strikingly revealed, and Japan was obliged to give-up many of the unequal privileges and special interest which had been acquired during a half-century. The treaties in effect made it possible for the US to be supreme in the Eastern pacific, and Japan in the Western pacific. With only three-fourth of American battleships and carrier strength, Japan could not carry aggresssion into the Eastern pacific, nor the entire American fleet would be sufficient, to carry an offensive into Japanese waters. The whole scheme however, depended on the unwilling renunciation by Japan of her forward policy on the Asiatic mainland. Regarding China, the principle of the "open door" was once more subscribed to by the great powers, no new disabilities were imposed, and a certain amount of lost autonomy was restored to the republic. China was given a breathing spell during which if she had the capacity, she might rebuild her weak national structure. The mutual decision to scrap planned or unemployed units meant a half to further capital ship construction. The naval arrangements concluded at the Washington conference partially eased the tension among the US, Great Britain and Japan. The Washington conference agreements dispelled Japan's dream of controlling China and establishing itself as the dominant naval power in the pacific-Japan's forward march was temporarily halted, and the world was relieved for a decade from the fear of general war. But the settlement reached at the conference was insecure as it depended entirely on the unwilling renunciation by Japan of her imperialistic ambition on the mainland of China. However, the settlement at Washington determined the political status of Asia for 10 years and regulated the controversies between Japan and the US until the Japanese invasion of Manchuria in 1931.

Mustafa Kemal Pasha and Turkey

A biography of Kemal (the name meant perfection and on whom the national assembly conferred the name of "Ataturk" father of the Turks) is entitled Tek Adam "Unique Man". There was certainly none other like him. The word Tek also means solitary, alone. This he was also. Ataturk had, by his singleminded, driving energy, carried through changes which had seemed impossible, at least at such a rapid pace. The adulation which was accorded him by his countrymen in his life time has not given place to a mature appreciation of his qualities. On the one hand there is a tacit assumption that he was something more than human, an attitude which leads to the dangerous conviction that any principle he ever enunciated is valid for all time. No doubt, under his leadership the nation had been firmly established. Westernisation had made great strides. Islamic polity had been firmly rejected and Islam was some what Turkified. On the other hand, many of those who fawned on the living lion have joined the ranks of the profession debunkers, who delight in exposing the weaknesses of the great. Turkey still lives in the long shadow he cast. This is a far cry from the sprawling, heterogeneous Ottoman empire out of which after World War I had shattered its remnant modern Turkey grew. Republican Turkey no longer bears the old imperial burden. Its Anatolian bulk, extending from the lush shores and good central plateau to Eastern highlands is essentially the Turkish homeland. The symbol of the republic, is its capital on the Anatolian Plateau, Anakara grown from a small town to a city.

Kemal Pasha forced the Turks to emerge from the crumbling ruins of the Ottoman empire and to became a nation, at a time when European and Asiatic people were lapsing into demoralisation and despair amidst the wreckage of ancient empires. With an unconquerable faith in the potentialities of his people, he drove them along the road to western civilisation. Once he declared in his speeches, "Nations which try to function with medieval minds, with primitive superstitions, in the presence of her might and majesty, are doomed to annihilation or, at best, to servitude or ignominy". His personal equipment for the modernisation of Turkey consisted of a fanatical belief in the Turks high destiny, an overriding strength of will, a quick wit, great powers of leadership and oratory. His achievement was made possible by a combination of various factors: the manifest political bankruptcy of the sultanate, the disunity of the allied powers, this his leadership and this support extended by the Turks.

The nineteenth century had witnessed the eclipse of many Islamic dynasties. But the Ottoman empire was the last surviving strongholds of Islamic political power, and its position was far from secure. The main stay of opposition to the Sultanate consisted of young army officers, whose professional training brought them into contact with the west, and whose professional pride made them bitterly resentful of the debilitating influence of the Sultan's autocratic rule. In the early years of the twentieth century revolutionary societies multiplied inside the empire. In 1908, the Salonica branch of the "society for union and progress" sent an ultimatum to the Sultan, demanding that the constitution be given effect and imposing a time-limit for convening the chamber of deputies. And the Sultan was forced to concede to their demands and proclaimed a new constitution. The nations of Europe, who had for so many years been sadly shaking their heads over the condition of the "Sick Man", rejoice with him now that he seemed to be on the road to recovery. In fact, the Young Turk revolution of 1908 had two objective, to curb Sultan Abdul Hamid's autocratic rule and to preserve the Ottoman empire's integrity. There was a widespread uprising against the Sutan, and Abdul Hamid was deposed by the assembly. After 1909 Ottoman Government was in flux. Mohammed V. reigned, but he did not rule. Ottomanism was the heritage of the Tanzimatera, postulating the equality of all Ottoman subjects. This was the creed of the Young Turk revolution of 1908, strengthened momentarily by the joyful fraternisation that followed restoration of the constitution. Yet, by 1909 the appeal of Ottomansism began to shade into Turkism. Meanwhile, during the Young Turk revolution of 1908, Kemal Pasha acted as chief of staff to the commander of the army that marched on constantinople and forced Abdul Hamid to grant a constitution. Under the leadership of Kemal Pasha, the nationalist movement grew strong and Turkey once again appeared as a world power with new vigour. Mustafa Kemal was born in Salonika in 1881 and lost his father during his childhood. He entered a school for prospective civil servants, and in 1893 he passed the entrance examination for the Salonica military school. Like so many young soldiers, he was an ardent opponent of the absolutism of Abdul Hamid. Graduating from war college in 1905, with the rank of staff captain, he plunged still deeper in to political intrigue. Mustafa was posted to Damascus, where he joined the "father land," the local revolutionary group, which he helped to reorganise as the "Fatherland and Freedom Society". He undertook the direction of propaganda and put the society into contact with his old friends of the Salonica headquarters of union and progress. Kemal served with distinction in the Balkan wars of 1911-12. The outbreak of First World War found him as military attache in Sofia, with the rank of lieutenant colonel. His leadership in the Gallipoli campaign, which had saved Istanbul, made him a national hero. Mustafa Kemal, now a brigadier and a pasha, was consequently sent to caucasus, where the spectacle of his success could not affront the minister's vanity. On October 30, 1918, the Ottoman Government signed the armistice of Mudros. The armistice terms opened the straits and its forts to the allied powers, stipulated demoobilisation of Turkish armies except for frontier defense and internal security forces and allowed the allies to occupy any strategic point in the empire if their security were endagered. The effects of the war went far deeper than simple military defeat. Allied forces were in control of Thrace, of the straits, and of Istanbul, and the Ottoman Government, was obliged to cooperate with the occupying powers. In 1919, British and then French troops occupied parts of south central Anatolia near the Syrian and Iraqi frontiers, Italian landed in south Western Anatolia, and Greeks were in Izmir. For many months after the armistice Mustafa Kemal remained inactive at Istanbul. His only dream was to get into Anatolia to organise the local nationalist into a force. But his dream seemed wildly improbable, for he was under allied surveillance.

From Severes to Lausanne

Meanwhile, secret war time agreements among the allies had laid down a scheme for partition of the Ottoman empire. The Ottoman Government was handed over the peace treaty by the allies. An independent Armenia and an autonomous Kurdistan were set up in Eastern Anatolia. The straits were demilitarised and made open to all ships, at all times. The region of Izmer was given over to Greek administration. The treaty, this death warrant was signed at sevres by the Government of Sultan Mohammed VI. From 1918-20 there had sprung into existence a nationalist movement that successfully battled against partition and foreign control. In 1919-20 it became better organised and was transformed into a Government in Anatolia. The movement found a leader and he was Mustafa Kemal Pasha. In 1919 Kemal addressed a circular letter to all militray and civil authorities whom he considered trustworthy. The letter contained "The territorial integrity of the fatherland and our national independence are in danger... It has been decided to hold a national Congress at Sivas...". He had rejected Pan-Turkism and Pan-Islam as illusory. The ministry of war indeed try to recall Kemal to Istanbul, but without effect. With the help of some friends in the government, Kemal secured as military inspector for Eastern Anatolia and embarked to aid in organising national resistance to the invaders in Anatolia.

Kemal went on to organise military resistance, to forge political cohesion among the Turks, and to gain diplomatic recognition for the nationalist movement. Mustafa Kemal was chosen to preside over the Sivas Congress, and it was decided in the Congres that a national assembly should meet to settle the national destiny. The grand national assembly should meet to settle the national destiny. The grand national assemble of Turkey began its first session at Ankara in 1920 with Kemal as its President. The Congress proclaimed to the world that sovereignty belonged to the nation.

Meanwhile Greek landing at Smyrna seemed to complete a ring of enemies around Turkish homeland–the allies at the strait, Greek at Smyrna and Izmir, Italian, British and French in the south, and a newly proclaimed Armenia in the East. With British naval support the Greeks had driven the nationalists out of Thrace and purshed eastward into Anatolia. Surprisingly, the nationalist troops drove French forces from Marash. Between 1920 and 1922, the Government of the grand national assembly managed to break the ring of enemies surrounding its territories. Success came mainly due to the growing dissention among the great power. Soviet Russia, at odds with all other powers, was willing to supply the Kemalists with war material and gold buillion. In 1921 Moscow and Ankara Government of the nationalist signed a treaty of friendship, by which the Ankara Government was given recognition. The French began openly to favour the Turks out of dislike for the Greek king and for British policy. Italy had never sympathised with the Greek venture. The allies proclaimed their neutrality in the Greco-Turkish war. In fact, the Greeks had expanded their area of control in series of attacks. In the beginning the Greeks drove the Turks back. In 1921 Ismet Pasha checked the Greek advance at Inonu. Finally, the Turks driven the Greeks out of Smyrna on September 9, 1922, the Turkish nationalist entered Izmir in triumph. The news of the victory was greeted with wild rejoicing. The grand national assembly promoted Mustafa Kemal to Marshal, and gave him the title of "Ghazi" (victorious). Few days later, an agreement was signed between France and Nationalist Turkey. By signing it, France had recognised the nationalist Government as the sovereign power in Turkey. Britain, who still recognised the Sultan's Government protested strongly, but no avail. A Greek army still remained in Thrace and the Turks marched northward upto the British line. At this point both sides wisely held their fire and agreed to negotiate. By the armistice of Mudanya the allied surrender to the demands of the nationalists.

When the allies issued formal invitation to Turkey to the peace conference to be held at Lausanne, in Switzerland they included both Turkish Government-Ankara and Istanbul. Divided counsels could only injure Turkish prospects at the forthcoming negotiations. The allied invitations precipitated Kemal's decision to abolish the Sultanate by separating it from the caliphate. After hours of discussion Kemal said "Sovereignty and Sultanate are not given by anyone to any one at the dictate of scholarship, or through discussion of debate. Sovereignty and Sultanate are taken by strength, by power, by force". The committee yielded to his forceful presentation. On November 1, 1922 the assembly declared the Sultanate had ceased to exist from 16th March, 1920. That was the date of the allies official occupation of Istanbul. The assembly also resolved that the Caliph was to be chosen, from the Ottoman line. On 17th November, the last Sultan Mohmmed VI fled away his palace. So passed into history, after six centuries, the Ottoman ruler. Hence when the Lausanne conference met in 1922, the Ankara Government was represented by Ismet Pasha, the foreign minister of the new government. The treaty of Lausanne was finally signed on July 24, 1923. The main provisions of the treaty were: the frontier with Iraq would be settled by subsequent discussion with Britain. The frontier with Greece was demarcated. Gallipoli was to be restored to Turkish soverignty, but the straits were to be demilitarised. The capitulation were to be totally abolished. It was a triumph of nationalism over the decision at Paris, and it was the only part of the peace settlement which was negotiated between equal and not imposed on the defeated. The conclusion of a genuine peace, gave the nationalist government sufficient prestige and stability. On October 13, 1923 Ankar was officially named the capital of Turkey. On October 29 the Turkish republic was proclaimed by the assembly, which then elected Mustafa Kemal Pasha as its first President. Ismet became the prime minister. Each move also symbolished the further cutting of ties with Ottoman past and its cosmopolitan capital and the golden horn. The republic now set out to make a new Turkey for the Turks. The first fifteen years of the republic, dominated by Kemal Pasha, brought rapid innovation in many fields. Innovation was easier because the Ottoman empire had established a trend towards westernisation of institution of thought, of custom. At the same time, the republic had inherited a capable elite of bureaucrats to guide its destiny. Above all, the Republic had driving leadership of Mustafa Kemal Pasha.

Modernisation and Westernisation of Turkey

The chief ingredients of Kemal's policies were the famous six principles Republicanism, Nationalism, Populism, Statism, Secularism and Revolution. In 1923, Kemal, to strengthen his own hand formed the party which became the Repubican people's party. It was the only political party and it served as a vehicle for Kemal's reform plans. His purpose was to make Turkey into a modern state on the western pattern. In his opinion, the virtues of the Turks had been strangled for centuries under the parasitical influence of the religion of the Arabs. One potential rival to the republic remained the caliphate. When Agakhan wrote a letter, Ismet Pasha in 1923 asking that the Caliphate be placed on a basis that would command the esteem of Muslim everywhere, and when this letter was published in Istanbul, Kemal decided to seize the opportunity. On 3rd March 1924, the grand national assembly, voted for the deposition of Abdulmecid, the abolition of the Caliphate and the banishment from Turkey of all members of the imperial family. At the same time two more blows were struck at the supremacy of Islam. The law of unification of instrucion gave into the charge of the ministry of public instruction all educational institutions within the boundary of the republic. Now the Medreses were under the direct control of the government. He replaced the ministry of Seriat and evkaf (Arabic Waqf) by a new department of the Prime Minister's office, the directorate of religious affairs. The religious courts were abolished. The changes were embodied in a new constitution. Its fundamental provisions were as follows: The Turkish State is a republic. The religion of the Turkish State is Islam. Sovereignity belongs to the nation. The grand national assembly of Turkey is the rightful representative of the nation. The official language of the State is Turkish. The assembly exercises its executive power through the president of the republic. The assembly has the power to keep a check on or to over throw the government. The judicial function is exercised in the name of the nation by independent courts in accordance with the law.

By analysing the structure of the new Turkish State, one can conclude that it was dictatorship. Kemal was the master, and few dared criticise him to his face. Those who unswervingly followed Kemal, there were many sincere republicans who disapproved of dictatorship. There were the Hocas, who were bitterly antagonistic to the government's laicist policy and had been ready even to have Mustafa Kemal as Caliph, rather than to see the total disapperatence of the Caliphate. These men began to beat the democratic drum and to wave the banner of liberalism as soon as the establishment of the republic showed them that any other form of opposition was foredoomed. A distinguished soldier Kazim Pasha take over the leadership of the rebels, and formed themselves into the progressive republican party. In 1925 a great insurrection broke out among the Kurds of the Eastern provinces. The Kurds are a wild, semi-nomadic Muslim people. The Turkish ministry of education describes the Turkish insurrection as the Eastern revolt. The revolt was due partly to resentment of Turkish rule and a positive desire for Kurdish independence, partly to outraged religious feeling at the abolition of the Caliphate. In spite of the suppression of the Kurdish movement, sporadic unrest continued in the East for many years. using its new power, the government took the occasion to close down a number of Istanbul newspapers, to arrest journalists, and to suppress the progressive party. The one party dominion was confirmed.

Kemal initiated several other secularising and westernising measures. The power of religion over the minds of the Turks had to be broken, or at least weakened, if Mustafa's plans were to succeed. The Muslim, those who believe that there is no God but Allah and that Mohammed is his messenger, is divided into two great sections, Sunnite and Shi'ite. The schism began soon after the death of Prophet Mohammed. The sunnites believe that the office of Caliph belongs to the man most capable of fulfilling its duties. Though Turkey pay no heed to this division, lumping all Muslims together, there is in Turkey a large Shi'te minority. Although many Turks had revered the Caliphate and deplored its passing, it was too remote and exalted an institution to mean much to the average Anatolian peasant. But the clothes he wore, especially his head dress, meant a great deal to him, distinguishing him as they did from the Christian. The Ulemas wore turbans, members of Terikats wore distinctive conical caps, officials and common men generally wore the Fez. Villagers usually wore a Fez with a cloth wrapped round it, turban-wise. In 1925 Kemal paid an official visit to the black sea region. He and the civilians who accompanied him wore Panama hats. In a meeting he pointed out that the traditional Anatolian male attire of full gown and baggy trousers took far more material than a suit of European cut, while the Fez, with its skull-cap beneath and its cloth wrapped round, was far more expensive than a European hat. The wearing of the Fez was made a criminal offence by law. Kemal was administering shock treatment to tear people away from traditional ways. The European hat was more than a symbol it was a psychological tool-perhabs the hat under a western hat would think western thoughts. All kinds of new and second hand European headgear found a sudden market in Turkey. One of the popular items was a vizored cap, which could be turned backward so the wearer, still covered, could touch his forehead to the ground during prayer. Kemal also lashed out at religious vestments in general, at dervish orders and worship at the tombs of popular saints. The veil was too delicate a matter for legislation. Kemal discouraged it, but left its disappearance to the law called fashion, which of course operated much faster in the cities than in the provincial towns and villages.

Three separate system of dating had been in use in the Ottoman Empire. For general purpose there was the Islamic calender, the era of which begins with the Prophet's departure from Mecca. All this tangle was swept-away with effect from 1926, by the adoption of the Gregorian calender for all purposes. At the same time the old oriental way of time-reackoning, starting from Sun-set, was replaced by the international method. Kemal also, was would not tolerate much longer the existence of Islamic law as the law of the land. In 1925 he opened the new school of law at Ankara. Les Dramatic but more fundamental were the new law codes. The process was brought to a climax with the adoption of the Swiss civil code, a penal code modeled on the Italian, and of a commercial code modeled on the German and Italian example. All these code came into effect from 1926.

Under the new civil code polygamy was illegal, and marriage became a civil contract. The husbands advantage under Islamic law in securing divorce was swept away. This was a major step in ensuring the legal equality not only of the sexes, but also of the sects. No doubt, there was still opposition to Kemal personally. In 1926, a plot to assassinate him during his visit to Izmir was discovered.

As striking as hat reform, but more far-reaching in its effects, was the alphabet change in 1928. Arabic characters, although providing a kind of short-hand still preferred by many Turks whose schooling pre-dates 1928, are unsuited to Turkish sounds, and are anything but phonetic. Because of their variations in form according to positioning in a word, the characters are difficult to learn. All proposals since the Tanzimat period to change to Latin characters had falled into void. Now Kemal forced the pace. First the international numerals were introduced in 1928, to replace the type of Arabic numerals common in Muslim countries. Then Kemal prodded the commission working on a phonetic modern alphabet to complete its task. In 1928 he announced the alphabet reform. Personally be went on tour, seting-up his black board and easel in village streets, giving spelling lessons to the croweds. But the language reform did not rest there. The Sun-language theory was propounded at the third Turkish linguistic Congress. It taught that all the languages of mankind derived from Turkish, so that in using any Arabic or Persian word they needed, the Turks were reclaiming their own. The history taught in pre-Republican Trukey had been mainly that of th Islamic dynasties, including the Ottomans. Now the study of Islamic history was dropped from school curricula, and the history of the Turks was taught instead. This innovation was beneficial to Turkish ego at a critical time. To revert to the language reform, one must remember that, although it was marred by many absurdities, it did service in mankind. Besides, the entire nation literally went to school for adults were obliged to learn the new writing as well as school children. Literacy rose, Newspapers, books increased in number after the initial difficulties of changover, and their circulation mounted with lowered printing costs. Other educational and cultural measures that followed also exhibited a strong natinalist purpose, as well as in varying degrees, a westernising and secularising purpose.

The major measures of secularisation had been carried out. The clause that proclaimed Islam the religion of the Turkish State was stricken from the constitution. Some of he cultural reforms of later years also had a secular connotation. The weekly day of rest, itself an innovation, was changed from Friday to the European style Saturday noon to Monday morning. Of course, this was a major of westernisation than secularisation.

Meanwhile, Kemal visited Istanbul, the first time he had seen the cosmopolitan city since he precipitous departure in 1919 to organise the nationalist movement in Ankara. It marked the end of the period of exile. In 1927 the republic's first systematic census taken under the direction of a Belgian expert in statistic.

Besides, formal education was supplemented by popular education, principally through the people's houses in all cities and towns. The house served as community centers to promote lectures, exhibition, dramas, sports events. Like the school the houses were vehicle for nationalism. Western forms of painting, sculpture and music were encouraged by exhibitions, prizes. In 1935, oriental music was banned from public concerts and radio broad-casts. The metric system of weights and measurements was strictly enforced. The Koran was also publicly read in Turkish translation for the first time in 1932. With the promulgation of the new Turkish civil code, the disabilities imposed on woman by Islamic law were swept away. The municipalities act, gave a women the right to vote at municipal election. Their political emancipation was completed in 1934, by a law entitling them to vote in the election of deputies and to stand for election themselves. A minor innovation of some interest was the request made in 1930 by the Turkish Government to the world at large, that only the Turkish name of cities should be used in addressing letters to Turkey. Later on, it was announced that letters addressed to the old name would not in future be delivered. It is noteworthy that in this matter the Turks nationalistic prode outweighted their strong desire to be western in all things. Another radical change which affected all Turks was brought about by the law making the use of surnames compulsory from 1925. Previously the Arab system of nomenclature had been in force. Mustafa Kemal himself became Kemal Ataturk and the title Pasha, Bey, Hanim (Lady) were declared obsolete, being replaced by the ill-conceived terms Bay and Bayan, for men and women respectively. In 1934 a new law forbade the wearing of distinctive dress by clerics of any religion outside their places of worship. Even beauty contests, unthinkable a few years before, were introduced. The seclusion of woman was undeniably on the wane. By 1933, thirteen women held judgeship. There was also an experiment in organising an opposition political party. The move was probably made at Kemal's suggestion. In the first decade of the republic, not much had been done to improve the economy of the country. But early in 1923 Kemal had promoted an economic conference. One of his recurring themes was that the plough share was mighter than sword. The burdensome tithe on agricultural produce was removed. Unfortunately Kemal was more concerned with social, cultural and political question than with economic ones. The principal economic theme was to avoid any kind of foreign economic domination. The doctrine of self-sufficiency led the young republic to avoid borrowing foreign capital, to buy up foreign owned rail roads in Turkey as fast as possible, and to develop agriculture, mining, and industry with indigenous capital. Custom barriers were raised to protect native industry. Commercial treaties were signed with many countries Extensive farm areas were settled with governmental aid in Anatolia. The government subsidised agriculture by the free grant of cattle, ploughs. In 1934 a five year plan was adopted for the building of state and private factories. The world depression caused Turkey to tighten import and currency control. A favourable balance of trade was achieved only through drastic cuts in needed imports, since exports also fell.

Turkish Foreign Policy Till 1939

Fortunately, Turkey had genuinely peaceful foreign relations, uncomplicated by the intervention of any great power. "Peace at home, pece abroad", was Ataturk's prescription. Turkey was the first of the defeated powers to repudiate a humiliating treaty and forced the allies to accept a treaty of her own. The main aims of Turkish's foreign policy were to ensure her own political security, to solve problems with her immediate neighbour, to form an alliance with Russia against the western states. The like mindeness of both Russia and Turkey led to the formation of an alliance. The Soviet Union won a great deal of goodwill by returning toTurkish sovereignity, the region of kars and Ardahan, by the Russo-Turkish treaty of friendship signed in 1921. Russia had been giving financial and military aid to the nationalists. Relations between them improved further after the diplomatic exchange in 1922-23. The two countries were brought even closer together by the question of Mosul. But Turkey never favoured the growth communism. The treaty of Lausanne left the destinies of Mosul to be settled by Turco-British discussion. As no agreement had been reached within the stipulated period the question was referred to the league council which decided to attack the disputed territory to Iraq. The Turks refused to accept this ruling, and they signed a pact of non-aggression and security with the USSR. However, Turkey was persuaded to conclude a treaty with Great Britain and Iraq (1926), accepting the league's decision. In 1932 Turkey became a member of the league of nations. In 1933 Turkey confirmed that the Turkish friendship for the Soviet Republic is rooted in Kremlin. This friendship was begun by Lenin and Mustafa Kemal and is now confirmed.

Meanwhile, Turkey and Afghanistan entered into a treaty of friendship in 1922 and agreed to help each other against the attack of imperialist powers. In the same year a triple alliance was concluded between Turkey, Iran and Afghanistan. After 1933 the chief aim of Turkey's foreign policy was to ensure the regional security of the middle East, for that purpose Turkey concluded the Sadabad pact with Iran, Iraq and Afghanistan in 1937. At the same time the Balkan pact was concluded by Turkey's efforts and with it the collective security system of the Balkan region came into existence. The greatest worry of Turkish statesmen in the 1930's arose from the aggressive policies of Bulgaria, and Italy, whose wartime designs on southern Anatolia had not been forgotten. Turkey therefore entered into a defensive alliance, with Yugoslavia, Greece and Rumania. The relations between the USA. and Turkey after the war were peculiar. Although the two countries never had declared war upon one another but diplomatic and commercial realtions had been revered. However, economic interest outweighed diplomatic considerations and a Turco-United States agreement, providing for the restoration of diplomatic relations was concluded in 1927. Besides, when in 1936 France announced the independecne of Syria and Alexandretta, Turkey lodged a strong protest with the league of nation. In 1937, the league of nations promised to protect the Turks in Alexandretta. In 1938 Turkey and Frnce entered into agreement, where by Franco-Turkish joined rule was instituted in Alexandretta. The fear of Italian aggression is referred to in the note which Turkey sent to Great Britain in 1936, asking for revision of the Dardandeeles Convention of 1923, which borbade the fortification of the straits. In response to this note, the Lausanne powers held a conference at Montreux, which, by the Convention of 1936, restored full Turkish sovereignity over the straits. The rise of Hitler and Mussolini's aggressive tendencies in the 1930s disturbed Ataturk, and he took several steps to preserve the status quo and improve the Turkish position. Turkey's good foreign relations were a consequence of Ataturk's unyielding resistance to any revival of Ottomanist, Pan-Turanian, or Pan-Islamic expansionism. The national state in its national frontiers was not revisionist. Turkey took advantage of France's desire for friendship with her to press for the cession of Hatay, the former sub-province of Alexandetta. France being eager to win Turkish support in coming struggle (World War II), raised no objection when Hatay voted of her forbearance in 1939, when the Anglo-Franco-Turkish treaty was signed at Ankara.

Probably, the negotiation over the Hatay was Ataturk's last public act. He had been ill since 1937 and on November 10, 1938, he died in the palace of Dolma-Bahche, once the summer residence of the Sultan. At 9.20 A.M. each November 10 activity in Turkey comes to a halt. For five minutes the country remembers in silence the moment of death of Kemal Ataturk, creator and first President of the Turkish republic. Turkey still lives in the long shadow he cast. The guiding principles which he laid down have fundamentally been followed: the inculcation of a Turkish national consciousness, the breaking of the hold of Islam over state, the westernisation of life and institution, a devotion to a republican form of government, and finally the pursuit of peaceful foreign relations. Indeed Turkey has fought her way up from the pit of defeat and despair, and now she stands in an honoured place amongst nations. To the free People of Asia she is a guide and an inspiration.

Chapter-XX

Imperial Japan upto 1945

JAPAN INTO THE MODERN WORLD

It was commodore perry of the US navy who compelled the reluctant Japanese to modify their policy of seclusion.By an agreement signed in a village later to become the city of Yokohama, the Japanese opened two small ports to American Vessels. The American example was soon followed by Great Britain, France, Russia and other powers. The Shogunate (Regents) lost face as a result of the treaties that it had been forced to sign. The foreigners being looked upon as intruders and the Samurai (Japanese Knights) class considered them an unsettling influence on the mass of the people, who, it was feared, would be corrupted by foreign ideas and customs. Ultimately dis-satisfaction crystallised in an Anti-Tokugawa alliance of four south western clans and under the emperor's banner they overthrew the last of the Shoguns and his supporters in a brief civil war (1867-68). This turn of events is known as the Meiji (Englishtened Rule) restoration and the emperor and his court moved from Kyoto to Yedo, renamed Tokyo (Eastern capital), where he took up residence in the Shogun's caslte. The members of the new government were Samurai retainers mainly from Satsuma and Choshu clans. This able oligarchy of clans warriors pushed Japan into the modern world. Rapid westernisation began. Japan was rapidly Europeanised-militarily, politically and educationally. The army was reorganised on the German pattern and the navy in accordance with the advice of the British. In other words, at the behest of their leaders the japanese turned their backs on much of their own old past. The watch words were progress and civilisation. Of the patriotic slogan," "revere the Emperor, drive out the barbaraians", the first part remained very much in force, but the second became a dead letter. The government helped the growth of private industries through subsidy. The government laid more stress on the development of heavy-strategic military and chemical industries in order to make Japan a powerful state. The radical changes brought about by the programme of modernisation were both stimulating and exciting. By the early 1890s, Japan was beginning to be an industrial power on a modest scale. In this progress the real pace-setters by the end of the century were four or five enormous concerns known as the Zaibatsu (Financial cliques), of which the most famous wer Mitsui amd Mitsibisi. Patriotic indoctrination was one hall-mark of the meiji educational system. A "rich country and a strong army" – this was the great slogan in Japan during the last part of 19th century. In the second half of the nineteenth century two issues dominated Japan's outlook on foreign affairs. These were the unequal treaties with the foreign powers, and Japan's relations with Korea. The Japanese considered Extraterriorial rights enjoyed by the foreigners as humiliating to national self-esteem. However, it was only on the eye of the tweneeth century that Japan was able to shake off what in the Jargon of to-day would be called' the shackles of semi-colonialism. Within a few weeks of an Anglo-Japanese agreement on treaty revision Japan was at war with China. The war arose over Korea. In the summer of 1894 Japan struck the first blow, at sea, before war declared. And within a few months the Japanese had driven Chinese forces from Korea, and captured port Arthur and Liaotung Peninsula in South Manchuria, and seized the port of Wei-hai-wei on the coast of Shantung. China had to agree to Japanese tgerms by the treaty of Shimonoseki (1895). This dramatic triumph of Japan alarmed the western powers of the "Yellow perile." Only a week after the peace treaty was signed, three powers, Russia, Germany, and France, advised Japan to give up, her claim to port Arthur and Liaotung Peninsula. This "Triple intervention," as it was called, was a body-blow to Japanese pride. Despite this diplomatic humiliation. Japan's international prestige was much enhanced by her rapid and decisive victory over China.

Victory against China was a tremendous boost for patriotic sentiment, and the prestige of the army and navy was now very high. Japan learnt an important lessons from the war, that she must have allies to support her in the ambitions beyond the national frontiers. A little later, Great Britain in order to checkmate the ambitions of Russia, she concluded a treaty with Japan in 1902. This treaty meant anointing an Asian powers as an equal to the western powers. meanwhile, Japan received an unpleasant shock when Russia obtained control of port-Arthur and the Russians began to increase their military and economic influence in Korea. This greatly disturbed the Japanese. As Russian power expanded in Korea, it become clear that Japan must either come to terms with Russia or face the likelihood of war. In 1904 the Japanese felt strong enough to put the quarrel to the test of battle and in the same year she declares war against Russia. Japanese land and sea war was ended by the treaty of ports-mouth, signed in 1905, South Manchuria, the Liaotung peninsula and Korea came within Japan's sphere of influence. It was the first occasion in modern time that an Asian country had defeated a European power. Emboldned by this victory, Japan went ahead with its aggressive exploits. She embarked on a blatant policy of imperialism which made her to annex Korea in 1910, seize shantung, and presented the Chinese with the so-called "twently-one demands." It aroused permanent resentment among the Chineses and the gravest suspicious among the Americans. In 1918 the aftermath of the Bolshevik revolution in Russia led to confusion and Civil war in Siberia, and Japan, together with other foreign powers, sent a military force to vladivostok. The Japanese contingent that moved west-ward along the Trans-Siberian railway, to hold in the establishment of an anti-Bolshevik front. But this Siberian venture was unpopular in Japan. The ferment caused by the events in Russia, the revolution of 1917, could not be entirely prevented from spreading to Japan, however, ruthlessly the authorities tried to stampout what they called dangerous thoughts. Japan's rulers looked upon Marxism as an evil to be dreaded like a contagious disease. But they could not ban completely all leftwing activities.

Japan between the Two World War

In 1919 at the Paris peace conference Japan was given a permanent seat on the council of the league of Nations. The German islands in the pacific were given to Japan in the form of a mandate. The Americans, who both preached self-determination and regarded themselves as the protectors of the Chinese, agreed reluctantly to this point about Shantung. Consequently relations between the USA and Japan deteriorated. The 1920s in Japan have often been regarded as a relataively liberal decade. Japans foreign policy was on the whole temperate and restrained. Besides, new international forces emerged in the post-war period. The US was calling for a new deal for China and an end to the pre-war power alliances, while the Japanese Government was beset by severe economic problems in 1920s and depended on the US Which limited the Japanese navy and affirmed the soverignity and independence of China. At the Washington conference, 1921-22, Japan agreed to carry out a limitation of naval armaments and also came to a settlement with China, where-by Shantung province reverted to Chinese control. The Anglo-Japanese alliance lapsed in 1921.

(For Washington Conference please see Chapter XIX)

After the Washington conference of 1921, political opinion within Japan turned against the liberal politics of the day. Politically and militarily, she rapidly developed her strength although it was tremendous strain on her resources. From 1924 onwards, it was the army that took all the initiative of expansion in Manchuria region, while the big business interests and the extreme nationalists gave it full support. Besides, the belief was widespread in Japan that the Washington conference had deprived Japan of what she had acquired by legitimate mean. There was also the conviction that at the root of all these was a racial basis. However, the militarists could not have it all their own way and democracy was really making headway. But in 1927, Baron Tanaka with the support of the Seiyukai party, became the Prime Minister of Japan. Tanaka outlined his continental policy in the Eastern region conference at Tokyo.

The broad outlines of the conference can be summed up as follows: Manchuria, Mongolia and the three north Eastern provinces of China were of special strategic and economic importance to Japan. Therefore, she had a special responsibility for maintaining law and order in these regions. This policy was carried out when Japanese troops were rushed to Tsinan, ostensibly to protect the Japanese living in Shantung province, when Chiang-Kai-Shek marched towards the north in 1928. Fighting broke out and the Japanese demanded an apology from Chiang and the immediate withdrawal of Chinese troops from Tsinan and Chiang had to submit to all the Japanese demands. This was the first clash between imperialist Japan and nationalist China. The death of Changetso-lin, the Manchrian war-lord in a train accident (caused due to a bomb explosion) was responsible for the resignation of Tanaka Government in 1928. Tanka's successors who were civilian, associated with industry and commerce, reverted to a more conciliatory policy with regard to China and to international politics. When the great depression curtailed world commerce, the Japanese economic struggle to maintain themselves became more severe. Besides, many senior Japanese naval officers strongly objected to the London naval disarmament treaty on the grounds that the agreed naval ratio between the US, England, and Japan, weakened their country's power of self-defense. On the other hand, Hamaguchi, the Prime Minister advised the emperor that the treaty be ratified, and this shocked many conservatives. A somewhat mutinous temper began to spread among army officers. In 1930 premier Hamaguchi was gravely injured when a young ultra-nationalist fanatic fired a pistol at him and few months later he died of his wound. Soon an extra-parliamentary ministry was set up with a naval officer, named Satio and efforts were made to promote imperialism abroad. The supporters of the army leadership employed the Manchurian question as an effective means of propaganda. Thus, the Manchurian issue tremendously influenced the Japanese politics and subsequently action in Manchuria occured in September 1931.

(For Manchurian incident please see subsequent pages)

Second Sino-Japanese War – (1937-45)

After Manchuria Japan wanted to conquer more of China's territories. Control of Manchuran led to pressure on North China. During the period of 1931-37 there was a great growth of militarism in Japan. The army became independent from civilian control. The political and economic weakness following the depression resulted in the growth of fascist elements. With the militarists in control of government at home, the forward continental policy was pushed on. On one retext or another Jehol, Chahar, Hupei were brought within the Japanese sphere of influence by winning over war-lords, and business interests of these areas. The times seemed propitious for a bolder adventure. The rise of Hitler absorbed the attention of Europe. The naturality act passed by the USA in 1935 announced to the world that America was not going to give up her policy of isolation. Russia was in a state of alrm on account of the anti-communist spirit of Hitler's statements and of the formation of Rome-Berlin axis. It was a favourable opportunity for a big step for-ward in China. Meanwhile Japan had left the league and repudiated the Washington naval agreement. And the army leaders proposed an entente cordiale with the Nazi Government of Hitler and in 1936 an anti-comintern pact was signed between Germany and Japan. After this Japan followed a forward continental policy to fulfil her ambitions in the Asiatic region. At midnight, July 7, 1937, there was a clash between some Japanese troops, who were out on their monoeuvres, with Chinese soldiers at Marco-polo bridge near the railway station of Lukuchiao quite close to peking. This was the "incident" which started the second Sino-Japanese war. Chiang-Kai-Shek and the nationalist government in Nanking had not put up a determined resistance against Japanese encroachments, because Chiang believed that he must give priority to the task of defeating the Chinese communists. Chiang once remaiked "The Japanese are a disease of the skin, where as the communists are a disease of the heart." But by the summer of 1937 this enmity had been temporarily put aside, for the Chinese nationalists and communists were in the process of forming a united front against the Japanese. The fighting in the north developed into full-scale undeclared war. The Japanese occupied Peking and began advancing south. Meanwhile, a new front was opened, in Shanghai, Chinese resistance was fierce, but eventually the Japanese forced their opponents to withdraw from the city. Advancing up the Yangtse valley the Japanese took Nanking by storm in December. However, Chinese resistance continued and the Japanese force were led farther to exhaust the enemy by luring him on deepr and deepr into the interior and thus lenthening the line of communication. But Hankow, the capital after the Nanking, passed into Japanese hands without much opposition. Canton, the chief city of the

South, also fell. China did not want to risk large armies in attempting to prevent the Japanese from achieving military objectives within their easy reach. Japanese aircraft, dominating the sky, raided as far west as Chungking, whch had became Chinag's capital. Some Chinese leaders came to terms with Japan, and a puppet government was set up in Nanking. But the war went on. In the course of it Japan's relation with America and Great Britain steadily worsened. The people of the two countries felt great sympathy with the Chinese in their ordeal. To a world not yet accustomed to the idea of mass air-bombardment Japanese raids on chinese cities seemed very shocking Japanese Russian relations, too, were extremely tense, being strained by serious armed clashes on the border of Manchukuo.

From the end of 1938 until 1945 the Japanese controlled the main cities and communications of Fastern. China, but their hold on the countryside remained weak. Meanwhile, the Japanese Government extended its control at home. Political parties were ended and Prince Konoye organised a national party. A totalitarian state made any expression of discontent become dangerous. The high command of the army and the totalitarian government at home were thinking by now of other expedients. A "Greater East Asia co-prosperity sphere," which was to be dominated by Japan as the champion of East Asia against western imprealism, was to be the next move in which the China affair and other continental adventure would all be merged. With a virtually Fascist Government now in power in Japan, it was likely that closer relations with Itlay and Germany would follow. When the second World War began in Europe in 1939, Japan remained strictly neutral. But Hitler's overwhelming victories in 1940 inevitably impressed and excited the Japanese army. The military leadership insisted that was accomplished in September 1940 with the signing of the tripartite Axis Pact. Now Japan-felt herself politically and militarily in a very strong position. The rapid conquest of Eastern China showed the stength of her armies. In South-East Asia the colonial territories of France, Britain and Holland seemed almost defenceless. This seemed an excellent opportunity for Japan to occupy these territories, secure the grateful support of the native population freed from their European rulers, and establish an empire looking to Japan as its head. The Germans were eager to persuade Japan to join them in their struggle against Russia in 1941. But Tokya adopted the policy of 'wait and see'. More tempting prospects lay elsewhere. The British, Dutch, and French colonial territories in South-East Asia contained rich resources, such as oil, tin. So when the Japanese forced France to allow them the use of certain bases in Southern Indo-China in July 1941 it seemed clear that this advance to the south would soon be followed by threatening action against malasiya and the Dutch East Indies. Accordingly the USA,

Britain, imposed an embargo on trade with Japan. After much internal debate and fruitless talks with America, Japan decided to break the trade embargo by force. Meanwhile, general Tojo, became prime minister in October 1941, it was evident that Japan was on the brink of war with America and Britain. Early on the morning of Sunday 7th December, 1941 waves of Japanese naval air planes attacked the American war-ships berthed at pearl Harbour, Honolulu. After the battle of midway in 1942, Americia's victory in the pacific, the tide of war no longer flowed in Japan's favour. During 1944 the prospects began to darken for the Japanese. Americans air-raids grew progressively heavier as the spring of 1945 advanced. At the end of July 1945, the Japanese Government was faced with the potsdam proclaimation. However, no response came from Tokyo. On the morning of 6th August, 1945 an American aircraft dropped an atomic bomb on the city of Hiroshima and on 9 August a second atomic bomb descended on Japan. Finally on 14-15 August Japan surrendered before the allies. The formal surrender ceremony took place on September 1945. Thus Japan which aimed at the establishment of an Asiatic empire surrendered unconditionally and the unequal contest ended disastrously. And Japan was under the allied occupation for six years from 1945-51. During this period general Mac.–Arthur exercised supreme powers. Finally, in September 1951 a peace treaty was signed at San Francisco between Japan and forty eight nations. The treaty came into force on 28th April, 1952 and on that day Japan became in an official sense an independent nation once again.

The "Manchurian Incident" of 1931

While the First World War was being waged there was a widely held hope that it would be a 'war to end war.' By proclaiming this idea the allies boosted their own morale and tried to quiten the consciences of those sections of their peoples who had doubt about the justification of war in general and of the First World War in particular. So general and terrible was the suffering caused, and so strong was the revulsion against war, that there was a common belief that in future no nations would venture upon, open violance in defiance of world opinion. These hopes soon proved to be illusory. Beginning in 1931, there was a series of aggressive actions, in various parts of the world, all following the same general pattern.

In Peking, 18 September 1931, the Chinese military ruler in Manchuria, Known as the young Marshal, was a guest at dinner of the British minister to China. The evening was interrupted by the arrival of news that fighting had broken out between Chinese and Japanese troops along the Japanese controlled south Machurian railway line near Mukden. On 21st September, the Chinese telegraphed to Geneva a direct appeal for the support of the league of nations. The Japanese aggression, they claimed was premeditated and was contrary to the league convenant. The "Manchurian incident" thus reached at international arena less than seventy two hours after the first shots were fired in Mukden.

The Japanese had been a self-contained, enclosed island people, until in 1853 the United States commodore perry forced them to open their door. During the 1850s, however pressure from the US and European countries forced Japan to trade with them. Within one generation Japan became a westemised statc with railways, schools, factories, upto date science, and even a new legal system. The success of the foreign intervention, together with growing political and economic discontent, in Japan, made the government very unpopular. In 1868 a brief and successful revolution ended the power of the ruling family, and political power was restored to the emperor, then a young boy named Meiji. The new emperor also in imitiation of the western powers, looked for possible expansion over-seas. This was all the more necessary because the new economic development was accompanied by a tremendous increase in her population. The obvious direction for Japanese expansion was China which still remained in a traditionally self-satisfied condition. In 1895, following a war with China, Japan forced upon the treaty of Shimonoseki by which she acquired formosa and the Liaotung Penisula which was the extreme tip of Manchuria. In 1902 Japan formed an (Anglo-Japanese) alliance with Britain. Even more significant was the overwhelming Japanese defeat of Russia in 1904-1905. According to the treaty of portsmouth, South Manchuria came within Japan's sphere of influence. During the years after 1905 a confident Japan exploited its new sphere of influence. The confusion in China following the downfall of the Manchu dynasty in 1912 seemed to Japan an excellent opportunity for expansion. Accordingly in 1915 Japan presented Twenty-one demands to Yuan-Shi-Kai, the president of the Chinese republic. The demands include the extention of Japanese privilege in Manchuria. Japanese aggressive policy towards China had been greatly helped during the period after 1915 by Chinese weakness and disunity. However, in 1928, it appeared that Chiang-Kai-Shek was going to end this situation. Many Japanese army officers believed that China must be exploited. Therefore, the Chinese war lord of Manchuria was assassinated at Mukden. It also marks the growing independence of the Japanese army from Civilian control. On the other hand, the Kuomingtang Government under Chiang-Kai-Shek was taking keen interest in Manchuria. The Kuomingtang Government infused nationalism among the Manchurians. China also decided to lay down railway lines in her own part of Manchuria, so that Japanese commerce facilities were undermined. China was also claiming that since Japan had agreed to respect her territorial integrity, therefore she had no right to advance in Manchuria. Above all, the Kuomingtang Government considered that both Manchuria and China were inseparable.

Historical Background

In these circumstances it was natural for Japan to attach great importance to the extention of her special interest in the fertile region of Manchuria . Manchuria's relations with Japan hinged upon certain basic factors about Japan's modernisation and emergence as a world power. When in 1868 the Emperor Meiji assumed his full imperial authority, he promised that "knowledge shall be sought among the nations of the world and thus the empire will be promoted." In learning from the west, Japan learned to play the foreigners game. Most swiftly and effectively this showed itself in empire building. Modernisation of government and economy, social and educational reform, all these changes led, logically to expansion. Japan achieved a lot within a short span of time-Japanese motives in colonising were mainly political and the search for prestige. It was all part of that task of winning intenational recognition which was the emperior's chief objective. Japan did in fact enter the circle of great powers after centuries of western contempt for the corruption, inertia, and backwardness of Asiatic civilisation. It was to be a basic formataive influence in the 20th century, not just for Asian nationalism generally, by the 1920's Japan had already become an example in Asia to all who wanted to defy colonialism and assert their own nationhood. By the treaty of portsmouth Japan acquired the South Manchurian railway and in 1910 Japan annexed Korea. By the famous twenty-one demands, China forcibly conceded Japanese demands in Manchuria and the Japanese got the right ot travel, reside and conduct business in Manchuria. Though, the twenty one demands was partially liquidated in the Washington conference (1921-22), yet the Japanese never abandoned their rights in Manchuria.

Importance of Manchuria for Japan

The strategic importance of Manchuria to Japan, is inherent in its situation. Economically, manchuria is mainly of value to Japanas as a secure though limited market in a world of shrinking opportunities, and as a basis of supply for some essential raw materials particularly the soyabean, but also important materials such as iron, coal and potentially considerable deposits of oil-shale. A very large amount of money has bene invested in Manchuria by Japan, a fact which makes the preservation of order and the prevention of competitive railway traffic matters of great importance. There is also the possibility of colonisation, though in this respect Japan could claim but little success hitherto, the population being overwhelmingly Chinese. However, it included, a considerable number of Koreans, and if the undisturbed settlement of these Japanese subjects could be promoted, it had been suggested that the pressure in Japan might be indirectly eased by emigration of Japanese to vacated areas in Korea. Besides, through the Kuomintang, in the later part, had turned against its former Russian advisers, the likelihood of an alliance between the communist doctrines in the North and the anti-Japanese propaganda of the Kuomingtang in the south remained a possibility which made the desire to impose between the two, a Manchuria which should be free from both increasingly felt in Japan. Above all, industrialised Japan wanted source of cheap raw materials, marketing for surplus manufactures, fields for investment of accumulated capital, food for workers, and outlet for surplus population. Manchuria, with its plentiful resources, undeveloped opportunities, geographic nearness and stratetgic location, tempted Japañ.

Causes of Conflict

The pressures within Japan were the product of the tremendous speed of change from a rural, rice growing economy to the high sophistication of modern industrial power. The world war provided an opportunity for Japan to use Asian markets because European could not send their finished goods to these countries. But after the war, when heavy tariff duties were imposed on japanese goods, a serious economic problem was created for Japan. She was insearch of a market for the disposal of her surplus goods. And manchuria was considered a good market. As the family exercised a protective influence which discouraged individual enterprise, this fact coloured Japanese economic and political development. It was reflected in the Zaibatsu, the giant business empires which controlled the whole area of Japanese economy. Like the family tradition, the Zaibatsu worked against the idea of democratic responsibility. They were deeply involved in party politics. Although its is not to be assumed that the right-wing business combines, favoured militarism in politics, the 1930s saw the growth of armaments combines, and the Zaibatsu grew rich during the war year.

Upto the time of the death in 1912 of the Emperor Meiji, Japanese political life followed a well-ordered pattern on the lines of the constitution adopted in 1889. The emperor exercised a reasonable authority in what he believed to be the best interest of the people. But gradually the emperor become a figure head, power came to lie with a number of factions. In the long run, the military elite emerged as the most effective faction, both in its method and popular appeal. Relying on their constitutional right of direct access to the Emperor as the source of their authority, the military succeeded in the 1930s in bypassing the cabinet and the politician. The Manchuria incident of 1931 was a preconceived plot by the army, planned and carried out by the local Kwang-tung army with the connivance of the general staff in Tokyo. The cabinet itself divided, tried vainly to restrain the army. By the beginning of thirties, political terror became the order of the day in Japan. Cabinet came and went, ministers were assassinated. Voices of opposition were silenced by a rising tide of militarism. Interal stresses in Japan played ultimately into the hands of the military elite. No single cause of militarism can be isolated. It was a product of the interplay of western and Japanese ideas and it was fostered by economic and social conditions which did not favoured the growth of organised moderate opinion. Civil administration had to act under the pressure of the military authorities.

Ever since the idea of divine mission of Japan had been enunciated, it had played into the hands of fanatics. After the First World War many ultra-nationalist sects grew up. They flourished in town and countryside preaching patriotism and sacrifice. It was this fanatical concentration of loyalty which explains what has been described aptly as the double patriotism of the militarist in Japan in the 1930s. The Government was under strong pressure from these nationalist. This forced Japan to follow aggressive policy.

Japan emerged in 1918 as a creditor nation, but by then, the world, as well as Japan had changed. Sensitive to shrinking markets and falling prices, the Japanese economy went through an uneasy decline from 1920 to a serious financial crisis in 1927. From this she was just recovering when the crash on wall street heralded the world depression. The American market for Japanese silk goods, the Asian and European markets for cotton almost vanished. The depression was the setting against which the Manchurian incident took place. Manchuria's growing population promised markets for her industrial exports, as a natural sphere of influence in the prevailing hostility of world economic conditions. Therefore, Manchuria invited asborption by Japan.

The question of Korean settlement has proved, one of the more serious causes of friction with the Chinese. The Koreans were regarded as a vanguard of Japanese penetration and absorption by the Chinese, their status and rights to acquire land were disputed. They were the victims of oppression and discrimination at the hands of the Chinese authorities, and their protection by the Japanese was resented. Besides, the relations of Japan and China were, ambiguous. In the growing confidence brought by modernisation, Japan believed she had a duty to lead the way for China to reform and renew herself. Progressive Chinese accepted the example of Japan. But by the end of the First World War, however, there were unmistakable signs that Japan aimed not at a partnership but a domination of China. Conditions in China in 1931 were turbulent. The right and leftwing members of the Kuomintang exchanged accusation of self-interest and treachery.

By 1931, so far as Japan was concerned, there external pressures now focused attention on Manchuria. They were the economic troubles caused by the depression, the shadow of militant communism in Russia with the ever present military threat of the Soviet army stationed on manchuria's northern border, and the emergence in China itself of a new nationalism, led by the anti-Japanese Kuomintang. The world was under the grip of economic depression. Unemployment, agrarian difficulties, disarmament, security, these were the matters which demanded the attention of the westerners. Japan felt the moment ripe for the realisation of her dream in Manchuria. For a variety of reasons, the Japanese army took the lead in Manchurian venture. Meanwhile the political power in Japan slipped from the hands of the civilian government in to those of the high command of the Japanese army. The Japanese Kwantung army made its own contribution of violence. The officers of that army wer professionally among the narrowest and ideologically the most extreme in Japan, far to the right even of the general staff in Tokyo. They saw themselves as guardians of a divine purpose to save Manchuria from military, communist and Chinese threats, and to open the eyes of the Japanese to the danger to their security. In 1931 two incidents that provided the Japanese army with a pretext for moving the manchurian question to the sphere of armed hostilities. Firstly, the murder of captain Nakamura, a Japanese officer, by Chinese soldiers in the interior of Manchuria and secondly rival railway line had been deliberately laid to challenge the monopoly of the Japanese controlled south Manchurian railway line. The Kwantung army on September 18, 1931 provoked yet, one more incident and the whole of Manchurian prize subsequently fell to Japan. During the night of 18 Septembers, 1931 the inhabitants of Mukden paid little attention to the fact that a loud explosion, followed by sounds of shooting, could be heard. In the morning the city was found to be in the hands of Japanese troops. Japanese armies speedily overran the entire territory, dispersing the forces of the Chinese governor and putting him to flight. Accordingly the Japanese forces seized possession of Mukden the capital of Manchuria, on the ground that Japanese treaty rights and vested interests had been violated. Infact, the incident occured due to the destruction by bomb explosion of a portion of one of the rails of the South Manchurian line. The damage done was not at all serious. The

Japanese claimed that the bomb had been set by Chinese soldiers, which was denied by the Chinese. The Chinese Government had immediately appealed to the league of nations.

The League and the Manchurian Incident

The league convenant was not to be exposed to its most searching test sice its birth. China's complaint against Japan was at first some what coldly received in the west. Japan had been a member of the league since its foundation. In Geneva, Japan put her case skillfully, and, in a sense sincerely, for in disclaiming all aggressive intentions against China, the Japanese civilian Government was honestly saying what it meant, even though its military advisers intended otherwise. For a time, at least, this ambiguity in the Japanese position worked as a delaying factor. Japan almost persuaded the league she was not in fact settling her dispute with Chine by force contrary to the covenant. In any case, most league members preferred to see it that way, for they had other, more pressing, worries nearer home. The military, got their way in Manchuria and the league could no longer ignore the breach of the covenant when, in late October, the Japanese delegate at Geneva refused to fix a date from withdrawing troops from Manchuria. At last in December 1931, the council agreed to a Japanese suggestion that a commision of inquiry be sent to investigate on the spot in Manchuria and China. The delay from October to December was not due to league inactivity, but no Coherent league view on the Far-Eastern problem had emerged.

The news from Mukden was not taken too serious in Washington. The troubles of the depression were in the forefront of American minds. As the weeks went by, the aggressive intention of Japan became cleared, stimson, the secretary of state declared that–USA will not approve any action which fundamentally disturbed existing treaty structure in the Far-East. The USA condemned Japanese action in Manchuria. Similarly, Britain was well aware that if, force were to be used against Japan, the main burden would fall on her own fleet in Far-Eastern waters. Public opinion in Britain was judged not to be ready to support war in such a cause. So, she put her main effort into using the league as a channel for conciliation between Japan and China. Britain considered the league as a useful forum for the exchange of ideas, a means of reconciliation. A simultaneous result of the Manchruian situation was, a great and univeral accentuation of the anti-Japanese boycott, accompanied by riots and violence. Anti-Japanese associations were founded and the most stringent rules against relations of any kind with Japanese were drawn up. The financial results to Japan were extremely serious. Meanwhile, in December 1931, the league had appointed an international commission, under the Chairmanship of Lord Lytton, to investigate the Sino-Japanese situation and recommend possible solution. Meanwhile, in February 1932 some Manchurian leaders at Mukden issued a declaration of independence and the new state was named Manchukuo. The head of the state was the last Manchu ruler Pu-Yi, who had abdicated the throne during the Chinese revolution of 1911. Virtually all governmental power was vested in his hands, but the government was under the direct control of Japan, manchukuo was independent in name, infact, it was a Japanese dependency. Japan concluded a treaty with the new government of Manchukuo and recognised it as an independent state. This recognition had the virtual effect of serving notice on the world that Japan would not accept any solution of the Manchurian question. Japan annexed the neighbouring area of jehol on the pretext that it was part of manchuria. Their armies now spread down to the great wall, ominously near to Peking. China negotiated for a demilitarised zone south of the wall, and for the next three years uneasy truce continued.

On 2nd October, 1932, the Lytton commission's report was published at Geneva. The commission recommended that the new state of Manchukuo was a political fiction. It proposed a settlement which should recognise the rights and interest of Japan in Manchuria. It also proposed that an autonomous regime should be set up in Manchuria under Chinese soverignity. It also advocated economic reapproachment between China and Japan. It further recommended the evacuation of the Japanese troops. Of course, the league did not brand Japan as aggressor nor did it consider the possibility of applying any sanctions against Japan. In the meantime, Japan had informed the league of her intention to withdraw from membership and in 1935, Japan officially ceased to be a member of the league.

The small powers of the world, who had found in the league's councils a first change to feel their way in international debate, were disappointed that the league had been used to so little apparent purpose by the great powers. Even the league's most ardent supporters could take little comfort and, for its critics, it merely seemed like an obvious lesson in failed pious hopes. Ahead lay the dangerous shallows of Nazism and the Italian attack on Ethiopia. The league entered those waters with its fabric strained and its timbers already leaking, though not without hope that repair and skillful seamanship might yet make it seaworthy. The open violation of league covenant was the prelude to the long and fatal series cluminanting in the Second World War of 1939. Whatever may be the fact that due to the so-called Manchurian incident, the military clique came to the front and civil authorities went to the background. Besides, after the Manchurian incident

USSR strengthened her position in the pacific and simultaneously concentrated on the defence of outer mongolia. The creation of Manchukuo provided a common frontier for Japan and the USSR, which affected the Russo-Japanese relation in future years.

"The Japanese conquest of manchuria," as carr has observed, "one of the most important historical landmarks since the First World War." It heralded the reemergence of the struggle for power not only in the pacific but in the world at large. The manchurian affair illustrates the new and interlocking relationship of Eastern and Western problems in between the war years. Important in itself to the domestic fortunes of Japan and China, the manchurian crisis also led out into the spheres of Russian and American interest. It drew Asian, American and European politics into a new relationship. However, it was Japan's misfortune that, in choosing the wrong side in the European struggle her bid for an independnet Far-Eastern sphere free from traditional European colonialism served in the end to destroy herself as totally as the dictators themselves destroyed the old Europe from which that colonialism had sprung.

Chapter XXI

Fascist Italy

After the First World War many of the old established powers of Europe were never again to attain the full extent of their former power. Germany had been humbled, Austria-Hungary had disintegrated, Russia had suffered revolution, the ottoman empire was on the verge of collapse, France had suffered relentless warfare and within Great Britain a social revolution of profound importance had taken place. Such ideas as democracy, self-determination, and a general liberation from earlier restrictions were now in the ascendant in the new Europe, but the events of the inter-war period were to show that these new ideas came too soon. The change from the authoritarian pre-1914 Governments to the more liberal forms after the war was too suden, and this change resulted in the emergence of totalitarianism in Europe. Italy was the first country that fell to totalitarian governments in the inter-war period. The rise of Fascism in Italy was directly related to the First World War and the settlement that followed. Fascism came to Italy as the post-war inflation stimulated an active and successful working class agiatation for higher fascism came from those who were afraid of red-revolution, Bolshevism, socialism and the classless society. After the great war Italy was politcally divided, undermined by internecine strife and rival faction, depressed by an unjust treaty of peace devoid of resources, with a totally disorganised economic system and that she was rushing towards anarchy. Italy was rescued from the post-war anarchy and set on the path of a reinvigorated national life by the fascist movement, which owed its origin to the expression of desire for order and stability. There object was to establish a new political and social order that might make it possible to undertake the task of reconstructing Italy.

Cause of the Rise of Fascism

More than any other country, Italy had entered the war with definite and limited objectives. These were contained in a bargain that would ensure their achievements when the war should end. The treaty of London of April 1915, concluded between the allies and italy before italy would agree to enter the war, defined these terms explicitly. Italy was to acquire the southern Tyrol, Trieste, the Istrian Pensiula, and a part of Dalmatia. One event that could not be foreseen when this treaty was concluded was that new states would emerge after war. One of these, Yugoslavia, made strong claims for a coastline of which a part had been promised to Italy. The Paris peace conference therefore, became the scene of bitter discontent, though she was one of the victorious allies. She had been denied even what she regarded as her treaty rights. Naturally the Government had to bear the blame for this failure.

This discontent was aggravated by social conditions. In comparison with other western powers, Italy was a poor country, and the long war had been a serious drain upon her resources. The general standards of living of the average Italian family were low, and there were few incentives for hard work and sacrifice. The Government had borrowed heavily and these debts had to be repaid. As the Lira (Italian currency) declined in value, the cost of living increased accordingly by atleast five times. There was massive unemployment as heavy industry cut back its wartime production and ex-serviceman had difficulty in finding jobs. Manhood sufferage and proportional representation were introduced in 1919 elections. But this made it difficult for any one party to gain an overall majority and coalition government were inevitable. As there was a coalition government, no consistent policy was possible. The instability of ministries was itself a cause of increasing discredit of parliamentary government. The government's prestige sank lower because of its failure to protect property, and many property owner's were convinced that the revolution was at hand. The most important element in the origin of the Fascist movement was what might be called a heresy of socialism. It is no accident that several leading Fascist, began their political carrier in the socialist movement Fascism after all was nurtured in the same conditions of 19th century industrial and social change which also produced socialism. It happened that many of the most ardent patriotic nationalist of the pre-war and post-war years were also radical socialist. They were deeply dissatisfied with the growing power of the great business combines. Besides, the econmic crisis of the post-war period led to the spread of socialism. To many the leaning towards communism proved more alluring than the empty talk of arm-chair politician of a shame democracy. Unemployment and lockouts in factories resulted strikes and seizure of factories by the socialist. The philosophy of communism was preached with vigor.

Benito Mussolini

These conditions, social, political, economic, breeding discontent among the people were suited to any politician who could persuade the people that he had a new system that would produce strong government, and general prosperity. They were the sort of conditions that might have favoured the spread of communism had not the middle classes been too strong to be wiped out. The solution to the Italian puzzle was provided by a very different type of political system, namely Fascism which always was intensely anti-communist. The first knowledge that most European had of Fascism was the news of Mussolini's "March on Rome." But this was only the tangible evidence of what had been seething and spreading for a long time. Mussolini was the man of the hour in the sense that his personal qualities were suited to take advantage of the situation.

Mussolini was born in 1883 in Romagna, an area of Eastern Italy renowned in the 19th century for its rebellious spirit. In his youth he had a reputations as a forceful man intent on securing his ambitions, and as rather a bully. His parents were not wealthy, but Mussolini in childhood received a fair education. He undertook a variety of jobs. He was an elementary school teacher, a mason, who carried on his shoulder heavy load of cement, a black-smith who bent iron bars on the anvil, a peasant, who turned up heavy sods with his spade. From his father he learned, and adopt, the ideas of extreme socialism. He had behind him a turbulent revolutionary carrier as a socialist agitator and journalist, editor of the leading socialist paper 'Avanti.' A pacifist in his early years, he developed violently anti-Boloshevik and intensely patriotic views which led him to enforce war as a means to Italian revival and to reassertion of her ancient historical role in the mediterranean. When Italy at last declared war against the axis, he shared the mood of national confidence and relief, "from to-day onwards, we are all Italian and nothing but Italians." In 1915 he was called into the army whence, after being wounded, he was invalided out, taking up again his work on his newspaper. Communism was at work in all the towns of italy. Strikes and mob rioting, breakdown of law and order, demolition, unemployment and a rising cost of living added to the toll of what war had already destroyed. The king was ineffectual and the parliamentary systems, weakened by multiparty divisions, lost the confidence of the peoples. Mussolini emerged as the strong man, ruthless and energetic enough to make a clean sweep.

In 1919 he founded the Fascist party in Milan with a socialist and republican programme and showed sympathy with the factory occupation of 1919-1920. The local party branches were known as Fasci di combattimente (the Fascist group of fighters) came into existence to face to dangers, the conservatism of the right and the destructiveness of the left. The word Fasces meant the bundle of rods with protruding axe which used to symbolise the authority and power of the ancient Roman consuls. The Fasci, recruited from the ranks of the unemployed, the discontented, the demobilised soldiers, were ready to break strikes, to raid and terrorise in the cause of law and order and, above all, to break up communist meetings. To Mussolini Fascism was not a party, but a movement. The nubulous character of the Fascist programme also helped to win adherents among those whose imagination readily succcumbed to the hypnotic influence of lofty sounding generalisation. Mussolini wrote "Fascism is a great mobilisation of material and moral forces. What does it aim at? We state without false modesty that it aims at governing the state. What is its porgramme? The programme needed for ensuring material and moral greatness of the Italian. "But it was a movement that has small, and not very encouranging beginnings. In the elections of Novemebr 1919 for the chamber of deputies, only two Fascists were nominated and both were defeated. Never the less, Fsaci were forming in other towns, and the movement spread throughout Italy. Later on, Mussolini became the defender of private enterprise and property, thus attracting much needed financial support from wealthy busiess interests. Beginning in late 1920 black-shirted squards of Fascist regularly attacked and burned down socialist headquartes. By the end of 1921, even though Mussolini's political programme was vague, he had gained the support of property owners in general. Though the founder of Fascism avoid formulating theoretical programme, Yet from the start, two of his objectives were manifest and they remained distinctive featurs of the movement. One was the need of strengtherning the authority of the state and the other was national syndicalism. Of course, Fascism had no Karl Marx no rationale of the improvement of the human lot. But Facism put more emphasis on action than on ideas. Fascist ideas originated in a number of 19th century thinkers, disillusioned by the failure of conventional politicians to achieve true national greatness. They put emphasis on creating a new national myth and seeking its fulfillment through an emotional response of the individual who was to sink his own material interest in a greater purpose.

The anti-Fascist group failed to cooperate with each other and made no determined effort to keep the Fascist out. The communist refused to cooperate with the socilaist. Giolitti, the prime minister held the elections in 1921, so that the Fascists, still unrepresented in parliament, might win some seats and than support his government. He was willing to overlook their violence. However, they won only 35 seats. The socialist refused to work with the government to curb Fascist violence. On the other hand, Mussolini tried to draw away the adherents of socialism to his side by organising syndicates (labour unions) for which he laid down the objectives. These included the control of industries by syndicates, and Eight hour a day, a capital levy and inheritance tax, economic council with legislative powers. In the meantime, Giolitti resigned, and the socialist tried to further their own ends by calling a general strike in 1922. The general strike played right in to the hands of the Fascist, who were able to use it by announcing that if the government failed to quell the strike, they would crush it themselves. When the strike failed Mussolini was able to pose as a saviour of the state from communism. At the sametime he make conciliatory speeches about the Roman Catholic church. So that the pope swung the church into line behind Mussolini-seeing him as an anti-communist weapons. When Mussolini announced that he had dropped his Republican amibitions, even the king became well disposed towards him. As about 50,000 black shirts converged on the capitals, the prime minister Facta was prepared to resist. But king Victor Emmanuel III refused to declare a state of emergency and instead invited Mussolini, who had remained nervously in Milan, to come to Rome and form a new government, which he obligingly did. Afterwards the Fascists fostered the myth that they had seized power heroically. But it had been achieved by the mere threat of force. The role of the king was important, he made the crucial decision not to use the army. Though many historians believe that the army would have had little difficulty in dispersing the disorderly and poorly armed black shirts. The reasons why the king decided against armed resistance remain something of a mystery. There is no doubt that he had a certain amount of sympathy with the Fascist aim of providing a strong government. Mussolini became the first ever Fascist premier.

Basic Principles of Fascism

A one party state was essential and there was no place for democracy. Fascism is the anti-thesis of democracy. Fascism was particularly hostile to communism, which accounts for much of its popularity. The Fascist political philosophy repudiates the basic principles of democratic government the right of the majority to rule. It poses the figure of the leader (Duce), a euphemistic term for dictator. Fascism rescued the state from the weight of faction, party interest and egoism of classes and restored dignity of the state. The Fascist Party members were the elite of the state and great emphasis was placed on the cult of the leader who would win mass support with thrilling speeched and skillful propaganda.

Military strength and violence were an integral part of the way of life Mussolini himself remarked peace is absurd. Fascism does not believe in it. Instead of peace, Fascism exalts war, for it teaches that war alone keeps up all the energies of man to their highest pitch, and sets the mark of nobility on those nations which have the courage to face it. Fascism support imperialism. The Fascist fostered the myth that they had seized power by revolution, they allowed the violent treatment of opponent and pursued an aggressive foreign policy. Economic self-sufficiency was vitally important in developing the greatness of the state. So the government must direct the economic life of the country. The exponents of Fascism believed that the age of laissez-faire is drawing to a close. Fascism made a compromise between socialism and capitalism. They presented before the proletariat the ideas of socialism. It denies the doctrine of the class struggle, which is the outcome of the economic conception of history. It contemplates the fusion of all classes in to a single ethical and economic reality. It claims that this unity of classes is realised within the unity of the Fascist corporate state, in which different interest are harmonised. The Fascist believed that the state is an end in itself, and every thing in the state, nothing outside the state and nothing against the state. A totalitarian system of government is a complete way of life in which the government attempted to control and organise with strong discipline as many aspects of peoples life as possible. This was necessary to promote the greatness of the state, which was more important than the interests of the individual.

Evolution of the Italian Fascist State

Mussolini's first government was, in fact, a coalition between the Fascists and some rightwing Italian nationalist. But this temporary partnership soon gave way to the realities of a personal dictatorship and one party state. Although, the monarchy, in the person of king Victor Emmanuel III, remained throughout the period, real power was concentrated in Mussolini's hand as, "Duce" or leader of Italy. After Mussolini the most powerful instrument within Italy was the Fascist grand council, a body of senior Fascist ministers on whom, the Duce relied. In building up power within Italy he had never given much attention to parliament. Once in power he discovered that he was unlikely to receive support within parliament unless he altered its structure. Consequently in 1923 and 1928 the electoral system was altered in such a manner that Fascist majorities were obtained. As per the electoral law, the party that secured most votes in an election should receive two-thirds of the seats in the chamber of deputies. Under this law in April 1924 fresh elections were held and these gave to the Fascist a substantial parliamentary majority. It was a victory won by corruption and by intimidating voters, but it served the Fascist'sf purpose. A semblance of parliamentary opposition was allowed at first but it was finally silenced after the murder of the socialist opposition leader Matteotti. This murder served to turn a section of Italian public opinion against Fascist methods and persuaded Mussolini that the time had come to impose the full rigour of Fascist control by every means at his disposal. This was a turning point that Mussolini openly repudiated any reconcilation with liberals. He said that "Italy wants peace, work and calm... I will give these things with love, if possible, by force, if necessary."

In the economic field, Mussolini was establishing the Fascist concept of the corporate state. Private property and capitalism continued, but under state control. The individual no longer faced risk alone, his interest, subordinated to the state was protected by and enlarged in it. In Fascist theory, work was a social duty, and process of production was a single whole, its aims being united and identified with the well-being of the producers and the promotion of the national power. To this end, the Italians were organised into corporations according to their occupations the relations between employer and employed being regulated by a national council of corporations. Fascist controlled unions had the sole right to negotiate for the workers and both unions and employers associations were expected to cooperate to settle disputes over pay and working conditions. Strikes and lockouts were not allowed. To compensate for their loss of freedom, workers were assured of such benefits as free Sundays, annuals holidays with pay, social security, sports facilities and cheap tours and holidays. The objective of the Fascist corporate state was prosperity in a highly competitive world, and it is not difficult to understand the appeal of such a programme in Italy. Prosperity in Italy did increase. A reduction was debt to the US was negotiated. The new regime justified itself in the most ambitious programme of public works Europe had everseen. New schools and hospitals, sports stadia, roads, bridges, railway station and irrigation projects gave promise of that 'Third Rome' which Mussolini offered to his peoples vision.

The papacy had been hostile to the Italian Government since 1870, though sympathetic towards Mussolini in 1922, Pope Pius XI disapproved of the increasing totalitarianism of Fascist Government. Though, Mussolini was an atheist, was well aware of the power of the Roman Catholic church, and put himself out to win over the Pope who was obessed with the fear of communism. The result was the "Lateran treaty" by which Italy recognised the Vatican city as a sovereign state, paid a large sum of money to the Pope as compensation for all his losses, accepted the Catholic faith as the official state religion. In return the papacy recognised the Kingdom of Italy. It was probably the most lasting achievements of Mussolini.

Methods of censorship and propaganda were freely employed. The press was subject to a severe Censorship. Propaganda was evident in all aspects of life, ranging from slogan painted on wall to systematic Fascist indoctrination in schools and among youth people. Anyone suspected of being anti-Fascist was liable to be rounded up and punished without a trial. Italy had become a one-party, totalitarian state dominated by the secret police. The army was enlarged and strengthened because war, and the glorification of war, was one of the main tenets of Mussolini's policy. The acid test of any regime is not whether it was fully totalitarian but whether its policies were effective. Did Mussolini rescue Italy from weak government, or was he, just a windbag whose government was as corrupt as previous ones? But the average Italian can have felt little benefits from the regime. Thus, the totalitarian regime of Benito Mussolini failed to achieve what it had promised.

Foreign Affairs

Italian foreign policy was somewhat confused. Mussolini knew what he wanted, which was to make Italy great, respected and feared. But he was not sure how to achieve it, beyond agitating for a revision of the 1919 peace settlement in Italy's favour. The Fascist need to make the national ideal a truly grandiose one led Mussolini to undertake a flamboyant policy of glorification, ill-suited to the means at his disposal and out of touch with the diplomatic realities of the day. Taking up the empire building, he put before the Italian people a vision of an Italian Mediterranean, rivalling the glories of ancient Rome. "I am all for motion", Mussolini once confessed, and his ambitions proved a disturbing factor in the sphere of international relations. Italy needed more territories, and the need was apparent after the USA had introduced the 1921 emergency immigration act which prohibited unrestricted immigrants from European countries to the USA. It was therefore necessary for Italy to look elsewhere for territories to accomodate her rising population. The search for territories brought her into open conflict with other countries. Mussolini said "we are hungry for land because we are prolific. . . ."

Besides, in his opinion the glory of Rome could be revived by pursuance of the policy of territorial expansion. He had no respect for league system, of collective security, territorial integirty of small states. Mussolini declared that the mediterranean was only a 'via' for Britain and France, while it was "Vita" for Italy. However, the mediterranean rather than forming a part of Italian empire, had become almost a prison for her. He was determined to proceed towards the Mediterranean without which Italy was half-independent. However, the mediterranean rather than forming a part of Italian empire, had become almost a prison for her. He was determined to proceed towards the Mediterranean without which Italy was half-independent. Italian aim appeared to be to link Libya with Ethiopia through Sudan.That would connect Italian North African empire and the Mediterranean with the Indian Ocean. Thus, as soon as he assumed the reins of power, Mussolini revealed his purpose to bring about a thorough reorientation of Italy's foreign policy. His foreign policy in the early years of Fascis regime brought remarkable successes.

The islands of Rhodes and Dodecannes which Italy had to transfer to Greece in 1920 was regained by Mussolini by the treaty of Laussane signed in 1923. The Corfu case threatened for a while to present a complicated situation. Mussolini in retaliation for the alleged murder on Greek soil of four Italian members of a boundary delimiting commission, bombarded the Greek island of Corfu. The crisis was eventually settled by a conference of ambassadors mainly at the initiative of Great Britain. Italy received a large sum of money as compensation and vacated the Corfu. This enhanced the prestige of Italy. Mussolini's handling of the affairs from beginning to end, was expressive of the new spirit of boldness that he claimed Fascism had introduced in to the notions general attitude to the world at large.

Franco-Italian and Yugoslavia Relations

The relations between Italy and France had been sore since the Paris conference. Italy held France responsible for the disregard to her just rights in the Paris conference. The creation of the Fascist dictatorship tended to throw Italy into opposing camps. France was a strong supporter of democracy. But Italy was now the exponent of a new dispotism, the anti-thesis of popular government, and a source of infection to other democracies. Fascist complained that opponents of their regime found ready asylum in France, further, they were encouraged by France to become naturalised citizens. Besides, on the main issue of post-war policy, Italy and France were in fundamental opposition, France was the protagonist of the statusquo powers, while Italy was sympathetic to the reaisionist cause. In addition to the antagonism of contrated political ideals and aims, there existed also causes of rivally in North Africa and western Mediterranean. In the French protectorate of Tunisia, the number of both French and Italian nationals was about equal. But France claimed that its nationals outnumbered the French, so Italy began to plead the cause of an oppressed nationality. Italy also demanded French territories of Corsica and Nice. The colonial aspirations of Italy are founded not merely upon the question of prestige, but also a need for an outlet for a supply of essential raw materials and for an outlet for her excessive increasing population. Mussolini also objected to France's alleged desire to bar, Italy's reasonably and logical aspirations at Tangier. Ultimately, Italy had another diplomatic victory when she got a share in the internationalised administration of the Tangier city. Besides, France in the quest for her security had concluded defensive agreement with countries of little entente, Yogoslavia, Czecoslovakia and Rumania which supported the status quo maintained by the treaty of Versailles. The rivalry between France and Italy over the creation of respective alliances became more and more intensified with the march of time. But during 1930's there was a marked improvement in France-Italian relations. This was due to Hitler's rise to power in Germany. The Laval-Mussolini pact was concluded and by its terms both agreed to settled their disputes by peaceful means. The improvement in the Franco-Italian relations had an adverse effect on the friendship between Italy and Yugoslavia. Fium had been a constant source of conflict between Italy and Yugoslavia. Italy considered Fiume essential for her territorial and commercial expansion in the Balkans. Italy forcibly occupied Fium, but Fiurg was recognised as a free-city by the treaty of Rapallo between Italy and Yugoslavia. But when Mussolini came to power a fresh treaty was concluded between Italy and Yugoslavia, at Rome and Italy, received the town of Fium and the adjoining territories remained with Yugoslavia. By the Nettiune convention where by the citizens of Yugoslavia gained some commercial rights in Italy, Italian were allowed to hold land in certain party of Yugoslavia. There was discontenment in Yugoslavia to this potential encroachment. The relations between the two further deteriorated due to the Marseilles murder.

Italy and Albania

Albania, one of the States the smallest in the Balkan Peninsula occupied an important place in the foreign policy of Italy. Albania emerged as a new state after Balkan wars of 1912-13. During the First World War Albania, was officially neutral, but the foreign powers used it as a battle ground. At the Paris conference Italy, sought an Albanian mandate, but her plea was turned down. A provisional government was set up in Albania in 1992. Later she became a member of the league. The provisional government failed to contain Chaos. It was succeeded by a Muslim chieftain named Ahmed Zogu. In 1928 Zogu proclaimed himself king of Albania, (king Zog I.) The new king tried his best to consolidate his power. Albanian national bank was founded to consolidate his power. Albanian national bank was founded with Italian help and many internal development projects were put in operation, with the cooperation of Italy. Both the countries signed the treaty of foreign relations of Albania whenever the latter so requested. An Italian company secured an oil concession from the King. To strengthened their bond of friendship, a military pact was concluded between the two. However, Albanian displayed an anti-Italian feeling. King Zog I refused the proposal for a custom union with Italy and closed all Private schools controlled by the Italian. He also tried unsuccessfully to reduce the influence of Italian officers in the army. The relations between the two countries began to deteriorate. By the end of 1938 Italy had become the master of Ethiopia. Rome-Berlin-Tokyo Axis had further strengthened Mussolini's position. So, he was not going to accept any reverse in Albania. By April 1939 war clouds were hovering on the European skies. Albania's anti-Italian attitude annoyed Italy and Italian troops launched attack on the Albanian coast and entered Tirana. Albania failed to resist and victor Emmanuel III proclaimed as King of Albania. The European power accepted fait accompli.

Annexation of Abyssinia

Mussolini's foreign policy was dominated by militant nationalism and blind imperialism. But Italy had avoided invading any other country's territory till Hitler adopted aggressive posture. By the end of 1935 Italy had made preparations for large scale aggression. Mussolini was determined to expand the "Fascist empire" through the glory of Italian arms. Mussolini's plan of military solution was put into operation on October 1935, when Italian troops invadedAbyssinia (Ethiopia). Abyssinia, a land-locked state wedged in the mountainous country between Somaliland and Sudan, was the only independent country in East Africa. The coveteous eyes of Italy, longing ever since her unification for imperialist expansion, had for long fallen upon Abyssinian natural resources, which ranged from pineapples to platinum. The Fascist Government advanced several arguments in favour of the Ethiopian expedition. Mussolini came to the conclusion that the acquisition of Ethiopia did not involve direct collision with a rival European power. The temptation of a forward policy in Ethiopia was strong, because of its potential wealth, as well as by the treaty of Ucciali (1889) the Italians had believed that they acquired a protectorate over Abyssinia until the denunciation of the treaty in 1893 and the disastrous defeat at Adowa in 1896. The defeat temporarily destroyed these dreams, and left only a rankling memory. But, France and Britain, had long recognised Italian interest in Ethiopia. Mussolini reiterated the nation's civilising mission and the backwardness of Ethiopia was depicted. Besides, acquisition of a new colony was necessary to accommodate her rising population. In 1925 an agreement was signed with England, whereby England was to receive free water right in Northern Ethiopia for the benefit of Anglo-Egyptian Sudan, in return for her giving Italy a free hand in Ethiopia. In 1928 a final effort to secure Italian interests by peaceful means took the form of an Italo-Abysinian treaty. With the rise of Nazi menace, it now appeared safe to follow Italian ends by more vigorous action. Hitler's policy of annexing Austria and French fear of Germany paved the way for a close friendship between France and Italy. By the Laval-Mussolini pact France not only awarded some portions of Addis-Ababa railway to Italy, but also she gave tacit consent to Mussolini's adventure in Ethiopia. The unruliness of the border tribes had given constant trouble to all Abysinian's neighbour and Italy thought of making these periodical acts of banditry an excuse for punitive action against the empire. At the same time the League of Nations was almost defunct after the Manchurian episode. So the time appeared opportune to Italy for an imperialistic venture. On Dec. 5, 1934 the wal-wal incident took place on the border of Abyssinia and Italian Somaliland. Although there were much Large number of casualities on the Abyssianian side, Italy blamed Abyssinia for the clash and demanded an apology and compensation from her. Abyssinia refused to accept her responsibility for the clash and requested that the dispute should be resolved through arbitration as provided the Italo-Abysinian treaty. Since Italy refused to accept the Abyssinian position the later appealed to the league on January 3, 1935 to settle the dispute. The council adjourned the question, requesting both sides to seek a settlement under their own treaty of 1928. However, the military preparation of Italy were so formidable apparent that there remained little doubt of her aggressive intentions. The Italian Government delayed the appointment of arbitrators. On March 16, the Ethiopian Government appealed to the league under Article 15. French foreign minister Laval and Sir Hoare of Britain obstructed all Ethiopian effort to initiate the League action. At the Stressa conference Britain, France and Italy attempted to make a common front against Hitler, who had repudiated the disarmament privisions of the treaty of Versailles treaty. Here Mussolini made it clear, in return for support to Britain and France, he expected a free hand in Africa. Neither France nor Britain made any objections, they were anxious to effect a rapproachement with Italy. From here on matters became worse rather than better. No doubt attempts were made to resolve the crisis in a way that would satisfy Italy, Yet preserve the independence of Ethiopia. British minister Anthony Eden in Rome suggested that Britain would cede from the British Somaliland the port of Zeila to Abyssinia, and in-return the latter would be persuaded to cede her Southern province of Ogden to Italy. This proposal was rejected by Mussolini. As Italy mounted pressure on Abyssinian Border, the delegates of Britain, and France met at Paris and suggested that Italy be given an economic mandate. Under the league, for the administrative and financial organisation of Abyssinia. In other words, this mandate could be a cover for Italian control over Abyssinia without resort to war. This proposal was also rejected by Mussolini. On September 1935, a League Commission of five proposed international assistance to Ethiopia, that is Italian domination. But Mussolini was determind to take Italy by Force.

Emperor Haile Selassi, reading the writing on the wall of Europe, made a desperate appeal to President Roosevelt. And requested him to find some way of making Italy observe her obligation under the Kellog-Briand pact. The appeal was rejected by the US, on the ground that the dispute was being considered by the league. The report of the leagues' conciliation committee suggesting a plan for the international development of Abyssinia with a recognition of Italy's special interest, and accepted in principle by emperor Haile-Selassie, was summarily rejected by Mussolini. While the council was at work, Italian troops advance into Ethiopia on 3rd Oct. 1935. The pretext for beginning this invasion was the Ethiopian with–drawal of its soldier from the border. According to Italy this strategic move, necessitated an immediate advance in order to protect Italian Somaliland against further aggression. On 7th Oct., 1935 the council of the league, unanimously adopted a report declaring that Italy had resorted to war in breach of the covenant.

The assembly on 11th Oct. concurred in the view adopted by the council. The problem of recommending and coordinating the sanctions to be imposed was entrusted to a committee. It was decided to raise the arms embargo against Italy. A comprehensive financial sanction was also imposed. The acceptness of imports from Italy was immediately afterwards prohibited. A very limited embargo on the export to Italy of certain important suppllies come in to force in November 18. From this the most important omission was oil, which was excluded ostensibly on the ground that the list was confined to commodities controlled by league powers. Thus was began the first grat experiment of the coercive powers of the league.

Ethiopia could have been saved easily by closing the Suez Canal, by imposing a naval blockade against Italy. But Britain and France were unwilling to apply military sanction, nor were they prepared to tighten economic sanctions. They could not risk war with Italy in defence of Ethiopia The French had all along stood for a league having overwhelming military force at its command to make collective security a reality. Britain had always opposed this conception, wanting the League to play the role of a mediator. Threatened by the rise of Nazi Germany, France had found a friend in the Fascist dictator. If Britain now chose to uphold collective security, it was not for any altruistic considerations, but for her own vital interest's, France was not eager to pull British chestnuts out of the fire, but she was prepared to cooperate with Britain as she could not dispense with British friendship. England also did not want to go too far to defeat Mussolini, for, after all Hitler's Germany was the real enemy and nothing must be done to weaken the anti-German front. Under the circumstance both France and England agreed to initiate some face-saving measures, as both were the so-called Champion of the league. Thus, the Anglo-French policy in connection with Ethiopia was nothing but a "deliberatly throwing dust in the eyes of the world." The application of sanctions was far from sufficient to compel Italy to vacate the occupied territory. Because the sanctions were half-hearted and lukewarm. Austria, Hungary refused to apply economic sanction against Italy. Hitler took advantage of the situation and regained a friend recently lost. At the same time, left to her fate, Abyssinia succumbed to the brutal might of Italy. Italian troops emerged victorious and marched into the Abyssinian capital Addis Ababa on May 5, 1936. The conquered country was annexed to into the Italian empire on May 9, 1936, and the king of Italy was proclaimed emperor of Abyssinia.

The Abyssinian episode marked a crucial turning point in post-war history. The triumph of Italian aggression, naked and unashamed, affected the world with fundamental consequences. Britain and France were demoralised, as they could neither save the covenant nor retained the friendship of Italy. Germany emerged as the principal gainer. She managed to regain the friendship of Italy which eventually led to the formation of the Rome-Berlin-Tokyo axis. To England, it meant the virtual destruction of the institution which successive government of different parties, had proclaimed to be the keystone of their foreign policy. Italy submitted her resignation from the League. Ethiopia was abandoned and the League committed suicide. After the conclusion of the Abyssinian war, Italy and Germany intervened in the Spanish civil war. It was in open defiance of the league. The axis between Italy and Germany was formed and consolidated. The Fascist axis continued to be strengthened and became a threat to world peace.

Chapter XXII

The Third Reich: Germany

(1919-39)

Strange but true! Germany an advanced country, fell into the hands of an irrational dictatorship. How did the formless and faceless figure, an epitome of the little man, gifted by demonic dynamism, possessing mesmeric power, swayed multitudes rescued Germany from the despair, led by his maniacal ambition dragged the world into another cataclysm is to be noted. That genius, he was none else than Adolf Hitler. How did Hitler secure control of Germany? Certainly a fact of interest. The year 1918 was intensely tragic for Germany. William II, the German Kaiser was forced to abdicate two days before the armistice in Nov. 1918. A weary and disillusioned people revolted against the form of government which had brought Germany to defeat. The most notable of thes revolts was a communist inspired rising at Kiel where Soviets were established. It was caused due to the breakdown of the German military machine, and the intoxicating effect of the Russian revolution. After the abdication of the Kaiser, Ebert, a moderate socialist, became president. After his coming to power a communist inspired rising took place in Berlin, known as the spartacist rising, led by Rosa Luxemburg and Liebknecht. It reached its climax in January 1919. 1919 witnessed further rising of a left-wing kind. Many of the soldiers who had fought in the war were bitter against their own government and denounced the "November criminals" for their betrayal. These soldiers were eager for the establishmeent of a right wing regime inside Germany. Amid this turmoil of political confusion from right and left the new republic was born, and throughout 1919 a national assembly met at weimer in order to devise an accptable consitution. The result of their meeting was the Weimer constitution, and the Republic which adopted this constitution is known as the Weimer Republic why a proud and gallant people trained to obedience, to war, to victory, and to government by authority, objected to anarchy, to defeat, and to government by discussion, there objection was more natural since all these seemed to be imposed by foreign dictation. The reaction was obvious. For the treaty of versailles had an even greater effect internally upon Germany than it had upon the rest of the world. It was Germany's determination to upset and to revise the treaty which armed the opponents of the newly born republic and nullified all the efforts of pacifists, democrats and man of goodwill in Germany.

The weimer republic lost popularity soon after its birth. When it accepted the humiliating treaty of verseilles. The republic was politically weak and the ecomonic crisis further worsened the condition. In this critical hour Hindenburg, the president of the republic was advised from all Quarters to appoint Hitler as chancellor, but he hesitated. He did not like this (Hitler) vulgar, loh form loud mouthed Bohemion corporate. In the end he felt he had no choice. Finally he choose Hitler as chancellor on 30 January, 1933. How and why Hitler kept his hold upon the German masses has been discussd in the subsequent pages.

The Weimer Republic

As per the Weimer constitution Germany remained a federation with power divided between the central government in Berlin and the provincial governments. The constitution provided for a parliament that was to consist of two houses, the Reichstag, the more important of the two. The Reichstag was to be elected by Universal suffrage and proportional representation. There was to be a president elected by universal suffrage for a period of 7 years and who occupied position of head of state. Elbert became the first president. He had the power to choose the Chancellor and rule by decree in times of emergency. In practise the Chancellor was more powerful than the president. The constitution established a supreme court and basic rights, such as freedom of speech, religion were guaranteed. For the first time Germany had a democratic constitution. The framers of the constitution were ever optimistic. To consider that a country could change from rigid autocracy of the Kaiser's Germany, with its Prussian militarist traditions, to a republic with universal suffrage was to expect too much in too short a time. Unfortunately the Weimer republic, born of defeat and with little positive support from the people, could hardly have had a more stormy beginning.

The new government accepted the humiliating and unpopular Versailles treaty, with its arms limitations, reparations and war guilt clause, and was thus always associated with defeat and dishonour. German nationalists could never forgive it for that. In Germany, there was a traditional lack of respect for democratic government and a great admiration for the army and the officer class as the rightful leaders of Germany. In 1919 the view was widespread that the army had not been defeated, it had been betrayed, stabbed in the back, by the democrats who had needlessly agreed to the Versailles treaty. However, the "Stab in the back" legend was eagerly fostered by all enemies of the republic. The parliamentary system laid down in the Weimer constitution had weaknesses, the most serious of which was that it was organised in a system of propertional representation so that all politicial groups would have a fair representation. On the other hand, the political parties had very little experience of how to operate a democratic parliamentary system, because before 1919 the Reichstag had not actually controlled policy, the chancellor had the final authority. Under the Weimer constitution the Chancellor was responsible to the Reichstag, but usually it failed to give a clear lead because the parties refused to compromise. The communists, conservatives, nationalist did not believe in the republic and refused to support the social democrats. Disagreements became so bitter that almost every party organised its own private army increasing the threat of civil war.

The first opposition came from members of the right who blamed the government for accepting the humiliating treaty of Versailles. They tried to displaced the government by force. There was a general strike in 1919. Social democrats crushed it with ruthless vengeance. While the new government was busy in setting up the new republic, at the same time in Bavaria there was a period of civil war, strikes and disorders took-place in most of the industrial areas. The social democrats allied with the conservative leaders to prevent a social revolution. On the other hand the government's policy of suppressing the communists encouraged the rightest. A new political party National Socialist German's workersparty came into existence in 1920. This new party was backed by the formerpan-German league, and more important by general Ludendorff. Besides, the nationalist party and the conservative people's party, representing the Prussian militarist and imperial interest, had been flourishing. In 1920 the rightist tried to displace the government by force, this was what is known as the Kapp Putsch (Coup), the force was provided by some remanants of the German army of the Baltic that had refused to disband. These, under the command of general Luttwitz, on 12-13th March 1920 marched into Berlin, occupied key points in the city and proclaimed Dr. Kapp, an active promoter of reactionary idea, as Chancellor of the republic. It is of interest to note that the Swastik was the badge of the movement, the first occasion on which the device was so used. Ebert, and his government, unprepared for this sudden invasion, fled to Stuttgart where they planned measures against the rebels. As might have been expected, the rising represented the views of one set of extremists only. The mass of the people, having had more than enough of violence, gave no support and when Ebert ordered a general strike of the worker the order was obeyed. Berlin was soon without public services, waters, electricity, transport. Ordinary life in the city became impossible. On 17th March Kapp and Luttwitz wre compelled to withdraw, and the putsch was over. It was not the last threat to the republic, rather the beginning. The communist led rising of the workers was a common feature. Munich and Bavaria became a breeding ground for nationalist agitation and a base from which to over-throw the republic. The nationalists showed open hostility to democracy in the Reighstag, political assassination were not uncommon. The Kapp affair did not end the attempt of reactionaries to avenge the betrayal of the fatherland. They instituted a reign of terror against individuals prominently identified with socialism. Jews and Catholics were attacked, and attempts were made upon the lives of Ebert. In 1922 W. Rathenau, successful industrialist, political philosopher, was assassinated. With a series of weak coalition government's from the outset and with a variety of Chancellor, the Weimer republic struggled for its life.

Another threat to the republic occurred in November 1923 in Bavaria, at the time when there was much public annoyance at the French occupation of Ruhr. The occupation of the Ruhr crated havoc in Germany. The French gained little, but their invasion disrupted the German economy. There occurred a catastrophic currency collapse. The large middle classes and professional classes in Germany were ruined as saving and pension became worthless. Germany was close to bankruptcy. The wartime inflation continued, was aggravated by the allied demand for reparation payments. Exports were difficult to sell. The mark was weak and its value fell steadily. In a short-sighted effort to solve immediate difficulties, government, simply issued paper currency and inflation resulted. It was easier to resort to barter than to try to keep up the useless flood of paper money. Bank balance became valueless, a suitcase became more useful than a purse for carrying one's money. There was a communist rising in Hamburg which was routed by the police. Left-wing and right-wing plot multiplied. Chancellor Cuno resigned and Ebert called on Gustav-Stresemann to form a new government. He took office in August 1923 with a widely based coalition to save the Republic. In November the Munich putsch (Coup) occurred. It was already too late and was also badly planned. Supported by the Veteran soldier General Ludendorff, who had already backed the Kapp putsch, it was organised by Adolf Hitler. Hitler intended to take control of Bavaria and then lead a nationalist attack on Berlin. However, police easily broke up Hitler's march and the beer hall putsch (so called because the march setout from Munich beer hall in which Hitler had announced his national revolution the previous evening) fizzled out. Hitler was arrested, on total for treason, Hitler stated that, the future of Germany means the annihilation of Marxism. Who is born to be a dictator will not be halted. I wish to be the drummer of the "Third Reich". Hitler was sentenced to five years imprisonment. Hunger, humiliation, hopelessness for the future, the prospect of etternal poverty, the reduction of Germany to a minor power, the restriction of her army, constant interference from outside, these were permanent features in Germany's life in the decade after the war. But the ray of hope brightened when the republic had at last produced an able politician in Stresemann.

Stresemann quickly overcame the threat of civil war, ordered a returned to work in Ruhr, pacified the French with a resumption of reparation payment and set about restoring the currency. From the appointment of Stresemannn, the outlook brightened, and he did much to restored confidence. He provided an element of stability to the republic. One of his major achievements in foreign policy was to persuade the French to leave the Ruhr.

The crisis of 1923 which had threatened to destroy the Weimer republic proved, to be the beginning of a new hopeful year. The economic situation improved dramatically in the years after 1924, largely thanks to the Dawes plan of that year which provided an immediate loan from the USA. The currency was stabilised, there was a boom in industries. The work of the Dawes plan was carried on a stage further by the Young plan agreed in October 1929. But the financial and economic situation was still critical for Germany. Following the wall street crash the economic crisis developed. The USA stopped any further loans. This shook the currency and caused a run on the banks, many of which had to closed. Factories had to close, and unemployment was increasing. Sadly for Germany, Stresemann, the politician best equipped to deal with the situation, died of a heart attack. On the other hand, Ebert death made it necessary to elect a new president and in 1925 Field Marshal Hindenburg took office. He was nearly eighty, but his aristocratic and military back-ground pleased the nationalist, he seemed to personify stability. Governments also seemed more stable. W. Maxe held office as Chancellor, with a coalition of moderate parties. Meanwhile, the social-democrats played the part of a normal democratic opposition and although the nationalist did well in the elections, they lost ground. The communist throughout kept 10 per cent of the seats. The Reichstag was not free from extremist parties but the moderates were making the system, work satisfactorily. After the defeat of Stresemann, the government of Chancellor Bruning reduced social services, unemployment benefits, and salaries of government officials, and stopped reparation payment. High tariff were introduced to keep out fareign food-stuff and thus help German formers while the government bought shares in industries. However, these measures did not produce immediate results. The government came under criticism from almost all groups in society. Thus, by the end of 1932 the Weimer republic had been brought to the verge of collapse.

In the 1920's Stresemann, a liberal minded man wished the end of German isolation and to restore her to a place of equality among nations. He sought to achieve his purpose by creating an atmosphere of goodwill. He was responsible for the discontinuance of passive resistance in the Ruhr. But his greatest was the negotiation of the Locarno treaties. Thus, the cloud began to lift. When the treaty of Locarno gave to France the security which was the goal of their policy, and to Germany the status which admitted her into the family of nations. She was elected a member of the League of Nations with a permanent seat in the council. Germany also signed the Kellog-Briand pact, which was designed to renounce war as an instrument of national policy. The removal of foreign garrisons from Germany was followed by the evacuation of occupied territories. Germany was accorded equality of status in the world disarmament conference. Yet, the domestic front in Germany was deteriorating, and the rise to power of a new political sect was entrusted with the destinies of the Germans. The Weimer republic had been faced with too many problem in too short a time. It had lost popularity soon after its birth when it accepted the humiliating treaty of Versailles. The republic was politically weak and the economic crisis further worsened the condition. There were too many parties and, with the exception of Stresemann, the leaders were of limited ability. After Stresemann, it is not too much to say that the fate of the German nation was hanging in the balance. Though no one could have foreseen it, the hand that determined how the balance would top was Adolf Hitler. Hindenburg, the president was advised from all quarters to appoint Hitler Chancellor, but he hesitated for snobbish rather than political reasons. He did not like this vulgar, low born, loud-mouthed Bohemian corporal. In the end he felt he had no choice. Finally he choose Hitler as Chancellor on 30 January 1933. How and why Hitler kept his hold upon the German masses ?

Adolf Hitler

For a decade before his (Hitler's) advent to power he had been an impassioned and much publicised champion of Germany's tearing up the treaty of Versailles, rearming itself and recapturing all "German" lands, and during the first five years of his dictatorship he achieved an impressive part of his programme, to the delight of Germans and Chagrin of foreigners. Moreover, in preparing for ultimate war he built up in conjunction with the capable Goering, huge military industries, which provided full employment for German workmen and satisfactory profit for employers. And in H. Schacht, who was appointed Minister of economy and President of the Reich bank in 1934, Hitler had a kind of financial wizard. Schacht initiated a complicated system of currency controls and barter trade with foreign countries, which enabled Germany to secure raw materials for its rearmament without overtaxing its people and it extended German economic and political influence in central Europe. The Nazi dictatorship was obviously restoring Germany to the position of a great power.

Why at all the Germans succumbed without any opposition to the overthrow of their rights? Paradoxically, the national socialist succeeded unexpectedly, when it was apparently on the wane. The leader of the movement was none else than, an Austrian by birth and a German by choice, Adolf Hitler. Hilter coming from the family of a minor custom official born on April 20, 1889 at Braunau. For many years his father had been known as Schicklgruber, and it was later in his life that he took the name of Hitler. Later in life Hitler revealed his satisfaction at this change of name, Schichlegruber had a somewhat comic sound, and contrasts very much with Hitler. At school he was an undistinguished boy, though he had a particular liking for history, largely on account of the extremely nationalistic type of history that he was taught. Having left school, he embarked on a number of casual occupation, and seemed unable to settle into anything definite. He was at various time a road-sweeper, an artist, a labourer, and a house painter. His free time was spent in reading on the racial, moral, social, economic, political problems confronting the German speaking people in Austria and Germany with the passing of time the spirit of German nationality grew stronger in him and the hatred of international socialism increased. Since he associated immorality and radicalism with Judasim, regarding socialism as a ruse of international jewry to control the worker. Hitler also became an anti-semitic. Before the First World War he moved into Germany, to Munich, a city to which he was to be much attached for the rest of his life. When the First World War started, he immediately volunteered for service. For the greater part of four years he was in or near the front line. He became a corporal and was a conscientious and brave soldier for he was awarded the iron cross. When the war ended in 1918 he was in hospital under treatment for gas poisoning.

His fellow soldiers testified later to his extreme disappointment in November 1918 at the decision of the Kaiser to seek an armistice. He remained in the army even after the war, and was employed by the military authorities as a spy within Germany to discover the opinion of the Germans. While thus, employed he attended a meeting of the workers party, a right wing party with strong views on race and nationalism, founded by a certain, A. Drexler, into which Hitler was admitted as seventh member. In 1920 this became the National Socialist German workers party with head quarter at Munich. The name National Socialist German workers party, then abbreviated to National Socialist, the first four letters in the German producing Nazi. Hitler, the greatest demagogue in history, possessed a remarkable gift for oratory. The policy of the party was vague, but was besically a mixture of nationalism and socialism, a blend which proved to be popular. The main target of their enmity were the jews and the Bolsheviks whom they blamed for the moral degradation of Germany, the treaty of Versailles and the Statesmen who had perpetrated it. The Nazi Party adopted the ancient symbol of the swastik as its own symbol. Roehm, Hess and Goering, all ex-officers joined the Nazi Party. A sinster portent of things to come was the creation of the S. A., or the brownshirts or (Stormtroopers), who present at Nazi meetings to lend a military appearance to the proceeding and to eject with violence any one who presumed to object. They were organised by Rohm.

In November 1923, when inflation, unemployment and strikes had been at their worst in Germany Hitler had attempted to overthrow the bavarian Government preparatory to a march on Berlin. This Munich beer hall putsch' had failed, however, and Hitler found himself in prison for treason and for some time the Nazi movement seemed dead. In prison he began work on Mein Kampf (my struggle), later the bible of Nazism, part an autobiography and part a pronouncement of Nazi ideas. Under the third Reich this book was to be found in almost every German household. The main idea that it advanced was the superiority of people of Aryan race over inferior races such as Jews, slaves, and the extermination of these inferior races was suggested. The ultimate goal of the Hitlerites was a third Reich, a greater Germany where in should be united all those of German blood including the Germans in Austria, Czechoslovakia, Poland. It propagated for the abrogation of the treaty of Versailles, revision of reparation, expulsion of non-Germans, decent living condition for the citizens, confiscation of war profits, nationalisation of trust, agrarian reforms, religious toleration for all sects, Rearmament, refutation of war-guilt and above all lebensraum (Living space), Eastern Europe must be conquered to provide this land. The Hohenzollern monarchy had failed at a crisis and could not be restored, the old military Junkerdom equally failed as it was aristocratic. The new Germany which Hitler promised was to be one which could select its elite from the people themselves, for all doors were to be thrown open to efficiency and merit. The new Germany could be appear to be a democratic society, but politically it was the anti-thesis of democracy. The state was strictly authoritarian. Under the absolute command of its leader of propaganda, Hitler was a master, the power of reception of the masses is small, their understanding limited, but their power to forget enormous. The framing of an attractive economic programme, the promise to destroy unemployment, was very much appealing to the masses. After the great depression of 1929 this programme was dangled before the eyes of the peoples as well as the brilliant oratory of the Nazi leader promised them a new heaven. The years 1924-29 saw little advance by Nazi Party as Germany returned to some measure of prosperity. The Nazi representation in the Richstag fell, by 1928 there were only 12 Nazi members. The economic depression which began in 1929 eventually created havoc for the democratic republic Business prosperity, which had been artificially stimulated, came to an abrupt halt. Desperately the government sought financial help. Economies in internal administration only swelled the ranks of the unemployed. In this circumstances, the democratic majority in Germany was rapidly whittled away. The communist party made gains, but principal gains were made by the Nazi Party. Influential and wealthy Germans gave support to the Nazis as a bulwork against communism. By posing as a party that would restore prosperity and discipline to Germany, Nazism made advance. The party had been refounded. One valuable recruit was Josef Goebbels, a highly intelligent journalist, who had real flair for propaganda. The brown shirted and jack-booted storm troopers (S.A.) was expanded and within the S.A. was formed the S. S., a select bodyguard for Hitler. The Hitler youth rally started. In the election of 1930 the Nazi polled 6 million votes and won 107-seats, and by July 1930 it had 230 members (out of 608). Nevertheless it did not possess an overriding majority. For two years from 1930-32, the Government of the German republic was perilously carried on by Bruning. In 1932 Hitler stood for the preidency against the 84 year old Hindenburg. President Hindenturg was reelected. Hitler was atleast a major national politician. The president was now senile, befuddled by the intrigues of army officers, landowner and industrialists, dismayed by the economic problems but still possessing as president the deadly power to make and unmake government, in a Reichstag where no one had a clear mandate to rule. Hindenburg appointed vonpapaen who tried in vain to gain more substantial support in two elections in 1932. The only significant result of the selections was that the Nazi Party became the largest single group in the Reichstag with 37 per cent of the seats in July 1932. The social democrats were the next largest party with the communists close on their heels. Von papen represented none of these. For a time he kept office by using emergency powers but at the end of the year, Hindenburg replaced him and called on Schleicher. The republic was now in its death agony. Even the ending of reparations could not save it. The president flounded ineffectively. Only the Nazis, who despised the system, could rely on substantial support in the Reichstag. The depression was acute and Hindenburg grabbed at what seemed to be the only workable compromise, appointing Adolf Hitler on 30 January as Chancellor. Hitler was at last in power, and to the discomfiture of his opponents he was in power in accordance with the letter of the constitution. Hitler promptly arranged another election for March 1933. The campaign was a vicious one, rival parties were handicapped, their meetings broken up, members battered and newspapers muzzled. On the eve of the elections the council chamber of the Reichstag was opportunely set on fire. The Nazi alleged that this act of incendiarism was intended as the prelude to a communist insurrection. The president consented to an emergency decree which suspended the constitutional guarantees of German liberties. Armed with the arbitrary powers, the government banned the Communist party. The opposition was weakened by arresting or expelling communist members. In July 1933 the coalitions was dissolved, and the Nazis gathered the reins of power in their own hand. Eighteen months afterwards, when Hindenburg died and, with him, the last remnants of the Weimer republic, Hitler assumed the title of Der Fuhrer (the leader) of the German Reich. Thus, Germany's brief honeymoon with democracy was at an end.

What did Nazi Stand For?

What the Nazi did not mean was nationalisation and redistribution of wealth. The word socialism was only included to attract the support of the German workers. Since it was likely that greatness could be achieved only by war, the entire state must be organised on a military footing. There was only one thing more irrational than the racist theories of the Nazi's and that was the acceptness on them. Yet it was its very Germanness that made Nazism so acceptable. Hitler offered the Germans a new messianic world view of a Germanic domination to which there was no physical limit. The idea of a purified race and a reunited German people achieving a world role to which they had an inalienable right had a logical simplifications which lend itself well to the broad simplifications of modern propaganda closely linked to racialism and the nation state was the Nazi doctrine of leadership. "Ein Reich, Ein Volk, Ein Fuhrer", in this triology, the leader was the medium of his people. In the Nazi creed, the race could only express itself through the leader. To further this principle, the Nazis planned to create an elite of leaders specially bred and educated, who would establish "authority of every leader downwards and responsibility upwards" which had once, in Hitler's words, made the Prussian army in its heyday the most wonderful instrument of the German people. It glorified war and considered international peace as coward's dream. Hitler had said "He who would live must fight". Nazis believed in the policy of reciprocity regarding disarmament. They champion the cause for the union of all Germans to form one great Germany, a Germany in which none but those of German blood whatever their creed, may be members of the nation. The chief arm of the Nazi was elite crops of stormtroopers and, through them the Gestapo (the state police), set up in 1933 under Goering. It ceveloped, under Himmler and Hey-drich, in to a weapon of terror having power of life and death, without appeal, over every German citizen. Besides, a highly sophisticated propaganda machine, organised by Goebbels, carried the Nazi message through every channel of communication. Hitler's youth movement held the key to the future of the purified German race. For girls there was the league of German maidens, dedicated to training for healthy motherhood and the perpetuation of the German racial myth. An elite of future leaders was trained in so-called Nazi order castles, on lines of Spartan dedication similar to those of the old medieval orders, where the virtues of total obedience and sacrific were inculcated.

What Made the Nazis so Popular?

The Nazi promised to overthrow the Versailles settlement, which was unpopular with most Germans. The Weimer republic was attacked for accepting the treaty. The degrading conditions of the peace settlement destroyed the self-respect of the Germans. They had drained the cup of national humiliation to its dregs, and their feeling grew embittered towards their victorious adveraries. To this were added the continuing hostile attitude towards of France, the quarrels over the Ruhr, the Rhineland occupation, reparations, and the wrangling over disarmament. The unjust treaty of Versailles was a national wrong, and they regarded it morally justified to repudiate the treaty. The unemployed youth that dreamt of a glamorous and secure future wanted the ending of reparation payment, the reacquisition of colonies. In fact they wanted to avenge the humiliation. The treaty of versailles gave the Nazi an opportunity to pose as super patriots, and to denounce as a traitor to every government which sought to remove the country's grievances by the method of conciliatory approach to the western powers. The propaganda of the Nazi against the treaty of Versailles led their rise to power. They wanted to build Germany into a great power again. This would include bringing all Germans (in Austria, Czechoslovakia, Poland) back in to the Reich. At the same time, imposition of a democratic form of government was vehemently opposed by the Germans. They were not only unfamiliar with this type of government, but also impatient with the bickering and time wasting that characterised the parliamentary system of government. Seeing the deteriorated and indisciplined condition of the parliament, the Germans remembered the days of Bismark. Between 1919-33 they saw the rise and fall of 19 ministries. They became convinced of the need for a strong man to restore German honour. The Nazi understood the pulse of the nation, Hitler, a demagogue, a resourceful agitator, a tireless worker and a competent organiser seized the opportunity.

The Nazi offered national unity, prosperity and full employment by ridding Germany of what they claimed were the real causes of the troubles, the November criminals (those who had agreed to the Treaty of Versailles). Great play was made in Nazi propaganda with the "stab in the back" myth. Wealthy land ownders and industrialists encouraged the Nazis because they feared a communist revolution and they approved of the Nazi policy of hostility to communists. The Nazi told the people that the aim of the communists was to capture power and then to surrender Germany before Russia. The widespread fear of coming communist revolution furnished the Nazis with the most effective plank in their platform, namely the slogan, "If the national party collapses, there will be another ten million communists in Germany." But there is no reason to suppose that the increase of communist strength was an indication that Germany was moving in the direction of Bolshevism. However, Hitler, exploited the situation in favour of the Nazi Party.

The Nazi Party storm troopers was attractive to young people out of work, it gave them a small wage and a uniform. The social democrats who had long dominated the Reich took no action against the Nazi armed bands. The men of the republic were imbeciles, cowards and gave Hitler the chance to grasping the reins of government. Besides, Hitler could rise to power because the social democrats and communists failed to build a common force against him. He took advantage of the weakness and disunity of the opposition. Similarly, the striking contrast between the government of the republic and the Nazi Party impressed people, the former was dull and unable to maintain order, but the Nazi promised a strong and decisive government. With economic crisis, it is doubtful whether Hitler would have had much chance of attaining power. It was the widespread unemployment and social misery which gained the Nazi mass support, not only among the working classes, but also among the lower middle classes, shopkeepers, civil servants, teacher, farmers. They worked upon the anti-capitalist feeling of the lower middle classes. The Nazi drew to their side the unemployed. Due to the economic blizzard the performance of the republic was discouraging. The depression also shook the pillars of the unstable regime in Germany. The wartime inflation continued, and was aggravated by the allied demand of reparation. Hitler successfully capitalised on miseries of the common men and discredited the government for failure and in-action in redressing the grivancess of the peoples. He assured employment tc the unemployed and he claimed to have a panacea for every economic malady. The Nazi exploited diverse elements of unrest which seething in a cauldron of disaffection. Hitler also took-full advantage from the anti-Jewish feeling of the Germans. The supporter of Nazism considered the Jews as a curse of Germany. The Jews were regarded as non-Aryan the Germans considered the Jews to be the cause of national crisis. The people extended their support to Hitler against the Jewish.

Hitler himself had extraordinary political abilities. He possessed tremendous will power and a remarkable gift for public speaking which enabled him to put forward his ideas with great emotional force. Germans began to look towards him as a messiah. He had the knack of giving expression to the mood of the people. their hidden longing and passion, so that his words had a deep impact on the mass. According to Hiden, "Though there were signs of economic improvement by the late summer of 1932, it was perhaps inevitable that the republic would collapse, since the powerful conservative groups and the army were prepared to destroy it. But it was not inevitable that Hitler should take its place, that need not have happened, papen, Hindenburg must take the blame for inviting him to became chancellor. He was appointed the chancellor on January 30, 1933.

Foreign Policy

What were Hitler's aims? The 'Mein Kampf' partially provides a vague outline of his foreign policy, which includes land must be conquered and settled by Germans. Hitler wrote that it was pointless to continue saying that Germany lacked food and raw materials, something must be done to solve it. The final solution lies in an expansion of lving space, of the bases for raw materials and for the feeding of our people. The German army must be fit for operations in four years time." All this is certainly vague. There is no evidenc to show that Hitler had a plan Of course, circumstance would dictate the pattern of events. Probably, Hitler was not contemplating general war, though Eastern expansion was the primary purpose of his policy. But German rearmanent suggest that Hitler was deliberately preparing to fight some kinds of war. The extent of Hitler's responsibility for the Second World War has been a matter of debate in recent year. What is certain is that from the first attempt to achieve power, he bitterly and hysterically, condemned the versailles settlement and made plain his determination to destroy it. It seems that Hitler set high hopes upon his ability to achieve most of his ends without fighting. In this he proved a sound judge of the political mood of the mid-thirties, in that he did not provoke France and Britain to make a firm stand until a large part of his ambition had been achieved. The method he used to achieve these ends were a mixture of deliberation and opportunism, of political and diplomatic pressure used with an unuscrupulous cyncism which heralded a new phase in international diplomacy.

Above all, Hitler aimed to make Germany into a great power again. The new regime preferred to take-rather than receive, and to keep the nerves of Europe on edge by creating an atmosphere of tension. He was not in favour of compromise, rather relied on force. He wished to extend the Reich to include all Germans who would then look to Eastern and South-Eastern Europe for "Lebensraum." It was also the irony of events that repeated concessions encourage third Reich to make each concession inturn the stepping stone of a fresh demand.

With the advent of Hitler's Nazi dictatorship, a new era inaugurated in the History of Europe. Hitler was resolved to rearm Germany, and to do so he had to repudiate the treaty of versailles. By the treaty of versailles, the league had been charged with the responsibility of following up the limitation on German armaments. After protracted delay a draft treaty for general disarmament had been prepared. In 1932 an international conference on disarmament was convened at Geneva. But Hitler withdrew German delegates from the disarmament conference. At the same time, he denounced the league and proclaimed Germany's secession from it which was later-on confirmed by a plebiscite. He intended to reestablished Germany as one of the great power of Europe. The first step towards these ends was taken when the German Government issued a decree restoring universal military service. The decree was accompanied by a statement that when under compulsion, Germany had submitted to disarmament the allies had declared this to be part of a policy of general disarmament, yet this general policy had never been carried out. Therefore, Germany refused to remain disarmed while surrounded by neighbours whose own armaments were increasing. Accordingly Germany rearmed herself which was certainly a breach of the treaty of Versailles. Germany's purpose was to use military force in order to assert herself as a power in Europe. And sooner or later this would involve a clash with some other nation that thought its security threatened.

Hitler signed a ten-years non-aggression pact with the poles, who were showing alarm in case the Germans tried to take back the Polish corridor. This was something of a triumph for Hitler. It ruined the French little entente which depended very much on Poland, and it guaranteed Polish neutrality whenever Germany should move against Austria and Czechoslovakia. With England, Germany signed a naval pact in 1935, whereby she agreed that the German navy should not exceed 35 per cent of the British navy. Its purpose was to allay British apprehensions that Germany might start another race in naval armaments. In this way it was hoped to induce the island power to give the land power a freehand in the continent. Besides, under the terms of the treaty of versailles, a plebiscite was to be held in the saar after in 1935. The population was to decide whether, they wished to join Germany or France, or remained under leagues rule. Ninety per cent voted for a return to Germany, and the saar was incorporated into Germany. This was a big boost for Hitler's prestige since it occurred aftet two years of Nazi rule by which time the character of Nazism was becoming apparent.

Another major abrogation of the terms of Versailles by Hitler occurred in 1936, when Hitler ordered German troops to enter the dimilitarised Rhineland. It was Hitler's first territorial aggression, and perhaps the most crucial of all. The move, a frontal challenge to the settlement of 1919 even more serious than his open rearmament of Germany. It was also a violation of the Locarno agreement, which Germany had made voluntarily. It was perhaps the biggest gamble of his career. There is little doubt that vigorous military repriasals taken by a strong French Government should at that moment, have checked Hitler for a time and may be forever. Their inaction may have been due to the general preoccupation with the contemporary Italian invasion of Ethiopia, but proved fatal, for encouraged Hitler to make further demands. At the same time, well aware of the mood of pacifism among his opponents, Hitler soothed them by offering a peace treaty to last for 25 years. In one move Hitler had transformed the whole military and diplomataic situation in western Europe. France was exposed to attack and Germany was more defencible against attack. The episode of 1936 was perhabs the last moment when a Second World War might have been avoided. As time passed, and as Hitler became stronger, he grew bolder in aggression.

The years 1936-38 have been described by Churchill as the loaded pause before the final Acts of Nazi aggression that precipitated war. The weakness of the league as a peace keeping force in the world was becoming more obvious. Hitler concluded the anti-comintern pact with Japan, which was directed against Russia. But the most important change in Germany's foreign relations was the reapprochment with Italy. Though both countries were totalitarian states, but they had been kept apart by a conflict views over the destiny of Austria. Italy became estranged from the democratic countries by their opposition to her conquest of Ethiopia. Italy came closer to Germany and Hitler availed the opportunity. The beginning of the Spanish civil war in 1936 not only diverted attention from events in central Europe but led to closer relations between Hitler and Mussolini. In October 1936 the Rome-Berlin axis came into being. Japan subscribed to the anti-comintern pact, and thereby Rome-Berlin-Tokyo associated together. The events of 1936 formed a watershed in international relations. The Spanish civil war also enabled the dictators to employ their armies in real warfare. Hitler's hoped that in an eventful European warefare, France would be isolated, surrounded by totalitarian powers. International relations deteriorated further during the Spanish civil war, as the non-intervention committee proved incapable of preventing widespread intervention in the war.

The Anschluss or the Annexation of Austria

Union between Austria and Germany was not a new idea. The union (Anschluss) movement went back to the days immediately following the First World War, and the initiative towards it had then come not from Germany but from Austria. Even the Austrian national assembly in 1919 resolved that German Austria was part of German Reich, which was greeted by the Germans as an historic manifesto. But the treaty of St. Germain, of September 1919, forbade any union between Austria and Germany. In spite of this, there always had been people in both Germany and Austria in favour of Anschluss. The proposal for an Austro-German custom union, put forward in 1931 had been opposed by the powers, mainly through fear that it would proved to be a prelude to a voluntary political union between the sister nation. The triumph of the Nazi in Germany had an immediate repercussion upon Austria, where there already existed a national socialist party which was now emboldened to adopt terrorist methods of assassination and bomb outrages. The Nazi Government of Germany openly encouraged the subversive elements in Austria in the hope of wrecking the republic. Dollfuss, the Austrain Chancellor, suspended the constitution and ruled as a dictator. He took steps to suppress the terrorist activities of the Austrain Nazis. In July 1934, the Austrian Nazis being instigated by the Germans attempted a putsch in which they murdered Chancellor Dollfus, but failed to establish themselves in power. This was due mainly to Mussolini's support of Austria. But the formation of the Rome-Berlin axis altered the balance of political power in central Europe. Now it could be only a question of time before Hitler renewed his attack on Austria.

After the conclusion of the Rome-Berlin axis, Hitler felt himself strong enough to act, and it was difficult to see who was likely to stop him. The league of nations, though nominally still in existence, was in practise defunct, the US still abstained from world politics, Japan. Italy, Germany had withdrawn form the League. France, the only continental power that might be disposed to challenge Germany, would be barred geographically by Italy and Germany from contact with Austria. Besides, the Austrian Nazi Party had a good deal of support. Thus, the time was ripe to use the Nazi army to overrun Austria. The new Austrian Chancellor schuschnigg, a prey to internal dissension, bereft of its Italian protector, and left to its fate by the western powers which contented themselves with formal declaration of their interest in the maintenance of Austrian independence, the republic proved unable to survive. In 1938 the Austrian Chancellor Schuschinigg received an invitation to visit Hitler. Schuschnigg, imagining this to be a normal meeting for friendly consultation found himself browbeaten by Hitler, who, after along harangue, delivered an ultimatum. A Nazi named Seyrs-in Quart was to be appointed Austrian minister for public security, all imprisoned Nazis were to be set-free, and German officers were to be accepted for service in the Austrian army. After some resistance the Chancellor was forced to sign his acceptness. He then was allowed to return to Vienna. There he tried to escape from the net, but no help was forthcoming either from within or from outside. Matters came to a head when Austrian Nazis staged huge demonstration in Vienna, which the government could not control. Realising that this could be the prelude to German invasion, Schuschinigg announced a plebiscite about whether or not Austria should remain independent. This was forbidden by Hitler, and the German army took up position along the frontier. Schuschinigg agreed to cancel the plebiscite, and then resigned, saying, "we are resolved that on no account–shall German blood be spilled." Seyss-Inquart was appointed Austrian Chancellor and he invited German troops to restore order in the country. On 12th March, 1938 German army entered Vienna. Two days later Hitler arrived in the city, greeted with all the usual paraphernalia of Nazidom, masses of saluting people, swastik hung from every possible point, and peals of church bell. After a triumphal drive in Vienna, Hitler addressed a gigantic audience from the balcony of the palace where the Hapsburg had resided while he slept in doss-houses.

Possession of Austria gave Hitler strategic control over the rail, road and river communication. It gave him contact with Italy, Yugoslavia, and Hungary, and opened up three sides of the Bohemian fortress of Czechoslovakia. Austria became the ostmark of Germany. The Austrian national bank and the army was absorbed by the Reich-bank, and the

Reichswehr respectively. Non-Nazis and Jews were arrested. Neither Britain nor France had the will to resist the Anschluss, although it was forbidden in the peace-settlement of 1919. Hitler's prestige as well as his material strength, were immensely enhanced. The success enlarged Hitler's violent ideas and inflamed his passion for further power.

Sudetan Land Crisis and Czechoslovakia–1938

Everything seemed to be shaping up auspiciously for Hitler by the beginning of 1938. The international situation was favourable. Hitler appointed the unscrupulous Ribbentrop as his foreign minister. No doubt, his forceful seizure of Austria was a flagrant case of aggression and treaty violation. But reassured by Chamberlain's appeasing policy, Hitler quickly followed up his success in Austria with preparations for aggression against Czechoslovakia. Historically, the Czechs have proved themselves to be a people of strong character, with energy, a capacity for industrial development. However, the inhabitants of the predominantly Czech territory, are not purely Czech. Czechoslovakia was a polyglot state, composed of Czechs, German, Slovaks, Magyars, Poles, Ruthenians. If one dissect the tadpole form which the state assumed on the map, the head, corresponding to Bohemia and Moravia, was a Czech brain, with a German skin. The body was Slovak, with a polish infection of the spine and a belly full of indigestible Magyars. The slender tail was Ruthenian. But there was considerable friction between the czechs of Bohemia and the Slovaks. But far more serious were the differences between the Czechs and the influential minority of Germans, the so-called "Sudetans", in Bohemia and Moravia. These Sudetans Germans, long used to a privileged position. In the old Hapsbug empire, were resentful, of being subordinated to the Slavic Czechs. Not only did that make nationalistic demands on the Czech Government, but they counted on the sympathy of their kinsmen in Germany.

The Sudetan land was the ridge of mountain territory on the border of Moravia and Bohemia. The Czech Government had been wise enough to treat this minority group liberally. It had full parlimentary representation and equal political facilities. It is true that the Sudetan minorities usually were, and there need never have been serious trouble if it had not been stirred up from outside. The rise of national socialism in Germany, stimulated national feeling and separatist activity among the Sudetan Germans. The Sudetan German party was formed in Czechoslovakia and it became the second largest group in the general election of 1935. The Sudetan German party under Konrad Henlein emphasised on the rights of the German. Germany encouraged the dissension and took advantage of it to conduct a vigorous diplomatic campaign against Czechoslovakia. The

Czechs were accused by the Gobbels propaganda machine of harsh mistreatment of the Sudetan Germans. The Czech Government promised cultural autonomy to the Germans, whereas, Henlein, with Hitler's backing, was now demanding for political autonomy. Henlein, was little more than Hitler's puppet whose antics combined with a Fuhrer's rumbling to persuade the powers that the question of Sudetan land was urgent. But there seemed to be no obstacle to self-government for the Sudetan Geramns, but Hitler wanted no such easy end to the crisis. Hitler poured verbal abuse on Czechoslovakia, deriding it as an artificial state of mixed nationalities and as an ally of the USSR. Meanwhile, Henlein was demanding not mere autonomy but their outright incorporation of Germany. Hitler was also openly delcaring that he would use force to liberte them if peaceful means failed. Europe was confronted with a fresh international crisis.

Riots in the Sudetan land caused the Czech Government to declare martial law, and Henlein fled to Germany. For the success of German intervention, much would depend upon the attitude of the other powers. France held one of the keys to the situations. But France was in a peculiarly embarrassing position. It was under treaty obligation to go to war in defense of Czechoslovakia, and yet it dared not to go to war without Britain. No doubt, Daladier, the French Prime Minister was a man of ability and vigour, but his foreign minister Bonnet, was a peace at any price man. The events of 1938 make up a deplorable story in which France and England, yielding to one after another of Hitler's demands. Anyhow, to avert the danger, the British Prime Minister Chamberlain visited the German Chancellor. The meeting between the two men, the fuhrer's mountain nest at Berchtesgaden is one of the most dramatic scene in contemporary history. On one side was the anxious, harassed businessman, the civilian figure with the umbrella, resolved to avoid the outbreak of war, if possible. On the other side was the crazed, paranoiac dictator, the fanatic of the Swastik, bent on war for the domination of the master race. But it was agreed that the principle of self-determination should applied, that meant that the inhabitants of the Sudetan land should be allowed to determine by their votes whether they would prefer to remain in Czechoslovakia or to be transformed to Germany. New boundaries were to be drawn according to the results of the voting. And Britain and France were to guarantee the new boundaries. A week later, at Godesburg on the Rhine, Chamberlain informed Hitler of this decison. He hoped for an excuse to invade Czechoslovakia and now demanded that his army should occupy the Sudetan land by 1st October before any plebiscite could be held. There was an atmosphere of impending war, but the Anglo-French Government were not prepared for war. Chamberlain returned to London as a defeated negotiator.

Munich Pact

At the very end of the month on September 28, 1938, partly through the proposal of Mussolini, it was agreed to hold a summit conference at Munich, to be atteed by Chamberlain, Daladier, Hitler, and Mussolini. At this conference war was avoided by the pursuance of the policy of appeasement. An agreement was signed by the four powers on September 30th. It provide for the transfer of Sudetan land to Germany, a process which was to be supervised by an international commission. By this secession Czechoslovakia not only lost a valuable defensive frontier, but also its major industrial region, while the communication system within the country was seriously disrupted. At the expense of Czechoslovakia, peace in Europe had been achieved. Chamberlain secured an assurance from Hitler that these territorial demands had been his last. However, the Munich agreement, a crying violation of international law, was concluded in an atmosphere of rude pressure and blackmail. Neither the Czechs, nor the Russians were invited to the Munich conference. The Czechs were told that if they resisted the Munich decision they would receive no help from Britain or France. When Chamberlain arrived back in London, he received a rapturous welcome from the public. He himself remarked "I believe it is peace for our time." Momentarily Europe breathed freely. The powers together had submitted completely to Hitler blustering threats, and in the process had consented to watch one of the truly democratic countries in Europe while it was crushed by a dictator. But chamberlain proudly declared. "This is the second time in our history that there has come back from Berlin to ten-Downing street peace with honour". Churchill bitterly criticised the policy and he commented, "Britain and France had to choose between war and dishonour. They choose dishonour, they will have the war."

But 1939 was to witness further acts of aggression, the breakdown of appeasement, and the outbreak of world war. International differences continued to centre in Czecholslovakia. Since Munich it had suffered further aggression by neighbouring countries, a large southern area was awarded to Hungary. Teschen in the north was taken by Poland. Hitler had made further demands, insisting that Germans within Czechoslovakia who were not then under German rule should be given special privileges. In March 1939 he stated that unless the remaining part of Czechoslovakia were accorded these privileges, the capital city of Prague would be bombed. Slovakia began to demand semi-independence, and when it looked as though the country was about to fall apart. Hitler pressurised President Hacha into requesting German help to restore order. Consequently in March 1939 German troops occupied the rest of Czechoslovakia. Britain and France protested but took no action. The guarantee of Czech frontiers did not apply because technically Czechoslovakia had not been invaded, as German troops had entered by invitation. However, the German action caused a great rush of criticism. For the first time even the appeasers were unable to justify what Hitler had done, he had broken his promise and seized non-German territory. Hitler' use of the name "Third German Reich" carried peoples mind back to the Reich which had been the Holy Roman empire, this had stretched across Alps into Italy and across the Rhine to Paris. It would seen that there was no limit to Hitler's ambition, that his real object, was "lebensraum", living space for Germans.

Memel, Danzig and Poland

European opinion had hardly rallied from the shock of the Czech annexation when German attention was turned to the Baltic-Lithuania region. The Lithuanian minister for foreign affairs was received by Ribbentrop in Berlin, and Lithuania decided to cede the Memel territory to Germany.

In the meantime both England and France embarked on a change of policy. Since Hitler's mounting collection of trophies suggested that appeasement led only to new crisis. Chamberlain resorted to guarantees, pledging Britain to defend Polish independence. At the same time, France strengthened her existing alliance with Poland. Chamberlain's pride had been injured and Halifax, the new foreign secretary of Britain, put his trust in a strong policy statement, hoping to deter the Nazis from further aggression.

Germany's last and decisive, act of aggression was her invasion of Poland. Under the treaty of Versailles, Poland was givn access to the sea by a corridor of territory, much of which had been German, which reached the Baltic at Danzig, though Danzig was to be a free city under league administration. One of Hitler's earliest aim was to annex Danzig to Germany towards the end of 1934. Nazis in Danzig obtained control of the city. From time to time Hitler's speeches included demands for the transfer of Danzig and for a strip of land across the corridor. So that road and rail communication could be established to link East Prussia to the rest of the Reich. After German successes against Austria and Czechoslovakia, Hitler renewed his demands. When the Polish government showed an unwilingness to accede to the German's demand, Gobbels progpaganda machine went in to action. Chamberlain had become disillusioned. Hitler's repeated breaches of promises were felt to be deliberate humiliation of Britain. On Hitler's side there was one fatal obstacle to his occupation of Poland. He was confident that he could defeat the poles, Britain was too remote to be effective in Poland's defence, France would follow Britain, but what would

Russia do? So reluctantly Hitler decided that he must make temporary terms with Stalin as a preliminary to attacking Poland.

The role of the USSR was now a vital one. Hitler exploited the Russians, as the Russians had bitter memories of their exclusion from the Munich conference, and Stalin suspected that the capitalist powers would have no regret if the Nazis were to launch an anti-communist war against the Soviet union. Molotov replaced Litivinow as the Soviet foreign minister and he seemed less anxious than Litvinov to reached an agreement with the west. On the other hand. France and Britain tried their best to win ever the Soviet Government, which ended in fiasce. Negotiation between Molotov and Ribbentrop culminated on August 23, 1939 and on that day the Russo-German non-aggression pact was signed. It was the one event which the diplomacy of the world had known could never happen. It has been called truly "the greatest diplomatic bombshell of the century," which exploded over a stunned Europe. On the surface, this was a ten year non-aggression pact, but it included secret clauses. The pact was a triumph for Hitler. The threat from Britain and France seemed irrelevant. For Stalin the pact held out the prospect of recovering much that Russia had lost after 1917, and of neutrality in any Europan war with Germany might fight with the west. He could, thus, preserve communism while the capitalist fought among themselves. However, it was a bizarre agreement a marriage of convenience between Fascism and communism. A week later the Russo-German non-aggression pact was signed, Hitler seized Danzig and attacked Poland on 1st September, 1939. Chamberlain lamented "Everything that I have worked for has crashed into ruin." The long struggle for peace in Europe had failed. The Second World War had begun.

Chapter-XXIII

Foreign Policy of the USA (1919-39)

The American peoples attained independence towards the end of the 18th century, their first thought was to avoid involvement in the bitter conflicts of the European powers. Americans were sceptical of the intentions of the European powers, as they were afraid of losing their newly owned independence if they got themselves involved into the intrigues and counter-intrigues of the European Government. Thus, the first president of America, Washington, in his farewell address, warned his countrymen to avoid entangling alliances with the Government of Europe. This advice was reiterated in President Jeffersons's inaugural address. All they wanted was to be left in peace to develop the riches of their country and to integrate it in the form of a federal nation state. After having demonstrated its resolve to keep away from the entangling alliance, the US moved one step further when president Monroe pronounced the dectrine that has come to be known as the "Monroe doctrine." There had been three guides to American foreign policy action, the USA should do business with Europe but should not involved in European power politics. Europe should abstain from power politics in the American continent. And both the USA and the European powers abstain from Asian power politics. During the 19th century American interests were well-served by these guidelines. But these failed to serve her interst in the 20th century, changes in the world, considerations of security and self-interest of American big business and the desire to assume the role of world leadership compelled America to come out of her isolationist shell and to interven by diplomacy and arms, in Asia, Europe, Africa, and Latin America. For a century after 1815 the US foreign policy was marked by three distinctive features, no entangling alliances, the Monroe doctrine, and equal trading opportunities for all in the colonial areas (Open door policy), fredom of the seas, and neutral rights. The annexation of Philippines in addition to the acquisition of dependent territories such as Alaska, Hawaii, and Puerto-Rico wer the only aberrations from the doctrine of anti-imperialism and non-intervention in the affairs of other nations. Yet, even before the intervention of America in the First World War, the US had acquired many characteristics of an imperialist.

When the First War broke-out in 1914 the interests of US dictated close relations with the allied powers. No doubt the allies were fighting to defend the statusquo, that is their possessions and colonies. When the war reached a stalemate and no decisive outcome seemed to be in sight, it became obvious to the policy makers of the American Government that their interests would best be served if Germany was defeated quickly. At the same time the US protested against German policy of destroying enemy ships. A few days later the British liner named Lusitania carrying some military supplies from Newyork was destroyed by German submarines. This incident sparked off great resentment in the USA. Finally, president Wilson defined the war aims of the USA "The world must be made safe for democracy, its peace must be planted upon the foundation of political liberty. We have no selfish end to serve. We desire no conquest, no domination..."

The USA had been deeply involved in the First World War and when hostilities ceased she seemed likely to play an important role in world affairs. President Wilson was an important figure at the Paris peace conference, his great dream was the league of nations through which the USA would maintain world peace.

The peace conference opened at Paris and Wilson headed the American delegation. He believed that once the treaty had been drafted, the senate would not dare to refuse ratification. This was a serious error of judgement. The major decision of the conference were thrashed out by a council of four. Their meetings consisted largely of a long battle between the Americans and the French man. While liberal idealists throughout the world looked to Wilson for leadership, the mass of the British and French peoples, embittered by the deaths of large numbes of young men of their country, demanded a peace of vengeance. However, Wilson's main victory was the establishment of a league of nations and Wilson was the principal author of the league convenant. However, there was no unity of policy among the states. While a united front of the satiated powers was not brought to life, no concrete alternative was projected. This happened as Wilson had to accept the reservations insisted upon by the allies against his 14 points. Besides the structure of the league had been, so distorted that in effect it meant a virtual dictatorship of the victorious great powers. So the league would not have served purposes even if it had been delivered properly The treaty with Germany was signed at versailles in June 1919 and submitted to the US senate in July. But the division of the senate made it impossible to secure a majority for the treaty.

In the presidential election of 1920, Harding, of the Republican Party became president. The new president declared the US foreign policy in these words "We seek no part in directing the destinies of the world. We are ready to associate ourselves with the nations of the world... but every commitment must be made in the exercise of our national soverignity." But the failure of the US to join the league meant not only that the league was born a cripple, but the US herself entered the troubled waters of the inter-war period like a ship with its ruder broken and drifting with the currents. Republican adopted the policy of cooperation without entangling alliances. The Republican Government believed in a policy of isolation. Throughout the 1920s and 1930's a majority of the American people remained unwilling to assume binding commitments to action against an aggressor or give support to other countries in the event of war. But, infact, the Harding, collidge, and Hoover administrations assumed world leadership in the promotion of disarmament, peaceful settlement of disputes, and economic stabilisation. This included some cooperation with world affairs was due not only to a general interst in peace but also to a rapid expansion of her foreign trade and overseas capital investment. Unfortunately, attempts made during the 1920's to bring about international harmony had only temporary results. The first and most successful American gesture in the cause of peace was the Washington conference of 1921-22, which was concerned with naval disarmament. The conference agreed on a five-powers naval treaty, by which the US and England accepted the principle of naval equality, and the capital ship tonnage of the world was fixed by a system of ratio. No agreement could be made about smaller ships, but as a result of the treaty there was no battleship construction by any power until 1930s. This was the only one of the various postwar disarmament conferences which actually brought about any disarming.

During the prosperous years of the 1920s, Americans tried to increase trade and profits by investment abroad in Europe, Canada and in central and south America, and it was inevitable that the US should take an interest in what was happening in these areas. There was, a serious dispute with Mexico whose government was threatening to seize American owned oil-wells, but a compromise solution was reached.

Allied war-debts to the USA caused much ill-feeling. During the war, American Government had organised loans to Britain and her allies. The European hoped that the Americans would cancel the debts since the

USA had done well out of the war but both Harding and Coollidge insited that repayments be made in full. The allies claimed that their ability to pay depended on whether Germany paid her reparations to them, but the Americans would not acknowledge any connection between the two. Eventually Britain was the first to agree to pay the full amount. Other states followed, and the USA allowing much lower interest rate depending on the poverty of the country. With the German financial crisis of 1923 the Americans had to change their attitude and admit the connection between reparations and war-debts, they agreed to take part in the Dawes and Young plan (1924, 1929) which enabled Germany to pay reparations. However, this caused the ludicrous situation in which America lent money to Germany so that she could pay reparation to Britain, France and others, so that they could pay their war-debts to the USA. The whole set-up, together with the American insistence on keeping high tariff, was a contributory cause of the world economic crisis, with all its far-reaching consequences.

The Locarno treaties of 1925 looked like the dawn of a new day in Europe. They were followed in 1928 by a more comprehensive attempt to exercise the threat of war. This was the pact of Paris, better known by its two co-sponsors Kellog, the US secretary of States and Briand, the French minister. By the pact of Paris virtually all the nations of the world, totaling 59, pledged themselves to outlaw war as an instrument of national policy. But the pact did not provide any method for enforcing obediance upon any nation violating its pledge and did not rule out defensive war. It illustrated in extreme form the illusion cherished by many Americans that noble moral gestures, not backed by force, could but an end to international power politics. Obviously, the abolition of war should have been followed by general disarmament. But none of the powers had faith in the Kellog-Briand pact to scrap its armed forces. Even after the Washington conference, competition had continued in the building of ships, and naval conference in 1924 and 1927 had failed to agree on any programme of limitation. In naval conference held at London in 1930 and 1932 the USA participated. The USA took an active part in the world disarmament conference at Geneva. She offered to cooperate with the league in the adoption of a general plan for disarmament in 1933. Meanwhile Hitler became ruler of Germany, and all hope of disarmament had to be abandoned. It soon became obvious that the only way to preserve peace was not by disarmament but by the rapid rearmament of all peace loving nations.

The First World War had changed the situation in Asia and, Japan had emerged as the dominant power in the pacific. The American attitude towards political developments in East Asia was different from that towards Europe. After the First World War Japan acquired from Germany, the leased territory of Kiachow in the Shantung province of China. She had become the only great power on the borders of China. This was highly disquieting to the US. After the occupation of Philippines island, the US had began to take increasing interest in the Far-East and look upon China as a potential market. The American-Japanese conflict thus introduced a new inflammatory factor in the politics of the Far-East. The situation prompted the US to summoned the Washington conference to check the rising power of Japan. The US was also anxious to end the quarrel between China and Japan. A threat to American policies in East Asia was presented by the aggrandisement of Japan against the mainland. After the Japanese found that their expansion in the North was blocked by the growing strength of the Soviet armies in the Far-East, they turned their eyes towards China. In 1931 when the Japanese began a full-fledged attack of conquest against China, and it seemed likely to prove successful, the US woke up to the danger to its interests. In 1932 the assistant secretary of State of the US, Henry sitmson despatched identical notes to Japan and China in which he declared that his government would not recognise the legality of any action which adversely effected the interests of the US or the integrity of China. When Japan launched an undeclared war against China in 1937, as Hartmann points out, the US did not move to undo what force has wrought. The Americans took shelter behind the wall of neutrality, but in fact they wanted, to quote Taylor, "the moral satisfaction of non-recognition and also material satisfaction of their profitable trade with Japan." They could do nothing to prevent China from the Fascist aggression. However, when Japan attacked pearl-Harbour in December 1941, the US had no other alternative but to declare war against Japan.

The most lasting diplomatic achievement of the 1920's was the improvement of relations with Latin America. At the end of World War I, American armed forces were occupying four caribbean countries, Cuba, Haiti, the Dominican republic, and Nicaragua. This "big-stick" policy had antagonised all of Latin America, and made it difficult for US business-man to secure markets and investment opportunities. But with the defeat of Germany and the decrease of international tension in the 1920's, the US could afford to relax her vigilence in the caribbean. Therefore America set out to conciliate Latin America by initiating a process of withdrawal. But the renewed US intervention in 1927 was condemned at the Pan-American conference held at Havana. However, it took time to convince the Latin Americans that the US had genuinely dropped the "big-stick." Throughout the 1920s they continued to ask what American troops were doing in Haiti and Nicaragua and whether they really intended to leave. So, the US faced belligerent criticism from the rest of th hemispher. Although the administratioin was not willing to give-up interventionism totally, it went a long way to meet these criticism. But as discontent against "Dollar imperialism" in Latin America gathered momentum, there occured a shift in US policy after the great depresion. In his first inaugural address in 1933, F.D. Roosevelt espoused the policy of good neighbour in these terms. "In the field of world policy I would dedicate this nation to the policy of the good neighbour, the neighbour who respect himself and, because he does so, respect the rights of others–the neighbour who respects his obligation....." This good neighbour policy in the sequel became primarily associated with the Latin American policy of the US. Henceforth, the US repudiated her rights of internvention and her military and fiscal controls in Latin American republics. Pan American conferences at Montevideo (1933), Buenos Aires (1936), and Lima (1936), and Lima (1938) Worked out new principles of inter-American law which developed after World War II into the organisation of American states (OAS). meanwhile, the US gave practical demonstrations of her sincerity, when there was a revolution in Cuba in 1933, she did not interfere and in 1934 she negotiated a new treaty dropping the platt amendment. She also gave-up her right to intervene in Panama and terminated her financial supervision over Haiti and the Dominican republic. Thus, the hated domination of the colossus of the north was replaced by a partnership among soverign equals. So, between 1919-41, the US did not go back to her pre-war policy of isolation from international affairs. But in the post-World War II period, since 1947, the US foreign policy took a revolutionary trend. This policy is characterised by a declaration of ideological war upon communism, and determined by a desire to set world pattern of free enterprise capitalism, and the USA self-appointment as a global custodian or a world policeman. As prof. Friedmann says "The European tension and emergences forced upon the US a dramatic revision of her foreign policy."

Chapter-XXIV

The Second World War-Causes and the World in 1945 and Afterwards

The Second World War, in its origins and events, was quite different from the first. While the question of responsibility for the First World War has caused mush controversy, there can be no doubt that the major responsibilities for the second rests heavily on one country, Germany, and one man, Adolf Hitler. The Second World War, like the first, began ostensibly about a quarrel concerning German national minorities in Eastern Europe. Minorities were used as livers. While Poland was invaded by the Germans, Europe faced-war the second time in two generation. Many who had in their youth survived the battle fields of the First World War now had to mortgage a span of their middle years in the demands of the second. The Frist World War, the twenty years of uneasy peace-keeping and the Second World War seemed in one sense to be part of a continuous single process. One war rather than two, in which Europe was involved in a self-destructive struggle centred in the unresolved problem of Germany. The history of the war, belongs only in part to the history of Europe, while paradoxically, the entire history of Europe was dominated by the war.

The treaty of Versailles is regarded as one of the causes of the Second World War. Germans felt that the provisions of the treaty of versailles represented a deep humiliation imposed on them which was all the more bitter as the Germans believed that they had not lost the war in fair combat. The war-guilt clause and the harsh economic clauses wounded the national pride and sentiment of German people. The treaty was unfair to Germany in apportioning the guilt of responsibility for the war to her and in imposing penalties of reparation and loss of colonial empire to which Germany was subjected. The allies imposed an almost complete disarmament. The allies were inspired by the feeling of revenge. They betrayed Germany and did not adhere to Wilson's 14 points which were fourteen disappointment. The treaty provided German imperialists and militarists the necessary fuel to revive their military strength. Of course, the treaty contained the seeds of a future war. The Second World War had its roots in the unwillingness of Japanese militarist, German Nazis and Italian Fascists to go to war to get their own way. Their countries had grievances, which militarists, strenuously encouraged. The flaws in the peace treaties were exploited to serve the purpose of unscrupulous leaders bent on power. They were determined to repudiate the provisions of the peace treaties. One reason for the dictators success in gaining the loyalty of their peoples was that they promised to tear the treaty provisions. No doubt, Germany was defeated in the war, yet her spirit was not broken. The Germans felt that they had been robbed of victory in the war because of the treachery of their leaders. This led them to believe in the legend of "a stab in the back." Similarly, the treaty of Versailles proved to be twenty years armistice. A definite guarantee of peace provided in the treaty of Versailles was the provisions regarding disarmament, but it was not based on reciprocity. When Hitler came to power, he unilaterally denounced the Military clauses of the treaty and introduced conscription. The totalitarian states raised the slogan of armaments and rearmaments. The letters of failure, written large over the portals of successive disarmament conference during the inter-war period. All the so-called big powers stock-piled arms and ammunition and they were gripped by the fever of militarism.

While the Nations of Europe were engrossed in restructuring and rehabilitating them selves in the post-war period, burden imposed by the reparation commission further sharpened the bitterness of the defeated powers. Germany was crippled economically. The reconstruction of Europe depended on the availability of finance. But the rebuilding of Germany depended on US finances, Whereas the US preferring to stay in its own cocon aspired to take its economy to greater height. But the American confidence crashed in 1929, and once the financial crash occurred it soon spread throughout the world, which caused great hardship to the masses. Millions of people lost employment, factories stopped working, banks failed, value of property sank. Peoples were so confused that they lost confidence in the rationality of political institution. Governments of the western countries that were caught in the economic crisis found it impossible to over-come the crisis by peaceful means. Gradually these nations found that reparation for war acted as a stimulant to economic revival. Almost all the countries resorted to imposition of high tariff to save their industries. Due to the economic blizzard the international trade came to a standstill position. Taking advantage of the economic crisis Japan attacked Manchuria which open the path to armed conflict.

To place the blame for the Second World War on others is to do no more than criticise a man for defending his property. It can be argued that weakness of their neighbours tempted the aggressors to strike. The league of nations showed many weakness and from its birth was severely handicapped by the non-membership of the USA. It lacked an effective weapon with which to resist aggression and when attempts were made to strengthen it they failed. The covenant of the league was ignored. There was lack of unanimity among the league members to impose economic sanction against a big power. The league had no machinery to enforce its decision, so it failed to maintain peace when quarrels involved big powers. The league system of collective security totally failed. Japanese conquest of Manchuria was followed by Italian invasion on Ethiopia, German annexation of Austria and Czechoslovakia. The search for collective security led to the signing of endless pieces of paper which undermined the importance of the league. Even worse, the pieces of paper were not honoured in time of crisis. But the only way to honour them was to go to war or at least to be prepared to go to war. There were occasions when the aggressors might have been deterred by a firmer show of resistance. Hitler might have been persuaded to retreat from the Rhineland. No doubt, Britain and France were also not free from pressing internal problems. They were bewildered by the rise of fanatical totalitarian regimes. In their eagerness to preserve peace the democracies were hoodwinked. Probably one of the most important single factors that enabled Germany to wage the most barbarous war in history was that Britain and France were at loggerheads over the execution of the peace-settlement. Thus, as Langsum has observed "many of the worst post-war Franco-German quarrels developed into Franco-British quarrels, to the obvious advantage of Germany". They also failed to tackle the problem of involving the USSR in a policy of collective security. besides, the horror of the First World War convinced the statesmen that if another war was to be averted emphasis should be given on pacific international order based and on co-operation. On the other hand in GErmany, italy, Japan and Spain, dictators came to power on a wave of popular nationalist enthusiasm. The aggressive nationalism manifested itself in imperialist conquest. Both Italy and Germany choose different political ideologies to pull up their nations. The main cause of the Second World War lay in the struggle between the Haves and Have nots. The treaty of Versailles had deprived Germany of her colonial empire and the German colonies were divided among the big powers. Great Britain and France had been the largest possessor of colonies, so they favoured the maintenance of statues quo. Whereas German imperialist would want a change in the status–

quo. Since a redivision of colonial world was not possible through peaceful means, the imperialist could hope to obtain sphere of influence only by wrestling them from the existing colonial powers. Hitler and Mussolini declared that the fundamental aim of their foreign policy was to reestablish a vast empire. The logic of imperalism is world domination through conquest and that mean war, hence the war-machine of the axis powers directed to that one end.

As Europe began to marchig towards war, the atmosphere became more vicious by the grandiose military design of Japan. It began its militarism during the last part of 19th century and she kept it up all through the crucial year. Japanese Fascism differed in several respects from its European counterpart. japan's militarism definitely showed Fascist traits. Most pronounced was the similarity of the foreign policies of the three Fascist powers. Each powers tried the solution of the three Fascist powers. Each powers tried the solution of domestic problems through foreign expansion and each based the right to such expansion on claims of superiority.

The western powers might be said to have undertaken the appeasement of Germany with a view to deflecting her anger against the west and turning it against the East. Some western statesmen hope that Hitler could be encouraged to turn his aggressive energies against the Soviet Union. Besides they feared that the communist Government of Soviet Russia was intent upon spreading communism all over the world, and with this intention Russia was not admitted in to the family of nations for a long time, and remained as an outcast. On the otherhand, the USSR often expressed its willingness to play a part in defending the weak. Russians argued that, in excluding the USSR from the Munich confenrence, the west showed its contempt and perhaps more sinister, a readiness to gang up with Hitler against communism. It was the final tragedy which made war in Europe inevitable, that Britain and France reached no agreement with Russia, but Germany did. Hitler was able to attack Poland, safe in the knowledge that the USSR would not interefere. Hitler declared "our enemies are little worms, I saw them at Munich." But Poland was only one of many victims. General war was avoided until 1939, because no country went to the rescue of the victims. Britain and France only enlarged a conflict which had already begun. Mussolini said "I want to make Italy great, respected and feared." The First World War caused by extreme nationalism and colonial scrambles. Behind these lay the problems generated by the capitalist system. And modernisation of Europe was based on geographicla discoveries, decline of feudalism and along with the emergence of national state, birth of secularism, and development of science. Thus, possibly the origin the Second

World War lay in the emergence of modernisation in Euope. So it is difficult to identify a single force as the villian of world peace. Similarly it would be wrong to hold every German responsible for the wickedness of the Nazis. The invasion of Poland need not have led to a world war, that it did has nothing to do with the selfishness and timidity of the British and French or the perfidious callousness of the Soviet Union. Hitler and those followed him bear the responsibility for the war. Many millions who died in Hitler's war did not die for Danzig, but they died as a result of Nazi Germany's insatiable lust for conquest. The ultimate responsibility lies with hitler that the war became one for German hegemony, whether continental or global, that it was fought with unamatched bruatality and was fuelled by visions of a pathological and immoral Utopia. Anyhow, a torch lit in the frontiers of Eastern Europe set the whole world aflame.

The World in 1945 and Afterwards

The enormous power and resources of the USA and the USSR combined with an all-out effort from Britain and her empire slowly but surely wore the Axis powers down. Italy was eliminated first and this was followed by an Anglo-American invasion of Normandy which liberated France, Holland and Belgium had crossed the Rhine to capture cologne. In the East, the Russians drove the Germans out and advanced on Berlin. Germany surrendered in May 1945 and Japan in August 1945 after the American had dropped atomic bombs on Hiroshima and Nagasaki. Thus, the greatest and the most devastating war in human history came to an end on 10th August, 1945, when the Japanese Government accepted the allies terms of unconditional surrender. The events of the six years war presented to the people and statesmen of the world problems on an unprecedented scale, unfortunately after the Second World War there was no great peace conference to draw up terms of settlement as there had been after the Napoleonic wars or the First World War. The reason for the absence of a general settlement was that by the time hostilities ended a serious rift had appeared among Germany's enemies. Perhaps the original fundamental differences had reappeared, that is between 'East' and 'West', between the communist Soviet union and the western, capitalist democracies.

Wreckage and devastation on a scale previously unknown bore witness to the colossal disruption brought about by the war. In continental Europe, the destruction of homes, factories, schools, hospitals and transport system was on an immense scale. Many nations suffered devastation equivalent to about three total production, reckoned in pre-war terms. The damage to factories and communications meant that it would take many years to return to pre-war condition. In Europe alone, there were an estimated 25 million people who had been displaced from their homes and were simply refugees. A vast resettlement operation was requird. When the war ended the allies made an enormous effort to being relief and reparation to those in need. Besides, without massive aid to repair their economies, most countries faced a grim future. Apart from the devastation, many were deep in debt. The end of the war brought a new struggle to re-establish at least the old standard of life. The war accelerated the demand for social change. At the sametime, the war which ended in 1945 left violence in its wake.

Scientist in all countires had experimented with new and more terrible weapons throughout the war. But the fissioning of atom bomb had been achieved by Germany first, USA developed it and bomb became available in July 1945. The first atomic bomb was dropped on the Japanese industrial town of Hiroshima on 6th August. The entire town was devasted and many were killed. Undoubtedly the atomic bomb shortened the war, yet, arguments soon raged about the morality of their use. Nuclear weapons heralded a new era in human destructiveness. American possession of such weapons created fear in the world The USA refused to share nuclear expertise with the Russians. Thus, a terrible arm race was under-way in which America and Russia were soon joined with Britain, France and China.

Instead of fostering a long period of friendship the Soviet-American victory was followed by an intensification of their previous suspicious and distrust which became known as the cold war. The rivalry of these two super powers has been the most important feature of international relations since 1945 and apparently a constant threat to world peace. Towards the end of the war the harmony that had existed between the USSR and the USA began to evaporate. The decade after 1945 saw the first phase of the cold war. The basic cause lay in the differences of principle between the communist states and the capitalist or democratic states which had existed ever since the communists had set up a Government in Russia in 1917. Only the need for self-preservation had caused them to sink their differences and as soon as it became clear that the defeat of Germany was only a matter of time, both sides, began to plan for the post-war period. Althogh no actual armed conflict took place between the two opposing camps, set the rival powers confined themselves in attacking each other with propaganda and economic measurs. Russia which was an out-cast from the family of nations, emerged as the most dominant power in Europe, America, after the Second World War became the leader of the free world and took all possible steps to stem the tide of communist expansion. Thus, from the Second World War there energed two great powers, the USA and the USSR and upon their uneasy relationship the future course of the world affairs was to depend. Their confrontation in that broken European context was symbol of Europe's changed role in the balance of world power. After Yalta conference, the soviet union had undoubtedly established a zone of communist influence wherever her armies had advanced in Eastern Europe. Then system of communist satellite states in Eastern Europe was contrary to the intention of war time agreements. It brought out a confusing feature of international diplomacy, that both communist and non-communist were using a common vocabulary of words such as self-determination, democracy, freedom, liberation, and using them with opposite meanings. However, at the time of the economic crisis in Europe, it was the Marshal plan which made the cold war division in to two world explict.

Besides, by 1945 a number of powerful distruptive influences had been brought to bear upon the older certainities of colonial empire. Chief among them were the appeal of communism, to the dispossessed and those who lived in undeveloped areas of the world, the steady growth of American influence and, with it, the anti-colonialism of a people proud of their self-made origins in the rejectioin of colonialism. So there was found a moral flaw inherent in the concept of empire and colonial rule. In a century which has been authority challenged in so many spheres of human relations, colonial rule represent an unwanted political authority. To be ruled by a foreigner, be he exploiter or benevolent administrator came to seen no better than an enslavement. To be ruled by one's own people, became the very touch stone of national pride. Political nation hood became self-justifying and initiative passed from the colonial rulers to those whom they ruled. It was the Second World War which opened an era of Decolonisation. Many countries in Asia. Africa, Latin America achieved independence in the years after 1945, with the passing of time and the steady increase in their numbers, the newly emergent nations began to be identified as a "Third World", not in any sense organised as such, but grouping towards some alternative role between the two rival system represented by the USA and the USSR. The third world nations wished to remain neutral or non-aligned in the struggle between the other two worlds, communism and capitalism. Usually poor and industrially undeveloped, the new nations were often suspicious of the motives of both the world and resneted their own economic dependence on the world's ealthy powers.

Germany had been partitioned after the Second World War. In the midst of the war, at the Casablanca conference, Preisident Roosevelt and Mr. Churchill, issued a declaration to which Stalin later subscribed, announcing that the objective of the war was to be the unconditional surrender of Germany, Italy and Japan. But it was agreed at the Yalta conference that Germany should be divided into zones of occupation, one alloted to each of the three powers, and that France should also be invited to takeover a fourth zone. It was further decided that drastic measures were to be taken for the complete demilitarisation, denazification of Germany. By the end of May 1945 the whole of German territory was occupied by the allies within the zones agreed upon at Yalta.

An international military tribunal was established for the trial of the war-criminals. The trials were held at Nuremburg. The Russians were determined to make their zone a communist satellite country. The French demanded reparation from their zone. In 1946 Britain and America put forward the idea of an amalgamation of the zones and formed Bizone which was later-on became Trizone, When the French agreed to co-operate with them. Differences between Russia and the other three powers led to the breakdown of the four power machinery for the control of Germany, preparations were set on foot for the creation of independent German Government. These preparation resulted in the formation of the Federal republic of Germany with its seat at Bonn, and in the East, the German democratic Republic with its seat in the Russian sector of Berlin. Thus, two German states came into existence. A separate peace treaty was signed with Japan at Sanfrancisco in 1951 and Japan recognised the independence of Korea, the allied occupation forces were to be withdrawn from Japan and she gave up all special rights in China.

Throughout world history war has been one of the greatest instrument for change. By 1945 all the allied governments were eager to see the establishment of the United Nations, and at Yalta arrangements were made for a meeting at Sanfrancisco. The UN charter was drawn up at Sanfrancisco. The aim of the UN was to preseve peace and to remove the causes of conflict by encouraging economic, social, cultural and educational progress throughout the world. It played an important role in a number of international crisis by arranging ceasefires, negotiations and peace-keeping forces. Its achivements in non-political issues is really praiseworthy. Above all, it spread the message of internationalism among the nations. They are concerned not to allow a repetation of the events of 1939-45, a period that, amid the horror of war, saw the birth of the UNO.

Chapter - XXV

The United Nations

"From 1945-1995 a long March in the life of an organisation which has sustained many ups and down in its career. On 24th October, 1995, the United Nations completed its fifity years marked by celebration commemorations throughout the world. In the last 50 years of its existence this world form has witnessed a stormy, cyclonic period of political upheavals, aggression and invasions. On 26th June, 1945, when the historic charter, endorsed by Fifty nations was enshrined in the United Nations charter, the fine forte of this world body reads "we the people of United Nations." But in reality it has little to do directly with people, except in a sentimental way. It has experienced an era of elevation and degradation. The 50th aniversary of the United Nations provided an opportunity to do some stock-taking. What has the United Nations achieved and where has it failed? Is the United Nations relevant, yes, if the United Nations did not exist, it would have to be invented. The history of this world organisation has sordid and dismal record of cold war politics. Heaps of resolution and floods of oratory weighing in tons, are the salient production of the United Nations. What to talk of peace and security, the very foundation of which it was created have been grossly and impudently thwarted on many occasions by the heavy-weights in the international politics.

While the Second World War was still going on and before the rot had started on the allied side, the big three, Roosevelt, Stalin and Churchill, had given considerable thought to the problems of the coming peace. Even before the United States had entered into the war, President Roosevelt and Prime Minister Churchill had, following their meeting at sea, issued the Atlantic charter. It pledged an idealistic programme of international peace, to the repudiation of territorial aggrandizement, and to the right of every nation freely to choose its own form of government. The Principles of the Atlantic charter were reaffirmed by the 26 allied states on 1 January, 1942 in the declaration by United Nations. The allied powers came together to mediate the process of creating a new world organisataion to save succeeding generations from the scourge of war, to establish respect for international law and to promote better standards of life in larger freedom. The allied powers were confident of creating a new and better world organisation for two reasons. One, the emerging super powers, the United States of America which was not a member of the league of Nation and the Soviet Union which withdrew from the membership of the league after a years, came together to create a new world organisation. And, secondly they were aware of the inadequacies of the league.

Draft proposals for the new organisation were prepared under the auspices of the four sponsoring powers (the United Kingdom, Union of Soviet Socialist Republic, United States of America and China) at conference held at Dumbeartonoaks, near Washington, in the autmn of 1944. The decision of this conference served as the basis for the draft of the charter of the United Nation. They reached agreement on all important matters except voting procedure, and that was setled by the big three at Yalta in February, 1945. The draft charter was then discussed, modified and improved, and finally signed by representatives of fifty states at the Sanfrancisco conference in April-June 1945. They turned the United Nations from a war time alliance into permanent peace time organisation for general international co-operation. It formally came into force on October 24, 1945.

The Preamble of the United Nations Charter

The Preamble of the United Nations contain all major purposes. The preamble began with the words "we the people of the United Nations". The United Nations charter contain 111 article. The various obligations proclamied in the preamble have no special Juridical character. Further the representatives to the United Nations were appointed by their respective government, which could not be said to be the legal equivalent of "the people". The charter has established a system of equal votes, expressing the sovereign equality of all the members. The United Nations is also to develop friendly relations among nations based on respect for equal rights and self-determination of people. In the preamble it it stated to be a principle and purpose of the United Nations to establish conditions under which justice and respect for the obligations arising from treaties and other sources of international law can be maintained. It gives expression to another basic democratic principle, that of the rule of law. In the preamble it is stated as a purpose and principle of the Organisation to promote social progress and better standards of life.

The signatories of the charter agreed to establish the United Nations Organisation in order to curb the anarchic tendencies in international life by a system of equal political rights, equal economic opportunities and the rule of law. And the charter out-law the use of armed force. The purpose are the aggregation of the common ends on which the minds of the signatories to the charter of the United Nations met. The United Nations shall maintain international peace and security. It shall take collective measures for the prevention and removal of threat to the peace. However, it is not the purpose of the United Nations to interfere in the internal affairs of member states. The purpose of the United Nations is world peace. The United Nations shall develop friendly relations among nations. The United Nations aims to achieve international cooperation in solving international problems of an economic, social, cultural and humanitarian character and in promoting human rights and for fundamental freedoms.

The United Nations shall function as a Centre for harmonising the action of nations in the attainment of these common ends. Besides, the organisation is based on the principle of the sovereign equality of all members. It further declared that the members are to settle their dispute through peaceful means. All members are to refrain from the use of force against the territorial integrity or political independence of other States.

Membership and Organisation

The United Nations is a voluntary association of more than 180 nations and it works for world peace and security and the betternment of humanity. Countries from all parts of the world belong to the United Nations. Each member country sends its representative to the United Nations headquarters situated in New York. It seeks the causes of war and tries to find ways to eliminate them. The United Nations has met with both success and failure in its effort. Article 4 of the charter states. Membership in the United Nations is open to all other peace loving nations which accept the obligation contained in the present charter. The admission of a State to the United Nations is effected by a decision of the General Assembly upon the recommendation of the security council. It is not possible to admit a new member without the unanimous support of the five permanent members (USA, Britain, USSR, France and China). According to Article 6 of the United Nations charter that a member states which persistently violates the charter may be expelled by the General Assembly upon the recommendation of the Security council. The charter provided for six main organs, the General assembly, the Security Council, the economic and social council, the trusteeship council, the secretariat, and the international court of Justice.

General Assembly

As all the members of the United Nations are members of the General Assembly, so the Assembly has been called the town meeting of the world. The importance of the General Assembly, the pivot of the organisation, lies in the fact that it is built around the principles of universality and equality of nations. The assembly elects its own president for the session. Besides, 13 Vice Presidents and Chairman of the seven standing committees are also elected by the General Assembly. The assembly must meet once in a year in the month of September. Each member, big ot small, has only one vote, but each member is entitled to have five representatives in the Assembly. The representatives act according to the direction of their respective government. Thus, the General Assembly is a diplomatic conference rather than a legislative body. There is also an interim committee, known as the little assembly. It meets when the assembly is not in session. the General Assembly operates by majority rule, some matters requiring a simple majority, others a two-third majority but not uanimous consent. Regarding voting procedure the charter distinguished between important questions and other questions. Decision on important questions shall be made by a two-third majority of the members present and voting Decision on other questions shall be made by a majority of the mambers present and voting.

Functions

The charter has endowed the assembly with the power to discuss any matter, within the scope of the charter. As part of this power, the assembly can consider any peace and security question for making appropriate recommendations. The General Assembly can make recommendations as well as initiate studies for the promotion of international cooperation. The Assembly can call the attention of the Security Council to situation which are likely to endanger international peace and security.

It can recommend measures for peaceful adjustment of situations likely to disturb freindly relations amongst nations.

It is designed as a body to discuss and to recommend but not to decide on problems of peace and security. It also receives and consider reports from the other organs of the UNO. It passes the budget of the organisation as well as of the specialised agencies referred in Article 57 of the charter. Though the assembly has extensive powers of discussion it cannot intervene in matters which are within the domestic jurisdiction of any state.

The Assembly is not vested with any, legislative powers. It cannot legislate for the members States. According to Article 11, the Assembly may formulate general principle of cooperation in the maintenance of international peace and security, including the principles governing disarmament. It has the right to initiate studies and make recommendations for encouraging the progressive development and codification of international system as are assigned to it under Chapter XII of the charter. The Assembly play an important role as an organ of political settlement, of peace making and peace saving.

The General Assembly has been entrusted with the task of supervising the UN, not only the Secretariat, but also the economic and social council, trusteeship council, the security council. The Assembly has some elective functions. It can elect the Secretary General, Judges to the International Court, and admits new members on the recommendation of the security council. However, the Assembly possesses exclusive power in other election cases like the election of non-permanent members of the Security Council, election of the members of the Social and Economic Council. It will have the right to propose amendments to the charter which must be adopted by two-third majority vote Besides, the economic and social council of UNO has to seek the approval of the General Assembly for calling international conferences, concluding agreements with the specialised Agencies.

The Assembly serves, "as a valuable setting for personal contacts, private meetings, exchange of views..." It provides a diplomatic meeting place. It were as a Centre for harmonising the actions of States. The assembly is a class by itself. If the Assembly is to function as a town meeting of the world, it must be universal. For several reasons the Assembly is increasingly being viewed as an organ for debate and concilliation, not for collective enforcement action.

Security Council

Under the charter the security council is assigned the primary responsibility for maintaining world peace and security. The charter authorises the security council to work for world peace, in two inter-related areas. they are peaceful settlement of disputes among nations and punitive collective action to restore or maintain international peace and security.

According to Article 23 of the charter the security council shall consist of 11 members (now 15) of which 5 are permanent members namely China, France United Kingdom, USA and USSR. The other non-permanent members of the security council are elected by the General Assembly for a term of two years. On 31st August, 1965 the General Assembly by an amendment of the charter increased the number of non-permanent members of the Council to 10. The five permanent members enjoy an exceptional status by virtue of special voting rights that is the power of "VETO". The justification for granting this exceptional status to 5 members lies in inscapable to fact of power differentials. Each member of the council has one vote. Decision of the security council on procedural matters shall be made by an affirmative vote of 9 members, but these 9 votes must include the concurring votes of the 5 permanent members. Thus, a negative vote by a permanent members on a matter which is not procedural (a substantive matter) has come to be known as `Veto'. Hence by its single negative veto any one of the big 5 can prevent the Security Council from taking a decision which has a support of majority of the council. The question that arise in this connection are, can a permanent member exercise his veto right by abstaining from voting or by being absent. It may be stated that a permanent members abstention from voting on substantive qeustion is not considered a veto. There is no enumeration of what matters falls into procedural or substantive question.

Functions

The Security Council is the enforcement wing of the United Nations. According to Article 28 of the charter. "The Security Council should be so organised as to be able to function continuously. The presidency of the Security Council is held in turn according to the alphabetical order of the names of its member states. The powers of the Security Council, the key organ of the United Nations, are primarily of an executive nature. The Council has been vested with the primary responsibility, for the maintenance of world peace and security. It can investigate any issue likely to jeopardise international peace and security. The member states are called to settle dispute by peaceful means. However, if the members are not in a position to settle their disputes peacefully, they have an obligation under the charter to refer the matter to the Council. The Security Council will seek a solution through negotiations, mediation, arbitration. But if the situation is serious, the Council under Article 39 of the charter shall determine the existence of any threat to peace or act of aggression. The Council may decide diplomatic, economic, military, sanctions against the aggressor state. Any country whether a member or not has the right to draw the attention of the Council to any threat to peace Besides, the Council has the power in the appointment of the Secretary General, in the admission of members and in the election of Judges to the international court of Justice. It also share power with the General Assembly regarding the regulation of armaments and possible disarmaments. Though the main function of the Council is to maintain world peace and security, but in recent times it has declined, decayed and defunct. Of all the organs of the United Nations none has shown a greater discrepancy between promise and performance then the Security Council. The Council was envisioned as the Central agency of the United Nations, but it has not been able to play its expected role. Instead of great powers unanimity on which the United Nations was predicted, the post-war years have brought major rifts and disagreements among the states. Perhaps the most significant development about the Security Council has been its relative decline in the work of the United Nations as a whole. The Council has, in effect, becomes an anachronism. But more fundamentally, the role of the Security Council was weakened by the emergence of collective defence arrangements, effectively detached, from the United Nations. Even in the realm of pacific settlement of disputes, the Security Council has had very limited effectiveness. As a result of differences of ideology, the USA and the USSR could not maximise their role as a peace keeping team in cases involving other states.

In the era of cold war the Security Council has had more frequent occasions to function in its diplomatic capacity. But it does not appear that the Council has functioned impressively as a forum for building among the great powers, as a diplomatic centre for the great powers. This is largely attributable to the attitudes exhibited by the two super powers. Yet, the security Council, which for some years seemed in danger of paralysis from the stresses and strains of the East-West conflict, has reemerged recently to resume the key role in the world politics, with the advent of something like nuclear stalemate, and a stable balance of power between the East-West, and disunity among the Western power, the attitude of the United States has changed. Besides, the emergence of a powerful Afro-Asian block has brought about a shift. In short, the usefulness of the Council has increased and is increasing. It is likely to be maximised further in the future if the great power recognise its diplomatic function as of primary, not of secondary, importance. It may became a more useful part of the machinery by which the powers, with the assistance of lesser powers, promote the development of a more stable basis for peace than the world has recently witnessed.

Secretariat

Article 7 of the charter describes the Secretariat as one of the Principal organs of the United Nations and Article 97 provides that the Secretariat shall comprise a secretary general and such staff as the organisation may required. The Secretary General is elected by the Security Council and General Assembly. The General Assembly reserves the right to reject the name by the Security Council, but it cannot make its own choice. It has to wait until another candidate is recommended by the Council. Initially a term of three years was suggested about the term of office of the Secretary–General. But it was argued that frequent elections effect the independence of the Secretary General. So, in January 1946 the assembly decided that the first secretary general should be appointed for a term of 5 years. The secretary general and his staff enjoy independent international status and member governments are expected not to interfere in their independent working. The appointment of the staff of the secretariat is made by the secretary general under the rules prescribed by the General assembly. The secretariat is organised on functional basis Till 1954 the secretariat consisted of an executive office of the secretary general and six departments and two services under Assistant Secretory General. According to Article 100 of the UN charter, the secretary general and his staff shall not seek or receive instructions from any other authority external to the organisations. In order to ensure that the staff could meet the requirement of a truly international service, effort is made to secure highly qualified personnel. Two principles are laid down by the staff regulations for recruitment, personal qualifications of the applicant and securing a balanced geographical distribution.

Functions and Powers

As the chief administrative officer of the UN, the Secretary General is to ensure the efficient working of the meetings of the organs and committees and also of such conferences as may be convened under UN auspices. The staff of other organs of the UN, except the international court of justice form part of the secretariat. The Secretary-General is overall responsible for the efficient working of the various organs. He helps in drafting of documents resolutions and gives legal and technical advice. In financial matters he assumes responsibility for the preparation of the annual budget of UN. He also assumes custody of UN funds and responsibility of their expenditure. He has the responsibility of consulting the specialised agencies to develop arrangements for common fiscal control and financial parctices. The secretary general may bring to the attention of the security council any matter which in his opinion may threaten the maintenance of international peace. He is to act as the eyes and ears of the organisation and its members. However, the scope of the secretary general's political power depends to a large extent on the personality of the office holder and the prevailing political conditions. He has a certain representational function where by he acts as agent of the UN. According to the UN charter every treaty and international agreement entered into by any member of the UN after the present charter comes into force shall be registered with the secretariat and published by it. He can purpose items for the agenda of the assembly and council. The powers of the secretary general demonstrates that, he is expected to be a world statesman, playing an important role in world politics. He is a spokesman, a negotiator, and an initiatior, who can gather the elements of common will which the UN contains and focus them on disputes and dangerous situation. He must also be a servant of the UN charter. Thus, he occupies a pivotal position in the world organisation.

The Economic and Social Council

It consists of 18(54 now) members elected by the General Assembly for 3 year terms of office. The Council is responsible under the General Assembly for carrying out the functions of the UN with regard to international economic, social, cultural, Educational, health and related matters. It coordinates governmental organisations established to deal with special problems. It may call international conferences on any subject within its jurisdiction.

Trusteeship Council

This council consists of all member statees administering trust territories, which were held by certain powers as a result of the Second World War or are dependencies which are volunatrily, included within the trusteeship system by an administering power. The council exercises supervision over the administration of the trust territories, through report from the administering states. It has the power to receive and examine petitions from individuals and organisations in the trust territories. Besides, the council is authorised to arrange periodic visits to trust territories to acquire first hand information about their conditions and problems. Inspite of criticism, the council has helped to reduce the colonial evils and in most of the cases accelerated the process of economic, social and political development in colonial area.

International Court of Justice

It is the principal judicial organ of the UNO. All members are lpso facto parties to the statute of the court. The jurisdiction of the court extends to cases submitted to it by the parties.

The Assembly or the council may request the court to give an advisory opinion on any legal question. The court consists of 15 Judges elected for a term of 9 years by the Assembly and the council. Retiring judges are eligible for reelection. The international court of justice has its permanent seat at the Hague. Cases are heard by full court, but it can also compose chambers composed of three or more judge to deal with specific cases. President and Vice-President of the court are elected for a term of three years. As the principal judicial organ of the UN the court has the primary responsibility to decide cases brought to it by the states. The jurisdiction of the court comprises all cases which the parties have agreed to submit a dispute to it. The court possess a quasi-compulsory jurisdiction. As per Article. 36, its jurisdiction covers all matters specially provided for... in treaties and conventions in force. The same article contain an optional clause where by members may declare that they recognise as compulsory *Ipso facto* and without special agreement, in relataion to any other state accepting the same obligation, the jurisdiction of the court in all legal disputes concerning the interpretation of a treaty, any question of international law. A state may concede compulsory jurisdiction of the court under the optional clause either conditionally or unconditionally for any period of time. Usually the states concede the compulsory jurisdiction of the court, subject to the condition that the other party to the dispute will also accept it. The advisory jurisdiction of the court is available to organisations but not states.

The cases which have come before the court are numerous, thereby indicating that the court fills an important place in the international organisation of the society of states. The record of the court since the year of its inception has been impressive. The court has handed down many decisions. But in a divided world, even law has lost its universality. The court has demonstrated a tenedency towards political rather than legal decision.

The Specialised Agencies

The UNO aims at promoting higher standard of living, solution of economic, social and health problems, Universal respect for human rights. The charter of the UN provides that the various specialised agencies, established by inter-governmental agreement are to be brought into relationship with the UN.

International Labour Organisation

It was creatd on 1st April, 1919 by the League of Nations. It try to secure humane conditions of labour for men, women and young people throughout the world. The organs of the ILO are the General conference, the governing body, the international labour office. The general conference is composed of 4 delegates from each member states, two representing the government, one the employer one the worker. A two-third vote is required for the adoption of a convention. The main aim of the ILO is the improvement of conditions of labour. That is to be achieved by the regulation of hours of work, prevention of unemployment, protection of workers against sickness. To work towards this goal it has assisted several countries in establishing technical training programmes and employment service organisation.

World Health Organisation

It came into existence in Sept. 1948. The membership of WHO is open to all members of the UN. Each member states has one vote. The main organs of the WHO are the world health assembly, the executive board and the secretariat. It aims at the health development of the child, and the enjoyment of the highest attainable standand of health is one of the fundamental rights of every human being. Its main functions are to prevent the spread of diseases, to cure the diseases once it has spread, providing help in preventing the diseases, helping the establishment of an environment, promoting good health. The WHO has achieved an admirable success in securing international cooperation in solving specific health problems. It has also played an effective role in checking epidemics.

Food and Agricultural Organisation

With the intention to promote international cooperation in the economic and social field, the FAO was formed in 1945. Its aims are to help nations to raise the standard of living, to improve nutrition of the people, to increase the efficiency of farming, to better the condition of rural peoples. It is composed of the representatives of member states, each member having only one vote. There is a council consists of 49 members elected by the conference. The Director General is appointed by the conference, FAO has a technical divisions dealing with agriculture, marketing, forestry, fisheries, rural welfare. During the post-war world food crisis the FAO played a significant role. The special problem of the FAO is hunger. It provides technical assistance to many countries to grow more food to control pests, to increase the yield of farm.

Unesco

It was initially started by England and France and later adopted by 143 members. Important organs of the UNESCO are the General conferences, the executive body and the secretariat. Its main purpose is to contribute to peace, and security by promoting collaborataion among the nations through education, science and culture in order to further universal respect for justice and for the human rights. Its major task includes education, natural activities, mass communication, technical aid to developing countries. The advancement by UNESCO of human welfare through education, science and culture promotes internatinal understanding which contributes to peace.

IBRD

The international bank for reconstruction and development, an important UN agency, was born as a result of the Britton woods conference held in 1944. The main objective of the Bank is to promote the international flow of all types of long-term capital for productive purposes, and to assist in financing the rebuilding of divested areas and the development of the resources of members states. It has been described as a bridge from war to peace. It was created to help restore economic health to the world.

United Nations Conference on Trade and Development

The UNCTAD came into existence in 1964. The purpose of this organisation is to narrow the gap between the rich and the poor nations. The backward countries have become dependent on advanced countries. The rich nations are expected to share their income with the poor countries. The widening economic gap would disturb world peace. The Algiers charter of 77 Nations, demanded that the international trade should be based on terms of equality. On the contrar the rich countries have erected tariff walls to protect their industries.

In addition to the above important organisations the UN has also a number of other specialised agencies. There are international monetary fund, international postal union, International civil aviation organisation, international trade organisations, ITU, UNICEF, WMO, IAEA. The UN in its early years, while responding to various problems which upset international peace did not go strictly by the letter of charter. In fact the UN displayed a dynamism worthy of a living institution. By choosing what might be called trial and error method, the UN applied different technique, keeping in view the peculiarities of each case.

The UNO and Political Disputes

Although the UNO has had mixed success, it is probably fair to say that UNO has been rather more successful than the League in its peace-keeping efforts, especially in crisis which did not directly involve the interest of the great powers. On the other hand, it has often been just as ineffective as the league in situations such as the Hungarian, Czech crisis, when the interests of one of the great power, deemed to be threatened and where the great power chose to defy the UNO. The best way to illustrate the organisations of the major disputes in which it has been involved.

(A) In 1946 UNO helped to arrange the granting of independence by Holland to the Dutch East Indies which became Indonesia. However, no agreement was reached about the future of West New Guinea which both sides to reopen negotiations, it was agreed in 1962 that the territory should become part of Indonesia. The transfer was organised and policed by a UN force. In this case the UN played a vital role in getting successful negotiations going, though it did not itself make the decision about West Guinea's future.

(B) The problem of the warring Jews and Arabs in Palestine was before the UN by Britain in 1947, and the resulting UN investigation decided to partition Palestine, setting up the Jewish State of Israel. The UN was unable to prevent a series of war between Israel and various Arab states. Though it did useful work arranging cease-fires and providing supervisory forces while UNRWA cared for the Arab refugees.

(C) The Korean war was the only occasion on which the UN was able to take decisive action in a crisis directly involving the interest of the great powers, when South Korea was invaded by communist North Korea in June 1950. The security council passed a resolution condemning North Korea and called on member states to send help to South Korea. However, this was only possible because of the temporary absence of the Russian delegates who would have certainley vetoed the resolution. Although the Russian delegates returned, it was too late for them to prevent action against going ahead. Troops of 16 countries were able to repel the invasion and preserve the frontier between the two Koreas along 38th parallel. Though it was claimed by the west as a great UN success, it was in fact overwhelmingly an American operation. The Korean war had important results for the future of the UN, one was the passing of the "Uniting for peace" resolution. Another was the launching of a bitter attack by the Russians on T. Lie, the Secretary General for his biased role in the crisis.

(D) The Suez canal crisis 1956 showed the UN at its best. When President Nasser of Egypt nationalised the Suez Canal, both France and England protested strongly and sent troops to protect their interest. At the same time the Israelis invaded Egypt from the East. A security council resolution condemning force was vetoed by England and France, when the matter passed to the General assembly which by a majority of 64 votes to 5 condemned the invasions and called for a withdrawal of troops. In view of the weight of opinion against them the aggressors agreed to withdraw provided the UN ensured a reasonable settlement over the canal and kept the Arabs and Israelis from killing each other. A UN emergency force moved and the prestige of the UN was greatly enhanced. However, the UN was not successful in the 1967 Arab-Israeli conflict.

(E) The Hungarian rising 1956, which occurred at the same time as the Suez crisis, showed the UN at its most ineffective role. When the Hungarians tried to exert their independence from Russian control, Soviet troops entered Hungary to crush the revolt the Hungarian Government appealed to the UN, but the USSR vetoed a security council resolution. The Assembly set up a committee to investigate the matter, but the Russian refused to cooperate with the committee. But the Russian ignored the UN, and nothing could be done.

(F) The Belgian Congo civil war which dragged on from 1960 until 1964 the UN mounted its most complex operation so far. When the Congo (zaire) dissolved into Chaos immediately after gaining independence, special UN Congo fund was established to help the recovery of the ravaged country. But the financial cost was so high that the UN was brought to bankruptcy. Big powers refused to pay their contributions towards the cost of the operation, as they disapproved of the way the UN was handling the situation.

(G) Cyprus has kept the UN busy since 1964. A British colony since 1878, the island was granted independence in 1960. In 1963 a civil war broke out between the Greeks, (who made of about 80% of the population) and Turks. A UN peace keeping force arrived in 1964, an uneasy peace was restored. In 1974 the Greek cypriots tried to unite the island with Greece, this prompted the Turkish cypriots to seize the north of the island and to expell all the Greek who happened to be living in that area. The UN has not been successful in finding an acceptable compromise.

(H) In 1947 the large province of kashmir between India and Pakistan was claimed by both States. In 1948 the UN had negotiated a ceasefire after fighting had broken out. At this point the Indians were occupying the southern part of Kashmir, and the Pakistani the northern part. For the next so many years the UN policed the ceasefire line between the two zone. When Pakistani troops invaded India in 1965, a war developed between Indian and Pakistani, the UN intervened and hostilities ceased. But he original dispute still remained and there seemed little prospect of the UN finding a permanent solution.

(I) In 1968 the Czech crisis took place. When the Czechs showed what Moscow judged to be too much independence. Russian troops were sent to enforce obedience. The security council tried to pass a motion condemning this action but the Russian vetoed it. There was nothing the UN could do inview of the Russian refusal to cooperate.

Role of the UNO

Since 1945 the records of the UN to-date swing between wild hopes and gloomy despair. The record also does not seem to prove that the organisataion would have been a greater success, if the security council had been more effective. The security council, a body originally designed to be cohesive and organised in such a manner as to act decisively, in practice, became exactly the opposite, because of the cold war politics within the world body. The permanent members did not mind brushing aside their obligataions under the charter. The veto power was used indiscriminately.

More often there was deadlock in the security council and its importance as an instrument for world peace declined.

Besides, the advent of atomic weapons and their subsequent modernisation and proliferation by the US and USSR elevated them to a new status of super powers. The new status symbolised their unmatched ability to destroy the world many times over with the use of nuclear weapons and their ability to influence events in all parts of the world. The resultant rivalry between the two was known as the cold war. This division was further institutionalised with the formation of military alliances. The conflict vitiated the entire gamut of inter-state relations for a long time. Surely there was no organ or activity of the UN which was free from the impact of the cold war or East-West rivalry. Particularly, the impact was considerable on the role of the security council. But the greatest hurdle in the just and fair functioning of the UN has been that it has been controlled and directed by powers. The UN has became an anti-communist alliance system rather than a non-partisan world organisation, promoting and safeguarding the larger interest of mankind. Besides, political events in the fifties, both outside and inside the UN had their impact on the UN. With the March of times, a large number of newly independent states were admitted to the UN. The new members were those which emerged from colonialism in Asia, Africa, the Caribean and the pacific, which were undeveloped and intensely nationalistic, and most of whom were adhering to a policy of non-alignment. Both the super powers were interested in wooing the newly emerging nations betterly known as the third world countries. The third world countries on their part looked up the UN as their gretest benefactor. On the otherhand, the big powers considered the third countries as pawn in the game of power politics.

Yet, the UN has certain weaknesses and difficulties. The UN is not a super state. Every member states retains their sovereignity and they are not bound by the decision taken by the UN. It also does not possess any coercive power to punish any aggressor state. At the same time there has been a lot of criticism of Article 2(7) which deals with the domestic jurisdiction which has not been properly defined by the UN charter. Above all, the financial crisis has further weakened the position of the UN.

But in recent years, the UN has proved itself as an indispensable institution. It has been repeatedly defied, by-passed and ignored, but it has contributed more, both directly and indirectly, to the maintenance of peace than has been realised. It has been the major coordinating agency for a vast number of organisations which are dedicated to the service of nations and peoples all over the world. More than five decades of the UN's multifaced activity provide convincing evidence that this organisation is viable, necessary and important for the cause of peace and international cooperation. The UN is now a universal institution, it had 51 members in its inception, but more than 180 to-day. It has been a useful instrument in settling conflicts, in containing the arms race, in defending the interest of the colonial peoples struggle for freedom.

In recent years the UN has devoted much attention to helping the developing nations in their economic growth and promoting democratic rules, probably its major achievement has been the adoption of the universal declaration of human rights proclaimed to be the common standards of achievement for all people. No wonder, in recognition of their past contribution and future potentialities, the UN peace keeping operations were awarded Nobel peace prize in 1988.

In evaluating the role of the UN the question therefore should not be how much the organisation can do, but what it can do. A politically meaningful and effective UN will be one in which the powers have achieved modus vivendi and have developed peaceful co-existence to a point at which cooperation became more important than competition. That is to say, the UN, can became an instrument of genuine peace, if the great powers act according to the principle laid down in the charter. It is true that the UN was designed by the then major powers to subserve their exclusive interests, of course, at present it is not controlled by one power or group of powers, although it is not immune to the influence of the mighty ones. Furthermore, the political processes of the UN should be understood more in terms of what it is rather than in terms of what it ought to be in an ideal situation which does not exist.

In this computer age, we expect instant solution to problems. The criticism against the UN has been that it sleeps over burning problems. The answer to such criticism is that the UN is not like a xerox machine to produce instant output. The effectiveness of the UN would depend on the cooperation offered by the community of nations. Given that cooperation the UN has always proved and will continaully prove its usefulness in preserving international peace and security. Besides, it has grown and adopted itself to a changing world are no mean achievement for an international organisation. In this dark labyrinth of international aberrations, the UN is the only oasis of hope for the humanity, which has recovered from the catastrophic calamities perpetrated by the devastating world wars. To prevent such a traumatic occurrence is the loftiest task and the objective before the UN and only in that lies the redemption of humanity.

Chapter-XXVI

From War to Cold War

The end of the Second World War in 1945 opened a new phase in world history and it changed the character of international relations. The world of the twentieth century was one of rapid and often startling changes which accelerated as the century progressed. It was no longer a world dominated by Europeans. Towards the end of the Second World War the harmony that had existed between the USSR, USA, and the British empire began to evaporate and all the old suspicions came to the fore again. After the defeat of the principal Axis powers, Germany and Japan, International relations were dominated by continuous rivalry between the USSR and USA, who could sustain the war and emerged more powerful after the war was over. Due to tremendous economic and military power at their disposal, they were designated as "Super Powers". Unfortunately, relations between the two super powers soon became so strained that although no actual armed conflict took place directly between the two opposing camps, the decade after 1945 witnessed the first phase of the "cold war". As a result, two power blocks came into existence led by the USA and the USSR representing two divergent and opposite ideologies. The cold war between the two super powers and their allies was a condition which was neither peace nor war, in which actual fighting was limited in scope and objectives. This meant that instead of allowing their mutual hostility to express itself in open fighting, the rival powers confined themselves attacking each other with propaganda and economic measures and with a general policy of non-cooperation. In other words, there began a period of zero sum game, in which the loss of one party was taken as a gain of the other party. It was a new technique of warfare which covered the entire world so far as the super power hostilities are concerned. The frontiers between west and East (communist states) were uneasy, the atmosphere was not free from tension, but no territories changed lands, and only few lives were lost in the US-

Soviet confrontation. The cold war was characterised by extreme hostility between the two factions, psychological warfare, and uninterrupted mutual vilification, in public international organisations such as the UN, but with little actual fighting. For about fifteen years there were repeated crisis in which war seemed imminent. But each contained the other. The basis of the co-existence was an unwritten but apparent acceptance that, at least in Europe, neither side would trespass on the territories of the other. This balance of power was achieved partly through fear, because both sides were well-aware of the destructive powers of nuclear weapons. As time passed on it seemed that the possibility of a Third World War became less likely, and the cold war gave way to what is called detente a period of relaxation of hostilities. However, it still continued in different forms and greatly modified by profound upheavals in different parts of the globe.

Origin and Evolution

The conflict and tensions between the communist states led by the USSR, and the anti-communist western power led by the USA was certainly dramatic. This state of affairs was known as the 'cold war', the phrase was coined by walter Lippmann. Of course, the battle cry was first raised in Churchill's Fulton speech, Misscouri on 5th March, 1946, in which he declared "From stettin in the Baltic to Trieste in Adriatic, an iron curtain has descended across the continent of Europe". Gobbles, a Nazi lieutenant of Adolf Hitler in editorial in Das Reich on February 25, 1945 warned that "red" Russia was out to conquer the world". Churchill urged strong Anglo-American alliance under which the western democracies could make a stand against the indefined expansion of the Russian power and doctrines. Churchill's battle cry became the bible of western democracies. The emergence of the socialist countries in Eastern Europe liberate from Nazi aggression by the Soviet Union was one of the revolutionary consequences of the Second World War However, this was unacceptable to the ruling elite of the western world. The USA having then atom bomb monopoly took upon herself the responsibility of leading the crusade. Henry Stimson's advice, resorted to atomic-blackmail method to keep the Russians out of Eastern Europe in order to put them under Anglo-American Control to preserve the crumbling capitalist regime. But it ended in a fiasco.

The basic cause of conflict between the two superpower lay in the differences of principle or ideology (capitalism and communism) which had existed ever since the communist had set up a government in Russia in 1917. After the failur of the intervention of the western power in Bolshevik Russia, President Hoover confessed to an American journalist "The ambition of myself is to stamp out Soviet Russia". Churchill urged that "communism should be strangled in its cradle". The relations between the west and the USSR remained tense throughout the inter-war period. Self preservation had caused them to sink their differences as soon as it became clear that the defeat of Germany was only a matter of time, both sides, began to plan for the post-war period. The Yalta conference held in February 1945 was attended by Stalin, Roosevelt and Churchill. At the same time generally thought to be a success, agreement being reached on several points. However, there were ominous signs over poland, when the Russian swept through Poland, pushing the Germans back, they had set up a communist government in lublin, even though there was a polish government in exile in London. It was agreed at Yalta that some members (non-communist) of the London based government should be allowed to join the Lublin Government, while in return Russia would be allowed to keep the strip of Eastern Poland which she had occupied in 1939. But, Roosevelt and Churchill refused to agree with Stalin's demands that Poland should be given all German territory East of the river oder and Neisse. The Potsdam conference held in July 1945 revealed a distinct cooling-off in relations. The representatives were stali, Truman and Churchill. The war with Germany was over. But no agreement was reached about her long-term future beyond what had been decided at Yalta (it was understood that Germany should be disaramed, denazified and democratised). At the potsdam conference, a system of four powers occupation of Germany and Berlin were agreed. For all practical purposes, Germany's sovereignity passed into the hands of the victors. In Churchill's dramatic phrase" a headless trunk had fallen on the table of the conquerors". But Truman and Churchill were annoyed because Germany East of the oder-Neisse line had been occupied by Russian troops and ruled by the pro-communist polish government. Besides, Truman did not inform stalin about the nature of the atomic bomb, though Churchill was told about it during the conference. A few days after the conference closed, the two atomic hombs were dropped on Japan and the war ended without the need for Russian aid. Besides, the Russian leadership had not forgotten the West's denial during the war period of a second front which was the very substance of suspicion between communist and non-communist allies. The secretive and ambiguous character of Stalin himself was undoubtedly a factor making for difficulty in war-time alliance. He presented even in the worst phase of German advance to the very gates of Moscow, a completely unshaken faith in Russian victory and an imperturbable example of hardwork and endurance as inspiring in its silent and different way as leadership of Churchill and Roosevelt. To his allies, he revealed a little of his mind.

Undeterred by the Fulton speech of Churchill, the Russian continued to tighten their grip on Eastern Europe. The Russian Red Army penetrated deep into the Balkans in the close years of war. Stalin intended to establish a regime sympathed to the Soviet Union in the countries of defeated enemies (Rumania, Bulgaria, Hungary) and of liberated allies Czechsolvakia, Yugoslavia, Albania) Communists were already strong in many of these countries, where they were respected for their resistance to Nazism and popular among those accustomed to poverty. Stalin set out to create community governments. Obedient to the wishes of Moscow from left-wing coalition and popular fronts. The west called these countries "Russian satellites" and Churchill called the division between them and the west as an "iron curtain". These political happenings in Eastern Europe, coupled with the lack of agreement between the powers on the future of Germany, raised the suspicion of the Western Government about the real intention of Russian under Stalin. From the western point of view, it was the action of the Soviet Government in occupying the countries of Eastern Europe, which was accountable in arousing their distrust and opposition. Thus, a genuine misunderstanding existed between Stalin and the western leaders in the sense that Stalin suspected an agreement to have been made on a sphere of interest by which he would not provoke communist coup in western Europe. In spite of this the Russians did not at once establish monolithic dictatorship in all the countries of Eastern Europe. Yet, the developments in Eastern Europe were interpreted by western leaders and intellectuals as an evidence of Russian expansionism. Their convictions were strengthened by events in Iran.

The confrontation between these two groups took an ideological form. The ideological division which emerged in 1946, was the opposition between East Europe and West Europe, between Soviet control and US influenced groups of states and also the opposing concepts of capitalism and communism. Stalin stood for the policy of socialism in one country, but in the post-war period a Chain of friendly socialist states was deemed to be necessary for the security of communist fatherland. Where as, the western were apprehending that communist was an expansionist, crusading ideology intent on bringing world revolution. On the other hand the communists regarded the western democracy as shameful, an instrument of the wealthy, and an aggression upon peoples democracy. In the words of Friedmann, "The social and political system of Soviet Union has become the direct enemy of American policy". Viewed in this light stalinism and democracy became mutually irreconcilable. Moreover, the emergence of power vacuum which invited the clash, the clash of economic interest, and the arms race between the two super powers was accelerated as each strove to insure itself against a surprise devastating nuclear attack from the other side further aggravating the situation.

COLD WAR-ITS VARIOUS DIMENSIONS AND PHASES

Truman Doctrine

The first pitched battle between the two camps was the Greek civil war. The American Government was informed that Britain could no longer afford to give assistance to Greece. The reaction of President Truman to this news was that the US must step in to offer aid to Greece. Under these conditions, George F. Kenan, the foreign policy planning staff of the state department, later on, the ambassador to Moscow, was of the opınion that the USSR's strength was on decline. He analysed the Soviet policy as a form of doctrinal imperialism and urged the US to adopt a counter policy of "containment", that is, the construction of strong-points around the vast periphery of the Soviet Union to hold its expansionist propensities in check. The cold war which dominated the international scene for about fifteen years, following the Second World War, was officially, proclaimed by the US President Truman on March 12, 1947. Britain which had intervened in the Greek civil war, was unable to crush the communists. In this situation the American President delivered his Truman doctrine speech. His speech received overwhelming support from the Congress, and by the end of May 1947, Congressional legislation had enacted financial aid to Greece and Turky. In his speech Truman launched a vigorous attack against the Soviet Union. Referring to Poland, Rumania he pointed out that the people of these countries have recently had totalitarian regimes forced upon them against their will. Truman said "our way of life is based upon the will of the majority and is distinguished by free institutions, representative government, free elections, guarantee of individual liberty, freedom of speech, and freedom from political oppression it must the policy of the US to support free people who are resisting attempted subjugataion by armed minorities or by outisde pressure. The seeds of totalitariam regimes are nurtured by misery and want. They spread and grow in the evil soll of poverty and strife. The free peoples of the world look upon us for support in maintaining their freedom. If we falter in our leadership we may endanger the peace of the world, and we shall surely endanger the welfare of our own nation". The sweeping terms of the doctrine thus anticipated Americans armed intervention in any part of the world to prevent the spread of communism. The prime object of American "policy became the containment of communism".

Marshall Plan

The US had made important contributions to the alleviation of economic crisis. The European recovery programme commonly known as the Marshal Plan, was the extention of the American policy of containing communism in the economic field in the European continent. The announcement of the plan led to a further deterioration of American-Soviet relations. Under-secretary of States, Dean Acheson speaking of Europe's economic weakness declared, "without outside aid, the process of recovery in many countries would take so long as to give rise to hopelessness and despair. In these conditions freedom, democracy and independence of nations could not long survive, for helpless and hungry people often resort to desperate measures". At first American assistance was poured into Europe through the United Nation's relief and rehabilitation administration *UNRRA), but in June 1947 secretary of states, George Marshall anounced in a speech at Harvard University a new programme of aid to Europe, the marshal Plan, as it came to be called, which lasted until 1952. Marshall said, "The US should do whatever it is able to do to assist in the return of normal economic health in the world, without which there can be no political stability. Our policy is not directed against any country or doctrine but against hunger, poverty, desperation and chaos. Its purpose should be the revival of a working economy in the world so as to permit the emergence of political and social conditions in which free institutions can exist". The announcement was significant. It was made after the declaration of the Truman doctrine and moreover, the American aid to war–from Europe was flowing through the UNRRA. Why then did the US attempt to by pass the UN to finance the recovery of Europe? A meeting was convened to consider the Marshall offer. On 16th June, 1947, "pravda,", the Russian newspaper, commented "Marshall's Plan announced in his speech at Harvard is despite its apparent novelty, only a repetition of the Truman plan for political pressure with the help of dollars, a plan for inter ference in the domestic affairs of other countries." Moreover, when the Marshall Plan came up for discussion, the Soviet delegates asked the conditions under which the US aid would be forthcoming and no answers came up. The Soviet bloc refused to accept the plan, as the aid programme would impair the economic independence and sovereignty of the European states by allowing certain strong powers of some European countries against others in whatever way proved profitable in establishing their domination." The Marshall offer was converted into a western European recovery programme. Molotov, the Russian foreign minister denounced the whole idea as "dollar imperilism". Seeing it as a blatant American device for gaining control of western Europe, which Stalin considered to be in the Russian sphere of influence, Russia rejected the offer and the iron curtain seemed a reality. The stage was now set for the intensification of the cold war.

The Cominform/Comecon

It was this situation which led to the establishment in September 1947 of a communist information bureau (comminform) at a meeting of Communist parties summoned in Warsaw. This was an organisation to draw together the various European communist parties of Europe. All the satellite states were members and the French and Italian communits parties were represented. Stalin's aim was to tighten his grant on the satellite states. The purpose of the organisation was to provide the institutional framework and even more the covered behind which Eastern Europe could be forced into a concentrated mould. The communists in power have always regarded education and agitation as an essential part of government and terror. The cominform provided the resources the most important being, its Journal, for this kind of activity. Besides, the Molotov Plan was introduced, offering Russian aid to the satellites, and another organisation known an comecon (council of mutural economic assistance) was set up to coordinate their economic policies.

The Communist Takeover in Czechoslovakia

The communist takeover in Czechoslovakia came as a great blow to the western bloc because it was the only remaining democrataic state in Eastern Europe. After the great war a coalition government was formed under the communist leader Gottwald. However, a crisis arose in 1948, elections were due in may and all the signs were that the communists would lose ground. They were blamed for the Czech rejection of Marshall aid which might have alleviated the continuing food shortages. The communists decided to act before the elections, already in control of the union and the policy. They seized power in an armed coup. While thousands of armed workers paraded through prague. All non-communist ministers resigned. The elections were duly held in May 1948, but there was only a single list of candidates (all communists) Benes, the president resigned and Gottwald became president. The western powers protested, but could hardly taken any action, because they could not prove Russian involvement, the coup was purely an internal affairs. The Bridge between East and West was gone, the iron curtain was complete.

The German Problem

No part of the world escaped the Chills of the cold war but upto 1949 its main effects were centred in the problems of Germany that the most immediate confrontation of the two power blocks took place. The powers could not agree on a solution to the German problem. The problem continued to produce a great deal friction between the West and the Soviet

Union in the years after 1945. The allies began by dividing Germany into four Zones of occupation in accordance with their agreements at Yalta and Potsdam. All former German lands east of the oder-Neisse line were incorporated into either Poland or the USSR. The city of Berlin was also divided into four sectors. These divisions were meant to destroy militarism and Nazism in Germany and prepare the way for reconstruction and democracy. An allied control council representing the four occupying powers directed German affairs. Early co-operation between them to bring relief to the suffering people, quickly turned into distrust. The Russians felt fully justified in seeking compensation for the huge losses they had suffered in the war. They proceeded to take what they could from their zone, to press Germans to forced labour and to demand a share in the spoils of other zones. Each side accused the other of breaking faith in the potsdam agreement to treat Germany as a single economic unit. Ideological differences inevitably became involved in their disputes. The USSR fostered communism in the Russian zone. The discussion on the council of foreign ministers reached deadlock on the question of Germany's future. Suspicion between the two sides hardened into a cold war with an almost total lack of cooperation between them. Political and economic divisions between the East and West hardened in 1947 when the Truman doctrine and Marshall Plan gave clear indication that the USA intended to remain involved in Europe, a major departure from the USA's traditional isolationism. The USA was bent on the containment of communism. The USSR too was determined to limit US influence and would not yield the areas to which Soviet authority had already spread.

The new currency for the western zones produced an immediate confrontation over Berlin. In March 1948, the Russians began harassing the communications of the western powers with their sectors of Berlin. On 24 June 1948 all land communications with Berlin were cutoff. The million citizens in the western sectors of Berlin seemed likely to starve. The west considered withdrawal, but that had the smell of appeasement. It was decided to ferry supplies by air, and for almost a year this was west-Berlin's only source of supply. Day and night, the air-lift went on and, in May 1949, Stalin agreed to raise the blockade. Although neither side gained from the confrontatin, but it made both sides even more stubborn. Their stubbornness became more prominent in the establishment of separate and independent states in Germany. In the west, the Federal republic of Germany came into existence, under chancellor Adenauer, with the capital at Bonn. With American support it established a leading role in the political and economic balance of western Europe. The communist response in East Germany was the Democratic people's republic, which was set up under Soviet protection.

Although discussions between West and East about a peace treaty for Germany continued to take place from time to time, neither side would abandon its own German State in order to bring about one, United German nations.

The West Consolidates

Whether the west-over-estimated the threat in 1948-49 is open to question. The communist world was not without its own troubles, as Stalin's bitter quarrel with Marshall Tito and the expulsion of Yugoslavia from the cominform showed, and the next few years were to see much internal conflict, within the communist world. The international situation was very tense and the Berlin blockade had taken its toll of confidence. As a result, twelve founder members, led by the USA, in 1949 formed the North Atlantic Treaty Organisation (NATO) with its head quarter in Paris for mutual defence against armed attack on any one of them, and to promote stability in the North Atlantic area. At the same time, Western Europe began to draw together through the council of Europe, through the Benelux custom union, and the Schuman Plan for pooling mineral resources, into the beginning of a regional unity which might serve to protect her from the political and economic as well as the military, Chills of the cold war.

[Effect of China's Revolation and the Korean War Policy of Containment in Asia]

The second phase of the cold war began in 1949, When the Soviet Union exploded the atomic bomb, which broke the American monopoly. On 1st October, 1949 the people's republic of China, under Mao-Tse-Tung, was proclaimed. This communist success, (which was an almost totally unexpected piece of news to the west) was among the crowded events of a crowded year, to prove a turning point in world affairs. It spelt the end of the long cherished American aim to stabilise China under. Chiang-kai-Shek. It faced the USA with the appalling prospect of an immense, if as yet untried, communist extention in the very head of Asia and on the dour step of occupied Japan. Overnight the communist cold war threat seemed almost doubled. The sheer physical size of Russia and China, and of their combined population, was a daunting challenge to the American policy of containment. The massive sucessful intrusion of communism in the Asia had, moreover, come at a time when the continent was in the throes of political and social upheavals.

The potentiality of China in the cold war was revealed at once in the Korean war which began in June 1950 with the invasion of South Korean republic by the communist forces of North Korea. A united force under American command, was sent to the frontier between the two koreas on the 38th parallel in order to restore international peace and security to support the freedom of South Korea and 'contain' the communist threat. In the struggle that followed, China came openly to the help of the North Koreans and it became clear that Stalin was using China to fight his battles for him in this area of Asia. President Truman insisted that conflict in Korea should remain a limited war, in keeping with the American policy of containment. And when General Mac-Arthur, tried to carry the struggle over into an out right war with China, on Chinese territory, he was overruled and dismissed. The Korean war ended, after an uneasy truce in 1952, by President Eisenhower.

Korea provided the unfortunate battle ground for one of the trials of strength which were to mark the course of the cold war. The Korean war was fought with all the ferocity of civil and ideological strife, and the outcome established the frontier along the same parallel where the war had started. If it could be regarded as a success for the "free" world, a finger of warning was raised against communism by a limited war, it nevertheless answered very few questions and posed many new ones.

The Korean war, together with the death of Stalin, may be said to mark the end of an evolutionary stage in a cold war, whose origin lies in the strains of wartime alliance. The two richest and most powerful survivors of the Second World War, the USA and the USSR, had marked out a course in world affairs in which political, economic, military and ideological pressures all played. Moreover, the diplomacy of cold war had revealed itself as a dangerous form of "brinkmanship" where the smallest error of judgement or failure of nerve could have world-wide consequences. In the years after 1953 the cold war conflict entered a more complex phase. A new generation of world leades was emerging. The simplifications of the immediate post-war, East-West division of 'two world' fast became blurred by the rise of newly independent states from among the old European colonial empires. The UN itself was transformed by the activities of a 'third world' of neutralist states in Asia and Africa many of which hoped to reject the blandishment of both sides in the cold war strugle. At the same time, nuclear rivalry between the two protagonists was fast approaching a climax in a state of statemate of bears which was the unhealthy and unexpected peace time off-spring of the war time ground alliance against the dictator.

SEATO, CENTO AND INDO-CHINA AFFAIRS

The year 1953 was a turning point in the history of the cold war when John Foster Dulles, the new Secretary of States, replaced Washington's policy of containment by the doctrine of liberation or rolling back communism, that is open threat of attack upcn the socialist countries. He described such tactics as "brinkmansltip". He still believed that an American nuclear blow from the air or even such a threat was capable of solving the problems of the enemies of socialism. Under his guidance, American built up the South East Asia Treaty Organisation (SEATO) in September 1954. The west discovered, that Russian communism was not the only communism against which to build barriers. The success of communists in China caused considerable anxiety to the USA. The communists were also successful in Korea. Communist guerrilla were very much active in Malaya, where the communists party had been banned since 1926 but where communism had gained popularity in resistance to the Japanese. The USA took the main burden of resistance Vigorous efforts were made to rebuild Japan in the image of the USA and to ring China with American bases. In the ANZUS. (A ustralia-New Zealand and USA) Pact of 1951, the USA gave guarantee of protection to the pacific countries. In 1954, the ANZUS powers, together with Britain, France, Pakistan, the Philippines and Thailand joined together in the SEATO, for collective action against aggression and subversion. Similarly the USA build up the middle East defense organisation in February 1955 with a view to crushing the national liberation ınovement in the Middle East and communist movement in general. Later on, in 1959 the central treaty organisation (CENTO) came into existence, which was built on the foundation of Middle East treaty organisation. Thus, CENTO was seen both in the East and West as another barrier against communism. This period also witnessed the beginning of Vietnam crisis involving both the super powers. The communists were in control of North Vietnam under Ho-Chi-Minh. The defeat of Japan in 1945 did not lead to the freedom for Indo-China (Vietnam). Ho-Chi-Minh's Vietnam Government was recognised by the USSR and China Vietnam was divided into two parts, at the 17th parallel. From this division developed the most prolonged confrontataion and bloodiest conflict between the USA and communism. USA took it upon itself to keep communism out of South Vietnam . But the long drawn conflict in Indo-China went in favour of the communist and the socialist Republic of Vietnam was proclaimed in 1976. It was a devastated land, blasted by years of savage conflict with the US, its soil polluted by US Chemical weapons, the communists had won the competition with the USA and the whole of Indo-China had gone communist after the US retreat.

A Thaw in the Cold War After 1953

There came a shift in Soviet policy following the death of Stalin. The death of Stalin brought to the forefront new leaders Malenkov, Bulganin and Nikita Khrushchev, who wanted to improve relations with the US. Their reasons were possibly connected with the fact that by 1953 the

Russians as well as the Americans had developed the hydrogen bomb. Recognising that the cold war had reached a dangerous stalemate and had to be liquidated, in the twentieth communist party Congress, held in Moscow. Khrushchev delivered a massive onslaught on Stalin and all that stalinism stood for. The possibility of the co-existence of capitalism and communism side by side was out lined, on the grounds that nuclear weapons were now making the older and simpler idea of permanent military war on capitalism meaningless. He emphasised that struggle with capitalism would go on, but with other weapons and in other spheres. He said that peaceful co-existence with the west was essential because there were only two ways, either peaceful co-existence or, the most destructive war in history. In 1955 the Russians gave up their military bases in Finland, and Bulganin attended a summit meeting in Geneva in 1955 where he met the US President Eisenhower. This summit did not produce any effective result, but it showed that the USA was gradually coming round to the principle of peaceful coexistence proclaimed by the Soviet Union. This was followed by cultural and political exchanges, mutual visits of the heads of government of the West and East and the "Camp David" spirit. The Soviet Union agreed to most of the important points in the Anglo-French disarmament plan in the sub-committee of the UN disarmament commission. The quarrel with Yogoslavia ended when Khrushchev paid a visit to Tito and the Cominform was abandoned, suggesting more freedom for the satellite states. Having stalled for years in the negotitations for a peace treaty with Austria, Russia now gave way on most of the points about which she had formerly prevaricated and agreed to the creation of an independent neutralised Austria. Probably Russia hoped in this way to enhance, the allurements of neutralisation for west Germany which had just joined the NATO alliance. It seemed that a new era of cordiality had begun for East-West relations.

Revolution in Eastern Europe and Warsaw Pact

Yugoslavia was the only satellite country that showed a spirit of revolt towards Moscow in the Stalin years. The actions of the new Russian Government at Moscow towards the satellites were typical of the period of thaw. Inside Poland many who had been imprisoned during the purges of Stalin's later years were released in 1956. The workers took this opportunity to indulge in strikes which developed into revolt that had to be suppressed by troops in July 1956. Nevertheless, the polish communist leader Gomulka, released from imprisonment, was able to make a popular stand against the Russians, and far greater degree of independence was allowed to him after the uprising. In Hungary a similar rising took place in 1956. In the earlier part of the year opposition to Rakosi mounted. In the prevailing climate of opinion Rakosi was compelled to resign. In October an all party government was formed under Imre-Nagy. In November Nagy declared that he would adopt a policy in Hungary similar to that taken by Tito in Yugoslavia and appealed for the assistance of the UN to maintain Hungarian independence. Prior to the formation of Nagy's Government came an Anti-Russian uprising centred in Budapest, which for three days was the scene of much rioting, deepening into civil war. Such insubordination could not be allowed by Russia and on November 4th, 1956, Russian tanks entered Budapest and with in a week, the revolution was at an end. The Russians appointed Jones Kadar as Prime Minister of Hungary. The events in Hungary were a cause of disillusion to many who disliked their communist leaders, as some hope had been cherised that the western powers might aid such a revolution. Infact, the western powers were concerned with the Suez affairs in the middle-East. The suppression of the revolution owed further that Russia intended to keep control of the satellites, and to keep them as communist states. Meanwhile, the Warsaw pact was signed in 1955 between Russia and her satellite states shortly after West Germany was admitted to NATO. The pact was a mutual defence agreement which the west took as a gesture against German membership of NATO.

Aim Race, ICBM, Sputnik

There was another major development of both ideological and strategic importance in Europe. Yugoslavia had refused some of Stalin's demands and was, in effect expelled from a communist bloc. She became, under Marshal Tito, a pioneer non-aligned country. This was the first hint that there could differences within the socialist world. Towards the end of 50s, the communist bloc began to witness a breach as manifested in the Sino-Soviet rift. Similarly, in the suez crisis France, Britain and Israel invaded Egypt. This is important in any study of bipolarity as both the USA and the USSR are agreed on the need to give some support to Nasser, of Egypt. Although it did not lead any irreparable breach in the Western alliance but it showed that there were moments when the allies could act differently due to the divergent perception of their individual interest. It seemed that there is differences within both the camps.

But the most important event which underlined the change in American foreign policy was that in October 1957. The soviet Union launched into space man's first artificial satellite (sputnik) to circle the earth and send back messages to its launchers. This event, besides filling Americans with a quick unnecessary dread and envy of Russian's technological superiority, showed that no spot on the globe was too-remote for the USSR to reach with its nuclear war-headed missiles (Inter continental ballastic missiles, ICBM) despatched was unerring the accuracy. As America speedily caught up in missile race and as both super powers buried their (ICBM) deep in concrete silos and in submarines which could disappear beneath the seas for months, America and Russia now achieve second strike nuclear capability. Neither super powers could hence-forth launch a surprise attack on the other and leave it entirely without the nuclear capability to retaliate with devastating effect. This meant that neither super-powers was quite so dependent on its allies as it had been in the past since both now had the means of striking directly. Hence taking into account the unparalleled destructiveness of all out nuclear war, the issue on which the super-powers were willing to fight each other to the death were gradually reduced until the only one left was that of their own national security

Berlin the Focus of East-West Tension

Beginning in 1958 a protracted crisis developed, in which the East German Government, encouraged by the Russia asserted that the old wartime occupation zones of Berlin which had been settled at potsdam in 1945 were now a dead letter, and that the whole of Berlin was self-evidently integral part of East Germany. At the sametime they putforward schemes for some amalgamation of the two Germany's which would be a prelude to German unification. The terms was unacceptable to the west. Russians threatened to completed separate peace treaty with East Germany. The western power had an important state in Berlin and did not intend to forfeit it, and the only terms on which they would discuss Germanreunification-free elections in both East and West Germany were unacceptable to Russia. The crisis continued on its uneasy way through 1959-60. Form time to time planes from the Germany were interfered world as they flew along the corridors which linked west Berlin to the outside world. With a rising flood of refugees to the West, the East Germans decided to 'seal' the frontier by building the Berlin wall, a physical barrier of concrete and barbed wire. The west made no attempt to demolish the wall, but Soviet and American ranks lined up against each other on either side of it, and dangerous incidents frequently added to the tension at the wall's official crossing place, check point "Charlie".

The U-2 Incident and the Cuban Missil Crisis

The building of the Berlin wall brought the crisis to a high peak of tension and, as a result, American forces were built up to new strength in Western Europe. In 1960 it was khrushchev's turn to feel aggrieved when an American U-2 spy plane was shot down over a thousand miles inside Russia. President Eisenhower declined to apologise, defending American's right to make reconnaissance flights and the affairs ruined the summit conference, which was about to begin in Paris. The event gave Khrushchev a good cause for self-righteous indignation in his condemnation of American spying.

The Cuba crisis brought the cold war into the very heart of the American hemisphere. In Cuba there was a communist government under Fidel Castro. Both the Soviet Union and Cuba meantime drew closer to each other. Russia began to supply arms to castro, ostensibly for Cuban defence. It was soon clear, as a result of air reconnaissance; that Cuba was building nuclear missile bases. By 1962 Kennedy, the American president had certain proof of the imminent delivery of Soviet nuclear missiles whose range would, easily, embrace the whole American continent. The moment of truth arrived. On 22nd October, 1962 President Kennedy, no longer able to ignore the threat to American safety, proclaimed a naval blockade of Cuba to put an end to this clandestine, reckless and provocative threat to world peace. After four days, the Russian leader indicated, through the UN, that they were ready to dismantle bases in Cuba if America would do so in Turky. But Kennedy did not answer. Finally, Khrushchev agreed unconditionally to remove the missiles. War had been averted and the crisis faded. But the crisis had important consequences. The enormity of what might have happened seemed to bring both sides to their senses and produced a marked relaxation of tension. A telephone link (the hot line) was introduce between Moscow and Washington to allow swift consultation. The Caribbean crisis demonstrated the futility of nuclear diplomacy and the hollowncess of the policy of confrontation. In fact, the sixites provided a comparative period of lult. in the relations between the two super powers.

Co-Existence–"The Thaw"

It is difficult to identify the exact moment at which the cold war began to 'thaw'. Although the 1960s opened inauspiciously with the summit fiasco in Paris and went on unpromisingly with the escalation of the war in Vietnam, the decade overall saw a considerable improvement in East-West relations. President Kennedy advocated peaceful co-existence of different states in the course of his speech at the American university, Washington on June 3, 1963. "Today... it is ironical but certain fact that the two strongest powers are the two in the most danger of devastation and we are both caught up in a vicious and dangerous cycle... in which new weapons beget counter weapons. Let us direct our attention to common interests and to the means by which those differences can be resolved...." In terms of US foreign policy, kennedy's speech heralded a radical departure from the established cold war dogmas. No subject was debated more earnestly after 1945 than disarmament, but nothing what ever was achieved until 1963, was reached by the three nuclear power at a meeting in Moscow. They agreed to cease testing nuclear weapons in the atmosphere or under water, with a view to limiting radioactive debris. Yet, the nuclear powers continued to test weapons underground. Further progress was delayed by an argument about an American plan to create a single nuclear force for NATO which, the USSR objected. The USA abandoned the plan and further discussion between Johnson (USA) and Kosygin (USSR) led to the singing of the Nuclear non-proliferation treaty in 1968. Its aim was to prevent the further spread of nuclear weapons. The nuclear powers undertook not to transfer such weapons to other states and an attempt was made to offer greater security to non-nuclear countries, and to discourage them from embarking on the manufacture of atomic bombs. Anyhow, the treaties of 1963 and 1968 could become the foundation for further agreement. The super powers edged towards peaceful co-existence and new impetus was added to the movement when Willy Brandt became the Chancellor of west Germany in 1969 and pursued the ostpolitik (Eastern Policy). His aim was to establish more normal relations across the iron curtain. To achieve this aim he accepted oder-Neisse line as the permanent boundary between West Germany and Poland, which was vital in easing relations between West-Germany and Eastern Europe. A non-aggression treaty was signed between Bonn and Moscow and he also accepted the existence of East Germany. In the meantime the four powers agreed on a pact on Berlin which eased communication within the city. East-West relations were now improving markedly, not only between Moscow-Washington but also between China and the West. Communist China was admitted to the UN in 1971. President Nixon visited peking in February 1972 and Moscow in May, adding to the growing good will by seeking at the same time to bring to an end the war in Vietnam.

Brezhnev, Nixon and their ministers scribbled their signatures, piling-up agreements and apparently burying past differences under expressions of goodwill. Both the leaders concluded the famous SALT (strategic arms limitation treaty) in 1972, fixing limits on missiles and their locations. Other agreements dealt with space research, trade and pollution. The US-Soviet commission set up to discuss trade produced many new commercial exchanges, and cooperation in space led to the Apollo-Soyuz link up in 1975. Besides, the European negotiations bore fruit in 1975 when in USA, Canada and the European nations met in Helsinki in the conference on security and cooperation in Europe (CSCE). Peaceful co-existence, it seemed, had been achieved, but had it actually been? However, certain problems like the Indian Ocean, Arab-Israel conflict, America's armed built up in Iran still persisted. The great powers tasted a new cold war, when Soviet forces invade Afghanistan in 1979. President Carter and his adviser Brezenski imposed economic embargo on many items and even the West (boycotted the Moscow Olympic in 1980. Gorbachev's (Russia) political philosophy ruled in the 1986 Reyjkavek summit and his Geneva programme of nuclear disarmament war partially achieved. In the meantime, Japan and Germany emerged as the two powerful forces in the economic sense. With the collapse of communist regime in East Europe in 1989 the Soviet bloc withered away. In 1991 the strategy arms reduction treaty was signed between Bush and Gorbachev. With the disintegration of Soviet Union, Bork Yeltsin (Russian Federation President) and President Bush made a formal declaration regarding the end of the cold war. An enlarged Europe with a unified Germany at its heart is as powerful a pole as the two super powers today. The world is moving slowly into a multi-power arrangements. The cold war has far-reaching repercussion in international relations. The UN became a platform for the rival propaganda and during the cold war period the shadow of Hiroshima deepened into a dark cloud of nuclear rivalry among the power. Naturally the death of the cold war led to the reconciliation between the two super powers which would facilitate amicable settlement of long standing disputes. Certainly it would lead to the birth of a new world free from military alliances and armament race. Probably the birth of the non-alignment movement was one of the greatest by-products in a polarise world politics. The third world countries became a prey at the hands of the big powers, but then the process of decolonisation speeded up.

Certain international crisis like the West Asia conflict, Indo-Pak problem and the difficulties in the formation of a generally acceptable disarmament treaty tended to produce tensions and crises in international scene. But the 'big' question still persists–Is the cold war over? Many optimists inclined a answer in the affirmative, and few in the negative. No doubt it is a matter of speculation only. Anyhow, it has disappeared and a new world order is in the offing.

Chapter XXVII

Foreign Policy of India

(1947-1971)

In the world that has over 185 Nation-States, who are most of the time interacting with each other, the importance of foreign policy cannot be underestimated. Each country identifies its national interests and subject to the availability and nature of determinats, formulates its foreign policy. India has pursued a carefully formulated foreign policy during the fifty period since independence. The policy of non-alignment adopted in view of the then prevailing cold war has successfully stood the test of time. India tried to maintain friendly relations with both the power blocks. India believes in peaceful settlement of international disputes, and friendly cooperation with all countries and particularly its neighbour.

According to J. Bandopadhaya, "basic determinants of foreign policy include geography, economic development, political traditions, domestic millieu, international millieu, military strength and national character".

India has the heritage of an ancient civilisation and culture. The foreign policy that India formulated after independence reflected our foreign policy makers had before them the teachings of Kautilya, the realist. They were also impressed by the Buddhist traditions of Ashoka, the great, who advocated peace, freedom and equality. India's foreign policy is determined largely in accordance with the ideals of our freedom struggle, Gandhian philosophy and the fundamental principle of Indian tradition of Vasudhaiva Kutumbak (the world as one family). Further, the personality of Nehru has had a direct impact.

India achieved independence on August 15, 1947, that immediately necessitated foreign policy making by this country. India became a member of international community. In 1948, the congress party stated in a foreign policy resolution, "The foreign policy of India must necessarily be based on principles that have guided the congress in past years. These principles are the promotion of world peace, the freedom of nations, racial equality and the ending of imperialism and colonialism—— With a view to advancing the cause of world peace and cooperation, India associated herself with the united Nations". Jawaharlal Nehru was the Prime Minister and foreign minister from 1947 till his death in 1964. The foundations of India's foreign policy were firmly laid by him. Like any other foreign policy maker, Nehru underlined India's national interest as the basic guiding principle. In a broadcast to the nation he had said on September 7, 1946, "We shall take full part in international conferences as a free nation with our own policy and not merely as a satellite of another nation. We hope to develop close and direct contacts with other nations and to cooperate with them in the furtherance of world peace and freedom...". Many people are amazed to see how India could manage to maintain friendly relations with countries on both sides of the so-called "iron curtain". In December 1947, Nehru declared with equal emphasis, "We intend cooperating with the United States of American and we intend cooperating fully with the Soviet Union". When India emerged on the map of the world as a Sovereign State in 1947, she was fortunate in having no traditional enemies and no vested interests in world affairs. India has never been in favour of participation in any military alliance either bilaterally or multi-laterally. It has always been opposed to any military alliance either bilaterally or multi-laterally. It has always been opposed to any military approach to world problems. Since the advent of the cold war the U.S.A and the Soviet Union have been engaged in an arms-race, including the building up of nuclear weapons and in forging military alliances against each other. India believed that this only helped accentuating tension between nations resulting into armed conflicts. Indian foreign policy has been an independent foreign policy not tied to any of the two contending power blocs. It was, however, not a neutral foreign policy. Infact, India has never been neutral on international issues. It has judged every issue on its merits. Nehru has opposed "trying to align ourselves (India) with great powers or that and becoming its camp-follower in the hope that some curmbs might fall from their tables". Indian foreign policy aimed at maintaining her freedom of political manoeuvre. India wants to be able to determine her foreign policy as independently of external commitments as is possible in this dependent world. Nehru's neutrality is far from being a scuttle from reality or a desire to keep out of trouble at all costs. Nehru is not an isolationalist.

Apart from friendship with all nations, which might have been influenced by the Gandhian doctrine as well as national tradition, there were two commitments which have since become the keynotes of Indian foreign policy, first to end racial discrimination and second, to help free the countries of Asia from political and social bondage. Having herself suffered all the evils of colonialism and imperialist domination, India was inevitably committed to this cause. According to W. Levi, "This sweeping aim to wipe out imperialism and racism every where is advanced in the belief that there can be no real freedom for any nation and no equality for Indians in particular as long as recial discrimination continues... closely related to this aim, and its final purpose, is equality of status for Asian nations in international councils".

Basic Principles of India's Foreign Policy

As early as 1925 the Indian National Congress had established the four cardinal points that determine India's path in world affairs today. These are opposition to imperialism and colonial rule, support of subject peoples and oppressed races in their struggle for freedom and equality, promotion of peace and abhorrence of war, and avoidance of foreign entanglements. The relationship India desires with other countries was splled-out in a statement of the Five Principles (Pancha Sheel). The Chinese and Indian Governments, on the initative of Jawaharlal Nehru, formulated the following scheme for the regulation of their relations with one another, Mutual respect for each other's territorial integrity and soverignity, Non-aggression, Non-interference in each other's internal affairs, Equality and Mutual benefit, and peaceful co-existence. Nehru said, "these principles indicate the policy that we pursue not only in regard to China or with any neighbouring country, or for the matter of that any other country. They also constitute a statement of wholesome principles and imagine that if these principles were adopted in the relations of various countries with one another, a great deal of the trouble of the present day world disappear". The most important aspect of panchsheel is peaceful co-existence. The principles contained in Panchsheel were, According to Nehru, a consequence of democratic outlook. The idea of peaceful co-existence is morally so correct that it allows all countries to follow their ideology without interfering in internal affairs of the other.

In the early years of independence the Indian foreign policy was described as "neutral" foreign policy by some people, because India wanted to keep herself away from the blocs, i.e. the Western and the Soviet blocs. But neutrality is a legal concept, and India has never been neutral in that sense. So the foreign policy of India should be called an independent foreign policy not neutral. The term "Non-alignment" got currency in the post-Bandung conference (1955) phase, and the first conference of the non-alingned group of countries was held in 1961 in Belgrade. The concept of non-alignment is India's greatest conribution to international relations. The policy of non-alignment was to keep away from bloc politics. Nehru said that, "India did not belong to any power blocs, India's non-alignment is a positive, or dynamic, neutralism, in which a country acts independently, and decides its position on each international issue on the merit of the Cause". The policy of non-alignment pursued by India provides the best conditions for realising India's aims, clearning up the remnants of colonial rule, industrialising the country and raising living standards. Non-alignment means refusal to acept definite commitments to or to join system of alliances or pacts. But it has nothing to do with neutrality or passivity. According to M.S. Rajan, "Non-alignment stands for abstention from power politics, for peaceful co-existence and for active international cooperation among all states-aligned or non-aligned". Non-alignment was adopted by India as a means of foreign policy in order to ensure fuller meaning and content to our newly achieved political independence. Non-alignment was not a result of ad hoc decision, rather, it was well thoughtout and well planned policy. Its ultimate objective was promotion of national interest.

The non-alignment Nehru stood for meant a struggle against the aggressive blocs set up as weapons of neo-colonialism, active opposition to the arms race, the cold war and the positions of strength policy. The government of India helped bring an end the wars in Korea and Indo-China, insisted on the withdrawl of U.S. and British troops from the Middle East resolutely condemned the establishment of SEATO. The goal of non-alignment is peace. That is why India has been a staunch supporters of disarmament and the ban on nuclear weapons from the very start. India has opposed the Western powers attempts to turn the U.N. into a weapon of their aggressive policy. India has always worked for disarmament at the international levels. When the charter of the United Nations was being framed, India kept itself closely associated with that process. In order to ahieve international disarmament, Article 11 of the charter said that the General assembly may consider the general principles of cooperation in the maintenance of international peace and security, including the principles governing disarmament and the regulation of armaments...". India supported the formation of Atomic energy commission in 1947 and sponsored 18 nations disarmament conference in 1962. The Valuable service rendered by India to the UNO to preserve the world peace were acknowledge by the U.N. Secretary General Hammarskjold. India pleaded for just solution of Arab-Israel conflict. India participated in U.N. military operation in Congo for the latter's unification. India has continuously supported the efforts for universalisation of the United Nations.

In the struggle against racialism and colonialism, India has historically played an important role, being in a way the heart of the oldest of the modern empires. The Indian struggle against recial discrimination in South Africa started long ago. India is committed to oppose the policy of apartheid pursued by South Africa. This policy of racial discrimination has jeopardized the political and civil rights of the coloured people of South Africa. India has raised her voice at Various international forums against this policy. India has supported the cause of the Negroes in the united States and the black majority in Rhodesia against the white minority. In 1952, India along with 12 other Afro-Asian countries, raised the question of apartheid at the U.N. and asserted that its practice not only constituted a flagrant violation of the U.N. charter, but also constituted a serious threat to world peace.

Anti-colonialism has been one of the main planks of Indian foreign policy. Indian leaders are proud of their anti-imperialist tradition and still proclaim themselves to be champions of the oppressed peoples in Asia and Africa. India stands for a policy of non-intervention in the internal affairs of other countries. In the recovery of Indonesian independence, India is supposed to have played an important part. According to Nehru, "Asia till recently was largely a prey to imperial domination and colonialism a great part of it is free today, part of it still remains unfree and it is an astonishing thing that any country still ventures to hold and to set forth this doctrine of colonialism whether it is under direct rule or whether it is indirectly maintained in some from or another. We, in Asia, who have ourselves suffered all these evils of colonialism and imperial domination have committed ourselves inevitably to freedom of other colonial countries". Now that colonialism and imperialism have been terminated, one may think that there is no relevance of this principle any more. But most of Afro-Asian countries are now being subjected to a new form of colonialism, commonly known as "Neo-Colonialism". India is determined to oppose neo-colonialism as it aims at exploitation which may eventually lead to political control. India's policy of freedom of depentent peoples has now acquired new dimensions as it seeks freedom from new form of economic slavery.

India firmly believed that economic development of the country was an urgent necessity. Soon after independence India devoted its energies to a planned development. India needed economic assistance as well as loans for numerous projects that it wanted to start in the process of multi-facted development of the country. The financial and technological help that we needed could come either from the U.S. or the Soviet Union. The business community in India as well as the government realised that the only country that could give substantial help was the U.S.A. Still the government did not want to compromise with the principle of non-alignment, independence and soverignity of the country. As the process of development was acclerated, India began accepting aid from the world bank and a number of other countries. India tried to maintain independence in decision making and foreign policy.

India was not merely satisfied to adopt policy of non-alignment but also tried to promote the spirit of cooperation and peaceful coexistance among the states professing different ideologies. It was in the spirit of peaceful co-existence and co-operation that India laid great emphasis on the settlement of disputes peacefully. Although India had to face wars imposed on her, its faith in pacific means is not shaken.

In so far as India's nuclear policy is concerned it is the same as before, unless nuclear powers ban nuclear tests and undertake to eliminate atomic stockpile's, India cannot accept discriminatory safeguards which inhibits peaceful nuclear programme.

India and the Super Powers

India tried to balance its relations with the super powers and other major powers right from its independence. Both the super powers with faith in their respective ideologies looked with suspicion towards each other. When India gained independence it had option to join either of the two power blocs. However, India decided to keep away form both these blocs, and adopted policy of non-alignment.

The history of India's relations with the United States has been marked by a series of ups and downs. Though India was indebted to Reosevelt for his support during the indpendence struggle, the U.S. took little interest in the region, till the rise of communism in China. From 1948 to the beginning of the Korean war in 1950, India committed to accept United State's advice over a large area of its foreign policy. The U.S. regarded India as the signpost of parliamentary democracy in the East and spared no pains to influence New Delhi in order to win its over to her side in the newly emerging cold war. But as the Korean war progressed, India showed her inability to support some American moves relating to the war which in India's view were likely to aggravate and prolong the conflict. India did not approve of the American policy of containment of communism against Soviet Union and China through a system of military alliances, and sought to promote a climate of peaceful co-existance and cooperation. India adopted a neutralist policy in the cold war politics. Pakistan became a member of both the military organisations (SEATO and CENTO) and received massive U.S. military and economic assistance. India regarded those military alliances as the extention of the cold war to Asia, and therefore opposed them gradually. Further, in the U.N. security council, U.S.A. had on Several occasions supported Pakistan stand on Kashmir. Thus, the U.S. took partisan approach on the Kashmir issue and the relations between the two countries came under heavy strain. However, the relations between the two countries in the economic, cultural and educational spheres continued to grow and the U.S. provided valuable assistance to India under the technical cooperation agreement of 1951.

The Sino-Indian conflict of 1962 introduced a new element in the Indo-U.S. relations. A common element of China's hostility towards the U.S. and India now induced a new mood in this country. The U.S. provided India with the useful moral and material help. Voices arose in India for an alliance with the U.S. against China. However, with the withdrawl of military forces by China from most of Indian territory and generally pro-Indian stand of the Soviet Union, India returned to the earlier Non-aligned position. The united States involvement in Vietnam and her military assistance to Pakistan increased during Johnson's presidency and they worsened the relations between the two countries. The use of American arms by Pakistan during Indo-Pak war of 1965 embittered Indo-U.S. relations. The pro-Pakistan attitude of the U.S. caused tension in Indo-U.S. relations. However, American leaders took no action in this regard and continued to maintain a pro-Pakistan stand. These worsening relations reahced their lowest ebb during the Bangladesh war and Indo-Pakistani war in 1971, when the Nixon administration openly supported Pakistan and even tried to intimidate India and weaken her war effort through the deployment of a naval task force (the fleet) and other provocative exercises. Sharp differences remained on U.S. arms supplies to Pakistan, the West Asian conflict and the war in Vietnam. The perception of the two countries of their interest in Asia in particular, and the developing countries and the world in general has for most of the time, been fairly divergent. The visit of secretary of state Henry Kissinger in New Delhi marked the beginning of the resumption of friendly talks between the two countries. The positive trend in Indo-U.S. relations that had become evident in recent years were consolidated. It is hoped that there will be better understanding and fruitful cooperation between the U.S.A. and India.

The Soviet Union had supported India's struggle for independence. After 1947 the developments in the international scene brought the two countries, further closer to each other. The Soviet leaders were impressed due to India's decision to recognise the people's Republic of China, its support to anti-colonial struggle at the U.N., its efforts to establish ceasefire in korea, its refusal to be a part of alliances against the Soviet Union etc. After the Korean crisis the relations between the two countries began to improve, though in the early phase of the crisis a serious tension had developed between India and the Soviet Union. When India accepted the security council resolution in June 1950 describing North Korea as the aggressor, the Soviet Union adopted a hostile posture. But later, when India strongly criticised the U.S. particularly General Mac Arthur, for having threatened China after penetrating deep into North Korea, the entire communist world was appreciative of India's stand. One area in which Soviet Union has solidly stood by India was in regard to India's dispute with Pakistan. The Soviet Union vehmently opposed the sending of foreign forces to Kashmir. The two countries adopted the identical position on the Suez crisis in 1956 and condemned the Anglo-French-Israeli aggression against Egypt. However, some misunderstanding developed between the two countries on the question of Hungary. But the relations between the two countries continued to grow despite the Hungarian episode. In 1961 when India used its armed forces for the liberation of Goa from the portuguese, Soviet Union extended full support to Indian position. During the Sino-Indian conflict in 1962, the Soviet Union practically stood behind India. When Pakistan attacked India in the Kutch area in 1965, the Soviet Union supported India and offered to mediate in the Indo-Pak dispute. It was on the initiative of the Soviet premier Kosygin that India and Pakistan signed an agreement at Tashkent which established peace in the Sub-Continent.

It is largely due to Soviet assistance that India has created a powerful public sector which today (1970-75) commands more than 25 per cent of her economy, and has laid foundations for an impressive industrial and agricultural development.

The 1971 Indo-Pak war clearly demonstrated that India has become self confident in her defence capacity. The reason is not far to seek. The public sector projects are, in many cases, in a position to switch on to defence production in times of emergency. But it is also to be admitted that the Soviet Union is India's main supplier of sophisticated defence equipment which were not forth coming from any other source. On 9th August, 1971 as a result of prime minister Indira Gandhi's State visit to the Soviet Union, the 20 year Indo-Soviet treaty was signed. The treaty provided a political and legal basis for further cooperation between the two countries in political, economic, cultural, technical and scientific fields. One important aspect of the treaty was the assurance that in the event of an attack or threat there of, the two sides shall immediately enter into mutual consultations in order to remove such a threat and take appropriate measures to ensure peace and security of their countries. The historic treaty was the culmination of a two and half decades of Indo-Soviet understanding and cooperation in many spheres which has been a model of peaceful co-existance between two different social system.

In the economic, scientific and cultural spheres also the relations between India and Soviet Union have consistently grown. Soviet Union assisted India in he setting up of the steel and iron factory at Bhilai. In 1963 India and Soviet Union entered into an agreement under which Soviet Union provided technical aid to India to explore and develop oil and gas. The iron and steel factories at Bokaro and Bhilai were further expanded with the help of Soviet Union. Relations between India and Soviet Union grew closer over the years.

India and the Common–Wealth

There is no doubt that the Republican India has a sort of unique relationship with the commonwealth, where, previously allegiance to the crown was supposed to be the only binding link between the self-governing countries. K.M. Panikkar has very ably pointed out that the policy of a state is determined by its geographical position, the object of all policy is territorial security, and this is governed predominantly by geographical factors. Panikhar has effectively developed the argument that whatever the political status of India, a close and intimate association in defence policy between the British empire and India is no less than essential for the security of India and is inevitable. When India became a sovereign republic in 1950, she retained her membership of the commonwealth, recognising the British monarch as titular head of that body, a sort of symbol of the common bond between independent member states. But the queen is not the sovereign in India, as she is in the dominions. There was some opposition in India, but Nehru was the chief defender of commonwealth link. He said it had obvious advantages. For one thing, the continuous exchange of information and consultations among commonwealth capitals is of great value in determining the day to day course of foreign affairs. India's adherence to the sterling bloc, with its currency backed by reserves in Britain, is another reasons. India sees some advantage in the field of diplomacy from her membership with the commonwealth is consistent with India's policy of friendship with all nations. During the Sino-Indian war (1962) some commonwealth countries were the first to come to her aid. Britain herself highly values India's membership of commonwealth because India is the most populous commonwealth country and is the largest democracy in the world. Membership of the commonwealth is also supposed to have affected the economic soverignity of India through the maintenance of the imperial preference. Economically India benefits from her membership of the sterling area. For some years after 1947 the commonwealth continued to be the vehicle for India's contacts with a wider international arena. In defending his decision not to repudiate commonwealth membership, Nehru told the Indian Parliament, "If we dissociated ourselves from the commonwealth, then for a moment we are completely isolated". The commonwealth provided means of cooperation among member states, and the form of cooperation most useful to India was economic assistance from developed to under developed members.

India and West Asia

India strove to forge friendly ties with the various countries in West Asia, i.e., Egypt, Iran, Iraq, Saudi Arabia, Turky, Sudan, Yeman, etc. West Asia holds about 60 percent of the world's oil deposits. This area connects two strategically important waterways–the straits connecting the Black Sea with the Mediterranean and the Suez connecting the Red Sea with the Mediterranean. India's commercial contacts with West Asia before the second world war brought export profits from sales of cotton textiles, jute goods, and tea, and also encouraged the settlement of Indians in great and small trading centres throughout the Arabian sea region. Post-independence policy towards the countries of West Asia and Arab World revealed the same basic objective of ridding the region of European colonialism. The creation of Israel out of the three-quarters of the British mandated territory of palestine in 1948 brought about a festering political sore which taxed the ingenity of all interested States. India's official response to the formation of new states was determined by the fact of an implaceable, unmitigated hostility manifested towards Israel by the Arab States. India's policy was conscientiously low-keyed. In 1950 India formally recognised Israel as a legal entity in the international community, but was reluctant to enter into close relations with the Jawish state. At the same time, India also expressed its disapproval of Israeli military retaliations and Israel's appropriation of additional territory and its alteration of the flow of the river Jordan's water. A close look at the palestine question, Arab-Israel dispute or Suez crisis, proves that India took a definite stand to side with the countries in the Arab world to promote peace and development of the the region.

Of all the disputes referred to the United Nations from West Asia probably the Palestine question was one of the most complex. The question of Palestine was first brought before the U.N. by Great Britain in April 1947, when it wanted the General assembly to take up the issue of the future set up of Palestine. A special committee was set up on Palestine. The committee submitted its report in August 1947 and recommended that Palestine should be divided into a Arab State, a Jewish State and a special area including Jerselum should remain under international government. Israel emerged as a state on the international horizon with the backing of the Western powers, but the Arabs were not ready to accept its existence. Subsequently, the problem of the homeland of the Palestine was raised with popular support and thus, the problem became more and more complicated. At every stage, India fully supported the Palestinian cause inside and outside the United Nations.

Suez crisis was one of the most explosive questions which threatened the peace of the world. In 1956 Egypt announced the nationalisation of the Suez canel and froze the Suez canel fund in Egypt. Great Britain and France took a serious view of the nationalisation. Rival claims were made and charges were levelled by the Anglo-French and Egyptian Government. India suggested that the Suez canel should be recognised as an integral part of Egypt. It supported the Egyptian case at the U.N., when the security council took up the issue for discussion. In October 1956, Israel, France and England attacked Egyptian positions in the Suez canel area. India expressed her sympathy for Egypt and urged immediate ceasefire. India played an active role in the resolution of the Suez crisis.

India's Relations with the People's Republic of China

The present Sino-Indian relationship has its roots in history. In the two thousand years history of their intercourse, cultural and commercial, there has never been any armed conflict between the two peoples. Buddhism spread to China from India defying the mountain barriers. During the last two centuries, the normal contacts between the two countries were lost due to the intergention of the Western powers, created mutual sympathy and identical interest against Western imperialism. Nehru, who visited Chungking in 1939, paid a high tribute to the brave Chinese people and emphasised Sino-Indian cooperation as the key to world peace and freedom. The Chinese too voiced their strong support for the cause of Indian independence. The political upheavals happening in the two countries in the post-war period, though of very different nature, do not seem to have affected the traditional friendship between the two nations. India was the first among the nations of the so-called free world to recognise the communist government of China, although ideologically the two government were poles apart.

The birth of the people's republic of China in 1949 changed the politics of the Asiatic continent, China seemed to represent a powerful anti-colonial force. It denounced the Western world as bourgeoisie and oppressive. The most important ingredient of China's foreign policy appears to be attain a great power status. Nehru advocated a policy of befriending China. On the other hand, China wants to establish hegemony in the region adjoining her borders. The communist controlled press indulged in slanderous attack against Nehru. He was called the running dog of Western imperialism. However, within one year of the establishment of formal relations, two accute problems embittered the relations between China and India. The first problem was concerned with the Korean war. During the Korean war India extended its supports to the U.N. and India's support for the U.N. military effort in Korea must have confirmed its identity with Western interest in the minds of the communist government in China. But by late 1952 China had accepted India's good offices and mediation efforts and seemed more anxious to cocnclude a ceasefire under terms suggested by India. Yet, China could not whole heartedly appreciate India's role in the Korean war.

The withdrawl of British power from the sub-continent in 1947 prepared the way for a reversal of the balance that had existed across the Himalayas. The birth of the people's Republic of China confirmed, reassertion of her authority in Tibet. India sent a note of protest, deploring the invasion of Tibet and China's use of force to settle the question of her relationship with the Tibetan. China considered Tibet as an integral part of China. India's traditional rights in Tibet came under immediate attack. The Nehru government was in a dilemma. The choice was between commitment to the lost cause of Tibetan independence, or of pursuing a friendly relations with China, and war with China was beyond practical consideration. Nehru choose the middle path and India reaffirmed Chinese suzerainty over Tibet. In 1954, India reached an agreement with China. The preamble of this treaty embodied Nehru's famous Panchsheel (Five principles of peaceful co-existence). The Chinese respected the terms of the treaty upto 1959. The five years following the conclusion of 1954 agreement may be described as the years of Sino-Indian honeymoon. In 1957, the Indian government discovered that the Chinese had built a road across the Aksai Chin of Ladakh and felt perturbed. Meanwhile, the Chinese violated the treaty of 1954 and suspended the autonomy of Tibet. Where they committed great atrocities. The Dalai Lama, the supreme temporal head of Tibet, fled to Delhi. In 1959 China occupied Longju and nearly 12,000 sq. miles of Indian territory in Ladakh. Frequent border violations were made by China. In 1960 the prime ministers of the two countries met at New Delhi, but no agreement could be reached and the 6 order incursion continued. The things took serious turn in 1962 when China launched a fullfleged attack on India in NEFA and Ladakh and took possession of large chunks of Indian territory. On November 21, 1962 China announced a unilateral ceasefire. The six Colombo powers (Ceylon, Burma, Indonesia, Cambodia, UAR and Chana) negotiated for fong to bring about a settlement but failed due to the uncompromising attitude of China.

On the other hand, during the Indo-Pak war of 1965, China supported Pakistan. But the Chinese attempts to exploit the Indo-Pak war to her own advantage was foiled. Even after the Tashkent agreement, China fully endorsed the Pakistani stand on Kashmir. India did not shift its policy on either Tibet or Taiwan in response of unremitting Chinese hostility. Upto 1971, India took a number of steps, to defreeze relations with China. There was also indication of slow but definite change in China's stand that might lead to a possible thaw. However, the sudden explosion in the then East Pakistan (Bangadesh) halted this process and fostered renewed bitterness. China wanted to play Pakistan against India and the Chinese interest lay in keeping India weak. However, in recent time the interest of both India and China in maintaining a trend of normalisation of their relations has been evident. Yet, the border problems between India and China still remained unsolved. But India has shown keenness to resolve outstanding disputes with China amicably. The Chinese leaders also responded favourably. Despite these development several causes of friction between India and China still exist.

Indo-Pak Relations

Two independent sovereign dominions were born in mid-August 1947. Although for centuries Hindus and Muslims had lived together in the sub-continent, the partition created unprecedented hostility between secular India and Islamic Pakistan. The partition has been described as the most unfortunate fact of post-war international politics. In a message on August 15, 1947 Nehru has said, "I want to say to all Nations of the world, that we stand for peace and friendship with Pakistan". This has been the main thrust of India's foreign policy for 50 years. India has consistently sought peaceful, cordial and friendly relations with Pakistan. However, Pakistan leadership has been harping on threats from India, and the alleged Indian desire to swallow her. In the past, India has made several offers of "No war pact" to Pakistan, but the latter has never responded favourably to Indian offer. Above all, the partition of the sub-continent in 1947 was responsible for the generation of ill-feeling between India are Pakistan.

The policy of confrontation was first executed when Kashmir was invaded by Muslim tribesmen who received Pakistani help. On October 26, 1947 the Maharaja of Kashmir signed an instrument of accession to the Indian union and the Indian troops were sent to Srinagar the next day. Thus, began the first armed hostilities between the two new born states. The government of India referred the Kashmir dispute to the U.N. In January 1948 the security council passed a resolution calling both sides to cease hostilities, and a U.N. commission for India and Pakistan was formed. The commission called for a ceasefire and the withdrawl of pathan tribesmen and Pakistani forces. India and Pakistan accepted the resolution, but Pakistan didnot withdraw its forces and formed the so-called Azad Kashmir in the occupied territory. Thus arose the Kashmir dispute which embittered the relationship between the two neighbours.

Pakistan had joined the Western bloc in 1954. It concluded a military pact with the U.S. and later jointed the South East Asia treaty organisation (SEATO). These organisations were aimed at what American called, "containment of communism". The military aid that the U.S. gave to Pakistan was meant for defence against communism. But in practice, Pakistan used the American wapons only against India. Pakistan at one stage tried to bully the western countries by raising the bogey of communism and threatening to walk over to communist bloc. At the same time, Pakistan sought friendship with China. Pakistan saw a wonderful opportunity of aligning itself with China, when Sino-Indian relations was in a deteriorating stage. During Chinese aggression on India in 1962 Pakistan fully supported its newly acquired friend. In March 1963 Pakistan and China signed a treaty by which Pakistan handed over to China a large slice of Indian territory in Kashmir under her illegal possession. China supplied large quantities of arms to Pakistan. Besides, the sharing of river waters became a major issue between India and Pakistan. Under a standstill agreement India had agread to supply water to the canals in Pakistan from the headworks in India against payment. This agreement lapsed as Pakistan failed to renew it. A fresh agreement was concluded whereby the two sides agreed to a progressive diminution of water supplies by Indian to Pakistan. India had to construct a dam at Bhakra to meet the irrigation needs of its territory. Pakistan unilaterally repudiated the agreement in 1950 saying that it was signed under duress. Mr. Blake, president of the world Bank, agreed to mediate between India and Pakistan on the sharing of waters. An agreement on sharing of waters was eventually conclueded in 1960. The dispute regarding sharing of river water was amicably settled. However, in 1968 Pakistan objected to the construction of Farakka barrage to control the water of the Ganges.

Hopes for an Indo-Pakistan detente were aroused when in 1964, president Ayub Khan of Pakistan met Lal Bahadur Shastri, the Prime Minister of India. But hopes were shattered when in 1965, Pakistan occupied Kanjarkot in the Rann of Kutch. On April 9, 1965 two pak battalions advanced into Indian territory and Indian forces repulsed the attack. On June 30, a cease fire agreement was signed by the two countries. Yet, Indo-Pakistani relations did not improve. Shastri was reluctant to go to war with

Pakistan. The corner stone of his foreign policy was to have good relations with all neighbouring countries. Shastri offered a no-war pact to Pakistan, but Pakistan did not respond to the offer. On August 1965, Pak infiltrators crossed into Indian territory. Pakistan was bent upon a solution of the Kashmir problem by means on force. This triggered off the first major was between the two neighbours. On September 1, 1965 Pakistan attacked Chhamb and on the 5th, fighting broke out on the Western border. Now Shastri had no choice, he had to attack pakistan to relieve the pressure in the area. As a result of the U.N. efforts, a ceasefire was ordered by the two countries on September 23. After the 22 days war, Lal Bahadur Shastri and Ayub Khan met at Tashkent, the metting was arranged on the initiative of the Soviet Prime minister Kosygin. In the Tashkent declaration both the leaders expressed their firm resolve to restore normal relations between their countries and to settle their dispute through peaceful means.

The Tashkent spirit did not last long. The partition of Pakistan and the emergence of Bangladesh as a separate nation in 1971 had been implied in the very nature of Pakistan as it had come into existence in 1947. East Pakistan was being exploited economically and politically by West Pakistan which created a strong demand for autonomy in that part of the country. The Awami-league led by Sheikh Mujibur Rahman won the election in East Pakistan. But Yahya Khan and Z.A. Bhutto were not at all willing to accept Awami league's demand for regional autonomy. A reign of terror was let loose in East Pakistan and Mujib was arrested. Large number of refugees from East Pakistan fled away to India. Mrs. Indira Gandhi, the Indian prime minister made sincere appeal to the Pakistan government but it was not heeded. All on a sudden Pakistan declared war on India on 3rd December, 1971. Fierce fighting broke out on both boarders-East and West. The war lasted two weeks. Indian soliders hand in glove with the Muktibahini of East Pakistan liberated Dacca on December 16, 1971 and the Pakistani troops surrendered. When the liberation of East Pakistan (Bangladesh) accomplished, India ordered unilateral ceasefire on December 17, 1971 in Western front. Then came the Simla summit between prime minister Indira Gandhi and Z.A. Bhutto, President of Pakistan. The two countries agreed to settle their differences throught bilateral negotiations. Bhutto supported early restoration of diplomatic ties between India and Pakistan. Both the country agreed to respect each others territorial integrity and soverignity. Though hopes generated by the Simla agreement has been shattered to a great extent by Pakistan's refusal to recognise Bangladesh. It cannot be denied that the Simla pact has a historic significance for exceeding matters of immediate concern to the two countries. It was the first time that two nations recently freed from colonial domination, had formally declared that they would not permit the interference of outsiders, but would settle their differences by peaceful means through bilateral negotiations.

India and the United Nations

India's foreign policy recognises the United Nations as the humanity's hope for a peaceful and secure world order. The Constitution of India, in Article 51, gives directive to the government to promote international peace and seek peaceful settlement of international disputes. The United Nations is an organisation of sovereign nations dedicated to the cause of world peace. Faith in the U.N. and cooperation with the world body is an important principle of India's foreign policy. A delegation led by Sir R. Mudaliar represented India in the San-Francisco conference. He signed the charter on behalf of India. India's commitment to the ideals of the U.N. was expressed time and again. India always, cooperated with all organs of the U.N., and faithfully discharged such responsibilities as it were assigned to him from time to time. These included India' role in peace-keeping in West Asia and the Congo. India has sereved a number of 2 year terms as non-permanent member of the security council. India's Mrs. Vijyalaxmi Pandit was elected as President of the 8th session of the U.N. General Assembly. Eminent Indian Jurists, such as B.N. Rau and Nagendra Singh, have served with distinction as judges of the International Court of Justice. India pleaded strongly for speeding up the process of decolonisation in Asia and Africa. India along with other likeminded countries, played a significant role in the release of French colonies of Tunisia, Algeria. India supported the cause of freedom of Cyprus. India fully supported the cause of independence of Namibia. Ever since the U.N.'s General Assembly adopted the Universal Declaration of Human Rights in 1948, India has cooperated in implementation of human rights related decisions and resolutions. India led the movement against apartheid both in the U.N. and outside. Further, India stands committed to total nuclear disarmament. India has signed the partial Test ban treaty.

Index

MAPS

THE FRENCH REPUBLIC AND ITS DEPENDENT REPUBLIC IN 1799

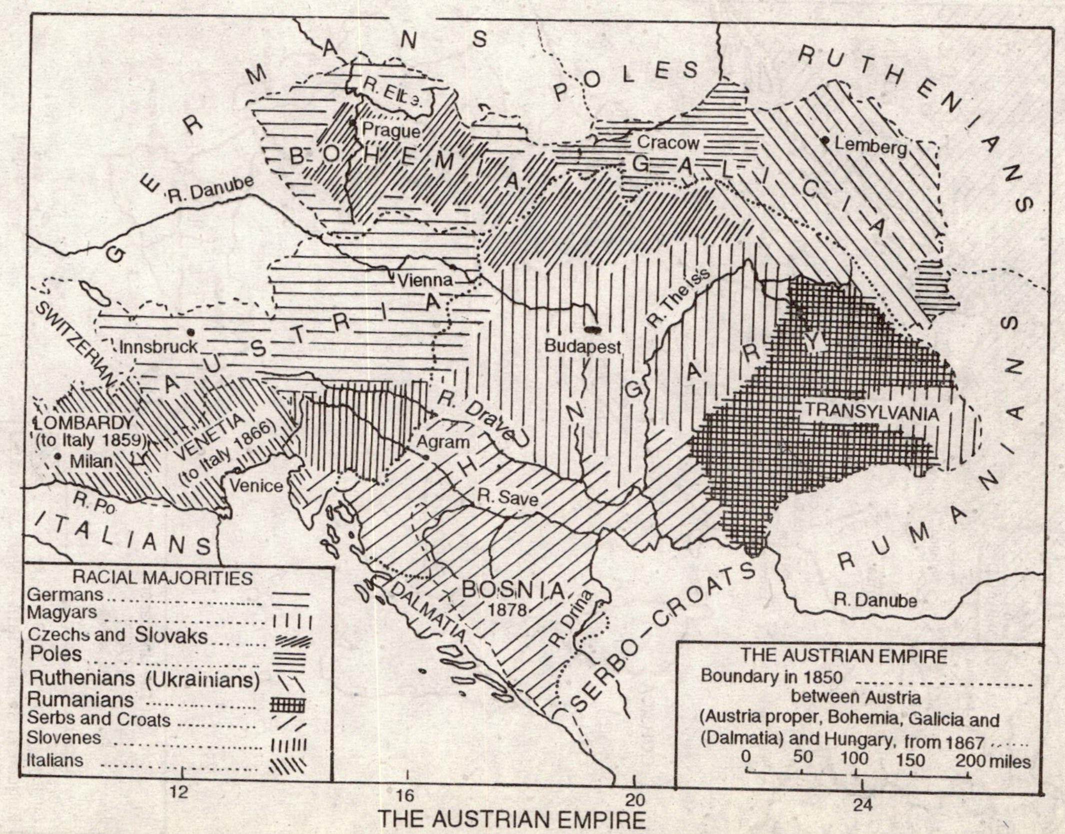

THE AUSTRIAN EMPIRE

AUSTRIA
SWITZERLAND
TYROL
SAVOY (to France 1860)
LOMBARDY
1859
VENETIA
(1866)
Trieste
Fiume
Magenta
Milan
R. Po
Peschiera
Solferino
Mantua
Verona
Custozza
Legnag
Venice
FRANCE
PIEDMONT
PARMA
(1860)
MODENA
R. Po
ROMAGNA
(1860)
Ravenna
REP. OF SAN MARINO
ADRIATIC SEA
BOSNIA
(Turkisn till 1908)
to France (1860)
Nice
Monaco
Genoa
LUCCA (1860)
(to Tuscany 1847)
Pisa
Florence
Leghorn
TUSCANY
(1860)
R. Tiber
UMBRIA
(1860)
MARCHES
(1860)
Ancona
Castelfidaro
PAPAL STATES
Elbe
CORSICA
(to Frence)
ROME
(1870)
Pontecorvo (Papal)
Benevento
(Papal)
Naples
Castellammare
NAPLES
SARDINIA
THE TWO SICILIES
(1860)
MEDITERRANEAN SEA
Massina
Aspromonte
Palermo
Calatafimi
Marsala
SICILY
Catania
Syracuse
Malta
(British)
The Unification of
ITALY
English Mile
0 50 100 200
Austrian territory in 1859
Kingdom of Sardinia, 1815—1859
Boundary after 1870
Acquisitions after the Great War
The dates (1860) are those of the uniox of the various states with the kingdom of Sardinia, forming together the Kingdom of Italy

NORTH
SEA
DENMARK
SWEDEN
BALTIC SEA
Heligoland
(German 1890)
Pruasian 1891)
Schleswing
Holstein
Lübeck
Hamburg
Bremen
MECKLENBURG
Pomerania
West
Prussia
OLDEN-
BURG
Hanover
HOLLAND
Brandenburg
Berlin
Posen
Vistula
R. Elbe
Westphalia
Saxony
R. Oder
Silesia
RUSSIA
BELGIUM
Rhine
Provi
Rhine
Nassau
Hesse-
Cassel
THURINGIAN
STATES
SAXONY
HESSE
Sadowa
Königgratz
Prague
1818
LUXEM
BURG
Frankfort
R. Main
(to
bavaria)
Lorr-
aine
(1871)
BAVARIA
FRANCE
BADEN
WURTTEMBERG
Hohenzollern
Alsace
R. Danuba
Vienna
Budapest
AUSTRIA – HUNGARY
SWITZERLAND
ITALY
ADRIATIC
SEA
TURKEY
English Miles
0 20 40 60 80 100 200
Prussian Territory in 1886
" Acquisitions in 1866
Boundary of German Confed. 1815-1866
Southern boundary of North
German Confedration, 1866-1871
Boundary of German Empire, 1871
The Formation of
MODERN GERMANY
1815 – 1871
a=Part of Luxemburg excluded from the
Confederation in 1839.
b=Part of Limburg nominally included in
the confederation in 1839

THE BALKANS, 1878-1914

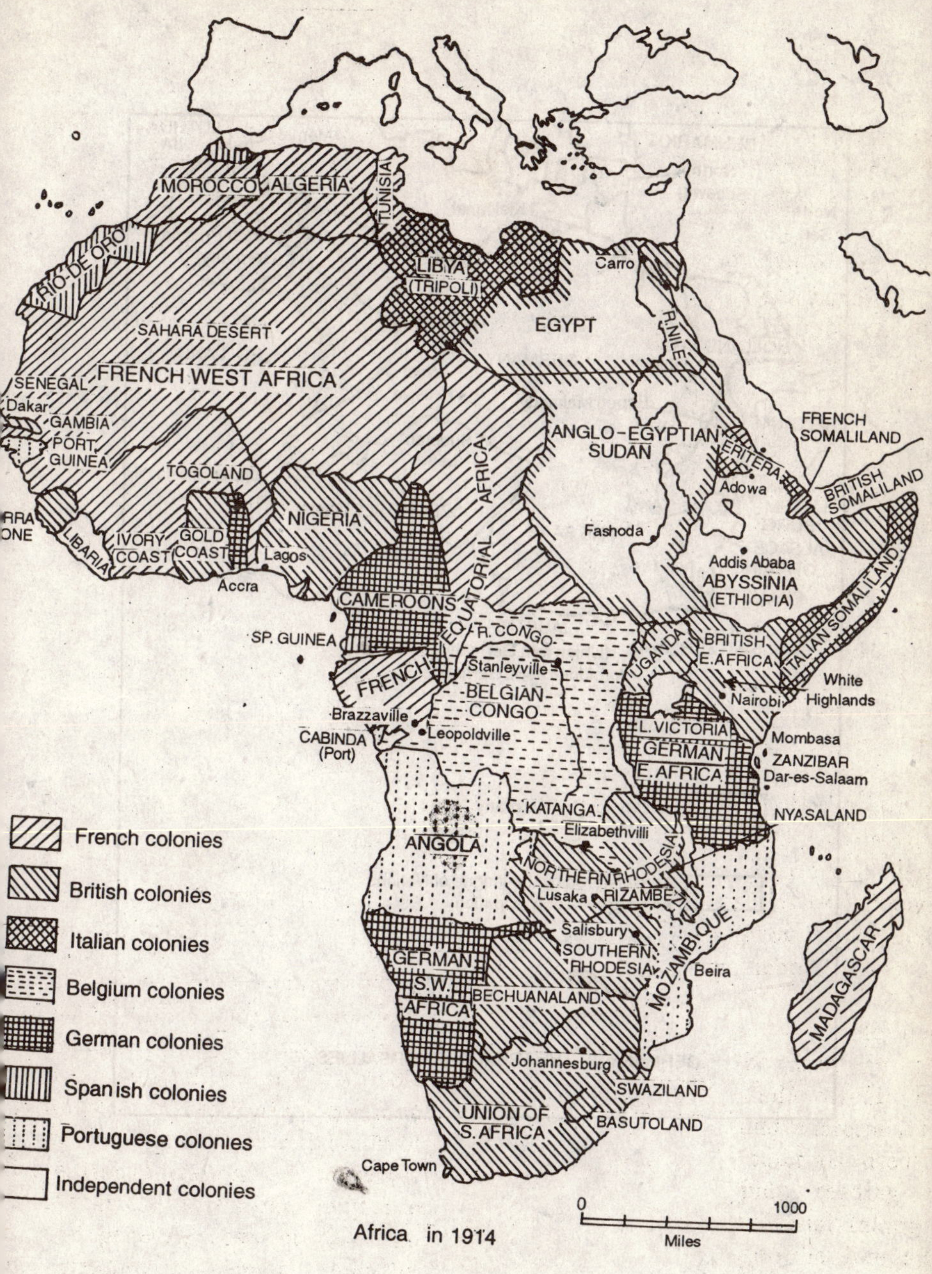

Africa in 1914

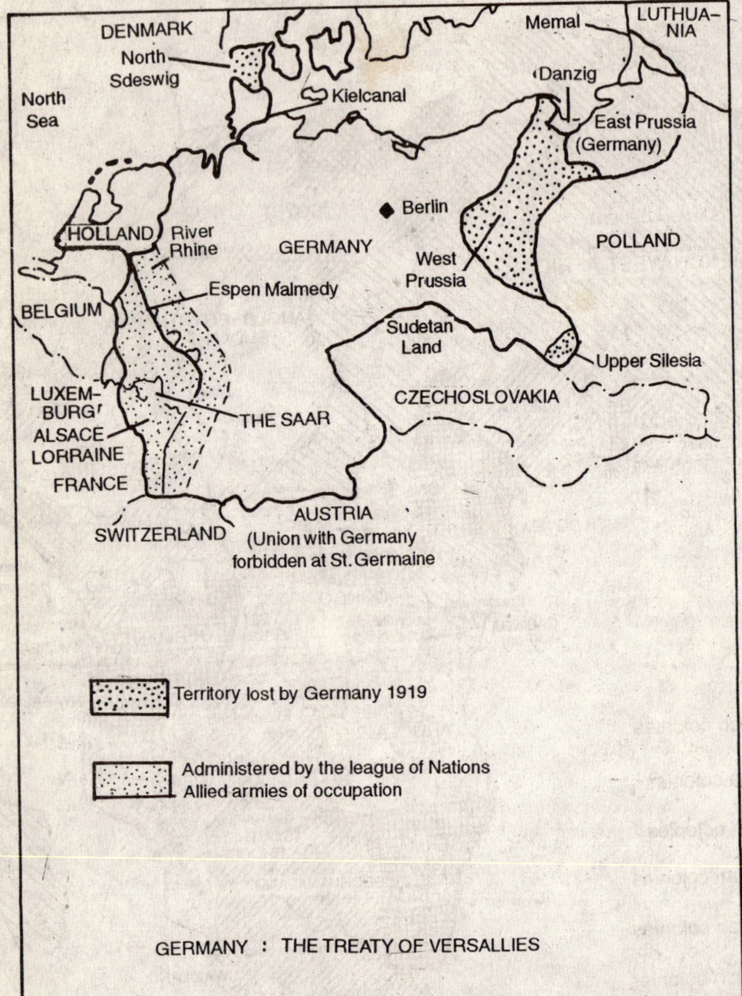

GERMANY : THE TREATY OF VERSALLIES

THE EXPANSION OF GERMANY 1933-39

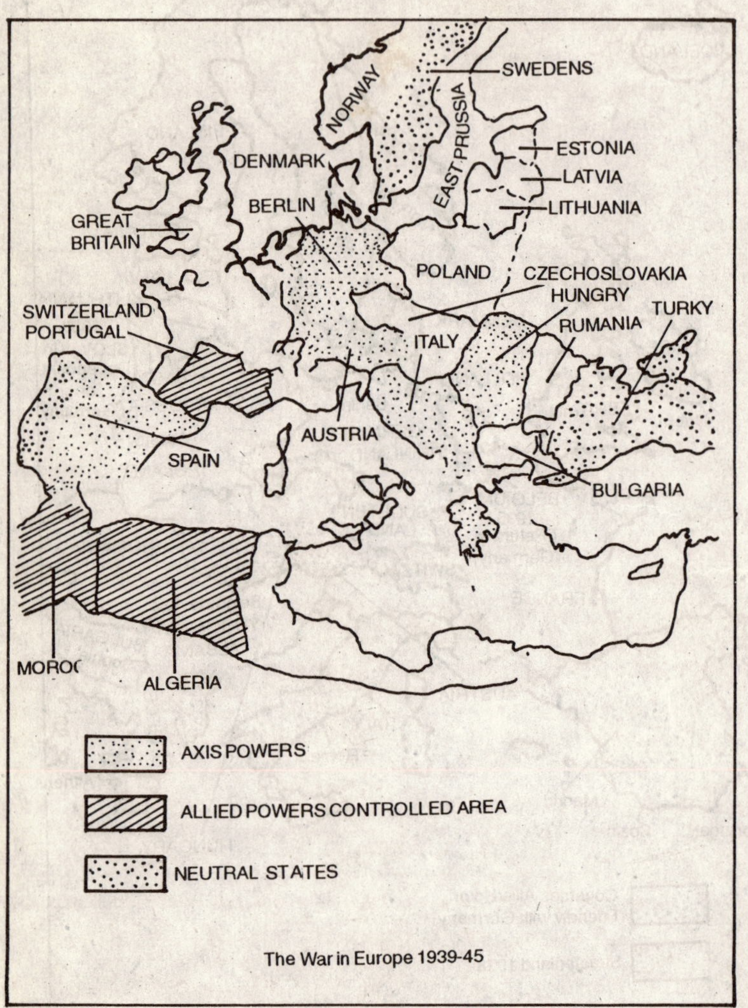

The War in Europe 1939-45

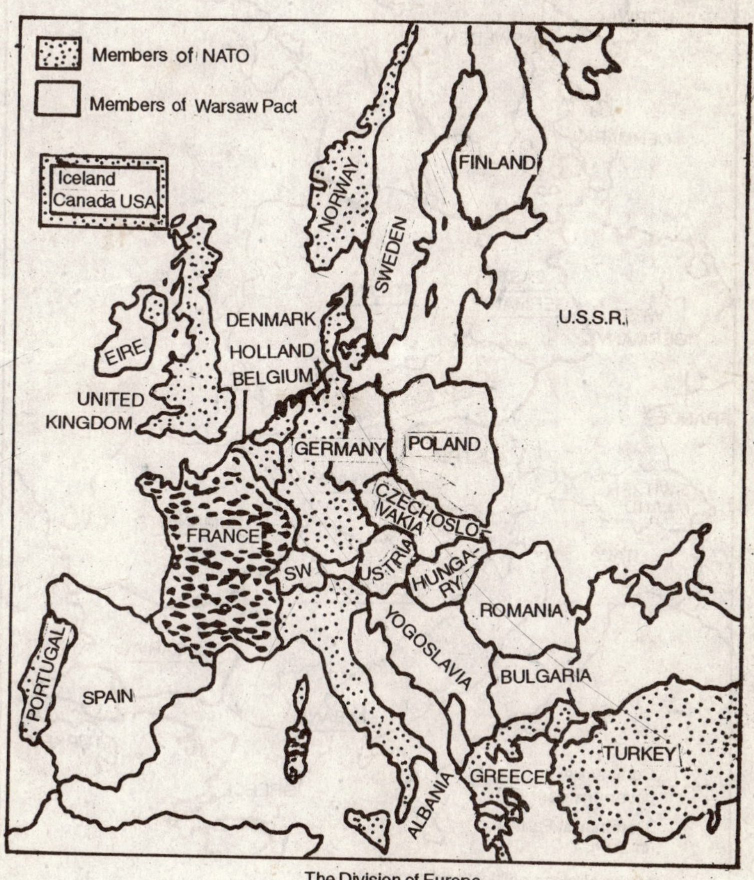

The Division of Europe

The European Communist bloc.